PERSPECTIVES ON

HEALTH

Getchell • Pippin • Varnes

Jefferson High School
Daly City, CA 94014

 D.C. Heath and Company
HEATH Lexington, Massachusetts/Toronto, Ontario

173

Executive Editor: Ceanne Tzimopoulos
Editor: Joanne C. Kryszpin
Editorial Development: Ann E. Bekebrede, M. Frances Boyle, Dottie Burstein, Fran Needham, Edwin M. Schiele
Program and Cover Design: Lisa Fowler
Design Development: Jane Bigelow-Orner *with* Penelope Peters, Camille Venti, Nancy Smith-Evers, Caroline Bowden
Composition in Quark: Ricki Pappo, Susan Geer, Greg Johnson
Cover Photography *(l to r):* D. Greco/The Image Works; Lori Baker/ airbrush helmet; Rhoda Sidney/The Image Works; © Dan McCoy/ Rainbow; Bill Gallery/Stock Boston; © Ulrike Welsch
Permissions: Dorothy McLeod
Production Coordinator: Pamela L. Tricca
Contributing Writers: Linda Adler, Margaret Cleveland, Toby Klang, Debra Osnowitz, Jo Pitkin
Readability Testing: J&F Readability Service

ABOUT THE AUTHORS

Leroy H. (Bud) Getchell, Ph.D., is a Professor in the Department of Kinesiology at Indiana University, Bloomington, Indiana, and former Executive Director of the National Institute for Fitness and Sport. Before joining Indiana University, Dr. Getchell served as Professor and Director of Adult Physical Fitness Programs in the Human Performance Laboratory at Ball State University, Muncie, Indiana. Dr. Getchell is a nationally-recognized lecturer and author on the subjects of exercise physiology, physical fitness, and wellness. He is the author of *Physical Fitness: A Way of Life, Being Fit: A Personal Guide,* and *The Fitness Book.* Dr. Getchell is a Fellow and former member of the Board of Trustees of the American College of Sports Medicine (ACSM). In 1991, he was selected as a Healthy American Fitness Leader, an award sponsored by the U.S. Chamber of Commerce, The President's Council on Physical Fitness and Sport, and Allstate Life Insurance.

Grover D. (Rusty) Pippin, Ph.D., C.H.E.S., a former high school science and health teacher and athletics coach, is now Professor and Director of Health Education at Baylor University in Waco, Texas. Dr. Pippin, a certified health education specialist, is a noted speaker and consultant in health and wellness. He serves as chairperson of the Board of Trustees of the Texas Association for Health, Physical Education, Recreation, and Dance, has served on the Board of Governors of the Texas School Health Association, and was the chairperson of the Texas Jump Rope for Heart task force. He has received special commendations for his outstanding contributions from the State of Texas, the American Cancer Society, and the American Heart Association. Dr. Pippin is currently vice president of the Health Division of the Southern District of AAHPERD.

Jill W. Varnes, Ed.D., a former high school health teacher and coach, is now Assistant Dean in the college of Health and Human Performance at the University of Florida in Gainesville. Previously she was employed as Health Education Consultant with the Florida Department of Education. Dr. Varnes is the author of numerous journal articles on health and is currently Principal Investigator on a cancer prevention project with the National Cancer Institute. She has held numerous offices in professional organizations including President of Florida AAHPERD, Vice President for Health of Southern District AAHPERD, and President of Southern District AAHPERD. At the national level, she has served on the Board of Directors for the Association for the Advancement of Health Education and the AAHPERD Board of Governors. Dr. Varnes is the 1994 recipient of the Association for the Advancement of Health Education's Professional Service Award.

REVIEWERS

MEDICAL REVIEWERS

This text was reviewed by Robert B. Kelly, M.D., and Jay Siwek, M.D. Dr. Kelly is associate professor of family medicine at Case Western University; chairperson of the Department of Family Practice at Metro Health Medical Center in Cleveland, Ohio; and is Medical Editor of the Patient Education Brochure series published by the American Academy of Family Physicians. Dr. Siwek is professor and acting chairperson, Department of Family Medicine at Georgetown University, Washington, D.C., and is Editor of *American Family Physician,* a journal published by the American Academy of Family Physicians.

CONTENT REVIEWERS

Kathleen M. Foell, R.D., M.S.
Consulting Registered Dietitian and Nutritionist
Foxboro, Massachusetts

L. Candace Jennings, M.D.
Orthopedic Surgery
Massachusetts General Hospital
Boston, Massachusetts

Carole A. Jordan-Belver, M.Ed.
Project Coordinator
AIDS Consortium of Texas Colleges and Universities
Southwest Texas State University
San Marcos, Texas

Marian Maguire, L.I.C.S.W.
Private Practice, Psychotherapist
Wellesley, Massachusetts

Warren L. McNab, Ph.D.
Professor of Health Education
College of Human Performance and Development
University of Nevada at Las Vegas

Alan E. Mikesky, Ph.D.
Assistant Professor
School of Physical Education
Indiana University Purdue University Indianapolis
Indianapolis, Indiana

Richard G. Schlaadt, Ed.D.
Professor and Director
University of Oregon Substance Abuse Prevention Program (SAPP)
Eugene, Oregon

REVIEW OF FIRST AID MANUAL

American Red Cross
of Massachusetts Bay
Boston, Massachusetts

MULTICULTURAL CONSULTANT

W. P. (Pat) Buckner, Jr., H.S.D., C.H.E.S.
Health Coordinator and Professor of Health Science and Allied Health
Department of Health and Human Performance
University of Houston
Houston, Texas

CONTRIBUTING CONSULTANT, SCOPE AND SEQUENCE

David M. White, Ed.D.
Associate Professor of Health Education
Department of Health, Physical Education, Recreation, and Safety
East Carolina University
Greenville, North Carolina

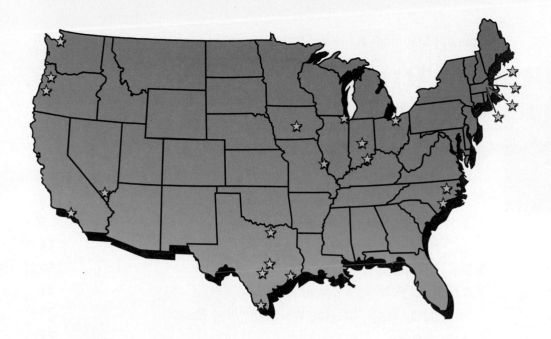

TEACHER REVIEWERS

Elaine Atherton
Project Coordinator
Los Angeles County Office of
    Education
Downey, California

Vicki Beveridge
Health and Physical Education
    Teacher
Ankeny High School
Ankeny, Iowa

Paul Blair
Health Teacher
Evergreen Junior High School
Redmond, Washington

Rebecca T. Davila, C.H.E.S.
Department Chair, Physical
    Education and Health
Lewisville High School
Lewisville, Texas

Velma Dukat
Health Teacher
Nikki Rowe High School
McAllen, Texas

Anna Mae Gahlinger
Director, Student Services
New Albany Floyd County
    Consolidated School
    Corporation
New Albany, Indiana

Donald Hallett
Assistant Director, Health and
    Physical Education
Swampscott Public Schools
Swampscott, Massachusetts

Carole P. Hancock
Department Head, Physical
    Education
Theodore Roosevelt High
    School
St. Louis, Missouri

Joe Harris
Health and Physical Education
    Teacher
Oberlin High School
Oberlin, Ohio

Arnold Mandell
Health and Physical Education
    Teacher
Dunbar Vocational High
    School
Chicago Public Schools
Chicago, Illinois

Ron Speck
Health Curriculum Specialist
Salem-Keizer Public Schools
Salem, Oregon

TABLE OF CONTENTS

Concept Mapping: A Study Strategy   **xvii**

UNIT 1

MAKING HEALTHY CHOICES

Chapter 1   WELLNESS: A WAY OF LIFE

1.1   Health Today

    Making A Difference *CAREER: Health Educator*   **6**

1.2   Making Healthy Choices   **9**

    Health Inventory   **14**

1.3   Accepting Responsibility   **16**

1.4   Your Role As a Consumer   **19**

    Being Well, Staying Well *Weighing Risks*   **23**

Chapter Review   **24**

Chapter 2   TAKING CARE OF YOURSELF   26

2.1   Protecting Your Skin   **28**

    Consumer Health *Using Cosmetics*   **31**

2.2   Structure and Care of the Teeth   **35**

2.3   Your Sense of Sight   **39**

    From a Cultural Perspective *Skin Color and SPF*   **43**

    Issues in Health *Thinking Critically About Teenagers and Advertising*   **46**

2.4   Your Sense of Sound   **48**

    Making A Difference *RESEARCH: Closed-Caption Television*   **50**

    Being Well, Staying Well *Tan Time*   **53**

Chapter Review   **54**

UNIT 2

MENTAL HEALTH   56

Chapter 3   DEVELOPING A HEALTHY PERSONALITY   58

3.1   Recognizing the Healthy Personality   **60**

3.2   Personality Development   **64**

    Making A Difference *PEOPLE Carol Gilligan*   **72**

3.3   Achieving Mental Wellness   **73**

    Consumer Health *Developing Your Self-Esteem*   **74**

    Being Well, Staying Well *Friendship for Sale*   **77**

Chapter Review   **78**

Chapter 4 HEALTHY EMOTIONS   80

4.1 Understanding Your Emotions   82
     Consumer Health *Advertising Techniques Use
        Emotional Appeal*   86
4.2 Dealing with Emotions   89
     From A Cultural Perspective *Valuing Diversity* 92
     Making A Difference CAREER *Sports Psychologist* 93
4.3 Anger and Violence   96
     Being Well, Staying Well *Saving Face*   99
     Issues in Health Feature *Thinking Critically About
        Violence Prevention*   100
Chapter Review   102

Chapter 5 MANAGING STRESS   104

5.1 Stress and Stressors   106
5.2 Stress and Its Effects on You   112
     Consumer Health *Managing Stress Without
        Speding Money*   115
     Making A Difference PEOPLE: *Suicide Peer
        Counseling*   117
5.3 Handling Stress In Your Life   118
     Being Well, Staying Well *Stressed Out*   123
Chapter Review   124

Chapter 6 UNDERSTANDING
MENTAL DISORDERS   126

6.1 Causes of Mental Disorders   128
6.2 Types of Mental Disorders   131
6.3 Treating Mental Problems   139
     Making A Difference RESEARCH *Light Therapy
        for SAD*   142
     Consumer Health *Obtaining Help*   143
     Being Well, Staying Well *Getting Help*   145
Chapter Review   146

SOCIAL HEALTH 148

UNIT 3

Chapter 7 **HEALTHY RELATIONSHIPS** 150

7.1 Acceptance and Cooperation 152
7.2 Dating and Marriage 156
    Making a Difference *CAREER: Marriage Enrichment* 159
7.3 Life Choices 162
    Consumer Health *Living on your Own* 162
    Being Well, Staying Well *Not Now* 165
Chapter Review 166

Chapter 8 **FAMILY ROLES AND RESPONSIBILITIES** 168

8.1 The Family Unit 170
    Making a Difference *PEOPLE The Humanitas Awards* 172
    Issues in Health *Thinking Critically About Open Communication* 176
8.2 Family in Crisis 178
    Consumer Health *Children's Toys* 179
    Being Well, Staying Well *Sticking Together* 185
Chapter Review 186

Chapter 9 **YOU IN THE COMMUNITY** 188

9.1 Community Health 190
    From a Cultural Perspective *Community Pride* 192
    Making A Difference *RESEARCH: Americans With Disabilities Act* 195
9.2 Special Health Concerns 196
    Consumer Health *Home Health Assistance* 198
    Being Well, Staying Well *Make An Effort* 201
Chapter Review 202

NUTRITION

204

Chapter 10 UNDERSTANDING NUTRITION   206
10.1 Nutrients That Provide Energy   208
10.2 Nutrients That Regulate   213
10.3 A Healthy Daily Diet   219
 From a Cultural Perspective *Culture, Diet, and Disease*   223
 Making A Difference *PEOPLE: David Kessler*   224
10.4 Identifying Nutritious Foods   225
 Consumer Health *Tips for Food Shopping*   227
 Being Well, Staying Well *Diet Change*   229
Chapter Review   230

Chapter 11 IDENTIFYING YOUR DIETARY NEEDS   232
11.1 Managing A Healthy Weight   234
 Consumer Health *Choosing a Weight-Loss Plan*   238
 Issues in Health Feature *Eating Disorders*   242
11.2 Diets for Individual Needs   244
 Making A Difference *CAREER: Nutritionist*   250
 Being Well, Staying Well *A Sensible Way*   253
Chapter Review   254

Chapter 12 DIGESTION AND EXCRETION   256
12.1 The Digestive System   258
12.2 Digestive Disorders   263
 From a Cultural Perspective *Lactose Intolerance*   265
 Making a Difference *RESEARCH: Laparoscopy for Gallstones* 268
12.3 Excretion   271
 Consumer Health *Antacids*   273
 Being Well, Staying Well *Facing Surgery*   275
Chapter Review   276

UNIT 4

Anatomical Plates are located between pages 300 - 301

PHYSICAL FITNESS 278

UNIT 5

Chapter 13 BONES AND MUSCLES 280
13.1 Bones—Living Organs 282
13.2 The Human Skeleton 285
13.3 Bone and Joint Problems 291
From a Cultural Perspective Therapy for Muscle Tension 294
Making A Difference RESEARCH: Joint Replacement Surgery 297
13.4 Muscles 298
Consumer Health Muscle Building 300
Being Well, Staying Well Broken Chances 303
Chapter Review 304

Chapter 14 CIRCULATION AND RESPIRATION 306
14.1 The Circulatory System 308
14.2 Circulation 312
14.3 Blood and Lymph 316
14.4 The Respiratory System 321
Consumer Health Humidifiers 324
Making A Difference RESEARCH: Organ Donation 325
Being Well, Staying Well Medical Directives 327
Chapter Review 328

Chapter 15 LIFELONG ACTIVITY 330
15.1 The Benefits of Fitness 332
Making A Difference PEOPLE: The Easy Access Project 335
15.2 Assessing Your Fitness Level 336
15.3 Designing a Fitness Plan 342
Consumer Health Athletic Shoes 347
Issues in Health Feature Thinking Critically About Steroid Abuse 350
15.4 Sensible Planning 352
Being Well, Staying Well Fitness for Life 355
Chapter Review 356

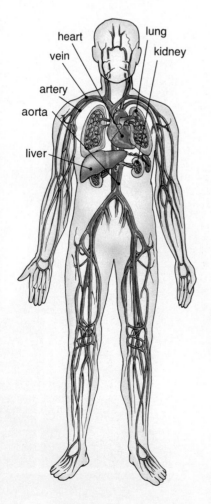

heart
lung
vein
kidney
artery
aorta
liver

THE HUMAN LIFE CYCLE

358

UNIT

6

Chapter 16 REPRODUCTION AND HEREDITY   **360**

16.1 Beginning of Life   **362**
    Consumer Health *The Cost of Raising a Child* **365**
16.2 Prenatal Care   **369**
    Making a Difference *CAREER: Midwives*   **372**
16.3 Heredity   **375**
    From a Cultural Perspective *Cystic Fibrosis* **378**
    Being Well, Staying Well *Becoming a Family* **381**
Chapter Review   **382**

Chapter 17 GROWTH AND DEVELOPMENT   **384**

17.1 The Endocrine System   **386**
17.2 Female Development   **393**
    Making A Difference *RESEARCH: Hormone Therapy* **398**
17.3 Male Development   **400**
    Consumer Health *Hair Loss*   **403**
    Being Well, Staying Well *Preventive Care*   **405**
Chapter Review   **406**

Chapter 18 UNDERSTANDING THE AGING PROCESS   **408**

18.1 Aging and Adulthood   **410**
    Consumer Health *Senior Citizens as Consumers* **414**
    Issues in Health Feature *Thinking Critically About Life Changes* **418**
18.2 Death and Dying   **420**
    Making A Difference *PEOPLE Alzheimer's Disease Support Groups* **424**
    Being Well, Staying Well *Saying Good-bye*   **425**
Chapter Review   **426**

UNIT 7

PREVENTING SUBSTANCE ABUSE 428

Chapter 19 COORDINATION AND CONTROL 430

19.1 The Nervous System 432
    From a Cultural Perspective *Tea* 437
19.2 Brain Activity and Sleep 440
    Consumer Health *Getting a Good Night's Sleep* 441
19.3 Nervous System Disorders 443
    Making a Difference RESEARCH: *The Miami Project* 445
19.4 How Drugs Affect the Body 448
    Being Well, Staying Well *Burning the Candle* 451
Chapter Review 452

Chapter 20 TOBACCO 454

20.1 Tobacco and People 456
20.2 Tobacco's Effects on the Body 461
    Consumer Health *Costs of Smoking* 462
20.3 Tobacco's Long-Term Risks 465
20.4 Quitting Tobacco Use 470
    Making a Difference RESEARCH: *Nicotine Patch* 473
    Being Well, Staying Well *In a Pinch* 475
Chapter Review 476

Chapter 21 ALCOHOL 478

21.1 Alcohol, The Problem Drink 480
    Consumer Health *Alcohol Advertising* 482
    Issues in Health *Thinking Critically About Staying Clean* 486
21.2 Intoxication 488
21.3 Alcohol's Long-Term Effects 493
    Making A Difference PEOPLE: *Alateen* 496
21.4 Alcohol and Society 498
21.5 Making Responsible Choices 501
    Being Well, Staying Well *Making A Contract* 505
Chapter Review 506

Chapter 22   **PSYCHOACTIVE DRUGS AND STEROIDS**   508

22.1   What is Drug Abuse   510
      Consumer Health *Over-the-Counter Drugs*   511
22.2   Commonly Abused Drugs   513
22.3   Drugs and Society   522
      Making A Difference *CAREER: Employee Assistance Counselor*   526
22.4   Preventing Drug Abuse   528
      Being Well, Staying Well *Talk It Out*   531
Chapter Review   532

DISEASES AND DISORDERS   534

Chapter 23   **INFECTIOUS DISEASES**   536

23.1   Causes of Disease   538
      Consumer Health *Staying Healthy while Traveling*   540
23.2   The Body's Response to Pathogens   542
23.3   Fighting Diseases   547
      Making a Difference *RESEARCH: Animal Viruses and Bacteria*   550
23.4   Common Infectious Diseases   553
      From a Cultural Perspective *Culturally Sensitive Medicine*   555
      Being Well, Staying Well *At the Beach*   559
Chapter Review   560

Chapter 24   **SEXUALLY TRANSMITTED DISEASES/AIDS**   562

24.1   The STDs Epidemic   564
24.2   Common Sexually Transmitted Diseases   568
24.3   HIV Infection and AIDS   575
      Making A Difference *PEOPLE: AIDS Action Committee*   579
24.4   Prevention and Treatment of STDs and AIDS   583
      Consumer Health *STD Support Groups—Finding Help*   584
      Being Well, Staying Well *An Open Mind*   587
Chapter Review   588

UNIT 8

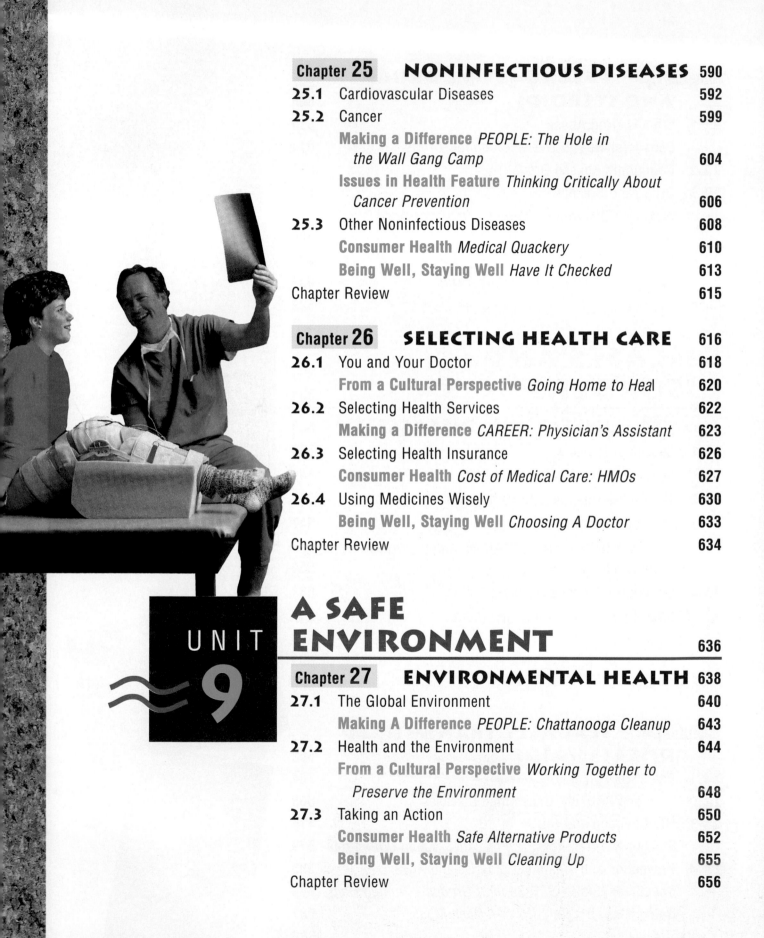

Chapter 25   **NONINFECTIOUS DISEASES**   590

25.1   Cardiovascular Diseases   592

25.2   Cancer   599

   Making a Difference *PEOPLE: The Hole in the Wall Gang Camp*   604

   Issues in Health Feature *Thinking Critically About Cancer Prevention*   606

25.3   Other Noninfectious Diseases   608

   Consumer Health *Medical Quackery*   610

   Being Well, Staying Well *Have It Checked*   613

Chapter Review   615

Chapter 26   **SELECTING HEALTH CARE**   616

26.1   You and Your Doctor   618

   From a Cultural Perspective *Going Home to Heal*   620

26.2   Selecting Health Services   622

   Making a Difference *CAREER: Physician's Assistant*   623

26.3   Selecting Health Insurance   626

   Consumer Health *Cost of Medical Care: HMOs*   627

26.4   Using Medicines Wisely   630

   Being Well, Staying Well *Choosing A Doctor*   633

Chapter Review   634

UNIT 9

A SAFE ENVIRONMENT   636

Chapter 27   **ENVIRONMENTAL HEALTH**   638

27.1   The Global Environment   640

   Making A Difference *PEOPLE: Chattanooga Cleanup*   643

27.2   Health and the Environment   644

   From a Cultural Perspective *Working Together to Preserve the Environment*   648

27.3   Taking an Action   650

   Consumer Health *Safe Alternative Products*   652

   Being Well, Staying Well *Cleaning Up*   655

Chapter Review   656

Chapter 28 **SAFETY** 658

28.1 Safety at Home and Work 660

    Making a Difference CAREER *Home Inspector* 663

28.2 Safety on the Road 665

28.3 Recreational Safety 668

    Consumer Health *Bicycle Helmets* 670

    Issues in Health Feature *Thinking Critically*
      About Crime Prevention 672

28.4 Safety During Emergencies 674

    Being Well, Staying Well *Safety First* 677

Chapter Review 678

FIRST AID MANUAL 680

HEALTH ALMANAC 710

    Medicines in Your Home 710

    Medical Specialists 711

    Warm-Up Exercises 712

    Household Hazards and Some Alternatives 713

    Calories, Nutrients, and Minerals in Select Foods 714

    Common Noninfectious Diseases and Disorders 715

    Common Infectious Diseases 717

GLOSSARY 720

INDEX 732

ACKNOWLEDGMENTS 746

SPECIAL FEATURES

MAKING A DIFFERENCE

CAREER

Health Educator **6**

Sports Psychologist **93**

Marriage Enrichment **159**

Nutritionist **250**

Midwives **372**

Employee Assistance Counselor **526**

Physician Assistant **623**

Home Inspector **663**

PEOPLE

Carol Gilligan **72**

Suicide Peer Counseling **117**

The Humanitas Awards **172**

David Kessler **224**

The Easy Access Project **335**

Alzheimer's Disease Support Groups **424**

Alateen **496**

AIDS Action Committee **579**

The Hole in the Wall Gang Camp **604**

Chattanooga Cleanup **643**

RESEARCH

Closed-Caption Television **50**

Light Therapy for SAD **142**

Americans With Disabilities Act **195**

Laparoscopy for Gallstones **268**

Joint Replacement Surgery **297**

Organ Donation **325**

Hormone Therapy **398**

The Miami Project **445**

Nicotine Patch **473**

Animal Viruses and Bacteria **550**

BEING WELL, STAYING WELL: DECISION-MAKING PRACTICE

Weighing Risks **23**

Tan Time **53**

Friendship for Sale **77**

Saving Face **99**

Stressed Out **123**

Getting Help **145**

Not Now **165**

Sticking Together **185**

Make An Effort **201**

Diet Change **229**

A Sensible Way **253**

Facing Surgery **275**

Broken Chances **303**

Medical Directives **327**

Fitness for Life **355**

Becoming a Family **381**

Preventive Care **405**

Saying Good-bye **425**

Burning the Candle **451**

In a Pinch **475**

Making A Contract **505**

Talk It Out **531**

At the Beach **559**

An Open Mind **587**

Have It Checked **613**

Choosing A Doctor **633**

Cleaning Up **655**

Safety First **677**

CONSUMER HEALTH

Using Cosmetics	**31**
Developing Your Self-Esteem	**74**
Advertising Techniques Use Emotional Appeal	**86**
Managing Stress Without Speding Money	**115**
Obtaining Help	**143**
Living on your Own	**162**
Children's Toys	**179**
Home Health Assistance	**198**
Tips for Food Shopping	**227**
Choosing a Weight-Loss Plan	**238**
Antacids	**273**
Muscle Building	**300**
Humidifiers	**324**
Athletic Shoes	**347**
The Cost of Raising a Child	**365**
Hair Loss	**403**
Senior Citizens as Consumers	**414**
Getting a Good Night's Sleep	**441**
Costs of Smoking	**462**
Alcohol Advertising	**482**
Over-the-Counter Drugs	**511**
Staying Healthy while Traveling	**540**
STD Support Groups—Finding Help	**584**
Medical Quackery	**610**
Cost of Medical Care—HMOs	**627**
Safe Alternative Products	**652**
Bicycle Helmets	**670**

FROM A CULTURAL PERSPECTIVE

Skin Color and SPF	**43**
Valuing Diversity	**92**
Community Pride	**192**
Culture, Diet, and Disease	**223**
Lactose Intolerance	**265**
Therapy for Muscle Tension	**294**
Cystic Fibrosis	**378**
Tea	**437**
Culturally Sensitive Medicine	**555**
Going Home to Heal	**620**
Working Together to Preserve the Environment	**648**

ISSUES IN HEALTH THINKING CRITICALLY ABOUT ...

Teenagers and Advertising	**46**
Violence Prevention	**100**
Open Communication	**176**
Eating Disorders	**242**
Steroid Abuse	**350**
Life Changes	**418**
Staying Clean	**486**
Cancer Prevention	**606**
Crime Prevention	**672**

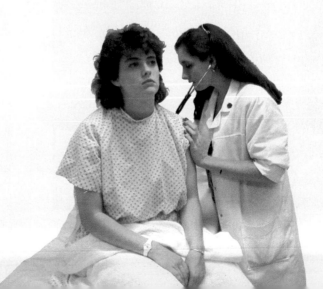

CONCEPT MAPPING—
A STUDY STRATEGY

Based on the work of Dr. 'Laine Gurley-Dilger.

How do you study? Do you reread a chapter over and over the night before a test, hoping you will remember all the information the next day? Do you take notes and try to memorize them? Perhaps you make flash cards of the information and quiz yourself. If your study method is one of the methods described here, you are learning by rote memorization. When you learn by rote memorization, information is stored in your short-term memory. Often this kind of learning only lasts a short time. Making a concept map or idea map helps you to transfer information from short-term memory to long-term memory and helps you to find relationships among ideas.

PROCESSING INFORMATION

A concept map is based on how you process or remember information. Look at this list of words. Read it over slowly for about 20 seconds, and then cover up the words. Recall as many as you can.

black	sweater	brown	shirt
cinnamon	dove	gloves	green
canary	garlic	parrot	pepper

Look at this second list of words and again memorize as many as you can in 20 seconds:

vanilla	yellow	horse	desk
chocolate	red	camel	table
strawberry	green	elephant	chair

Which list was easier to remember? The second list was easier to remember because the words are grouped. The groupings or categories linked the words together and helped you remember them. For example, the category *flavors* helped you remember *vanilla, chocolate,* and *strawberry*. Grouping words also reduces how much information you must memorize. For example, by using what's in your long-term memory and recognizing four groups in the list, you could more easily memorize twelve concepts.

You can also look at groups of terms and give them a name that represents their main idea. For example: math, science, English, history, and art are all *school subjects*. Try to find the main idea for these terms:

Canada, Egypt, Mexico, USA are _____

banjo, guitar, violin, piano, and drum are _____

CONCEPT MAPPING

Concept mapping helps you figure out the main ideas in a piece of reading material. A concept map can also help you understand that ideas have meanings because they are connected to other ideas. For example, when you define a pencil as a writing utensil, you have linked the idea or concept of a *pencil* to the ideas of *writing* and *utensil*. Look at the following words:

| car | tree | raining | thundering |
| dog | cloud | playing | thinking |

All of these words are concepts because they cause a picture to form in your mind. Are the following words concept words?

| are | when | where | then |
| the | with | is | to |

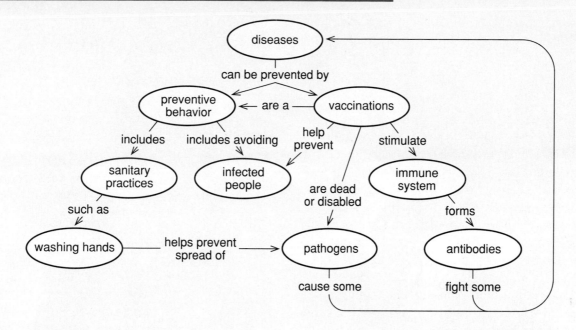

No. These are linkage words. They connect, or link, concept words together. In a concept map, words that are concepts go in circles or boxes, and words that are linking the concepts go on a line connecting the circles or boxes.

How is a concept map different from note-taking or making an outline? If you outlined page 547 it might look like this:

Fighting Diseases—Preventive Behavior

I. Avoiding sources of pathogens
  A. Avoiding infected people
  B. Sanitary practices (example: wash hands)
II. Vaccinations
  A. Are doses of dead or disabled pathogens
  B. Stimulate immune system to form antibodies
  C. Help your body respond to invasion to avoid infection

Now look back at page 547. Would you want to reread that page over again, trying to learn all of that information for a test? Would you prefer the slightly shorter outline? Or would you rather study a concept map like the one above, especially if you had made it yourself? If you made the map, your long-term memory would already know parts of that map. Reviewing the map would make studying easier.

HOW TO MAKE A CONCEPT MAP

• *First, identify the main concepts by writing them in a list. Then put each separate concept from your list on a small piece of paper. You* will not have to use this paper technique once you make a few maps, but it is helpful at first.

The next step is to put the concepts in order of most general to most specific. Examples are most specific and will go at the bottom.

• *Now begin to rearrange the pieces of paper on a table or desk top. Start with the most general main idea.* If that main idea can be broken down into two or more equal concepts, place those concepts on the same line. Continue to do this until all the concepts have been laid out.

• *Use lines to connect the concepts. Write a statement on the line that tells how the concepts are connected.* Do this for all the lines connecting the concepts.

• *Do not expect your map to be exactly like anyone else's map.* Everyone thinks a little differently and will see different relationships between certain concepts. Practice is the key to good concept mapping. Here are some points to remember as you get started:

1. A concept map does not have to be symmetrical. It can be lopsided and have more concepts on the right side than on the left.
2. Remember that a concept map is a shortcut for representing information. Do not add anything but concepts and links.
3. There is no perfect or single correct concept map for a set of concepts. Errors in a concept map occur only if the links between concepts are incorrect.

Making Healthy Choices

Chapter 1
Wellness: A Way of Life

Chapter 2
Taking Care of Yourself

Why is wellness considered to be a way of life?

Why is consumer awareness especially important for teenagers?

Do you do anything that might put your health at risk?

CHAPTER 1

Wellness: A Way of Life

"If you can imagine it, you can achieve it. If you can dream it, you can become it."

William Arthur Ward

BACKGROUND

William Arthur Ward was born in Louisiana in the early 1900s. He has written several books and materials on philosophical thought. What is philosophy?

Striving to reach your own personal best is a lifelong pursuit. It involves sorting out values and making them work in a world that is full of variety, wonder, and challenges. Reaching your personal best depends a great deal on the choices that you make.

Sometimes it is difficult to identify the right choices. The answer lies in listening very closely to your own body, mind, and emotions. By being aware, and by learning as much as you can about what makes your whole self work and thrive, you can strengthen your chances for a long, healthy, and ultimately happy life.

As you go through life, you will experience changes that will cause you to reevaluate what is best for you. It is important to remember that no one else can make these important choices and decisions for you. You have infinite power over your own health and your own life. Listen carefully to yourself. Because if you can imagine what you want to be, you can indeed become who you want to be.

Create your own Wellness Journal. Use it at the beginning and the end of each chapter to assess your commitment to a healthy life and to set goals for improvement. Number the first page of your Wellness Journal from 1–12. Respond to the following statements by writing *yes* or *no*.

1. I eat a balanced and healthy diet.

2. I usually get between 7–8 hours of sleep a night.

3. I participate in regular exercise at least three times a week.

4. I have people in my life with whom I feel comfortable sharing my emotions.

5. I accept my feelings as part of who I am, and I am not overwhelmed by my emotions.

6. I always use a seat belt.

7. I never ride in a car with anyone who has been drinking alcohol or using illegal drugs.

8. I take time to be alone when I need to be alone.

9. I avoid situations that put my health at risk.

10. I am happy with my relationships with others.

11. I am not afraid to say no to my friends when they are engaging in activities that might affect my health.

12. I am able to recognize false promises made by advertisers.

Review your responses and consider your strengths and weaknesses. Save your checklist for a follow-up activity at the end of the chapter.

HEALTH TODAY

What comes to your mind when you hear the word *health?* Do you think of the way a person looks? Or maybe you think about the way a person acts. Most people would probably agree that **health** is a state of well-being. However, what defines a person's state of well-being has changed considerably over the years.

HEALTH: PAST AND PRESENT

In the past, a healthy person was someone who was considered to be free of disease or illness. In the early 1900s, the leading causes of death were infectious diseases caused by things such as bacteria and viruses. If you had lived then, your chance of dying from pneumonia would have been three times greater than your chance of dying from cancer. Diseases such as pneumonia, influenza, and tuberculosis served as a constant threat to people of all ages. Therefore, it is not surprising that in the early 1900s, the emphasis of health was on freedom from illness.

MEDICAL ADVANCES   Over the years, medical science began to unfold the mysteries of life-threatening infectious diseases to identify their causes. Through improved working and living conditions and new medicines, most of the diseases eventually were brought under control. As a result, many of the diseases that were common 70 to 100 years ago now can be prevented or cured and, in some cases, are nonexistent.

MAIN IDEAS

CONCEPTS

✔ The definition of health has changed considerably over the years.

✔ Wellness is a state of physical, intellectual, emotional, and social well-being.

✔ Advances in medical care and an approach to life that focuses on prevention have helped to increase the average life span of people.

✔ There are four major factors that determine one's health.

VOCABULARY

health	heredity
wellness	gender
life expectancy	

Figure 1-1   Why might the leading causes of death differ across age groups?

THE TEN LEADING CAUSES OF DEATH, 1900 AND TODAY

1900	Today		
All Ages	**All Ages**	**Children Ages 1–14**	**Youth Ages 15–24**
Pneumonia/Flu	Heart Diseases	Accidents	Accidents
Tuberculosis	Cancer	Cancer	Homicide
Inflammations of the Digestive Tract	Stroke	Homicide	Suicide
Heart Diseases	Accidents	Heart Diseases	Cancer
Stroke	Lung Diseases	HIV Infection	Heart Diseases
Kidney Diseases	Pneumonia/Influenza	Pneumonia/Influenza	HIV Infection
Accidents	Diabetes Mellitus	Suicide	Pneumonia/Influenza
Cancer	Suicide	Lung Diseases	Lung Diseases
Childhood Diseases	Infectious Diseases	Meningitis	Stroke
Diphtheria	Liver Diseases	Birth Defects	Birth Defects

SOURCE: National Center for Health Statistics

Today, poor health is highly related to the way we live. With most infectious diseases under control, diseases that can be directly linked to life-style are now among the leading causes of death. These diseases are shown in Figure 1-1. Many of these diseases can be avoided. Therefore, the health focus of today is on **wellness** —a positive, whole-health approach that includes your physical, intellectual, social, and emotional well-being. Wellness means striving to live your life to its fullest potential and acting in healthy ways to prevent, or decrease the chances for, unnecessary illness.

LONGEVITY   The practice of preventive behavior and advances in medical technology and living conditions enable you to enjoy a better and longer life. Controlling diseases has greatly increased the life expectancy of people around the world. **Life expectancy** is the measure of the average number of years that a group of people may expect to live. If you had been born in the United States in 1900, your life expectancy would have been only 47 years. Today you can expect to live for 75 years, as long as you maintain good health. Some researchers predict that through continued medical advances and the practice of preventive behaviors, the average life span of your children and grandchildren may approach 85 years.

A "can do" attitude about life can positively affect your overall health. What do you think it means when a person has a "can do" attitude?

WHAT DETERMINES HEALTH?

The United States Centers for Disease Control (CDC) have identified four major factors that determine your health. They are personal health behavior, your physical environment, hereditary influences, and the quality of health-care services that are available to you. Figure 1-2 shows the estimated percentage that each of these factors contributes to the leading causes of death.

HEALTH BEHAVIOR   Personal health behaviors contribute to over 50 percent of all major causes of death. Health behavior refers to patterns of behavior that affect your health now and as you get older. Therefore, your personal life-style greatly affects the quality of your health. Over the years, research has identified a variety of behaviors that promote good health and tend to increase the average length of life. These behaviors include:

- Sleeping 7 to 8 hours daily
- Eating breakfast daily
- Rarely eating between meals
- Maintaining a healthy weight
- Reducing fat and salt in meals
- Getting regular physical exercise
- Avoiding the use of tobacco and alcohol
- Appropriately using only legal medications

■ HEALTH FACTORS AND DEATH

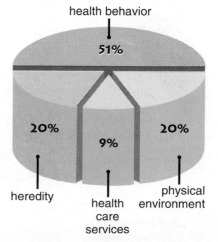

Source: Centers for Disease Control

Figure 1-2   Which of the four health factors has the greatest impact on death rates in the United States?

For some people, the wide-open spaces on a farm provide a relaxing environment.

PHYSICAL ENVIRONMENT Your physical environment is your surroundings—any place in which you live, work, and play. The conditions of your physical environment can directly affect your health. The quality of air both inside and outside may influence your chances of developing lung disorders. Too much noise, crowded living places, and infected food or water are other factors in the environment that can affect your health.

HEREDITY Sometimes your ability to prevent diseases may be limited by hereditary factors. **Heredity** [*huh RED ut ee*] is the biological passing of physical traits from parents to their children. If several members of your family have died prematurely of heart disease, you may be at a higher risk of heart disease than someone whose family members have been free of heart disease. However, hereditary effects on your health often can be reduced by choosing responsible health behaviors. For example, eating properly, exercising regularly, and controlling your weight are steps you can take to reduce the chances for developing heart disease.

MAKING A DIFFERENCE

CAREERS HEALTH

Health Educator

Barbara Vincent helps children and teenagers stay healthy. She teaches them about healthy habits and attitudes, and about practicing preventive medicine. Through her teaching, she makes them aware of dangerous health risks.

Vincent is a health educator. She works with school children and their parents, leading workshops, advising them on current health issues, and involving the community in problems and issues that involve her school district.

Health educators can be found in many settings. They practice in schools, at colleges, in medical settings, at local, state, and federal agencies, in health organizations, and in businesses.

Health educators must complete professional studies in health education. More than 250 colleges and universities in the United States offer these degrees. Training involves courses in biological and social sciences, psychology, and education, with an emphasis on health. The number of people getting degrees in health education is growing rapidly.

Once settled in a practice, a health educator's duties vary with the needs of the setting. In a medical setting such as a hospital, nursing home, or clinic, a health educator works with patients and families to implement treatment and answer questions about their health. In a community setting, such as an agency like the Department of Social Services, a health educator works with department members to educate them about current health issues or regulations. He or she may also work with subscribing families to inform them about proper health care. In a business setting, health educators may oversee stop-smoking, weight-management, and stress-reduction workshops.

The rewards of being a health educator are many. Professional practice is as varied as the individuals with which a health educator works. Dedication to good health

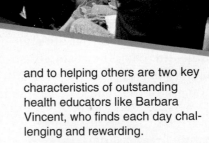

and to helping others are two key characteristics of outstanding health educators like Barbara Vincent, who finds each day challenging and rewarding.

1. Why is there a growing demand for health educators throughout the country?

2. Why does being a health educator require strong leadership skills and good personal health habits?

HEALTH-CARE SERVICES The quality of the health care you have available to you also helps determine the quality of your general health. Regular medical and dental care can help to prevent many health problems. Preventing an illness usually is easier than curing an illness.

STRIVING FOR PERSONAL WELLNESS

As you have read, the concept of health has changed a great deal over the years. Today more and more people are becoming aware that the major factors that determine health are personal choices. The key to health lies in your ability to achieve balance in your life. Reaching a point of balance involves understanding four dimensions of wellness that affect your health.

- *Physical wellness* refers to the health of your body. Physical wellness is achieved through exercise, proper nutrition, preventive care, and avoidance of abusive substances.

- *Intellectual wellness* encourages you to continue gathering knowledge through stimulating learning experiences. As you challenge your mind, you improve your mental potential and ability. Good intellectual health helps you to solve problems.

- *Emotional wellness* is achieved through awareness and acceptance of your feelings and self-image. An emotionally well person is able to demonstrate self-expression, self-control, self-evaluation, and enthusiasm for life.

- *Social wellness* refers to relationships with others. It involves your ability to make friends, to cooperate with others, and to be a productive member of a community and society.

The strength within and balance among all of these dimensions determines the strength of your well-being. To understand this idea, think of wellness as a wheel with four equal sections that contribute to the roundness of the wheel. When all of the dimensions of the wheel are equal or close to equal, a person will roll smoothly through life. When the dimensions of wellness are in a reasonable balance, a healthy life is more possible than when the dimensions are out of balance.

HEALTH IN THE YEAR 2000

Achieving personal wellness should be everyone's goal. However, access to the information and resources that help a person achieve wellness is not always easy to obtain. Concern has grown over the general well-being of our nation as a whole. In response to this concern, health officials have developed health-related goals for the nation to reach by the year 2000. The published document, entitled *Healthy People 2000,* includes three major goals.

- Increase the span of a healthy life for Americans

- Reduce the health [differences] among Americans

Figure 1-3 *Wellness does not mean that you have to be the best. It means that you strive for your personal best and for balance. What happens when the dimensions of wellness are out of balance?*

- Achieve better access to preventive health services for all Americans

    from *Healthy People 2000: National Health Promotion and Disease Prevention Objectives*

To reach these three broad goals, specific objectives in 22 areas related to health were also established. The objectives address overall health concerns, as well as those related to age, income, race, and **gender** [*JEN dur*]—the classification that refers to whether you are male or female.

Throughout this book are references to some of these objectives. These references indicate that the information you are reading can help you improve your own health, which also can help improve the overall health of the nation. As you read each objective, ask yourself what you can do to help meet the goal in order to make the United States a healthier nation by the year 2000.

THE SOCIOLOGY OF HEALTH

For some Americans, obtaining good health is a greater challenge than it is for others. National health statistics indicate that health care is closely related to socioeconomic status, or the amount of money a family or individual earns. In other words, the rich are likely to be healthier than the poor.

The poor often lack adequate health insurance. Without the benefit of insurance, health care is expensive. For the poor, feeding their families and providing adequate housing may be greater priorities than health care. For many, taking time off from work to visit a doctor or clinic can be costly or threatening to job security. For others, transportation to a health-care facility may be difficult to arrange.

The health crisis in America is an issue that concerns all people. Everyone must work hard to change what has become a pattern of poor health among low-income citizens.

SUMMARY

Health is the state of your well-being that includes how you feel physically, intellectually, emotionally, and socially. Healthy people take an active role in determining their health status. Being aware of the factors that influence health will help you make decisions that can lead to balance in your life. Practicing preventive behaviors now will help the nation reach its goal of better health for all Americans by the year 2000.

LESSON 1.1 **USING WHAT YOU HAVE LEARNED**

REVIEW

1. How has the definition of *health* changed from 1900 to now?
2. List the four major factors that determine health.
3. Give three examples of positive health behaviors.

THINK CRITICALLY

4. The intent of *Healthy People 2000* is to encourage people to practice preventive behavior in 22 different areas. How does this intent support the philosophy of wellness?
5. Why might it be difficult for a person to be truly healthy if he or she does not have balance in his or her life?

APPLY IT TO YOURSELF

6. Your life expectancy is greatly affected by your life-style. What are some choices that you might be able to make now that can improve your chances for a long, healthy life?

MAKING HEALTHY CHOICES

As you learned in Lesson 1, wellness is a state of physical, intellectual, emotional, and social well-being. It is a way of life that requires you to take a positive and active role in your own health. Some of the factors that determine health may be beyond your control. Your heredity and at times your physical environment are not things you can change. However, there are many factors that affect your health that you can control. You can take responsibility for making appropriate choices about your health behavior. This responsibility involves weighing the risks connected to the decisions you make.

UNDERSTANDING RISKS

Risk can be defined as the degree of danger that goes along with a situation. All risks have possible negative outcomes. However, many risks also have positive outcomes and can lead to personal growth. For example, suppose that you want to learn how to ski. You may have some concern about the possibility of injury while learning to ski. However, the sense of enjoyment that comes from being able to ski may be worth the risk of injury. By being in good physical condition, you can reduce the risk of injury. The feeling of accomplishment from learning a new skill and defeating a fear can increase your confidence. The increased confidence will help you face new challenges.

Health risks are based on what has happened to a number of people in the recent past. **Epidemiology** [ep uh dee mee AHL uh jee] is the study of factors that cause illnesses in an effort to determine their chances of occurring. Knowing this information helps scientists identify how illnesses can be prevented. This information also can help you make healthy decisions about your own behavior. For example, research indicates that 80 percent of all cancers are related or partly related to things over which you have some control. Therefore, you can reduce your risk of developing cancer by practicing healthy behaviors. These include such things as eating a balanced diet that includes fiber and not smoking.

RESPONSIBILITY TO SELF To reduce your risk of illness, disease, or accident, you first need to assess the way you live. Based on your daily living habits or behaviors, what are your chances for health problems?

MAIN IDEAS

CONCEPTS

✔ Risky behavior can directly affect your health.

✔ The Wellness Continuum illustrates the relationship between health and risk behaviors.

✔ A system for making decisions can help you handle times of conflict.

VOCABULARY

risk	chronic
epidemiology	values
evaluate	

Not everyone agrees about what is considered risky behavior. It is important to recognize the risks that will help you grow.

As Velina and her friends walked out of the pizza house, they passed a bakery with monster chocolate chip cookies in the window. Although her friends all chose to get some cookies, Velina fought the temptation. She had made a very important decision a while back. Her family had a history of diabetes—a serious condition where the body cannot use the sugar in the blood properly. Velina recently had learned that the type of diabetes in her family can be brought on by being overweight. Because she had a higher than normal risk of developing diabetes, Velina decided she would work hard at maintaining a healthy weight. Her efforts included cutting back on the amount of food that she ate. Limiting what she ate wasn't always easy. However, Velina knew that the decisions she made now would help her in the future.

Velina evaluated the risk involved and acted on it. To **evaluate** means to consider all of the information that is available to you. In deciding to change her eating habits, Velina acted on her evaluation in order to reduce her personal health risk.

Another way to reduce risks is to learn to identify and avoid high-risk situations. One example of avoiding a high-risk situation is choosing not to ride in a car driven by someone who has been drinking—when the risk of having an accident increases.

RESPONSIBILITY TO OTHERS   Just as you act to reduce health risks to yourself, you can also act to reduce health risks to others. You should be aware of how your behaviors may harm other people. For example, if you have a sore throat or cold that can spread to others easily, it is your responsibility to avoid contact with others until the danger of spreading your illness is no longer possible.

THE WELLNESS CONTINUUM   Not all risks are life-threatening, but they may prevent you from living to your full potential. Just as there are degrees of risk, there also are degrees of health. The relationship between health and risk is shown on the Wellness Continuum [*kun TIN yuh wum*] in Figure 1-4. As you progress toward the right end of the continuum, you reduce your health

Figure 1-4   Practicing disease prevention brings health to the neutral zone. Taking an active role in promoting health leads to wellness. Where would you place yourself on the continuum?

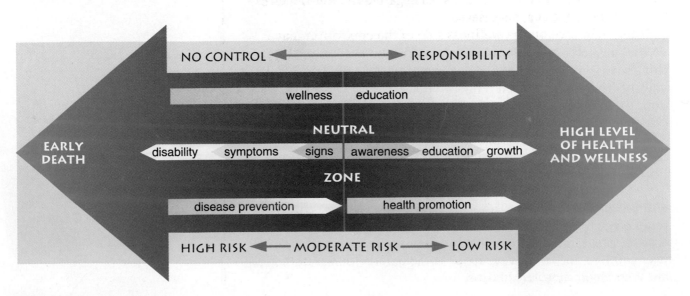

THE DECISION-MAKING MODEL

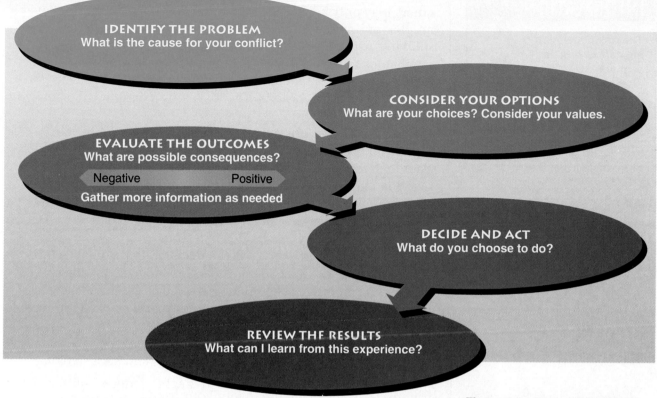

IDENTIFY THE PROBLEM
What is the cause for your conflict?

CONSIDER YOUR OPTIONS
What are your choices? Consider your values.

EVALUATE THE OUTCOMES
What are possible consequences?

Negative   Positive

Gather more information as needed

DECIDE AND ACT
What do you choose to do?

REVIEW THE RESULTS
What can I learn from this experience?

Figure 1-5 *Every day of your life you make decisions. Making good decisions requires a method and practice.*

risks. At the same time, you move in the direction of a higher level of physical, intellectual, social, and emotional health. The left end of the continuum represents a move toward high-risk behaviors and possible early death.

The area in the middle of the continuum is called the neutral zone. People in this area are not ill, but they are not especially well either. They may appear to be fine and yet never seem to have much energy. Although the health risks at the middle of the Wellness Continuum are not immediately dangerous, they are **chronic** [*KRAHN ik*], or long-lasting. Disorders that result from chronic health behaviors can be just as negative in later life as disorders caused by a serious disease.

People who live on the wellness side of the continuum have learned to make the most of their strengths and accept any limitations. They tend to feel good about themselves and care about their health. The reward for high-level wellness is the ability to live at your full potential.

MAKING DECISIONS

Avoiding risky behavior requires that you make decisions. Decision making is not something that is new. You make hundreds of decisions every day. Most of the decisions you make are simple and come naturally. For example, when you woke up this morning, you made a decision to get out of bed. When you left your room, unconsciously you made the decision whether or not to follow your usual morning routine.

Many decisions you are faced with making require more thought and consideration. Some may have life-threatening consequences; others may only appear to at the time. You may feel conflict over a number of issues. Common issues for many young people include smoking, drinking, relationships, and dating, to name a few. It often helps to have a system for carefully evaluating situations. Figure 1-5 shows a model for decision making that can help you make wise health decisions. The following example will show you how the model works.

Imagine that you are getting together with a group of your friends on Friday night. Several of these friends smoke cigarettes. You do not smoke, but lately you have been tempted to try smoking. You feel a great deal of pressure to join in with your friends. Your mother smokes, but your father does not. However, both have made it known that they do not want you to smoke.

IDENTIFY THE PROBLEM   What is the decision that you have to make? What is the cause for your conflict? Identifying the specific problem is important. The problem, or the conflict you face, is whether or not to join in with your friends and smoke cigarettes.

CONSIDER YOUR OPTIONS   What are your options? You have many options. You can go along with your friends and start smoking. You can avoid the conflict by breaking away from this group of friends. Or you can choose to join your friends but still avoid smoking. You are torn by a bond with your friends, respect for your parents, and your own value system. **Values** are beliefs and standards that you feel are important. Your values are based on a combination of what your parents have taught you, what society considers to be right, and on your own evaluation of what is right and wrong. In this situation, as you consider your options, it is important that you consider your values about smoking cigarettes.

EVALUATE THE OUTCOMES   Think about all of the potential positive and negative outcomes for each option. Consider the outcomes if you decide to smoke. You would be in danger of violating your parents' trust. You would be making yourself vulnerable to the potential dangers of smoking. You also may feel that you would gain the approval of your friends.

Many of the decisions you have to make revolve around your friends and their acceptance of you.

Now consider the outcomes if you choose not to smoke. You would feel good that you didn't deceive your parents. You would be avoiding some potential health risks that come from smoking. You would avoid the feelings of guilt. You also may feel left out of sharing something with your friends.

You may decide that you need more information before you can make a firm decision. You could go to the library to read information about the effects of smoking on health. You can also discuss your conflict with people you respect.

DECIDE AND ACT   Once you determine which option will be best for you, a decision can be made. If you feel the negative effects of smoking are stronger than the benefits, you will decide not to smoke. You could go out with your friends and firmly state that you choose not to smoke. Or you may choose to find another group of people to do things with.

Making the right decisions about your health can give you a sense of accomplishment, enhance your self-esteem, and develop your confidence.

REVIEW YOUR DECISION   Once you have acted, it is important to think about the results of your decision. Taking this last step in the model may either confirm your original decision or cause you to revise your thinking. There are times when you will make a decision that you later regret or that you realize was the wrong decision. It is important to remember in such cases that few decisions are final. Had you decided to smoke with your friends, only to regret the decision afterward, you could now make the decision to change your behavior and quit smoking.

You can use this model to look closely at any health decision. Evaluating all of the possible outcomes will help you see all sides of even very difficult problems. By evaluating the outcomes before you act, you can learn to make decisions that will help you lead a full and healthy life. On the following pages, you will find the Personal Health Inventory. Your results on the inventory may help you identify some areas of your behavior that may be a problem for you. Take the Personal Health Inventory now and again when you finish the course. It will show you if what you have learned about health and wellness is helping you make healthy choices.

LESSON 1.2 **USING WHAT YOU HAVE LEARNED**

REVIEW

1. What can you do to reduce a health risk?
2. What is the relationship between risk behavior and wellness?

THINK CRITICALLY

3. A person's values should always be considered when making decisions. What could happen if a person is faced with a difficult decision and fails to consider his or her values?
4. Epidemiologists identify the rates of occurrence for illnesses. Why is this type of information helpful to people?

APPLY IT TO YOURSELF

5. Identify where you would place yourself on the Wellness Continuum and explain your reasons for the placement.

SUMMARY

Your health depends a great deal on the decisions you make about risks in your life. Most risks are minor and don't have an immediate impact on you. Other risks may be more life-threatening. Learning how to make the right decisions about your health requires that you understand the elements of decision making. Making good health decisions and forming good lifelong health habits now will help you maintain a high level of wellness throughout life.

PERSONAL HEALTH INVENTORY

On a separate sheet of paper, or in your Wellness Journal, write the numbers from 1 to 47. For the first section on heredity, write *yes* or *no* for each disorder.

HEREDITY

One of my close relatives has had:

1. heart disease	5. glaucoma	9. overweight
2. high blood pressure	6. asthma	10. clinical depression
3. cancer	7. alcoholism	
4. diabetes	8. schizophrenia	

For the remainder of the inventory, write *usually* (or *always*), *sometimes*, or *rarely* for each statement. Respond to each statement with the word that best describes your typical behavior, not what you think you should do.

MENTAL HEALTH

11. I allow myself to cry.

12. I express feelings such as love, fear, and anger constructively.

13. I have friends or relatives with whom I discuss problems.

14. I keep anxiety from interfering with my activities at school or at home.

15. I do not let stress build up and give me headaches or an upset stomach.

16. I have hobbies that help me get away from daily tasks.

NUTRITION

17. I eat a wide variety of foods, including breads and cereals, fruits and vegetables, meat and milk.

18. I avoid foods high in refined sugar.

19. I avoid adding salt to my food.

20. I avoid eating foods that are high in fat.

21. I eat breakfast.

22. I select and eat only healthy snacks.

PHYSICAL FITNESS

23. I do vigorous exercise such as running, swimming, brisk walking, or biking at least 3 times a week.

24. I exercise to build muscle strength and endurance at least 3 times a week.

25. I stretch to build flexibility.

26. I warm up and cool down when I exercise.

27. I enjoy some exercises or strenuous sports that I can continue with throughout my life.

28. I maintain a healthy level of body fat, neither too much nor too little.

29. I get 7 to 9 hours of sleep each night.

PERSONAL AND HEALTH CARE

30. I brush and floss my teeth daily.

31. I always use sunscreen when I am out in the sun for extended periods of time.

32. I have my teeth checked twice a year.

33. I see my family doctor every two years for a complete checkup.

34. When under medical treatment, I follow my doctor's instructions about activities and using medications.

35. I avoid using nonprescription drugs, including tobacco and alcohol.

36. I have my blood pressure checked once a year.

37. I know the seven warning signs of cancer.

38. I practice monthly self-examinations for cancer (breast exam for girls; testicle exam for boys).

PUBLIC HEALTH

39. I walk, bike, or use public transportation whenever possible.

40. I recycle such items as cans, paper, glass, clothes, and books.

41. I avoid polluting the air with unnecessary smoke.

SAFETY

42. I use safety belts when driving or riding in a car.

43. I always wear a helmet when riding a bike.

44. I follow water safety procedures and can save myself or others from drowning.

45. I use safety precautions when working with power tools, firearms, and other dangerous equipment.

46. My home has safety features such as smoke detectors, outlet caps, and nonskid rugs.

47. I know first aid methods to help others in an emergency.

SCORING

1. Questions 1–10: Give yourself 1 point for each question you answered *yes,* 5 points for each question you answered *no.* Questions 11–47: Give yourself 5 points for each question you answered *usually* (or *always*), 3 points for each *sometimes,* and 1 point for each *rarely.*

2. Add up all your points. The total is your inventory score.

3. Your score relates to the Wellness Continuum as follows.

175 or higher   You are at low risk. You are practicing many good health behaviors.

80 to 174   You are in the neutral zone. You may not be ill, but you are at risk for long-term health problems. You are not getting everything you could out of life.

79 or lower   You are at high risk. In what sections did you answer *rarely* and *sometimes*? Pinpoint areas that need your attention, and find ways to lower your risk.

No matter what your score, you can make changes to increase your health. As you read this book, look for ways in which you can change your behavior to lower your health risks and improve your level of wellness. Now is the time to develop positive health habits.

ACCEPTING RESPONSIBILITY

The information in this book can help you not only to increase your awareness about health, it also can help you plan ways to make healthy living an important part of your daily life. Making good grades on your health knowledge exams does not guarantee you good health. Health knowledge will benefit you only if you use it to make informed choices about your health. Good health is the result of caring enough about yourself to identify and change behaviors that may be harmful to your health.

CHANGING YOUR BEHAVIOR

Making changes in your life is never easy. Changing your health behaviors can be especially difficult because they often are learned behaviors that developed over a long period of time. There are three main factors that are necessary to make a change in your personal behavior.

- *Recognition*   Before any change in behavior can begin to take place, you have to be aware of the need for the change. However, recognition alone often is not enough to make you change. For example, a person may be aware that a life-style that includes little or no physical activity can cause many health-related problems. Yet this information may not greatly affect his or her exercise habits.

- *Motivation*   Recognizing the need for change is useless unless you want to change. People are motivated to change by several factors, including desire or fear. For example, if you cut fat from your diet because you want to have more energy and maintain a healthy weight, you are motivated by desire. However, if the reason for your change in diet is to avoid a heart attack and early death, you are motivated by fear. Unfortunately, even motivation is not always enough to keep you from practicing risky behaviors.

- *Commitment*   True change depends on how committed you are to making the change. Success depends on realizing who is really in control—you.

Change is an ongoing process in life. Expecting any change to happen overnight is unrealistic. Change takes time and patience. Being healthy means being in control and actively managing your everyday life. As you make changes in your health behavior, it is important to remember that there will be times when you stumble. Your choices may not always be the right ones at the time. You should not expect perfection, nor can you expect to achieve all your health goals. However, the sense of accomplishment you can realize from making a healthy change in your life can affect you in other ways as well.

MAIN IDEAS

CONCEPTS
✔ Changing any behavior requires recognition, motivation, and commitment.
✔ Self-esteem and a realistic self-concept are important factors in determining your mental well-being.
✔ The teenage years are times when a person's values are shaped and challenged.

VOCABULARY

self-esteem   self-concept
peers

Change takes recognition, motivation, and commitment.

A SEVEN-STEP PLAN TO CHANGE

A simple system often can help in changing a behavior. Avoid skipping steps and remember to stick with the system.

1. Identify one target behavior. Concentrating on one behavior increases your chances of success.

2. Identify the circumstances of the behavior. How were you feeling? When is it more likely to occur?

3. Analyze the information for patterns.

4. Set specific goals.

5. Develop a plan of action.

6. Record your progress.

7. Forgive yourself when you slip. Identify what caused you to slip and decide what you will do the next time.

SELF-ESTEEM

Caring about yourself enough to want to be the best you can will help you change any harmful behavior. How you feel about yourself is known as your **self-esteem**. It refers to the confidence, pride, and respect that you have for yourself. People with good self-esteem feel comfortable in social situations. They relate well with others. People with good self-esteem make the most of what they have. They seize opportunities to grow and use their skills to fulfill their goals. They approach each day with enthusiasm.

People with good self-esteem, however, do not see themselves as perfect. They are aware of their weaknesses and limitations, but they build on their strengths. Having good self-esteem helps a person handle setbacks and accept responsibility for mistakes as well as successes.

Tony sat on the back porch thinking about that day in school. "What a disaster!" he thought. Tony had to introduce a guest speaker for an all-school assembly. He hadn't really prepared what he would say, and when his time came to speak, Tony's mind went blank. He couldn't even remember the speaker's name. "I'm so embarrassed," Tony thought.

At first, Tony thought about skipping school the next day to avoid facing other students. But he knew that wouldn't do any good. He'd have to face the music sooner or later. "It's no big deal," he said. "I made a mistake. It's not as though no one will ever speak to me again. I'll live through it." Tony also made a promise to himself that he would never be unprepared again.

You are at an age when you are developing and changing in every dimension of wellness. You are becoming more independent and you are beginning to shape your values. You also are at an age when you begin to accept responsibility for your actions. Nobody else can make your everyday decisions. Your health is not determined by teachers or parents. It is heavily influenced by your

STRATEGIES FOR LIVING

Steps for improving your self-esteem.

1. Learn to accept yourself for who you are.

2. Don't be too harsh on yourself.

3. Be open to new experiences.

4. Encourage yourself to learn something new.

5. Do something positive for someone else.

6. Focus on being positive.

7. Be rational and realistic with yourself.

8. Remind yourself of your personal strengths.

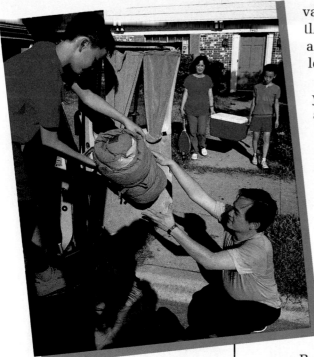

Active involvement with family members can affect the development of self-esteem and self-concept.

values and the choices you make. Tony was able to accept that his decision not to prepare for the assembly had been a bad one. He was willing to accept the consequences and learn from his mistake. Tony had accepted responsibility.

This is also a time in your life when being accepted by your **peers** is important. Your peers are other people who are like you in age, status, or interests. We all tend to select friends with similar values. At times, your values may be tested or questioned by others. For example, you may have to decide whether or not to defend a friend who is involved in a violent situation. Establishing your own values for good health will make it easier for you to act responsibly in a situation where your values are being tested. Having a level of self-esteem that assists you in being comfortable and confident will ensure that you make decisions that will be favorable rather than harmful to your health.

SELF-CONCEPT

People who believe in the importance of practicing good health behaviors are secure in holding to their own values. They have a good self-concept. Your **self-concept** is your view of yourself and your role in life. If you have a good self-concept, you are aware of who you are and what you believe. You also have a realistic picture of both your strengths and your weaknesses. Recall that awareness is the first step toward good health in the Wellness Continuum. You need to have a realistic view of yourself and your world in order to make good health decisions. Accepting yourself and knowing your strengths and weaknesses are vital for the achievement of wellness.

LESSON 1.3 USING WHAT YOU HAVE LEARNED

REVIEW

1. Why is commitment important to a person when making behavior changes?
2. What is meant by a realistic self-concept?
3. Compare and contrast self-esteem and self-concept.

THINK CRITICALLY

4. Parents and guardians are an important influence on the development of a child's values. How do parents and guardians pass values on to children?
5. Self-esteem and self-concept are closely related to making changes in behavior. How does each help motivate a person to make changes? How can making changes have a positive effect on a person's self-esteem and self-concept?

APPLY IT TO YOURSELF

6. Identify two personal health behaviors that you feel may need to be changed. How do these behaviors affect your ability to make decisions that influence your life-style?

SUMMARY

Being well-informed about health is the basis for making sound health decisions. How you feel about yourself, how you see yourself, and your efforts to maintain a healthy life-style provide the basis for your wellness. However, this means having goals that are realistic for you. It means being committed to maintaining healthy behaviors that are reasonable for you. A person with a realistic self-concept is well aware of personal health behaviors that can be improved. A healthy person is committed to maintaining or improving his or her health behaviors.

YOUR ROLE AS A CONSUMER

Many important decisions you make involve the purchasing of products and services that can affect your health. **Services** are the skills and talents of a person that have value. For example, your doctor performs a highly-skilled service for which you pay a certain fee. Many products and services have been developed specifically for teenagers. Therefore, you need to be a wise consumer. **Consumer health** focuses on helping you make responsible decisions about products and services that can affect your health. A key step in becoming a wise consumer is understanding what influences your consumer decisions.

WHAT INFLUENCES YOUR DECISIONS?

Each time you purchase a product or a service, you should be making an informed purchase. That is, your purchase should be based upon the identification of a true need and the collection of complete information about all available products that could meet your need. However, decisions are not always made in such a manner. Consider the last piece of clothing that you purchased. What factors influenced your decision? Is it something everyone else wears? All purchases you make are based on several factors.

NEED   When the soles of your shoes are completely worn out, you have a definite need to buy new shoes. However, people's needs vary. What you may consider to be a worn-out pair of shoes may be considered almost new to your parents. Your need may be based on style, while your parents may be thinking of practicality.

PRICE   The price of a product or service depends on several things. Name-brand items are usually more expensive than a comparable store-brand item. This does not mean that the name-brand product is better. Its price usually includes the cost for advertising the product. The price of a particular service can be influenced by the degree of skill that is required to perform the service. For example, doctors perform services that require advanced education and a great deal of skill. The fees you pay to a doctor reflect the need for the doctor's expertise.

CONVENIENCE   In the past twenty years, one of the fastest-growing areas in the market has been the service industry. This growth has tapped into peoples' needs for their lives to be made easier. Buying a take-out pizza may be much more convenient than buying all of the ingredients and making the pizza. Buying because of convenience can be helpful, but it also can be expensive.

Many of your purchases can affect your self-esteem in subtle ways. A desire to "fit in" sometimes can create a false need for a product.

COMMON ADVERTISING TECHNIQUES

Techniques	Description
Pleasure Appeal	This technique uses people, places, or things to associate a happy feeling with a product.
Omission	The advertisement only identifies the best things about the product. It omits information.
Snob Appeal	The product is associated with success.
Bandwagon	Advertisers imply that everyone is using the product.
Repetition	Repeating words or phrases in a commercial keeps the product on people's minds.
Individualism	The message of the ad is that using the product provides the user with a sense of uniqueness.
Romance Appeal	The ads suggest that the product will bring love and romance into a person's life.
Bait-and-Switch	A promotional ad brings the consumer into the store with the intent of getting the person to buy more expensive products.

Figure 1-6 Advertisers use many methods to create a need in consumers. Can you think of an example of each of the techniques listed?

QUALITY   Sometimes a person is willing to purchase a product that may not be made as well as another product and may be less expensive as a result. However, a higher price does not mean that a product is necessarily of better quality than a less expensive product. Only careful examination of the product or service will determine its quality.

DESIRE   Perhaps the most important influence on your purchasing decisions is your personal desire. How much do you *really* want something? Your desire for a product can be greatly affected by pressure from your friends or family. It also can be affected by **advertising,** a method of calling your attention to a product.

Each year, billions of dollars are spent on advertising products and services. The purpose of advertising is to keep a company's products in front of you in hope that you will buy the product when your need arises. However, sometimes through clever use of advertising techniques, a need and a desire for a product or service can be created. Figure 1-6 identifies several advertising techniques.

FRAUD/QUACKERY

A serious problem in the health field revolves around people or companies that take advantage of the fears of others. The problem has existed for as long as the fear of disease and illness has existed. **Health fraud** is the promotion or selling of health-related products or treatments that have little or no healing power. This deceptive practice also is referred to as **quackery** [*KWAK uh ree*]. Health fraud, or quackery, takes advantage of people's fears by promising quick cures or hopeful remedies for anything from ingrown toenails to fatal diseases. The people who are most vulnerable to quackery include:

• teenagers, who are concerned with self-image

• the elderly, who are worried about their failing health

- people living with life-threatening illnesses
- the poor, who often lack affordable health care

Quackery is both illegal and dangerous. The patient who invests in a useless treatment or remedy can lose more than just money. The person also loses time. For someone suffering from a serious illness, that time could be spent seeking treatments that have been proven to be helpful. As a health consumer, be aware of the common signs of quackery, as shown in Figure 1-7. Another key step in protecting yourself from quackery is to know your rights as a consumer.

CONSUMER RIGHTS

In 1962, Congress enacted four basic rights to protect the consumer from fraud. These four rights provide standards that must be followed when producing or selling a product or service. Consumer rights protect the consumer from fraudulent practices and also carry a certain responsibility for all consumers.

THE RIGHT TO CHOOSE   You have the right to choose from a variety of products and services. This right protects you from the possibility of one company or person dominating the market by preventing any competitors from selling their products or services.

THE RIGHT TO BE HEARD   You have the right to speak out when you are not satisfied with a product or service. Consumer complaints have helped companies enact service policies designed to create customer satisfaction, such as return policies.

THE RIGHT TO SAFETY   You have the right to be protected from products and services that may lead to illness, injury, or other health problems. Government agencies such as the Food and Drug Administration (FDA) and the Environmental Protection Agency (EPA) establish guidelines for product safety. You are responsible for using the product in the way it was intended.

STRATEGIES FOR LIVING

Suggestions for avoiding consumer fraud.
- Look for specific information.
- Carefully consider any statistical information that is quoted.
- Be aware of the emotional appeals that are being made.
- Avoid products or services that promise miracle results.
- Avoid any product or service that promises something for nothing.

Figure 1-7   Why have the methods of quacks been successful?

COMMON CLAIMS MADE BY QUACKS

Method	Description	The Catch
Diagnosis by Mail	Offer to analyze a description of symptoms	Most accurate way to diagnose an illness is through a thorough examination.
"Free Trial Offer"	30-day trial period of product	People continue to use product out of habit only to be charged later with much higher costs.
Limited Supply	The only opportunity to purchase the product	Pushes customer to act before checking out the product.
Testimonials	Supportive statements from people	No evidence of accuracy of statements.
Guarantee of Cure or Satisfaction	Promise that the product will work or consumer's money is returned	Not even doctors will guarantee a cure. Quacks rarely return the money. Many are unable to be found after initial purchase.

Clever promotions can make it difficult to make decisions.

THE RIGHT TO BE INFORMED   You have the right to make a consumer decision based upon correct information. This information includes truthful advertising and information about all costs.

Since 1962, two new rights have been added. You also have the right to consumer education and the right to redress, which means that you have the right to have a wrong corrected. Various local, state, and federal agencies can help you with this. There also are many private organizations that are dedicated to consumer protection. For more information about groups in your area that can help with consumer problems, contact your local or state consumer affairs office.

MAKING RESPONSIBLE CHOICES

The best way to avoid making decisions that can threaten your health is to base your decisions on complete information. Be aware of the techniques that are being used to convince you to use a product or a service. You can follow the steps in the decision-making model to help you make wise decisions about products that can affect your health.

- *Identify the Problem*   Should you buy the product?
- *Consider the Options*   Carefully identify all of your options.
- *Evaluate the Outcomes*   Is there a potential health risk? What are the risks involved for each option? What are the potential positive and negative consequences?
- *Decide and Act*   Base your decision on careful consideration of all of the risks and of your own feelings.
- *Review Your Decision*   Don't be afraid to change your mind if you find that you made a poor decision.

LESSON 1.4   USING WHAT YOU HAVE LEARNED

REVIEW

1. Identify and explain the five factors that can influence your purchases.
2. What is quackery?
3. Why is it important to know your consumer rights?

THINK CRITICALLY

4. Why might desire for a product be the most important factor that affects purchasing decisions?
5. Quackery is a problem that has been around for many years. Why are the elderly at special risk for quackery?

APPLY IT TO YOURSELF

6. You are an advertising executive for a major soft drink company. How would you plan your campaign in order to create a desire among teenagers to purchase your company's product?

SUMMARY

Many of the decisions you will make throughout your life will be about the purchase of products and services. Some of these purchases will affect your health. Consumer health focuses on helping you make decisions about health-related purchases. By becoming an informed consumer, you can learn to avoid making purchases that serve no actual health benefit.

Weighing Risks

One Saturday, Jarvis went over to Pete's house just to hang out. It was a great day. They were out in the driveway shooting hoops when Sam and Rich came over. "It's a beautiful day, guys. Let's go climbing," said Rich.

"Great idea!" said Pete, "I'll get my gear." Jarvis had heard much about his friends' adventures on a sheer rock cliff just outside of town. He had heard that the climb was challenging and that the view from the top was spectacular. But Jarvis had never done any rock climbing as his friends had. All of his friends had taken a climbing course, and they knew all of the techniques.

"Jarvis, why don't you come too?" asked Sam. Jarvis was a little surprised. "I've never climbed," said Jarvis. "I wouldn't know what to do."

"Come on Jarvis. You'll love it!" said Pete. "We'll show you everything you need to know. Take a chance. You only live once you know."

Jarvis didn't want to refuse. He had been thinking about taking the climbing course, and this was a chance to try it—with experienced climbers! He knew his friends were responsible and would guide him along. But inside, he was pretty scared. "What if I slip," he thought. "What if they go on ahead of me and I don't know what to do?" He really wanted to go, and he didn't want them to think he was afraid.

PAUSE AND CONSIDER

1. **Identify the Problem.** What is Jarvis's conflict?

2. **Consider the Options.** What are Jarvis's options?

3. **Evaluate the Outcomes.** What could happen if Jarvis goes climbing with his friends? What could happen if he doesn't go climbing?

Jarvis followed Pete into the house. "Hey Pete, you know, I've never done this before. You guys know what you're doing."

"It's not hard, Jarv. Just follow us. We'll help you. Honest." Jarvis trusted his friends. But he just didn't feel right about going without some background training. "I really want to go, Pete, and I do trust you guys. But I'm not sure I trust myself without a little real training. As a matter of fact, I've been thinking of taking the same course."

"Look Jarv, it's up to you. We're going to have a blast up there. We can see the whole city and beyond."

"It's tempting. Really. But I better not. Sorry, Pete."

"Hey, your loss, Jarv. But I can understand your feelings. I might not have gone before I had the training. If you don't know what you're doing, climbing can be really dangerous. We'll go after you take the course," said Pete.

"Sounds good," said Jarvis. "When you come down, why don't you and the guys stop by. I want to hear all about it." Jarvis was relieved to hear Pete agree with his decision.

DECIDE AND REVIEW

4. **Decide and Act.** What choice did Jarvis make? What did he base his decision on? Do you think it was a good decision?

5. **Review.** Were there any other options Jarvis could have considered? What would you do in the same situation? Would you be willing to take a risk in order to join the group?

CHAPTER 1 ~ Review

PROJECTS

1. Create a medical history based on interviews with family members or guardians. Ask them to recall any major illnesses, causes of death among family members, and general health trends. When you have finished, assess the areas that might affect your life. Determine if there are behaviors that you should avoid or encourage based on your heredity.

2. Make a list of the physical activities in which you participate—playing sports, raking leaves, cleaning the house, dancing. Alongside each activity on your list, indicate whether the activity is one of no, some, or a great deal of risk. Then list all the possible risks for each activity. Pick your favorite activity, and write an essay that compares its health benefits and health risks.

WORKING WITH OTHERS

With a partner, review several different kinds of magazines and cut out advertisements that promote products that interest you. Then role-play a scene in which one person is the salesperson for the product you have chosen. The other person plays the buyer who asks pointed questions about the safety, durability, and need for the product. At the end of the activity, decide if the product is indeed one that you would buy.

CONNECTING TO...

HISTORY Research a major disease such as tuberculosis, polio, small pox, influenza, or diphtheria and trace its history and origins throughout time. Write a report about your findings. Include the impact of the disease on communities. Discuss the most recent research and the steps that are being taken to eliminate the disease.

USING VOCABULARY

advertising	health	risk
chronic	health fraud	self-concept
consumer health	heredity	self-esteem
epidemiology	life expectancy	services
evaluate	peers	values
gender	quackery	wellness

Complete the following paragraph using vocabulary words from Chapter 1. Create your own paragraph using words that were not used in this activity.

__(1)__ is a state of being that encompasses physical, intellectual, social, and emotional __(2)__. Wellness depends on many factors including healthy choices, environment, and __(3)__. The way you see yourself can affect your personal health. A healthy __(4)__ can help you develop a realistic attitude about achieving better health. By recognizing your own __(5)__ and by assessing the __(6)__ involved with all activities, you can hope to live a long, healthy life. In fact, the __(7)__ of a person living in the 1990s has greatly increased since the turn of the century, due to better health practices, better living conditions, and medical advances. Another, important area of concern for maintaining a healthy life is to be wary of __(8)__ that may promote health products that may be "too good to be true." A wise health consumer will __(9)__ the risks involved with using a product.

CONCEPT MAPPING

Copy and complete the concept map shown below. Information on concept mapping appears at the front of this book.

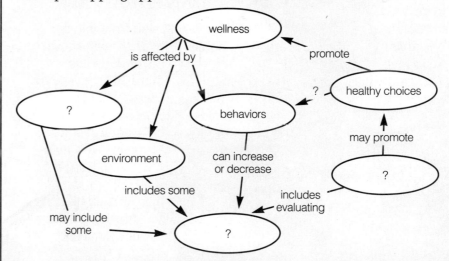

THINKING CRITICALLY

INTERPRET

LESSON 1.1

1. How did diseases like pneumonia, influenza, and tuberculosis define health at the turn of the century?

2. What is the main cause of poor health today?

3. Why has life expectancy changed since 1900? Why do health experts feel that life expectancy will continue to change?

4. What might be some positive benefits to maintaining healthy behaviors?

LESSON 1.2

5. What are the positive aspects of risk-taking? What are the negative aspects?

6. What can a person do to reduce the risk of cancer?

7. What are the important steps in evaluating a health risk?

8. How do values influence your ability to assess health risks?

LESSON 1.3

9. Why is recognition an important step when changing a health habit?

10. How does positive self-esteem affect health?

11. Why do peers play an important role in health behaviors?

LESSON 1.4

12. What is consumer health?

13. What are the four original consumer rights?

14. What is meant by the right to redress?

APPLY

LESSON 1.1

15. The leading causes of death can vary when broken down by different factors, such as age, socioeconomic status, and medical history. Why might these factors affect health?

16. Of the eight health behaviors that promote good health and tend to increase average length of life, which two behaviors do you think are most important? Why?

LESSON 1.2

17. Where on the Wellness Continuum is a 15-year-old boy who eats a high-fat diet, spends much of his time watching television, and gets very little exercise?

18. Homicide is the second-leading cause of death among 15 to 24-year-olds. What might be three ways of reducing the number of deaths from this cause?

LESSON 1.3

19. What are two things you can do to help improve another person's self-esteem?

20. A 16-year-old girl has a very bad temper that often interferes with her ability to get along with other people. Use the three-step model for changing behavior to help the girl.

LESSON 1.4

21. Why do you think that teenagers are particularly at risk to advertising quackery?

22. What are some products that you have been tempted to buy as a result of clever advertising? What steps did you take to evaluate the product to determine if it was right for you?

COMMITMENT TO WELLNESS

FOLLOW-UP

SETTING GOALS

Look back at your completed Commitment to Wellness checklist. Find your yes answers and review your strengths for overall wellness. Next, look at your no answers. What areas seem to be the weakest for you? Under your list in the Wellness Journal, create two columns titled *strengths* and *weaknesses*. For each item in the *strength* column, write down reasons why you consider that item to be easy for or important to you. For example, if you said *yes* to "I eat a balanced, healthy diet," explain why you consider it to be a strength and why eating a balanced diet is important to you. Under the *weaknesses* column, make a list of small ways that you can begin to change those behaviors. For example if you wrote *no* next to "I get between 7–8 hours of sleep a night," brainstorm ways that you can work towards getting a little more sleep at night such as " finish homework no later than 10:00 P.M."

WHERE DO I GO FROM HERE?

Once you have determined your strengths and weaknesses, you may want to find out further information about areas that you want to work to change.

FOR MORE INFORMATION ABOUT WELLNESS, CONTACT:

National Wellness Institute
1319 Fremont Street
South Hall
Stevens Point, WI 54481

25

CHAPTER 2 ~

Taking Care of Yourself

"Sight paints a picture of life, but sound, touch, taste, and smell are actually life itself."

Tom Sullivan

A medical error destroyed Tom Sullivan's eyesight very soon after he was born. Tom learned to use his other senses in ways that sighted people can only imagine.

Your senses keep you in touch with your world. Taking responsibility for your own health includes caring for your senses as well as eating the right foods and getting enough exercise. This chapter will give you important information about how to care for your skin, teeth, eyes, and ears.

Most teenagers care about having blemish-free skin. But you may not have thought much about the effects of sun on your skin. Each time you are in the sun and don't take appropriate precautions, you increase your risk of developing skin cancer.

Proper care of your teeth, eyes, and ears involves professional checkups or screenings on a regular basis. Proper care also involves protecting yourself against eye injuries and hearing loss. Your responsibility goes beyond simply knowing what to do if you are injured or have a disease. You must take an active role in preventing injuries, avoiding disease, and staying healthy.

BACKGROUND

Tom Sullivan is an author of several books, including *If You Could See What I Hear.* Sullivan's upbeat and energetic style of writing has helped to open the eyes of many sighted people to his world.

SELF-
ASSESSMENT

How well do take care of your personal health? Use the following checklist to take a closer look at your personal health practices. In your Wellness Journal, or on a separate sheet of paper, respond to the items below. Write *yes* for each item that describes you all or most of the time.

1. I brush and floss my teeth every day.

2. I protect my eyes in bright sunlight by wearing sunglasses that filter ultraviolet rays.

3. When I play the radio or stereo, I keep the volume low enough to talk without having to yell.

4. I use a sunscreen when I am going outdoors.

5. I help prevent skin infections by washing regularly.

6. I go for a dental checkup at least once a year.

7. I protect my eyes from injury by wearing safety goggles when working with anything that creates flying debris.

8. I wear ear protection when I am around very loud noises.

9. I avoid working at video display terminals for long periods of time.

10. Before I apply anything to my skin, I carefully read the ingredients to avoid an allergic reaction.

Review your responses and consider areas on which you may need to collect more information. Save your personal checklist for a follow-up activity that appears at the end of the chapter.

PROTECTING YOUR SKIN

Your skin is the largest organ of your body. An **organ** is a body part made of different types of tissues—groups of cells—that work together to perform certain functions. Your heart, your lungs, your stomach, and your brain are organs. Like these and all other organs in your body, your skin is made of living cells. It also contains some nonliving parts.

THE STRUCTURE AND FUNCTIONS OF THE SKIN

As you can see in Figure 2-1, your skin consists of two layers, the epidermis and the dermis. The **epidermis** [ep uh DUR mus] is the thin, outer layer of the skin. The cells at the surface of this layer are dead. These dead cells are continuously rubbed off by your clothing, by washing, or by any movement that causes friction. Living cells at the base of the epidermis are constantly dividing to make new cells. The new cells push older cells to the skin's surface, replacing the dead cells that you shed. The epidermis also produces the nonliving parts of your skin—your hair and nails. Notice the hair follicles in Figure 2-1.

The **dermis** [DUR mus] is the thick, inner layer of the skin. It contains most of the specialized structures you see in Figure 2-1—the blood vessels, the nerve endings, and the sweat and oil glands. Below the dermis is the subcutaneous layer, a layer of tissue that binds the skin to your body. Your body also stores fat in this layer.

Your skin performs four main functions: protection, sensation, temperature regulation, and waste removal.

PROTECTION Your skin is your body's first line of defense against disease. Hardened cells on the skin's surface help keep bacteria, viruses, fungi, and other disease-causing organisms from entering your body. In addition, your skin is coated with an oily substance called **sebum** [SEE bum]. Sebum is produced by the oil glands in the dermis and reaches the surface of the epidermis through tiny openings called **pores**. Sebum contains an acid that also helps protect you against disease-causing organisms.

Your skin protects your body in other ways, too. It holds moisture inside your body so tissues and organs do not dry out. Melanin, the brown pigment in the epidermis that gives your skin its color, helps block out the harmful ultraviolet rays in sunlight. Even the nonliving parts of your skin are protective. Your nails shield the sensitive tips of your fingers and toes. Hairs keep dust and dirt out of your eyes, ears, and nose. Your eyebrows and eyelashes help shade your eyes from bright light.

This highly magnified view of human skin shows a hair poking through the outer layer of cells.

SENSATION Notice the different types of receptors shown in Figure 2-1. A **receptor** [*ree SEP tur*] is a nerve ending that receives information about the environment and sends that information to the brain. The receptors in your skin sense pain, cold, heat, contact (light touch), and pressure (firm touch). This sensory information keeps you constantly aware of the conditions around you and also enables you to avoid dangers such as burning yourself badly when you touch a hot object. You can learn more about sensory receptors by reading about the nervous system in Chapter 19, "Coordination and Control."

TEMPERATURE REGULATION To function well, your body must stay at a fairly constant internal temperature of about 97–99°F. Sweat glands and blood vessels in the dermis work together to help maintain this normal temperature. The sweat glands produce perspiration [*pur spuh RAY shun*], which is made of water, salts, and body wastes. When your body is hot, the sweat glands increase their production of perspiration. The perspiration is released through the pores onto the surface of the skin. At the same time, blood vessels in the skin dilate. This dilation allows more blood to come near the skin surface to release heat. The perspiration evaporates by absorbing the extra body heat, and your body cools.

When your body is cold, the sweat glands decrease their production of perspiration. The blood vessels contract, which keeps

Figure 2-1 *This diagram shows the structure of skin. How many types of receptors can you find?*

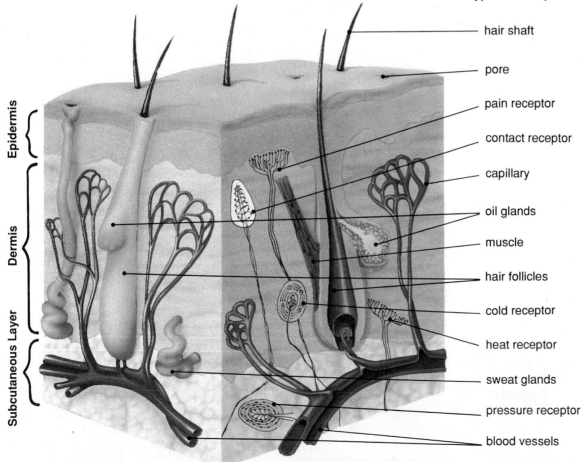

Epidermis

Dermis

Subcutaneous Layer

- hair shaft
- pore
- pain receptor
- contact receptor
- capillary
- oil glands
- muscle
- hair follicles
- cold receptor
- heat receptor
- sweat glands
- pressure receptor
- blood vessels

FOR YOUR INFORMATION

Dandruff forms when the scalp sheds dead skin cells. You cannot prevent this natural process, but you can keep dandruff under control by shampooing frequently and by using an anti-dandruff shampoo.

warm blood away from the cold skin surface. These processes help retain your body heat. In addition, the hairs on your skin trap warm air and hold it close to your skin. Also, the fat stored in the subcutaneous layer acts as insulation in cold weather.

WASTE REMOVAL Your body takes in food, water, and air and uses these materials in body processes such as building new cells, moving, and breathing. These processes create waste products that your body cannot use and must eliminate. Some of the waste products—salts, urea, and extra water—are carried by the blood to your skin and eliminated in perspiration.

COMMON SKIN PROBLEMS

Disease, infections, injury, and environmental conditions are often the cause of skin problems. Many problems can be avoided with good skin care or prevented with simple first aid. For more serious problems, consult your family doctor or a dermatologist [*dur muh TAHL uh just*], a doctor who specializes in skin problems.

DRY SKIN Most teenagers have oily skin, not dry skin. However, weather conditions—wind, sunlight, and dry air—or heated indoor air in winter months may cause your skin to become dry and flaky. Scrubbing lightly with a washcloth when bathing will help remove flakes of dry skin. Protecting the skin with a moisturizing lotion will help prevent drying and restore lost moisture.

ACNE Acne is very common in teenagers because it results from the natural changes that occur during physical development. These changes make the oil glands produce an excess of sebum. When excess sebum accumulates and hardens in a pore, a blackhead forms, as shown in Figure 2-2. When bacteria grow in the trapped sebum, the blocked pore becomes inflamed and filled with pus, forming a pimple.

Most teenagers eventually outgrow their acne problems, although some people still have acne in adulthood. For many years, scientists thought that eating greasy foods or chocolate caused acne, but recent research has shown that foods rarely cause acne. However, acne may become worse as a result of eating some foods. If eating certain foods seems to increase your skin problems, avoid those foods.

Figure 2-2 Blackheads and pimples develop when pores become blocked and inflamed. What causes the blockage?

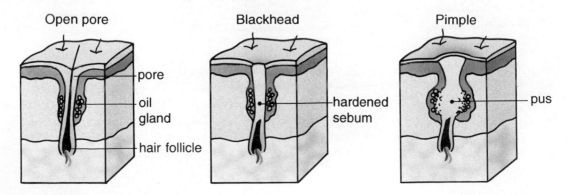

Open pore — pore, oil gland, hair follicle

Blackhead — hardened sebum

Pimple — pus

DERMATITIS Dermatitis [*dur muh TY tus*] is a condition characterized by red, swollen, itchy patches on the skin. Dermatitis may be caused by an allergy, which is a reaction of the body to an irritating substance such as certain foods or medicines. Contact dermatitis results when an irritating substance touches the skin directly. Some common irritants are detergents, soaps, fabrics, perfumes, hair dyes, deodorants, and make-up. The sap of certain plants such as poison ivy, poison oak and poison sumac also causes contact dermatitis. The only way to prevent contact dermatitis is to identify and avoid the irritating substances.

PSORIASIS Psoriasis [*suh RY uh sus*] is characterized by patches of pink to purple-colored skin covered with grayish-white scales. The patches generally do not itch or cause any pain. Although there is no known cure, psoriasis can be treated with medicated cream. You cannot catch psoriasis from someone who has it.

SKIN INFECTIONS Skin infections result when disease-causing organisms penetrate the skin, perhaps through a break such as an insect bite, a scratch, or a scrape. The First Aid Manual at the back of this book tells you how to treat cuts and bites to avoid infection.

Two common skin infections are ringworm and athlete's foot. Ringworm appears as round, red, scaly patches on the skin. Ringworm is caused by a fungus, not a worm. It gets its name from its appearance. Ringworm can be spread from one person to another or from a pet to a person. It is not serious and is easily treated.

Athlete's foot is an irritating and sometimes painful fungus infection that attacks the skin between and under the toes. The fungus causes the skin to become red, flaky, and itchy. Athlete's foot spreads easily from one person to another in locker rooms, around swimming pools, and in other damp areas. Drying your feet well, using an antifungal cream, and wearing absorbent cotton socks usually stops the infection and prevents its return.

CONSUMER HEALTH

Using Cosmetics

Cosmetics, like foods and drugs, are regulated by the Food and Drug Administration (FDA) to ensure that they are safe to use. However, many cosmetic labels are misleading, and if the cosmetics are used incorrectly they can cause harm.

Some labels tell you that a product is "hypoallergenic," "fragrance free," or "natural." "Hypoallergenic" probably indicates that the cosmetic company has eliminated some irritating ingredients. The label "fragrance free" means that no ingredient has been added to create a pleasant smell. However, other ingredients in the product may cause allergic reactions. The label "natural" on a cosmetic has no meaning.

Here are some tips for making sure the cosmetics you buy and use are safe and fresh.

- Use a disposable applicator when trying makeup at a store.
- Wash your hands before applying any cosmetic product.
- If a product has dried up, throw it away.
- Throw out any cosmetics that have changed in odor, consistency, or color. Throw out mascara three months after opening it.
- Read the ingredients on the product label carefully. Do not rely on the headlines on the label, for they can be misleading.

The ABCD danger signs in moles and birthmarks

Consult your doctor or a dermatologist immediately if a mole or birthmark shows any of these danger signs.

Asymmetry—
One half is
unlike the
other half.

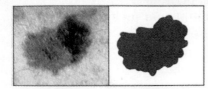

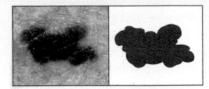

Border is
scalloped or
irregular.

Color is
varied from
one area
to another.

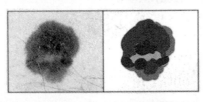

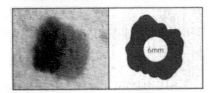

Diameter is
larger than a
pencil eraser
(6 mm).

SOURCE: AMERICAN ACADEMY OF DERMATOLOGY

SKIN CANCER   **Cancer** is an abnormal, uncontrolled growth of cells that invade and destroy healthy tissue. There are different types of skin cancer. Some begin as small pink growths that increase in size and damage surrounding tissue but do not spread to other parts of the body. Other skin cancers begin as lumps and spread to other parts of the body.

The most serious type of skin cancer, called melanoma [*mel uh NOH muh*], usually begins as a mole or birthmark that becomes irritated, bleeds, or changes color, size, or shape. Melanoma can spread quickly to other parts of the body. Most moles and birthmarks are harmless, but if you notice that one has changed, see a doctor immediately. Skin cancer can be cured if it is identified and treated early.

The best way to avoid skin cancer is to limit your exposure to harmful ultraviolet rays in sunlight and from sunlamps. According to the American Cancer Society, sunburns during childhood and the teenage years greatly increase the risk of developing skin cancer later. Half of the people who develop skin cancer are between the ages of 15 and 50. The risk of developing skin cancer increases with the number of years you have been exposed to ultraviolet rays and the number of sunburns you have had.

Choose skin-care products carefully to avoid substances that irritate your skin.

CARING FOR YOUR SKIN

A glowing, smooth skin is one of the first things you notice about a person. You can keep your skin healthy and attractive by practicing good health habits, including eating balanced meals and drinking plenty of water every day. Some additional care may be needed to clear up acne or to treat dry skin or oily skin. In addition, caring for your skin involves making choices that will reduce your risk of developing skin cancer.

GENERAL CARE   Regular washing keeps your skin clean and free from odor. Natural moisture in the skin keeps it smooth and flexible. Creams or lotions that hold in moisture help protect against dry skin. For oily skin, washing with a low-fat soap or cleanser may reduce oiliness.

Your skin-care program should include the careful choice of soaps, cleansers, make-up or after-shave lotions, and other grooming products to avoid substances that irritate your skin. Girls who use make-up should be sure to remove it every day. Liquid foundation and face powder can clog the skin's pores and contribute to skin irritations.

Beyond these simple procedures and products, you do not need specialized skin-care products or treatments. In fact, some products and treatments can contribute to skin problems rather than prevent them. In general, it is best not to use any specialized products unless recommended by a doctor.

Body odor occurs when bacteria come in contact with perspiration. Bathing or showering daily removes bacteria and perspiration and helps prevent body odor. Deodorants and antiperspirants also help prevent body odor. In addition, antiperspirants reduce the amount of perspiration that is produced. It is important to remember, though, that neither deodorants nor antiperspirants take the place of regular washing.

TREATING ACNE   Mild cases of acne can be treated simply by keeping the skin clean and using an acne medication that contains benzoyl peroxide. Dermatologists recommend washing with a very mild soap or cleanser. If acne is more serious, a doctor can prescribe a medication such as an antibiotic lotion. Do not pick or squeeze pimples and blackheads. Squeezing is likely to increase the problem because it damages skin tissue and can cause the infection to spread. Make-up, creams, and lotions that contain oils also can worsen the problem because they contribute to clogged pores. Severe cases of acne may cause permanent scarring. If your acne is severe, you should consult your family doctor or a dermatologist.

PROTECTION FROM ULTRAVIOLET RAYS   Some exposure to sunlight is needed to stimulate the production of vitamin D, which is necessary for healthy bones and teeth. As you learned earlier, though, exposure to ultraviolet (UV) rays in sunlight increases your risk of developing skin cancer. Sunlight contains two types of UV rays, called UVA and UVB. The UVB rays are most responsible for causing sunburn and skin cancer, although the UVA rays can damage your skin, too.

To protect your skin, follow the guidelines listed on the next page. In particular, *always* use a sunscreen when you are outdoors, even when you are not sunbathing. A **sunscreen** is a lotion that blocks out some of the sun's UVB rays and reduces skin damage.

Sunscreens are graded by a number, called the **sun protection factor (SPF)**, that shows how much protection they provide against UVB rays. The higher the SPF number, the greater the protection. Suppose, for example, that your skin usually burns

Always make sure you use a sunscreen and a sun block when you are sunbathing.

STRATEGIES FOR LIVING

The following guidelines are recommended for using a sunscreen.

- Develop a regular routine of using a sunscreen every day.

- Use a sunscreen every time you go outdoors, even if it is only for a brief trip to the store.

- Apply the sunscreen to your face, ears, neck, chest, back, abdomen, upper and lower legs, arms, hands, and feet each morning before you get dressed. It is best to apply it 45 minutes before you go outside. (You can apply make-up over a sunscreen.)

- Reapply the sunscreen once or twice a day if you stay outside.

- Limit your exposure to the sun when the rays are most intense—between 10:00 A.M. and 3:00 P.M.

- Use a sunscreen on cloudy days, too. The sun's burning rays can penetrate the clouds.

- Appropriate clothing and a hat also offer good sun protection and should be used along with a sunscreen.

ADAPTED FROM AMERICAN ACADEMY OF DERMATOLOGY

after 15 minutes in the sun. If you used a sunscreen with an SPF of 10, you could stay in the sun about 10 times as long before your skin would burn (10 X 15, or 150 minutes). People with fair skin should select a sunscreen with an SPF of 15 or higher. People with darker skin may be safe with a lower SPF. Remember, though, that the SPF applies only to UVB rays. Two sunscreens with the same SPF number may provide different amounts of protection against UVA rays.

Whenever you are outdoors, you should also use a sun block on your nose, lips, and other sensitive areas. A **sun block** is a thick cream that completely blocks both types of UV rays. Because sun blocks do not allow any light at all to reach the skin, they are not SPF-rated.

SUMMARY

Your skin protects your body from disease, senses conditions in your surroundings, regulates your body temperature, and removes body wastes. Common causes of skin problems include disease, infections, injury, environmental conditions, and, in teenagers, the physical changes that occur during development. Taking good care of your skin affects your health as well as your appearance.

LESSON 2.1 # USING WHAT YOU HAVE LEARNED

REVIEW

1. Name three living structures found in the dermis.
2. Describe two ways you can help prevent body odor.

THINK CRITICALLY

3. When you are outdoors, you should use both a sunscreen and a sun block. Why is it necessary to use both?
4. When your body is hot, your skin produces more perspiration. In your own words, describe how evaporation of perspiration helps control your body temperature.

APPLY IT TO YOURSELF

5. Suppose that you suddenly develop a red, itchy rash on your arms and legs, and your doctor tells you that you have contact dermatitis. Describe what you would do to try to identify the cause.

STRUCTURE AND CARE OF YOUR TEETH

Like your skin, your teeth are made of living cells and nonliving parts. Unlike most other tissues, though, your teeth cannot repair themselves if they are damaged or diseased. Strong, healthy teeth are important to your health as well as to your appearance. Good dental care can help your teeth last for your entire lifetime.

THE STRUCTURE AND FUNCTIONS OF THE TEETH

Your teeth prepare food for digestion by cutting and grinding it into pieces small enough for you to swallow. As you can see in Figure 2-3 *right*, there are four types of teeth in your mouth. Each type performs a different function.

- The **incisors** [*in SY zurz*] are sharp front teeth that bite and cut food. Notice that their biting surface is shaped like the tip of a chisel.
- The **canines** [*KAY nynz*], also called eyeteeth, are pointed teeth that tear food into smaller pieces.
- The **premolars** [*pree MOH lurz*] are flat teeth with double points that tear and crush food.
- The **molars** [*MOH lurz*] are large, flat teeth with several rounded points that grind food into bits.

Each tooth has two main parts, the crown and the root. The **crown** is the part that you can see above the gum line. The **root** is the part below the gum line that fits into the jawbone. You can see these two parts in Figure 2-3 *left*.

The crown is covered by **enamel** [*ih NAM ul*], a hard, nonliving, dense, white material containing calcium. Enamel is the hardest material in your body and helps protect the inner part of

MAIN IDEAS

CONCEPTS
✔ Different types of teeth perform different functions.
✔ Brushing and flossing remove the plaque that causes tooth decay and gum disease.
✔ Caring for your teeth includes having regular dental checkups.

VOCABULARY

incisor	enamel
canine	dentin
premolar	pulp
molar	plaque
crown	cavity
root	calculus

Figure 2-3   Which type of tooth is shown at the left?

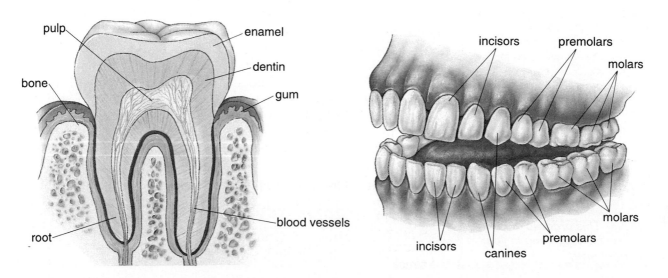

How old were you when you lost your front teeth?

the tooth from decay organisms. Inside the enamel is a softer material called dentin. **Dentin** [*DENT un*] forms the body of the tooth and extends down into the root. Inside the dentin is the **pulp**, the soft inner tissue that contains blood vessels and nerves. The blood vessels carry nutrients to the tooth's living cells and carry waste products away. The nerves are sensitive to heat, cold, pressure, and pain.

You probably remember when your "baby teeth" began to fall out and permanent teeth grew in to replace them. That process is almost complete for you now. Your second molars—the next-to-last back teeth—probably grew in when you were about 12. Your third and last molars, called wisdom teeth, will grow in sometime between age 17 and adulthood, if there is space for them behind the second molars. You will then have a full set of 32 permanent teeth.

COMMON DENTAL PROBLEMS

The most common dental problems are tooth decay and gum disease. Other dental problems involve the spacing and position of the teeth.

TOOTH DECAY   The process of tooth decay is shown in Figure 2-4. Decay begins with plaque on a tooth's surface. **Plaque** [*PLAK*] is a material made of saliva, food particles, and bacteria. The bacteria break down starches and sugars in the food particles, producing an acid that eats into the tooth's enamel. This eventually causes a **cavity**, a hole in the enamel. If left untreated, the decay spreads deeper, into the dentin and perhaps even into the nerve-filled pulp, which can be extremely painful.

GUM DISEASE   In most cases, gum disease is caused by plaque or **calculus** [*KAL kyuh lus*], which is hardened plaque. In the early stage of gum disease, the gums become inflamed and swollen and may bleed easily during brushing. In the later stage, the inflamed gums pull back from the teeth, forming pockets where pus collects. Without treatment, the disease eventually destroys bone tissue in the jaw, and the teeth loosen and fall out or have to be removed. If you notice that your gums bleed easily or that teeth are loose, you should see a dentist.

LEUKOPLAKIA   White patches on the gums, tongue, lips, or inner cheeks may be a sign of leukoplakia [*loo kuh PLAY kee uh*]. This disease is not a form of cancer, but it may lead to cancer. Early detection and treatment can cure leukoplakia. If you notice white patches in your mouth, see a doctor or dentist so a tissue sample can be taken and examined for cancer cells.

ORAL CANCER   Oral cancer may occur in several forms, including sores or lumps in the mouth. It is more likely to be cured if it is identified and treated early. The best way to help prevent oral cancer is to avoid using any form of tobacco, especially smokeless tobacco, or drinking alcohol.

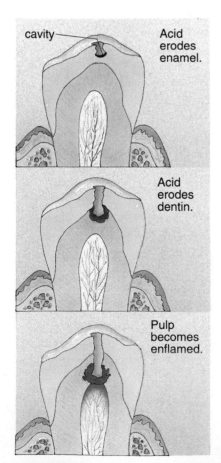

cavity

Acid erodes enamel.

Acid erodes dentin.

Pulp becomes enflamed.

Figure 2-4 This process of tooth decay may be happening in your mouth right now.

TMJ PROBLEMS

TMJ stands for "temporomandibular joint," the place where your lower jaw connects with the rest of your skull. Some common symptoms of TMJ problems are clicking or grinding noises in the joint, headaches, limited joint movement, and soreness or pain when chewing. Stress-related habits such as clenching or grinding your teeth contribute to the problems. Learning how to relax the jaw can help ease the symptoms. Some people with TMJ problems are helped by wearing a special mouthpiece at night. If the problems become severe, surgery may be necessary.

ORTHODONTIC PROBLEMS   Orthodontics [*or thuh DAHN tiks*] is a branch of dentistry that specializes in correcting irregular teeth—teeth that are crowded too closely together, turned, or in abnormal positions. A person with irregular teeth cannot bite, chew, and grind food correctly. Irregular teeth are also difficult to clean thoroughly, so tooth decay and gum disease may result. Irregular teeth can be repositioned over time with braces.

Wisdom teeth sometimes do not grow in correctly because there is not enough space behind the second molars. A wisdom tooth might grow in only partway, at an angle, or might even be blocked under the gum, causing pain and swelling. In this case, the wisdom tooth would have to be surgically removed.

CARING FOR YOUR TEETH

Good dental care begins with a healthy diet that contains enough calcium. Calcium is needed to build strong teeth, particularly the protective outer layer of enamel. Keeping your teeth clean helps prevent tooth decay and gum disease.

GENERAL CARE   Cleaning your teeth removes the food particles and bacteria that form plaque. A thorough cleaning involves both brushing and flossing. Brushing cleans the exposed surfaces of

HEALTHY PEOPLE 2000

Increase to at least 45 percent the proportion of people aged 35 through 44 who have never lost a permanent tooth due to dental caries or periodontal disease.

Objective 13.3
from *Healthy People 2000: National Health Promotion and Disease Prevention Objectives*

Wearing braces for a few years provides a lifetime of benefits.

your teeth. Flossing cleans between the teeth and under the gum line. Brushing and flossing also help keep your breath fresh. You should brush thoroughly at least twice a day and floss once a day. Try to brush after every meal and snack, too—or at least rinse your mouth with water.

Scientists have known for many years that fluoride [*FLOR yd*] helps prevent tooth decay. Fluoride is a tasteless, odorless chemical that occurs naturally in soil and water. When it is taken into the body or applied to the teeth, fluoride makes tooth enamel harder, increasing its resistance to decay. In some cities, the drinking water contains fluoride naturally; other cities add fluoride to their water supply. Fluoride is also widely available today in toothpaste.

A newer method of decay prevention involves applying a plastic sealant to the chewing surfaces of the teeth. The sealant prevents decay-causing acids from breaking through the tooth enamel.

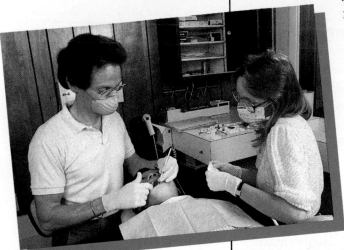

Having regular dental checkups prevents small problems from becoming worse. How often do you visit a dentist?

DENTAL CHECKUPS Dental checkups are vital for preventing tooth and gum disease. You should have checkups regularly—once or twice a year, or as often as your dentist recommends. Regular visits enable the dentist to discover and treat problems early, before they become more serious and require more costly treatment.

A checkup usually includes a thorough cleaning to remove calculus. The dentist also looks for early signs of gum disease and may X-ray the teeth to find problems that cannot be seen directly. If the dentist finds a decayed place in a tooth, that part of the tooth can be removed and replaced with a filling. Removing the decay prevents the bacteria from causing more damage to that part of the tooth.

SUMMARY

Your teeth cut and grind food to prepare it for digestion. A tooth's shape is related to its function. Tooth decay and gum disease can be prevented by brushing and flossing every day, using a toothpaste that contains fluoride, and having regular dental checkups.

LESSON 2.2 USING WHAT YOU HAVE LEARNED

REVIEW

1. Name the four types of teeth, and describe the shape and function of each type.
2. How does fluoride help prevent tooth decay?

THINK CRITICALLY

3. You notice a bump under the gum in the back of your mouth, just behind the last tooth on the bottom-right side. The gum does not bleed, but it hurts when you chew on that side. What might be causing this?
4. Both brushing and flossing are needed to clean your teeth thoroughly. Why is just brushing not enough?

APPLY IT TO YOURSELF

5. Imagine that you are the parent of a 14-year-old boy who has very irregular teeth. He insists that he doesn't want to wear braces. What could you say to convince your son of the long-term value of wearing braces?

YOUR SENSE OF SIGHT

Your eyes are delicate organs. The bones of your face guard them from injury. Your eyelashes and eyelids screen out dirt and bright light. Tears keep the eyes' surface moist and clean. Your eyes are also complex organs, with many internal structures that function together to produce vision.

HOW YOUR EYES SEE

As you read about the eye, follow the path of the light rays in Figure 2-5. Vision begins with light rays striking the **cornea** [*KOR nee uh*], the clear covering at the front of your eye. The cornea bends the light rays so they pass through the **pupil** [*PYOO pul*], the round opening in the center of your eye.

CONTROLLING THE AMOUNT OF LIGHT   The colored circle surrounding the pupil is called the iris. The **iris** [*EYE rus*] controls the size of the pupil, and the pupil's size controls the amount of light entering the inner eye. In dim light, muscles in the iris relax to make your pupil larger and allow in more light. In bright light, the muscles contract to make your pupil smaller and block out some light.

MAIN IDEAS

CONCEPTS

✔ The eyes convert light rays into nerve impulses that the brain interprets as sight.

✔ Serious eye diseases should be identified and treated early to prevent eventual blindness.

✔ The eyes should be protected against injury by wearing goggles and other safety headgear.

✔ Regular vision checkups are an important part of eye care.

VOCABULARY

cornea	nerve impulse
pupil	nearsightedness
iris	farsightedness
lens	astigmatism
retina	color blindness
rod	glaucoma
cone	cataract

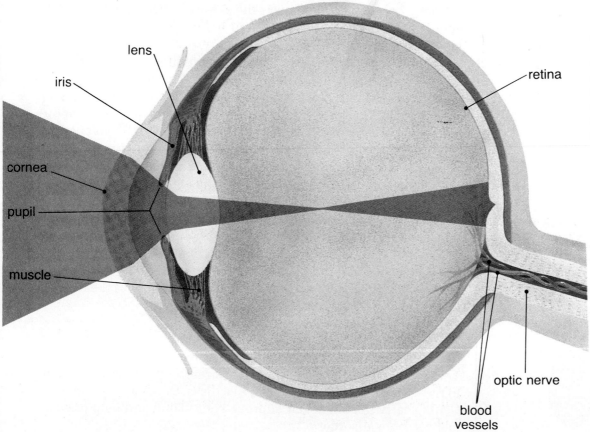

Figure 2-5
This diagram shows the structure of the eye. Notice the space between the cornea and the lens.

lens
iris
cornea
pupil
muscle
retina
optic nerve
blood vessels

Compare this photograph with the drawing on the previous page. What structures can you identify here?

FOCUSING THE LIGHT RAYS   The light rays pass through the pupil and into the curved lens behind it. The **lens** bends the light rays so they come together at a point inside your eye. To focus the rays correctly, the lens must change shape as you look at objects closer or farther away. The muscles attached to the lens relax or contract to change its shape.

The space between the cornea and the lens is filled with a watery fluid. The inner part of the eye is filled with a transparent, jellylike fluid. The pressure of these fluids against the eyeball keeps it from collapsing, much like the air inside a basketball keeps the ball from collapsing. From the lens, the light rays pass through the jellylike fluid and strike the retina at the back of the eye.

SENSING LIGHT AND COLOR   The **retina** [*RET ih nuh*] is the light-sensitive tissue that lines the inner eye. The retina contains two types of receptors that are sensitive to light, rods and cones. **Rods** are very sensitive to light but can only distinguish black from white. The rods enable you to see forms in dim light, but not colors. **Cones** can distinguish colors but are less sensitive to light. You can see colors well in bright light, but the dimmer the light, the less color you can see.

CREATING NERVE IMPULSES   Light striking the retina causes chemical changes in the rods and cones. These changes produce **nerve impulses**, electrical signals that are transmitted along nerves. Nerve fibers at the base of the rods and cones pass the impulses to the optic nerve, which connects the eye with the brain. The optic nerve transmits the impulses to your brain.

INTERPRETING IMPULSES   You do not *see* anything until the impulses are interpreted by your brain. The brain "decodes" the impulses and processes them to get meaningful information. This processing allows you to interpret the image, which appears on the retina upside down and reversed, in its proper orientation. This happens so quickly that you are not even aware of it most of the time. It is only when you see something that is unfamiliar or that does not "make sense" that you become aware of thinking about what you see.

Your brain also coordinates and interprets the impulses it receives from both eyes at the same time. When you look at an object, each eye sees it from a slightly different view, as shown in Figure 2-6. With your eyes looking straight ahead, each eye is able to view objects within an oval-shaped pattern. The two patterns overlap, but they are not identical. The overlapping of the two different views enables you to judge depth.

Figure 2-6   You can judge depth only in the area where your eyes' views overlap.

COMMON EYE PROBLEMS

Your eyes are valuable organs. For this reason it is very important to recognize vision problems and eye diseases when they occur. Getting early treatment can improve your vision and help prevent many serious disorders.

NEARSIGHTED

FARSIGHTED

VISION PROBLEMS   The most common vision problems are near-sightedness and farsightedness, shown in Figure 2-7.

- With **nearsightedness**, a person sees closer objects clearly, but objects at a distance look blurred.
- With **farsightedness**, a person sees distant objects clearly, but objects that are closer look blurred.

Both nearsightedness and farsightedness are caused by the eye-ball being shaped incorrectly. In nearsightedness, the eyeball is too long from front to back, so the retina is too far from the lens. In farsightedness, the eyeball is too short from front to back, so the retina is too close to the lens. In both cases, light rays do not focus on the retina correctly. How nearsighted or farsighted a person is depends on how badly the eyeball is misshaped. Also, a person's vision may not be the same in both eyes.

Both nearsightedness and farsightedness can be corrected by wearing a curved lens in front of the eye—a glass or plastic lens in an eyeglass frame, or a contact lens. The lens bends the light rays entering the eye so that they focus correctly on the retina.

Figure 2-7 Nearsightedness and farsightedness are the most common vision problems.

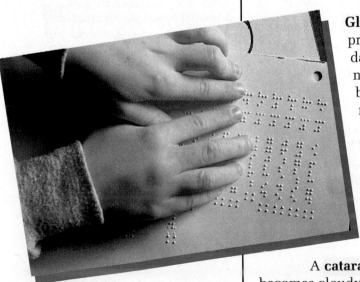

Can you see a number in each circle? If not, you may be color-blind.

Another common vision problem is **astigmatism** [*uh STIG muh tiz um*], a condition that causes blurred vision at all distances. With astigmatism, the cornea or the lens is irregularly shaped, causing light rays to focus unevenly on the retina. Astigmatism also can be corrected by wearing a lens.

People whose vision is so poor that it cannot be corrected with lenses are said to be legally blind. Touch and other senses can compensate for impaired vision.

One vision problem that cannot be corrected is **color blindness**, a hereditary disorder in which the person cannot distinguish between certain colors. Most people with color blindness cannot distinguish between red and green; both colors look brown.

EYE DISEASES   Two common but easily treated infections are a sty and pinkeye. A sty is an infection at the base of an eyelash. If treated with warm compresses, a sty usually drains and heals in about a week. If it does not drain with compresses, it should be drained by a doctor. Pinkeye is an inflammation of the eyelid's inner lining caused by infection with bacteria or a virus or by an allergic reaction or irritation due to pollen, make-up, or another substance. A doctor may prescribe medicine to help cure the infection or relieve the inflammation.

A detached retina occurs when the retina tears away from the inner eyeball, producing a blind area at the tear. In young people, the most common cause of a detached retina is a sudden blow to the head, which might happen in a car accident or while playing sports. Early signs of a detached retina include seeing flashes of light and not being able to see "out of the corners" of your eyes. If the problem is identified early, surgery can reattach the retina. Without treatment, the retina can continue to tear away, eventually causing total blindness in that eye.

Another serious eye disorder is glaucoma. **Glaucoma** [*glaw KOH muh*] is caused by increased pressure of the fluids inside the eye. This pressure damages the retina and eventually leads to blindness. Because the vision loss is gradual, it may not be noticed until the damage is severe and permanent. The causes of glaucoma are not fully known, but the disorder is sometimes hereditary. It is very important that people with a family history of glaucoma have regular eye examinations. A simple test that measures the pressure in the eye can detect glaucoma before permanent damage occurs. The disease can usually be controlled with medicated eye drops or corrected with surgery.

A **cataract** [*KAT uh rakt*] is a condition in which the lens becomes cloudy and blocks light entering the eye. Cataracts are most common in older people because of the cell changes that occur with aging. However, in rare cases, an eye injury, eye infection, or diabetes may cause a cataract at any age. The only treat-

FOR YOUR INFORMATION

Over-the-counter eye drops may temporarily sooth irritated eyes, but they can hide symptoms of serious eye infections and diseases.

Braille writing uses patterns of raised dots to symbolize letters and numbers.

Skin Color and SPF

Exposure to the sun is the primary cause of skin cancer—the most prevalent cancer in the United States today. At one time, it was believed that only those of Scandinavian or Northern European descent need worry about protection from the sun. Now scientists readily agree: while it is true that those with darker skin are better protected from the sun's damaging effects, everyone, including those with the darkest complexions, is susceptible to skin cancer. Skin reddened or darkened from exposure to the sun is damaged.

The problems that lead to skin cancer begin even before the adolescent years. It is important for everyone to recognize how his or her skin reacts to exposure to the sun and treat it accordingly. For those who live closest to the Equator, daily sun protection should be a part of their personal routine. Even for those farther from the Equator, sun protection is very important. Those who work outside daily, no matter where they live, should use sun screen every day. Scientists agree that everyone should use a lotion and lip protector with a sun protection factor (SPF) of 15 or more. Those with fairer skin should use lotions with an even higher SPF.

Skin cancer is among the most easily prevented cancers. By protecting your skin from the damage of the sun, you can prevent skin cancer.

---

ment is surgery to remove the clouded lens and replace it with a clear lens made of plastic.

One common cause of blindness is scarring of the cornea from disease or injury. Surgery can restore the person's sight by replacing the damaged cornea with a healthy cornea taken from a donor who has recently died. This surgical procedure is called a corneal transplant.

CARING FOR YOUR EYES

Good eye care includes protecting your eyes against irritations, infections, and injury. Regular checkups are important to identify vision defects and eye diseases at an early stage.

GENERAL CARE   Personal cleanliness is important in protecting your eyes from infection and disease. Because infections can be spread on hands, avoid touching or rubbing your eyes. If you must touch the area around your eyes, make sure your hands are clean. Never share a towel or washcloth with someone who has an eye infection.

Some make-up, face creams, cleansers, and soaps can be very irritating if they come in contact with delicate eye tissue. Itchy, red, or watery eyes may be a signal that something is wrong. If you have any of these symptoms, see a doctor.

Another important aspect of caring for your eyes is protecting them from injury. Always wear safety goggles when you are handling chemicals, working with power tools, or in other situations that may cause injury. During sports, wear appropriate headgear to protect your head against blows and a face mask to protect your eyes. If you need to wear eyeglasses while playing sports, wear goggles over them to prevent shattering an eyeglass lens and cutting your eyes.

Wear protective goggles when you work with power tools and machines such as this grinder.

WORKING WITH A VDT

Working with a video display terminal (VDT)—a computer screen—can cause eyestrain. The symptoms of eyestrain include blurred vision, a headache, and a burning feeling in your eyes. Eyestrain results when your eye muscles become overtired from focusing on a close or unclear object for too long. To prevent eyestrain when you are using a VDT, take frequent breaks and focus your eyes on distant objects. Also adjust the room lighting or the VDT's location to eliminate glare on the screen.

VISION CHECKUPS A vision problem may develop so gradually that the person does not even notice it for awhile.

Sharell had been having trouble seeing the board in her algebra class. She didn't seem to have any difficulty in her other classes or when she was reading or working on her leather projects. Sharell also noticed that she wasn't fielding or hitting as well in softball as she did last year.

Because she had never had a vision problem before, at first Sharell might have thought that she was just out of practice at softball and that her algebra teacher's writing was too small.

One day after practice, Sharell's softball coach asked what was the matter, and Sharell explained what was happening. The coach asked Sharell where she sat in her classes. When Sharell thought about it, she realized that she sat at the back of the room in algebra but near the front in her other classes. Sharell decided to talk with her parents and ask to have an eye exam. Two weeks later, she was back in top form on the softball field and in algebra class—wearing new glasses to correct her nearsightedness.

If you notice any change in your vision, you should have a vision checkup right away. Even if you do not notice a change, you should have your eyes examined every two to four years so that if a problem develops, it can be identified early.

To check your vision, the doctor will have you read rows of letters on a wall chart or in a viewer. The letters in each row are smaller than those in the row above. The farther down on the chart you are able to read, the better your vision. Normal vision is said to be 20/20, which means that you can read at 20 feet what people with normal vision can read at 20 feet. If your vision is 20/40, you have to be at 20 feet to read what people with normal vision can read at 40 feet. The doctor will test each eye separately and then both together.

What is the eye doctor checking?

After checking your vision, the doctor will look into each eye to check the clarity of the cornea, lens, and fluids and the condition of the retina. If necessary, the doctor will also measure the fluid pressure inside each eye to check for early signs of glaucoma.

When you apply for a driver's license, you will be required to have a very simple vision check. In most states, a person must have *corrected* vision—vision while wearing lenses—that is 20/40 or better in order to get a driver's license. These license checkups are not a substitute for a doctor's examination.

CORRECTIVE LENSES If you have a vision problem, the doctor will give you a prescription for corrective lenses. The extent of your vision problem and the types of activities you participate in should determine whether eyeglasses or contact lenses are the better choice for you. Some people get both and switch between them for different activities.

If you use prescription sunglasses, choose ones with lenses that protect your eyes from the sun's ultraviolet rays. UV rays can damage your eyes as well as your skin.

Several different types of contact lenses are available. Ask your eye doctor to explain the advantages and disadvantages of each type. Whichever type you choose, it is essential to follow your doctor's instructions for cleaning and sterilizing them. Contact lenses that are dirty or that carry bacteria can cause serious eye irritations and disease. If the lenses irritate your eyes or blur your vision, see your eye doctor immediately.

LESSON 2.3 USING WHAT YOU HAVE LEARNED

REVIEW

1. Describe the functions of the iris and the pupil.
2. What is meant by 20/20 vision?
3. Why does a doctor check fluid pressure in the eye during a vision checkup?

THINK CRITICALLY

4. Working with a video display terminal can cause eyestrain. What should you do to protect against eyestrain when you are working with a VDT?
5. People who apply for a driver's license are given a simple vision check. What is not included in this vision check that is included in a complete eye examination?
6. Think about what you do that may place your eyes at risk—your study habits, your sports or other recreational activities, your exposure to sun or other bright light. List these risks and suggest some things you might do to decrease their impact on your eyes.

APPLY IT TO YOURSELF

7. Your father and your older sister are farsighted. You haven't noticed any problems with your own vision, but you wonder whether you might become farsighted, too. What are some examples of problems you might notice that could be signs of becoming farsighted?

SUMMARY

The eyes collect and focus light rays, convert them to nerve impulses, and send the impulses to the brain for interpretation. Nearsightedness and farsightedness are common vision problems that can be corrected by wearing lenses. Eye injuries and diseases require medical treatment. Many eye problems can be avoided through good personal care, including wearing safety goggles, a face mask, and protective headgear when appropriate.

Teenagers and Advertising

HEALTHY PEOPLE 2000

Eliminate or severely restrict all forms of tobacco product advertising and promotion to which youth younger than age 18 are likely to be exposed.

Public health concern about tobacco advertising is based on the premise that such advertising perpetuates and increases cigarette consumption. Cigarette advertising may increase cigarette consumption by recruiting new smokers, inducing former smokers to relapse, making it more difficult for smokers to quit, and increasing the level of smokers' consumption by acting as an external cue to smoke.

Objective 3.15

from Healthy People 2000: National Health Promotion and Disease Prevention Objectives

Close your eyes for a moment and bring to mind a familiar television commercial or advertising jingle. Did the advertisement that came to mind encourage teenagers to participate in health threatening or life-threatening, activities such as smoking, drinking, and behaviors associated with drinking?

Consumers can resist the false promises offered by advertising. By understanding the nature of promotion and by analyzing the ads that they find particularly appealing, they can begin to make healthy and informed choices ensuring their participation in the health goals for the year 2000.

READING BETWEEN THE LINES

Promotion of harmful products, particularly tobacco and alcohol, takes many forms. Magazines offer traditional advertising that includes glossy photographs of young hikers enjoying an invigorating climb and a rewarding smoke. Tobacco companies distribute whole catalogs of items to buy. Huge billboards serve as a backdrop to sporting events like golf, tennis, and skiing competitions. T-shirts, hats, and banners adorn the stages of rock concerts or the car racing arena. Viewers and participants at these events are thus exposed to hours upon hours of promotion. Many of these viewers are under 20 years old.

Tobacco promotion is just one villain in the advertising melodrama. Products ranging from candy to cars to cosmetics to cereals make claims that are often blatantly untrue or misleading due to omission of the dangers associated with their use. Along with many products comes the promise of carefree life-styles, sexual appeal, and scenes that mix products like alcohol with risky behaviors such as skiing and scuba diving.

All age groups are susceptible to advertising. However, researchers feel that teenagers may be among the most vulnerable when it comes to product advertising, particularly ads that sell tobacco and alcohol. The sense of invulnerability and immortality is strongest among people aged twelve through twenty. In fact, during those crucial years, patterns and habits are formed that extend throughout life.

Many individuals and groups are working together to restrict advertising of potentially harmful products to teenagers. But it is teenagers who must make the final choices about what products they buy and use.

EXERTING CONSUMER POWER

Teenage consumers have a tough job sorting fact from fiction in advertisements. Many products are valuable and their advertisements are truthful. But some are not, and determining whether an ad is truthful or not requires intelligent scrutiny. The following strategies may help you to make informed choices about consumer products.

1. Look at the claims being made by an advertisement. Is the claim realistic?

2. Is the advertiser appealing to the emotions of consumers? What promises are being made? What problem will be solved by using this product?

3. Analyze the product based on your own experiences and expertise. Would using the product pose a health risk?

4. Use consumer guides, which evaluate thousands of products. These guides analyze the safety, effectiveness, and reliability of products.

5. Discuss the use of products with your friends. Discover which products are most effective for them.

6. Remember that you always have a choice about what products you buy and use.

WHAT DO YOU THINK?

1. Think about the products you use daily, such as shampoo, cosmetics, clothing, sports equipment, magazines, or electronic devices. What caused you to buy these products? What role did advertising play in your choice of products?

2. In what ways do you think advertisers should be responsible to consumers?

3. Make a list of advertising slogans. Analyze each slogan and discuss its emotional appeal. What is the product promising? Is the advertisement misleading in any way?

where the fla

YOUR SENSE OF HEARING

MAIN IDEAS

CONCEPTS

✔ The ears convert sound waves into nerve impulses that the brain then interprets as sound.

✔ Structures in the ears help provide you with your sense of balance.

✔ Prolonged exposure to loud sound is a common cause of hearing loss.

VOCABULARY

eardrum
eustachian tube
oval window
cochlea
semicircular canal

Listening to your favorite song, enjoying the cheers of your teammates when you sink a basket, moving out of the way of an ambulance before you even see it—all are possible because of your sense of hearing. Your ears also play an important role in enabling you to walk, ride a bike, dance, climb a ladder, or do any other activity that requires balance.

THE STRUCTURE AND FUNCTIONS OF THE EAR

In the previous lesson, you learned that your eyes receive light rays and convert them to nerve impulses that your brain interprets as sight. In a similar way, your ears receive sound waves and convert them to nerve impulses that your brain interprets as sound. In addition, specialized structures in the ear help provide your sense of balance. As you read about hearing and balance, locate the structures in Figure 2-8.

HEARING Your outer ear is shaped to collect sound waves moving through air. The waves then pass along a short passageway called the external auditory canal. This canal is lined with hairs and with specialized glands that produce earwax. The hairs and wax help prevent dirt, bacteria, and other material from going deeper into your ear.

The auditory canal ends at the **eardrum**, a thin membrane across the opening to the middle ear. The sound waves make the eardrum vibrate. Behind the eardrum are three tiny bones—the smallest bones in your body—commonly called the hammer, the anvil, and the stirrup, named for their shapes. Vibrations pass from the eardrum to each bone in turn.

The middle ear is filled with air that enters through the eustachian tube. The **eustachian tube** [*yoo STAY shun*] connects the middle ear with the back of the throat and nose. This connection keeps air pressure equal on both sides of the eardrum so it does not rupture when outside air pressure changes, as on an airplane or in an elevator.

Between the middle ear and the inner ear is an opening called the **oval window**, also covered by a thin membrane. When the stirrup vibrates, it makes the membrane vibrate, and this vibration is passed on to the fluid in the cochlea. The **cochlea** [*KOHK lee uh*] is a spiral tube containing receptors that sense vibrations. When the fluid vibrates, it moves tiny hairs lining the cochlea. Receptors at the base of the hairs change these vibrations to nerve impulses. The impulses travel along the auditory nerve from the ear to the brain.

As with the eye and vision, you do not *hear* until the nerve impulses are interpreted by your brain. The brain can tell which direction sound waves are coming from because impulses from

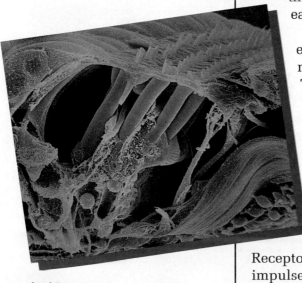

Inside your inner ear are tiny hairs like these.

one ear travel to one part of the brain, and impulses from the other ear go to another part. In addition, the brain also "decodes" the loudness of sounds and their pitch—how high or low they are.

BALANCE   Have you ever become very dizzy on a carnival ride? If so, you experienced the workings of your semicircular canals. The **semicircular canals** [*seh mee SUR kyuh lur*] are curved tubes in your inner ear that help provide your sense of balance. They play no role in hearing.

The semicircular canals are filled with fluid and lined with tiny hairs. When you move your head, the fluid moves, and the movement of the fluid causes the hairs to move. The hairs are connected to nerve cells that send impulses to the brain. The brain interprets the impulses and coordinates that information with information from your eyes and your muscles. Together, this information tells you the position of your body, whether you are moving, and if so, how fast and in which direction. When you get off a carnival ride,

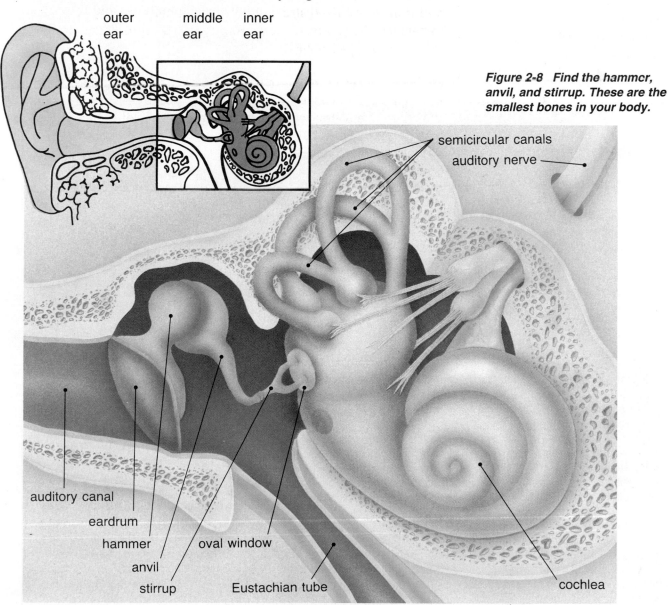

Figure 2-8 Find the hammer, anvil, and stirrup. These are the smallest bones in your body.

outer ear   middle ear   inner ear

semicircular canals
auditory nerve

auditory canal
eardrum
hammer   oval window
anvil
stirrup   Eustachian tube   cochlea

you may still feel dizzy because the fluid in your semicircular canals is still moving. After you stand still for a while, the fluid stops moving, and the dizziness goes away.

COMMON EAR PROBLEMS

Although the delicate parts of your ears are enclosed within your skull, they still can be damaged. Hearing loss from ear infections or other factors is not uncommon.

EAR INFECTIONS Most often, ear infections occur when bacteria or viruses travel from the nose or throat, up the eustachian tube, and into the middle ear. Besides being painful, an ear infection causes fluid or pus to collect in the middle ear, which can distort or block your hearing. Fortunately, most ear infections can be cured quickly with antibiotics. To help prevent ear infections, blow your nose as gently as possible when you have a cold. Blowing too hard can push the bacteria or viruses up the eustachian tubes and into your ears.

MAKING A DIFFERENCE

RESEARCH HEALTH

Closed-Caption Television

For many Americans, television is a part of day-to-day life. Breakfast is accompanied by the news, Saturday morning invites the unmistakable tinny music of cartoons, and evenings bring movies, music videos, drama, or comedy.

Until 1980, over 20 million deaf and hearing-impaired people were unable to receive the full benefits from television programs. They could see what was happening on a show but could not hear the story. However, since 1980, a technology called closed-captioned television has made it possible for the hearing impaired to enjoy regular television programming.

Captions for programs are created in places like the National Captioning Institute in Washington, D.C., or the Caption Center at PBS station WGBH in Boston, and by several private organizations. Captioners work from a script or from videotapes using a computer-enhanced typewriter which allows them to type over 200 words a minute. The true challenge for a captioner is to work with long-running live newscasts such as a press-conference or special event. In such cases, captioners must work at even greater speeds to deliver the news in print across the television screen.

In order to receive closed-captioned television, the viewer needs a decoder box that hooks up to a television. For many hearing-impaired individuals or for families with a hearing-impaired child, the cost of a decoder is too expensive. However, in April of 1990, the Federal Communications Commission ruled that, as of July, 1993, all televisions over thirteen inches must carry a built-in decoding device.

Deaf and hearing-impaired people are not the only community that enjoys closed captioning. Immigrants to the United States often invest in the device to help learn English. People who are semiliterate are finding that closed-captioned television greatly increases their ability to read.

1. How does the FCC ruling affect closed-captioned television?
2. Why is closed captioning a good learning aid for people who don't read or speak English very well?

HEARING LOSS In most cases, hearing loss is caused by an infection, an obstruction, or nerve damage. In a severe middle-ear infection, the eardrum can be damaged or even rupture. If large scars form when the eardrum heals, they will prevent the eardrum from vibrating easily. A severe infection also may damage the three small bones in the middle ear. Either condition can cause permanent hearing loss.

An obstruction in the ear blocks sound waves. If obstruction is the cause of the impairment, the hearing loss usually is not complete. Obstruction may be due to a buildup of wax or a bone blockage. Abnormal bone growth that causes hearing loss is an unusual inherited condition that affects both ears. Surgery usually can correct the problem.

Normally, earwax produced in the auditory canal works its way to the outside, where it can be removed easily. Sometimes, though, excess wax collects and hardens in the canal, blocking sound waves. If this happens, special eardrops can be used to soften the wax so it will work its way out. If a softener does not work, the wax should be removed by a doctor.

Damage to nerve cells in the cochlea also causes hearing loss. This type of hearing loss is permanent and cannot be corrected. Hearing loss caused by nerve damage usually affects hearing in both ears. The most common cause of this type of hearing loss is prolonged exposure to loud sound. For this reason, people who work in noisy environments—in a factory or outdoors at an airport, for example—wear protective earmuffs.

Hearing loss from nerve damage or from an obstruction may develop very gradually. The person may not even realize that he or she has a loss until it becomes serious. If you notice that your hearing has changed recently, you should see your doctor or an audiologist [*aw dee AHL uh jist*], a specialist who diagnoses and treats hearing problems.

CARING FOR YOUR EARS

Taking good care of your ears—and your hearing—is very important. Ear infections should be treated promptly because even a minor infection can lead to hearing loss. Although some types of hearing loss cannot be prevented, you can protect your ears against nerve damage. The guidelines listed at the right will help you protect your hearing.

GENERAL CARE Never try to clean inside your ear with a cotton-tipped swab, hairpin, or other object. Inserting an object into your ear can push wax further into the canal and pack it against the eardrum, blocking your hearing. An object also could puncture the eardrum and allow infection to enter the middle ear. Only a doctor should ever insert an object into the ear. You can, of course, use a swab or washcloth to clean your outer ear.

PREVENTING HEARING LOSS The best way to prevent hearing loss from nerve damage is to limit your exposure to loud sounds. Loudness is measured in decibels [*DES uh belz*]. At 70 decibels,

STRATEGIES FOR LIVING

To protect your hearing, follow these guidelines.

- Try to avoid noisy places. If you cannot, then carry ear plugs with you and wear them when sounds become too loud. Ear plugs will not block out all sound, but they will reduce the loudness to a safe level.

- If you have to be in noisy places often, give your ears a rest from time to time by finding a quieter place.

- Keep the volume of stereos and radios turned down to a comfortable level. If you listen through earphones, keep the volume low enough so that you can still make out normal sounds around you. If the earphones are drowning out all other sounds, the volume is too high.

SOUND LEVELS

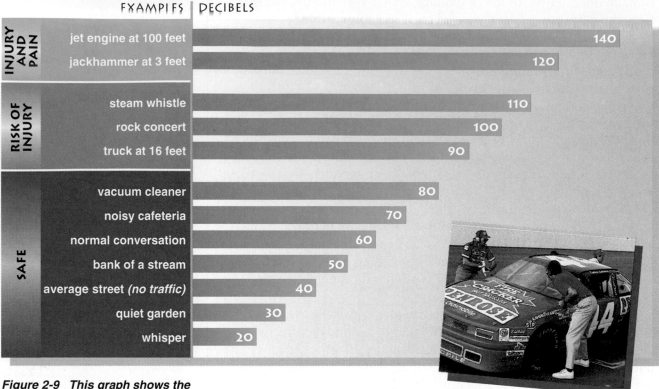

	EXAMPLES	DECIBELS
INJURY AND PAIN	jet engine at 100 feet	140
	jackhammer at 3 feet	120
RISK OF INJURY	steam whistle	110
	rock concert	100
	truck at 16 feet	90
SAFE	vacuum cleaner	80
	noisy cafeteria	70
	normal conversation	60
	bank of a stream	50
	average street *(no traffic)*	40
	quiet garden	30
	whisper	20

Figure 2-9 This graph shows the loudness levels of some common sounds. How loud do you think your gym classes are?

SUMMARY

The ears receive sound waves, convert them into nerve impulses, and send the impulses to the brain for interpretation. The ears also help you maintain your balance. An ear infection should be treated promptly so it does not lead to hearing loss. Hearing loss from nerve damage may be prevented by avoiding continued exposure to loud sound.

sounds become annoying; at 85 or 90 decibels, they become damaging. The length of time you are exposed to loud sounds is as important as the loudness of the sounds. Listening to music at 95 decibels for two or three hours is as damaging as hearing a much louder sound for only a short time.

LESSON 2.4 USING WHAT YOU HAVE LEARNED

REVIEW

1. In which part of the ear are vibrations converted to nerve impulses that are interpreted as sound?
2. Identify three causes of hearing loss.
3. What three sources provide information to the brain to give you your sense of balance?

THINK CRITICALLY

4. The eustachian tube connects the middle ear with the back of the throat and nose. What is the function of this connection? How could it contribute to an ear infection?
5. Identify a continuous, loud sound that you experience often. Describe what, if anything, you could do to avoid that sound. How could you protect your ears against it?

APPLY IT TO YOURSELF

6. Your friend listens to tapes with earphones. You think he keeps the volume turned up too high. What would you say to try to convince him to turn the volume down?

Tan Time

The end-of-school dance was two weeks away; and Josie, Benita, and Carol wanted to get together to discuss plans for the party that would follow the dance. Benita called Josie one Saturday morning and told her that she and Carol were going to the neighborhood pool to plan the party. Benita explained, "We can talk and work on our tans at the same time. Meet us there."

Josie agreed. It was going to be a hot day, and she welcomed a chance to lie by the pool and visit with her friends. She knew she only had a few minutes to catch the bus.

When she got to the pool, Josie discovered that she had left her sunscreen at home. She knew Benita and Carol wouldn't have any. They never seemed to think they needed it. Josie considered going to a nearby drugstore. But she didn't want to miss anything with her friends. Josie thought about the risk of sunburn. She hated to get a burn. Josie had been real careful to use sunscreen ever since a neighbor had developed skin cancer. "Oh, we're probably not going to be out that long. I could just be careful," Josie thought.

PAUSE AND CONSIDER

1. **Identify the Problem.** What was Josie's conflict?

2. **Consider the Options.** What are Josie's options?

What could Josie do to enjoy her day with her friends and protect herself from the sun?

3. **Evaluate the Outcomes.** What might happen if Josie remained with her friends and did not use a sunscreen? What consequences would she face if she took the time to get some sunscreen?

"Oh it's just this once," Josie thought. "It's not that big of a deal. I'll just be real careful."

When Josie got to the pool, she found her friends already engaged in a lively discussion about plans for the party. She sat down and joined them, excited to share her ideas with them. A couple of hours later, they were still talking—planning a list of what foods they would serve. Josie was beginning to feel the sting of the sun on her back. When she went into the changing room, she looked in the mirror and discovered that she was beginning to burn. "Oh no. What a mistake," she thought.

When she came out, she told her friends it was time to get out of the sun, and that she had already been out too long without sunscreen. "Oh come on. We've hardly been touched," said Carol.

"Look, you're just not showing your burn yet. I've been out

too long already," said Josie. "If I stay out any longer, I'm going to peel for a week. I have to go. Why don't you come to my place to continue our plans?" She was worried that Carol and Benita would continue making plans without her. Instead, they agreed. Everyone decided to continue their discussion at Josie's house over lunch.

DECIDE AND REVIEW

4. **Decide and Act.** What decision did Josie make? Was it the correct decision? Why did she decide to leave the pool?

5. **Review.** What other choices did Josie have? What did Josie do once she realized that her first decision wasn't working out? What would you do if faced with the same options?

PROJECTS

1. Using a variety of materials, create a 3D model of the skin, eye, ear, or a tooth. Base your model on the art in this chapter or on other resources.

2. Learn about seeing-eye dogs or hearing-ear dogs. Try to interview a blind or hearing-impaired person who uses a dog as a helpmate. What does the dog do to assist the person? How was the dog trained? What training did the person need? If you cannot interview someone, contact agencies for the blind or hearing-impaired, or do library research. Write a report, give an oral presentation, or create a display to share what you have learned.

3. Find out more about warts. What causes them? Are they contagious? Can you catch them by handling a toad? What are "satellite" warts? What are the methods of treatment?

WORKING WITH OTHERS

Work with two or three partners to find out how different animals see and hear. Each partner should choose a different animal and do library research on his or her own. Find out what types of structures the animal has for sensing sound (or vibrations), light, and color. Then, working together as a group, create a classroom display that illustrates how different animals see and hear compared with humans.

CONNECTING TO...

SCIENCE   Borrow a sound level meter from a physical science teacher. Use the meter to measure the sound levels in several different areas of your school, and at different times of the day. Which area or time is usually the quietest? Which is the noisiest? Create a bar graph similar to Figure 2-9 in this chapter.

USING VOCABULARY

astigmatism	enamel	pores
calculus	epidermis	premolar
cancer	eustachian tube	pulp
canine	farsightedness	pupil
cataract	glaucoma	receptor
cavity	incisor	retina
cochlea	iris	rod
color blindness	lens	root
cone	molar	sebum
cornea	nearsightedness	semicircular canal
crown	nerve impulse	sun block
dentin	organ	sun protection
dermatitis	oval window	factor (SPF)
dermis	plaque	sunscreen
eardrum		

Questions 1-10. On a separate sheet of paper, write T or F to indicate whether each statement is true or false. For each false statement, change the <u>underlined</u> term to make the statement true.

1. A(n) <u>organ</u> is a nerve ending that receives information about the environment and sends that information to the brain.

2. <u>Plaque</u> helps protect the inner part of the tooth.

3. The <u>iris</u> bends light rays so they come together on the retina.

4. Lenses cannot correct <u>farsightedness</u>.

5. Acne results when oil glands produce too much <u>sebum</u>.

6. Ear infections often happen when bacteria and viruses travel up the <u>cochlea</u> and into the middle ear.

7. The sharp front teeth that bite and cut food are called <u>molars</u>.

8. Increased fluid pressure inside the eye causes <u>astigmatism</u>.

9. The <u>epidermis</u> is the thin, outer layer of the skin.

10. Red, swollen, itchy patches on skin are signs of <u>calculus</u>.

CONCEPT MAPPING

Work by yourself or with others to create a concept map for *personal care*. In your map, use as many of these concepts as you can: *cleanliness, corrective lenses, ears, eyes, infection, loud sound, personal care, skin, teeth, UV radiation.* You may include other concepts related to personal care in your map. Information about concept mapping appears at the front of this book.

THINKING CRITICALLY

INTERPRET

LESSON 2.1

1. Which of the skin's four functions depends on receptors?

2. Explain how the skin helps protect your body against disease.

3. What can you do to prevent dry skin?

4. What is melanoma? Describe its warning signs.

5. Identify two ways to reduce your risk of developing skin cancer.

LESSON 2.2

6. What happens to tooth enamel when plaque is not removed from teeth?

7. How do brushing and flossing help prevent tooth decay and gum disease?

8. Why should you see a doctor or dentist if you notice white patches in your mouth?

9. Describe three common symptoms that someone with TMJ problems might experience.

10. Why should you have regular dental checkups?

LESSON 2.3

11. Your eyes receive light rays and convert them to nerve impulses. What must happen for you to actually see anything?

12. How are objects seen by a nearsighted person? a farsighted person?

13. Is "color blind" an accurate term? Explain your answer.

14. If a detached retina is not treated promptly, what could eventually result?

LESSON 2.4

15. Your ears collect sound waves and transmit them to the inner ear, where they are converted to nerve impulses. Beginning with the outer ear, name the structures that transmit sound waves, in the order in which they function.

16. Which structures in your ears play no role in hearing? What function do these structures perform?

17. Why are middle-ear infections common in people who have a cold?

APPLY

LESSON 2.1

18. Your younger brother has just started to develop acne. What advice would you give him to help control the acne and care for his skin?

LESSON 2.2

19. One cause of tooth loss is gum disease. Describe how gum disease develops and leads to tooth loss without treatment.

LESSON 2.3

20 Your aunt says she doesn't need to go to an eye doctor because she gets a vision test every three years when she renews her driver's license. Is she right? Explain your answer.

LESSON 2.4

21. A friend listens to loud rock music for two hours every day as he does his homework. What would you tell your friend to convince him to discontinue this bad habit?

COMMITMENT TO WELLNESS FOLLOW-UP

SETTING GOALS

Review your responses to the Commitment to Wellness checklist that you completed at the beginning of this chapter. Make a chart with four columns labeled *Skin, Teeth, Eyes,* and *Ears* to represent the four personal-care [areas] discussed in this chapter. In each column of your chart, mark Y if you responded *yes* to a checklist item about that area of personal care or N if you answered *no.*

Look at the Ys and Ns in each column and across all four columns. Do you see any patterns? For example, are there one or two areas of personal care that are stronger for you? Are your strengths and weaknesses fairly evenly divided across all four [areas] of personal care? Think about your strengths in personal care. How did you develop your good habits? What practices have you been using that you could also apply to your weaker areas? Jot down ideas about how you could make that healthy practice a regular part of your personal-care routine.

WHERE DO I GO FROM HERE?

Unlike some other forms of cancer, skin cancer is not uncommon among young adults. Develop and implement a plan for protecting yourself against harmful UV rays.

FOR MORE INFORMATION ABOUT SKIN CANCER, CONTACT:

American Cancer Society
1599 Clifton Rd NE
Atlanta, Georgia 30329

Mental Health

Chapter 3

**Developing a
Healthy Personality**

Chapter 4

Healthy Emotions

Chapter 5

Managing Stress

Chapter 6

**Understanding
Mental Disorders**

What influences in your life have helped you to be the person that you are?

What does it really mean when people say that they are "stressed out"?

Why are some people better than others at keeping their cool under pressure?

57

Developing a Healthy Personality

"Never let us be discouraged with ourselves."

François Fénelon

BACKGROUND

François Fénelon was a French author and priest. In the late 1600s he argued that women should be allowed a better education.

To belong is to feel a part of the group, to feel accepted, to feel safe and secure. But many children, teenagers, and even adults may feel that belonging seems to be reserved for the smarter, the stronger, the more beautiful, and the wiser.

To truly belong, a person must first feel a sense of belonging to him or her self. Acceptance of one's self—one's own intelligence, beauty, wit, and talents—is the first step in belonging. No one is everything. No one has everything. But everyone has unique talents and thoughts that define them and make them special and worthwhile.

What are your unique talents? Where did they come from? A closer look at your background can tell you a lot about why you are the way you are. Your unique heredity, social influences, role models, and placement in the family all combine to create a special individual—you. And you are worth accepting, loving, and celebrating. Never again will another person exactly like you ever live in the world and work, love, create, play, and contribute in just the way that you can and do. Indeed, you do belong.

On a sheet of paper in your Wellness Journal, write your responses to the following statements.

1. Most of the time I feel good about who I am.
2. I have confidence in myself.
3. I accept that I cannot be perfect nor all things to all people.
4. I accept differences in other people and understand that those differences make people special.
5. I believe in taking responsibility for my actions.
6. I try to be honest in my dealings with others and with myself.
7. I do not engage in stereotyping individuals.
8. I know how to accept praise for a job well done.
9. I know what I believe and what I value.
10. I accept that others will not think and feel exactly the way I do.
11. I understand the factors that influence my personality development.

Review your responses and consider what might be your weaknesses and strengths. Save your list for a follow-up activity that appears at the end of the chapter.

RECOGNIZING THE HEALTHY PERSONALITY

Positive mental health is an important part of wellness. The wellness continuum discussed in Chapter 1 relates to more than just physical health. In order to function at your highest level, you must feel good mentally as well as physically.

WHAT IS MENTAL HEALTH?

Mental health is a state of well-being of the mind. Having self-esteem is a vital part of mental health. Self-esteem means liking yourself and being able to stand up for what you believe is right. Does this mean that you never worry or never have a problem? No, but it is easy to understand that mental health depends on feeling good about who you are and having confidence in yourself.

THE MENTALLY HEALTHY PERSON   Who you are is reflected in your personality. Your **personality** is the mix of how you feel, think, and behave that makes you different from anyone else. Personalities, like bodies, can be healthy or unhealthy. Usually society regards mentally healthy people as those who accept themselves. They are people who live life with constantly renewed appreciation. They largely determine their own actions and afford others the same right. Mentally healthy people may question but tend to trust their own thoughts and feelings. They are creative and capable of forming close ties with others.

Good mental health helps you participate in life with energy and enthusiasm.

DIFFERENT APPROACHES   Scientists who study human behavior, including personality, are called **psychologists** [*sy KAHL uj justs*]. Over the years, psychologists have developed theories about how the personality is shaped. Each theory is based upon one or more of the common approaches psychologists take to describing a personality. Four major approaches to explaining the personality are psychoanalytic, trait, social-learning, and humanistic. Each approach explains personality development from a different point of view.

The *Psychoanalytic Approach*, developed by Sigmund Freud, focuses on the development of the child and subconscious motivations. The word *subsconcious* refers to a part of the brain that is not accessible to thought. According to Freud, every action, emotion, and thought is the result of subconscious wishes or fears.

Trait theorists define personality development in terms of specific traits, that is, personal qualities that are characteristic of the behavior of the individual. For example, while one individual might exhibit an aggesssive trait, another's behavior might be observed as passive.

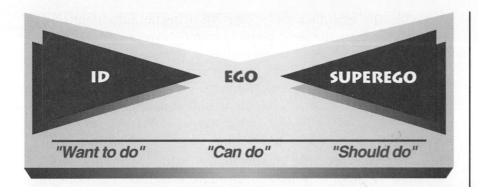

Figure 3-1 *Explain the place-ment of the ego between the id and the superego in this diagram.*

FREUD'S THEORY AND HUMAN INSTINCTS

Freud believed that humans are born with basic instincts of aggression that must be controlled in order to maintain a safe and civilized society. He divided the personality into three main systems: the id, the ego, and the superego. These are diagrammed in Figure 3-1. Instinctive behaviors belong to the most basic part of the personality called the id. The id is the part of the personality that seeks fun or pleasure, that is, the "want to do" part. The superego serves as a person's con-science and helps bring behavior into line with the values of society. It is the "should do" part. The ego represents reality. It puts boundaries on the impulses of the id by taking into account the values of the superego. The ego provides balance.

The *Social-Learning Approach* revolves around reinforcement. Actions that lead to rewards are likely to be repeated and those that lead to punishment are less likely to be repeated.

The *Humanistic Approach* to personality development is based upon the belief that each person is born essentially good and worthy and has the potential to develop into a fully empowered person.

In their studies, psychologists have found that the factors that shape your personality can be divided into two major groups: hereditary and environmental. Hereditary factors are the character-istics or traits that were passed down, or inherited, from your par-ents. Environmental influences on your personality include your physical and social surroundings and your life experiences.

HEREDITY AND PERSONALITY

Heredity is the biological passing of characteristics from parents to offspring. Physical characteristics such as height and color of eyes and hair are determined by heredity. Other characteristics such as shyness, ability to adapt, mood, and activity level can be noted in infants as young as 3 months old. This early setting of characteris-tics suggests a strong link to heredity.

Children often have levels of intelligence that are similar to those of their parents. **Intelligence** is the ability to learn and to adapt what you know to changing situations. To determine the role of heredity

HEALTHY PEOPLE 2000

Reduce to less than 10 per-cent the prevalence of men-tal disorders among children and adolescents

Objective 6.3
from *Healthy People 2000: National Health Promotion and Disease Prevention Objectives*

PERSONALITY TRAITS

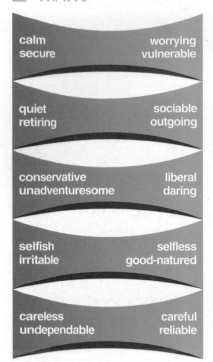

calm secure	worrying vulnerable
quiet retiring	sociable outgoing
conservative unadventuresome	liberal daring
selfish irritable	selfless good-natured
careless undependable	careful reliable

Figure 3-2   Which pair in each of the five sets of traits do you think best describes you?

An older admired person can have a powerful influence on a younger child.

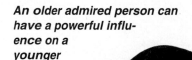

in intelligence, scientists study identical twins because identical twins have exactly the same heredity or genetic make up. Results have shown that identical twins tend to have very similar levels of intelligence. This similarity in intelligence is found even when twins grow up in different surroundings. These findings suggest that heredity plays a very strong role in determining intelligence.

INSTINCTS   Certain types of behavior are inherited by all people. These behaviors are called **instincts**. An instinct is an inherited pattern of behavior that does not need to be learned. For example, all babies are born knowing how to nurse. Humans are thought to have few true instincts.

PERSONALITY TRAITS   Some scientists suggest that people are born with certain characteristics that describe their personalities. Think about someone you know. How would you describe his or her personality? What words come to mind? Using certain adjectives to describe ourselves or others is one way of using personality traits to present a picture of people. Which of the word pairs in each set of words shown in Figure 3-2 best describes you?

If you chose the adjectives *sociable* and *outgoing* to describe yourself, you are probably considered an extrovert. An **extrovert** [*EK struh vurt*] is a person who is very outgoing. If you described yourself as quiet and retiring, you are likely to be considered an introvert. An **introvert** [*IN truh vurt*] is a person who prefers being alone rather than in a crowd. Extroverts and introverts may differ in their approach to life but neither is better than the other. Most psychologists recognize that few people are totally extroverted or introverted.

ENVIRONMENT AND PERSONALITY

Even though you were born with many traits that influence your personality, you develop other characteristics because of your particular environment. Your family, your school, and your community are parts of your environment. How you behave in response to your environment is called learned behavior.

The process of teaching behavior based on the beliefs and habits of the family and community is called **socialization** [*sosh uh luh ZAY shun*]. It includes the passing along of one's cultural heritage through the teaching of religion, traditions, dress, and ways of behaving toward other people. Whatever your cultural heritage, it has an effect on the development of your personality. Parents begin the process of socialization from the time a child is born, and school and the community add their influence as the child grows. There are several pathways through which socialization occurs.

- **Conditioning** is the shaping of behaviors by means of rewards and punishments. When a child is praised for kindness, the child is likely to continue behaving in that way.

- **Modeling** is the process of learning by watching and imitating another person. The person whom someone watches and imitates is called a role model.

- Expanding horizons play a crucial role in the development of personality and intelligence as a child grows. Exposure to people and places beyond the home, varied opportunities for learning, and new activities and experiences greatly influence the development of personality and intelligence.

Your **gender**, whether you are a boy or a girl, was determined before you were born, but as you grow it plays an important role in your personality development. The effect of gender on personality is largely due to the expectations of society about how males and females should behave. For example, girls are sometimes expected to be quieter and more passive than boys. Because of this expectation, people are more willing to accept aggressive behavior from boys than they are from girls.

Expectations for certain ethnic or gender groups may be the result of stereotyping. **Stereotyping** is thinking that all members of a large group share the same characteristics in a fixed way. Think about examples of stereotyping that you have observed. When you stereotype someone, you fail to recognize the person's uniqueness.

Some of the stereotypes that limit opportunities for women are being broken.

A COMBINATION OF INFLUENCES

Most scientists agree that heredity plays a very important role in the development of personality. They also point out that a person's surroundings greatly influence the way in which inherited characteristics are expressed. For example, a child of musical parents might exhibit an interest and talent in music. It would be difficult to determine how much of this interest and talent is due to heredity and how much is the result of the child's home environment where music might be a part of everyday life. Therefore, scientists agree that personality is the result of a combination of environment and inherited characteristics.

LESSON 3.1 **USING WHAT YOU HAVE LEARNED**

REVIEW

1. Describe two influences that affect personality development.
2. How do instincts differ from learned behavior?

THINK CRITICALLY

3. Explain how personality is affected by heredity and how it is affected by environment.
4. Describe one incident in your life that helped you to learn socially acceptable behavior through conditioning, and one incident that helped you to learn through modeling.

APPLY IT TO YOURSELF

5. In what ways has your personality been influenced by your cultural background?

PERSONALITY DEVELOPMENT

MAIN IDEAS

CONCEPTS

✔ Social scientists have different theories about the way personality develops.

✔ Personality development is closely related to experiences during various stages of life.

✔ Having a strong sense of self is important to being your own person and setting your own goals.

VOCABULARY

adolescence
gender identification
peer
values
maturity

Individuals develop at their own pace. Just as psychologists disagree about what most influences personality, they also have different ideas about the way personality develops. Most agree, however, that there are certain needs that must be met for children to grow up and become mentally healthy adults.

THEORIES OF DEVELOPMENT

Four of the best-known theories of personality growth were developed by Sigmund Freud, Jean Piaget, Erik Erikson, and Abraham Maslow. These men believed that personality is formed in a series of stages that typically occur at the ages shown in Figure 3-3.

Freud's theories about the importance of the subconscious in personality development are the basis for the psychoanalytic approach to the personality. His theories center on how instincts or drives propel development. Freud suggested that if a child has difficulty in one stage of development, the difficulty could affect later stages of development. Freud identified five developmental

◆ STAGES OF MENTAL DEVELOPMENT

Age	Birth to I	1 to 2	2 to 3	3 to 6	6 to 7	7 to 11
Freud Psychological Stages	**Oral Stage:** the child focuses on its mouth; is not aware of being separate from its mother		**Self-Control Stage:** child learns to control its body, including toilet training	**Self-Awareness Stage:** child becomes aware of self and its sexual identity; becomes aware of other people	**Socialization Stage:** child begins to identify with role models; boys identify with fathers, girls identify with mothers	
Piaget Intellectual Stages	**Sensorimotor Stage:** child has not learned to speak; thoughts expressed through actions; learns that objects exist even when out of sight		**Preoperational Stage:** learns to speak by imitating others; later learns to read and write; has not yet learned to think logically; learns by trial and error		**Concrete Operational Stage:** child views events from different perspectives; develops simple reasoning and problem solving abilities	
Erikson Social Development Stages	**Basic Trust or Mistrust:** child's feelings of being loved result in trust; or mistrust leads to chaos		**Autonomy or Shame and Doubt:** praise for learning and control of bodily functions bring independence; or criticism and neglect lead to shame and doubt	**Initiative or Guilt:** praise for efforts leads to initiative, with development of memory and desire to begin learning adult roles; or criticism results in guilt	**Industry or Inferiority:** feelings of worth and competence result in desire to learn and be productive; or lack of industry or sense of self-worth leads to feelings of inferiority in comparison to others	

stages from birth to the middle of adolescence. **Adolescence**, from about age eleven to the late teens, is the time when children develop adult physical characteristics, gain a sense of their identity, and grow emotionally.

Jean Piaget, a Swiss psychologist, was influenced by Freud's work as he worked on his own theories of development. Piaget's studies focused on the stages of intellectual development outlined in Figure 3-3. He found that the responses of children of similar age to questions on a variety of subjects were very comparable.

As a Social-Learning theorist, psychologist Erik Erikson studied development in terms of social reinforcement. According to Erikson, a person's development depends on his or her social interactions at key points in life. Thus, Erikson's eight stages, shown in Figure 3-3, are called social developmental stages.

Another important theory of development came from the work of Abraham Maslow. Maslow, a Humanistic psychologist, classified human needs into different levels, as shown in Figure 3-4, page 66. Maslow suggested that human needs can be shown in the form of a pyramid. Lower, or more basic needs, must be met before higher needs can be satisfied. For example, Maslow believed that it is very hard to develop a sense of belonging to a family or the community if the need for food and shelter is not met.

Figure 3-3   What differences between the developmental stages of Freud and Piaget and the stages of Erikson are revealed by this table?

11 to 12	12 to late teens	Young Adult	Middle Adult	Late Adult
Full Awareness Stage: adolescent becomes curious about opposite sex; is fully aware of self and prepares for adulthood				
Formal Operational Stage: adolescent develops complex reasoning and problem solving abilities; beliefs and values take shape				
	Identity or Role Confusion: sexual maturation and questions about identity lead to development of friendships; or inability to separate from family results in adult role confusion	**Intimacy or Isolation:** shares self with others; or inability to commit self leads to isolation	**Generativity or Stagnation:** has desire to contribute to community; or is self-absorbed	**Integrity or Despair:** accepts fact of death and remembers life fondly; or fears death and feels sense of failure

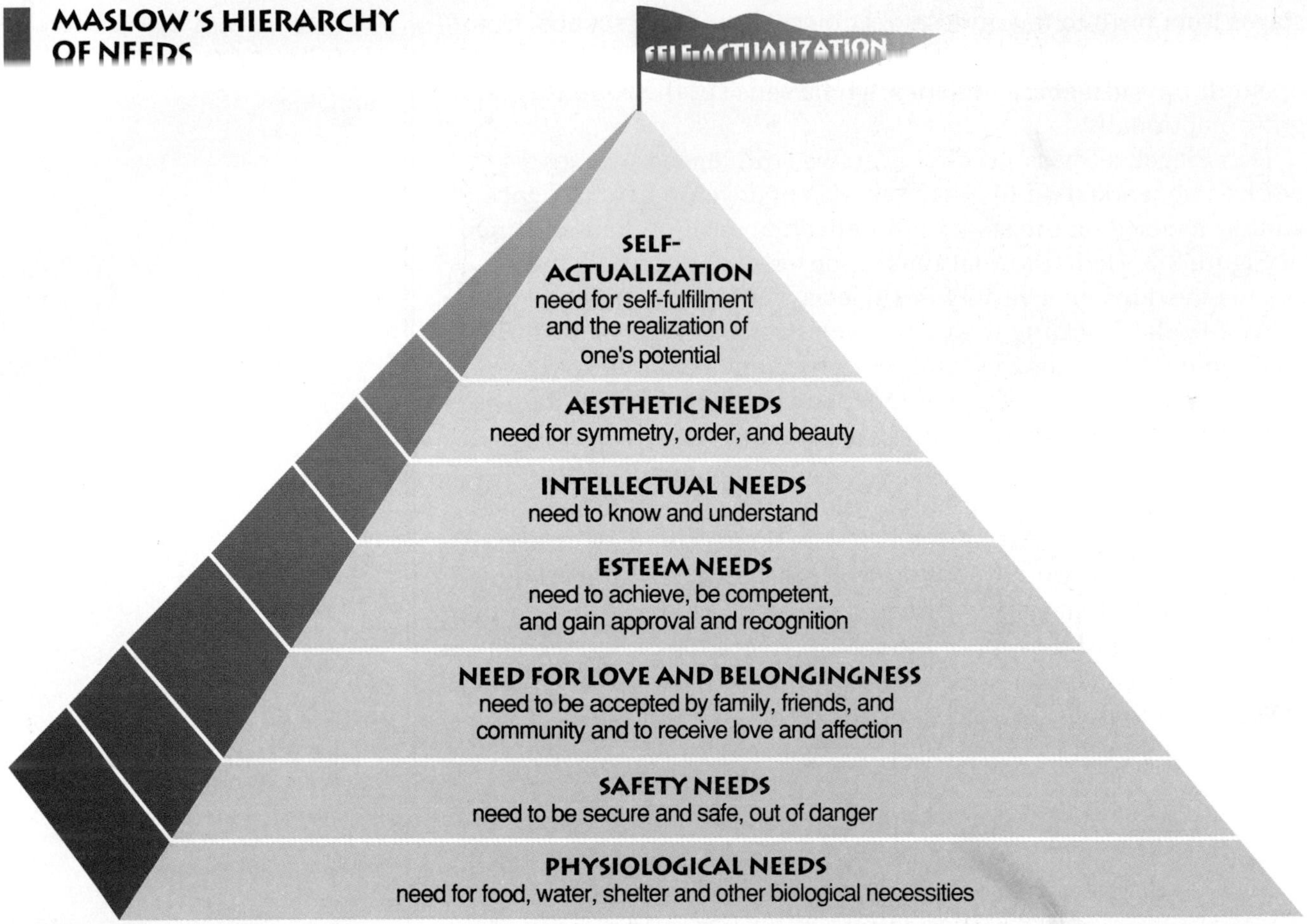

SELF-ACTUALIZATION

SELF-
ACTUALIZATION
need for self-fulfillment
and the realization of
one's potential

AESTHETIC NEEDS
need for symmetry, order, and beauty

INTELLECTUAL NEEDS
need to know and understand

ESTEEM NEEDS
need to achieve, be competent,
and gain approval and recognition

NEED FOR LOVE AND BELONGINGNESS
need to be accepted by family, friends, and
community and to receive love and affection

SAFETY NEEDS
need to be secure and safe, out of danger

PHYSIOLOGICAL NEEDS
need for food, water, shelter and other biological necessities

Figure 3-4   Does your own
development seem to follow this
hierarchy of needs?

There are many other theories of human development. Those presented here are some of the better known, or those that provide the foundation on which other psychologists have built new theories. No one theory of psychological development is accepted by everyone. But these theories and the theories of other scientists have led to a general understanding of how people grow and develop mentally.

DEVELOPMENT DURING PRE-ADOLESCENCE

Physical, social, and mental stages of development from birth to adulthood are somewhat similar for everyone. Recent research supports the belief that even very early experiences influence later development.

INFANCY   Studies have shown that, in addition to food, shelter and consistent care, infants need love and affection. Babies who are not held and comforted are likely to have difficulty trusting others. In later life, they may find it difficult to form attachments to others. On the other hand, babies who are touched, spoken to, and cared for can begin to build trust. They feel safe and start to learn that they can depend upon other people.

Babies soon begin to notice the world around them and learn to recognize things and people by sight and sound. They begin to

FOR YOUR INFORMATION

To become a psychologist you must earn a degree in psychology. Psychologists work in the fields of teaching, research, and counseling.

Children eagerly take on increasing challenges as they grow if they have a sense of security and trust.

explore their world, to crawl, to walk, and to speak. Encouragement at this early stage of life gives a child a sense of well-being and an eagerness to learn. This is the foundation for the development of self-esteem.

CHILDHOOD   Early in life, the child develops a need for independence. Self-confidence, desire for achievement, and sense of self all continue to develop during childhood. The child's environment and heredity affect the development of these characteristics.

Children gain a sense of achievement by successfully carrying out new activities such as doing puzzles, helping at home, and learning to read. Self-control also becomes important. Self-control means being able to control your actions. Learning not to grab a favorite toy from a playmate requires self-control.

During early childhood, children learn that boys and girls are different. This process is called **gender identification**. Parents are usually the chief models for gender identification, although other adults can also serve as models. Freud's theory suggests that girls are likely to identify with their mothers and boys with their fathers. Siblings, the media, and the community also play important roles in gender development. Children tend to accept as appropriate the roles in which they see males and females functioning. If boys and girls see both men and women in many different and nontraditional roles, they will tend to model the observed behavior. Therefore, many more options will be available to them. Erikson's and Piaget's theories suggest that socialization and intellectual processes allow the child to model whatever behaviors he or she finds most comfortable.

HEALTHY PEOPLE 2000

Increase to at least 75 percent the proportion of providers of primary care for children who include assessment of cognitive, emotional, and parent-child functioning.

Objective 6.14
from *Healthy People 2000: National Health Promotion and Disease Prevention Objectives*

Adolescence is a time when you begin to examine your goals and your attitudes.

DEVELOPMENT DURING ADOLESCENCE

As an adolescent, you may notice that at one moment you may feel on top of the world; at the next moment you can be angry, lonely, or sad for no clear reason. These sudden mood swings occur in part because your body is changing as you grow into adulthood. Changes in mood also can occur because you are trying to become an independent person. During this stage of development, most teenagers ask themselves three key questions.

- Who am I?
- What do I believe?
- Where am I going?

WHO AM I?   As a child, you may not have spent much time questioning your thoughts and feelings. Now you may worry about things that never seemed to bother you before. You may even be wondering who is the real you. This wondering is natural as you search for your own identity. Your identity derives from the particular parts of your personality that you and others recognize as being you. Your identity is who you are and who you wish to become.

Trying to understand yourself and express yourself fully can be both scary and exciting. You may sometimes feel like a stranger to yourself. You also may feel distant from people and activities you once enjoyed. Adolescents begin to look beyond their own families for new role models. Friends, teachers, or other people often offer new ideas and challenges. Because you may want to be with people who are like yourself, belonging to a group of people your own age becomes more important. People who are alike in one or more ways—usually in age and interests—are called **peers**.

Belonging to a peer group is important, because sharing experiences with friends and feeling accepted by them helps you to learn more about yourself. As you build a sense of your own identity and begin to believe in the person you are, you will be better able to resist pressure from your peers. Peer pressure is the urging from others to do what the crowd is doing. Not all peer pressure is negative, although often it may seem that way. Teenagers sometimes influence each other to volunteer their services to their community. However, at other times, they may feel pressure to smoke or drink alcohol because others are smoking or drinking. Sometimes no one encourages you to join in, but you just feel that you should. In both cases, peer pressure is at work. It is important for you to make your own decisions and avoid being talked into something you do not want to do. Giving in to peer pressure, when you think you should not, can influence how you feel about yourself.

WHAT DO I BELIEVE?   This question involves a search for values. **Values** are the rules and standards that you feel are important to live by. The question also addresses the role your conscience plays in the way you behave. Your conscience is the part of you that distinguishes right from wrong and can be associated with what Freud termed the superego. As a child, you probably accepted what your parents taught you. As a teenager, you may want to know the reasons behind your parents' opinions and rules. You are becoming more aware of the values held by other people, and you wonder about your own beliefs.

You may question what you believe about politics and social problems. You also are probably concerned about such personal issues as what makes a good friend, how important it is to be honest or hard-working, and how to please yourself without hurting others. Your adult personality will probably be a mix of some of the values you grew up with and some that you come to adopt during adolescence.

WHERE AM I GOING?   This question is characteristic of adolescence. In childhood, you probably lived within a very organized environment. As a child in school, you may have lined up and marched to lunch with your class. You depended often on others to help you with problems. Now as a teenager, you want to experience the freedom of making your own choices, but you may find it to be a struggle.

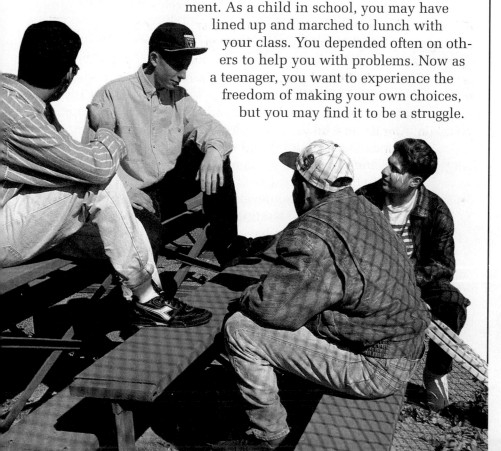

The values that you will adopt for your life need careful thought and discussion with others.

You will have better mental health if you can follow these suggestions.

- Determine to be healthy and work to achieve that goal.
- Understand that you must relate to the larger world.
- Try to understand others and have compassion for them.
- Give of yourself in the service of others.
- Be a true friend to those who care about you.
- Try to be flexible when circumstances change.
- Adopt the attitude that you are in control of your mind and body.

Although Annie was grateful to her mother for helping her get a summer job in the hospital, she was also a little concerned about how she would like working there. After speaking many times with her mother, who was a doctor, Annie was not sure that she wanted to work in a hospital. Nevertheless, she gave it a try.

After a few weeks it was clear to Annie that she did not enjoy hospital work. She didn't like the environment and some of the tasks she had to do. But Annie felt that she needed to continue because she didn't want to disappoint her mother, and she hated being a quitter.

As an adolescent, you will be trying to choose a way of life that suits your abilities and personality. What do you think Annie should do?

Annie finally decided to talk about her dilemma with her mother. They agreed that since Annie had tried hospital work and found that it was not right for her, she should try something different. One of Annie's friends knew of a job opening in the summer recreation program. Annie decided to apply for it.

Adolescents often try different paths before finding one that seems right. Such exploration is helpful in increasing your self-knowledge and preparing you for adulthood. Even as an adult, your goals may change as your interests change.

DEVELOPMENT DURING ADULTHOOD

Although adults are often referred to as "grown ups," their development is far from complete. Throughout the period of life following adolescence, you will experience continuing challenges that will result in change and growth. You are probably looking forward to entering adulthood with a healthy mixture of enthusiasm and anxiety. The transition will be smooth if you have successfully dealt with the challenges of adolescence.

Each stage in life brings challenges. Identify some challenges faced by the individuals in this photo.

YOUNG ADULTHOOD   During this period of your life you will become responsible for yourself and your actions. You may finish college or trade school or get a job and support yourself. Some young adults leave home and get a place of their own. Others continue to live at home. Goals during young adulthood usually relate to achievement in the working world, marriage, and starting a family.

Young adults have reached a certain level of emotional **maturity**, which is the state of being fully grown. People who are mature know themselves fairly well and are able to make long-lasting ties with others. They can make responsible decisions and understand what may result from their actions. For some young adults, however, the twenties and thirties continue to be a confusing time. These young people may find that they need to look further before reaching a clear understanding about how they wish to live.

MIDDLE ADULTHOOD   This period of life, from about age 40 to 65 or 70 years, often brings new satisfactions and new concerns. Doing well in a job can provide a great sense of achievement. However, as family resonsibilities increase and other responsibilities develop, this stage in life may be a time of financial worry.

Middle adulthood often is a time for reviewing life goals. At this stage in life, you will have a better understanding of yourself and the world in which you live. It may be clear to you what you can and cannot accomplish. This knowledge must be balanced against earlier hopes and dreams.

Even if you have achieved much of what you set out to accomplish by middle adulthood, you may find a need to identify new goals. Erikson's Generativity or Stagnation Stage describes the desire to give service to the community that many people feel during this time of life. Entering a new adventure, even a difficult one, often brings exciting new challenges and new drive.

LATE ADULTHOOD   In later years, usually after age 65 or 70, the fact that life will not go on forever becomes clear. This recognition can make late adulthood a very difficult time. However, many mentally healthy people find that the later years are rewarding and can present many new challenges. People who have learned that life carries both happiness and sadness are likely to enjoy the present and remember the past fondly. According to Erikson, most older adults view this stage of their lives in one of two ways. They may look upon their lives as failures and fear the approach of death, or they may accept death as a natural process while remembering the good things of their lives.

LESSON 3.2   USING WHAT YOU HAVE LEARNED

REVIEW

1. What is the foundation of Piaget's theory of development?
2. What is meant by the term *values*?
3. What is a peer group? Explain how belonging to a peer group can influence the development of your own set of values.

THINK CRITICALLY

4. Erikson's first stage of social development identified the importance of providing an infant with a sense of trust. How might this development of trust help the child as he or she gets older?
5. A person who has achieved Maslow's self-actualization stage has already satisfied the first six levels of human needs. Refer to Figure 3-4 and describe what you think such a person might be like in terms of his or her behavior and way of life.

APPLY IT TO YOURSELF

6. How can you use the information you learned about psychological development to help you set goals for adulthood?

SUMMARY

The work of psychologists and other social scientists has added much to the understanding of personality development. This work has shown how people grow and develop in stages. Each stage presents new questions and challenges. At each stage, certain needs must be met for individuals to develop and maintain a healthy personality.

Carol Gilligan

Harvard University psychologist Carol Gilligan believes that women think differently than men. Through her research, she suggests that women's behavior is based on a different set of moral values than those on which men base their behavior. A person's behavior and value structure is called moral development.

Gilligan began her research in response to psychologist Lawrence Kohlberg's theories of moral development. Kohlberg studied the ways that boys and men view rules in society. He suggested a "justice" morality that values individual rights, freedom, independence, and honor. Kohlberg's theory of moral development has three levels. At the first level, a person has no sense of rules and acts on the desire for reward or to avoid punishment. At the second level, a person understands rules and conforms to them in order to obtain approval. At the third stage, a person understands rules, and makes choices about whether to obey or disobey the rules based on individual principles about whether the rule is right or wrong. In his research, Kohlberg concluded that women rarely progress beyond the second level, therefore they are less mature in their moral development than men. Carol Gilligan disagrees.

Gilligan believes that the moral development of women is as mature as that of men, only different. From her research she concludes that women's moral development is based on the relationships that foster concern and caring for the self and for others. Her theory of moral development also has three levels. At the first level, a person is concerned with self and survival. At the second level, a person remains concerned with self, but is also concerned with being responsible and with the feelings of other people. At the third level, a person has high self-esteem and is concerned with self and balanced efforts toward what is best for all.

Gilligan believes that society's standards for moral development are based on Kohlberg's male model. She sees that, at around 12 years old, young women begin to checker their speech with "I don't know" and "This might be stupid but...." Gilligan believes that the use of these phrases signals a decrease in self-esteem and confidence because women's values are not taken as seriously as men's. The effects can last a lifetime.

Many consider Gilligan's work on moral development to be revolutionary. Gilligan and her supporters believe that all people can benefit from acknowledging both value systems.

1. Why would someone with low self-esteem precede questions and statements with "This might be stupid but . . . "?

2. What possible far-reaching consequences could Carol Gilligan's work have for psychologists?

Kohlberg's versus Gilligan's understanding of moral development

Kohlberg's levels and stages	Gilligan's levels
Level I	**Level I**
Stage 1 Obey rules to avoid punishment	Concern for the self and survival
Stage 2 Obey rules to get rewards, share in order to get returns	
Level II	**Level II**
Stage 3 Make decisions based on others' approval/disapproval	Concern for being responsible, caring for others
Stage 4 Rigid conformity to society's rules, avoid censure for rule-breaking	

Level III	Level III
Stage 5 Obey rules because they are necessary for social order, but the rules could be changed if there were better alternatives	Concern for self and others as interdependent
Stage 6 Behavior conforms to internal principles (justice, equality) and sometimes may violate society's rules	

ACHIEVING MENTAL WELLNESS

Your personality develops as a result of hereditary and environmental influences. As you mature and begin to take charge of your life, you will identify ways to make your life better. Doing so may mean making changes in your own behavior. Identifying areas that need to be changed should be the result of careful thinking and decision making. To make decisions, you need to recognize the characteristics of a healthy personality.

THE HEALTHY SELF

Identifying specific traits of a mentally healthy person can be difficult. However, many people agree that the mentally healthy person has a realistic self-concept, likes and trusts others, and takes responsibility for his or her own actions.

SELF-CONCEPT   Your **self-concept** is your view of yourself and your role in life. When you have a realistic self-concept, you can see yourself in a balanced way.

June's mother came into her room. She was concerned because it was after midnight and June was still up working on an English project that was due the next day. This was the third time this month that June had stayed up late to finish a school project.

"Why didn't you start earlier? You have had this assignment for a month," said her mother.

"I tried, but I just didn't have an idea," complained June. She felt frustrated. If she weren't such a perfectionist, she thought, it would be easier to get the project done more quickly.

Do you agree with June's assessment? Is her frustration really related to her wanting to complete the project well?

June tried to go back to her work, but she was unable to concentrate. She knew that her mother was not pleased with her. As June thought about her mother's words, she realized that her mother was right. If she really cared about doing a good job on her project she should have started earlier. June began to see that being a procrastinator was her problem, not being a perfectionist. She needed to change the way she managed her assignments. June resolved to set up a schedule for completing future assignment and to stick to it.

If your picture of yourself is not clear, it may be helpful to examine your thinking and your actions, as June did, to see if you are being honest with yourself.

FORMING RELATIONSHIPS   Being able to form close trusting relationships with other people is another sign of good mental health. People who cannot relate well to others are likely to feel lonely and unhappy. An inability to trust others often

MAIN IDEAS

CONCEPTS

✔ Understanding your strengths and weaknesses is important to good mental health.

✔ Self-examination is important for knowing who you are.

✔ You can change things about yourself once you have decided to do so.

VOCABULARY

self-concept
self-examination
attitude

Thinking honestly about who you are can provide greater understanding and acceptance as well as the determination to change.

Developing Your Self-Esteem

A healthy self-esteem is an important part of feeling good about yourself, the people around you, and your purpose in life. The key to a healthy self-esteem rests in appreciating your own worth, and acting responsibly toward yourself and others. Self-esteem does not depend on the clothes you wear, the car you drive, or the friends you keep. Advertisements that suggest you will be a better or happier person if you buy certain products are not aimed at you, they're aimed at your wallet, and their product will not improve your self-esteem. Self-acceptance and a sense of humor can go far in establishing and keeping a healthy self-esteem.

If you feel good about yourself, others will feel good about you, too. Even on your worst days, do something to make yourself feel good. Try an experiment. For one month, say only positive things about yourself. You will be amazed at your changed outlook. You may also notice that others respond to you differently, too.

There are a few ways you can work toward bolstering your self-esteem. Set realistic goals. Stay active and resist boredom. Read a book, go to a play, a ballet, a concert—activities that take you outside of yourself. Find a hobby you will enjoy, even if you think your friends might think it is silly or weird. Above all, try to be optimistic. Remember, you are responsible for your actions and reactions. Trust your instincts. You will find that you know yourself best.

stems from failures in relationships in childhood. If you think you are unlovable, it is hard to love others. You may feel that you do not deserve love.

RESPONSIBLE BEHAVIOR   Certain ways of behaving cause certain results. Responsible behavior includes not blaming others for the results of your actions. You must be able to anticipate the consequences of your behavior, then choose the action that will achieve the result you desire. When you decide for yourself how you will behave, you are more likely to accept responsibility for what happens. When June accepted that her own procrastination was the problem, she was open to making a change.

MAKING CHANGES

How do you know when change is necessary? Maybe you feel as if you have lost control of your life. Or possibly you recognize an aspect of your behavior that you don't like or has been causing you repeated problems. If you ever feel this way, you may wish to do some self-examination. **Self-examination** means stepping back and taking a look at yourself. This can be done alone or through talking

QUESTIONS FOR SELF-EXAMINATION

- Do I have problems that I ignore or count on someone else to solve for me?
- Are there some things about my behavior that I would like to change?
- Does peer pressure cause me to do things I would not otherwise choose to do?
- Does my physical health seem to be affected by how I feel about myself?

with friends or someone else you trust. You have the freedom to accept yourself as you are, or you can work toward changing parts of yourself that you think need improvement.

Once you have identified problem areas, you can begin to make changes. Sometimes just realizing you have a problem helps you to change. However, change will not happen overnight. Progress will be slow, but the effort will be worth it. If you decide that you want to make some changes, you can use the Seven-Step Plan to Change given in Chapter 1, page 17.

CHANGING ATTITUDES   Self-examination includes looking at your attitudes. An **attitude** is your state of mind toward something in particular or toward life in general. Your attitude is an outlook on something. A positive attitude toward life is the ability to see the best in a situation and to expect that good things are to come. A negative attitude toward life is always expecting that the worst will happen.

If your self-examination shows that you have a negative attitude about something, it may be helpful to think about how you developed that attitude. Suppose you lack confidence in your ability to make new friends. Perhaps when you examine this attitude you will see that it came from a few bad experiences when you were new in your school or neighborhood. Or it may have come from some earlier family experiences.

The Strategies for Living feature on this page gives some suggestions for changing attitudes. Following them can bring about change. When you notice that you are beginning to change, recognize and enjoy the rewards that an improved attitude can bring. In this way your positive attitudes will be strengthened.

ACCEPTING YOURSELF   Your picture of who you are can be greatly influenced by how others react to you. In deciding whether to accept or to try to change some of your behavior, remember that no one is perfect. All people have faults. Often people try to behave in ways that they think others will accept. However, trying to be someone you are not can hurt your self-esteem.

STRATEGIES FOR LIVING

Suggestions for making a change in attitudes

- Act as if you have the attitude you want to develop.
- Build on praise you receive from persons you respect.
- Try to avoid dwelling on your mistakes.
- Recognize and value your achievements.
- Recognize your good characteristics and the benefits you have that others do not.
- Decide that you can have more control of your life.

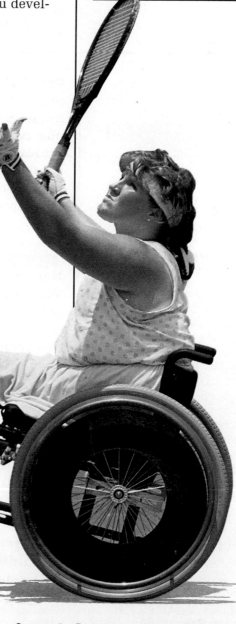

The attitude you have toward life helps determine your degree of happiness.

In order to form trusting relationships with others, you must first accept and appreciate yourself.

Saud had always been fairly shy and reserved. As he was entering his freshman year, Saud's parents urged him to get more involved in activities at school so that he would meet more people and make more friends. Saud felt as if he was letting his parents down. "Maybe they're right," he thought. "Maybe I am missing out on something."

Saud decided to give sports a try that fall. He went out for the soccer team and knew right from the beginning that it wasn't what he wanted to do. However, his parents seemed to be happy about his decision. After a week Saud thought about how unhappy he was. He realized that he just wasn't an athlete and really didn't want to be. That night he told his parents that he felt pressured by them to be someone he just wasn't. They agreed that the most important thing was for Saud to be true to himself, and that he should quit the soccer team. Saud also agreed that he wouldn't rule out trying some other activities at school.

Saud was responding to what other people thought he should be, not what he wanted to be. His experience made him realize that he was happy with himself as he was. You should consider trying to change only if the desire to change comes from within you. It takes courage to try to change. It also takes courage to accept yourself as you are, as Saud did. Changing your behavior and accepting yourself are both ways of growing.

SUMMARY

People who are mentally healthy usually have a realistic self-concept, they like and trust other people, and they take responsibility for their own actions. Self-examination can help you discover some facts about your behavior that you may wish to change. Change is not easy and can be frightening, but it can also be healthy and rewarding. The most important thing is accepting and valuing yourself for your own uniqueness.

LESSON 3.3 ## USING WHAT YOU HAVE LEARNED

REVIEW

1. How would you go about doing a self-examination?
2. What is meant by self-concept? Why is a realistic self-concept important to good mental health?

THINK CRITICALLY

3. Think of someone you know who has a negative attitude toward life. Identify two incidents that reveal that attitude. Suggest two strategies he or she could use to change.
4. According to Freud's theory, one part of the subconscious mind, the id, constantly seeks pleasure. In the light of Freud's theory, why are enjoyable habits hard to break?

APPLY IT TO YOURSELF

5. When you have acted on suggestions made by others about ways of changing your behavior, did you feel good about the change? Give one example of a positive result. Have you ever felt that you were acting a role rather than acting like yourself?

Friendship For Sale

BEING WELL, STAYING WELL

DECISION FOCUS MAKING

Kendra, Tina, and Marcie went to the mall one rainy Saturday afternoon. The three of them wandered from store to store browsing.

The three girls walked into a gift shop. Kendra remembered that her mother's birthday was coming up. She decided to buy a card for her. While she was busy looking at cards, she could hear Tina and Marcie laughing and whispering in the next aisle. Kendra paid for her card and called to her friends, "Come on, I'm starved. Let's get something to eat." "Okay," Tina and Marcie agreed.

While they were eating, Kendra asked, "Hey, what were you laughing about in the store?" Tina and Marcie burst out laughing. Marcie pulled a pair of earrings out of her pocket and asked, "Aren't these pretty?"

"Yeah," answered Kendra. "When did you buy those?"

"Silly," said Marcie. "I didn't buy them. I stole them."

Kendra felt sick. She had never stolen anything in her life. She knew they could all get in a lot of trouble if they got caught. Kendra didn't know what she should do. She felt really uncomfortable about spending the rest of the day with Tina and Marcie. "What if they steal something else," she thought. Kendra didn't want to go home either. She enjoyed doing things with Marcie and Tina. They were two of the most popular girls in the class. Kendra was worried that they might think she was a "goody-two-shoes."

PAUSE AND CONSIDER

1. *Identify the Problem.*
   What was Kendra's conflict?

2. *Consider the Options.*
   What were the options Kendra had for handling her mixed feelings about Tina and Marcie's action?

3. *Evaluate the Outcomes.* What would happen if Kendra told someone about what had happened? What would happen if Kendra just went along with the theft and said nothing?

Kendra was scared to say anything else to Tina and Marcie. She knew she would risk their friendship. But she had to say something.

"Hey, I really don't like it that you stole those earrings. My father runs a small store downtown and every time someone steals something, it costs him money. Besides, stealing is just plain wrong."

"Oh Kendra, relax. That's a big store. They aren't going to miss a pair of earrings. You're being a real drag."

Kendra swallowed hard. "Well, I'm just not comfortable with this. I'm leaving."

"Fine," said Tina. "Leave. We'll be sure to remember what a bore you are."

Kendra picked up her belongings and said good-bye. She knew she may have just lost her friendship with Tina and Marcie. But she just didn't believe in stealing. If they couldn't accept her as she was, were they really worth having as friends?

DECIDE AND REVIEW

4. *Decide and Act.* What choice did Kendra make? What risk did she take in speaking up to her friends?

5. *Review.* What other ways could Kendra have handled the situation? What would you have done if you had been in Kendra's situation?

PROJECTS

1. Pick a person whom you admire and whom you consider to be a role model. What do you admire about this person? If the person is someone you know, interview the person and find out about his or her family background, childhood, and adolescence. What factors do you think contribute to the personality of your chosen subject? Write a brief biography of the person highlighting his or her background and personality.

2. Sigmund Freud is often considered the founder of psychoanalysis. Find out more about Freud and his work. Write a report that describes his work and present arguments that reflect your agreement or disagreement with his findings.

WORKING WITH OTHERS

Well-known psychologists have developed theories to explain human behavior. With a partner, choose a psychologist, such as Carl Jung or Carol Gilligan, and read more about his or her theory about human behavior. Each partner should identify three common behaviors that people often try to change, such as smoking, laziness, or impatience. Use the psychologist's theory to explain why the behavior may have developed.

CONNECTING TO...

ENGLISH There are many books on the market that claim to help people deal with difficult psychological issues or achieve a healthy personality. Some of these self-help books are more helpful than others. Find a book that covers a subject you may want to know more about. As you read it, make lists of points with which you agree and disagree. Present a book report to the class analyzing the strengths and weaknesses of your chosen book.

CHAPTER 3 ~ Review

USING VOCABULARY

adolescence	heredity	personality
attitude	instinct	psychologist
conditioning	intelligence	self-concept
extrovert	introvert	self-examination
gender	maturity	socialization
gender identification	modeling	stereotyping
	peer	values

1. The name given to a scientist who studies personality
2. Patterns of behavior that do not need to be learned
3. A person who is outgoing and sociable
4. The time when children develop adult physical characteristics
5. The biological passing of characteristics from parents to children
6. The process of teaching behavior based on the beliefs and habits of the family and community
7. The rules and standards that a person lives by
8. People who are alike in more than one way, usually in age and interests

CONCEPT MAPPING

Copy and complete the concept map shown below. Information on concept mapping appears at the front of this book.

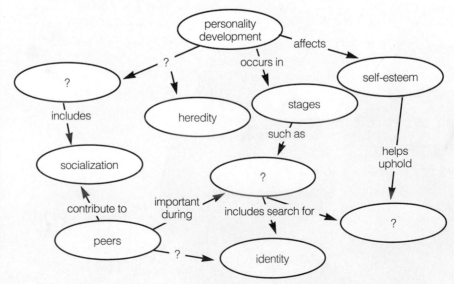

THINKING CRITICALLY

INTERPRET

LESSON 3.1

1. What are some of the attributes of mentally healthy people?

2. What are the four major approaches that explain personality?

3. Who developed the Psychoanalytic Approach to studying human behavior?

4. What are two factors that determine personality?

5. What are the characteristics of the id, ego, and superego?

6. What are two examples of traits that a person might inherit?

7. How does socialization affect personality?

8. Why do some people think that females are more passive than males?

LESSON 3.2

9. What effect does a safe and secure infancy have on a person's later development?

10. What is a peer group?

11. What are some qualities of a mature person?

LESSON 3.3

12. What are some strategies a person can use to change his or her attitude toward something?

13. What influence does attitude have on the way a person views her or his surroundings?

APPLY

LESSON 3.1

14. One boy in a certain family always seemed to take a leadership role among his siblings. His sisters tended to follow his lead. What factors might account for this situation?

15. How would exposure to many different life-styles affect learning through modeling?

LESSON 3.2

16. How do you feel when you see an adult acting in a childish way? What reasons might there be for the adult's behavior?

17. Why do you think it is impotant that teenagers think about the key questions *Who am I?*, *What do I believe?*, and *Where am I going?*

LESSON 3.3

18. After self-examination, a person might decide to try to change some part of his or her behavior but accept other parts. What do you think might be some factors that would influence whether a person would decide to try to change?

COMMITMENT TO WELLNESS FOLLOW-UP

SETTING GOALS

Refer to the Personal Commitment to Wellness checklist at the beginning of this chapter. Review your responses. As you go through the list, see if any of your responses have changed as a result of reading Chapter 3. If so, write a few sentences that describe your changed feelings.

If you find that some of your responses have not changed and you think that it is important that they do, recognize that change often does not happen quickly. Write the items you want to change in your Wellness Journal. Then think about what you can do to help change your thinking about yourself in that area. Frequently refer to these strategies for change as you continue to work toward achieving a healthy personality.

WHERE DO I GO FROM HERE?

If you need help in dealing with your self-assessment, talk with any trusted adult or peer who knows you well. Talking with someone can help you see and appreciate your strengths and recognize where your weaknesses lie. Your guidance counselor may be able to help, or she or he can refer you to a professional who can.

FOR MORE INFORMATION, CONTACT:
American Psychological Association
1200 17th Street N.W.
Washington, D.C. 20036

Healthy Emotions

". . . everything can be taken from a man [person], but one thing: the last of the human freedoms—to choose one's attitude in any given set of circumstances, to choose one's own way."

—from *Man's Search for Meaning*, by Viktor Frankl

BACKGROUND

Many of author Viktor Frankl's writings reflect his thoughts and experiences during his confinement in a concentration camp during World War II. Can you find anything else that he has written?

During times of trouble, it can be very easy to find blame or fault with someone or something else. In reality, how you are affected by incidents in your life is up to you. You can be angry, sad, happy, or frightened. Each of these is an emotion. Although you cannot always control your feelings, you can control how you behave in response to your feelings.

People experience many different emotions. How people express their emotions is also different. For example, some fans at a basketball game may express themselves harmlessly by cheering, booing, or shouting comments. Others may deal with their emotions in an unhealthy way—picking a fight in the crowd or feeling sad or depressed for hours after a game is lost.

Feelings can be very complex. Your emotions can affect you physically, mentally, socially, and intellectually. Knowing constructive ways to handle emotions is an important part of mental health.

When you learn to choose your attitudes, you realize real freedom.

SELF-
ASSESSMENT

How in touch are you with your emotions? Use the following checklist to take a closer look at yourself. In your Wellness Journal, or on a separate sheet of paper, number from 1 to 10. Respond to the following statements by writing a *yes* for each item that describes you all or most of the time.

1. I try to express my feelings in a constructive way.
2. I do not let jealousy harm my relationships.
3. I would be able to let myself grieve if someone close to me died.
4. I am able to laugh at myself when I make mistakes.
5. When I feel guilty, I realize that I am not a bad person, but that I should change my behavior.
6. I can talk to my parents or friends about the things that upset me.
7. I know when I am using defense mechanisms.
8. I avoid situations that might lead to violence.
9. I do not try to "save face" by fighting.
10. Emotional pressure does not interfere with my ability to make decisions.

Review your responses and consider what might be your strengths and weaknesses. Save your personal checklist for a follow-up activity that appears at the end of the chapter.

UNDERSTANDING YOUR EMOTIONS

Understanding your emotions is important to your mental health. **Emotions** are the strong, immediate reactions that you feel in response to an experience. They tell you whether what you experience is frightening or comforting, soothing or painful. If you are aware of your emotions, you can learn to express yourself constructively. For example, you may sometimes feel annoyed about a rule that seems pointless to you. If you understand why you are angry, you may be able to avoid responding inappropriately. You will be able to express your feelings more clearly.

People in all societies and of all ages have emotions. Often they affect people in similar ways, such as the body's responses to emotions. People who feel worried often have frowns on their faces or furrowed brows. Their muscles are tense. People who feel afraid may sit with their arms folded and legs crossed, as if they are protecting themselves. Other emotions cause physical changes. Your heart rate speeds up when you are angry. You perspire more when you are nervous. Emotions are powerful—they can make you sick, and they can help you to heal.

Some emotions, such as love, feel good. They enable you to feel attached to other people. They add to your sense of strength and give you a sense of hope. Other emotions, such as fear, can feel bad. They keep you from feeling pleasure and can even produce a sense of loneliness or emptiness. However, emotions are not necessarily good or bad. How you deal with the feelings is what matters. In fact, difficult emotions can sometimes be handled in such a way that the result is good. You experience each feeling in your own way, and you may choose to express or to hide that feeling.

LOVE

A strong affection or deep concern for another person is love. It can be communicated in many different ways. Love can be expressed through words or through touch or other actions that show caring and concern. Love often grows with time. All people have the ability to give love and the need to receive it.

Just as love is expressed in a variety of ways, there are also several types of love. Friendship is one form of love. Good friends feel trust and loyalty toward each other and share interests. They eventually grow to appreciate the loyalty. Such feelings and behavior are a form of love. The caring among parents, children, and brothers and sisters is another type of love. Members of a family can develop a strong bond that grows out of many years of living together. The love in marriage is one of the deepest kinds of love two people can share. This type of love involves commitments to each other about all parts of life.

Some types of love are not felt toward individuals. You may love your country, for example. Respect for its values and the opportunities it offers may result in a patriotic feeling. Affection

MAIN IDEAS

CONCEPTS

- ✔ It is important to understand your emotions.
- ✔ There can be constructive ways to handle anger.
- ✔ Fear and guilt can be useful emotions.
- ✔ Grief can be a very healthy emotion.

VOCABULARY

emotion   grief
hostility   guilt
anxiety

Every day, you witness a wide range of emotions in the people around you.

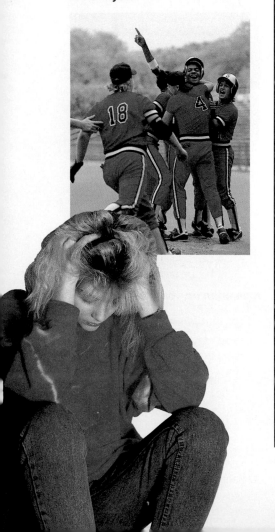

Love is an emotion that grows out of trust and appreciation. Friendship is a type of love that takes time to grow but can last forever.

for humanity is another kind of love. It leads to a desire to be helpful, from assisting a stranger across the street to working toward improving your community.

ANGER

All people feel anger at times. Anger is a strong feeling of displeasure that can range from annoyance to complete fury. It usually causes a physical reaction. Besides an increase in heart rate, you may tremble or your face may feel very warm.

RECOGNIZING YOUR FEELINGS   Anger may take different forms. Sometimes people feel angry out of frustration. Frustration is a feeling of disappointment. You feel frustrated when things are not the way you would like.

Hostility is another feeling of displeasure. It is a negative way of expressing an emotion. Hostility is feeling and behaving in an unfriendly way. People may show their hostility by making nasty comments or by going against the ideas of others. For example, if you feel hostile toward someone you may refuse to speak to that person, or you may not listen to his or her ideas.

Anger can sometimes be helpful. For example, if you see a friend being treated unfairly, you may feel angry. This anger may cause you to defend your friend.

Your anger is your own learned response to a situation. Other people do not cause it. Anger always can be handled in a constructive way. If anger is not handled constructively, the effects usually are harmful.

How often do you feel like this?

After working hard mowing lawns all summer, Rico was able to buy a bicycle. One day he went to get his bike to ride to the ball field. He found the front wheel twisted out of shape. Rico discovered that his younger brother, Pablo, had taken the bicycle that morning without asking. Pablo had run into a fire hydrant and twisted the wheel.

Suggestions for managing anger.

- Recognize your own anger and that of others.
- Be understanding with a person expressing anger.
- Always listen carefully to what an angry person is telling you.
- Try to express respect along with the anger.
- Notice your own reactions, especially your physical reactions.
- Focus your attentions on the present problem, and avoid thinking of old grudges or wounds.

SOURCE: THE INSTITUTE FOR MENTAL HEALTH INITIATIVES.

A tragedy often can leave a person feeling fearful and anxious about the future.

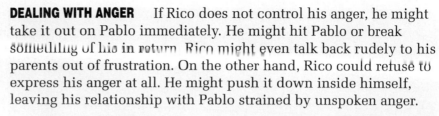

DEALING WITH ANGER   If Rico does not control his anger, he might take it out on Pablo immediately. He might hit Pablo or break something of his in return. Rico might even talk back rudely to his parents out of frustration. On the other hand, Rico could refuse to express his anger at all. He might push it down inside himself, leaving his relationship with Pablo strained by unspoken anger.

Rico grabbed his tennis racquet and left the house. He hit tennis balls against the wall of the garage for a long time. Then he went to see his best friend and told him what had happened. Later that evening, Rico sat down with Pablo for a talk. He told Pablo how angry he was about what Pablo had done. Pablo apologized for the damage and for not having told Rico what happened. Pablo also agreed to use his allowance to get Rico's bicycle fixed.

Rico chose constructive ways to handle his anger. Physical activity and talking with another person both help to get the anger under control. Waiting to talk with the person who made you angry is also a good idea. When you have calmed down, you can explain more clearly why you are angry. It is then easier to see that your anger is not with the person, but with the person's behavior.

FEAR

You feel fear when you believe you are in danger. It can make you break into a sweat, your heart beat rapidly, or your hands and feet go cold. Your muscles often get tense because your body gets ready to defend you against the threat.

Sometimes fear results from known dangers, such as fire or an accident. Fear of real threats to your safety can be a helpful emotion. It warns you to jump out of the way of a moving car, or it can lead you to take precautions.

Fear can also be caused by something less easily understood—a fear of the unknown. This feeling is sometimes called **anxiety**. Often it is fear of being hurt, or failing, or of losing something important to you. Anxiety makes you feel nervous and ill at ease. Your blood vessels may dilate, causing you to blush. It can cause changes in your digestive tract and leave you with a tight feeling in your stomach. You feel in danger, and you are not certain that you can handle it. Sometimes people have trouble figuring out what causes their anxiety. Some common causes are tests in school, a first date, or performing in front of people.

A COMMON REACTION   Everyone feels fear at one time or another. Since fear cannot always be avoided, it is useful to know how to deal with it in a healthy way.

Rachel was given an assignment to make a brief speech to her English class. As the day for her speech approached, Rachel became more and more anxious. What if her speech was boring? What if her mind went blank in the middle of it? She got so nervous that preparing for the speech became difficult. Rachel's heart beat faster just thinking about it, and her mind kept wandering.

Rachel could become so afraid of making the speech that she cannot sleep well, or she may lose her appetite. She may even feel sick and stay home on the day of the speech. On the other hand, Rachel might pretend that she feels fine about the speech and not study very hard. She may walk to the front of the class and suddenly feel overwhelmed by the anxiety she has tried to ignore.

Rachel decided to discuss her fear about the speech with her parents. Her parents reminded her of other difficult events that she had gotten through in her life. Together, the three of them agreed on a good study schedule for Rachel. They also had Rachel practice giving the speech in front of the family.

Open communication with someone you trust can help reduce feelings of fear.

DEALING WITH FEAR Rachel dealt with her fear in a healthy way. By admitting her anxiety and talking it over with her parents, she gained a better understanding of the emotion. Once the reason behind the anxiety was clear, it was easier to create a plan for reducing it.

When you feel fearful, it is best to admit the emotion and express it to someone who cares about you and that you trust. Then you can develop a plan to deal with the threat you feel—whether real or imagined.

JEALOUSY

Jealousy is an emotion that is related to fear. Jealousy is the fear of losing something you already have. People feel jealous, for example, when they are afraid of losing someone's love. Imagine that your best friend has been spending more time with other people than with you. This may make you feel jealous, thinking it means your friend no longer cares about you. Occasional jealousy is natural, but it should be kept under control. If it is not controlled, relationships with others can be harmed.

GRIEF

The death of someone you love, the divorce of parents, or the loss of a close friend are three events that can result in grief. **Grief** is a deep sorrow that is caused by the loss of someone or something.

Advertising Techniques Use Emotional Appeal

Have you ever watched a commercial for candy bars or thirst quenching drinks and then craved that product? If you have not, your powers of resistance are strong! Advertising is designed to appeal to the emotions of consumers. Do you want status or success? Buy this slick car. Do you want romance? Use this frothy mouthwash. Do you want to feel special, apart from the crowd? Wear this knockout perfume. Do you want to perform well at a sport? Drink this cool drink.

If these products could really deliver all that they promise, there would be no need for advertising. Word of mouth would be all the advertising a product would need. Often, it is hard to resist the temptation to buy things advertisers say you need, especially if the advertisement appeals to your weak spot. Become a discerning buyer. Here are a few tips for evaluating a product before you buy.

- Identify your own needs. Do you really need the product?
- Disregard the come-on. Will using this product really make a difference in your life?
- Check a consumer satisfaction guide before you buy a product. Why spend money on something that has built-in problems or flaws?

Crying over a loss can be a healthy release of feelings of grief.

A NATURAL EMOTION The loss can be so painful that you are left with an empty feeling. Although grief can be painful, it should not be seen as a negative emotion. Instead, it should be recognized as a natural emotion that most people will experience. It can serve as a good reminder of your ability to love and form friendships. There are both healthy and unhealthy ways to deal with grief.

Michael always had a special relationship with his grandfather. Whenever he visited, his grandfather took the time to talk with Michael. He often had good advice for Michael and told him stories about his own childhood. Sometimes they went to a ball game together. One day Michael came home from school to find his mother upset. His grandfather had become ill. A few days later, Michael's grandfather died.

HANDLING GRIEF Michael might respond to the loss of his grandfather in different ways. He might become so sad that he cannot think of anything else. On the other hand, Michael may refuse to think about his grandfather, since it makes him cry. While pretending to feel no pain, Michael may decide that the risk in caring for someone is too great.

At first, Michael could not believe his grandfather was gone. Then he felt terrible pain during the first weeks after his loss. He cried often and could not sleep. He also began to feel angry at the world in general. Michael was even angry with his grandfather for leaving him. He found it hard to do his school work or to do things with his friends. In time, he began to talk with his friends about how he felt. Although Michael did not feel like going out, he began to make himself do it. After a while, he grieved less. He still missed his grandfather, but he began to enjoy his memories of the good times they had shared.

Michael managed grief in a healthy way. It hurts to lose someone important, but it can hurt worse to pretend that the loss does not matter.

To better understand people's reactions to death and dying, psychiatrist Elisabeth Kübler-Ross and other researchers have studied terminally ill patients and their families. Kübler-Ross identified five stages of reactions that terminally ill people commonly go through as they deal with approaching death.

1. *Denial:* The person rejects the diagnosis of a terminal illness: "No, not me. It can't be true." Denial functions as a defense against the shocking news.

2. *Anger:* After accepting the diagnosis, the person feels anger, rage, envy, and resentment: "Why me?" The anger may be directed toward a religious deity and toward other people.

3. *Bargaining:* The person makes promises and uses good behavior in an attempt to postpone the inevitable outcome.

4. *Depression:* The person feels hopelessness and sorrow over the impending loss of everyone and everything he or she loves.

5. *Acceptance:* Finally, the person contemplates his or her approaching death with quiet expectation, free from the difficult emotions that characterized the earlier stages.

These stages are similar to the grieving process that people go through when a loved one dies. Grief can occur in response to other types of losses, too, such as the break-up of a relationship or losing one's home in a fire. Some researchers have suggested that the grieving process may include more than five stages, as shown in Figure 4–1. When you feel pain from a loss, you should allow yourself to experience the grieving process. Sharing your feelings with others and staying involved in your regular activities will help ease your pain.

Figure 4-1 Someone experiencing grief may not go through all of these stages and may not experience them in the order shown.

THE GRIEVING PROCESS

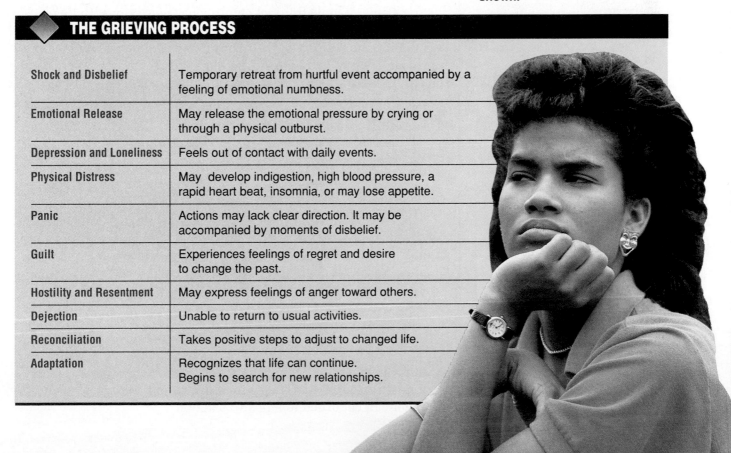

Shock and Disbelief	Temporary retreat from hurtful event accompanied by a feeling of emotional numbness.
Emotional Release	May release the emotional pressure by crying or through a physical outburst.
Depression and Loneliness	Feels out of contact with daily events.
Physical Distress	May develop indigestion, high blood pressure, a rapid heart beat, insomnia, or may lose appetite.
Panic	Actions may lack clear direction. It may be accompanied by moments of disbelief.
Guilt	Experiences feelings of regret and desire to change the past.
Hostility and Resentment	May express feelings of anger toward others.
Dejection	Unable to return to usual activities.
Reconciliation	Takes positive steps to adjust to changed life.
Adaptation	Recognizes that life can continue. Begins to search for new relationships.

Guilt is an emotion that can cause you to review many of your decisions.

GUILT

People feel guilty when they behave or think in ways that do not match their values. **Guilt** is a feeling of having done something wrong. Stealing, for example, is an action that clearly conflicts with the standards of society. Thoughts that cause guilt are more difficult to recognize than actions. For example, many people feel guilty when they are angry at someone they love, even though their anger may be reasonable at that time.

Guilt can be a helpful emotion. It can help you to live according to your conscience. It can help you recognize when you have not lived up to your standards, and then you can decide to do better. Everyone feels guilty sometimes. Learning to tell whether guilt is reasonable—and how to deal with it—will help your overall mental well-being.

Karen had just bought a new outfit to wear to a school dance. She knew that her older sister had a pair of earrings that were perfect with the outfit. However, Karen also knew that her sister would never let Karen borrow the earrings. So when no one was home, Karen slipped into her sister's room and took the earrings. Later that evening, she began to feel bad about having taken the earrings.

Karen did not sleep well that night. In the morning, she decided to tell her older sister what she had done. Her sister pointed out that even though stealing was wrong, she appreciated Karen's honesty. Karen had taken positive steps to correct her mistake.

Karen handled her guilt in a constructive way. She dealt with her problem right away. Taking steps to right the wrong were good ways of dealing with her guilt.

Sometimes people think of emotions as mysterious. But emotions can be understood. The ability to understand and express your emotions builds your self-confidence and helps you to communicate well with others. It also helps you to understand others better. These abilities contribute to your mental health.

LESSON 4.1 USING WHAT YOU HAVE LEARNED

REVIEW

1. What are two ways of dealing with anger constructively?

2. Describe some physical changes that might occur when you experience fear.

THINK CRITICALLY

3. Recognizing how you feel about something or someone doesn't always feel good. Yet it is very healthy. Why is this better for you than if you were to ignore the feelings?

4. Why was Kübler-Ross's research of the emotions of dying patients important for understanding grief?

APPLY IT TO YOURSELF

5. Imagine that you become angry because your brother has been unjustly accused of doing something wrong. Explain how your anger can be turned to a positive action.

SUMMARY

All people experience emotions. Learning to understand and express your emotions in a constructive way is a sign of good mental health. Hiding or ignoring painful emotions only makes it harder to deal with them later.

DEALING WITH EMOTIONS

Some emotions, such as anxiety and grief, can be difficult to face. Even when you handle a difficult emotion in a healthy way, you may still feel pain. Most people develop ways to protect, or defend, themselves from feeling too much pain. Such methods are called **defense mechanisms**. Because defense mechanisms hide unwanted feelings, people very often are unaware that they are using these protective techniques. A person can become dependent on a defensive way of dealing with problems but not know it.

Defense mechanisms often serve a good purpose and even may be necessary for survival. However, they can be used too often. It is very easy to rely on the protection of a defense mechanism rather than to face the real cause of the pain or discomfort. When a defense mechanism continues to protect you from your true feelings, it stops being helpful.

Feelings must run their natural course. When a painful feeling is ignored for too long, it can be more difficult to work through the pain. Each individual must find his or her own balance between emotions and defense mechanisms. It is important to find out whether defense mechanisms are working for or against the long-term goal of mental well-being.

REPRESSION

The most basic of all defense mechanisms is **repression**. In repression, the painful thoughts or feelings are pushed away from conscious thought. When Rico discovered that his brother Pablo was the one who had caused the damage to Rico's bike, he eventually talked with Pablo and the two worked out a solution. However, suppose Rico feels very protective of his younger brother and never lets himself get angry with Pablo. Rico might unknowingly repress his anger and probably would allow the situation to pass without expressing his feelings.

Working with other people to solve problems can be very constructive. It can help reduce anxiety and can create a healthy environment.

Psychiatrist Sigmund Freud considered repression to be the most important of the defense mechanisms. He argued that the repressed feelings usually come out in some other form and cause feelings of anxiety. To deal with these feelings, a person then relies on another defense mechanism. Therefore, it can be said that other defense mechanisms assist repression.

RATIONALIZATION

Rationalization [ra shun uh lih ZAY shun] is the act of making an excuse for a behavior. It is an attempt to preserve self-esteem and to avoid feelings of guilt. People are rationalizing when they make up a reason for something. They may do this because the real reason is more difficult to face. People who rationalize are often unaware that they are hiding from the truth. Their actions seem right and reasonable to them.

Rachel was anxious about her speech because she was afraid she would fail. Suppose Rachel insists that she is unable to go to school that day and convinces everyone, including herself, that it is because she has the flu. She is rationalizing.

Rationalization can help you maintain self-respect for a time. For example, if you are regularly late for school, you might have many reasonable excuses for your lateness. One reason might be that your alarm clock is unreliable, or that you have to wait your turn in the shower. These may be true statements, but they fail to address the underlying cause of your repeated tardiness. Facing reality and being honest about your feelings are better ways to build self-confidence.

COMPENSATION

Covering up faults or weaknesses by trying to excel in other areas is known as **compensation**. For example, someone may become the class clown in order to hide a fear of being unpopular. Compensation often occurs when people feel insecure or expect too much of themselves.

Karen borrowed the earrings because she is shy with boys and feels that dressing well will make her more popular. Karen is using a negative form of compensation. She is compensating for what she considers to be a personal weakness by replacing it with something she thinks will be approved of by others. It would be better if she were to try to make friends by being natural and cheerful. Clothes and earrings will not eliminate her shyness or attract true friends.

In some families, problems such as alcoholism can cause continual friction among the members. One of the children may react to the tension by trying to compensate for the family's shortcomings. He or she may focus on becoming a star athlete or an honor student. The child may be trying to shift attention away from the family. The child, in effect, is saying "Look at me! I'm perfect, and so is my family."

"Seriously! I'm not trying to rationalize this. The dog ate it!"

Many former athletes use compensation in a positive way by finding other ways to stay involved in sports.

In some situations, compensation can be a helpful defense mechanism. It can lead you to develop skills in another area. For example, a person who is not very talented athletically may compensate for this lack of ability by becoming very good at another activity, such as music or drama, or both.

PROJECTION

Rico was angry at his brother Pablo for wrecking his bicycle. Suppose Rico represses his feelings of anger and doesn't talk to Pablo for several days, without realizing that he is doing this. After a while, Rico imagines that Pablo is angry at him instead. He uses this as an excuse for continuing to be rude to Pablo. Rico is projecting.

Projection is seeing your own faults or feelings in other people, even when they do not have them. By projecting his own feelings onto Pablo, Rico was able to justify his own behavior. People who use this defense mechanism may do it quietly and internally or openly. Projection is used when people do not like what they see in themselves. By projecting their faults onto someone else, their own behavior is easier to accept.

Occasional projection is common and does not have to be a problem. When used often, it can keep you from facing opinions you actually have about yourself. As a result, it can keep you from changing possible bad behaviors.

IDEALIZATION

Sometimes people admire someone so much that they see the person as perfect. This defense mechanism, known as **idealization**, allows people to see others as they want them to be, but it keeps them from seeing others as they really are. Idealization often takes the form of hero-worship of film or music stars whose real personalities and faults are hidden in a cloud of glamour.

Idealization is important in growing up because it can help you set personal goals. However, it often means you are exaggerating the good qualities of the other person. Not seeing people as they really are can lead you to expect too much from them. You may be severely disappointed when you discover they have some faults.

DAYDREAMING

People often daydream in order to escape the frustration or hurt of difficult situations. **Daydreaming** is the creation of make-believe events that seem more pleasant or exciting than the real world. It is the living out in your mind of things you wish would happen. For example, you may wish to become better friends with someone you do not know well. If you are too shy to do anything about your wish, you might spend a lot of time imagining the friendship. Using your imagination in this way protects you from the anxiety of trying to develop real friendships. Your imagination serves as a defense mechanism.

Daydreaming can help a person focus on positive outcomes and thereby set realistic goals.

Emotions can be confusing and can cause a person to search for easy solutions.

Daydreams can be fun. They can also give you ideas for achieving your goals. They are obstacles when they serve as a substitute for reality. When used in this way, daydreams can keep you from taking action to meet your goals.

REGRESSION

Regression means acting less maturely than you usually would. People are regressing when they sulk or throw tantrums instead of expressing disappointment maturely. Often they act this way because they feel neglected and want attention. Regressive behaviors often were first learned as a small child.

Suppose Rico is so upset about his broken bicycle that he kicks it. Instead of discussing his anger, he goes into his room and slams the door. He refuses to eat dinner with the family. Rico is using regression.

Everyone feels like escaping back to childish behavior sometimes. However, it is more helpful to deal with disappointment or seek attention in mature ways. After all, when the sulking or the tantrum is over, the situation that produced it has not gone away and still must be handled.

DENIAL

Imagine that Michael finds the loss of his grandfather so hard to take that he refuses to believe it. He continues to speak of his grandfather as if he were still living. Michael is using denial.

Denial is the refusal to recognize reality. People are using denial when they behave as if something is true, when in reality, it is not true—or vice versa. This defense mechanism protects them from facing an unpleasant fact that they cannot yet accept.

Denial, as you learned earlier in this chapter, is the first stage in the grieving process. In this process, denial is a natural stage through which to pass. However, when denial is used to avoid other emotions, it is rarely helpful. It can prevent you from accepting reality and from seeking help for a problem.

Although denial most often is used to avoid feelings that must be dealt with, it can be used constructively. For example, a lawyer sometimes must refuse to accept what may appear to be strong evidence against his or her client. By denying the obvious and continuing the search, more facts may be found that can help to prove the client's innocence. Can you think of how this behavior might apply to relationships as well? Imagine that someone tells you that your closest friend was saying bad things about you. Would you believe this other person or deny what is being said? How would this affect your relationship with your friend?

As with all defense mechanisms, it is important to recognize when you are using denial. Failure to do so can prevent you from making healthy changes. This is especially true when you deny the end of a relationship. Although it may be very painful to face a broken relationship, it is important that it not interfere with your ability to form new relationships. Denial will only cause you to express your feelings in ways that may be hurtful to yourself and to others.

MAKING A DIFFERENCE

CAREERS HEALTH

Sports Psychologist

In the past fifteen years, athletes and their coaches have started to turn to sports psychologists in an effort to gain a competitive edge over opponents. One way a sports psychologist can help athletes is by teaching them how to keep their emotions under control. This allows the athlete to focus more productively on his or her performance rather than let anger or fear get in the way.

Fear and anger are two common emotions experienced by many athletes. At times, as the result of an injury, external distractions, or maybe from a fear of failure, an athlete suddenly may be performing poorly. Sometimes he or she may begin thinking irrationally about the causes for the performance and start blaming it on the officials, the coach, or a cheating opponent. A sports psychologist can help the athlete relax and look at the problem rationally. Once the problem is looked at in such a way, logical solutions can be explored and the athlete can focus on these.

A sports psychologist has an advanced degree in psychology or a related field. He or she specialized in the psychological aspects of athletics and of sports in general. However, emotions such as anger and fear are common among everyone, not just athletes, and can interfere with everyday performances. The skills learned through sports psychology can be easily applied to everyday life—control emotions, focus on the task at hand, and make decisions based upon clear thinking.

1. What is one way that a sports psychologist can help an athlete reach peak performance?
2. How might anger interfere with an athlete's performance?

SUBLIMATION

When Rico discovered his broken bicycle, his anger made him feel like striking someone. Instead, he got his tennis racquet and hit tennis balls for a while. By using his angry energy to get exercise, Rico was using a defense mechanism called **sublimation** [sub luh MAY shun]. This is the replacement of undesirable impulses with acceptable behavior. People are sublimating when they use their strong or angry feelings to do something else instead of hurting others. For example, a student who becomes angry about a new school rule that seems unfair could turn his or her anger to a positive action. He or she could seek an opportunity for all students to discuss the school rule with the school administration. Sublimation can be one of the most useful defense mechanisms. It channels energy that could be hurtful into a useful activity. However, it is only successful if the anger can be completely released.

DISPLACEMENT

Shifting the feelings about one person or situation to an object or another person is **displacement**. People are using displacement when they take out an emotion such as anger or guilt on an innocent person. It usually occurs when they feel unable to face the person who brought out the emotion in them. So the emotion is directed at someone else.

Figure 4-2   *Many defense mechanisms are constructive. However, all have risks.*

COMMONLY USED DEFENSE MECHANISMS

Defense Mecanisms	Example	Risk
Reaction Formation Behaving in a way that is directly opposite to the way you feel.	You are very angry over someone's comment. You act as though what they said did not matter.	The internal conflict can be uncomfortable. You may doubt your own behavior.
Negativism Always seeing the negative side to situations. This protects you from potential failure.	You refuse to take on a challenging task with the belief that it could not possibly succeed.	It can keep you from trying new things and may interfere with chances for success.
Denial Refusing to accept the obvious.	You refuse to accept the end of a relationship, and continue on as though the two eventually will get back together.	It can prevent you from moving on to new and possibly healthier relationships with other people.
Rationalization Assigning a rational explanation to your own irrational behavior.	You eat a double cheeseburger, large fries, and a thick shake and claim that you've earned it after a strenuous physical workout.	It only postpones feelings of guilt. Eventually you will have to deal with the consequences.
Idealization Admiring someone else to the point that the person appears to be perfect.	You model yourself after a professional athlete that you admire, denying any faults in the person that may be obvious to others.	When you realize that the person is not perfect, it can lead you to mistrust others.

If you are angry with your parents, but end up shouting at a younger brother or sister, you are displacing your feelings. Displacement can keep you from correcting the original situation.

REACTION FORMATION

Sometimes people hide their true feelings from themselves by acting in a manner opposite to the way they would like to act. This behavior is called **reaction formation**. For example, a person might really admire a classmate and wish to become a friend of him or her. However, if the person has had difficulty making friends in the past, he or she might fear rejection. That fear could lead the person to act as if he or she disliked the classmate. He or she might say unkind things or act as if he or she wanted nothing to do with the individual.

When people behave in this way, they are usually unaware that they are acting in a manner opposite to their own desires. They may have rationalized believable reasons why they should dislike their classmate. Often it is difficult for people to discover their true feelings. However, when a person can confront his or her underlying feelings, healthy changes can be made.

CHECKING YOUR DEFENSES

People commonly rely to some degree on these and other defense mechanisms listed in Figure 4-2. Some are more helpful than others. People who depend too heavily on unconstructive defense mechanisms most likely will experience more severe problems at a later time.

Understanding defense mechanisms helps you to recognize those that you commonly use and to identify how you use them. What situations make you defensive? Which mechanisms do you use most often? Do you practice defenses that are rarely constructive? You may want to try to lower your defenses. This means facing some difficult feelings, but it also means personal growth.

What other ways are there to deal with angry feelings?

LESSON 4.2 USING WHAT YOU HAVE LEARNED

REVIEW

1. Give two example of defense mechanisms.
2. How are sublimation and displacement similar?

THINK CRITCALLY

3. When a person relies too heavily on defense mechanisms, it interferes with personal growth. Explain why this is so.
4. Identify two strategies that people can use to avoid dependence upon defense mechanisms.

APPLY IT TO YOURSELF

5. Imagine that you learn that your best friend is going to a long-awaited concert with someone else. You respond by saying that you really don't want to go anyway. Explain the defense mechanism you are using.

SUMMARY

Most defenses are best used as temporary relief. In the end, it is healthy to recognize and to deal with your true feelings. Some defense mechanisms can be helpful, while others are rarely constructive. Self-examination may reveal that you need to use fewer defense mechanisms than you think. Admitting and dealing directly with your emotions will enable you and your relationships to grow.

MAIN IDEAS

CONCEPTS

✔ Violence is a negative expression of emotions.

✔ Fear and anger can lead to violence.

✔ Most incidents of violence can be prevented.

VOCABULARY

violence
homicide

ANGER AND VIOLENCE

What does the word violence mean to you? Do you think of the action you see on certain television programs or in movies? Is violence what you see on the news or read in the paper? Maybe you think of what happens on the streets of your neighborhood, in school, or even in your own home. **Violence** is the use of force to injure or abuse another person or damage property. Verbal abuse, sexual abuse, fighting, and murder are all forms of violence.

Perhaps you or someone you know has been a victim of violence. As a teenager in the United States, you are at high risk. Current statistics indicate that for people 15 to 24 years of age, homicide is the second most common cause of death. **Homicide** is the intentional killing of one person by another.

In some communities, violence may be a part of daily life. People begin to feel that nothing can be done to stop it. They live with the fear that at any time they may become the target of random violence. However, the majority of violent incidents can be avoided. Most acts of violence take place between people who know each other. For example, almost half of the homicides in the United States begin as arguments.

CAUSES OF VIOLENCE

Most acts of violence can be avoided if the people involved can control their behavior and search for alternative solutions to conflicts.

The best solution to family disagreements is to resolve the conflict together.

Paul is eating lunch in the school cafeteria. Two boys he knows slightly are sitting nearby. One of them starts talking loudly about Paul's poor pitching in the recent baseball game. Paul tries to ignore the boys. He knows that his pitching was not as good as usual that day, but he knows that he just had an off day. He feels embarrassed because other people in the cafeteria can overhear the conversation. As the boys continue their remarks, Paul can feel his anger growing. He finally gets up and walks out of the cafeteria.

If Paul had responded to the boys, he might have ended up in a fight. Even if he had won the fight, he would probably have been suspended from classes and from baseball for fighting at school. Paul kept his behavior under control and decided that walking away from the situation was the best thing for him to do.

ANGER AND FEAR Anger is the most common cause of violence. Angry arguments may end in violence if people do not find other ways to resolve their disagreements. When people let their anger get out of control, an argument can turn violent.

Anger is a factor in almost all violence, but some violence has additional causes. Fear can be another cause of violence. People fear what they are unfamiliar with or do not understand. In some cases, racial violence may be the result of fear.

PEER PRESSURE   Peer pressure can be a factor in violence between young people. While teenagers are establishing their identities, they also are trying to fit in with their peers. Many feel safer and more accepted if they join a group or gang. Often conflicts or disagreements between groups can get out of control—resulting in violence. As a member of a group, you may feel pressure from your peers to take part in conflicts with other groups of teenagers.

Friends can pressure you to resort to violence in other ways as well. Do you have a friend who encourages you to "stand up for yourself" rather than helping you find a way to work out a conflict? Many teenagers say they fight in order to "save face," or to uphold their reputations. If your self-esteem is low, you may feel you cannot risk the poor opinion of anyone. Finding a constructive way to solve a conflict is a much more effective way to gain the respect of others and to raise your self-esteem.

SUBSTANCE ABUSE   Alcohol and drugs often contribute to violence. Each affects the way a person deals with anger. An argument that might otherwise have ended quietly can escalate into violence and even death when alcohol or drugs are involved. Alcohol is a factor in more than half of the homicides in the United States. Violence in the home is often related to use of drugs or alcohol.

WEAPONS   Access to weapons such as knives or handguns is a factor that makes it more likely that a violent incident will result in death. As the heat of a conflict grows, the weapon may be seen as an easy solution. However, all too often it leads to tragedy. When guns are used, innocent bystanders may also be killed by stray bullets.

PREVENTING VIOLENCE

Everyone feels angry at times. Think about the things that make you angry or frustrated. Did you ever get so angry that you wanted to strike someone? What did you do about your anger?

Often violence is learned from watching others. If your family, your friends, or people you see in movies deal with strong emotions in harmful ways, you might not learn to use your emotions positively. There are ways to "let off steam" without becoming violent. It is important that you learn to deal with anger, hostility, or frustration in positive ways.

Violent confrontations can be avoided by keeping emotions under control.

HEALTHY PEOPLE
2000

Reduce by 20 percent the incidence of weapon-carrying by adolescents aged 14 through 17.

Objective 7.10
from *Healthy People 2000: National Health Promotion and Disease Prevention Objectives*

Remember that sublimation is a useful defense mechanism for handling these feelings. It is a method of turning angry feelings into something positive. When Paul walked out of the cafeteria, he was still angry. He could sublimate his anger by spending some extra time in baseball practice. Therefore, his extra work would help him improve his skills, at the same time, helping him to release his anger. Can you think of ways you might sublimate anger? The Strategies for Living feature on the previous page identifies several other effective ways to defuse a conflict.

SEEKING HELP

Everyone feels angry at times. If you find it more and more difficult to deal with your anger, and you notice that your angry feelings are becoming more frequent, don't be afraid to seek professional help.

You should also find help if your fear of violence begins to get out of control. Some people, especially those who live in high-crime areas, are so afraid of becoming victims of violence that it becomes difficult for them to function. If you think you need help, speak with your parents, a teacher, or the school guidance counselor for advice on where you can go for help in your community.

SUMMARY

Violence is more likely to occur between people who know one another than between strangers. Anger, fear, peer pressure, and the desire to save face can lead to violence. Alcohol use, drug use, and access to weapons contribute to violence. Much violence can be prevented by learning how to handle emotions in a positive way.

LESSON 4.3 USING WHAT YOU HAVE LEARNED

REVIEW

1. In which age group is homicide the second leading cause of death?
2. Explain how fear can lead to violence.

THINK CRITICALLY

3. Look at the cartoon on this page. Choose at least two of the examples identified by the cartoonist as carriers of information. Explain how each may help to encourage violence.
4. Explain how sublimation can help you redirect your anger.

APPLY IT TO YOURSELF

5. As a parent, two of your children are arguing with a great deal of anger. What would you do to prevent the situation from becoming violent?

Saving Face

It was Saturday night. Dave and his friends, Tom and Jake, met up with some other kids from school at the local pizza place. Earlier, their school's basketball team was knocked out of first place by the crosstown rival, East High. The game was close and very rough. It got so bad that a fight almost broke out in the stands.

As Dave and his friends sat waiting for their pizzas, it was obvious that Tom and Jake were still very angry. While telling the story to some of the others, Dave noticed that the emotions of the group were growing. He heard someone say something about "payback time."

Several students from East High stopped in and ordered pizzas to go. Tom shouted some rude comments at them. As the East High students left, they shouted back some comments. This angered Dave and his friends even more. Dave noticed that Jake seemed especially angry. Tom and Jake got up to follow the East High students out to their cars. Tom turned to Dave and said, "Let's go. Let's teach them a lesson."

Dave wasn't sure what he should do. He had as much school spirit as anyone, but he really didn't see the sense in getting into a fight. "It was just a game," he thought.

"It isn't worth someone getting hurt over." But he didn't want his friends to think he was a coward.

PAUSE AND CONSIDER

1. *Identify the Problem.* What is Dave's conflict?

2. *Consider the Options.* What are his options? What do you think Dave should do?

3. *Evaluate the Outcomes.* What are the possible positive results of either option? What are the possible negative outcomes?

As a few of his friends started to get up, Dave noticed that there were others who seemed to be hesitating. "Hey, forget it." Dave said. "What's the big deal? Let it drop."

"What's the matter? Don't you have any pride?" shouted Jake.

Dave laughed and said, "Oh, I have plenty of that. What I don't have is food, and I'm hungry. I came here to eat, so let's eat. You know I never let anything come before food."

There was a silence that felt as though it lasted an hour. Dave could feel that everyone was watching to see what would happen.

After a brief, but tense, pause, Jake laughed nervously and said, "Yeah, you're probably right. It's not worth the effort. Let's eat."

Dave was relieved. He knew he had taken a chance by standing up to Jake, but at the time, he felt it was the right thing to do. Now he was sure it had been right. Before too long, everybody was laughing as though nothing had happened.

DECIDE AND REVIEW

4. *Decide and Act.* What method did Dave use to calm the situation? Why can this method be effective?

5. *Review.* If you had been in Dave's situation, what would you have done to prevent the fight? What makes your method effective?

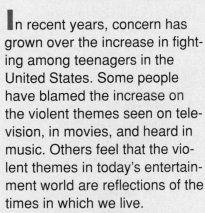

THINKING CRITICALLY ABOUT

Violence Prevention

HEALTHY PEOPLE 2000

Reduce by 20 percent the incidence of physical fighting among adolescents aged 14 through 17.

Physical fighting among adolescents is often considered a normal and sometimes even necessary part of growing up. Fighting, however, results in hundreds of homicides and uncounted numbers of nonfatal injuries among adolescents each year. Fighting is the most immediate [preceding] behavior for a great proportion of the homicides that occur in this age group and in many instances may be considered a necessary if not a sufficient, cause.

Objective 7.9
from *Healthy People 2000: National Health Promotion and Disease Prevention Objectives*

In recent years, concern has grown over the increase in fighting among teenagers in the United States. Some people have blamed the increase on the violent themes seen on television, in movies, and heard in music. Others feel that the violent themes in today's entertainment world are reflections of the times in which we live.

Regardless of the many complex reasons for the increase in teen violence, the trend poses a threat to the overall health of the country. Nationwide studies indicate that violence is a problem that touches everyone—not just those living in large cities. The number of incidents of teen violence can be reduced. As a teenager, your behavior can play an important role in meeting the health goals for the year 2000.

UNDERSTANDING CONFLICTS

Conflicts with others are common. It is unrealistic to expect everyone to agree all of the time. How you choose to handle the conflict is what is important. By understanding what leads up to most fights, you may be able to avoid a fight or help to prevent one. Often, there are steps that lead to a fight.
–First, there is usually a history between the individuals involved. They may have known each other for a few seconds, a few months, or for several years. Rarely does a fight break out between two people who have no connection with each other.
–Second, some form of conflict arises. The conflict may be over what one of the people has said or over something one of them

has done. Each person's perception of the other's intent is critical. For example, conflicts can arise over what are intended to be innocent comments. –Finally, a specific incident usually sets off the fight. The actual physical fight begins when one of those involved touches the other in an aggressive way. One person might push the other or may just grab the person's arm.

Friends and peers can play an important role in preventing or encouraging a fight. Have you ever encouraged a friend to "stand up for him- or herself," or encouraged the friend to "get even" with another person? Peers can also encourage a fight by spreading rumors about what someone may have said— even if the rumors are upsetting. Remember, real friends would not do anything to cause each other hurt.

PLAYING A POSITIVE ROLE

The most positive action friends and peers can take is to help defuse potentially violent situations and prevent fights. Although there are no strategies that work perfectly in all situations, the following suggestions may be helpful.

1. When observing a potential fight, intervene early in the conflict, before emotions are out of control. Speak in a calm voice.

2. Help those involved to identify the problem and to recognize that their angry feelings are natural.

3. Encourage each person to describe his or her feelings about the conflict using "I messages." In other words, have each person state his or her feelings from a personal view instead of accusing or blaming the other person. Remember, emotions are caused by personal responses to an event, not by the event itself.

4. Help identify positive solutions to the problem that everyone can accept.

5. Encourage the positive behavior. Remember that when a friend or peer steps away from a fight, he or she should be complimented, not ridiculed. Avoiding a fight takes far greater courage than getting into one.

WHAT DO YOU THINK?

1. Read the following statement. *The increase in violence among young people is caused by living in a violent society.* Do you agree or disagree with this statement? Support your answer.

2. Identify at least three common situations among adolescents that can result in fights.

3. Use one of the situations you identified in item two to create an imaginary conflict between two people. Write a brief paragraph that describes the conflict. Then develop two strategies for preventing the conflict from turning into a violent fight.

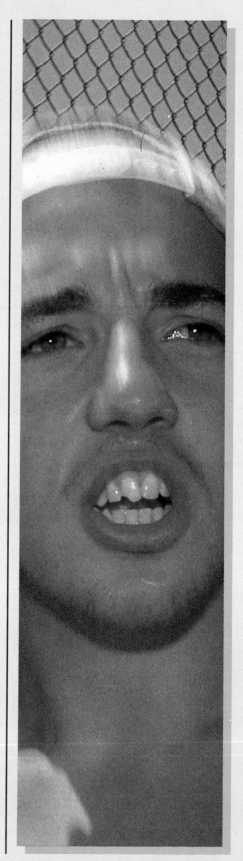

CHAPTER 4 ~ Review

PROJECTS

1. Organize a mime production in which only body language and gestures are used to convey a particular emotion. For each performance, have spectators guess the emotion illustrated.

2. Design a campaign to stop violence in and around your school. Include descriptions of how you would educate your friends and peers about the causes of violence and strategies for preventing it. For example, you might mount a poster campaign, hold an assembly, or ask school officials to pass some new safety rules.

WORKING WITH OTHERS

Plan a one-day workshop with your classmates on Coping with Loss. (Consult with your teacher for guidance and suggestions.) Divide up into four groups. Each group should focus on one of the following: the stages of grief; the changes that occur with divorce or the death of a parent (financial, social changes); how to cope with loss (i.e. the death of a peer and losses other than death); developing a library of resources on the topic of loss and arranging for a speaker on the topic.

CONNECTING TO...

ART   Use photography or cartoon drawings to create a humorous mural showing characters who are using defense mechanisms in a negative way. Also illustrate characters who use defense mechanisms, such as compensation and sublimation, in a positive way.

USING VOCABULARY

anxiety
compensation
daydreaming
defense mechanism
denial
displacement
emotion

grief
guilt
homicide
hostility
idealization
projection
rationalization

reaction formation
regression
repression
sublimation
violence

On a sheet of paper, identify the vocabulary word that matches each of the following phrases. For vocabulary words that are not used, write a phrase that correctly uses the word.

1. making an excuse for a mistake or failure
2. covering up faults by trying to do extra well in other areas
3. seeing your own faults or feelings in other people
4. replacing an undesirable impulse with an acceptable behavior
5. living out in your mind things you wish would happen
6. acting in a childish or immature way
7. refusing to recognize reality
8. expressing your anger by attacking an innocent person
9. feeling badly about something you have done
10. pushing your feelings back to avoid dealing with them

CONCEPT MAPPING

Copy and complete the concept map shown below. Information on concept mapping appears at the front of this book.

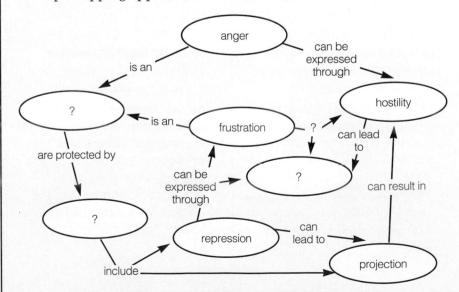

THINKING CRITICALLY

INTERPRET

LESSON 4.1
1. Why is it important to be able to express your emotions?
2. How might friendship be a form of love?
3. What are two helpful ways to deal with anger?
4. Describe some physical effects of anxiety.
5. Why is jealousy considered to be a form of fear?
6. What is one positive aspect of grief?
7. How might guilt be a positive emotion?

LESSON 4.2
8. How can defense mechanisms serve both positive and negative purposes?
9. What purpose does rationalization serve to the person using it?
10. How is projection related to self-image?
11. What is the difference between projection and displacement?

LESSON 4.3
12. How does peer pressure influence violence?
13. How do alcohol and drugs contribute to violence?

APPLY

LESSON 4.1
14. Jane confided in a friend that her grandmother, who lives with Jane and her parents, makes her angry by turning up the TV volume so that she can hear and by setting the heat at 78° F. Why might Jane's anger be considered to be irrational? As Jane's friend, what advice would you give her?

15. Maria is fifteen years old and an excellent student. Each day Maria works as a hospital volunteer, helps care for her six- and eight-year-old siblings, and cooks for her mother, who works. Lately Maria has felt overwhelmed by her responsibilities and angry at her younger siblings. How can you explain Maria's feelings? What changes might restore a sense of balance in Maria's life?

16. Months after John's younger brother died in a boating accident, John was confused by his conflicting emotions. Sometimes he felt angry at his brother, and other times he felt like crying over the loss. What is happening to John? How might he help himself?

LESSON 4.2
17. Talia's favorite uncle was a respected composer. After her uncle died, Talia began putting some extra effort into her composition courses at the conservatory she attended. How might Talia have been coping with the death of her uncle? Was her method constructive? Why or why not?

LESSON 4.3
18. Denzel and John are two of the best free throw shooters on the basketball team. One day after algebra class, Tracy overhears John telling Denzel that he, John, is the better player. Tracy goes over to defend his friend Denzel. Words are exchanged and John and Tracy begin shouting at each other angrily. What can Denzel do to defuse the situation?

COMMITMENT TO WELLNESS
FOLLOW-UP

SETTING GOALS
Look back at your Commitment to Wellness checklist. Review your responses to each of the items on the checklist. Identify two of the items on the checklist that you feel are strengths of yours. Write a brief story for each of these statements that provides an example of an incident that could cause such responses. Describe in detail the process you use to work through each of the situations you have identified.

After you have completed your work, think of ways that you can turn weaknesses into strengths. For example, if you answered no to *I do not try to "save face" by fighting*, think of how you can learn to back down from confrontations.

WHERE DO I GO FROM HERE?
Violence among youth is growing at a rapid rate. Many schools are organizing peer programs for teen violence intervention.

FOR MORE INFORMATION, CONTACT:
National School Safety Center
Pepperdine University
Malibu, CA 91362

CHAPTER 5

Managing Stress

"When you get into a tight place and everything goes against you, till it seems as though you could not hang on a minute longer, never give up then, for that is just the place and time that the tide will turn."

Harriet Beecher Stowe

BACKGROUND

Harriet Beecher Stowe was a well-known writer whose books and articles often reflected the political sentiment of the times.

Stress is a natural part of life. It is something that a person must deal with at every stage of his or her life. As a child, you may have felt stress over having to share a toy with another child. The first day of school may have caused you to feel nervous and sick to your stomach. As a teenager, changes to your body, the desire to be accepted and liked by others, and relationships with special friends may be areas of concern. In every stage of adulthood, you will continue to face situations that can cause you stress.

The conclusion is obvious—stress will always be in your life. The key to surviving stress is learning how to handle it. How you deal with stress is very important in determining your degree of happiness. Will you allow it to eat away at you? Will you let it interfere with your relationships? Will you recognize stress for what it is and use it to help you grow?

There will be moments in your life when you may think that the tide will never turn. Stressful moments will feel as though they have no end. It is important during such times to remember that indeed the tide does turn. Bad times do get better. Taking time to recognize—and deal with— the cause of stress is what makes all the difference in the world.

SELF-ASSESSMENT

In your Wellness Journal, or on a separate sheet of paper, make a list from 1–11. As you read each of the following statements, respond by writing *yes* next to the statements that describe you most of the time.

1. I understand the sources of stress in my life.
2. I am aware of my physical responses to stress.
3. I try to see problems as a challenge.
4. When everything around me seems overwhelming, I try to accomplish one small task to help me get back on track.
5. I have someone to talk to when I begin to feel stress.
6. I take time out each day to relax and free my mind and body of stress.
7. I engage in regular exercise at least three times a week.
8. I am able to laugh at myself.
9. I try not to overreact to comments made to me.
10. I am committed to meeting my daily goals and I do my best to remain focused.
11. I follow a healthy, balanced diet.

Review your responses and consider what might be your strengths and what might be your weaknesses. Save your personal checklist for a follow-up activity that appears at the end of the chapter.

STRESS AND STRESSORS

How often do you feel your face becoming flushed, your heart beginning to pound, or your muscles becoming tense? When changes such as these suddenly occur in your body, you know that something is happening to you. These physical reactions happen to everyone in response to the stresses of everyday life.

WHAT IS STRESS?

According to Dr. Hans Selye, **stress** is your body's response to physical or mental demands or pressures. The physical or mental demands that cause the stress are called **stressors**. However, the word *stress* is commonly used in place of the word *stressor*. Physical stressors might be hunger, thirst, or cold. Fatigue from overwork can be a physical stressor. A mental stressor might be an argument with your family or the loss of someone you love. The physical responses of your body to stressors, regardless of the type of stressor, include increased heart rate, elevated blood pressure, and the release of certain hormones.

During the teen years, relationships with peers can be a major source of stress, but teachers, parents, grades, sports, jobs, and money can all cause feelings of stress. Often you experience more than one stressor at a time. Stress is not always related to negative life events. Stress also can be related to positive life events. Driving on your own for the first time can be a stressful but memorable experience.

NEGATIVE AND POSITIVE STRESS

Whether a stressor has a positive or a negative effect on you is related to how you view yourself. How you see yourself is the result of all your experiences and how you have handled them. Past experiences help to determine whether you will respond to new challenges in your life positively or negatively.

DECISION FOCUS MAKING

Jackson and Martha were scheduled to give oral presentations to their class. Both were very worried. Martha was sure she couldn't do it. She could see herself stumbling over her words and being totally embarrassed in front of the class. Jackson was equally concerned, but he decided that the best way to avoid making mistakes was to be well-prepared. He carefully researched his topic. Then he practiced his presentation using a tape recorder to identify problems. Martha was so certain that she would fail that she couldn't even prepare her presentation. When she got up to speak her heart was pounding, she had a lump in her throat, and her hands felt clammy. She knew that her worst fears would be realized. When she couldn't answer a question her teacher asked her, Martha became so upset she quickly ended her talk.

Outward signs of stress can be very obvious. You also react to stress internally.

Jackson also was very nervous when his turn came. He suffered the same symptoms as Martha. But Jackson was familiar with his material. As he began his talk, he became more confident and comfortable.

Jackson's nervousness motivated him to a positive response. He used stress to his advantage and earned the reward of achievement. For Jackson the stressor had a positive effect. Positive use of stress is called **eustress** [YOO stres]. Because Martha had less confidence in herself, she did not take positive action to overcome her anxiety. For Martha the same stressor had negative results. Negative use of stress is called **distress**. It was the way in which Jackson and Martha dealt with stress, not the stressor alone, that determined whether the stress was positive or negative. You can learn to use stress to your advantage. Stress is much like spice or flavoring in foods. Without it you can still live, but you don't enjoy life as much.

HOW DO YOU RESPOND TO STRESS?

People respond to stress differently. One person may feel the need to escape from the day-to-day problems by watching television for hours, while someone else may be unable to sit long enough to watch one program. The following are some common physical and emotional signs of stress.

Emotional Signs	**Physical Signs**
Irritability	Pounding heart
Aggressive behavior	Trembling feeling
Easily startled	Grinding of teeth
Nervous laughter	Dry mouth
Trouble sleeping	Excessive perspiration
Overeating or undereating	Aching neck or lower back
Accident prone	Frequent colds
	Cold hands or feet

THE STRESS RESPONSE

In his studies of stress, Dr. Selye found that your body adapts to a stressor through a set pattern of physical reactions. He termed this adjustment the General Adaptation Syndrome. The three stages in the General Adaptation Syndrome are alarm, resistance, and exhaustion.

ALARM   As soon as you recognize a stressor, your body reacts. This quick physical warning is the **alarm stage,** or the fight or flight response. When you feel fear, your adrenal glands release adrenaline. **Adrenaline,** also called epinephrine, is a hormone that causes a rush of energy in times of excitement. Your heart rate and breathing speed up. Blood rushes from your stomach and other internal organs to your arms, legs, and brain. The adrenaline prepares you to fight with your greatest energy or to flee at your top speed.

Can you relate the cat's reaction to sudden surges of adrenaline you have experienced?

RESISTANCE The second stage of stress, called the **resistance stage**, starts when your body fights or flees. During this stage, your body works to resist a threatening stressor. Even though you may not be able to fight or run, your body responds as if it were in danger. In many cases your body continues to do so even after the stressor is gone.

In the resistance stage, you handle stress by using the psychological defense mechanisms that you learned about in Chapter 4, "Healthy Emotions." Defense mechanisms are sometimes called coping mechanisms. **Coping** means acting to deal with a problem or difficulty. Using a coping mechanism such as humor or denial may help you control certain symptoms of stress. For example, you may be able to face a bad situation by joking instead of losing your temper. But you might not be able to stop your nervous perspiration. Few people can consciously stop all of the physical symptoms of stress.

EXHAUSTION If stress lasts too long, you may move into the third stage of stress. In the **exhaustion stage**, the body's defenses against stress are used up. You are unable to fight, flee, or resist the stressor. During the exhaustion stage, you have a greater chance of becoming ill than when your body is well rested.

COMMON STRESSORS

Stress, especially mental stress, can accumulate. Overwhelming stress can destroy a person's physical health and mental well-being. Scientists have categorized different types of stressors. Generally these common causes of stress can be grouped into four areas: life changes, traumatic events, conflicts, and daily hassles.

LIFE CHANGES Scientists have developed various scales to judge the level and effects of certain life events. One scale, developed by R. Dean Coddington, is shown in Figure 5-1. It lists 42 events that happen in the lives of many students. Coddington asked senior high students to rate the events according to the amount of stress they thought each event caused. The measure of the amount of stress is called a life change unit. Figure 5-1 shows the average number of life change units for each event as determined by the students in Coddington's study. Notice that some events are positive changes. Others are negative. Some stressors are physical, while others are mental.

TRAUMATIC EVENTS Earthquakes, floods, fires, serious accidents, or physical assaults are obvious stressors. Any of these events can cause extreme distress and the need for an

When you face a crisis, you can be overwhelmed or you can take control.

RANKING OF STRESSORS BY SENIOR HIGH STUDENTS

Life Event	Life Change Units	Life Event	Life Change Units
Getting married	101	Being suspended from school	50
Being pregnant and unwed	92	Having a newborn brother or sister	50
Experiencing the death of a parent	87	Having more arguments with parents	47
Acquiring a visible deformity	81	Reaching a moment of outstanding personal achievement	46
Going through parents' divorce	77	Observing an increase in the number of arguments between parents	46
Becoming an unwed father	77		
Becoming involved with drugs or alcohol	76	Having a parent lose his/her job	46
Having a parent go to jail for a year or more	75	Experiencing a change in parents' financial status	45
Going through parents' separation	69		
Experiencing the death of a brother or sister	68	Being accepted at the college of your choice	43
Experiencing a change in acceptance by peers	67	Beginning senior high school	42
Having an unwed pregnant teenage sister	64	Experiencing the serious illness of a brother or sister	41
Discovering that you are an adopted child	64	Experiencing father's increased absence from home due to a change in his occupation	38
Having a parent remarry	63		
Experiencing the death of a close friend	62		
Having a visible congenital deformity	62	Experiencing the departure from home of a brother or sister	37
Having a serious illness requiring hospitalization	58	Experiencing the death of a grandparent	36
Moving to a new school district	56	Having a third adult added to the family	34
Failing a grade in school	56	Becoming a full-fledged member of a church	31
Not making an extracurricular activity	55		
Experiencing the serious illness of a parent	55	Observing a decrease in the number of arguments between parents	27
Breaking up with a boyfriend or girlfriend	51	Having fewer arguments with parents	26
Having a parent go to jail for 30 days or less	50	Having your mother begin to work outside the home	26
Beginning to date	51		

* Average of the rankings given to these events by 913 students.

extended period of coping. Survivors of traumatic events may develop a condition called **post-traumatic stress disorder**. Some symptoms of post-traumatic stress disorder are loss of interest in former friends and activities, extreme anxiety, and reliving in dreams and memories the traumatic event that brought on the condition. Post-traumatic stress disorder may develop immediately after the event, or it may show up months or years later triggered by a recent stressful experience.

Figure 5-1 Would you rate these stressors in the same way?

Jefferson High School **173**
Daly City, CA 94014

CONFLICTS   Internal conflicts cause stress because they require a person to make a choice between two or more options.

Carrie and Jasmin were sitting on Carrie's bed reading fashion magazines and trying to picture themselves in the new daring clothes. "Wow!" shouted Jasmin, "that's some dress. I'll bet Cody would really take notice if you wore that!" Carrie looked at her friend. Just the mention of Cody's name brought a lump to her throat. Even Jasmin, who was Carrie's best friend, didn't understand why she had broken off with Cody. There were times when Carrie wasn't sure herself. But she knew that she wasn't ready for the serious relationship Cody wanted. Besides, Cody was becoming more and more possessive, and Carrie didn't like that at all. She had a lot of friends, and she liked doing things with all of them. These last few months of dating Cody had been fun, but she didn't like being given the third degree about what she did every minute she wasn't with him. Carrie had thought hard about how she would tell Cody. But when the time came, it still hadn't been easy because she really cared about him.

Carrie was experiencing a conflict within herself. She still liked Cody, but she did not like the way he was treating her. She finally decided that the stress of breaking off the relationship was better for her than the constant stress of dealing with Cody's possessiveness and his interest in a more intimate relationship. Each time you need to make a decision you are faced with some stress. The amount of stress is directly related to the importance you put on the decision. That is why it is important to gather as much information as possible about all of your options. Then compare the expected outcomes of different decisions before you act.

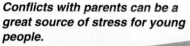

Conflicts with parents can be a great source of stress for young people.

DAILY HASSLES   Your everyday interactions with the world around you may be more stressful than major life events. Examples of daily hassles include an argument with your family, transportation problems, the alarm clock not going off, or losing your homework. Each of these irritating events may be unimportant compared to a major life change. But the accumulated effects of a number of these daily events over a period of time can have a serious impact. The events you consider daily hassles will vary with your age, gender, or stage in life.

SPECIAL POPULATIONS AND STRESS

Social scientists study groups of people to determine if group characteristics affect the responses of members to stressors. Group characteristics might be your age, where you live, your family income, or your ethnic background. The results of these studies indicate that different groups identify different stressors as being most important.

- Violence and crime are greater sources of stress for people who live in urban areas than they are for people who live in rural areas. People in rural areas have other sources of stress, such as money and weather problems.

- Concerns over money affect all groups. However, if your family has a comfortable income, stress from losing your part-time job will not be as great as it will if your job is a necessary source of support to your family.

- Age makes a difference. Think about some of the things that may have caused you stress when you were younger. These may be occasions such as staying home alone at night or going shopping for the first time without an adult.

- Stressors may be associated with being a member of a particular racial or ethnic group. Groups that preserve their unique clothing, foods, and ways of behaving may experience special stress in a society that has difficulty accepting differences.

Some individuals appear to be able to withstand even extreme distress and remain healthy. Psychologist Suzanne Kobasa characterizes these people as having the "hardy personality." Persons who have the traits of the hardy personality look upon change as desirable and challenging. They are not overwhelmed when inevitable changes take place in their lives. They see change as a challenge and an opportunity for growth. Also people with hardy personalities are committed to their activities. Their strong sense of purpose helps them overcome the negative effects of stress. Finally, these individuals are in control of their lives. Of course, no one is in complete control. But hardy personalities tend to assume control whenever possible and act rather than react to circumstances. People who exhibit these three characteristics—openness to change, commitment, and control—have an approach to life that helps them stay healthy in spite of what may seem like overwhelming stress.

LESSON 5.1 USING WHAT YOU HAVE LEARNED

REVIEW

1. What is stress?
2. What is the difference between eustress and distress?
3. Explain what happens in each of the three stages of stress.

THINK CRITICALLY

4. Explain why daily hassles may be more stressful than a major life event.
5. You may have experienced stress before the start of a competitive athletic event, or before you began to speak in front of your class. Keep in mind how the stress affected you and explain the statement "Moderate stress and accomplishment go hand in hand."

APPLY IT TO YOURSELF

6. Hardy personalities are able to withstand stress and stay healthy. Describe one way in which changing a behavior might make you more resistant to the negative effects of stress.

HEALTHY PEOPLE 2000

Increase to at least 40 percent the proportion of worksites employing 50 or more people that provide programs to reduce employee stress.

Objective 6.11
from *Healthy People 2000: National Health Promotion and Disease Prevention Objectives*

SUMMARY

Stress is the body's reaction to a physical or emotional strain. The body's response to stress occurs in three stages: alarm, resistance, and exhaustion. The effect of stress on the individual depends on how well the person is able to cope with stressors. The common stressors people experience are life changes, traumatic events, conflicts, and daily hassles. Being open to change, committed to your activities, and feeling in control of your actions allows you to deal more effectively with stress.

STRESS AND ITS EFFECTS ON YOU

MAIN IDEAS

CONCEPTS

✔ Personality type is related to how people experience stress.

✔ Many physical disorders are caused by stress.

✔ Stress can lead to depression and suicide.

✔ Teenagers can take steps to help themselves and others cope with depression.

VOCABULARY

Type A personality
Type B personality
psychosomatic illness
migraine headache
cholesterol
depression
overgeneralization
personalization

Everyone experiences stress every day. Stress is a natural and inescapable part of life. Positive stress can add new dimensions of accomplishment and enjoyment to your life, but distress can lead to physical illness or even suicide. Your response to stressors depends upon your personality and how well you learn to manage stress.

PERSONALITY TYPES

Some people thrive on challenge. As soon as one goal is reached they eagerly seek another. Other people take life more easily. They work slowly and methodically, being satisfied with lower output. Scientists who study the effects of stress on health often refer to these two primary personality types as **Type A** and **Type B**. Someone with a Type A personality is very productive. She or he often feels there is not enough time to do everything and has difficulty relaxing. People described as having a Type B personality are relaxed, cooperative rather than competitive, and satisfied with lower output. The characteristics of Type A and Type B are illustrated in Figure 5-2. As you can see, Type A and Type B are extremes. Most personalities are combinations of different degrees of both types.

STRESS AND YOUR HEALTH

Your personality type influences how you deal with the tasks you need to accomplish, and how you deal with your tasks partly determines the amount of stress you feel. When stress is excessive, your body may respond by becoming ill. Severe, prolonged distress can result in a number of physical health problems.

PSYCHOSOMATIC REACTIONS   Some physical disorders that result from stress are psychosomatic. A **psychosomatic illness** [*sy kuh suh MAT ik*] is a physical disorder caused by stress rather than by disease or injury to the body. Psychosomatic illnesses are real physical problems that are triggered or complicated by stress. A psychosomatic illness is not imaginary, as many people believe.

There are many kinds of psychosomatic illnesses with which you may be familiar. Sleep disorders are common examples. While worrying about something may make it hard for some people to sleep, others may deal with stress by sleeping much longer than usual. Skin disorders also are common stress responses. Studies have shown that the onset of cold sores, acne, and hives can often be linked to stress.

Digestive problems also may be psychosomatic. The immediate response to stress includes slowing down the digestive process. This change may cause "butterflies" in the stomach. Nausea, vom-

It is important to know the effect of stressors, both large and small, on your health and well-being.

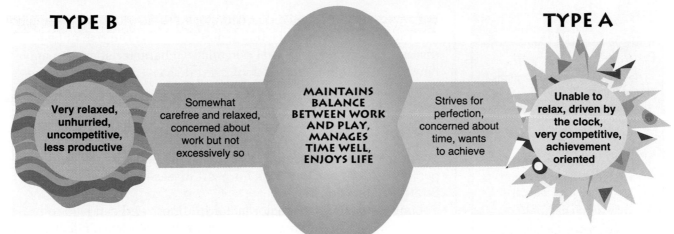

TYPE B

Very relaxed, unhurried, uncompetitive, less productive

Somewhat carefree and relaxed, concerned about work but not excessively so

MAINTAINS BALANCE BETWEEN WORK AND PLAY, MANAGES TIME WELL, ENJOYS LIFE

Strives for perfection, concerned about time, wants to achieve

TYPE A

Unable to relax, driven by the clock, very competitive, achievement oriented

Figure 5-2   Where would you place yourself on this continuum?

iting, diarrhea, and constipation are common results of distress. An ulcer is an example of a digestive ailment that is often related to stress. An ulcer is a hole or sore in the intestine just beyond the stomach or in the lining of the stomach. Stress causes the amount of acid in digestive juices to increase. At the same time, the stomach's resistance to the acid is decreased, thus increasing the risk of developing an ulcer.

Various types of headaches can be physical symptoms of stress. Tension headaches are caused by muscles that contract in the neck and scalp. A **migraine headache** is a very severe headache that can be triggered by stress. A migraine headache can be preceded by temporary vision problems and often is accompanied by nausea. When arteries to the brain constrict as a result of stress, the supply of blood to parts of the brain may decrease and cause temporary vision problems or other symptoms. Then the arteries dilate again and pressure on the nerve endings in the artery walls causes the severe throbbing of a migraine headache.

Some psychosomatic illnesses arise as a result of brain and body interactions that are not well understood but have been clearly demonstrated. Other disorders occur when the body becomes less able to resist infection. Such disorders can range from the common cold to serious infectious diseases.

THE IMMUNE SYSTEM   Scientists recognize that there is a connection between stress and the body's ability to resist infectious disease. But because the immune system is so complex, it is difficult to understand exactly how stress affects the system. Nevertheless, studies show that your body spends a great deal of energy when it is under stress, which leaves you very tired. When you are exposed to a disease organism, your immune system is activated to fight the disease. If your body is exhausted, the immune system may respond less quickly to the presence of a disease organism, and you are likely to become ill. You can learn more about the immune system in Chapter 23, "Infectious Diseases."

HEART DISEASE   The heart and blood vessels can also suffer from high levels of stress. Mental and emotional stress cause your heart rate, blood pressure, and cholesterol levels to increase. **Cholesterol**

HEALTHY PEOPLE 2000

Reduce to less than 35 percent the proportion of people aged 18 and older who experienced adverse health effects from stress within the past year.

Objective 6.5
from *Healthy People 2000: National Health Promotion and Disease Prevention Objectives*

The following are suggestions for modifying Type A behavior.

- Don't wear a watch.
- Cancel a task and go for a walk instead.
- Play a game with your younger brother or sister and let yourself lose.
- Take a long bath.
- Read a novel for fun.
- Ask someone to do you a personal favor.
- Ask someone a personal question and listen to the answer.
- Think about distrustful or hostile thoughts you may have and examine them to see if they are accurate.
- Recognize what is important in your life and take time to enjoy those things.

FOR YOUR INFORMATION

Sometimes an unsuccessful suicide attempt is an unconscious cry for help and attention. Every attempted suicide should be followed by special counseling.

is a waxy, fatty substance that can block the flow of blood through the arteries. All of these factors tend to increase the risk of heart disease. Research shows that personality characteristics also may have some effect on one's risk of heart disease. Some studies suggest that people with a Type A personality who also demonstrate a great deal of hostility may be at high risk for heart disease. However, other factors such as smoking, high blood pressure, eating a high fat diet, and lack of exercise are more important in determining risk. Some suggestions for changing the behaviors of Type A personalities to decrease risk for heart disease are listed in the Strategies for Living.

Long-term stress is a major factor in illness and can lead to premature death. Therefore, it is important that you learn effective ways of coping with stress. With each experience of stress, you will become either more or less capable of dealing with its effects. Whether you become more capable or less capable depends on how you handle each stressor.

CHRONIC FATIGUE SYNDROME

Chronic fatigue syndrome (CFS) is a condition in which a person experiences long-term feelings of abnormal bodily exhaustion. The illness is accompanied by other symptoms similar to those of mononucleosis—weakness, fever, headache, and sore throat. People with CFS may be unable to work or participate in their usual social activities. CFS can be difficult to identify because there is no clear-cut laboratory test for diagnosis. Although medical experts disagree as to whether there is a link between CFS and stress, persons who have CFS are usually treated for their mental as well as their physical conditions.

TEEN SUICIDE

Adolescence is a period of great stress. It is a time of accepting many physical changes and taking on new responsibilities. These changes can cause a great deal of anxiety. You may feel angry, frustrated, confused, or depressed. **Depression** is a feeling of sadness, worthlessness, helplessness, or isolation. In its milder forms, it is often called "the blues." Feelings of depression may be triggered by many different stressors—illness, injury, loneliness, changes in body chemistry, or the loss of someone you care about.

Everyone feels depressed or lonely from time to time, but these feelings usually do not last very long. When depression does last a long time, or when many things go wrong all at once, some teenagers may suddenly feel that nothing can ever go right again. They may even have thoughts of suicide. Teenagers who feel hopeless enough to consider suicide need to understand that they need help from family, friends and sometimes professionals. In the not-too-distant future things will be better. When that time comes, they well be glad that they are still alive.

THE FREQUENCY OF SUICIDE According to the United States Public Health Service, as many as ten percent of 14- to 17-year olds report having attempted suicide at least once. Suicide rates in the United States vary a great deal depending upon age, gender, and ethnic background. Figure 5-3 illustrates these differences. You will note that the adolescent rate is low compared with other groups, but as a cause of death in this age group, suicide ranks third.

HELPING YOURSELF AND OTHERS Some teenagers who consider suicide are loners who have problems making or keeping friends. Without friends, they lack the social support they could use to help them manage their problems. These teenagers may not have a positive self-image and they may tend to overgeneralize problems. **Overgeneralization** is drawing a broad conclusion from too little evidence. For example, a boy who loses his first girlfriend and concludes that no girl will ever like him is overgeneralizing.

People who consider suicide are often very critical of themselves. They may feel guilty or worthless. Failing in school, skipping classes, or having a hard time concentrating confirms their bad feelings about themselves. People who are very critical of themselves may personalize a problem. **Personalization** is the act of taking a general remark as if it were meant for only one person. Or it can mean interpreting an incident as if only one person were involved. For example, teenagers might feel guilty if their families have money problems. They may feel that they should be able to help more, or that they are burdening their parents. They are personalizing, making themselves feel responsible for events that are out of their control. When people have negative feelings like these, they may become very depressed and begin to think about suicide.

Teenagers who experience strong feelings of depression over a period of one or two months need to seek medical advice. Some of the symptoms of depression are loss of interest in friends, school and activities, changes in sleep patterns, major changes in eating

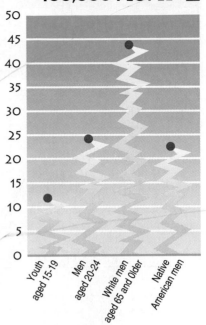

SUICIDES PER 100,000 PEOPLE

Figure 5-3 **Which group has the lowest suicide rate?**

CONSUMER HEALTH

Managing Stress Without Spending Money

Relieving stress recently has become a money-making industry. Companies are offering stress-reducing products and services that may help with the symptoms of stress, but these products often come at a high cost.

Massage, biofeedback therapy, and self-help seminars can help relieve some of the symptoms of stress. Stress-reducing vitamins can supplement a diet with missing vitamins and nutrients. However, these megavitamins provide no more vitamins than two or three helpings of vegetables or fruits a day. Instead of investing in expensive over-the-counter stress reducing vitamins, simply add more vegetables and fruit to your diet.

Beware of miracle cures and false promises. Stress is a part of everyday life, but there are things you can do every day to relieve it. Here are a few tips:

- Stress-reduction services or products cannot eliminate the stressors in your life. They may only help reduce the effects of stress.

- Exercise regularly. All of the experts agree that exercise is a productive and efficient way to reduce stress.

- Eat a balanced diet and avoid alcohol, caffeine, and nicotine.

- Be organized. Disorganization, chaos, messiness, and procrastination can produce stress.

- Learn your limits and say no when you cannot handle an extra responsibility or take on another task.

STRATEGIES FOR LIVING

These strategies may help if you have a friend in a severe crisis.

- Take your friend's crisis seriously.
- Get help immediately, but do not leave your friend alone.
- If you are talking on the phone, keep talking until you can get someone else to call for the police or fire department.
- Do not deny that your friend has a problem.
- Listen to your friend carefully.
- Avoid statements such as "Don't worry," "There's nothing to worry about," or "Your problem is not really that bad."

- Ask specific questions about the problem.
- Afterwards, talk about the crisis with someone to relieve any of the emotions you may be feeling.
- Ask your school guidance counselor to arrange a discussion group to help you and others deal with your feelings.
- Remind yourself and reassure your friend that in time the bad feelings will pass. But it requires patience and a day-by-day effort to face the problems.

patterns, feelings of hopelessness, and reliance on drugs to ease these symptoms. If these symptoms are present, professional counseling may be necessary. Many teenagers will want to talk with their parents first, but others may find it difficult to explain personal problems to their parents. A school psychologist or a school guidance counselor can help. A teacher or other adult may be able to recommend someone who can help.

Sometimes young people find themselves caught up in a friend's crisis and do not know how to stop it. Some tips on helping a friend in a severe crisis are given above. Many towns have suicide hot lines or suicide prevention centers to help people who have thoughts about suicide. Telephone numbers for such places are usually listed at the front of the telephone book. If your town does not have these resources, find someone who will listen and help—a parent, teacher, clergy member, or even someone your age. Make sure your friend knows that there are people who care.

LESSON 5.2 USING WHAT YOU HAVE LEARNED

REVIEW

1. What is meant by *depression*?
2. List three examples of psychosomatic illnesses.
3. Describe the characteristics of Type A and Type B personalities.

THINK CRITICALLY

4. Why is it helpful to talk with trusted peers and adults about feelings of depression that you might have?
5. Suicide rates often increase during very stressful times. Why do you think this happens?

APPLY IT TO YOURSELF

6. Describe an incident from your own life when you personalized something someone said to you. How did you regain a realistic viewpoint of the incident?

Suicide Peer Counseling

Suicide is one of the leading causes of death among teenagers in the United States. This sad and often violent end to life causes devastating hurt to all who know and love the person who has died.

Estimates are that as many as 40 percent of teenagers across the country consider suicide at some time. Fortunately, far fewer attempt it. Help is available for troubled teenagers. Suicide-prevention programs show teenagers that suicide is not a way to cope with feelings of alienation, frustration, or confusion.

Peer Counseling Programs are available in most states. The Peer Counseling Program involves teenagers who want to help their peers. After they have completed many hours of training, these teenage volunteers are equipped to answer hotline phones and make referrals for anyone who calls, 24 hours a day. They are trained to listen and to guide their callers into constructive alternatives to suicide. The peer counselors are supervised by trained social workers or counselors. People at hotlines are empowered to intervene if they hear a caller making plans to take his or her own life.

Suicide prevention classes are offered in hundreds of schools and are mandated in several states. These classes reach about forty percent of all teenaged students and they offer important education about suicide awareness. The first step in suicide prevention is awareness of the warning signs of suicide. The warning signs are talking about suicide; writing about suicide; losing interest in friends, school, hobbies, sports, personal appearance, or food; giving away favorite possessions; dropping all social inhibitions; behaving irrationally, violently, or becoming suddenly accident prone; carrying pills or a weapon; or being depressed for a long time. These signs do not nec-

essarily mean that a person is thinking of suicide. However, they do warrant attention and often action, such as telling an adult or referring the person to Peer Counseling or to a 24-hour hotline service.

One way to work toward suicide prevention is to understand some of the causes of suicide. Most often, suicide results from aggravated stress. As teenagers take on more adult roles, they feel pressure to be attractive and accepted, to succeed in school and in sports, and to appear self-sufficient and in control of their lives. Some teens feel overwhelmed by these pressures and by the physiological and emotional changes they experience during this time of their lives.

Another stressor that can be overwhelming is loss. The loss of a parent through death or divorce, or of a close friend who moves away, disrupts the support structure in the life of a teenager. Loss of self-esteem and confidence can result.

A third stressor is one that affects everyone but is particularly hard on teenagers. It is the emphasis on success. Parents may expect more of a child as he or she becomes a teenager. Some young people take on part-time jobs, increasing the pressures of their daily lives. Success breeds confidence, but with so many pressures, a teenager may feel he or she isn't living up to a parent's expectations or to his or her own expectations.

Everyone, particularly teenagers, needs to understand that the stresses that seem overwhelming today will be resolved in time. Stress, even in its severest form, is a normal part of everyday life. With

prevention services like the Peer Counseling Program and in-school prevention classes becoming more readily available, students can get help during difficult and challenging times. Many teenagers who were thinking of suicide have been helped—by a peer or a trusted adult—to help themselves meet the challenges that are part of every teenager's life.

1. Why do you think Peer Counseling Programs would be particularly effective in helping prevent suicide among teenagers?

2. What constructive steps do you take to counteract depression or low self-esteem in yourself or others?

HANDLING STRESS IN YOUR LIFE

The best time to develop healthy habits for reducing stress is when you are not under much stress. Although you cannot know exactly what stressors you will face in the future, you can begin now to develop some ways to decrease your level of stress.

RECOGNIZE YOUR REACTIONS

Earlier in this chapter you learned about some common stressors that you deal with every day. For example, emotional conflicts often affect the decisions you make and daily hassles cause annoyance and frustration. You may think that these inescapable upsets are not having an affect on you. But stress can affect you in many ways. Have you ever suddenly flared up angrily at a friend and then wondered why you had done so? Do you find yourself breaking out with acne or developing a tension headache at just the wrong time? Do you sometimes have anxious dreams or nightmares? These are some of the ways your body might tell you that stress is mounting. Recognizing what your body is telling you is the first step in managing stress.

BIOFEEDBACK One way that people are learning to recognize how their bodies react to stress is through the technique of biofeedback. During one type of biofeedback therapy, an electromyograph is attached by wires to different parts of the body. The electromyograph is a machine that monitors the activity of muscles and allows a person to observe, by means of colored lights or different sounds, how he or she responds to certain stimuli. Biofeedback can help people learn to recognize how stress affects their bodies and how to counteract those effects. For example, a headache sufferer might learn to relax the muscles that tighten and cause a headache. Biofeedback therapy also has been used to help people lower high blood pressure and control asthma.

MENTAL AWARENESS Most stressful situations can be dealt with directly by using a problem-solving strategy. The decision-making steps identified in Chapter 1, "Wellness: A Way of Life," can be adapted as a method for dealing with many stressful situations. Using a decision-making strategy forces you to be aware of all aspects of a situation. If you understand your problem and work out a plan of action, you are less likely to experience frustration and a fear of failure that often leads to stress. To understand this point, consider the following example. Suppose you are anxious about finding a part-time job.

- *Identify the Problem* How can you find a part-time job?

- *Consider Your Options* You could learn about available jobs through the

MAIN IDEAS

CONCEPTS
- ✔ Everyone experiences stress.
- ✔ Maintaining physical health is important in coping with stress.
- ✔ Relaxation, time management, and the support of friends help reduce stress.
- ✔ Positive thinking and laughter can defuse stress.

VOCABULARY
endorphin
cognitive appraisal
self-fulfilling prophecy

What activities are helpful to you in dealing with stress?

help-wanted ads in the newspaper. Your teachers and other people can tell you about jobs they know about. You can call businesses to find out what jobs are open, and you can find out what jobs are available at the state employment agency.

- *Evaluate the Outcomes*   Think about the positives and negatives of each job that is available.
- *Decide and Act*   Select your first choice of the available jobs and go out and apply for it.
- *Review Your Decision*   Has the part-time job you obtained fulfilled your expectations? If not, you may want to take what you have learned into consideration when you next begin a job search.

MAINTAIN PHYSICAL HEALTH

The first step toward reducing the effects of stress on the body is to stay in good health. Good eating habits, plenty of rest, and adequate exercise help you stay in good physical condition.

NUTRITION   During times of distress, it is important to pay close attention to your nutritional needs. Being well-nourished promotes a feeling of well-being and provides the energy needed to cope with stress. Eat balanced meals when you are hungry. However, it is best to eat more lightly during times of high anxiety because the digestive system slows down in response to stress. Avoid skipping meals. Becoming overly hungry may result in overeating when you do eat. Be careful to avoid overindulging in certain foods that have a high fat content such as ice cream or chocolate. You may have seen multi-vitamins advertised as "stress vitamins." These products contain vitamins C, E, and B-complex, but they have not been shown to improve people's ability to cope with stress.

The physical activities you enjoy help keep you healthy and also relieve stress.

PHYSICAL ACTIVITY   Exercise is a good defense against stress. Increasing your physical activity stimulates the release of **endorphins** [en DAWR funz]. Endorphins are a type of chemical released by the brain to reduce pain. During exercise the level of endorphins circulating in the blood is higher than at other times. These chemicals are thought to be responsible for the strong feeling of well-being and relaxation experienced by long-distance runners.

RELAX

Some part of each day should be reserved for relaxation. Even a few restful moments after lunch or dinner can have a refreshing effect. Listening to music, reading a book, working on a hobby, or sharing time with a friend are good ways to relax.

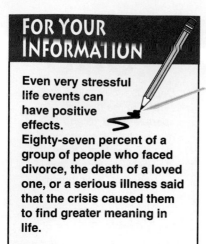

Are you in control of your time, or do you need to take charge?

Playing sports is another way to relax as long as you do not become too competitive. However, during stressful moments, a feeling of relaxation is not always easy to attain. There are several techniques that you can use to help you to relax.

PROGRESSIVE RELAXATION   Relaxation techniques are useful in relieving stress, especially when stress has made your muscles tense. Try lying on your back with your arms at your sides. Focus your attention on each part of your body in turn. For example, relax your arms gradually from your fingers to your shoulders until your arms feel heavy. Then do the same for your legs, relaxing them from your toes to your hips. Continue until your entire body feels totally relaxed. This exercise is good for a short break or for falling asleep at night.

VISUALIZATION   Another method of relaxing is called visualization. Some people describe visualization as giving yourself permission to daydream. Begin by picturing yourself in pleasant surroundings— lying on a sunny beach, or relaxing in the cool air of a mountain, or even floating on a cloud. Try to feel your imaginary environment with all five senses. Putting yourself mentally into another place can help you to focus on the positive side of any stressful situation rather than on the negative. Athletes, actors, and musicians frequently use another form of visualization to rehearse an approaching performance. As they imagine themselves performing at their peak, they promote positive expectations for themselves.

NURTURE SOCIAL SUPPORT NETWORKS

When stress begins to mount, it is important to have a group of trusted friends or family members to act as your social support network. Your support network consists of the people with whom you have built strong ties at home, at school, or in your community. Strong relationships are built over a period of time by the mutual sharing of both happy and sad feelings. It is important to begin to build a support group before stressful situations arise. Building friendships is easier when things are going well. Then when you find yourself being overwhelmed by distress, your support group may offer ideas that will help reduce stress. At the very least, they can often give encouraging support or help you see your situation from a new perspective.

MANAGE YOUR TIME

Moderate amounts of stress can help you achieve your goals. Stress motivates you to learn, to change, or to take action. However, if you feel good about your accomplishments, you may try to take on too much. In order to maintain good mental and physical health, it is important to know how much you can do without feeling stress. It also is important to learn to manage your time so that you can meet all your responsibilities. You may find the following time management strategy helpful for reducing stress.

- Set your priorities. Identify what tasks must be done and put them in order of importance.
- Schedule your tasks. Find the most efficient way of accomplishing each of them.
- Establish intermediate goals. If you are working on a large project, break it into smaller steps. Set deadlines for each step and finish one step before starting the next.
- Be realistic in estimating your time. Once you have decided how much time you need, add another 15 percent of the total for unanticipated problems.
- Identify your ultimate goal and break it down into smaller tasks. Decide what tasks you can accomplish in shorter periods and fit them into small blocks of time.
- Don't put off getting started. Everyone has favorite ways of procrastinating. Try to figure out what yours are, and avoid resorting to them.
- Leave time for recreation and relaxation.
- Learn to say "no." You do not have to do everything.

ALLOW FOR SETBACKS

Some people seem to bounce back from setbacks in achieving their goals. They may even turn setbacks into new opportunities. This is not always easy to do, especially if you have focused on a goal for a long time. However, each setback can be used as an opportunity to review the goal and make modifications.

Mario and Roland are good athletes and best friends. They both were recruited to play football at the state university in the fall. Mario passed all the National Collegiate Athletic Association guidelines for eligibility, but Roland was injured in a motorcycle accident and had to spend three weeks in the hospital. His absence from school caused him to fall behind in chemistry. Roland knows that if he doesn't pass chemistry he will not be eligible to play his first year. He wouldn't even be able to practice with the team during his first year.

When Roland failed his chemistry final, he was very angry. It was hard for him to feel good about his friend's good fortune. Mario would have a head start on the team while Roland would have to watch from the stands. He even thought about going to a junior college so that he could play right away.

"Hey, Roland, look on the bright side." said Mario.

"What bright side?" asked Roland.

"You could have been hurt so badly in the accident that you couldn't play ball at all. You could have been killed. Instead, you just got delayed."

"I guess you could look at it like that," laughed Roland. "Besides, I really want to go to State. I'll be able to focus on my studies and get off on the right foot with school. So you look out. Next year I'll be back and I'll be better!"

A good laugh is good for your health.

CHANGE YOUR THINKING

Good friends often are able to help us put things into perspective. When Mario reminded Roland that things could have been much worse, he helped Roland to deal more effectively with this setback. As a result, Roland changed his thinking about what had happened. This process is called **cognitive appraisal**. It means to think about an event using logic and knowledge rather than emotion or limited information.

POSITIVE SELF-TALK   Often you talk yourself into anxious feelings about an upcoming event or a task that you must complete. You may compare yourself to others whom you admire and find yourself inadequate. As these negative thoughts creep into your mind, they can unconsciously prevent you from performing at your best. If you think you cannot do something, unknowingly you may exert less effort. As a result your thought may come true. This behavior is called a **self-fulfilling prophecy**. Too much anxiety about failure will make you afraid to try new things. However, just as negative talk can interfere with your performance, positive self-talk can help you reach your goals. It is important that your positive talk also be stated realistically. For example, rather than declaring that you will get an A on a test in a class that has been a problem for you, think about the test in small steps. "I am prepared for the test." "It will be difficult, but I know I can do well." Positive statements will help you reach your goals with far less stress.

DEFUSE STRESS   Laughter is an important way to defuse stressful situations and feelings. Each time you laugh, your body responds both physically and psychologically. Physically, laughing uses many muscles. It increases your rate of breathing and your heart rate and it actually causes the release of endorphins. Psychologically, you respond by feeling more at ease, less tense, and less negative about a situation. Being able to laugh at yourself is the most natural and effective stress reliever you can have.

LESSON 5.3   USING WHAT YOU HAVE LEARNED

REVIEW

1. What are two ways of relaxing?
2. Why is good nutrition important in dealing with stress?
3. What are endorphins?

THINK CRITICALLY

4. Explain why a social support network is important to you when you face a stressful situation.
5. Explain how visualization can help to reduce stress.

APPLY IT TO YOURSELF

6. Choose a life change event from Figure 5-1 that you think you might encounter in the near future. Describe strategies that you could use to reduce the effect of the stressor.

SUMMARY

Being able to identify what causes stress for you is an important first step in learning to manage stress. People who are able to use stress in a positive way maintain their physical health through good nutrition, exercise, and adequate rest. They know how to manage their time, and they maintain close ties to family and friends. A positive self-image and a positive outlook on life are insurance against the negative influence of stressors.

Stressed Out

Jamal was busy these days. His senior year brought a lot of homework and papers to write. Also, he had just started working more hours. Jamal was having a hard time just keeping up with his homework.

Jamal was tired most of the time. As the weeks went by, his temper got shorter and shorter. He hardly spoke to anyone at school and spent any free time he had at the library. He was really pushing himself.

One morning in English class, his teacher handed back a paper Jamal had worked hard on. When Jamal looked at his grade, he couldn't believe it. He had gotten a D. He was furious. Jamal had always done well in Mr. Barrett's class, and now he was having a hard time accepting this setback.

In study hall, Jamal showed his paper to a couple of his friends. "Can you believe this? I am so mad!"

"Go tell him off, Jamal," said one friend. "You don't have to take this from him."

With his friends encouraging him, Jamal stormed off to Mr. Barrett's office. Just as he got to the door, Jamal stopped for an instant. "Wait a minute," he thought. "Don't do something foolish. Mr. Barrett has always been fair to me. But he had no right to give me this grade."

He turned and saw his friends down the hall. Jamal was torn. He knew he would feel a lot better if he could just vent his anger. But what about his relationship with Mr. Barrett? "Maybe I should just drop it."

PAUSE AND CONSIDER

1. *Identify the Problem.* What is Jamal's conflict?

2. *Consider the Options.* What are Jamal's options for dealing with his frustration?

3. *Evaluate the Outcomes.* What would Jamal's friends think if he "gave it" to Mr. Barrett? What could happen to the good relationship between Jamal and Mr. Barrett?

Jamal realized that he was overreacting. He decided it would be better to keep his cool. When he met with Mr. Barrett, Jamal asked him why he had given him such a bad grade. Mr. Barrett explained that Jamal hadn't really addressed the assigned topic. Once Mr. Barrett further explained it, the problem was clear to Jamal. "You know," Jamal said, "things have been really stressful for me lately."

"I thought so, Jamal. You just don't seem to be your usual self. Anything I can do to help?" Jamal explained what he had been going through. Mr. Barrett offered some suggestions for how Jamal might lighten his work load. When he left Mr. Barrett's office, a couple of Jamal's friends were waiting to hear what happened.

"We had a good talk," Jamal laughed. "Everything's squared away now. You know, Mr. Barrett is okay."

DECIDE AND REVIEW

4. *Decide and Act.* How did Jamal deal with his anger toward Mr. Barrett? Was his choice a healthy one?

5. *Review.* What other ways might have Jamal used to approach Mr. Barrett? How did stress affect Jamal's behavior?

PROJECTS

1. Researchers have determined that the release of endorphins during exercise can greatly reduce the effects of stress. Gather further information from the library and write an essay that describes the physical and psychological effects of exercise on stress. Include in your essay a description of any personal experience you may have had with "runner's high," the feeling of well-being that follows the release of endorphins as you exercise.

2. Find out about the characteristics of Type A and Type B personalities. Create a chart, based on your research, that compares the characteristics of these two extreme personality types. At the bottom of your chart, write your own conclusions as to the influences that may cause a person to be mostly Type A or Type B.

WORKING WITH OTHERS

Make a list of some of the sources of stress in your daily life. For each stressor, identify why it is a source of stress. Then develop some strategies for reducing the stress each item causes you. Exchange your list with a partner. Evaluate each other's strategies and make addtional suggestions.

CONNECTING TO...

MUSIC The stresses of grief, loss, and hardship are often the subjects of popular songs. Think of a song that you like that is about a hardship. Then write a paragraph that describes the songwriter's portrayal of the stressor. Does the song reveal a healthy approach to stress, or is the stress overwhelming?

USING VOCABULARY

adrenaline	overgeneralization
alarm stage	personalization
cholesterol	post-traumatic stress disorder
cognitive appraisal	psychosomatic illness
coping	resistance stage
depression	self-fulfilling prophecy
distress	stress
endorphin	stressor
eustress	Type A personality
exhaustion stage	Type B personality
migraine headache	

On a separate sheet of paper, identify the vocabulary word that matches the following definitions.

1. the physical or mental demands that cause stress

2. positive use of stress

3. the initial physical reaction to stress

4. the disorder characterized by extreme anxiety, reliving a traumatic event, and general loss of interest in day-to-day events

5. the physical reaction that works to resist a threatening stressor

6. a personality characterized by relaxed, cooperative behavior

7. the physical reaction to stress that lowers the body's resistance to illness

8. the act of drawing a broad conclusion from too little evidence

9. the act of taking a general remark as if it were meant for only one person

10. negative thinking that can actually cause a negative result

CONCEPT MAPPING

On a separate sheet of paper, create a concept map for *stress*. In your map, use as many of these concepts as you can: *accomplishment, decision making, health, humor, negative stress (distress), positive stress (eustress), relaxation, social support, stress, stressors.* You may use additional concepts related to stress in your map. Further information about concept mapping appears in the front of this book.

THINK CRITICALLY

INTERPRET

LESSON 5.1
1. What are two stressors with which you often deal?
2. List three physical responses to stress.
3. What determines whether stress is positive or negative?
4. What happens in your body during the alarm stage of stress?
5. At what stage of stress is a person most likely to become sick?
6. What are three characteristics of a "hardy personality?"
7. How does a person with a hardy personality view stress?

LESSON 5.2
8. List three characteristics of a personality that is a balance between Type A and Type B.
9. Name two psychosomatic illnesses that can be linked to stress.
10. Explain how stress affects the heart.
11. Why do you think that hostile Type A personalities are more prone to heart disease than others who are not Type A?
12. What is one strategy that a teenager could use to help her or him deal with overwhelming stress?
13. Explain what is meant by personalizing a problem.

LESSON 5.3
14. How can biofeedback help a person who is suffering from the physical symptoms of stress?
15. How can maintaining good physical health reduce stress?
16. How can visualization change feelings of negative stress into positive stress?
17. How can humor play a part in defusing stress?

APPLY

LESSON 5.1
18. What are the stressors that occur regularly in your life? Are you often late? Do you sometimes miss a deadline? What steps can you take to eliminate these stressors from your life?
19. What physical or psychological symptoms of stress have you observed in yourself? What are some ways that you can work to lessen these symptoms?

LESSON 5.2
20. When a friend is facing a crisis, why is it important that you take him or her seriously?
21. Why do you think stress is talked about a great deal in the world today?
22. Why are depression and suicide closely linked to each other?

LESSON 5.3
23. Explain why it is important for you to build a network of trusted family members and friends.
24. Give at least two reasons for agreeing or disagreeing with the following statement: Some stress is necessary to well-being, and a lack of stress can be harmful.

COMMITMENT TO WELLNESS
FOLLOW-UP

SETTING GOALS

Look at your evaluation of the statements at the beginning of this chapter. Which areas are your strongest? Which are your weakest? Next to each statement that you consider to be a weak area for you, write down the question, "What would make this behavior easier for me? " Answer this question by suggesting specific behaviors. For example, if meeting your daily goals and doing your best to stay focused is particularly difficult for you, think of ways that you can lessen some of your daily responsibilities. Can you share your responsibilities with another person? Can you set more realistic goals for yourself? Can you make a daily schedule that will help you organize your day? Ask yourself specific questions for each of the areas you want to improve. Each week, check your goals to assess your progress.

WHERE DO I GO FROM HERE?

Learning how to cope with stress is the subject of many books. Ask your guidance counselor to recommend books or essays that have been written about stress and stress management.

FOR MORE INFORMATION, CONTACT:
National Institute of Mental Health
Public Inquiries Branch
Room 15C-05
5600 Fishers Lane
Rockville, Maryland 20857

Understanding Mental Disorders

"The art of living lies less in eliminating our troubles than in growing with them."

Bernard M. Baruch

No one lives a completely carefree life without encountering trouble of one kind or another. The search for a life free of trouble and free of personal problems often can only result in greater problems. A person can learn to view troubled times as challenges and to do his or her best to cope with problems. Although problems, at times, can be overwhelming, they also can become an important source of personal growth.

During your lifetime, you will encounter many problems—some small, some large. Sometimes you will be able to solve a problem easily and on your own. At other times, you may need help. Each and every time you meet a challenge head-on, you learn something new about yourself. You learn to identify your strengths. You also learn to recognize areas that may need to be strengthened. A healthy attitude toward solving your problems can help you get on with the art of living.

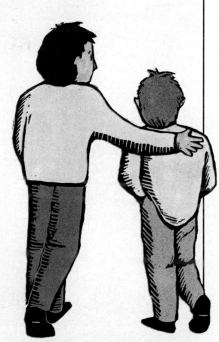

SELF-ASSESSMENT

Begin thinking about your personal behavior by responding to the following statements. On a separate sheet of paper, list the numbers from 1 to 10. Write *yes* next to the numbers of statements that apply to you and *no* next to the numbers of statements that do not apply to you.

1. I have more good experiences than bad experiences each day.
2. I am usually satisfied with the work I do and how others respond to my work.
3. I experience "blue moods," but they usually do not last very long.
4. I feel comfortable with the way I express my emotions.
5. I enjoy spending time with my family and friends and make an effort to do so.
6. I would seek out professional help if I thought I needed it for a mental health problem.
7. I take time to tell others that I appreciate what they do for me.
8. I am a good friend who can be relied upon in a time of crisis.
9. I am satisfied with the way I deal with daily problems.
10. I believe that I demonstrate charactersitics of an emotionally healthy person.

Review your responses and consider what might be your strengths and weaknesses. Save your personal checklist for a follow-up activity that appears at the end of the chapter.

CAUSES OF MENTAL DISORDERS

MAIN IDEAS

CONCEPTS

✔ Many people experience some degree of emotional distress during their life-times.

✔ Society dictates the bound-aries of acceptable and unacceptable behavior.

✔ Mental disorders stem from physical and emotional problems.

VOCABULARY

organic disorder
degenerative disease
functional disorder
mental trauma

Many years ago, it would have been considered inappropriate for a woman to express political views in public.

You live at a time when technological advances and social changes occur so rapidly that sometimes you might feel confused or upset by the world. In everyone's life, there is a time when he or she feels anxious, depressed, unreasonably angry, or unable to deal with what life offers.

The range of emotions that people feel is vast, and so is the range of how people deal with mental health challenges. When your feelings prevent you from taking part in daily life in your usual way, then you may be suffering from mental distress.

At one time, people thought they could "catch" mental illness just as easily as a cold or the flu. Some people stayed away from neighbors with mental illness. Mental disorders are not passed from person to person like the common cold.

WHAT IS EMOTIONALLY HEALTHY BEHAVIOR?

Mental health or mental wellness is affected by emotional and intellectual wellness. Emotional wellness contributes positively to mental health. Conversely, someone who is not feeling emotionally well may exhibit behaviors related to mental distress or illness.

DEFINED BY SOCIAL NORMS   Generally, behaviors that are accepted by a society are determined by the majority of the members in the society. In the United States, few people claim to hear voices, so society finds such a behavior unacceptable. In some African com-munites, on the other hand, hearing voices is accepted as a sign of high-level communication.

Acceptable behaviors, as defined by societies, change over time. Similarly, people's attitudes toward certain behaviors also change over time. For example, forty years ago, it was not acceptable for women to speak out on political or economic issues. Today women are effective change-makers in the boardroom and in Congress. While it is more common and more acceptable for women to be involved in politics than it was before, some people still have neg-ative attitudes toward them.

Although every society has its own ideas about what is right or wrong, healthy or not healthy, acceptable or unaccept-able, psychologists have established guidelines for evaluating mental health in most societies.

EVALUATING MENTAL HEALTH   Although there are no absolute rules, psychologists consider the following characteristics when evualuating a person's mental health.

• *Perception of reality*   Usually, individuals are able to realistically assess and interpret the world around them. They do not misinterpret other's intentions, and they do not overrate or underestimate their own abilities.

- *Self-awareness*   No one completely understands his or her own feelings or behavior. However, well-adjusted people have more self-knowledge than those who suffer from a mental disorder.
- *Control over behavior*   Well-adjusted people are usually able to control their behavior and are capable of restraining aggressive impulses. Feelings of aggression often can lead to violence.
- *Self-esteem and acceptance*   People who are well-adjusted feel accepted by those around them, appreciate their own self-worth, and do not allow their opinions to be swayed by the group without consideration.
- *Ability to form relationships*   The mentally well person is sensitive to the feelings of others and is able to form positive relationships with other people.
- *Productive attitude*   Well-adjusted individuals are enthusiastic and energetic about life. They are willing to meet challenges, take on tasks, and learn new skills that lead to personal growth.

Most people do not display all of these characteristics all of the time, but the mentally well person will demonstrate the characteristics most of the time. For those who do not, the first step in regaining mental wellness is to understand the causes of the problems.

ORGANIC CAUSES OF MENTAL DISORDERS

Scientists have divided mental disorders into two general classes: organic and functional. **Organic disorders** are those caused by a physical problem that impairs brain functions either permanently or temporarily. This can result from physical illness such as an extremely high fever, from abnormalities of brain chemistry, or from a degenerative disease of the nervous system. A **degenerative disease** [di JEN uh rut iv] is characterized by progressive deterioration of tissue over several years.

Changes in mood or reasoning can be signs of a physical illness or a mental disorder. A physical checkup is extremely important when a person feels very depressed for no reason or notices a sudden change in personality. If a physical illness causes worrisome mental symptoms, the physical illness needs to be treated first. For example, a brain tumor may cause changes in personality, the ability to think, and speech. The mental disorder cannot be helped unless the tumor is treated.

Your body produces chemicals that are needed for various functions. For example, your brain contains many natural chemicals that allow you to process information. A chemical imbalance in your brain can affect normal thinking, feelings, attitudes, and behavior. An imbalance sometimes occurs when your body produces too much or too little of a chemical. This problem may be an inherited trait, or it may have developed over a period of time. Drugs—legal and illegal—also can cause chemical imbalances in the brain.

When something goes wrong with the complex chemical processes within the brain, a person's mood can change dramatically. Sometimes the mental change caused by the imbalance is permanent. At other times, it lasts until the chemical imbalance is corrected or controlled.

A PET scan (Positron Emission Tomography) is a computer-generated image of chemical activity in the brain. PET scans are used to identify organic problems. The PET scan below compares a normal brain (top) to the brain of person with Alzheimer's disease. Red and yellow areas indicate brain activity.

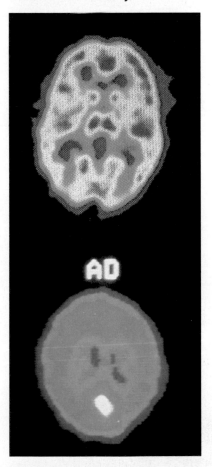

FUNCTIONAL CAUSES OF MENTAL DISORDERS

Mental disorders that stem from a person's environment are called **functional disorders**. Painful childhood experiences and severe stress are two environmental factors that can lead to mental disorders.

The shock of a serious accident can be very traumatic for the victims.

There are different theories about learning and behavior. Among them are the theories of psychiatrist Sigmund Freud who believed that childhood experiences were the most important influences on a person's mind. As you may remember from Chapter 3, "Developing a Healthy Personality," Freud felt that at each stage of development children have certain conflicts to resolve. If these conflicts are not resolved, they can affect the personality later in life. Frequently, conflicts in childhood revolve around family, friendships, or school.

Extreme stress also can lead to mental disorders. As you read in Chapter 5, "Managing Stress," many events in life lead to stress, including problems in the family, at work, or with friends. Mental stress makes people feel anxious, exhausted, and off-balance. Most people can cope with a certain amount of stress. But sometimes the stress is so great that a person cannot function normally.

Sometimes stress may be sudden and very powerful, as when someone experiences a trauma. A **mental trauma** [*TROW muh*] is a violent or tragic experience that can severely affect a person's mental health. For example, witnessing a relative's death in a car accident or the horrors of wartime can cause emotional distress.

Sometimes people with mental disorders act unpredictably. However, many people with mental disorders are able to function in society. With proper diagnosis and treatment, most emotional problems can be resolved or controlled.

SUMMARY

Research indicates that the causes of mental disorders can be organic and functional. Organic disorders result chiefly from physical abnormalities or chemical imbalances. Functional disorders are emotional problems that stem from environmental factors, such as stress or painful childhood events. A mental disorder can result from a combination of physical, behavioral, and environmental factors.

LESSON 6.1 USING WHAT YOU HAVE LEARNED

REVIEW

1. Explain the difference between organic disorders and functional disorders.
2. Describe three of the characteristics of a mentally healthy individual.

THINK CRITICALLY

3. Society establishes the boundaries of acceptable behavior. What is an example of something teenagers do today that might have been considered unacceptable in the early 1900s?
4. People with mental disorders often are portrayed in movies and books in a frightening way. How might this hurt the public's acceptance of the mentally ill?

APPLY IT TO YOURSELF

5. As a volunteer at a mental health halfway house, you have to work very closely with the residents of the home. Why is it important that you have a basic understanding of their illnesses?

TYPES OF MENTAL DISORDERS

Everyone has occasional problems dealing with emotions or relating to other people. But when these difficulties last for a long time or interfere with normal daily activities, a person's mental health may be threatened. Millions of people experience some degree of mental disability. The road to recovery from mental illness begins with identifying the problem.

CLASSIFYING BEHAVIOR

Psychologists do not always agree about ways to classify behaviors. But most scientists recognize the advantages to establishing a classification system. Such a system can provide mental health workers with a way to share information about symptoms. If an individual's behavior fits a particular group, then professionals have a point from which to start when deciding how to help the person.

However, establishing categories of behavior can be a problem. For example, an individual's condition may be overlooked if the symptoms do not fit neatly into a specific category. Also, a label is not an explanation for the behavior, how it began, or why it continues.

The American Psychiatric Association developed a classification system to identify the symptoms of various mental disorders. Many of the disorders are discussed in this lesson. The symptoms for each disorder are not exact. People diagnosed with the same disorder may exhibit varying degrees of symptoms. The severity of the symptoms is what determines the severity of the illness.

NEUROSES AND PSYCHOSES REDEFINED

Mental health professionals once organized all mental disorders under the broad categories of *neuroses* and *psychoses*. People exhibiting symptoms of a neurosis displayed persistent anxiety and personal unhappiness. They recognized their fears as irrational and were able to function in society, although with some limitations. Neurotic disorders rarely required hospitalization. Psychotics were defined as those people who had lost touch with reality and were overwhelmed by their fears. Treatment often included medication and hospitalization. The term *psychotic* is still used in descriptions of some behaviors. *Neurosis* and *psychosis* now are considered too vague to be helpful for the diagnosis of a mental disorder.

ORGANIC DISORDERS

Mental illnesses that involve impaired brain function due to chemical imbalance or physical abnormality are called organic mental disorders. Some disorders may show up in childhood, while others develop over many years and appear in adulthood.

MAIN IDEAS

CONCEPTS
✔ Social scientists have established categories of mental disorders.
✔ Classifications of mental disorders are based on the exhibited symptoms.
✔ Some problems are mild and affect a person for a short period, while other problems can be severe enough to affect a person's ability to function in society.

VOCABULARY

dementia	phobia
delirium	obsession
hallucination	compulsion
hyperactive	hypochondria
hypoactive	delusion
mania	amnesia

Most people experience some degree of emotional distress at some time in their lives.

DEMENTIA   A severe and irreversible loss of mental ability is called **dementia** [*dih MEN shuh*]. People with dementia may have great difficulty remembering names or conversations, and often lose their sense of judgment. They also may become quiet and withdrawn. Dementia is most common among elderly people and therefore, sometimes is called senile dementia.

Some older people who have senile dementia also suffer from Alzheimer's disease. People with this degenerative disease often become confused, emotionally unstable, and have trouble remembering recent events. The only treatment is emotional support, understanding, and a simplified environment. You can learn more about Alzheimer's disease in Chapter 18, "Understanding the Aging Process."

DELIRIUM   People who suffer from a condition called **delirium** [*dih LIR ee um*] rapidly become confused and lose their awareness of the environment. Delirium can result from poisoning, high fever, intoxication, or withdrawal from drugs or alcohol. It also can be caused by fear or trauma. Delirious people are not sure what day it is, where they are, or who they are.

Another sign of delirium is **hallucination**, or seeing, hearing, or sensing something that does not exist. For example, people who are hallucinating may see spiders on walls when none are there, or they may hear voices when no one is speaking.

DEVELOPMENTAL DISORDERS

Some forms of emotional distress begin to show in early childhood. This category includes mental retardation, speech disorders, and hyperactivity.

Autistic children often appear unaware of what is happening around them.

AUTISM   A very rare childhood disorder is infantile autism [*AW tiz um*], a condition in which the child is emotionally unresponsive and detached from his or her surroundings. Autistics turn within themselves and often are unable to react normally to people or to their environment. Repetitive, rhythmic movement is a common behavior pattern among autistic children.

ATTENTION DEFICIT DISORDER   Attention Deficit Disorder (ADD) is a fairly common disorder that is characterized by a child's inability to maintain concentration. Frequently, the child is hyperactive. A **hyperactive** child is in constant movement and can be distracted very easily. Some children may be hypoactive. **Hypoactive** children show signs of low activity and excessive daydreaming. Because ADD children have difficulty completing tasks and following instructions, they often have learning difficulties. Early treatment of this condition reduces stressful symptoms and can lead to improvement.

MOOD DISORDERS

Most people experience many moods. During one day, they may feel happy, sad, and angry. However, a mood disorder is a serious condition in which a single, often painful, mood rules the whole personality. Doctors today know a great deal about mood disorders and how to help people. Mood disorders often result from chemical imbalances that can be treated with prescribed medications. These conditions usually involve either clinical depression or alternating periods of depression and excessive elation.

CLINICAL DEPRESSION   Clinical depression is a disorder in which there are ongoing deep feelings of helplessness, worthlessness, and hopelessness. People with clinical depression lose interest in their usual activities. They feel guilty about small matters and have a low opinion of themselves. Clinically depressed people often do not eat enough, or they eat too much. They often have trouble sleeping, or they sleep too much. They may have difficulty concentrating and thus perform poorly at school or work.

A person who has a parent, brother, or sister with clinical depression is more likely to develop clinical depression than a person whose relatives have not had this emotional problem. Whether the cause for this relationship is hereditary or environmental is unclear. However, personal efforts and environmental changes can help overcome any possible hereditary factor.

People suffering severe clinical depression often have thoughts of suicide. In such cases, these people have given up hope of ever feeling better. The risk of suicide increases when a clinically depressed person abuses alcohol or other drugs that depress the nervous system. Fortunately, most periods of severe depression last no longer than three months. The majority of people who suffer from clinical depression eventually recover, either on their own or with professional help. About ten percent of people diagnosed with clinical depression do not recover.

ADOLESCENT DEPRESSION

Once thought to be an adult disease, clinical depression among teenagers is of great concern to health professionals. Symptoms include:

- Down or irritable mood most of the day, nearly every day
- Noticeable changes in appetite and weight
- Difficulty sleeping at night or sleeping during the day
- Daily fatigue
- Long-term feelings of guilt or worthlessness
- Concentration problems
- Persistent thoughts of death or suicide

Signs of depression can be worrisome. However, they are of greatest concern when they last for an extended period of time, such as several months.

PHOBIAS

Name	Fear of
Acrophobia	heights
Aerophobia	flying
Agoraphobia	public places
Aquaphobia	water
Claustrophobia	closed spaces
Mikrophobia	germs
Nyctophobia	darkness
Ophidiophobia	snakes
Phonophobia	speaking aloud
Thanatophobia	death
Triskaidekaphobia	number 13
Xenophobia	strangers
Zoophobia	animals

Figure 6-1   Phobias can be very intense for some people. What might bother someone with Triskaidekaphobia?

MANIC-DEPRESSION   Mania—a wildly elated and impulsive mood—is the direct opposite of depression. Manic individuals talk rapidly and feel jittery and on edge. They often report that they feel out of control. For example, they may buy things they know they cannot afford. Although manic people appear very happy, their extra energy can lead to violent behavior. Mania also ends in emotional and physical exhaustion. Therefore, it is very rare for mania to occur without depression.

Manic-depression, also called Bipolar Affective Disorder, is a condition in which mania and clinical depression alternate in cycles. People with this condition experience periods of severe depression and extreme elation, along with their normal moods. These periods come and go and are unpredictable.

ANXIETY DISORDERS

Anxiety is a normal reaction to stress. It becomes a problem when the feeling is long-lasting and keeps a person from feeling any pleasure, or interferes with daily living. Anxiety disorders are a group of conditions in which anxiety is the main symptom or is the result of trying to control certain behaviors.

GENERALIZED ANXIETY AND PANIC DISORDERS   Generalized anxiety is a constant state of tension with no single cause. Different people have different symptoms of generalized anxiety. Some shake or tremble. Others perspire and have pounding hearts, cold hands, and dry mouths.

Panic disorder is a sudden attack of terror that seems to have no cause but is usually connected with certain situations. Panic disorder feels like anxiety, only much worse. The symptoms of a panic attack may include chest pains, increased heart rate, trembling, dizziness, and difficulty breathing. Everything around people with this disorder seems unreal, and they may have no definite idea of why they are frightened. In their efforts to control the terrible feeling of panic, people sometimes develop phobias.

PHOBIA   A **phobia** is a constant, unreasonable fear of a situation or object. Figure 6-1 lists some common phobias. When phobic people are in the presence of whatever they fear, they are overcome with anxiety. Therefore, they try to avoid the fearful situations. For example, claustrophobia is the fear of small enclosed

WHAT ARE YOU AFRAID OF?

Most people are afraid of something. However, the source of people's fears appears to change with age. For example, injections, doctors, and darkness cause the greatest fear in young children. Social situations, snakes, and heights are often reported by teenagers as their greatest sources of fear. As a person ages, crowds, death, injury, and illness are the most common causes of fear. Of course a fear is not a phobia unless it is so intense as to interfere with a person's day-to-day life.

spaces. Claustrophobics often have difficulty riding in elevators. Phobias are learned behaviors that often are the result of an event that created a feeling of panic. For instance, a person who was severely frightened while driving a car may develop a phobia about driving.

OBSESSIVE-COMPULSIVE DISORDER   Obsessive-compulsive disorder involves the presence of unwanted thoughts, emotions, or behaviors. **Obsessions** are persistent thoughts that interrupt normal thinking. **Compulsions** are urgent, repeated behaviors and are quite often connected to obsessions. In such cases, the anxiety that is created by the obsessive thoughts can only be relieved through a particular compulsive act. For example, a person who is overly worried about contracting a serious illness may develop an obsession about cleanliness. The obsession may cause the person to wash his or her hands after touching anything. Immediately after washing, the person begins to worry again. Individuals with severe symptoms of obsessive-compulsiveness are often unable to carry out their usual daily activities.

POST-TRAUMATIC STRESS DISORDER   Experiencing a traumatic event can cause severe stress for a long time. People who have difficulty coping with this type of stress may develop post-traumatic stress disorder. Symptoms include bouts of anger, nightmares, lack of interest in activities, and severe anxiety. Post-traumatic stress may develop immediately after the disaster happens, or weeks or months later.

This disorder became a widely accepted diagnosis as a result of the symptoms displayed by the Vietnam War veterans. Once referred to as "shell-shock" or "combat fatigue," wartime experiences left some veterans unable to cope with the daily pressures of civilian life.

After major disasters such as earthquakes or terrible accidents, some communities now send teams of mental health professionals to the damaged area to talk with survivors. They hope that by talking with people about their feelings immediately after a trauma, the victims will be able to cope better with the stress and avoid long-term emotional problems.

 Mary worked for ten years as an emergency medical technician (EMT). Then the events of one particularly hard day strained her own ability to cope with the stress of her job as part of a trauma team. Mary began to suffer headaches and nightmares. After a couple of weeks, the troubling symptoms had not gone away. Mary began to worry about her effectiveness on the job. As an EMT, she needed to be alert and have a clear mind.

After consulting her physician, Mary concluded that the stress of her work was a major cause of her headaches and sleeplessness. She asked for, and was granted, a leave of absence from work. Mary decided to talk with a specially-trained team of peers and mental health workers. After several sessions, Mary's headaches and nightmares became less severe. In time, Mary was able to resume her duties and to avoid developing a more serious problem.

Daily pressure in a life-threatening environment can cause long-term emotional problems for some soldiers.

SOMATOFORM DISORDERS

A somatoform disorder [*suh MAT uh fawrm*] is a condition in which there are physical symptoms, but no physical illness. Although people with such disorders may believe that they are suffering from a real disease, medical tests reveal that there is no organic cause for their conditions.

Hypochondria [*hy puh KAHN dree uh*] is one type of somatoform disorder. People with hypochondria strongly believe that they are ill when illness is neither present nor is it likely to develop. Hypochondriacs often complain about multiple pains that come and go. Even doctors cannot make a hypochondriac accept that they are healthy. Hypochondriacs change doctors frequently in order to find a treatment for their imagined disease. New health information often triggers new symptoms.

Psychosomatic disorders are real physical problems that have been caused by stress or anxiety. The presence of actual disorders distinguishes them from hypochondria. Migraine headaches caused by worry or nausea caused by stage fright are examples of psychosomatic disorders.

Health information should increase awareness rather than create a panic.

PERSONALITY DISORDERS

Personality traits that prevent people from interacting with others in a healthy way are called personality disorders. People with personality disorders behave inappropriately and have immature and inappropriate ways of coping with stress or solving problems. They may have trouble adapting to life and forming friendships. A personality disorder can be very difficult to change.

ANTISOCIAL PERSONALITY DISORDER People with antisocial personality disorder have little sense of responsibility, no respect for the rights of others or concern for other people, and show no signs of a conscience. People with this disorder believe that society's rules should not apply to them. They may appear confident, sincere, and charming, while inside they feel cheated and believe they deserve whatever they can get.

PARANOID PERSONALITY DISORDER Individuals with paranoid personality disorder [*PAR uh noyd*] have an unfounded suspicion and mistrust of others. They often keep their suspicions to themselves. In severe cases, their relationships may be damaged by their mistrust. Even after their suspicions are proved wrong, people who suffer from paranoia may believe that they are being followed and may go so far as to change the locks on their doors.

People with paranoid personality disorder often suffer from delusions of persecution. **Delusions** are strong beliefs in things that are not true or real. The paranoid person may feel he or she is being cheated, spied upon, followed, poisoned, drugged, maliciously maligned, or harassed. People suffering from persecutory delusions often feel that others are "out to get them." They are resentful, angry, and might turn to violence against people they have identified as the enemy.

SCHIZOID PERSONALITY DISORDER   Schizoid personality disorder [*SKIT soyd*] involves a condition of deep withdrawal from other people. Persons with this emotional disability do not have warm feelings for other people, yet criticism from others can easily hurt them. The schizoid may become withdrawn. Schizoid persons keep their feelings and thoughts to themselves. They have little desire to be involved with others—yet they feel lonely because they do not think other people have anything to offer them.

COMPULSIVE PERSONALITY DISORDER   When someone is constantly concerned with rules or standards, they may suffer from compulsive personality disorder. People with this disorder have difficulty changing the way they do things. They may lack a sense of humor and cannot express warm, loving emotions. Unable to really enjoy themselves, people who have a compulsive personality can only express grim satisfaction when things seem right to them. When they are unable to control others, they become angry. Often these people overwork—valuing work above all else and leaving them little time for family and friends.

PASSIVE-AGGRESSIVE PERSONALITY DISORDER   Passive-aggressive personality disorder causes people to strongly resist cooperating with others. Such resistance is not out in the open, but is expressed indirectly and can severely hamper relationships. Passive-aggressive people do not openly refuse or express their anger. Instead, they show their resistance by being unreliable. For example, a passive-aggressive person may routinely forget commitments and responsibilities.

Constant cleaning can be a compulsive behavior. Compulsive behavior often is a response to a need for a feeling of control.

DISSOCIATIVE DISORDERS

Conditions in which the personality suffers sudden changes are called dissociative disorders [*dis OH shee uh tiv*]. People with these disorders may have periods where they forget who they are or they may have developed an entirely new self.

Dissociative disorders are rare and usually result from terrible experiences, such as accidents or severe family circumstances. They also may result from extreme stress. By dissociating, these people are able to avoid facing extremely stressful events. Dissociating also helps people avoid feelings with which they cannot cope. They lose touch with their real selves, thereby protecting themselves from emotional and physical pain.

AMNESIA   The sudden inability to remember basic personal information is called **amnesia** [*am NEE zhuh*]. Most cases of amnesia result from emotional trauma. People with amnesia forget their names and where they live. They may not recognize family members or friends. For example, a fire that kills all but one person in a family may produce amnesia in the one who survives.

MULTIPLE PERSONALITY DISORDER   A very rare illness is multiple personality disorder. This is a condition in which a person develops two or more separate personalities. The central personality

Reduce to less than 10 percent the prevalence of mental disorders among children and adolescents.

Objective 6.3
from *Healthy People 2000: National Health Promotion and Disease Prevention Objectives*

usually is unaware of the existence of the other personalities. What the person most likely *is* aware of are periods of time that are missing in his or her life. It is during those times that one of the other personalities is awake, or in control. Each personality often is very different from the others and reflects a particular emotion. In one case of multiple personality disorder, a young woman was a kind and friendly person. Her second self was an unpleasant, noisy boy. Her third self was a quiet, frightened seven-year-old girl.

Multiple personality disorder usually results from severe childhood abuse or severe emotional trauma. To cope with the abuse or trauma, the individual subconsciously develops another self to handle his or her feelings. The new personalities cover up the pain felt by the central personality.

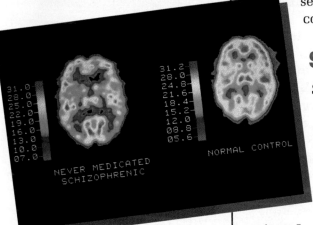

A PET scan of a schizophrenic brain (left) and a normal brain shows the imbalance in brain chemicals of schizophrenics.

SCHIZOPHRENIA

Schizophrenia [*skit suh FREE nee uh*] is a severe mental disorder that usually lasts throughout life. The illness appears to be linked to a disturbance in brain chemistry. Schizophrenia is characterized by extreme distortions of or withdrawal from reality. Symptoms of schizophrenia include deep confusion, odd behavior, and the apparent lack of touch with reality. Some schizophrenics have hallucinations, especially those of hearing voices. In some cases, people with schizophrenia feel that they have magical powers or that others can read their thoughts. Some withdraw from people. Others talk to themselves. Schizophrenia usually begins between the ages of 15 and 25. It may come and go throughout life or, in severe cases, require lifetime hospital care. Although the exact causes continue to be a mystery, research does indicate a strong hereditary factor.

SUMMARY

Mental disorders are organized into categories determined by common symptoms. The broad categories include organic disorders, developmental disorders, mood disorders, anxiety disorders, somatoform disorders, personality disorders, dissociative disorders, and schizophrenia. Some disorders are more severe than others and are relatively uncommon. Most people commonly exhibit some mild symptoms of less severe disorders.

LESSON 6.2 USING WHAT YOU HAVE LEARNED

REVIEW

1. Name one advantage and one disadvantage to categorizing mental disorders.
2. Describe the difference between a hypochondriac and someone who has a psychosomatic disorder.

THINK CRITICALLY

3. Scientists have divided mental disorders into categories to help them diagnose and treat people with mental disabilities. Compare and contrast two major categories of mental disorders.
4. Emergency medical workers have very stressful jobs that often require quick thinking. Identify two other jobs that can be very stressful. Explain why the jobs could lead to emotional problems.

APPLY IT TO YOURSELF

5. A friend of yours is complaining about being the constant target of unfair treatment. You tell your friend that he only feels this way because he has a paranoid personality. Why should you be careful about diagnosing another person's mental health?

TREATING MENTAL PROBLEMS

Everyone experiences times of anxiety. For some people, the anxiety can be overwhelming. For others, it may be just severe enough to be a nuisance. Problems cannot always be handled alone. It is a sign of emotional maturity, not weakness, to ask for help. Seeking psychological help for emotional problems is as important as seeking medical help for a cold. For most people, treatment rarely interferes with their normal activities. For people with more serious mental problems, hospitalization and medication may be necessary.

FINDING HELP

The most important step toward recovery from mental illness is recognition that a problem exists. By recognizing the signs early, a person can prevent the development of worse mental distress. It is important to take notice of long-lasting signs of emotional distress. You should be aware of changes in yourself or your friends, such as difficulty coping with everyday tasks; feeling angry much of the time; poor concentration or memory loss; withdrawal from friends and family; or deep feelings of hopelessness. It is particularly important to acknowledge signs of clinical depression, especially if someone frequently talks about suicide or death.

The next step is having the strength to ask for help. Parents, the school nurse, a doctor, a member of the clergy, a teacher, or the school counselor can help identify the right person to talk with or the best place to go for help. Help may be found by working with a mental health professional with a private practice. Or it may be found in public programs, such as community centers.

COMMUNITY MENTAL HEALTH CENTERS   Community mental health centers offer various services. Some centers have workshops about mental disorders. Or they may provide advice on the most suitable treatment for a particular mental problem and offer treatment. Many community health centers have special programs for teens or facilities where teenagers can meet and discuss problems with each other and with counselors. Youth centers also may provide counseling for personal problems.

HELPLINES   Many people who need help turn to telephone helplines that exist for a variety of problems. A **helpline** is a confidential telephone service that provides information and advice to people with personal problems. Crisis centers exist all over the country offering immediate help over the telephone. For example, people considering suicide can call one of these centers. Staff members listen as long as the distressed person needs to talk. If necessary, they can send someone to the caller's home and then try to arrange for professional assistance.

MAIN IDEAS

CONCEPTS

✔ Sometimes people need help solving their problems.

✔ There are many resources available for people suffering from emotional distress.

✔ Various methods can be used to help people regain their mental and emotional health.

VOCABULARY

helpline
psychotherapy
psychoanalysis
unconscious
behavior modification

Treatment at community health centers often includes sessions of group discussion.

Professional	Description
Psychiatrist	A medical doctor who specializes in the treatment and prevention of mental disorders. Able to prescribe medicine
Psychoanalyst	A therapist specially trained in the techniques and theories of psychoanalysis. Has undergone personal analysis while treating several clients under supervision
Clinical Psychologist	A person with a doctorate degree (Ph.D) in psychology. Learns to administer and interpret psychological tests, conduct psychotherapy, and conduct research
Counseling Psychologist	A person who earns a master's degree or a Ph.D. with graduate training similar to that of a clinical psychologist. Focuses on problems of adjustment rather than disorders
Psychiatric Social Worker	A professional with a master's degree in social work (M.S.W.) and special training in psychotherapy.
Pastoral Counselor	A member of the clergy trained in individual and group counseling techniques. May add a spiritual component to counseling sessions

Figure 6-2   A number of health professionals are specially trained to help people with mental disorders. Which professional is able to prescribe medication?

OUTPATIENT CARE   Many general hospitals have outpatient psychiatric centers. People with problems can make an appointment to be tested for treatment. These centers offer the services of professionals trained in psychiatric care. Many hospital emergency rooms provide immediate care for persons undergoing mental crises. Often, a variety of professionals work together to provide the best possible care. Figure 6-2 identifies some of the health-care professionals trained to help people with mental disorders.

PSYCHOTHERAPY

A common way to treat mental disorders is through **psychotherapy** [*sy koh THER uh pee*]. Psychotherapy is the treatment of emotional problems through sessions of personal discussion between a person and a therapist [*THER uh pist*]. The therapist has been trained to treat mental illnesses and may be a psychologist, a psychiatrist, or a psychiatric social worker.

Psychotherapy helps people understand their thoughts, feelings, and actions. A therapist may use different types of psychotherapy and different techniques to fit a particular person's problem. There are several types of psychotherapy.

PSYCHOANALYSIS   A process that helps a person reveal unresolved conflicts is **psychoanalysis** [*sy koh uh NAL uh sus*]. According to Sigmund Freud, unresolved conflicts are the source of mental disorders. Many of these unresolved conflicts may lie in the person's **unconscious,** the part of the personality that is hidden from the person's awareness. The psychoanalyst tries to discover the unresolved conflicts by having the person look at his or her childhood experiences, dreams, fantasies, and attitudes. Through psychoanalysis, doctors try to improve a client's self-awareness by decreasing the person's conflicts.

PSYCHOANALYTIC PSYCHOTHERAPY   The techniques of psychoanalysis have changed since Freud first introduced his theories. Psychoanalytic psychotherapy represents some of the changes. It emphasizes rational problem solving to change behavior and places less emphasis on the importance of unconscious motivation. The therapy sessions are usually shorter and less frequent than sessions of traditional psychoanalysis. The therapist and the client discuss childhood relationships and experiences and how they affect current relationships. Psychoanalytic psychotherapists focus on helping the client recognize what can be done to make healthy behavioral changes. The goal of sessions is to strengthen the client's self-esteem and confidence.

Some people prefer the privacy of one-on-one sessions with a therapist over group sessions. The entire session focuses on the individual's thoughts and concerns.

BEHAVIORAL THERAPY   Another form of psychotherapy helps individuals change their personal behavior. Behavior therapists try to change problem behavior rather than focus on the underlying reasons for the problem. Behavioral therapy is based on methods of learning and conditioning to encourage healthy changes in behavior—a process called **behavior modification**. The following are three methods of behavioral therapy.

- *Systematic desensitization* is effective in eliminating phobias. Clients are taught how to combat their anxieties by learning to relax. The clients gradually conquer fear by experiencing or imagining the fearful situation and then overcome it by relaxing.

Dan's claustrophobia had become so serious that it began to interfere with his job. He recently had been assigned to an exciting project that would sometimes require him to work in small spaces. Dan knew that he would not be able to work on the project with his present condition. Dan decided he needed to overcome his fear if he wanted to continue working in his field. He decided to start seeing a therapist who had been recommended by a good friend.

The therapist helped Dan change his habit of avoiding small, enclosed places. The therapist taught Dan how to relax through a conscious effort. Dan would imagine himself to be in a small room and try to relax at the same time. By repeating this many times, Dan learned to link small places with relaxation.

- *Reinforcement* uses conditioning techniques that reward positive behavior with praise or treats, or punish unacceptable behavior. The client is conditioned to connect the reinforcements with the behaviors. If treatment is successful, the client is likely to choose behavior that has been positively reinforced.

- *Modeling* is another method of changing behavior. Observing people who behave in an acceptable way can help people learn appropriate responses. Modeling allows people to watch someone else successfully go through a situation that may create a great deal of anxiety.

HEALTHY PEOPLE 2000

Increase to at least 30 percent the proportion of people aged 18 and older with severe, persistent mental disorders who use community support programs.

Objective 6.6
from *Healthy People 2000: National Health Promotion and Disease Prevention Objectives*

COGNITIVE THERAPY   The combination of behavior modification techniques and methods of changing interpretation of experiences is called cognitive therapy. The word *cognition* indicates that the person uses logical thought processes to make judgments. Therefore, cognitive therapists help people recognize that their thoughts and interpretations of events may be distorted. The therapist has the client focus on developing a realistic attitude and a positive outlook on life.

GROUP AND FAMILY THERAPY   Many mental disorders can be helped through group therapy. In group therapy, a psychotherapist meets at the same time with several people who have similar problems. Groups often consist of six to twelve people. They try to talk about their problems freely and honestly and advise each other. Therapy groups are formed to treat many kinds of emotional distress. By sharing similar experiences, these people are able to deal with the feelings that affect their current behavior. Family therapy is one form of group therapy in which all the members of a family work together to address problems of the family.

MAKING A DIFFERENCE

RESEARCH HEALTH

Light Therapy for SAD

Each winter, millions of Americans suffer from depression, anxiety, lethargy, and extreme sadness. They eat more, work less, and hardly socialize at all. They are suffering from a phenomenon known as Seasonal Affective Disorder (SAD), or the winter blues. SAD strikes hardest the people who live farthest from the equator. The farther a person lives from the equator, the fewer hours of winter daylight a person experiences. Only one or two percent of the residents of Florida have it; as many as ten to eleven percent of people in Maine have SAD.

Twenty years ago, medical researchers began to notice a pattern in the complaints of their patients in the wintertime. The researchers began to treat their patients with bright lights, or phototherapy, for one or two weeks every winter and found that phototherapy relieved the symptoms of the winter blues.

Those afflicted with SAD seem to have a delay in the regular secretion of melatonin, a hormone which helps regulate sleep. Bright light therapy can trigger the release of melatonin, causing a more restful sleep and refreshed awakening.

Some researchers theorize that the incidence of SAD has increased as more and more people spend their winter days indoors in artificial light, thus missing the bright days of winter. Some SAD sufferers seem to feel better if they take a walk outside during daylight hours.

1. If you live where winters are severe, suggest some ways you and your friends might spend more time outdoors during daylight hours. How might this affect your health in winter?

2. If you live where winters are mild and there is little difference between winter and summer activities, write a few paragraphs to describe what your life would be like if you stayed inside all winter.

Obtaining Help

At one time or another, everyone needs a boost for their mental health. Some emotional disturbances can be eased through personal evaluation and behavior modification, self-help books, or talks with a trusted friend. Other more serious emotional disturbances require the help of a professional.

Prolonged depression or anxiety that interferes with day-to-day functioning, thoughts of suicide, or an attempted suicide are signs that professional help is needed. Drugs or alcohol abuse and hallucinations, memory loss, or incoherent speech require professional attention. Witnessing an accident, losing a friend or relative, or having a crime committed against you may also lead to the need for help.

Seeking professional help is a sign of strength and health, not weakness or disease. Knowing where to look is an important first step. Finding the professional that can offer the best help often depends on the cause of the problem or problems. For example, a person who is seeking help during drug rehabilitation would be best served by a therapist that specializes in drug counseling. Many adolescents who are in therapy see mental health professionals who focus on the problems of teenagers.

One way to identify the right professional for a problem is to talk with others who have sought help and may be able to recommend a therapist. Another suggestion is to speak with a school counselor or a doctor. Many communities also have confidential referral programs.

PLAY THERAPY   Therapists use play therapy to study and then treat emotional distress in children. The children often show their thoughts, feelings, and conflicts while playing with toys or puzzles. For example, a girl who unknowingly feels unloved by her father may break a male doll. To her, the doll may represent her father. By observing this behavior, a therapist can develop strategies for helping the child.

DRUG THERAPY

A biological view of inappropriate behavior assumes that mental disorders are caused by the biochemical or physiological problems within the brain. At times, psychiatrists find it necessary to use drug therapy, or medicines, to treat mental disorders. Tranquilizers, antidepressants, and other medicines may be used to treat clients with severe depression, manic-depression disorders, panic attacks, and schizophrenia.

Medicines for mental disorders need to be monitored closely and should be used only under the supervision of a psychiatrist. Medicines can correct chemical imbalances in a person and reduce the symptoms of a mental disorder. They enable many people to feel better and lead normal lives. Although many personality problems still need to be resolved through psychotherapy, drug therapy can greatly assist treatment.

HOSPITALIZATION

For some people with mental illness, the disorder is so severe that they are no longer able to function in society. Often they have become a threat to themselves or to others. In such cases, hospitalization is necessary.

A SAFE ENVIRONMENT   Hospitalization provides protection for patients and their families. Patients receive specialized care in a safe environment. Their environment is controlled and their time

FOR YOUR INFORMATION

Group therapy has been very effective in helping adults who grew up in homes with an alcoholic.

during their stay is structured. Patients are nearly always in the company of a member of the staff. If there is a high risk that a patient may harm others, he or she may need to stay in a special ward until the behavior can be controlled.

Psychiatric hospitals have staff psychiatrists and psychologists who specialize in different mental disorders. Other staff members are specially trained to help psychiatric patients. A major role of psychiatric nurses, for example, is to provide patients with emotional support. They also administer the medicines prescribed by psychiatrists and observe changes in a patient's behavior.

Psychiatric social workers provide family support, family therapy, and may conduct individual therapy as well. Some social workers specialize in psychiatric care but are not trained therapists. Such social workers often work closely with family members to help them assist in the patient's recovery.

Art therapy can be a very effective method for helping a child express his or her feelings of distress.

TREATMENT While in the hospital, a patient with an emotional disorder will receive extensive treatment. This includes diagnosis, psychotherapy, and, when needed, drug therapy. Many patients also receive recreational and occupational therapy.

Recreational therapy helps patients express themselves through pleasurable activities, such as sports and crafts. One form of recreational therapy is art therapy, which was developed in the late 1960s. By expressing themselves through painting or drawing, people communicate their feelings nonverbally. A therapist can begin to understand a person's problems by studying his or her creative work. Psychotherapy is then used to help that person deal with his or her problems.

Occupational therapy helps patients overcome their problems by teaching them practical skills. Therapy is individualized to meet each patient's needs.

SUMMARY

There are many effective treatments for people with mental illnesses. Community mental health centers, helplines, and outpatient psychiatric centers are available to help people with mental problems. The type of treatment needed by a person depends entirely on the severity of the illness. Psychotherapy is the most common treatment. However, for many people with emotional problems, drug therapy or hospitalization may be necessary.

LESSON 6.3 USING WHAT YOU HAVE LEARNED

REVIEW

1. Describe two symptoms of mental distress.
2. What is the difference between a psychiatrist and a psychologist?

THINK CRITICALLY

3. Compare and contrast psychoanalysis and behavior therapy.
4. Treatment through group therapy has grown considerably over the past 20 years. Why might group therapy be more successful than individual therapy for many people?

APPLY IT TO YOURSELF

5. Imagine that for the past month, your closest friend has withdrawn from everyone and refuses to leave the house. What would you say to your friend to convince him or her to seek the help of a professional?

Getting Help

Maria broke up with Alan after two years of dating. "You're just not as much fun anymore, Alan. All you ever want to do is sit around and watch television." Maria also had said that Alan had become too critical of everything and that he was always down.

Alan's inactivity grew worse. He never went out on weekends, and he never called anyone. His closest friend, Thomas, kept asking Alan to go out, but Alan never felt up to it.

One day at school, Thomas approached Alan in the hall and said, "What is happening with you? You look terrible! I'm worried about you. You've got to snap out of this. Get on with it! Man, you need help!" Alan just walked away.

Later, Alan thought about what Thomas had said. "What does he mean 'you need help?' I'm not crazy! What I need is for people to just leave me alone!"

Alan knew that he had been a little depressed lately, but he blamed it on the breakup with Maria.

That night, Alan couldn't sleep. He kept thinking about his life. "What a mess!" he thought. Alan found himself thinking about suicide. "Would that be the answer?"

The next day in school, Alan was walking by the guidance office when he noticed a pamphlet on the bulletin board. It was about clinical depression in teenagers. "What if Thomas is right? Maybe I do need help," he thought. But Alan was afraid. "Would that mean I'm crazy?"

PAUSE AND CONSIDER

1. *Identify the Problem.*
   What is Alan's conflict about seeking help?

2. *Consider the Options.*
   What could Alan do about feeling bad all the time?

3. *Evaluate the Outcomes.*
   What might happen if Alan decides to seek help? What might happen if he chooses to wait it out?

Alan took one of the pamphlets about clinical depression and stuck it in his jacket. That night in his room, he looked it over. He saw that there was a 1-800 number on the back. The pamphlet said that all calls were kept confidential.

Alan decided to call the number. His dad was out, so Alan could have some privacy. When he called, the counselor on the other end was really nice. "No, you're not crazy," said the counselor. "Calling this number was one of the healthiest things you could have done."

They talked for an hour. The counselor gave Alan several options for getting help. At the end, they agreed to touch base in a couple of days. Alan felt that he had taken a step in the right direction.

DECIDE AND REVIEW

4. *Decide and Act.* How did Alan deal with his depression? How did the privacy of the helpline help Alan?

5. *Review* What else could Alan have done to help himself through his depression? What were the signs that he was suffering from clinical depression?

PROJECTS

1. It is now generally accepted that the brains of people with schizophrenia are different from the brains of nonschizophrenics. Investigate several of the following theories about the cause of these brain differences: heredity, nutrition, stress, infectious diseases, and family interaction. Which are the more generally accepted theories?

2. Develop a list of facilities and other resources available in your community to help people with mental disorders. You could interview a psychiatrist, a psychiatric nurse, a psychologist, a psychiatric social worker, or an art therapist. You might also visit a hospital or mental health clinic to find out what kinds of treatment are offered to patients and whether occupational and recreational therapy are available.

WORKING WITH OTHERS

Form groups of three people. One person should play the part of a teenager who has become withdrawn and is no longer interested in school or activities with friends. The other two people should play the parts of estranged friends who are concerned with the first person's behavior and who want to help. Explore different reasons for the behavior, different ways to approach the friend, and different ways to recommend counseling.

CONNECTING TO...

SCIENCE Psychiatrists and psychologists often engage in research to discover what causes different mental disorders. Choose one of the disorders discussed in this chapter. Investigate the research that has been conducted to learn more about the disorder. Write a one-page summary of your findings.

USING VOCABULARY

amnesia
behavior modification
compulsion
degenerative disease
delirium
delusion

dementia
functional disorder
hallucination
helpline
hyperactive
hypoactive
hypochondria
mania

mental trauma
obsession
organic disorder
phobia
psychoanalysis
psychotherapy
unconscious

On a separate sheet of paper, identify the vocabulary word that matches each of the following definitions.

1. progressive deterioration of tissue over several years
2. inability to remember basic personal information
3. an irrational, overwhelming fear
4. a wildly elated, impulsive mood
5. seeing, hearing, or sensing something that does not exist
6. violent shock that is damaging to a person's mental health
7. constant movement and the inability to concentrate
8. treatment that focuses on identifying unresolved conflicts
9. severe and irreversible loss of mental ability
10. emotional problem that stems from a person's environment

CONCEPT MAPPING

Copy and complete the concept map shown below. Information on concept mapping appears at the front of this book.

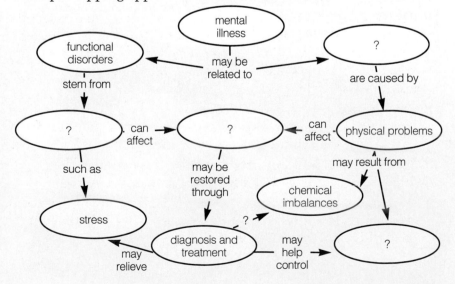

THINKING CRITICALLY

INTERPRET

LESSON 6.1

1. Explain how society determines what is acceptable behavior.
2. Describe four characteristics that psychologists consider when evaluating a person's emotional well-being.
3. What is the difference between a functional disorder and an organic disorder?
4. Why do many doctors consider past experiences when identifying the causes of a person's emotional problems?

LESSON 6.2

5. Compare the symptoms of mood disorders with those of personality disorders.
6. What is the difference between dementia and delirium?
7. What are the characteristics of a mood disorder?
8. Identify the symptoms of clinical depression. Given these symptoms, how is it possible for a person to be both manic and clinically depressed, as in manic-depression?
9. How does a compulsion differ from an obsession?
10. What is thought to cause multiple personality disorder? Why does an individual develop different personalities?

LESSON 6.3

11. Name three symptoms that indicate someone needs to seek professional help to solve their problem.
12. What is the goal of psychoanalytic psychotherapy?
13. Name and discuss one positive and one negative aspect of drug therapy.
14. At what point would a person with a mental disorder be hospitalized?

APPLY

LESSON 6.1

15. A 14-year-old boy has recently been involved in starting small fires in old buildings, stealing food and inexpensive objects for "the thrill of it," and hurting household pets. What might this boy's behavior mean? What may happen if he doesn't receive proper treatment?

LESSON 6.2

16. At four years of age, Carlos would neither cuddle nor make eye contact with his parents or siblings. Most of the time he stared blankly into space and rarely responded to questions. Based on this description of his behavior, what disorder might you suspect that he has?
17. Ten-year-old Tony has been diagnosed with attention deficit-hyperactivity disorder. Explain what Tony's symptoms might be and why the symptoms may cause him stress.

LESSON 6.3

18. Name three undesirable habits or behaviors and describe how they might be changed through behavior modification.
19. Some police trauma teams carry stuffed animals with them to give to a child at the scene of an accident. Why might it help the child to have a stuffed animal to hug?

COMMITMENT TO WELLNESS

FOLLOW-UP

SETTING GOALS

Review your responses to the Commitment to Wellness Self-Assessment statements from the beginning of the chapter. List your positive responses in your journal. Alongside each item, identify what events in your life may have helped you develop these strengths.

Now focus on the items you consider to be weaknesses for you. Choose one area you would like to improve. How can you use your positive skills to improve this weakness? Develop a set of small, attainable goals that will help you reach your ultimate goal. Each smaller goal should be progressively more challenging. Decide how you will reward yourself as you reach each goal. Develop a realistic timetable for yourself for improvement. Check your progress from time to time to determine whether you need to revise your plan.

WHERE DO I GO FROM HERE?

Emotional problems can be difficult to recognize. They also can be very difficult to face. You may wish to further investigate topics that have been raised in this chapter.

FOR MORE INFORMATION, CONTACT:

National Institute of Mental Health
5600 Fishers Lane, Room 6C-12
Rockville, MD 20857

Social Health

Chapter 7
Healthy Relationships

Chapter 8
Family Roles and Responsibilities

Chapter 9
You in the Community

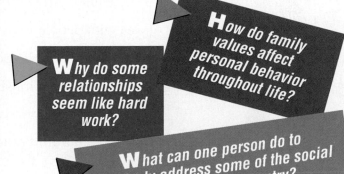

How do family values affect personal behavior throughout life?

Why do some relationships seem like hard work?

What can one person do to positively address some of the social problems in our country?

Healthy Relationships

"Nobody sees a flower—really. It is so small, we haven't time, and to see takes time. Like to have a friend takes time."

Georgia O'Keeffe

BACKGROUND

Painter Georgia O'Keeffe (1887–1986) was influenced by the desert landscape of the Southwest. Her paintings often include animal bones, flowers, and rocks. Try to find one of her paintings in an art book or in an encyclopedia.

Whether in good times or bad times, all people need other people. Because you cannot meet all of your own social, physical, intellectual, and emotional needs, you must reach out to others for love and support. Throughout your life, you continually initiate and build relationships with many different people—from coaches and store clerks to a spouse or your own children.

During the course of your life, you form different types of relationships. When you were a very young child, for example, you first had relationships with family members who cared for you. Then, as you grew older, you began to make friends in your neighborhood and at school. As an adult, you will likely develop relationships in your community and at work, as well as with people with whom you share emotional ties.

Think of all the people you will interact with today. Some of these relationships may be important to you; some may simply be unavoidable. You may enjoy some relationships but find others frustrating or even painful. Although building and maintaining healthy relationships can be difficult, this process is the key to your social health.

SELF-ASSESSMENT

How healthy are your relationships with others? Use the following checklist to take a closer look at your relationships. Number a separate sheet of paper from 1–12 and respond to the items below by writing *yes* for each item that describes your relationships all or most of the time.

1. I have close friends whom I know I can count on.
2. I communicate openly with my friends and family.
3. I can say *no* to my friends when I do not want to participate in their activities.
4. I accept and respect differences among people.
5. When I date someone, the other person's values are very important to me.
6. I understand what responsible behavior in a dating relationship includes.
7. I work well with others.
8. I do not belong to a group that excludes others.
9. I feel comfortable in most of my relationships.
10. I am able to resolve conflicts in my relationships.
11. I try to be trustworthy.
12. I avoid or end negative relationships.

Review your responses and consider what might be your strengths and weaknesses. Save your personal checklist for a follow-up activity that appears at the end of this chapter.

ACCEPTANCE AND COOPERATION

Every day you come into contact with many people—a bus driver, a math teacher, your best friend, your cousin, or another student in your art class. You share some moments and common experiences with each person. A **relationship** is a bond or connection that you have with another person.

Every relationship is unique. The kind of relationship that you have with someone depends on what that person is like and how you feel about him or her. The way you relate to another person may be influenced by your personal needs, social expectations, your experiences in relationships, what you have seen others do in relationships, and your values and attitudes.

Because you live in a social world, relationships are inevitable. To get the most out of your interactions with others, you need to develop skills that will help you build positive connections that meet the challenges and responsibilities of each relationship.

YOUR NEED FOR RELATIONSHIPS

Having relationships is important to your social, physical, emotional, and intellectual health. Strong relationships with other people give you a sense of belonging and security. Emotional intimacy—mutual closeness and deep caring—gives support and love, particularly when times are tough. Without connections with others, people feel isolated, lonely, and frequently become depressed.

Alfred Adler, a twentieth-century psychologist, believed that all people are naturally social. According to Adler, all people have a natural urge to adapt positively to social environments. He stressed the importance of social interaction, especially during childhood, in the development of an individual's personality.

Your relationships with others affect you. How you view yourself is often influenced by how others view you. You learn and practice communication skills in relationships, and you are introduced to new experiences, ideas, and activities. Positive relationships contribute to self-esteem, build confidence, and give you an opportunity to express your opinions and feelings. Of course, one relationship alone cannot give you all that you need; neither will one type of relationship. Experiencing different types of relationships will help you interact effectively in a variety of social situations.

TYPES OF RELATIONSHIPS

Just as there is more than one kind of person, there is more than one type of relationship. Some last; others do not. Some relationships change over time. As you read about relationships, think about different types of relationships that you have experienced.

MAIN IDEAS

CONCEPTS
✔ Relationships contribute to social, physical, emotional, and intellectual health.
✔ There are different types of relationships.
✔ Open communication, a sense of self, cooperation, respect, and acceptance help build healthy relationships.

VOCABULARY
relationship
acquaintance
friend
platonic friendship
communication
peer pressure
cooperation
prejudice

Relationships give people a sense of belonging and acceptance. What positive feelings do you get from relationships?

ACQUAINTANCES An **acquaintance** [*uh KWAYNT unts*] is someone you are familiar with but not especially close to. Although you regularly come into contact with an acquaintance, you may not share thoughts and feelings. Most acquaintances are people you know because you attend the same school or live in the same community. Having acquaintances can give you a sense of belonging.

PROFESSIONAL RELATIONSHIPS You form professional relationships with people in order to achieve your goals in school or at work. In school, teachers guide you and help you learn new skills and concepts. Professional relationships, such as those with teachers, coaches, employers, and colleagues, help you develop self-esteem and confidence in areas of your life that are important to you.

When you team up with others, you must be willing to listen and to cooperate. Whether you want to learn to drive a car or to use a computer, positive professional relationships can help you reach your goals. Like acquaintances, professional relationships may develop into friendships.

FRIENDS Picture the cafeteria during lunch. Your classmates probably sit with **friends**—people who enjoy being together and who share similar interests, goals, and attitudes. Friendship involves some or all of these qualities: enjoyment, caring, loyalty, trust, sharing, reliability, understanding, respect, and consideration.

You may have both casual and close friends. These friends may be male or female. Casual friends, such as a lab partner or a soccer teammate, share common interests and everyday experiences. Casual friendships often develop because they are convenient. In time, casual friends may become close friends.

A close friend is someone you trust enough to share feelings, thoughts, and secrets. You can be yourself with a close friend, but he or she may make you feel hurt or angry at times. Your feelings for this person should motivate you to resolve these conflicts.

Your friends may be people of the opposite gender. Casual and close friendships with people of the opposite gender are called **platonic friendships** [*pluh TAHN ik*]. Platonic friends do not have romantic feelings for one another, yet they may develop strong relationships and emotional intimacy.

INTIMATE RELATIONSHIPS Intimate relationships are closer types of relationships than are friendships. People who share deep thoughts and feelings, such as family members or couples who date or marry, have intimate relationships. Intimate, platonic friends may become physically attracted to one another and eventually develop physical intimacy.

Intimate relationships involve love and trust. The more that two people are willing to share, the greater the level of emotional or physical intimacy that develops between them. Having an intimate relationship requires a strong commitment to the other person.

FOR YOUR INFORMATION

Healthy relationships fulfill many different needs. The give-and-take in a relationship is essential to your personal growth.

Teaming up with other people in professional relationships can help you reach your goals.

Open communication is essential to any healthy relationship.

BUILDING HEALTHY RELATIONSHIPS

A healthy relationship is one in which both people feel good about the interaction. Building healthy, lasting relationships is an important goal. Most healthy relationships grow and change over time. For example, casual friends may become close, or platonic friends may develop an intimate relationship. Because changes in relationships can create tension, you must learn to communicate openly and to resolve conflict in a positive way.

OPEN COMMUNICATION   Think about important news you want to share. Whom will you tell and why? The act of sharing thoughts, feelings, and information is called **communication.** People who trust each other and are honest with one another have open communication. They can talk out problems and avoid conflicts. Open communication brings people closer together.

How do you feel when a friend is not completely honest with you? Sometimes people use communication that is neither honest nor open—lies, flattery, false promises, teasing, threats—to get what they want, to get attention, or to control others. To build healthy relationships, you need trust and open communication.

MEN AND WOMEN SPEAK DIFFERENT LANGUAGES

Dr. Deborah Tannen has studied the different communication styles of men and women. She has found that men often speak to "report," while women speak to build "rapport." For example, men use questions and answers as an opportunity to exchange information. Women, on the other hand, use questions and answers as an opportunity to build relationships through negotiation and conversation. Rather than become angry or misunderstand each other, Dr. Tannen suggests that men and women learn to understand each other's different communication styles. Do you agree?

MAINTAINING A SENSE OF SELF Many people, especially teenagers, are affected by **peer pressure**, or the strong influence of people their age. Negative peer pressure influences you to do things that you know are wrong or harmful. It is important to maintain a sense of self—your values, your goals, your beliefs, your identity—to avoid negative peer pressure.

What you put into a relationship is up to you. To have a healthy relationship, you must know and trust yourself and set your own limits. You must be able to stand up for what you believe.

COOPERATION Cooperation, or working together, makes tasks and goals easier to accomplish and helps friendships grow. When you cooperate, you share equally. One person does not do everything alone or do more or less than is fair. Cooperation is essential in all relationships.

ACCEPTANCE AND RESPECT Different ethnic and cultural backgrounds, as well as family and community influences, shape a person's personality, beliefs, values, ideas, attitudes, and biases. While it is important to take pride in your own background and beliefs, it also important to respect and accept other people's backgrounds and beliefs. To achieve a mutual respect, you must take pride in yourself and express your values in a way that is not hurtful to others.

Prejudice [*PREJ ud us*], an opinion based on ignorance, shows a lack of acceptance and respect. Rejecting people because they are different from you, or subjecting someone to hurtful and annoying verbal or physical treatment shows prejudice and lack of respect. Some people have difficulty accepting and respecting others' views and different ways of life without feeling as though they are placing less value on their own. Accepting other people does not mean that you value someone else's experiences over your own, however. Rather, learning to understand differences can help you better appreciate your own uniqueness.

To build healthy relationships, you have to accept and respect other people's differences and learn to cooperate with each other.

LESSON 7.1 USING WHAT YOU HAVE LEARNED

REVIEW

1. Why do people need relationships?
2. Name and describe four types of relationships.
3. Name and describe four qualities that help build healthy relationships.

THINK CRITICALLY

4. Relationships can be both healthy and unhealthy. What are some ways to determine whether a relationship is healthy?
5. Why is it difficult to resist negative peer pressure?

APPLY IT TO YOURSELF

6. Identify a specific relationship you have had that was important to you. Explain how you worked to build a healthy relationship with this person.

SUMMARY

Relationships are the unique bonds or connections between people. Having acquaintances, friends, and professional and intimate relationships builds self-esteem and confidence and helps people feel loved and secure. To have healthy relationships that grow and last, people must communicate openly, maintain a sense of self, accept and respect others' differences, and cooperate with each other.

DATING AND MARRIAGE

A large percentage of young people are likely to marry before the age of 45. You will have had your first date long before that. Dating helps you learn more about yourself and about developing new friendships. What you learn about yourself and others through the experience of dating will help you when you are ready to make important decisions about getting married and having children.

ATTRACTION TO OTHERS

Most people usually begin to feel attracted to others during adolescence. **Adolescence** [*ad ul ES uns*] is the period of development that occurs from about age eleven to the late teens. Boys and girls reach physical and sexual maturity during adolescence. They grow taller and heavier, and develop characteristics typical of adult men and women. As their bodies suddenly begin to produce large amounts of sex hormones, adolescent boys and girls experience many new feelings, including an emotional and possibly a sexual interest in other people. You can read about specific physical changes that take place during adolescence in Chapter 17, "Growth and Development."

People who are attracted to members of the opposite gender are said to be **heterosexual**. People who are attracted to members of their own gender are said to be **homosexual**. Discovering sexual feelings during adolescence can be confusing, but feeling affection for someone of the same gender should not necessarily be interpreted as an indication of homosexuality. It is common and natural for people to feel affection for both men and women. Most people form friendships with people of both genders throughout their lives.

Typically, adolescent boys and girls initially develop strong friendships with members of the same gender and then later feel attracted to the opposite gender. This attraction may begin at any time during adolescence. When feelings of sexual interest in others do begin, these feelings often take the form of crushes or infatuations. An **infatuation** [*in fach uh WAY shun*] is an intense but short-lived period of interest in another person.

Although the feelings can be overwhelming, few lasting relationships develop from an infatuation. These intense feelings are usually one-sided and are often directed toward people who are distant and out of reach. Having infatuations, nevertheless, is a sign that a person is developing the ability to form strong attachments.

DATING

As young people become more confident and decide to act on their attraction to others, they may begin to date. When you date someone, you make specific plans to do something, such as eating

Why do few lasting relationships result from infatuations?

For Better or For Worse® by Lynn Johnston

lunch together or attending a concert. Dating gives you an opportunity to share your interests, social activities, and experiences with a person of the opposite gender.

Many people become interested in dating during adolescence, but not all people begin dating at the same age. One person, for example, may be more interested in participating in sports or playing in a band than in dating. Another person may have to wait until an age set by his or her parents to begin dating. Because people who are attracted to one another often feel shy around one another, they may delay dating. Dating is a big step for most young people.

When young people are ready to date, they often begin dating in groups, attending sports events, dances, parties, or movies with other people of both genders. Many young people feel more comfortable dating in a group. Group dating may help you meet one special person with whom you want to become closer.

GOING STEADY   Most young people prefer to date several different boys or girls before choosing one special partner. But sooner or later, you may develop a special relationship with one person and begin going steady. Going steady means that you will only date the other person. Although couples can develop a strong friendship and a sense of loyalty to one another, going steady with someone may cause some problems.

One problem faced by couples is jealousy and possessiveness. When a person feels insecure, he or she may try to control the other person. By dating only one person exclusively, you may miss a chance to learn more about others and about yourself.

Steve and Anne have been going steady with each other for about a year. Anne has left for college in another state. She does not want Steve to date others. But Steve would like to start dating other girls.

Many young people feel more comfortable dating in a group. Why?

Another problem that young couples encounter is the question of whether to be physically intimate. They may have strong feelings that they want to express, but they may not feel prepared to deal with all of the physical and emotional consequences.

Jim and Michelle, both juniors, have been going steady since they were 15. Lately, Jim has been trying to talk Michelle into having a sexual relationship. Michelle wants to continue seeing Jim but feels that he is challenging her personal values.

Young people frequently face negative peer pressure to become physically intimate. A young person may be pressured by a partner who feels ready for physical intimacy. Deciding whether to be physically intimate requires maturity and responsibility.

RESPONSIBLE BEHAVIOR   Dating not only helps you learn about yourself and others, but it is also a way for you to develop responsibility. For example, when you agree on certain dating rules with your parents, observe curfews, and show courtesy to a date, you are behaving responsibly. Sometimes going steady forces young people into decisions they are not yet prepared to make. Many difficult situations call for couples to be mature and responsible. Because couples have made an emotional commitment to one another, they have to learn to work out differences and respect one another's values.

Steve tells Anne that he cares for her but is not ready to make such a serious commitment. Anne is relieved because she also wants a chance to date others while she is in college. She realizes that she and Steve can still date when she comes home.
Michelle is afraid that Jim will break up with her, but she tells him she just isn't ready for a sexual relationship. Jim says that he understands. He admits to Michelle that he isn't ready either but figured they were expected to be physically intimate by now.

Both couples—Anne and Steve and Jim and Michelle—honestly discussed their feelings to resolve their conflicts and respected one another's values. Dating can help you value other people and their goals as well as develop skills and attitudes that will help you form positive relationships.

ISSUES OF CONCERN

Young people have many different concerns about dating and about forming new relationships. Some worry about whether they are attractive. Others wonder how to start relationships or how to end them. Most of these concerns take care of themselves as a person begins to date and feels more comfortable with the other person. However, dating and relationships also involve an awareness of some very serious issues.

VIOLENCE   Sometimes people find themselves in violent or threatening situations. The crimes of sexual harassment, stalking, and

Treating each other with respect and courtesy promotes responsible behavior. In what other ways are dating relationships strengthened by respect and courtesy?

FOR YOUR INFORMATION

By 1992, 24 states in the United States had passed laws making stalking illegal.

Marriage Enrichment

Many married couples want to give their marriages a boost. Many of these couples have attended marriage enrichment programs. Marriage enrichment programs are weekend or intensive day-long workshops in which couples talk about issues related to their marriages in a safe and private environment. The workshops are usually led by couples who have gone through the program themselves. The leaders are ordinary people who are devoted to helping others strengthen their marriages.

The program usually begins with presentations by the leaders about topics such as communication, work, sex, and money. The participating couples may then be asked to respond to the presentations by writing in a journal. They do not share their journals with other members of the group. Instead, they read their partners' answers and then discuss them. For many couples, the experience raises new issues in an environment that is intended to nurture communication.

Some couples report that they hear and see new aspects of their spouses.

Marriage enrichment programs serve about eight million people in the United States each year. Marriage counselors and psychologists agree that such programs could benefit every married couple. Unlike therapy, marriage enrichment programs work to address problems before the problems are big enough to harm the marriage.

1. Why might it be difficult for some couples to decide to attend a marriage enrichment program?
2. What are some ways that a marriage enrichment program might help a couple strengthen their marriage?

---

date rape can cause both emotional and physical harm. **Sexual harassment** [HAR us munt] occurs when someone is subjected to unwanted verbal or sexual advances by a person who takes advantage of feelings of superiority or power. Sexual harassment, which occurs when one person does not respect another, may take place at jobs or in schools. A person who is sexually harassed can try to stop the behavior by confronting the harasser or by documenting what happens in order to file a complaint or pursue legal action.

Another kind of harassment is called **stalking**. Stalkers may follow someone with whom they are obsessed. They may also send unsolicited letters or make annoying telephone calls. Some stalkers may even try to harm their victims. A person who receives unwanted attention from a stalker should notify local police.

Forcing someone to have sexual contact is **rape**, a serious, violent crime. In about 80 percent of all cases, rape victims know their attackers. Attackers can be neighbors, co-workers, classmates—even dates. **Date rape**, or acquaintance rape, occurs when someone is forced to have sex by a date or an acquaintance. Although date rape can happen to anyone at any age, it most often happens to young people between the ages of 15 and 25.

HEALTHY PEOPLE 2000

Reduce rape and attempted rape of women aged 12 and older to no more than 108 per 100,000 women.

Objective 7.7
from *Healthy People 2000: National Health Promotion and Disease Prevention Objectives*

Teenagers are seldom ready for the responsibilties of parenthood.

Date rape happens for a variety of reasons. For example, some people expect to have sex on a date and will not take *no* for an answer. Others receive confusing messages or misinterpret the relationship. Rape, for any reason, is an illegal act of violence.

Victims of date rape may feel upset, angry, depressed, guilty, or ashamed. Some may feel that they did something wrong and are somehow to blame for the violence against them. However, victims are not at fault. Victims of date rape should report what happened to the proper authorities and then seek professional help.

TEENAGE PREGNANCY Teenagers have the physical ability to create new life. For this reason, sexual responsibility is very important. More than 500,000 babies born in this country each year have teenage mothers, and the number of births to younger and younger girls is increasing. Pregnancy for a teenager, especially under the age of 18, can be a health risk for the mother and the baby.

Because sexual feelings are normal, thinking ahead about how to deal with these feelings is important. Teenage pregnancy often occurs because couples have not seriously thought about the consequences of sexual behavior or because they do not know the facts. Setting ground rules and limits for sexual behavior in a relationship is a sign that you are ready for serious, responsible dating.

Teenage couples with children rarely marry. The couple often is unable to provide financial support for a family. Even if the mother and father do marry, teen marriages are more likely to end in divorce than the marriages of older couples. The children of such marriages usually remain with their mother.

Being a mother at any age is hard work, but for teens it may be overwhelming. Most teenage mothers soon realize that they are not ready to care for a baby 24 hours a day. The responsibility of a baby may overwhelm them. The emotional and economic pressures of raising a child often force teenage mothers to drop out of school to take care of their babies. Abstaining from sexual activity during teenage years is the only sure way to avoid unwanted teenage pregnancy.

SEXUALLY TRANSMITTED DISEASES Some diseases can be transmitted through sexual contact. In the United States, more than 13 million new cases of sexually transmitted diseases (STDs) occur each year—many among young people between the ages of 15 and 24. If diagnosed, most STDs can be treated. Untreated STDs can cause serious health problems or even death.

The most effective way to avoid both pregnancy and STDs is to delay having a sexual relationship. If you wait to become physically intimate, you eliminate your risk of causing a pregnancy and lower your risk of contracting an STD. You can read more on these topics in Chapter 24, "Sexually Transmitted Diseases/AIDS."

MARRIAGE

Do you plan to marry? Most people who marry in the United States will do so between the ages of 23 and 26. A rising divorce rate suggests that many couples are marrying before they are ready or for the wrong reasons. The decision to marry should be made carefully. Couples must seriously consider whether they can make a life together.

COMMITMENT   When couples discuss marriage, it should be because a strong love has developed. The romantic, head-over-heels feeling should have grown into a more mature, steady relationship. Couples should know each other well, and they should have seen their partners at their best and at their worst. The commitment that two people make when they decide to marry means that they are willing to work out differences.

COMPATIBILITY   Compatibility [*kum pat uh BIL ut ee*] is also important for a successful marriage. Compatible people get along well, can discuss problems, and enjoy similar interests and activities. When you marry someone, you must be able to live in the same home, make decisions together, and grow as a couple.

Having similar backgrounds and educational experiences can contribute to the success of a marriage. Decisions about social activities, rearing children, and religious practices are easier to make when couples have similar backgrounds. Although couples from widely different backgrounds have successful marriages, their marriages usually need more discussion and compromise.

ADJUSTMENTS   Successful couples learn to handle conflicts by compromising and making changes. **Compromise** is the process by which two people with opposing views on an issue settle their differences. Both must give in a little to solve a problem. Decisions about household duties and money can be major sources of conflict for couples. Therefore, compromise is important.

Marriage may not be the right choice for everybody. Some people like to live alone or feel that their friends satisfy their need for companionship. If you do decide to marry, however, you must be willing to work hard to create a lasting bond.

Why are commitment, compatibility, and compromise essential ingredients for a successful marriage?

LESSON 7.2   USING WHAT YOU HAVE LEARNED

REVIEW

1. What does dating help people learn?
2. Name three things that can help make a successful marriage.

THINK CRITICALLY

3. More teenagers are infected with STDs than any other age group. Why do you think the infection rate is so high among teens?
4. Young people generally begin dating in high school. What are some advantages and disadvantages of dating?

APPLY IT TO YOURSELF

5. Imagine that a younger brother or sister wants to start dating. How can you use your experiences in relationships to help your brother or sister develop a healthy dating relationship?

SUMMARY

When adolescents begin to feel attracted to others, they may start to date. Dating can help people learn about themselves and about developing new relationships. However, it can also raise issues of concern. If couples decide to marry, they must be committed, compatible, and willing to compromise in order to have a healthy relationship.

LIFE CHOICES

How many people that you know are married? How many are single? How many have children? There are many different choices that you will have to make about your life. Making these choices requires you to understand who you are and to think about what kinds of relationships you want.

MARRIAGE AND CHILDREN

One of the most important decisions a married couple makes together is whether to have children. Children bring great joy and great responsibility. Because children demand a great deal of time, both parents need to share the responsibility. Most couples budget carefully when they have children. From the hospital costs for delivering a baby to clothes and food, a new child is a big addition to the family budget.

POSTPONING PARENTHOOD   Deciding when to have children and how many to have are matters of family planning. Family planning involves deciding when children will be born and how many children there will be in a family. By careful family planning, couples can be financially and emotionally prepared for a new child.

Preventing pregnancy, usually by preventing the union of the egg and sperm, is called **contraception.** Sometimes, despite family planning, unwanted pregnancies do occur, causing a great deal of stress. Support and assistance are especially important at this time. Decisions about what to do should be made thoughtfully by both parents with the advice of family members and professionals.

CHILDLESS COUPLES   Some married couples do not have children. They may be physically unable to have children, or they may not want children. Some couples feel that they cannot afford the great

---

CONSUMER HEALTH

Living on Your Own

Sooner or later you will leave your parents' home and set up housekeeping on your own or with friends. Living on your own can be fun and it can be a challenge. To start out on the right foot, understand that living on your own means being responsible for your own needs and managing your money wisely.

Before you move away from home, decide on your goals. Set up a budget that shows all of your

expenses including rent, utilities, food costs, transportation costs, entertainment, and savings. If you have a special hobby or interest that costs money, factor that in, too. Try to be generous in your estimates. Coming up short every month can only lead to trouble.

Next, figure out whether the job you have will cover your expenses and leave you some savings. If it does not, reevaluate your needs or find a higher paying job. A financial problem does not fix itself, and time can only make matters worse.

When you set out to look for a place to live, ask questions of your potential landlord. Before you sign a contract, read every word and be sure you understand the contract and feel comfortable signing it. Do not sign under pressure.

Be very careful using credit. Credit companies charge high interest rates each month and it is difficult to budget for monthly payments. If you do have a credit card, use it sparingly—only in emergencies—and pay the entire balance each month.

expense of raising children. Other couples may prefer to maintain their independence and freedom. Before couples marry, they should openly discuss their feelings and attitudes about having children.

PARENTHOOD Before becoming parents, married couples should think carefully about their reasons for wanting to start a family. A couple should really want to have children. They should have a happy, stable marriage.

Couples should be emotionally and financially ready to support a family. They should understand the responsibilities of becoming parents and be committed to providing a loving home for their children. Parents should be willing to share the responsibilities of caring for their children. They should realize that in addition to bringing much joy, children require a great deal of time and hard work.

Sometimes it's best not to force difficult decisions!

DELAYING MARRIAGE

One hundred years ago, the average age for marriage was 26 for men and 22 for women. Today, the average ages are nearly the same. However, more adults than ever before delay getting married until they are in their thirties. About 16 percent of women and 27 percent of men between 30 and 34 have never married.

One reason that people wait to get married is that they are involved in other aspects of their lives, such as attending school or pursuing careers. Because making a commitment to another person takes time and energy, it can be difficult to juggle a job or school with marriage. Some people decide to wait to marry until they are better able to handle the financial and emotional demands of marriage.

Another reason that some people delay marriage is that they feel they have not yet met the right person. Although many young people express the desire to get married, they want to be certain that they find a compatible partner. Because it is more acceptable today for young people to live on their own, they do not feel pressured to rush into marriage.

SINGLE PARENTHOOD

About one quarter of all children under age 18 live with one parent, usually their mothers. Some adults choose to be single parents, but others find themselves raising children alone as a result of divorce or the death of a spouse. A **divorce** occurs when a married couple agrees to legally end their marriage and live apart. There are over one million divorces each year, and nearly one half of all marriages now end in divorce. Most single parents have been divorced.

Almost everyone involved in a divorce—husband, wife, children, families, friends—faces emotional challenges. Divorced people must adjust to living alone and to dating. Some divorced spouses who have not had outside employment while married must enter or re-enter the workforce.

STRATEGIES FOR LIVING

Areas to consider for marriage compatibility

- cultural background
- attitudes about having children
- attitudes about careers
- beliefs, interests, values and goals
- ideas about where to live
- attitudes about raising children
- educational experiences
- attitudes about chores
- attitudes toward money

Single parents who have custody of their children shoulder many responsibilities alone. For example, some single parents must support themselves and their children on one income. Although the number of men who are single parents is increasing, the vast majority of single parents are women. While divorced single parents may receive financial assistance from their former spouse, some have additional financial pressure if a spouse fails to help.

Raising children without financial support can be difficult, yet single parents also deal with the lack of emotional support. Making important decisions alone can be stressful. Single parents who must both work and raise children may at times feel lonely or overwhelmed.

REMAINING SINGLE

Although most Americans get married at some point in their lives, millions of men and women remain single. Being single has advantages and disadvantages. For example, single people have more freedom and control over their choices. On the other hand, single people face financial and social pressures.

Many single people offset household expenses by living with a roommate. Finding compatible roommates is not easy; therefore, single people may choose to live with a friend or acquaintance. They also may use a roommate-matching service in the real estate or classified sections of newspapers. Some single people live with their parents in order to meet expenses. More than 32 percent of single men and 20 percent of single women between ages 25 and 34 live with their parents.

Because most people get married, single people may often feel pressured to follow suit. However, many single people develop a strong network of friends. Friends help them make decisions, give them a sense of belonging, and provide companionship.

Maintaining social ties with others is especially important for single people.

SUMMARY

No matter what choices you make in your life, you will have relationships. Strong friendships, professional contacts, and intimate relationships are signs of good social health.

Among the choices that people make is the decision to marry or to remain single. An important decision for couples who marry is whether to have children. Single parents often face extra financial and emotional pressures.

LESSON 7.3 **USING WHAT YOU HAVE LEARNED**

REVIEW

1. What are some of the responsibilities parents have?
2. List some of the difficulties of single parenthood.

THINK CRITICALLY

3. The United States has the highest divorce rate in the world. What are some changes that might occur in families as a result of divorce?
4. According to recent statistics, the marriage rate is declining. Why do you think more people are deciding to remain single or delay marriage?

APPLY IT TO YOURSELF

5. Imagine that you are a single parent whose child has just become engaged. How can you best help your child make sound decisions about marriage and children?

Not Now

Susan and Kevin had been going out together for six months. Ever since their first date, they had been together every Saturday night. They got along well. Everybody thought of them as a couple that would last forever.

Susan really liked Kevin but he had begun to pressure her to become physically intimate. Susan was very nervous about their growing relationship. She had always had a good time with Kevin. But Susan just didn't feel she was ready for physical intimacy. She wanted to take the relationship more slowly. Besides, there were just too many issues to consider. Teen pregnancy, sexually transmitted diseases, and AIDS were all reasons to wait. Susan was embarassed to talk about these issues with Kevin. She wondered if he'd break up with her.

Each time Kevin had pressured her, Susan had handled it casually by suggesting they do something else. But lately Kevin was being persistent, and she knew she'd have to say something. She really didn't feel that she was ready for sex. However, Susan was worried that she would lose Kevin if she kept refusing. One night when they were out, Kevin suggested that they go back to his house. "My parents are gone for the weekend, " he said. "Why don't we go to my place."

BEING WELL, STAYING WELL

PAUSE AND CONSIDER

1. *Identify the Problem.* What is Susan's conflict?

2. *Consider the Options.* What are her options?

3. *Evaluate the Outcomes.* What could happen if Susan doesn't let Kevin know how she feels? What might happen if she talks to Kevin about her feelings?

Susan tried her ususal tactic of casually rejecting Kevin's suggestion and changing the subject. But Kevin was persistent. "Come on," he said, "I thought you cared about me."

"Kevin, I do like you a lot. I think I love you. But I'm just not ready now. Our relationship means a lot to me. Sex is not something I want to rush into. I know in my heart that it would be wrong for us to get more intimate right now."

Susan paused for a moment and then continued, "I enjoy being with you more than any-one else. You are my closest friend. For me, that's enough. Sometimes I even think about us getting married some day. But for now, I just want to enjoy our time together without any complications. That's just how I feel. I hope you can accept that."

"Wow," Kevin said. He was silent for a while and then spoke. "Yeah. I can accept that. In fact, I feel a little relieved. I really wasn't sure how you felt."

Susan and Kevin talked for several hours. They talked about relationships, about peer pressure, and about issues, such as AIDS. At the end of the evening, both felt as though they knew each other better than they had before. They also recognized that their friendship had really grown that night. It had grown out of open communication and honesty.

DECIDE AND REVIEW

4. *Decide and Act.* How did Susan and Kevin resolve the conflict together?

5. *Review.* How else might Susan have let Kevin know how she felt? Why are such situations often difficult for couples?

PROJECTS

1. Create a bulletin-board display to illustrate different types of relationships. Find and then label magazine and newspaper pictures illustrating acquaintances, friends (casual, close, platonic), and intimate and professional relationships. Try to find pictures that show healthy, positive relationships.

2. Write an advice column giving teenagers practical information about the merits or drawbacks of dating. First, choose one specific topic, such as how to turn someone down without hurting his or her feelings. Then research your topic. Before you write, you may want to look at examples of advice columns.

3. Find recent statistics that tell how many households in your state are two-parent families, how many are single-parent families, how many are couples without children, and how many are single with no children. Use the data you gather to make a simple bar graph or pie chart.

WORKING WITH OTHERS

Work with a group of three to five classmates to simulate a radio talk show about having healthy relationships. Each group member should be responsible for one or more of these tasks: brainstorm discussion topics, write questions and answers, role-play the host who answers listeners' calls, or role-play a few listeners who ask questions. Encourage classmates to pose their own questions as well.

CONNECTING TO...

SOCIOLOGY Investigate marriage during a specific time in the past, or in a different country today. Find out why people got married, what terms they agreed to, what vows they exchanged, what formal ceremonies they held, and so on.

CHAPTER 7 ≈ Review

USING VOCABULARY

acquaintance	date rape	peer pressure
adolescence	divorce	platonic friendship
communication	friend	prejudice
compatibility	gender	rape
compromise	heterosexual	relationship
contraception	homosexual	sexual harassment
cooperation	infatuation	stalking

Identify the vocabulary word that matches each phrase. With the remaining terms, create matching exercises for a partner to complete.

1. someone who is familiar to you but not especially close
2. people who are attracted to members of the opposite gender
3. strong influence of others who are the same age
4. process by which people with opposing views settle differences
5. a special bond or connection with other people
6. unwanted verbal or sexual advances
7. method used to prevent pregnancy
8. intense but short-lived period of interest in someone
9. legal ending of a marriage

CONCEPT MAPPING

Copy and complete the concept map shown below. Information on concept mapping appears at the front of this book.

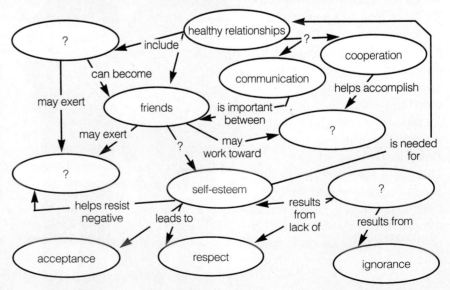

THINKING CRITICALLY

INTERPRET

LESSON
7.1
1. How do healthy relationships contribute to your social health?

2. Why do you think people generally have more acquaintances than close friends?

3. What should you do if a relationship you are having with someone is not healthy?

LESSON
7.2
4. How are dating and going steady alike and different?

5. Which issue of concern—violence, pregnancy, or STDs—do you think is most important to teenagers? Why?

6. Explain how commitment, compatibility, and compromise can help build a successful relationship.

LESSON
7.3
7. What are some advantages and disadvantages of delaying marriage?

8. Why do single parents often have more difficulty raising children than two parents?

9. Name two challenges faced by people who remain single.

APPLY

LESSON
7.1
10. Darnell, an excellent swimmer, has just moved to your community from another state. How might Darnell begin to develop new friendships in your high school?

11. Jan's friends skipped math class so they could shop at the mall, but Jan chose not to go. When one of her friends, Amy, called to find out about the next day's math assignment, Jan would not help her. She said she thought it was wrong to skip class, and she didn't feel comfortable helping. Do you think Amy and Jan have a healthy relationship? Why or why not?

LESSON
7.2
12. After Juan and Maria went out on two dates, Juan could not stop talking about her and put her picture in his wallet. Juan started hanging around the department store where Maria had a part-time job. Do you think Maria should be concerned? How should she deal with the situation?

13. Your best friend is attracted to someone who has been pressuring your friend to have a sexual relationship. What advice would you give for resisting the pressure for sexual involvement but maintaining a healthy relationship?

LESSON
7.3
14. Joan and Vic have been going steady for a long time. Vic just started graduate school, and Joan is working at her first job. Why might this couple delay getting married?

15. Sondra lives with her mother, a nurse who works the night shift, and two younger brothers. Sondra's father has remarried and lives in another town. Describe two problems Sondra's mother might face.

16. Craig, who is going to turn 35 next month, has decided to remain single after ending a steady relationship with Barbara. Name two kinds of pressure that Craig might face. What choices can he make to help alleviate each of these pressures?

COMMITMENT TO WELLNESS

FOLLOW-UP

SETTING GOALS

Look back at your completed Commitment to Wellness checklist. Find your yes answers to determine your strengths in having healthy relationships, and find no answers to determine your weaknesses.

Now make a two-column chart with the headings Strengths and Weaknesses. In the first column, write short phrases that describe your strengths in the area of relationships, such as can resolve conflicts. Then describe your weaknesses in the area of relationships in the second column.

After you complete your chart, think of ways that you can turn weaknesses into strengths. For example, if you said you don't work well with others, think of how you can learn to cooperate by sharing tasks fairly.

WHERE DO I GO FROM HERE?

Once you have analyzed your strengths and weaknesses in having relationships, you may want to investigate further how you can continue building and maintaining healthy relationships. To help you reach your specific goals, you might seek the advice of parents, teachers, a school counselor, or the following professional organization.

FOR MORE
INFORMATION CONTACT:
Youth Counseling League
138 East 19th Street
New York, NY 10003

Family Roles and Responsibilities

"Guided by my heritage of a love of beauty and a respect for strength—in search of my mother's garden, I found my own."

Alice Walker

BACKGROUND

Alice Walker is a critically acclaimed African American novelist. She is best known for her book *The Color Purple*, on which the popular movie was based. In her work, Walker often explores the complex relationships among family members.

When you hear the word *family*, what do you think of at first? For Alice Walker, love of beauty and respect for strength were the telling characteristics of her family.

Families change over time. Younger members grow up and leave the family. Some family members die, and others join the family through birth, adoption, or marriage. Some marriages end, and the family structure changes. New marriages create new families.

All families face challenges. Most face a crisis from time to time. Financial worries, illness, loss of a job, domestic violence, substance abuse, death of a family member— these and many other circumstances strain family relationships and resources. The keys to meeting the challenges of family life are understanding your own role in your family, accepting responsibility for yourself, and caring for other family members.

Whatever its structure and character, within your family lies the potential for your future. You have an important role to play in shaping what the future holds.

THINKING CRITICALLY

INTERPRET

LESSON 8.1

1. Identify the most important features of a family.
2. What are some ways that dual-income families find care for their children?
3. What are two reasons that a couple may adopt a child?
4. How is foster care different from adoption?
5. In what ways do parents help children prepare for adulthood?
6. What changes typically occur during the launching stage of the nuclear family's life cycle?
7. In what ways might a boomerang child disrupt his or her family?

LESSON 8.2

8. How can financial worries strain a family relationship?
9. In what ways can additions to a family cause stress?
10. What is child abuse?

APPLY

LESSON 8.1

11. Although the nuclear family is still a typical family structure, today's families also commonly include single-parent families, blended families, extended families, and childless families. Why do you think family structures have changed so much over the years?
12. Why do you think custody is usually granted to the mother in a divorce settlement? Do you think this is fair? Explain your answer.
13. The parents and children in every family have roles and responsibilities—some spoken, some assumed. What would be the benefit of talking openly about the expectations of parents and children?

LESSON 8.2

14. Why does gang membership appeal to some teenagers?
15. Domestic violence is against the law. Why do you think family members often do not report acts of violence?
16. Substance abuse affects others besides the abuser. Describe two ways in which members of the abuser's family might be affected.

COMMITMENT TO WELLNESS

FOLLOW-UP

SETTING GOALS

Look at your responses to the checklist you completed at the beginning of this chapter Which checklist statements reflected your strengths? Which reflected your weaknesses?

Choose two checklist statements that you would like to change from *no* to *yes.* Copy these statements in your Wellness Journal. Below each statement, list five specific actions you could take to achieve that goal. For example, if you decided to work on doing chores without complaint or reminders, some specific actions you might list are putting a list of your chores where you'll see it every day, rewarding yourself at the end of the week for each day you completed your chores successfully, and trading a chore with another family member for variety once in a while.

WHERE DO I GO FROM HERE?

If you need help in solving a problem or resolving a conflict within your family, your school guidance counselor may be able to help. Besides offering advice, a counselor can suggest books and articles you can read to help develop better strategies for coping with problems.

FOR MORE INFORMATION, CONTACT:

Clearinghouse on Child Abuse and Neglect Information
P.O. Box 1182
Washington, D.C. 20013-1182

You in the Community

"By mutual confidence and mutual aid, great deeds are done, and great discoveries made."

Homer

People have always lived and worked together in communities. Through the cooperation of its citizens, whole communities have built cities, changed laws, and improved the standard of living for everyone.

If someone in your family is sick or suffering, it affects every member of the family. In the same way, if some part of your community is sick or suffering, it affects every member of the community. For this reason, it is important to be aware of the health concerns of your community so that you can do your part to lend support when it is needed.

Homelessness, violence, poverty, and poor health care are just some of the difficult challenges of everyday life in most communities. These problems may not show up in your house, but they may exist next door or down the street. Those who are facing these problems cannot solve them alone. They need help from other community members who are willing to lend support and aid. Each and every effort—no matter how small—can greatly affect the quality of life for many individuals and for a whole community.

SELF-
ASSESSMENT

How aware are you about public health issues? On a sheet
of paper or in your Wellness
Journal, write *yes* or *no* in
response to the following
statements.

1. I regularly participate in
   volunteer activities in my
   community.

2. I am aware of the public
   health issues in my community.

3. I have regular check-ups
   with my physician and I
   perform self-examinations
   to detect any changes in
   my body.

4. I practice strong preventive health care by making
   healthy choices and avoiding high risk behaviors.

5. I do not engage in any
   behaviors that would promote violence of any kind.

6. I never use alcohol.

7. I feel confident about my
   self-worth and I have
   strong, supportive relationships.

8. I make my own decisions
   about activities my peers
   encourage me to join.

9. I am respectful and consid-
   erate of the special needs
   of those who may be differently abled than I am,
   including the elderly.

10. I know where to turn for
    help if I have a physical or
    emotional problem.

Review your responses and
consider what might be your
strengths and your weaknesses. Save your personal checklist for a follow-up activity that
appears at the end of the
chapter.

COMMUNITY HEALTH

At this point in your life, you may be discovering how the choices you make can influence your health and well-being. To make good decisions—choices that lead to a healthy, productive life—you need information.

Community efforts can influence your behaviors. For example, if your community wages a campaign to encourage the use of bicycle helmets, you are more likely to strap on your helmet each time you hop on your bike.

SOCIETAL PROBLEMS

In order to meet the Healthy People 2000 objectives for promoting positive health behaviors, communities must face some difficult problems. They include poverty, homelessness, alcoholism, violence, a polluted environment, and access to health care. Facing problems like these and finding ways to solve them require the talents, time, and hard work of the individuals that make up the community—individuals like you.

POVERTY A very large number of people in the United States live in families whose income is below the federal poverty level. People who live in poverty are at greater risk for serious health problems. In fact, low income is considered a risk factor in almost all chronic illnesses. Poor families are unlikely to have continuous health care. Often, money to buy food is limited. Some children whose families cannot provide a nutritionally balanced diet suffer from severe levels of malnutrition. Children whose immune systems become weakened by a lack of nutrients may require hospitalization because their bodies cannot fight infection. Pregnant women living in poverty often suffer from lack of prenatal care. Without adequate care, the health of both mother and infant is at risk.

HOMELESSNESS When you think of someone who is homeless, you may have an image of an adult without family, friends, or shelter. Yet shortages of low-income housing and cutbacks in benefits have caused entire families to join the ranks of the homeless. The number of homeless people has increased in recent years. One conservative estimate is that in 1991 there were 600,000 homeless in the United States. About thirty percent of these were children in families, and 5 percent were teenagers, usually runaways. The homeless live in emergency shelters, cars, abandoned buildings, or on the streets.

Many of this country's homeless people are

There are many ways for citizens of a community to help homeless people. Have you ever volunteered to help?

women with children. Children of homeless women often are unable to attend school regularly. Homeless children also have high incidences of malnourishment, asthma, and lead poisoning. Babies born to homeless women, who have had little or no prenatal care, tend to weigh less, may be mentally deficient, and have more congenital problems than children born to women with homes.

Of recent concern to health officials is the relationship between homelessness and tuberculosis (TB). **Tuberculosis** is a contagious lung disease caused by bacteria spread on airborne droplets that are released when a TB sufferer coughs. TB is associated with the kinds of conditions found among the homeless: poor hygiene, poor nutrition, lack of health care, and crowding. People living with TB sufferers in poorly ventilated shelters are especially at risk.

Many cities try to provide a place for homeless citizens to sleep. However, this is not a long-term solution to the problem of homelessness.

ALCOHOL USE   In our society alcohol is the most frequently abused drug. Alcohol use decreases a person's ability to make good decisions. It increases the tendency to engage in unsafe or high risk behaviors. For example, alcohol use is a frequent factor in motor vehicle and boating accidents. It also plays a role in fatal intentional injuries such as suicide and homicide.

Although alcohol abuse continues to be a serious problem, media campaigns and community groups are actively addressing the problems of education and treatment, especially among young people.

TEENAGERS AND ALCOHOL USE

Some facts as they relate to teenagers and alcohol:

- Almost 17 percent of the students surveyed in a recent poll had never tried alcohol.

- The legal drinking age in all states is 21.

- Penalties for using fraudulent identification to obtain alcohol can be severe—involving at *least* arrest and a fine.

- A person 21 or over who provides alcohol to a minor is also subject to stiff penalties. For example, in Texas the penalty could be a $2,000 fine and a year in jail.

- Although 92 percent of students in a recent survey said that a person should never drink and drive, almost one third have accepted a ride from a driver who had been drinking.

VIOLENCE   Tied closely to misuse of alcohol and other drugs is the increase in violence in our society. Each year in the United States, millions of people are victims of violent crimes. At highest risk are people aged 12 to 19 years. Those who live in inner cities and in poverty are most vulnerable. Gang-related violence is on the rise in many American communities. Women also are at risk. According to a 1992 report from the surgeon general's office, violence is the leading cause of injury to women aged 15 to 44.

FOR YOUR INFORMATION

In the early 1990s, an estimated 36 million people in the United States had no health insurance.

Community Pride

Important cultural anniversaries and events can be reasons to celebrate for everyone in a community. Community pride is a major aspect of community health and celebrations that give people a chance to display their pride are important to the health of the entire community.

One celebration that has become a regular event in western and southern cities like San Diego, Los Angeles, Austin, and San Antonio is Cinco de Mayo—the fifth of May. Cinco de Mayo marks the anniversary of the Mexican defeat in 1867 of invading French troops under Napoleon II. In Mexico, Cinco de Mayo is a national holiday. In the United States, it has become a celebration of dances, parades, and speeches commemorating Mexican heritage.

On June 19, African-Americans in Texas celebrate Emancipation Day—the day General Gordon Granger arrived in Galveston to establish federal control over the state and he announced to the slaves in Texas that they were free. In some communities, Emancipation Day is the high point of a 3-day celebration of community pride that includes parades and a variety of other activities.

Cinco de Mayo celebrations demonstrate and promote pride in the Latino community and in Mexican heritage. Emancipation Day celebrations serve the same functions among African-Americans and their neighbors in Texas.

ACCESS TO HEALTH CARE   A primary goal of the health objectives for the year 2000 is to increase access to preventive services for all citizens. Preventive services include immunizations, appropriate screening for health problems, and counseling. In the early 1990s in the United States, almost 18 percent of the population had limited access to health care. Access may be limited by lack of money, lack of transportation, or cultural barriers.

THE ENVIRONMENT   You may often hear people express concern for the environment and the long-term effects of human action on the environment. There is good reason for concern. Some factories still dump toxic wastes into rivers and streams. Smog and acid rain threaten many parts of the world. Lakes are being poisoned with pesticides.

For decades, scientists have been warning about the health consequences of human actions on the environment. People are now realizing that they must do many things differently in order to ensure a healthy environment for future generations.

PUBLIC HEALTH: RESPONDING TO PROBLEMS

The effort to protect and improve the health of a group of people is called **public health**. In today's world, this effort extends beyond the control of infectious disease and the inspection of food and water. Today, the public health system must address health issues related to poverty and homelessness. It must be responsive to victims of violent acts and reach out to families affected by problems of alcohol abuse.

Health experts have learned that the best way to fight the lifestyle diseases of today is through organized preventive efforts. To this end, public health agencies work with individuals and organizations to find better ways to prevent injury and diseases.

FUNCTIONS OF A PUBLIC HEALTH SYSTEM   In today's world, a public health system works on many levels and in many areas of health.

HEALTHY PEOPLE 2000

Increase to at least 90 percent the proportion of people who are served by a local health department that is effectively carrying out the core functions of public health.

Objective 8.14
from *Healthy People 2000: National Health Promotion and Disease Prevention Objectives*

A public health system investigates diseases, and it controls epidemics. An **epidemic** refers to a public health problem that occurs in greater numbers of people than would normally be expected. In order to prevent a contagious disease from spreading, a quarantine may be imposed. A **quarantine** is a drastic step that isolates sick people from others. In the case of tuberculosis, quarantine may mean voluntary TB hospitals where patients can receive supervised drug therapy and nutritious meals.

The functions of today's public health system go beyond the investigation and control of infectious diseases. Today, the public health system is also working to understand and manage noninfectious diseases, such as cancer and heart disease. These so-called life-style diseases appear to be related to health choices that people make every day.

The public health system has three specific functions: investigation, prediction, and control. You can see how each of these functions is carried out by studying Figure 9-1, which shows the involvement of each public health function in issues related to smoking and lung cancer.

The public health system must provide services to all members of the community.

LEVELS OF PUBLIC HEALTH

Many communities provide health care through local public health departments. You may have received a vaccination at your local health department, or you may have used some of the services provided by a neighborhood health-care center. What you may not realize is that there is a large network of public health units in the United States and throughout the world. Although these units do not come under one agency, they all work together toward a single goal—to keep the world community healthy and safe.

STATE AND LOCAL The public health departments at the local and state level have several functions. One is to provide direct service to people who need preventive health care. Another function is to inspect water, restaurants, hotels, and other public places to ensure that they are clean and safe.

Many communities have established public health centers where citizens can go for free primary health care. This care generally includes physical examinations, immunizations, and routine medical tests.

Non-profit neighborhood health centers offer low-cost medical care in a community-oriented setting. Neighborhood health centers often sponsor after-school recreational activities and programs designed especially for

PROBLEM: LUNG CANCER AND SMOKING

INVESTIGATION

- Conduct basic research into the cause of lung cancer

Agencies and organizations involved:
National Cancer Institute (federal)
American Cancer Society (private)

PREDICTION

- Compile data collected during investigation
- Analyze data to generate statistics

Agencies and organizations involved:
Office of Health and Smoking (federal)
American Lung Association (private)

CONTROL

- Try to influence life-style choices through ad campaigns and warnings
- Pass legislation to restrict smoking in public places

Agencies and organizations involved:
Public Health Service (federal)
Environmental Protection Agency (federal)
American Cancer Society (private)
American Lung Association (private)
Businesses and restaurants (local)

Figure 9-1   How many different agencies work together in this example?

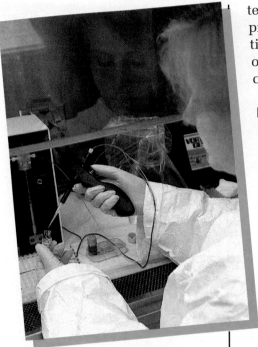

Public health agencies conduct research to improve the quality of health care worldwide.

teenagers. For example, in the Codman Square Center in Boston, a program for pregnant teenagers helps to establish a caring relationship between the pregnant teen and an older woman who was once a pregnant teenager herself. Another program organizes the community's residents against crime.

NATIONAL   The United States Department of Health and Human Services (DHHS) is the agency most responsible for public health at the national level. This agency is headed by the Secretary of Health and Human Services, a member of the President's cabinet. Within the DHHS is the Public Health Service, headed by the surgeon general. The Public Health Service is an umbrella for several important health agencies, including the Centers for Disease Control, Food and Drug Administration, National Institutes of Health, Agency for Toxic Substances and Disease Registry, and Indian Health Service.

Government health agencies, together with private voluntary organizations such as the American Lung Association, the American Heart Association, and the American Cancer Society, use their national presence to promote positive health behavior. All of these organizations conduct research and work with policy makers to encourage legislation that will protect and promote the health of all citizens.

INTERNATIONAL   Countries often work together to solve health problems. The need to work together usually takes place after a major disaster. Most often, efforts are combined through the United Nations (UN). The UN is an organization of over 170 nations that works for peace, health, and good living conditions worldwide. One UN agency—the World Health Organization (WHO)—was established to serve as a clearinghouse for medical and scientific information. In addition, WHO provides assistance to many countries during health emergencies.

SUMMARY

Health behaviors are influenced by the community in which you live. In communities where there is poor access to health care and where there are other problems, it is more difficult to practice positive health behaviors.

Public health began as an effort to prevent the spread of infectious diseases. Today, local, state, and national governments and international agencies continue that effort, investigate noninfectious diseases, and address health problems related to societal issues such as homelessness, poverty, and pollution.

LESSON 9.1   **USING WHAT YOU HAVE LEARNED**

REVIEW

1. Why are people who live in poverty at risk for serious health problems?
2. List the major functions of the public health system at local, state, and national levels.

THINK CRITICALLY

3. What do you think are the major factors that influence teenagers' attitudes about alcohol use?
4. Why do you think there are so many different organizations concerned with public health? What might be done to ensure that all people who need help have easy access to it?

APPLY IT TO YOURSELF

5. Imagine that you are a teacher in an area where layoffs have just occurred and poverty is high. You suspect that some of your students may be homeless. As their teacher, how might you help?

Americans with Disabilities Act

In July of 1990, the Federal Government changed the lives of about 43 million Americans by passing the Americans with Disabilities Act. The act makes discrimination against those with hearing, visual, physical, or developmental disabilities against the law. With the passage of the act, everyone has equal access to jobs, public facilities, retail establishments, transportation, and communication.

Before the bill became law, many disabled Americans were not able to participate normally or actively in many aspects of society. For example, many people with disabilities were barred from working because they could not get to or into places of work. Today, because of the Americans with Disabilities Act, citizens with disabilities who want to work will be given an opportunity to compete for jobs.

Some people opposed the Americans with Disabilities Act because they felt that it would cost too much money to make all buildings accessible. In fact, however, construction and implementation of accessibility costs very little, under $1,000 per compliance.

Compare the cost of making the workplace accessible to the cost to private citizens or government agencies of supporting citizens denied a chance to work. Some estimates place the cost of social security disability insurance, welfare allotments, worker's compensation insurance, and various forms of private insurance for disabled Americans at close to $170 billion per year. Much of the government's portion of this cost can be eliminated when jobs become more readily available as the Act's requirements take effect. Soon, the approximately one million people in wheelchairs, twenty-two million hearing impaired and deaf Americans, and almost two hundred thousand sight impaired or blind people will be able to enjoy complete access to the marketplace.

Telephone companies now provide relay services to their deaf and hearing impaired customers so that they may communicate with those who are hearing. Access to public transportation, buses, subways, trains, and airplanes has increased drastically. Retail stores and restaurants have installed wider doorways, ramps, and bathrooms accessible to people in wheelchairs. Theaters, stadiums, libraries, and museums have provided entryways for those in wheelchairs, too, as well as services for their hearing and sight impaired clients.

Other, more subtle, changes have also taken place as a result of the Americans with Disabilities Act. Because of compliance, those living with disabilities are becoming more a part of everyday society. They are therefore enjoying a wider and broader acceptance by those who may not previously have been exposed to them. The Americans with Disabilities Act has helped people living with disabilities become a vital and contributing portion of the population.

1. Describe the terms of the Americans with Disabilities Act.

2. Walk around your home and school. Make a list of features that would be barriers to someone in a wheelchair. What are some things that could be done to eliminate those barriers?

SPECIAL HEALTH CONCERNS

As you read in Lesson 1, communities have special health issues that must be addressed. Many of these issues affect a community as a whole. Other issues affect particular groups, such as women, men, teens, and the elderly. Your age, gender, income, and ethnic background all play a role in your health status.

WOMEN'S HEALTH

Until the late 1980s, most of the medical research conducted in the United States had been done on men. The findings were then applied to both men and women. Scientists today recognize that what is true about disease in males may not be true about disease in females. Women have unique health concerns that need to be investigated more thoroughly.

Since 1989, the National Institutes of Health (NIH) has set aside funds for the investigation of health problems of special concern to women. In 1990, the NIH issued new guidelines to ensure that women would be adequately represented in all NIH-funded research that applies to women. Yet, even with improved funding of medical research, scientists are still far from answering some of women's major health questions or finding cures for the major diseases affecting women.

CANCER   Until 1986, breast cancer was the leading cause of cancer death among women. Today, lung cancer kills more women than any other form of cancer. This is largely due to the increase in cigarette smoking among women. Breast cancer and cancer of the reproductive system are also of special concern to women.

One in every nine women will develop some form of breast cancer during her lifetime. This statistic has motivated many women to put pressure on the government to fund areas of basic research so that a cure might be found. In the meantime, more women are relying on screening measures such as monthly self-examination and mammograms. A **mammogram** is a special X ray of the breasts. It is a method of detecting breast cancer, not a method of preventing it.

Cancer of the uterus develops in the lining of the uterus. It is one of the most common cancers among women in the United States. It is also one of the most curable, if caught early.

Cervical cancer is another common cancer affecting women's reproductive organs. However, since 1970, there has been a steady decline in the number of deaths due to cervical cancer. This decline is the result of increased screening using the Pap test. The **Pap test** is a method for distinguishing normal cells from abnormal cells from a woman's cervix. The Pap test detects 95 percent of all cervical cancer.

Ovarian cancer can be deadly. Its symptoms often are vague and may be dismissed as signs of stress. An annual pelvic examination is recommended as the best screening device for diagnosis. You

While mammograms cannot prevent breast cancer, they can help detect the disease early enough for effective treatment.

can learn more about the female, as well as the male, reproductive systems in Chapter 17, "Growth and Development."

OSTEOPOROSIS   In the United States alone, osteoporosis affects some 20 million people, mostly women. **Osteoporosis** is a skeletal disease that causes loss of bone tissue. The result is brittle bones that can fracture easily. Osteoporosis contributes to at least 1.3 million broken bones a year. Mobility becomes restricted, and some people find that they can no longer care for themselves. For this reason, osteoporosis is a major public health problem.

VIOLENCE   Women of every age, class, and ethnic background are victims of violence. According to the Federal Bureau of Investigation (FBI), one in three American women is assaulted in her lifetime. Although this is an alarming statistic, it has challenged some women to work to bring about reform and to learn ways of protecting themselves. Today it is estimated that more than 1,000 helplines, shelters, and programs serve battered women across the country. Neighborhood groups have organized safehouse or greenlight programs that provide places for women to turn for safety and protection. Groups also have worked for legal reform that makes it easier for women to report crimes of violence and obtain convictions in court.

MEN'S HEALTH

Studies show that most men do not actively seek care unless they are sick. Neighborhood health centers and public health clinics are trying to change this attitude among men. Clinics and health centers are reaching out to the young men in communities to increase their awareness of the need for preventive care. The clinics and centers are making available educational programs about family life, careers, and diseases that are related to life-style behaviors.

CANCER   Before the age of 60, more women than men develop cancer. After age 60, there is a dramatic change in the male to female ratio. For men, two of the most commonly occurring cancers are prostate cancer and testicular cancer.

Prostate cancer appears most frequently in men aged 60 to 80. It is one of the most curable cancers if detected early. A physical examination by a doctor is one method of detection. A new blood test to detect prostate cancer also may be used as a screening method.

Testicular cancer often begins in the cells that produce sperm. The first sign is a hard painless lump on the testicle. Testicular cancer is most common in men between ages 15 and 35. Therefore, young men should learn how to do the monthly testicular self-exam. You can learn more about prostate and testicular cancer in Chapter 25, "Noninfectious Diseases."

Why do you think men are less likely than women to seek preventive health care?

Home Health Assistance

Living at home has many advantages for an elderly or handicapped person. Living at home also can pose many challenges.

There are several services that can help a person living at home who requires special care. Visiting nurses or doctors can pay a visit to check on the person, help administer medicines, or perform therapeutic functions. Home health aides can help prepare meals and per-

form light housekeeping for those unable to do it for themselves. Specialized therapists can come into the home regularly to administer therapy that the client needs. Neighbors, family members, or volunteers can work as part of a telephone check-in network. For senior citizens who have a chronic condition, or are at risk of falling, personal monitoring devices help. If unable to get to a telephone to call for help, the person just needs to push a button.

You can help a person living at home maintain independence and a

fully integrated life by participating in one of many volunteer efforts. Various social agencies ask volunteers to pay visits to those confined to their houses to read, take drives, deliver meals, or just to talk. By helping others in this way, you are enriching your own life and that of others.

HEART DISEASE   Today, coronary heart disease (CHD) is the number one killer among both men and women in the United States. However, in men, the disease appears much earlier than in women. One of the largest studies ever done on CHD found that heart disease occurred in 1 out of 6 men aged 45 to 49, and 1 out of 5 men aged 50 to 54. Yet studies also have shown that, among serious illnesses, heart disease is the most responsive to changes in health behaviors. Positive health behaviors such as getting regular exercise, reducing stress, and not smoking can help to prevent CHD or, in some cases, reverse its effects.

TEEN HEALTH

It can be both exciting and frightening to be a teenager today. Not only is your world changing but so are you, both physically and emotionally. The way you relate to the world beyond school and family also is changing. Now you must struggle with the realities of peer pressure and your own sense of right and wrong. Decisions are not simple and clear-cut. As you get older, your actions can make a real difference in the world. In order to decide which actions to take, it is important to have accurate information and people upon whom you can rely for good advice.

SELF-ESTEEM   According to some psychologists, self-esteem, or the way you feel about yourself, is related to three things: confidence, competence, and relationships. When you feel confident, you have a sense of self-worth. You believe that who you are is of value.

Competence—the skill or ability to do something well—can lead to high self-esteem. In some schools, praise and rewards have been used to help raise the level of self-esteem among students. However, this approach has not been entirely successful. High self-esteem follows accomplishment, not flattery or rewards.

At this stage of your life, what you think about yourself is also influenced by your relationships with other people. If you like who you are most of the time, then you believe that others will like

FOR YOUR INFORMATION

High school females are at greatest risk to start smoking, and more females smoke than do males in this age group.

you, too. Adolescents with low self-esteem are more likely to practice health-harming behaviors if they believe their friends would approve of these behaviors.

PEER PRESSURE   Peer pressure can be positive or negative depending on the behavior that is being promoted. Whenever you feel pressured to do something, stop and think about whether *you* really want to do it.

Peter had always found it difficult to make friends. When members of a group in school befriended him, Peter was flattered by their promise of loyalty and friendship. Before long, however, some of the kids were urging Peter to join them in the use of drugs. Peter wanted their friendship badly. Yet he did not want to use drugs.

Like Peter, you may have trouble saying no to friends who may encourage you to do things you do not feel are right. But many communities are making it easier for you to choose healthy alternatives. For example, some communities have alcohol and drug-free places of entertainment just for teenagers. Organizations such as Students Against Driving Drunk (SADD) work to support *not* drinking and driving as the approved behavior in a community.

Peter was lucky. A concerned school counselor discovered the group's attempts to pressure several students to use drugs. She suggested that these students attend some of the workshops sponsored by the school's "Just Say No" club. Through the positive peer reinforcement of the club, Peter gained the confidence to say no to drugs, and he made several friends who had been struggling with some of the same issues.

What organizations in your community help teenagers find healthy alternatives to drug and alcohol abuse?

VIOLENCE   Today many young people must cope with the realities of violence. In the early 1990s, homicide was the second leading cause of death for young people. Violence is not confined to some parts of the city. Violence occurs in suburban and rural areas as well—anywhere there are issues such as poverty, unemployment, drug abuse, or family problems.

The increase in gang violence is of special concern to many communities and public health officials. For young people who may be feeling isolated and alone, gangs may provide a feeling of belonging. To help prevent violence, health-care providers can talk with students about how to handle anger and how to resist peer pressure to become involved in gangs. In some communities, law enforcement officials, health officials, and community leaders have formed assistance programs to help young people stay focused on positive life-styles.

SPECIAL POPULATIONS

There are about 35 million people with disabilities in the United States. A **disability** is a condition that affects a major life activity, such as walking, hearing, or seeing. People who are alcoholics or

HEALTHY PEOPLE 2000

Increase to at least 50 percent the proportion of elementary and secondary schools that teach nonviolent conflict resolution skills, preferably as a part of quality school health education.

Objective 7.16
from *Healthy People 2000: National Health Promotion and Disease Prevention Objectives*

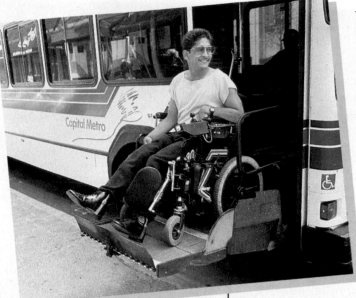

In what ways is your community helping people with special needs live productive lives?

who are living with AIDS also are considered disabled. Public health professionals are concerned with prevention of disabilities as well as finding ways to enhance the lives of those who already have a disability.

THE MENTALLY CHALLENGED   Until very recently, many mentally ill and mentally retarded people were largely hidden, usually in institutions. Today, government agencies and private organizations are trying to return the mentally challenged to the community. In many communities, for example, the mentally challenged live in special group homes where they prepare meals, hold jobs, and earn money. In this kind of setting, they become productive members of society.

In the 1980s and early 1990s, the trend was to deinstitutionalize as many of the mentally ill as possible and to control their illnesses with medications. Community outreach efforts provide counseling services and assistance for monitoring drug treatments. These maintenance programs help some mentally ill people obtain housing and employment while receiving treatment.

THE ELDERLY   As a group, the elderly suffer from high rates of poverty and poor health. The combination of these two problems often limits mobility and quality of nutrition for older people. Programs such as "Meals on Wheels" deliver nutritious food for some elderly people who are incapable of preparing their own meals. In some large cities, a special branch of the public transit system provides transportation for the frail or disabled elderly. Private nonprofit organizations serve a similar function. Such programs allow many elderly people to maintain their private homes and independent ways.

SUMMARY

Society today faces a number of troubling health issues. As a result, public health officials and local and state organizations are focusing attention on many of these issues. Studies have indicated that some health concerns of women are different from those of men. Teenagers and other special populations, such as the mentally and physically challenged and the elderly, all have special health concerns. Communities and official organizations are working to recognize the health needs of all groups.

LESSON 9.2   ## USING WHAT YOU HAVE LEARNED

REVIEW

1. Why is osteoporosis a major public health problem?
2. What preventive factors would decrease the death rate in heart disease?

THINK CRITICALLY

3. Some health officials feel that low self-esteem is the cause of many problems among young people. Why might this be true?
4. Scientists are just beginning to discover health factors that affect women differently than men. Why is research on the health differences of men and women important?

APPLY IT TO YOURSELF

5. You are a single parent living in a high-crime area with your 16-year-old son. How would you counsel your son to deal with the potential for violence? Why?

Make an Effort

As part of a community service project at school, Lucy was a volunteer at a local shelter for the homeless. It wasn't an easy place to work because she saw a lot of emotional pain and problems. Yet, Lucy enjoyed lending a hand to people who needed her.

At the end of the spring semester, Lucy's time at the shelter ended. She had grown to admire the staff at the shelter, and she felt good about the work she had done. "You've been a great help, Lucy," said the director. "If you are able to work the time into your schedule, we would love to have you continue on here." "I'd like to," said Lucy. "I think I can fit it in."

Lucy also was a very good tennis player. She belonged to a youth recreation team that played in tournaments throughout the year. The heaviest part of the competition was during the summer. Occasionally, Lucy missed a match to help at the shelter. She also had cut back on her practice time in order to work at the shelter.

One day, the coach of the team approached Lucy after practice. "Lucy, you are one of our best players, but your lack of practice is showing. Your game is starting to suffer. I'm thinking about replacing you for this next tournament. I need someone who is going to be committed to the team."

Lucy felt torn between tennis and working at the shelter. She loved playing tennis, but her work at the shelter meant a lot to her. She didn't want to lose her place on the team—her teammates were counting on her. But the people at the shelter were counting on her as well.

PAUSE AND CONSIDER

1. *Identify the Problem.* What is Lucy's conflict about working at the shelter?

2. *Consider the Options.* What has Lucy identified as her options?

3. *Evaluate the Outcomes.* What would happen if Lucy quit working at the shelter? What would happen if she quit the team?

Lucy didn't see why she couldn't do both. "What I need to do is prioritize my time better," she thought. Lucy decided to figure out a way that she could do both, at least part-time.

The first thing Lucy did was talk to the director at the shelter to see what could be worked out. Lucy explained to the director about her tennis commitment. "I know tennis may not seem as important as people in a crisis, but it's a real outlet for me. I've been doing it a

long time," she explained.

"Lucy," said the director. "Your commitment to the shelter is heartwarming, but you need to take care of the rest of your life as well. If that means you are here only one hour each week, it's a valuable hour. Whatever time you can give us is appreciated. Don't feel guilty about cutting back on your hours." Together they identified some blocks of time that Lucy would work. Lucy was pleased. She would be able to do both of the things that she enjoyed so much.

DECIDE AND REVIEW

4. *Decide and Act.* How did Lucy handle her dilemma?

5. *Review.* What would have been the consequences if Lucy had quit either the tennis team or working at the shelter? What other ways might Lucy have solved her problem?

PROJECTS

1. The Department of Health and Human Services is a federal agency headed by a member of the President's cabinet. Create a chart listing the parts of the Department of Health and Human Services and their functions. How are the departments represented in your community?

2. Does your community support recycling? Investigate your community's recycling efforts and evaluate the effectiveness of these efforts. What could be done to improve the participation of the members of your community? How does your community dispose of harmful products such as oil, asbestos, or toxic chemicals? Create a report on your community and offer suggestions for improving recycling and disposal efforts.

WORKING WITH OTHERS

With a partner, research the provisions of the Americans with Disabilities Act (ADA) of 1990. Then conduct research to see how the ADA has encouraged change in your community. How has the ADA affected schools? The workplace? Retail stores? Public facilities and transportation?

CONNECTING TO...

SOCIAL STUDIES The World Health Organization offers assistance to communities world-wide who may be suffering from an epidemic of disease or famine. Investigate the workings of the WHO. Prepare a report that describes your findings. In your report, be sure to include answers to the following questions. What are three major areas of concern for the WHO today? How is the health issue affecting the populations of other countries? What are the plans for helping the affected countries or communities?

USING VOCABULARY

disability	osteoporosis	quarantine
epidemic	Pap test	tuberculosis
mammogram	public health	

On a separate sheet of paper, write the vocabulary word that fits each definition below.

1. The isolation of an individual or group afflicted with a contagious disease.
2. The effort to protect and improve the health of a group of people.
3. An outbreak of disease that occurs in a great number of people.
4. A contagious respiratory disease caused by airborne bacteria.
5. A skeletal disease that results in brittle bones.
6. A test that can determine the presence of abnormal cells on a woman's cervix.
7. A condition that affects the life activity of an individual.
8. An X-ray test used to detect the presence of tumors in a woman's breast.

CONCEPT MAPPING

Copy and complete the concept map shown below. Information on concept mapping appears at the front of this book.

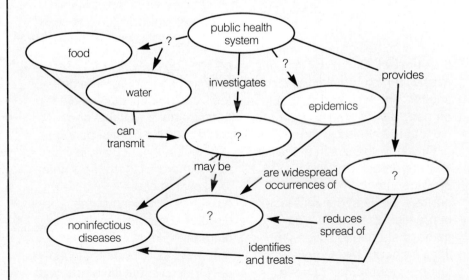

THINKING CRITICALLY

INTERPRET

LESSON 9.1
1. How can community efforts influence behavior?

2. In what way can poverty put the health of a woman and her newborn at risk?

3. Why is the incidence of tuberculosis on the rise?

4. What are some of the reasons that health care is inaccessible to large portions of the American population?

5. What are the three functions of the public health system?

6. What international organization serves as the umbrella for worldwide health concerns?

LESSON 9.2
7. What measures have contributed to the decline in the death rates for breast and cervical cancers among women?

8. What are community health centers doing to encourage preventive health practices among men?

9. Why might heart disease be considered one of the easiest health threats to control?

10. What are some reasons that are cited for the increase in violence that has been seen among high school students in the United States?

11. What is one positive result of deinstitutionalizing people who are mentally or physically challenged?

APPLY

LESSON 9.1
12. Statistics show that women and children represent most of the homeless population. Why do you think this is so?

13. Why might some people in inner cities be at greater risk of violence than others?

14. Tyler and his family recently ate at a restaurant. Tyler's father had raised some concern about the cleanliness of the place. Yet, they stayed to eat. Later that evening, several members of Tyler's family came down with severe stomach cramps and vomiting. They suspected that the food at the restaurant was contaminated. What could Tyler's family do to be sure that something such as this did not happen to other people?

LESSON 9.2
15. What steps could be implemented by public health officials to try to reduce violence against women?

16. When conducting a monthly breast exam, Lea discovered a small lump on her breast. What steps should Lea take, and why?

COMMITMENT TO WELLNESS FOLLOW-UP

SETTING GOALS

Look at the list of statements in your Wellness Journal from the beginning of Chapter 9. Which areas need improvement? Which areas do you feel good about?

Make a list of the statements to which you answered no. Rate the behaviors you want to change by first the one about which you feel most strongly. Second on your list would be the item that is your second priority, and so on. For each item on your list, write and complete the following statements.

a. The reason I want to change this behavior is

_____.

b. I can begin changing this behavior today by

_____.

c. A person I can enlist to help me change this behavior is

_____.

d. I will be able to write a yes next to this behavior by

_____.

WHERE DO I GO FROM HERE?

Your local health department can help to answer any questions you may have about health concerns in your community. A listing of government agencies, including the health department, can be found in your community's telephone book.

FOR MORE INFORMATION, CONTACT:

National Association of Community Health Centers
1330 New Hampshire Avenue, NW Suite 122
Washington, DC 20036

Nutrition

Chapter 10
Understanding Nutrition

Chapter 11
Identifying Your Dietary Needs

Chapter 12
Digestion and Excretion

How can you eat foods that you like and still be healthy?

Why is nutrition an important aspect of wellness?

What can you do to maintain a weight that is right for you?

CHAPTER 10

Understanding Nutrition

"Nothing in excess, moderation is best in all things."

—a saying from ancient Greece

Your body needs food for life and good health. Eating the right kinds of foods in the right amounts helps you to look your best, feel your best, and perform at your best. Too much or too little of any major nutrient can have a negative effect on your growth and development, your resistance to disease, and even your life span. No one food provides all the nourishment you need to keep your body going. Eating a variety of foods is important to your health.

Foods come in many colors, textures, and flavors. Today a wide variety of foods can be found in the United States. Foods from around the world are available year-round in most supermarkets. Some people may eat Chinese-style food one day, Italian-style the next, and Mexican-style the following day. This variety not only makes eating enjoyable, but it also provides the opportunity for good nutrition, which is an important part of physical well-being.

BACKGROUND

Like many sayings common in our culture, this one is attributed to the Greeks of ancient times. Modern scholars have a list of 10 ancient Greeks who are thought to have promoted the wisdom of moderation.

SELF-ASSESSMENT

What nutritional choices do you make every day? Use the following checklist to take a closer look at your choices about food and nutrition. On a sheet of paper, or in your Wellness Journal, number from 1 to 10 and respond to the statements below by writing a *yes* for each statement that describes you all or most of the time. Write a *no* for those statements that do not describe you.

1. I eat a wide variety of foods and enjoy trying new foods.
2. I make a conscious effort to eat well-balanced meals.
3. I use what I know about food labels to carefully select foods.
4. I try to limit my eating of foods that I know are high in fat.
5. I include fruits and vegetables in my daily diet.
6. I try to eat a good breakfast each day.
7. I usually select snack foods that are low in fat and sugar.
8. I drink six to eight glasses of water each day.
9. I keep a record of the foods I eat in order to ensure that I eat a balanced diet.
10. I know what the daily requirements of fat, sodium, and calcium are for someone my age.

Review your responses and consider your strengths and your weaknesses. Save your personal checklist for a follow-up activity that appears at the end of the chapter.

NUTRIENTS THAT PROVIDE ENERGY

Nutrition is the process by which the body takes in and uses food. Foods that promote good nutrition contain **nutrients**, which are substances within foods that the body needs to work properly. There are six types of nutrients—carbohydrates, fats, proteins, vitamins, minerals, and water. Together they supply energy, promote growth and repair of body tissues, and regulate body functions. Each nutrient is important in one or more of these ways.

Carbohydrates, fats, and proteins provide energy and perform other important functions. You need energy for all activities, from riding a bike to taking a test to breathing and sleeping. When your body uses carbohydrates, fats, and proteins, energy is released. This energy is referred to as **Calories**. You may have learned about calories as a measure of heat energy in science class. A food *Calorie* is actually a kilocalorie, which is equal to 1,000 calories. It is written as Calorie, with a capital *C*. Calories are useful in comparing the energy available from different foods when you are deciding what foods to eat. For example, a small apple contains only 80 Calories, while a slice of apple pie contains almost 350 Calories.

CARBOHYDRATES

It's the night before the state championship swim meet. The boys' and girls' swim teams are having a pre-competition dinner with their coaches. Pasta with tomato sauce, thick slices of crisp Italian bread, and fresh vegetables are on the buffet table along with bananas and pineapple for dessert. The coaches chose this menu for the dinner because it is high in carbohydrates, the body's major source of energy. During the next day's meet, the swimmers will need all this energy to fuel their muscles.

Athletes are not the only people who need carbohydrates. Everyone needs them. **Carbohydrates** are the sugars and starches found in foods. They are made up of carbon, hydrogen, and oxygen. Dietary guidelines suggest that nearly 60 percent of your daily caloric intake should be from carbohydrates. There are two general types of carbohydrates—simple and complex.

Eating a meal rich in complex carbohydrates builds up energy needed for competition.

SIMPLE CARBOHYDRATES   The different forms of sugar, which are called simple carbohydrates, are easy for the body to process.

HOW MANY WAYS CAN YOU SAY SUGAR?

A List of Names and Descriptions of Various Forms of Sugar Often Found in Foods

Brown sugar	Crystals of molasses syrup
Confectioner's sugar	Finely ground sucrose
Corn syrup	Liquid made from cornstarch
Dextrose	Glucose or glucose and water
High fructose corn sweetener	Syrup made from cornstarch
Honey	Mixture produced by bees, made of fructose, glucose, and water
Invert sugar	Liquid made by breaking down sucrose
Maltose	Formed in the breakdown of starch especially in seeds from grains—sometimes called malt sugar
Maple sugar	Sap of sugar maple trees—made of sucrose, fructose, and glucose
Molasses	Residue from processing sugarcane or beet juice into sucrose crystals
Raw sugar	Residue from evaporating moisture from sugarcane juice

SOURCE: THE AMERICAN DIETETIC ASSOCIATION

Figure 10-1 Each of these items is a form of sugar. No one form is better for you than the others.

These sugars are fructose and glucose (found in fruits and vegetables), lactose (found in milk), and sucrose (found in sugarcane and sugar beet). Sucrose, the most common form of sugar, is refined, or purified, to produce table sugar. The most important sugar to the body is **glucose** [*GLOO kohs*]—the form of sugar that goes directly into the bloodstream and provides quick energy. All other sugars must be changed into glucose by the body before the cells can use them. The cells use glucose as their primary source of energy. Glucose that is not needed immediately is converted by the body to **glycogen,** a form of starch stored in the muscles and liver, or it is converted to and stored as body fat.

COMPLEX CARBOHYDRATES   Starches are complex carbohydrates that are made up of many units of glucose or other sugars, which form long chains. These chains must be broken down by the body into single units of glucose before they can be used. Starches take longer than sugars to be broken down into glucose. Therefore, starches provide energy to the body over longer periods than do simple sugars. Breads, cereals, pasta, and potatoes contain starch. They also contain other important substances such as protein, vitamins, minerals, and fiber.

Another complex carbohydrate is **dietary fiber,** which comes from the non-digestible part of plants. There are two types of dietary fiber: soluble and insoluble. Insoluble fiber absorbs water and helps to provide needed bulk to the diet. It is found in whole grains and the skins and seeds of fruits and vegetables. Soluble fiber combines with waste and other substances to assist in their removal from the body. It is found in oat bran, barley, beans, apples, carrots, and other vegetables.

FATS (LIPIDS)

The nutrients that contain the most concentrated form of energy are fats, which are a type of **lipid** [*LIP ud*]. Lipids are substances that are somewhat similar to carbohydrates, but they contain less oxygen and they do not dissolve in water.

Fat is one of the essential nutrients. To function well, your body needs at least a small daily intake of fat. One gram of fat provides more than twice as much energy as one gram of carbohydrate. Fats are part of many body tissues and are important as carriers of other nutrients, such as vitamins. Fats also carry the flavor of foods—making foods tastier. Because they are digested more slowly than other nutrients, they make you feel satisfied for a longer time. However, the consumption of fat should be monitored closely.

CONCERNS ABOUT FATS   Although fats are important nutrients, many people in the United States eat more fat than they really need. Current dietary guidelines suggest that no more than 25 to 30 percent of the daily caloric intake should come from fats. However, national studies show that people in the United States get nearly 40 percent of their Calories from fat. Most people are aware of the visible fats such as margarine, butter, and the fat on meats. But many other foods contain hidden or invisible fats. For example, cookies, pastries, nuts, cheese, and milk products all contain fat that isn't readily apparent. Figure 10-2 shows the percent of Calories from fat found in some common foods.

TYPES OF FATS   The major kinds of fats are saturated and unsaturated—terms that refer to the number of hydrogen atoms in the fat. Most foods contain combinations of these types of fat.

- **Saturated fats** are usually solid at room temperature. They contain the maximum number of hydrogen atoms. Butter, hydrogenated shortening, and animal fats tend to be high in saturated fats. Tropical oils such as coconut oil and palm oil are also high in saturated fat. These tropical oils are often used in commercially prepared products such as cookies, pastries, and whipped toppings. Studies have shown that a diet high in saturated fats can lead to an increased chance of heart and blood vessel disease, obesity, and some types of cancer.

- **Unsaturated fats** are those fats that are liquid at room temperature. Olive oil and peanut oil are called monounsaturated fats because they lack one pair of hydrogen atoms. Fish oils and most vegetable oils, such as corn, soybean, and sunflower oils, are called polyunsaturated fats because they lack two or more pairs of hydrogen atoms.

CHOLESTEROL   Eating foods high in fats, especially saturated fats, may increase the level of **cholesterol,** a waxy, fat-like substance produced by the body. Cholesterol is part of cell membranes and nerve tissues. It is also used by the body to form vitamin D and other hormones. Cholesterol is found *only* in foods that come from

"Percy the Pig"—300 pounds of lard—shows how much fat a family of four consumes in a year!

FOR YOUR INFORMATION

- There are 4 Calories in a gram of carbohydrate.
- There are 4 Calories in a gram of protein.
- There are 9 Calories in a gram of fat.

animals, such as butter, eggs, and meats. Although cholesterol is found in food, it is not an essential nutrient because the body produces cholesterol in the liver. As cholesterol levels in the body increase, the risk of heart and artery diseases increase. Some of the cholesterol tends to be deposited on the walls of the arteries, thereby reducing the flow of blood to the cells supplied by those arteries.

Cholesterol is transported in the blood in two forms. **LDL** is the "bad" form that tends to deposit cholesterol on the walls of the blood vessels. **HDL** is the "good" form that removes cholesterol from the cells and brings it back to the liver and intestines to be recycled or excreted. You should know your total cholesterol level and the ratio of LDL to HDL. Exercise has been proven to raise HDL. Low-fat diets lower LDL.

PROTEIN

Proteins are substances found in every cell. Muscles, skin, and organs such as the lungs and brain all contain protein. The body needs proteins to build and repair all body tissues. Protein is also an important part of red blood cells. Proteins are made up of carbon, hydrogen, oxygen, and nitrogen atoms that are formed into basic units called **amino acids**.

ESSENTIAL AMINO ACIDS   There are 20 different amino acids. Nine of them are considered essential amino acids—that is, they must be supplied in the foods you eat. The other eleven amino acids can be produced by your body.

Figure 10-2   Which foods in this graph contain a higher percentage of calories from fat than you had thought?

PERCENTAGE OF CALORIES FROM FAT IN COMMON FOODS

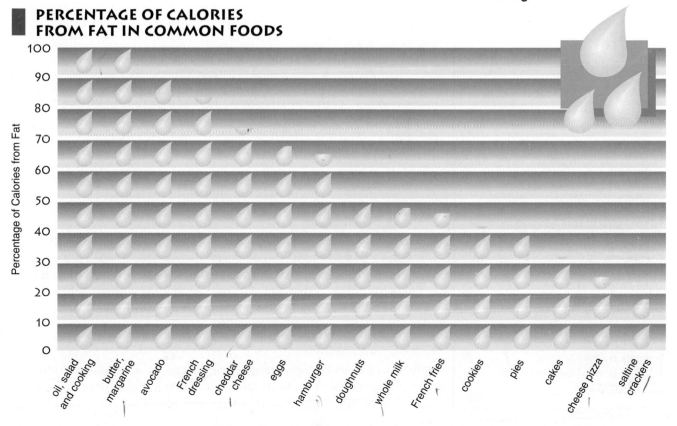

Ways to cut down on fat in your diet

- Bake, broil, poach, or steam foods.

- Eat more poultry and fish than red meat.

- Trim fat from meat; take skin off of poultry.

- Decrease portion sizes of meat and poultry or substitute with legumes.

- Use nonfat or low-fat dairy products.

- Use reduced-Calorie or oil-free salad dressings and mayonnaise.

- Use herbs, spices, and lemon juice to season foods instead of butter and cream sauces.

- Reduce saturated fat by using margarine and oils instead of butter.

- Limit foods with hidden fats.

- Eat less of foods with added fats such as sauces, gravies, and butter.

SUMMARY

Carbohydrates, fats, and proteins are the nutrients that provide the body with energy. Each of these nutrients also affects the body's use of other nutrients. Some carbohydrate, fat, and protein should be included in your daily diet. However, too much or too little of any of these nutrients can be harmful. It is important to eat an adequate amount of protein containing the nine essential amino acids and to eat in moderation foods that contain fat.

Proteins are classified according to whether or not they contain essential amino acids. Foods that contain complete protein are those that provide all the essential amino acids in the right amounts needed by the body. Complete proteins come from animal foods such as poultry, fish, eggs, meat, milk, and milk products. An incomplete protein lacks some of the essential amino acids. Vegetables and grains are examples of incomplete protein foods. **Legumes** [*LEG yooms*] are plants such as peas, beans, and peanuts that bear seeds in pods. Legumes are excellent non-animal sources of incomplete protein.

PROTEIN REQUIREMENTS You need to get all the essential amino acids daily and in the right amounts. Too little of even one essential amino acid can limit your body's use of other amino acids. If you eat foods with incomplete proteins, you can still obtain the proper amounts of all the essential amino acids by eating a mix of incomplete protein foods. Two examples of food combinations that combine incomplete proteins to provide the essential amino acids are beans and rice, and peanut butter on whole-wheat bread.

If you eat more protein than your body needs, the excess is broken down. Part is excreted through the kidneys as waste and the rest is converted to glucose and ends up stored as fat. The extra protein stored as fat is not needed by most people and can lead to an overweight condition.

Too little protein in the diet causes the body to use up its own protein, thereby weakening the muscles and organs. Similarly, when the body does not have enough carbohydrates, the body breaks down both stored fat and protein and changes them into glucose, robbing the body of protein it needs. This is one reason why diets that are extremely low in carbohydrates or Calories are dangerous. People who limit their food intake in order to avoid gaining weight must be careful that the foods that they select are a balance of all the nutrients needed to maintain good health.

LESSON 10.1 USING WHAT YOU HAVE LEARNED

REVIEW

1. What does *nutrition* mean?
2. Name the six classes of nutrients found in the foods we eat.
3. Why should a person eat complex carbohydrates?

CRITICAL THINKING

4. Why should there be a balance of carbohydrate, fat, and protein in one's daily foods?
5. Dietary guidelines suggest increasing the amount of complex carbohydrates in the diet and decreasing the amount of fats. Explain why following these recommendations can improve one's health.

APPLY IT TO YOURSELF

6. A few of your friends are planning to go on a weight-reduction diet that allows them to eat only fruit. What would you say to persuade them against using that diet plan?

NUTRIENTS THAT REGULATE

Vitamins, minerals, and water are not digested by your body. However, unlike carbohydrates, fats, and proteins, they do not provide Calories. Instead, vitamins, minerals, and water are released from the foods you eat and are absorbed by the body's tissues. They work with carbohydrates, fats, and proteins to promote growth and regulate body processes.

VITAMINS

Your ethnic background probably has a major influence on the foods you eat today. Staple foods of different cultures often can be traced back to ethnic homelands. The type of animals that were raised and the crops that could be grown in your ancestors' region determined what they ate. Those foods became a traditional part of your culture.

However, sometimes due to changes in their food supply, people suffered from mysterious diseases that did not respond to traditional treatment. While searching for the causes of these diseases, people noticed that eating certain foods cured some of them. These foods seemed to contain substances that prevented or cured the diseases. These substances were named *vitamines*—meaning a vital amine. Today, these substances are called vitamins and the diseases they prevent are known to be caused by vitamin deficiencies. A **deficiency** is having too little of a necessary substance. Figure 10-3 lists some diseases that develop because of a lack of a particular vitamin.

Vitamins are compounds found in living things and are needed in small amounts for life and growth and to prevent diseases. Vitamins help build bones and tissues. They also help change carbohydrates and fats into energy. Because the body cannot make most vitamins, they must be supplied by the foods you eat. Vitamins are classified into two groups. Figure 10-3 identifies the vitamins in each of these groups.

FAT-SOLUBLE VITAMINS   Fat-soluble vitamins dissolve in fat and can be stored in the body. They are found in oils, some green vegetables, whole milk, and eggs. Your body can actually manufacture vitamins A and D, but not without your help. When you eat foods high in a substance called beta-carotene, your body converts it to vitamin A. Beta-carotene is found in carrots, sweet potatoes, cantaloupe, and dark green leafy vegetables. Normal exposure to sunlight on your skin helps the body make vitamin D. Milk fortified with vitamin D is another important source of this vitamin.

WATER-SOLUBLE VITAMINS   Water-soluble vitamins dissolve in water. Because water-soluble vitamins are not stored by the body to any extent, foods rich in these vitamins must be eaten more

Various ethnic backgrounds have contributed to the diets of all Americans.

Vitamin	Sources	Functions in Body	Signs of Toxicity	Signs of Deficiency
FAT-SOLUBLE VITAMINS				
Vitamin A	Orange, yellow, red, and dark green vegetables, liver, fortified milk, margarine, and egg yolk	Maintains healthy eyes, skin; bone growth and tooth development; possible aid in cancer protection	Nausea, vomiting; dry skin, rashes, hair loss; headache, fatigue	Nightblindness, eye infections; rough skin; respiratory infections
Vitamin D	Fortified milk, eggs, liver, exposure of skin to sun's ultraviolet rays	Promotes absorption of phosphorus and calcium to build and maintain bones	Loss of appetite; headache, nausea, weakness, calcification of bone and soft tissue	Rickets (poor bone development), malformation of teeth
Vitamin E	Wheat germ, whole grains, vegetable oils, legumes, nuts, dark green leafy vegetables	Protects red blood cells; stabilizes cell membranes	General digestive discomfort	Rupture of red blood cells; anemia, nerve abnormalities
Vitamin K	Green leafy vegetables, kale, cabbage, liver; made in body by intestinal bacteria	Assists in normal clotting of blood	Anemia, jaundice	Slow clotting of blood, hemorrhage especially in newborns
WATER-SOLUBLE VITAMINS				
Thiamin (B₁)	Pork, legumes, whole-grain and enriched cereal products, liver, dark green vegetables	Aids in release of energy from food, promotes normal nerve functioning	Rapid pulse, weakness, headaches	Beriberi (inflamed nerves, heart failure); mental confusion; irritability, muscle weakness
Riboflavin (B₂)	Milk, eggs, liver, leafy green vegetables, whole-grain or enriched cereals	Essential for growth; releases energy from foods; supports normal vision and healthy skin	Unknown	Cracks at corners of mouth; scaling skin; sore tongue; sensitivity to light
Niacin	Legumes, fish, liver, whole grains or enriched grains and cereals	Important in energy metabolism; maintains healthy skin and nervous system	Liver dysfunction; flushed skin, especially on face	Pellagra; diarrhea; depression, mental confusion; mouth soreness; skin rashes
Vitamin B₆ (Pyridoxine)	Pork, poultry, fish, liver, eggs, green leafy vegetables, legumes, whole grains	Metabolism of fats and amino acids; helps in formation of red blood cells; promotes normal functioning of nerves	Nerve damage, fatigue, headache, difficulty in walking	Anemia; skin irritations; irritability; muscle twitching (nervous tics)
Folacin (Folic acid)	Leafy green vegetables, liver, yeast, whole grains, legumes	Important in the synthesis of proteins and red blood cells; helps prevent birth defects	Diarrhea; insomnia	Anemia; diarrhea; depression; fatigue; inflamed tongue
Vitamin B₁₂	Foods from animal sources (liver, meats, fish, poultry, eggs, milk, cheese)	Necessary for formation of red blood cells; maintains healthy functioning of nervous system	Unknown	Pernicious anemia; fatigue; degeneration of nervous system
Pantothenic acid	Widespread in most foods (liver, whole grains, legumes, nuts)	Release of energy from foods; synthesis of many body substances	Diarrhea; water retention	Weakness, fatigue; nausea, vomiting; susceptibility to infection
Biotin	Liver, dairy products, egg yolks, legumes, nuts, whole grains	Energy release; amino acid metabolism; fat and glycogen synthesis	Unknown	Skin disorders; weakness, fatigue; muscle pain
Vitamin C (Ascorbic acid)	Citrus fruits, cantaloupe, tomatoes, potatoes, strawberries, peppers, dark green vegetables	Promotes healthy gums and teeth; aids in iron absorption; aids in healing of wounds; maintains connective tissue	Diarrhea, nausea; dependency	Scurvy (slow healing wounds, bleeding gums, loose teeth); bruised skin; anemia

often than foods with fat-soluble vitamins. Fruits and vegetables are good sources of water-soluble vitamins.

Vitamin supplements are not necessary if you eat a variety of healthful foods each day. In fact, too much of some vitamins over a long time can be harmful to the body. For example, large amounts of vitamins A and D taken over a long period can be **toxic,** or poisonous. Figure 10-3 also identifies the symptoms of taking too much of some vitamins.

MINERALS

Minerals are simple substances found in the environment that are essential to the body's functioning. Table salt, for example, provides two minerals in the diet, sodium and chlorine. Minerals are used to regulate a wide range of body processes, from bone formation to blood clotting. They are also important to the body's structure. Most minerals are either quickly used or lost in waste products. Therefore, you must eat mineral-rich foods daily to replenish your supply. Iron is an exception—it tends to be kept and recycled by the body, except when there is blood loss. Figure 10-4 identifies many of the minerals the body needs.

MAJOR MINERALS   Your body requires larger amounts of some minerals than others. These major minerals include calcium, phosphorus, magnesium, potassium, sulfur, sodium, and chlorine.

Calcium keeps the nervous system working well and is needed for blood clotting. Together with sodium and potassium, calcium helps you maintain a normal heartbeat. Calcium and phosphorus provide strength and hardness to bones and teeth. Research indicates that a lack of calcium during the teenage years and early adulthood may result in a bone disease called **osteoporosis** later in life. This disease, which is characterized by very brittle bones, develops more commonly in older women and less frequently in older men. Consuming needed calcium and staying physically active throughout your lifetime can help prevent this bone disease in later years.

Sodium and potassium help regulate the passage of fluids in and out of cells. People rarely suffer from too little sodium in the diet. However, too much sodium in the diet may aggravate high blood pressure or **hypertension**, increasing the risk of heart attack, stroke, or kidney disease. Research studies have suggested that hypertension may be hereditary in many people. For example, hypertension often occurs in African-American families. People who are at risk for high blood pressure should be especially careful to limit their sodium intake. Table salt is one source of sodium in the diet. Most sodium we take in comes from foods. Processed foods such as canned or dried soups, soy sauce, and luncheon meats often contain large amounts of sodium. People who take medication for hypertension need to be careful to get enough potassium, because some medications may cause potassium to be

Vegetables are good sources of vitamins.

HEALTHY PEOPLE 2000

Decrease salt and sodium intake so at least 65 percent of home meal preparers prepare foods without adding salt, at least 80 percent of people avoid using salt at the table, and at least 40 percent of adults regularly purchase food modified or lower in sodium.

Objective 2.9
from *Healthy People 2000: National Health Promotion and Disease Prevention Objectives*

Figure 10-3   (opposite page) Folic acid may help prevent some cancers. What are good sources of folic acid?

lost from the body. A deficiency of potassium can lead to muscle weakness and abnormal heart beat.

TRACE MINERALS   The majority of the minerals needed for the body to function are only required in very small, or trace, amounts. These trace minerals include iron, iodine, manganese, zinc, copper, and fluorine.

Iron is a vital part of **hemoglobin** [*HEE muh gloh bun*]—a substance in red blood cells that carries oxygen to all parts of the body. Insufficient iron may cause **anemia**, a disease in which the body has either too few red blood cells or too little hemoglobin. As a result, too little oxygen is carried to the cells of the body. People with iron-deficiency anemia are pale, tend to feel weak, may tire quickly, exhibit shortness of breath, and may have a hard time concentrating. Girls and women need to be careful to eat iron-rich foods, especially if they are limiting their caloric intake.

Iodine is needed for the thyroid gland to function properly. The thyroid gland produces hormones that control how quickly chemical reactions occur in your body. Too little iodine causes the thyroid gland to enlarge. The sign of an enlarged thyroid gland is a swelling in the neck, a condition called a goiter. The primary sources of iodine in the diet are seafoods and iodized table salt.

Figure 10-4   Use the information in the table shown here to explain in what ways a person who stops using table salt can obtain enough iodine.

MINERALS

	Mineral	Sources	Functions in Body	Signs of Toxicity	Signs of Deficiency
MAJOR MINERALS	Calcium	Milk and milk products, sardines and salmon eaten with bones, bean curd, dark leafy green vegetables	Builds bones and teeth; blood clotting; muscle contraction; nerve impulse transmission	Excess blood calcium; urinary stones; constipation	Stunted growth; rickets; soft bones; osteoporosis; slow blood clotting; convulsions
	Phosphorus	Found in most foods, especially milk, egg yolk, meat, poultry, fish, whole-grain cereals, legumes, carbonated soft drinks	Part of every cell; bone and tooth development; energy transfer; helps maintain acid-base balance	Draws calcium out of bones; muscle spasms; lowers blood calcium level	Deficiency usually does not occur
	Magnesium	Whole grains, milk, dark leafy green vegetables, nuts, legumes	Aids in bone growth; energy metabolism; protein metabolism; muscle contraction	Rare except in the case of people taking medication containing magnesium	Growth failure in children; mental and muscular disorders
	Sodium	Salt, soy sauce, processed foods, dairy products, cured meats	Regulates water balance outside cells; transmission of nerve impulses	Hypertension; edema	Muscle cramps; weakness; nausea; dehydration
	Potassium	Meat, milk, legumes, vegetables and fruits—especially potatoes, bananas, oranges, dried fruits	Maintains fluid balance; necessary for contraction of muscles and heartbeat; transmission of nerve impulses	Muscular weakness; respiratory failure; abnormal heartbeat	Muscular weakness; paralysis and confusion; can cause death
	Sulfur	All protein foods	Protein and amino acid metabolism; detoxification of body fluids	Unknown	Unknown
	Chlorine	Table salt; processed foods	Aids in digestion	Unknown	Stunted growth; muscle cramps

WATER

Water is your most abundant nutrient. It is found in every cell, in the spaces around the cells, in the fluid tissues of the body, and in body cavities. Water carries dissolved nutrients throughout your body and assists in all of its functions. These functions include digesting foods, removing wastes, regulating your temperature, and cushioning sensitive parts of your body, such as your brain.

Each day you lose two to three quarts of water when you urinate, perspire, and breathe. If this water is not replaced, you face the risk of **dehydration**—the loss of water from body tissues. Dehydration weakens the body and may cause muscle cramps. Severe dehydration can cause death.

When minerals are dissolved in your body, they break apart into charged particles called ions. For example, table salt in water breaks into two ions, a positively charged sodium ion and a negatively charged chloride ion. The ions formed in body fluids are called **electrolytes**. These ions play a central role in water balance in the body. The body's electrolytes help control the flow of water into and out of cells, and from the blood and other tissues to the cells and spaces around cells. The kidneys help keep the body's total electrolyte content in balance. A person who eats more table

FOR YOUR INFORMATION

Your intake of iron can be increased by cooking foods such as spaghetti sauce in cast-iron pans. Some of the iron on the pan's surface is removed by the acid in the food and absorbed by the food that you eventually eat.

◆ MINERALS

	Mineral	Sources	Functions in Body	Signs of Toxicity	Signs of Deficiency
TRACE MINERALS	Iron	Red meats, liver, whole-grain and enriched cereals and breads, dark leafy green vegetables, dried fruits, legumes, dark molasses	Formation of red blood cells; helps transport oxygen	Liver dysfunction	Anemia: fatigue, weakness, paleness of skin, reduced resistance to infection, inability to concentrate
	Iodine	Iodized table salt, seafood, seaweed food products, vegetables grown in iodine-rich soils	Assists in function of the thyroid gland which regulates growth and metabolic rate	Enlarged thyroid	Goiter; cretinism
	Zinc	Seafood, meats, liver, poultry, whole grains	Formation of enzymes; aids in wound healing; promotes normal growth and development; helps in taste and odor perception	Vomiting; loss of copper from body; interference with absorption of copper; impaired immune response	Growth retardation; delayed wound healing; poor taste sensitivity; loss of appetite
	Copper	Shellfish, liver, nuts and seeds	Formation of red blood cells; aids in absorption of iron; production of several enzymes	Rare	Anemia; bone and nerve disorders; change in structure and color of hair
	Fluorine	Fluoridated drinking water, seafood, tea	Strengthens bones and teeth	Mottled teeth	Increased dental decay
	Manganese	Whole grains, vegetables, tea	Component of enzymes; important in brain function; maintains bone structure	Rare	Poor growth; nervous system disorders; reproductive abnormalities
	Selenium	Fish, shellfish, liver, meats, milk, eggs, grain	Part of an enzyme that works with vitamin E to prevent cell damage	Digestive system disorders; fingernail changes; hair loss	Rare

Drinking water before, during, and after competition is essential for top performance.

salt than his or her body needs, for example, will get rid of the excess sodium and chloride ions in the urine.

Thirst, or the desire to drink fluids, usually determines your fluid intake. Under normal conditions, you should drink at least six to eight large glasses of water each day. Beverages, soups, and water in foods help you meet this requirement. During very hot weather, while exercising, or when involved in any strenuous activity, you will need to increase your fluid intake beyond the level of your thirst in order to replace water loss.

More water than normal is lost through diarrhea and vomiting. If either condition lasts for a long period, or when children have these conditions, medical help should be sought. In severe cases of diarrhea and vomiting, and in other medical emergencies, both water and electrolytes must be monitored and replaced.

SUMMARY

Vitamins, minerals, and water are nutrients that work with the energy-providing nutrients to be sure that the body functions properly. Water is the most vital nutrient because it provides the means for all other nutrients to be carried throughout your body. Eating a variety of foods in the right amounts is usually all that is needed to get your daily supply of vitamins and minerals.

LESSON 10.2 ## USING WHAT YOU HAVE LEARNED

REVIEW

1. What is the main difference between fat-soluble vitamins and water-soluble vitamins?
2. In what ways can you be sure to get enough iodine?
3. Why is water so important in the body?

CRITICAL THINKING

4. What are some things you can do now to help prevent osteoporosis later?
5. Very few foods contain vitamin D, therefore, most milk has been fortified with vitamin D. Why do you think milk was chosen for fortification?

APPLY IT TO YOURSELF

6. Defend this statement as it applies to your dietary need for vitamins and minerals: "If a little is good, a lot is not better."

A HEALTHY DIET

If you live to be 100 years old, you will have eaten about one hundred and ten thousand meals. That's about 1,100 per year, not including snacks. Is it any wonder that what you choose to eat can become almost automatic? Good nutrition, however, is not automatic. It involves selecting a variety of foods, following good health guidelines, and eating only what your age and activity levels require. What you eat each day should provide enough of all the nutrients that are needed for your growth and activities.

THE FOOD GROUPS

In Lesson 2, you read that food choices from an ethnic homeland were determined by what people could farm or catch. Knowing what to eat was easy then; people simply ate what was available. Today there are many choices. It is not always easy to choose, and sometimes you may not be certain if you are making healthy choices. Nutritionists provide guidelines for making food choices by grouping foods and recommending a number of servings from each group. In 1992, the United States Department of Agriculture (USDA) issued the *Food Guide Pyramid* to go along with the

MAIN IDEAS

CONCEPTS

✔ It is important to select a variety of foods each day.

✔ Using The Dietary Guidelines for Americans can help you make the right food choices for your daily needs.

✔ Snacks are often an important part of the daily diet.

✔ What you eat now may help prevent cancer and heart disease in later years.

✔ You can eat a well-balanced meal at fast food restaurants.

VOCABULARY

vegetarian
complementary proteins

Figure 10-5 What is the purpose of the Food Guide Pyramid?

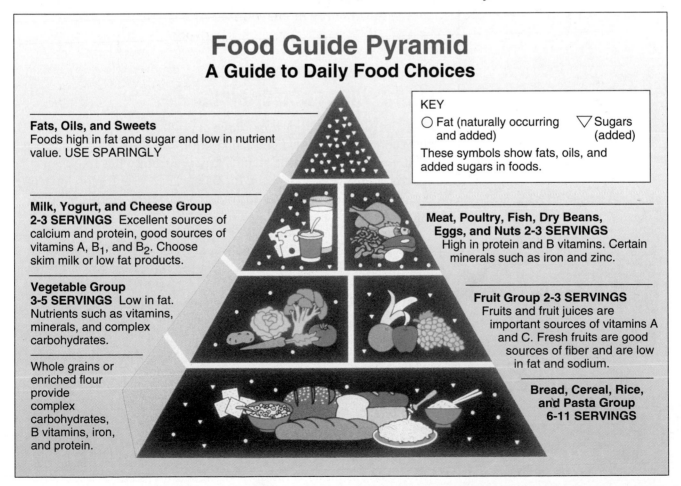

Food Guide Pyramid
A Guide to Daily Food Choices

Fats, Oils, and Sweets
Foods high in fat and sugar and low in nutrient value. USE SPARINGLY

KEY
○ Fat (naturally occurring and added)   ▽ Sugars (added)
These symbols show fats, oils, and added sugars in foods.

Milk, Yogurt, and Cheese Group
2-3 SERVINGS Excellent sources of calcium and protein, good sources of vitamins A, B$_1$, and B$_2$. Choose skim milk or low fat products.

Meat, Poultry, Fish, Dry Beans, Eggs, and Nuts 2-3 SERVINGS
High in protein and B vitamins. Certain minerals such as iron and zinc.

Vegetable Group
3-5 SERVINGS Low in fat. Nutrients such as vitamins, minerals, and complex carbohydrates.

Fruit Group 2-3 SERVINGS
Fruits and fruit juices are important sources of vitamins A and C. Fresh fruits are good sources of fiber and are low in fat and sodium.

Whole grains or enriched flour provide complex carbohydrates, B vitamins, iron, and protein.

Bread, Cereal, Rice, and Pasta Group
6-11 SERVINGS

SOURCE: United States Department of Agriculture

Dietary Guidelines for Americans. The pyramid is made up of six sections. Nutritious foods are divided into five of the six groups and arranged in the pyramid according to the number of servings needed daily. No one group is more important than another in maintaining good health. Fats, oils, and sweets are placed at the tip of the pyramid to emphasize how little you need of them. They should be used only sparingly.

Foods containing ingredients from two or more food groups are called combination foods. There are many combination foods that provide both Calories and good nutrition. For example, chicken chow mein, beef tacos, pizza, and sukiyaki are combination foods that are good nutrient sources.

DIETARY GUIDELINES FOR AMERICANS

There is a strong relationship between what you eat and your health—not only for today, but in the future as well. Selecting a well-balanced diet is important, but not always easy. The USDA's Dietary Guidelines for eating a balanced diet can help.

1. Eat a variety of foods.
2. Maintain a healthy weight.
3. Choose a diet low in fat, saturated fat, and cholesterol.
4. Choose a diet with plenty of vegetables, fruits, and grain products.
5. Use sugars only in moderation.
6. Use salt and sodium only in moderation.

MAKING WISE FOOD CHOICES

When you skip a meal or don't have enough to eat, do you feel lightheaded or shaky? Do you feel anxious or cranky? The feelings that you get are warning signals that your body has not been given enough fuel. Skipping meals because you are too busy or because you are trying to limit your intake of Calories is not a good health practice and usually results in overeating at the next meal. The human body is a wonderful machine, but it needs the proper care to function at its peak. Part of proper care is eating the right kinds of foods at the right times.

AN IMPORTANT MEAL   Breakfast is the meal most often missed, yet research suggests that it is a very important meal. At breakfast time, the body has gone 12 to 14 hours without food. Breakfast can provide you with necessary nutrients that will be used throughout the day. Eating a good breakfast also reduces irritability, decreases nervousness, and provides you with energy that enables you to do better in school.

A well-balanced breakfast might include a glass of orange juice, a bowl of cereal or 2 slices of whole-grain toast, and a glass of milk. A breakfast shake or some other breakfast foods

Get a good start for the day by eating a healthy breakfast.

may be more appealing. They are fine as long as they supply essential nutrients. If you miss essential nutrients at one meal, you need to make them up with a well-chosen snack or at the next meal.

NON-NUTRITIVE SUBSTANCES

Some foods and beverages contain substances that provide no nutrition and are not considered nutrients. Some of these are:

- *Caffeine* Coffee, tea, chocolate, and some soft drinks contain the stimulant caffeine. A stimulant is a drug that speeds up the body's mental or physical activities. While some people enjoy moderate amounts of caffeine, it often produces undesirable side effects in other people. These side effects may include feelings of nervousness, edginess, irritability, and hyperactivity.

- *Artificial sweeteners* Originally developed for people with diabetes, artificial sweeteners have grown in popularity among weight-conscious people. Several studies have shown that the use of artificial sweeteners does not directly result in weight loss. The safety and effects of long-term use of these substances remain controversial.

- *Alcohol* Although Calories are released when the body metabolizes it, alcohol is not a nutrient. Alcohol contains empty Calories and can prevent the body from burning Calories that should be burned.

- *Fat substitutes* In 1990, fat substitutes came into use in frozen desserts and other food products that are not heated. Fat substitutes contain no cholesterol, and may help those people needing to cut down on fat and cholesterol. Concern has grown about the effects on the body of these substances over a long time. Also, people may simply eat more of these fat-like foods instead of following the Dietary Guidelines for Americans.

1 slice of bread; 1 oz of ready-to-eat cereal; 1/2 cup of cooked cereal, rice, or pasta

1 cup of raw leafy vegetables; 1/2 cup of other vegetables, cooked or chopped raw; 3/4 cup of vegetable juice

1 medium apple, banana, orange; 1/2 cup of chopped, cooked, or canned fruit; 3/4 cup of fruit juice

1 cup of milk or yogurt; 1½ oz of natural cheese; 2 oz of processed cheese

2-3 oz of cooked lean meat, poultry, or fish; 1/2 cup of cooked dry beans; 1 egg or 2 tbs of peanut butter count as 1 oz of lean meat

Source: The United States Department of Agriculture

Figure 10-6   What is considered a serving?

SNACKING   Snacks can play an important role in your daily diet, especially during your teenage years when your body has high nutritional needs. Select nutrient-dense foods—foods that are high in complex carbohydrates, vitamins, and minerals and low in fat, sugar, and salt. Nutrient-dense foods may come from the five food groups below the top of the Food Guide Pyramid. Good snack choices are whole-grain breads, cereals, low-fat yogurt, fruits and raw vegetables, popcorn without butter and salt, and pretzels without salt. Poor snack choices are chocolate, potato chips, pastries, and cola drinks.

Snacking is not unhealthy as long as the foods you eat are nutrient-dense.

Figure 10-7   Using the table shown here of typical fast foods, choose a meal that is nutrient-dense yet low in fat and sodium.

VEGETARIAN DIETS   For a variety of reasons, some people choose to limit or completely eliminate certain foods from their diets. People who choose to eat no animal foods are **vegetarians.** There are several types of vegetarians.

- *Vegans,* or strict vegetarians, eat no animal foods of any kind.
- *Semi-vegetarians* eat fish, poultry, eggs, and dairy products but avoid red meat.
- *Lacto-ovo vegetarians* eat eggs, milk, and milk products but do not eat red meat, fish, and poultry.

A vegetarian diet is healthy as long as it contains all the essential nutrients. Vegetarians need to eat **complementary proteins**—a mixture of two or more sources of incomplete proteins that provides all the essential amino acids. Selecting complementary proteins is especially important for children and teenagers who follow vegetarian diets, because the amount of protein needed during rapid growth is higher than at other stages of life. Young people also need to make sure they are getting enough Calories to meet all their energy needs. Strict vegetarians will have to use supplements in order to get enough vitamin B_{12}, which is found only in animal products.

A well-planned vegetarian diet can be an excellent diet. Because they consume less fat overall, vegetarians are less likely to be overweight or to suffer from diseases linked to high fat consumption.

FAST FOOD COMPARISON

Food	Calories	Total Fat (g)	% Calories from Fat	Sodium (mg)
Hamburger patty on bun	260	9.5	32	500
1/4 lb Hamburger patty with cheese, lettuce, tomato, and sauce on a bun	520	29	50	1150
French fries	220	12	49	110
Fried chicken breast on bun	490	29	53	780
Chef's salad with strips of ham, turkey, and sliced egg	230	13	51	490
Garden salad	110	7	57	160
Croutons	50	2	36	140
Blue cheese dressing	70	7	90	150
Lite vinaigrette dressing	15	0.5	30	75
Chocolate shake	390	11	25	240
Low-fat milk	120	11	35	130
Orange juice	80	0	0	0

* Quantities are for one average size serving

SOURCE: McDonald's Corporation, 1989

Culture, Diet, and Disease

More and more people today are concerned about the food that they eat and its effects on good health. The emphasis has shifted from eating foods rich in fat and cholesterol to eating foods that are fresh and high in fiber. Some of the information available about healthy foods is a result of research about the relationships between diet and health in different cultures.

Heart disease and cholesterol problems are infrequent in many of the countries of Asia—China, Japan, Cambodia, Thailand, and Indonesia. The regular diets in most of these countries do not include excessive amounts of meat, refined sugar, or fats. Instead they are characterized by fresh fish and vegetables and foods high in fiber like fruit and whole grains.

Researchers have found that Americans are beginning to enjoy the tastes of many Asian cultures and are adopting their healthier eating habits. However, some American foods are also being adopted in other cultures! It is not surprising to discover that heart disease is on the rise among people who are introducing fatty foods into their diets.

FAST FOODS Fast foods are a part of modern society. Some fast-food restaurants specialize in foods such as chicken, pizza, or hamburgers. While meals from these restaurants provide protein and may be adequate in most B vitamins, they often contain a lot of fat. Fast-food meals also tend to be low in calcium, vitamin A, and folic acid. Deep-fat fried foods such as french fries and onion rings are high in fat and sodium. In fact, the sodium content of many fast-food meals is too high.

It is possible to eat a balanced meal at a fast-food restaurant if you use the information you have learned about nutrition. When ordering food, try coleslaw or a salad instead of french fries. Order milk instead of a soft drink. Take advantage of the salad bar offered in many places. No matter where you go, it is possible to eat a well-balanced meal if you choose foods wisely.

LESSON 10.3 USING WHAT YOU HAVE LEARNED

REVIEW

1. Identify the six food groups included in the *Food Guide Pyramid*. From which group is it suggested you eat the most servings per day?
2. Name three snacks that are low in fat.
3. What can vegetarians do to ensure that they obtain the proper nutrients?

CRITICAL THINKING

4. Why are fruits and vegetables so important in your diet today and possibly in future?
5. What danger comes from skipping a meal or meals?

APPLY IT TO YOURSELF

6. Using the Food Guide Pyramid, plan a day's menu for yourself that would meet the minimum daily requirements from each group. List specific foods and amounts for each meal or snack.

SUMMARY

Good nutrition means eating a wide variety of foods in moderation each day. Snacks are an important part of your diet but they need to be selected carefully. Following the USDA's Food Guide Pyramid and the Dietary Guidelines makes it easy for anyone to have a well-balanced, healthful diet.

David Kessler

David Kessler believes that change should begin at the top. In February of 1991, when he was appointed head of the Food and Drug Administration (FDA), Kessler weighed 205 pounds and he rarely exercised. Today, he weighs 140 pounds and runs for at least 30 minutes a day.

Kessler's personal transformation was not the only change he made. In his position as head of the influential FDA, Kessler began to wage a battle against food manufacturers who were misleading the public. Foods labeled with *lite, healthy, no cholesterol, only one Calorie,* and *low-sodium,* among other claims, were lulling consumers into a false sense of fat-free, low-salt security. In reality, many of these foods contained more fat and salt than their regular counterparts. Many experts, including Kessler, felt that deceptive labeling was hurting consumers. Diabetics and patients advised to cut salt intake rely on the honesty of food manufacturers as they make their dietary decisions. But instead of helping people make healthy decisions, dishonest labeling was jeopardizing the health of some people and costing Americans millions of dollars in unnecessary health care.

Kessler's interest in health did not begin with his appointment as head of the FDA. As a graduate of both the Harvard Law School and the Harvard Medical School (degrees he earned at the same time), Kessler worked double-time to ensure the health of those around him. A specialist in pediatrics, Kessler did his residency by night at Johns Hopkins Hospital in Baltimore, Maryland. During the day, he worked as a consultant on food and drug legislation for the director of the Labor and Human Resources Committee in Washington, D.C. By the late 1980s, Kessler had become aware of what he thought might be major problems in the FDA. In 1991,

when he became head of the Food and Drug Administration, his first battle was to challenge food manufacturers on their labeling practices. Kessler soon earned the title "Eliot Knessler," after the FBI prohibition enforcer, Eliot Ness, portrayed in an old television series, *The Untouchables.*

The list of food labeling offenders was huge and the task monumental. But Kessler, along with a team of over 8,000 employees, set up a plan with three phases that requires food manufacturers to accurately state the contents of their products.

- Phase I, begun early in 1991, requires nutritional content labels for fresh products such as fruits, meats, and vegetables. Distributors are not required to place the labels on the products. Instead, the contents can be posted on a counter or wall near the place where the products are sold.

- Phase II, started in the fall of 1991, requires labels to mean exactly what they say.

- Phase III, begun in 1992, provides standard definitions for such labels as *high-fiber* and *low-Calorie.* These changes will not happen overnight, and there surely will be court battles by manufacturers trying to prove that their products are labeled properly. But manufacturers will adopt standard labels.

The relabeling of food products, including fruits and vegetables, is expected to cost manufacturers close to $600 million during the next two decades. However, the labeling reforms are expected to help all Americans maintain better control over their diets. In the long run, these reforms could reduce health-care costs by billions of dollars. David Kessler's work may well result in a healthier America.

1. In what ways do you think David Kessler's work will result in a healthier America?

2. How do you think David Kessler's work might directly affect your life?

IDENTIFYING NUTRITIOUS FOODS

Applying what you know about nutrition when you purchase food is not always easy because there is so much information that must be considered. Food labels can help you make good choices if you know how to read and understand them.

FOOD LABELING

Imagine a grocery store full of products covered with blank labels and marked with only a price. How would you know what you were buying? Fortunately, food products are labeled. The labels give you a variety of information about what you are buying.

PRODUCT IDENTIFICATION   The Food and Drug Administration (FDA) regulates the labeling of foods. To identify food products, the FDA requires that the following information be listed somewhere on the package.

- The name of the product, which must state the predominant food first. For example, a product labeled *Beef and Gravy* has more meat than a product labeled *Gravy with Sliced Beef.*
- The style, or the form of the product, such as *sliced* peaches, *whole kernel* corn, or *peeled, ground* tomatoes.
- The name and address of the manufacturer.
- The net weight, or weight of the contents only.

INGREDIENTS   The FDA requires that ingredients in a product must be listed in descending order by weight. Before this requirement became law, some foods such as catsup, mayonnaise, and peanut butter had a *standard of identity*. The FDA required each of these types of food to contain specific amounts of certain ingredients, but the individual ingredients did not have to be listed on the label. This situation caused problems for people with allergies to certain substances or who wanted to avoid eating certain foods.

NUTRITIONAL INFORMATION   Nutritional labeling first appeared on foods only when a nutrient was added to a food or a nutritional claim was made. To help consumers, some manufacturers voluntarily listed nutritional information such as the number of Calories and the amounts of other nutrients such as carbohydrates, protein, fat, and certain vitamins and minerals contained in the food.

FOOD ADDITIVES   When you look at a food label, you may notice some long chemical names. Many are names of food **additives,** substances added to food to improve nutritional value, maintain freshness, or improve a food's appearance, texture, or taste. The most common food additives are sugar, salt, and corn syrup. Others are citric acid, mustard, baking soda, and pepper. Food additives can be classified in the following ways.

MAIN IDEAS

CONCEPTS
✔ Nutrition knowledge can help you make good decisions when buying foods.

✔ Food labels contain valuable nutritional information to help you select your foods.

✔ Food additives commonly are used in many foods.

✔ Advertising and marketing strategies can greatly affect your purchase of foods.

VOCABULARY
additive

Figure 10-8 Nutrition panels have four sections. How have the new labeling guidelines helped consumers?

Nutrition Facts
Serving Size 1/2 cup (114g)
Servings Per Container 4

Amount per serving	
Calories 260	Calories from fat 120

} 1

	% Daily Value *
Total Fat 13g	**20%**
Saturated Fat 5g	**25%**
Cholesterol 30mg	**10%**
Sodium 660mg	**28%**
Total Carbohydrate 31g	**11%**
Sugars 5g	**
Dietary Fiber 0g	**0%**
Protein 5g	**

} 2

Vitamin A 4% • Vitamin C 2% • Calcium 15% • Iron 4%

} 3

* Percents (%) of a Daily Value are based on a 2,000 calorie diet. Your Daily Values may vary higher or lower depending on your calorie needs:

Nutrient		2,000 Calories	2,500 Calories
Total Fat	Less than	65g	80g
Sat Fat	Less than	20g	25g
Cholesterol	Less than	300mg	300mg
Sodium	Less than	2,400mg	2,400mg
Total Carbohydrate		300g	375g
Fiber		25g	30g

} 4

1g Fat = 9 calories
1g Carbohydrates = 4 calories
1g Protein = 4 calories

SOURCE: Health and Human Services Department

- *Preservatives* are additives that prevent food from spoiling. For example, salt is a preservative added to hams and pickles to prevent growth of molds and bacteria. Calcium propionate prevents the growth of mold in bread.

- *Enriched* foods are those that have nutrients added to help replace those that were lost during processing. For example, niacin, thiamine, riboflavin, and iron are added to enrich flours and cereals.

- *Fortified* foods are those that have vitamins and minerals added that are not naturally present. For example, milk is usually fortified with vitamin D.

- *Emulsifiers* are substances that make foods smooth. Ice cream and peanut butter often have emulsifiers added to them.

- *Leavening agents* are substances such as baking soda that make breads and cakes rise.

Over 2,800 additives have been approved by the FDA for use in the United States. In most cases, additives are not harmful. However, some people are sensitive to certain chemicals and may have allergic or even toxic reactions to some additives. Therefore, it is important for consumers to read food labels carefully.

PRODUCT DATING   Dates on foods help consumers determine the freshness of perishable packaged products. Various forms of product dating, called open dating, are used:

- *Freshness date*   Often found on baked goods. This date tells the last day a product should be used to ensure peak quality.

- *Sell or pull date*   The last date a product should be sold. The product will continue to be usable for its typical use period after purchase.

- *Expiration date*   Foods eaten after this date may no longer be flavorful, or they may be dangerous to your health.

It is important that you know the meaning of each kind of dating, and that you handle and store food properly after purchase.

LABELING REFORMS

In 1990 the FDA and the USDA began a major reform to make food labels more accurate and consumer-friendly. By 1993 new regulations were in place. In announcing the changes, health officials said that the new label's purpose was "to help consumers select healthier diets." The labeling changes addressed four main areas: serving size, nutrition labeling, descriptive terms, and health claims. Two of these changes directly affected the information provided on the nutrition panel. A sample nutrition panel is shown in Figure 10-8.

SERVING SIZE   Determining serving sizes is an area that was often confusing or misleading when reading food labels. In the past, serving size was determined by the manufacturer. Nutrition labels

Getting the Best Buy

When comparing two different food products, the one that is nutrient-rich, lower in fat and sodium, fresher, and which has undergone less processing probably should be your choice. However, cost and convenience also are important factors.

You can check product costs by comparing the net weight and the unit price. The unit price is the cost per unit of measure, usually expressed in pounds or ounces. When comparing products' unit prices, make sure that the units you are comparing are the same. Remember that the cheapest food may not be the best bargain nutritionally, nor is the most expensive item better because it costs more.

Convenience also may matter when selecting foods. For example, a person with very little time to prepare a meal may choose to use canned vegetables instead of fresh vegetables, or pieces of boneless chicken instead of using the whole chicken. Although fresh vegetables may provide more nutrients than canned vegetables and the whole chicken may be less costly than boneless pieces, the preparation time may make them inconvenient to use.

Be a healthy consumer. Be aware of the dietary guidelines, read labels carefully, and compare prices before making a purchase. Knowing what you are getting is important to good health.

today have a standard serving size that is determined by the FDA. The serving size of a product reflects an accurate estimate of what people eat. It must be given in measures common in households in the United States, as well as in metric measures.

NUTRITION LABELING   The law requires nutrition labeling on all processed foods that are sources of nutrients. The nutritional information on the nutrition panel is separated into four key sections.

1 *Calories*   The number of Calories in one serving must be identified, as well as the amount of the Calories in one serving that come directly from fat.

2 *Percentage of daily recommended consumption*   Manufacturers of products must provide information about the amount of total fat, cholesterol, sodium, and carbohydrates, among other elements. This information identifies the percentage of recommended daily amounts for each item. The percentages are based on a 2,000 Calorie-per-day diet.

3 *Vitamins and Minerals*   The percentage of daily requirements for selected vitamins and minerals must be included.

4 *Recommended amounts*   A reminder of the recommended daily amounts of each item is included. This information is shown for the daily caloric recommendations for women (2,000) and men (2,500).

Changes in the other two areas of concern standardized the claims that can be made about a product.

DESCRIPTIVE TERMS   Products are designed to get your attention. Brightly colored boxes and package designs grab your eye. Words or phrases on the package may imply that the food in the package has a certain health benefit. Words or phrases such as *Fortified!* or *No Cholesterol!* capitalize on the public's health concerns.

The FDA has identified nine basic terms that can be used only to indicate specific information about certain nutrients in the

Products marked with special labeling cannot have the nutritional value of their ingredients misrepresented.

Food labels provides information that can help you plan and serve nutritious meals.

SUMMARY

Reading and understanding the information on food labels is important. The FDA and the USDA have taken steps to ensure that consumers get the right information. When making food choices, nutritional needs must be considered carefully along with cost and convenience.

product. These terms are *low, high, free, source of, reduced, light (lite), less, more,* and *fresh.* For example, if *light* is used on the label of ham that has 50 percent less sodium than it used to have, it must be labeled *light in sodium.* Therefore, a consumer cannot interpret the label as meaning that the product has less fat.

HEALTH CLAIMS Labels can make health claims if the product contains certain nutrients that have been proven to affect health conditions. As research continues into the relationships between certain foods and diseases, more claims may be allowed. Health claims presently allowed are those that cite relationships between:

- calcium and osteoporosis
- sodium and hypertension
- fat and heart diseases; fat and cancer
- fiber-containing foods and cancer; fiber-containing foods and heart disease

The food labeling reforms were intended to help consumers make better food choices.

Isaac wanted a good snack food he could eat on the run. In the supermarket, he bought a box of granola bars made with honey and oats. "Oats are nutritious and honey is better for you than refined sugar," he thought. At home, when he read the food label he saw that honey was not the only form of sugar in the bars. Also, the low fiber content indicated that the oats were not whole rolled oats. Isaac was really discouraged when he noted that about 40 percent of the Calories in one bar were from fat. The bars turned out to be less nutritious than he had thought. Isaac decided to return the bars and look more carefully for a healthy snack. "This time," he thought, "I'll read the label before I buy the product."

LESSON 10.4 USING WHAT YOU HAVE LEARNED

REVIEW

1. List four things that are required on a food label.
2. Explain the difference between *enriched* and *fortified.*

CRITICAL THINKING

3. Many food products have a date marked on them. How does that date help consumers make healthy purchases?
4. Labels often provide more than just the required information. Design a label for a box of cereal. Place an asterisk (*) beside the information that is required by law. Include any other information that will make the label helpful to consumers.

APPLY IT TO YOURSELF

5. As an adult, you probably will shop for food more often than you do now. Select items for a day's menu. For those items that are prepared foods, examine the food labels and compare the nutritional information on them with the nutritional information on substitute products. Compare the unit costs.

Diet Change

Vikki was on the cross-country team, and she was being very careful about what she ate. Vikki wanted to eat well-balanced, healthy meals that would help her maintain her energy and strength. She knew such a diet consisted of a lot of fresh vegetables and fruit, carbohydrates, and protein. She also knew that she needed to go easy on the fats and sweets—a task that wouldn't be easy.

Dinnertime at Vikki's house was always fun. Her father and stepmother loved to cook. They were always trying something new. However, Vikki's family was truly a meat-and-potatoes crowd. Dinner usually included a heavy meat dish, potatoes, and one vegetable. But even the vegetable was usually dripping in butter. There was almost always something rich for dessert.

Vikki had always enjoyed eating with her family. But now she worried that her family's diet was too high in fat. She was concerned that the diet was not quite the right eating plan to help her maintain her energy for cross-country. Her awareness of her own diet also made her think about the unhealthy eating patterns of her family. Vikki wondered how she could change her family's diet so that everyone would benefit.

PAUSE AND CONSIDER

1. **Identify the Problem.** What is Vikki's dilemma?

2. **Consider the Options.** What are some of the choices Vikki has that would meet her needs for a balanced diet and still please her family?

3. **Evaluate the Outcomes.** What might happen if Vikki does not eat meals with her family? What could happen if she continues to eat the meals prepared by her parents?

Vikki decided to ask her parents to help her with her diet. She explained to them that she needed to reduce her fat consumption in order to stay lean and competitive. Vikki challenged her parents to find new recipes that were low in fat.

Vikki knew that her family's eating habits would not change overnight. She understood that changing a lifetime of eating takes time and a gradual introduction to new foods. Vikki offered to help plan and shop for meals. She told her parents that she wanted to help prepare some meals.

While preparing the meals, Vikki would offer some ideas to cut down on fats, such as using a non-stick spray for frying and using lemon juice on the vegetables instead of butter. She introduced her family to several pasta and vegetable dishes. For a birthday present, Vikki gave her father a cookbook about easy preparation of

nutritious meals. Six months later, Vikki's family was enjoying a wider variety of foods than ever before.

DECIDE AND REVIEW

4. **Decide and Act.** What decision did Vikki make to meet her needs for a well-balanced eating plan?

5. **Review.** How else might Vikki have solved her nutritional dilemma? What consequences could those choices have had on the rest of her family? How would you go about helping your family members change some of their eating habits?

PROJECTS

1. If your school has food-vending machines, a snack bar, or both, take a look at the food choices that are offered. Make a chart of the selections offered and put together balanced combinations of the foods. If balanced combinations are not possible, what would you change in the selections offered? Consider asking the student council and school administration that your recommendations be put into effect.

2. Practice your label-reading skills by comparing the nutritional information of two different brands of a particular food, such as whole wheat bread, a box of cereal, or a can of chili. Examine the food label of each brand. How many Calories does a serving of each contain? How many grams each of protein, carbohydrates, and fats are contained in a serving? How many Calories are from fat? What is the first item in the list of ingredients? What other information does each label provide?

WORKING WITH OTHERS

With a partner, research the staple foods of another country. Find the recipes for two food dishes that are customary to your particular country. Evaluate the nutritional value of each dish. As a class, combine the recipes that are nutrient-rich to create an ethnic cookbook.

CONNECTING TO...

SCIENCE   Choose one of the following disorders or diseases and research the connection that each has with nutrition: *electrolyte imbalance, cancer, heart disease, hypertension, breast cancer, hypoglycemia, gout, acne, eczema, muscle cramps, nervous tics, ulcer.* Research and explain how a person's diet can affect the condition positively or negatively?

USING VOCABULARY

additive	dietary fiber	mineral
amino acid	electrolytes	nutrient
anemia	glucose	nutrition
Calorie	glycogen	osteoporosis
carbohydrate	HDL	protein
cholesterol	hemoglobin	saturated fat
complementary proteins	hypertension	toxic
	LDL	unsaturated fat
deficiency	legume	vegetarian
dehydration	lipid	vitamin

On a separate sheet of paper, identify the vocabulary word that matches each of the following phrases. For those vocabulary words that are not used, write a descriptive phrase that correctly applies the word's meaning.

1. people who do not eat red meat

2. protein alternatives such as beans or peas

3. occurs if you do not drink enough water

4. form of starch stored in the muscles and liver that provides energy to the body

5. blood condition in which the body has either too few red blood cells or too little hemoglobin

6. the unit of measure for food energy

7. heart disease and certain types of cancers are closely linked to eating too much of this substance

8. "good" substance in your blood that returns cholesterol to the liver for recycling

9. provided by eating protein foods such as milk, poultry, fish, or red meat

10. substances found in the environment that are necessary for the body's functioning

CONCEPT MAPPING

Work by yourself or with others to create a concept map for *carbohydrates*. In your map, use as many of the following concepts as you can: *balanced diet, carbohydrates, energy, simple carbohydrates, complex carbohydrates, glucose, good health, life activities.* You may use additional concepts related to carbohydrates in your map. Further information about concept mapping appears at the front of this book.

THINKING CRITICALLY

INTERPRET

LESSON 10.1
1. Of the six types of nutrients that your body needs, which ones provide energy? Which class provides the most energy?

2. Dietary fiber may be effective in reducing the risk of diseases such as cancer? What foods are good sources of fiber?

3. Why is limiting fat intake important? What percent of your daily caloric intake is suggested to come from fat?

4. Using the graph in Figure 10-2, arrange the following foods in ascending order according to the amount of Calories derived from fat: cheddar cheese, French fries, cheese pizza, whole milk, hamburger, saltine crackers, and margarine.

LESSON 10.2
5. Identify three sources of complex carbohydrates that also provide beta-carotene.

6. What can a person who suffers from anemia do to improve his or her condition?

LESSON 10.3
7. What foods provide complete proteins? How can complementary proteins be used to provide the essential amino acids?

8. Why does the USDA recommend that your diet contain a greater percentage of carbohydrates than of fats or proteins?

LESSON 10.4
9. Compare the advantages and disadvantages of using additives in food products.

10. How do food labels help consumers make informed choices?

11. Why do consumers need to pay close attention to food labels?

12. Why do you think the FDA requires that all food labels include information about the percentage of Calories from fat?

APPLY

LESSON 10.1
13. Explain why natives of the Arctic and Greenland, whose diets contain a high level of fish, whale, and seal oil rather than butter and beef fat, might have a low incidence of heart disease.

14. What nutritional advice would you give to people who participate in strenuous physical activity?

LESSON 10.2
15. Sam's father and grandfather both suffer from hypertension. What modifications, if any, would you recommend that Sam make in his eating habits?

16. Electrolyte imbalance can be a serious threat to health. Why is it related to dehydration?

LESSON 10.3
17. Give an example of a meal you could select at a fast-food restaurant that would be enjoyable and still follow the dietary guidelines.

18. Using the Food Guide Pyramid, plan a day's menu for a lacto-ovo vegetarian that would meet the minimum daily requirements from each group. List specific foods and amounts for each meal or snack.

LESSON 10.4
19. How might the food label changes have affected the marketing methods of food manufacturers?

COMMITMENT TO WELLNESS

FOLLOW-UP

SETTING GOALS

Look back at your completed Personal Commitment to Wellness checklist. Review your response to each item on the checklist. Identify at least two areas of your daily diet that need improvement. Use the following system to make changes. Reduction of candy in diet is used as an example.

1. Create a diary of your progress throughout your plan for change.

2. Identify your present level of consumption by keeping a detailed record of your daily candy consumption for one week. Include information about the time of day you eat candy, and what happens right before and after you eat the candy.

3. Identify ways to break the routines that may precede your candy consumption.

4. Tell your friends about what you're trying to do and encourage their help.

5. Evaluate your progress after two weeks and make any necessary revisions.

WHERE DO I GO FROM HERE?

A great deal of information exists about the affects of diet on your health.

FOR MORE INFORMATION, CONTACT:

Human Nutrition Information Service
6505 Belcrest Road
Room 325A
Hyattsville, MD 20872

231

Identifying Your Dietary Needs

"Some people live to eat, others eat to live."

Benjamin Franklin

For people who "eat to live," food is a way of nourishing the body and fueling the mind. For them, the idea of well-balanced meals and daily exercise is a fact of everyday life.

But for those who "live to eat," food has more value than just nutrition. Most people enjoy the social aspects of eating with family and friends. Preparing tasty foods is a way of showing care and love. Many of those who "live to eat," however, eat to stave off emotional hunger such as anger, boredom, low self-esteem, loss, and feelings of inadequacy. For them, the food they consume and the amounts of food that they consume are daily obsessions.

A healthy eater is one who understands his or her dietary needs and meets those needs most of the time. Moderation is the key to a healthy mind and body. Identifying your own personal dietary needs is an important step in achieving and maintaining overall physical and mental health.

How healthy is your perspective on food? On a sheet of paper or in your Wellness Journal, write *yes* or *no* in response to the following statements.

1. I eat well-balanced meals and exercise regularly.
2. I am comfortable with my present weight.
3. I try not to let emotional feelings trigger my appetite.
4. I do not succumb to "miracle" weight-loss diets or supplements.
5. I do not hide food and eat it secretly.
6. I do not engage in binge-purge eating.
7. I try to lower my caloric intake when I am less active.
8. I am supportive of those around me who are trying to lose weight.
9. I do not criticize another person because of his or her weight.
10. I discourage friends from participating in fad or trendy quick weight-loss diets.

Review your responses and consider what might be your strengths and weaknesses. Save your list for a follow-up activity that appears at the end of this chapter.

233

MANAGING A HEALTHY WEIGHT

In our complex society, managing a healthy weight is not easy. In some situations, even when you know how to select the right foods, these food choices may not always be available. Everyone is different—each person has a different natural shape and healthy weight. Some people appear to be able to eat anything they want, while others must closely monitor their Calories. Maintaining a healthy weight requires an understanding of several important factors.

WHY YOU EAT

Often the urge to eat is the result of an outside stimulation. Remember the last time you smelled freshly baked bread, saw a juicy apple, or tasted lasagna? Your senses—smell, sight, and taste—all help trigger your desire for food. You eat for a number of reasons. One of the first steps of a good weight management program is to identify the reasons for eating.

PSYCHOLOGICAL REASONS   One of the reasons for eating is your **appetite**—your desire for food. Your appetite is a learned response to external influences that can cause you to eat. For example, sometimes you eat certain foods because of a social custom, such as having turkey on Thanksgiving Day. You may eat other foods because of a family custom, such as having black beans and rice and plantains on Fridays. If you visit another country or another region of the United States, you may enjoy trying new foods. Yet at some point, you may find yourself craving some of the foods you usually eat at home.

Some people eat when they are lonely or bored. Others eat because eating is a habit connected with an activity, such as always eating popcorn at the movies. Sometimes people eat in order to be polite and sociable, for example, eating cake at a birthday party. Still others eat when they are under stress, such as before a big test.

Carmen walked from her room to the kitchen for the fourth time in 30 minutes. She looked first in the refrigerator and then in the cupboard. She didn't see anything that she really wanted, but she took two chocolate chip cookies from the package anyway. She knew why she was eating—she had to complete a short story that was due the next day. Carmen realized that she was only eating in response to stress. She put the cookies back and started to work on writing her story.

Carmen was not eating because her body needed food. She has learned to use eating as an excuse to put off doing a task. Studies on appetite and hunger indicate that appetite may have more impact on what you eat than does hunger.

MAIN IDEAS

CONCEPTS

✔ People often eat for reasons other than hunger.

✔ Managing body weight involves a balance between diet and exercise.

✔ Successful weight-loss programs involve gradual weight loss through permanent changes in eating behavior and exercise habits.

✔ Eating disorders such as anorexia nervosa and bulimia are serious health problems that require psychological evaluation and counseling.

VOCABULARY

appetite
hunger
metabolism
basal
  metabolism
overweight
obesity
lean body
  mass
underweight
anorexia
  nervosa
bulimia

Often food is used as a reward. Describe a situation that you have experienced in which food was a reward.

PHYSICAL REASONS   **Hunger** is the body's physical need for food. It is regulated internally by physical sensations that tell you to eat food until you feel full. Some people have no difficulty separating hunger from appetite. They eat when they are hungry, stop when they feel satisfied, and do not eat again until their brain sends them a physical signal. In these people, hunger and the feeling of being satisfied work together to help their bodies receive the nutrition they need without overeating.

Other people, however, do not pay attention to the hunger signals for eating. They may eat so fast that their stomach is full before the brain has a chance to begin the process to signal them to stop eating. They also may continue eating after their hunger is satisfied because their appetite is stimulated. For example, some people eat dessert even though they are full because it is tempting and appealing to them.

People eat for many reasons. Do you eat only when you are hungry?

METABOLISM

The next step in weight management is to understand **metabolism** [*muh TAB uh liz um*] —the means by which your body releases the energy in food and uses it to build and repair body tissue. Metabolism involves two processes that work at the same time. One process breaks down larger substances into smaller substances. For example, glycogen is broken down into glucose from which the body releases energy. The other process of metabolism brings smaller substances together to form new substances used in the growth and repair of cells and tissues.

One factor that determines your energy needs is your **basal metabolism** [*BAY sul*], which is the amount of energy needed by the body when at rest and fasting to carry out basic life functions such as breathing, circulating the blood, and maintaining body temperature. Basal metabolism varies with age, size, gender, physical activity, and body type. For example, a muscular person generally will have a higher basal metabolism than a non-muscular person of the same weight.

Figure 11-1   People are born with an inherited body type based on skeletal frame and body composition. Most people are unique combinations of the three body types shown here. It is difficult to alter body type even with diet and exercise.

Teenagers are experiencing rapid growth and need more Calories than adults. A fifteen-year-old boy may need to take in as many as 3,000 Calories each day to be sure that he is getting enough energy. The BMR or basal metabolic rate— the rate at which the body uses energy to support its basal metabolism—of males is faster than that of females due to more-muscular bodies and larger bones. Teenage girls tend to need fewer Calories than boys.

Ectomorph
Elongated and slender

Mesomorph
Muscular, medium build

Endomorph
Rounded body with short arms and legs

The other factor that determines your energy needs is your level of physical activity. For example, a construction worker or a professional athlete will use more energy than a person who sits at a desk all day. Teenagers involved in organized or recreational physical activities after school may need additional Calories.

WEIGHT CONTROL

Balancing the amount of energy in what you eat with the total amount of energy expended by your BMR and activities is the key to weight management. When people are unable to achieve or maintain this balance, they have a weight problem.

OVERWEIGHT AND OBESITY   If you eat more Calories than your body needs, you will store the extra energy as fat. If you do this often, you will add excess body fat. A person who is more than 10 percent over the recommended weight for his or her age and height is considered **overweight**. **Obesity** is the condition of being at least 20 percent over the highest recommended weight. Research indicates that heredity, overeating, and lack of enough exercise are the major causes of overweight and obesity. In rare cases, obesity is caused by an improperly working thyroid gland, which results in a lower rate of metabolism than normal. Obesity has been linked to many health problems including high blood pressure, heart disease, some forms of diabetes, breathing difficulties, kidney and gallbladder disease, and problems during and after surgery. Scientists estimate that about one half of the adult population in the United States is moderately overweight to obese.

With the growing interest in fitness in the United States, body weight is no longer considered to be a reliable measure of body fat. Instead, a more accurate assessment is one that includes a measure

Figure 11-2   Calorie intake and energy use affect your weight. You can increase your energy use with physical exercise.

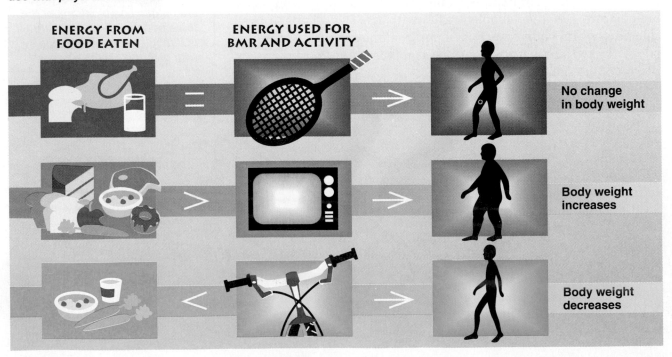

of body composition, which provides a more specific estimate of body fat. Muscle is more dense than body fat. Therefore, while your weight on a scale may be more than is recommended on a standard height-weight chart, you may not be overweight or at risk for related health problems. Chapter 15, "Lifelong Activity," explains the testing for body fat. Fitness testing in your physical education class may include such a test.

FAD DIETS Each year millions of dollars are spent on weight-loss programs—most of which are unsuccessful. At times, a new weight-loss plan seems to appear on the market each week. These plans often appeal to people because they promise quick and easy weight loss. However, most of these plans, or fad diets, are nutritionally unbalanced and often eliminate a group of foods. While some fad diets produce an initial weight loss, the weight is quickly regained once a person stops following the diet.

AMY

By Jack Tippit

©1992 Cowles Syndicate, Inc.

"If you'd eat a salad every now and then you'd be healthier and keep your weight down."

Reprinted with special permission of King Features Syndicate

By the time she reached sixteen, Angie had lost and regained about 75 pounds on several diets but she only weighed five pounds less than when she first decided that she needed to lose some weight two years ago. As she sat reading an article about yet another celebrity's easy weight-loss plan, Angie was feeling angry at herself. "Why does it seem so easy for everyone to lose weight but not for me? Wait a minute," she thought. "It's easy to lose the weight. I've certainly shown that I could do that over the years! So, why haven't I been able to keep it off?"

Angie's experience is not unusual. Many people use quick weight-loss plans then regain the weight. This loss-and-gain cycle, called yo-yo dieting, can be dangerous. People who lose and regain weight several times are at a much higher risk for heart disease and other fatal diseases than those whose weight remains steady. Many studies today indicate that just losing weight is not the answer to being healthier. It is only when the weight loss is maintained that health is enhanced. In addition, fad diets have been known to contribute to high blood pressure, strokes, vitamin deficiencies, and even heart failure.

Diet pills, diuretics, and other diet aids only bring about a short-term weight loss, and they can also be dangerous. Laxatives and diuretics rob the body of vital water and can lead to dehydration. Diet pills often contain caffeine, which can make some people feel jittery and may cause a sudden rise in blood pressure. Some diet aids are also habit-forming, which will make them difficult to stop taking. Generally be wary of any weight-loss program that promises quick results with little effort. A weight-loss program only works if you are committed to changing behavior over time.

LOSING WEIGHT WISELY Your best guide to weight management is daily exercise and a well-balanced, low-fat diet.

STRATEGIES FOR LIVING

Ways to control weight and decrease caloric intake

- Gradually cut back on the serving size of high-Calorie foods and eat only one serving of all foods.

- Eat less fat and more complex carbohydrate foods.

- Broil, steam, or bake foods instead of frying them.

- Cut back on the use of salad dressings, sauces, and butter.

- Choose low-fat or non-fat dairy products.

- Avoid packaged snacks, cookies, pastries, and other baked goods.

- Exercise daily or at least five days per week.

- Choose hobbies and other activities that don't involve food.

Choosing a Weight-Loss Plan

The secret to losing weight is really no secret at all: increase your exercise and lower your intake of food. It is a successful formula. Yet millions of consumers seek cures that promise fast, painless weight loss—if you only buy a product or service.

A successful weight-loss program should not deprive you of the foods you like. It should focus on behavior changes and help curb the behaviors that trigger overeating. Foods in each of the essential food groups should be part of the plan. Single-food weight-loss plans that emphasize just one food group, or plans that recommend less than 1,200 Calories a day, or promise a weight loss of more than two pounds a week, are unrealistic. In the long run, they are unsuccessful, and they may be dangerous.

Adopting new eating habits and sticking with them is difficult to do alone. Support groups that encourage talking about nutrition and help you avoid the pitfalls of overeating may be the most useful plans to help you lose weight.

For many people, weight loss is a matter of changing poor eating habits, so seek a program that you can live with for the rest of your life. Remember that it took a while for the weight to add up, and it will take a while for the weight to go away. With commitment and support, weight loss can be successful.

As Angie thought about the upcoming school year, she really felt she wanted to lose weight. But she wanted to do it the right way this time. She talked with her mother and together they decided Angie would see a doctor for a complete physical. Then, along with the doctor's input, Angie identified a weight-loss plan.

A successful plan for weight loss combines a reduction in Calories with an increase in exercise. To lose weight you must eat fewer Calories than your body is using so that your body will start to use the energy it has stored as fat. A sound weight-loss program follows *The Dietary Guidelines for Americans.* It should include at least 1,200 Calories per day, which allows you to lose no more than one to two pounds each week.

It is not healthy to lose weight too quickly. If you eat too few Calories, you will not get all of the nutrients that your body needs. In quick-loss programs, much of what is lost at first is water and then **lean body mass**—the protein in your muscles, organs, and

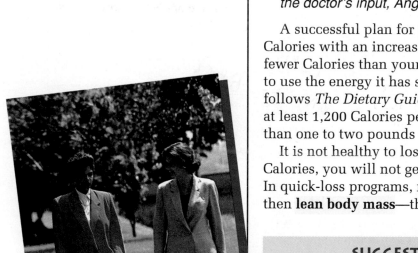

Regular exercise can help you lose fat.

SUGGESTIONS FOR WEIGHT LOSS

Here are some things you can do to help you lose weight.

- Try to set small goals, such as losing five pounds.
- Reward yourself with something that you enjoy besides food when you reach a goal.
- Take a walk instead of eating when you are upset or worried.
- Avoid eating while watching television, reading, or listening to music.
- Leave the table as soon as you have finished eating.
- Eat your meals at regular times every day.
- Eat slowly, and enjoy the taste of each bite of food.
- Avoid skipping meals. You are more likely to overeat at the next meal.

bones. When you go off the diet and back to your old eating habits, the lost weight is quickly regained as water and fat. Lean body mass can only be regained through exercise.

Angie and her mom talked about Angie's eating and exercise habits. They decided that Angie's snacking habits were a problem. Many of her snacks were high in fat and sugar. The first few days were not easy—she had to break her habit of eating while on the phone or watching television. She also started walking at a good pace for thirty minutes five or more days a week. After four weeks, Angie was pleased with how well she looked and felt—she had lost almost eight pounds!

It is a good idea to check with a doctor before starting any weight-loss program. If you find you have trouble losing weight on your own, ask for support from someone who shares your concern about weight, or consider joining a weight-loss support group. Remember there is no magic to weight loss. Find a program that suits your needs over a long time. Eventually you will find that you are not only pleased with losing weight, but that you also feel better.

GAINING WEIGHT WISELY   In spite of the preoccupation of many Americans with losing weight, there are other people who have the opposite problem—gaining weight. People who are more than 10 percent under the recommended weight for their height and age are said to be **underweight.** An underweight person may have just as much difficulty gaining weight as an over-weight person has losing weight. Many factors contribute to being underweight. Teenagers are often underweight because they have grown very rapidly and their bodies have not yet filled out. An under-weight person's BMR may be faster, so that most of the food eaten is used to meet immediate energy needs. For some people, emotional distress may decrease the appetite. Eating patterns established early in life can also contribute to being underweight.

DECISION FOCUS MAKING   *At fifteen, Jacques was taller than he was the year before, but his growth spurt did not include much of an increase in body weight. His grandmother described him as gangly. Jacques wished he were heavier and had more muscle, but his attempts to gain weight had not been successful. No matter how many milkshakes or extra servings he consumed at mealtime, his weight stayed the same. His concern about being underweight began to make him moody and withdrawn. In health class, the teacher presented a lesson about weight management, and Jacques realized that this was the first time he had heard about how to gain weight. The teacher suggested eating high-Calorie, nutrient-dense foods and using strength training as a way to increase muscle mass and body weight. After class, Jacques asked his teacher for more information about selecting the right high Calorie foods and a good program for strength training.*

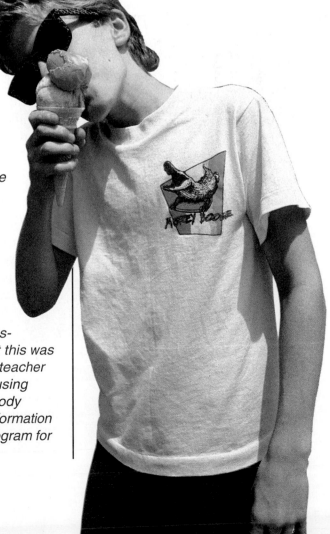

If you are trying to gain weight, choose nutrient-dense snack foods such as frozen yogurt instead of high-fat snacks such as ice cream.

Before you start any program to gain weight, check with a doctor to be sure you have no medical reason for being underweight. The doctor or a dietician may also recommend a sensible way to gain weight. For example, your doctor might suggest:

- Increased servings of high-Calorie foods from the carbohydrate and protein groups at meals.
- Snacks high in nutrients and Calories, such as dried fruits, nuts, and dairy products.
- An extra sandwich and milk after school or before bedtime.

Adding about 500 Calories a day usually will be sufficient to gain about one pound a week. At the same time, you should continue to exercise regularly. Strength-training programs such as lifting weights will increase body weight with muscle mass rather than fat. Getting proper rest and using appropriate methods for coping with stress, such as those identified in Chapter 5, "Managing Stress," will help your body store the extra Calories.

EATING DISORDERS

With the overemphasis today on being thin, some people have developed dangerous eating behaviors. Eating disorders are both an emotional problem and a nutritional problem and lie within the behavioral make-up of the person. Not eating or eating too much often are symptoms of emotional difficulties. The most common eating disorders are obesity caused by overeating, anorexia nervosa, and bulimia.

OBESITY   Obesity that is caused by overeating is considered to be an eating disorder. Recently, studies have been conducted to more clearly define the relationship between eating behavior and obesity. These studies have not been successful in determining which came first—the use of food as a way to cope with emotional problems, or the obesity which led to emotional problems. Researchers agree that the reasons for overeating are different in many individuals.

ANOREXIA NERVOSA   Anorexia nervosa [*an uh REK see uh nur VOH suh*] is an eating disorder characterized by constant dieting, severe weight loss, and the illusion of being overweight in spite of the weight loss. Ninety percent of anorexics are females who view themselves as too heavy, even when others see that they are very thin. It is currently estimated that each year one out of every 250 females aged 12 to 18 years will show some symptoms of anorexia.

The warning signs of anorexia nervosa are dry skin, brittle hair, loss of body fat, and the wasting away of muscle tissue. At mealtime, anorexics often make up excuses for not eating, or they may shift the food around on their plate to make it appear that they are eating. They may wear bulky or loose clothing and exercise excessively. Other signs of the condition are dehydration, fainting, irregular heartbeat, and in females, loss of

Admission of a problem by a famous person can help bring attention to eating disorders.

menstrual periods. Many anorexics must be hospitalized due to their condition.

BULIMIA   Bulimia [*byoo LIM ee uh*] is characterized by eating large amounts of food and then purging the body of food by making themselves vomit or by using laxatives. Sometimes anorexics are also bulimic because they purge as well as starve themselves. Most bulimics are girls or young women who are of average weight or slightly overweight. They tend to gain weight easily and live in constant fear of becoming obese.

Due to repeated vomiting, bulimics often have open sores in their mouths, their throats are often red, and their teeth decay because of the constant exposure to acids in their vomit. As with anorexics, bulimics need to be under the care of a doctor.

Anorexics and bulimics have several traits in common. They have trouble feeling good about their bodies no matter how good they may look. They have an intense fear of being fat. They are insecure and try to be perfect in everything—many are overachievers. There are combinations of factors that contribute to these traits, including the person's mental state, family relationships, and cultural background.

Effective professional treatment for eating disorders includes psychological counseling and nutritional counseling as well as intense medical treatment. A family approach to evaluation and treatment is particularly useful. While many individuals who develop eating disorders recover, they may have caused irreparable damage to their bodies. For example, the bones of anorexics become less dense and may be more likely to fracture easily. Some anorexics do not respond to treatment. Still others may not receive treatment and death may result. As many as fifteen to twenty percent of anorexics may die from their condition.

LESSON 11.1 USING WHAT YOU HAVE LEARNED

REVIEW

1. Compare the differences between appetite and hunger.
2. What are the factors that determine one's body weight?
3. Why is it difficult for some people to gain weight?

THINK CRITICALLY

4. Body weight is often used as one measure of health status. Explain why the term *overweight* might not be an accurate way to describe the health status of some individuals.
5. People often associate weight-control with losing weight, however, some people are trying to gain weight. Compare and contrast the process of weight-loss with the process of weight-gain.

APPLY IT TO YOURSELF

6. Keep a diary of your eating habits for one week. Record everything you eat as well as the time of day, the occasion, and how you feel for each time you eat. Analyze the results for any patterns in your eating behavior. In what ways were your food choices influenced by having to write about what you ate?

SUMMARY

People eat for many reasons other than to stay healthy. A healthy weight is something that is different for each individual—even for people that are the same age and have the same level of activity. Your health and longevity may be related to the amount of fat that your body stores. If you are underweight or overweight, you will need to modify gradually both your caloric intake and your physical activity. People suffering from eating disorders need both medical and psychological treatment to recover.

Eating Disorders

HEALTHY PEOPLE 2000

Increase to at least 50 percent the proportion of over-weight people aged 12 and older who have adopted sound dietary practices combined with regular physical activity to attain an appropriate body weight.

Overweight occurs when too few calories are expended and too many consumed for individual metabolic requirements. The results of weight loss programs focused on dietary restrictions alone have not been encouraging. Physical activity burns calories, increases the proportion of lean to fat body mass, and raises the metabolic rate. Therefore, a combination of both caloric control and increased physical activity is important for attaining a healthy body weight.

Objective 2.7

from *Healthy People 2000: National Health Promotion and Disease Prevention Objectives*

For many Americans, weight loss is an obsession—and for every second of every day, one more person resolves to "go on a diet." Bookstores are teeming with volumes that promise quick success with little effort. Low-fat, high-protein, liquid, and single-food diets all promise a variety of good things. However, weight loss cannot be achieved overnight. Weight loss can be accomplished and maintained safely by combining sound eating practices with a regular exercise program.

Over one million people suffer from an eating disorder—anorexia nervosa, bulimia, or compulsive eating. Changing the dietary habits of these people requires more than cutting down on fat intake or stepping up an exercise program.

Overweight and eating disorders most often appear during the teenage years. Your understanding and management of these issues can affect the health goals for the year 2000.

BEYOND WEIGHT LOSS

Everywhere you look, the message is clear: thin is in, and fat is out. The message suggests that a thin person is in control of his or her life and a fat person cannot hope to measure up. What happens to overweight people receiving this message? They may feel undervalued as people, judged completely on appearance rather than on characteristics such as intelligence, creativity, or talent.

For the compulsive eater, food serves as a comfort. The

THINKING CRITICALLY

INTERPRET

LESSON 11.1

1. What is the difference between appetite and hunger?
2. What are some psychological reasons that people eat?
3. What are the two processes at work in metabolism?
4. Why is the BMR higher for males than females?
5. What percentage over "normal" body weight is considered obese?
6. What are the major causes of obesity?
7. What complications can arise as a result of obesity?
8. How much of the population of the United States is considered overweight?
9. Why don't fad diets work?
10. What is the best way to lose or maintain weight?
11. What role can exercise play in weight loss?
12. How can lean body mass be replaced once it is lost?
13. What are some factors that contribute to underweight?
14. What are some common characteristics of people with eating disorders?

LESSON 11.2

15. What impact does age have on body weight?
16. What might happen if a woman follows a weight-loss plan while she is pregnant?
17. What are electrolytes? How can they be replenished if lost?
18. Why did the FDA ban the use of sulfites in salad bars?

APPLY

LESSON 11.1

19. Why do you think eating disorders are most common among women?
20. What factors do you think might contribute to 50% of the population of the United States being overweight?
21. Why do you think so many people continue to follow fad diets when there is so much evidence that they do not work?
22. Why do you think some people are so preoccupied with weight?

LESSON 11.2

23. Why do you think a pregnant woman should be especially careful about her diet?
24. Why do you think some people choose dietary supplements rather than a healthy diet to help them build strength? Do you think this is a good choice? Explain?

COMMITMENT TO WELLNESS

FOLLOW-UP

SETTING GOALS

Consider your responses to the self-assessment checklist at the beginning of Chapter 11. Are you comfortable with your body weight? If so, what steps do you take to maintain that weight? How balanced is your eating plan? If not, identify the steps you can take to moderate your eating plan sensibly? It might help to talk over some of your feelings about your weight with a trusted friend who can work with you to "coach" you as you work toward achieving and maintaining a balanced eating plan.

WHERE DO I GO FROM HERE?

Obsession with weight and body image is a serious problem among teenagers, male and female.

FOR MORE INFORMATION, CONTACT:

The National Institute of Diabetes and Digestive and Kidney Diseases
Building 31 Room 9A04
Bethesda, MD 20892

Anorexia Nervosa and Related Eating Disorders, Inc. (ANRED)
P.O. Box 5102
Eugene, OR 97405

National Eating Disorders Helpline
1-800-873-8732

CHAPTER 12

Digestion and Excretion

"You are what you eat."

Adelle Davis

What makes you unique is your one-of-a-kind combination of heredity, learning, and personality—and the choices that you make every day. What you eat is one of the many choices that determine who you are. Even the smallest choices can greatly affect your health, your feelings, and the internal workings of your body.

Imagine that you are preparing a picnic lunch. You want to take chicken, some bread, a salad, and some snacks. How can small decisions about your picnic lunch affect your health? You can choose to grill the chicken instead of frying it. You can bring a whole-grain bread instead of bread made from bleached white flour. You can bring nutritious snacks such as fruit and popcorn instead of sweets and salty chips. You can bring a thirst-quenching mixture of fruit juice and sparkling water instead of ordinary soda.

These small choices make a big difference in how your body is nourished. Together, many small decisions have a great effect on your entire well-being. Your body, your mind, and your emotions are all nourished by the foods you eat.

THE FUNCTIONS OF THE DIGESTIVE SYSTEM

The main functions of the digestive system are the breakdown of food into simpler substances and the absorption of these substances into your bloodstream. The digestive system also performs the job of elimination—getting rid of the waste that is left after the nutrients in food have been absorbed.

DIGESTION The process by which the body breaks down carbohydrates, proteins, and fats into substances that your cells can absorb and use is called **digestion**. There are two kinds of digestion—mechanical and chemical. Mechanical digestion is the process of chewing, mashing, and breaking food into smaller pieces. Chemical digestion is the process of changing food into simpler substances chiefly through the action of enzymes. **Enzymes** are proteins that cause a rapid chemical breakdown of complex substances.

ABSORPTION AND ELIMINATION The process by which nutrients from digested food move into the bloodstream is called **absorption**. Periodically, your body must get rid of the waste material remaining in the intestine after absorption has occurred. The process of releasing solid waste from your body is called **elimination**.

DIGESTION IN THE MOUTH

The digestion of the chicken, bread, and other foods in your picnic lunch begins as soon as you take your first bite. As food enters your mouth, mechanical digestion begins. During mechanical digestion, your teeth tear, grind, and chop the food into smaller pieces. Your tongue mashes soft food and mixes it with saliva, a liquid that moistens food, making it easier to swallow.

Three pairs of salivary glands, shown in Figure 12-1, secrete saliva, which contains amylase. Amylase [*AM uh lays*] is an enzyme that begins the chemical digestion of complex carbohydrates, such as the whole grain bread in your picnic lunch.

Once you have chewed your food and it has softened in your mouth, your tongue rolls it into a ball and pushes it to the back of your throat. The process of swallowing is shown in Figure 12-2. As you swallow, a small flap of tissue called the epiglottis [*ep uh GLAHT us*] covers the opening to your windpipe. This prevents food from entering. The food passes into the **esophagus** [*ih SAHF uh gus*], a tube that connects your mouth and stomach. In much the same way that your fingers squeeze toothpaste from a tube, the walls of the esophagus squeeze behind your food, pushing it toward your stomach. This squeezing action is the result of peristalsis. **Peristalsis** [*per uh STAWL sus*] is a wavelike contraction of muscles that pushes food through your alimentary canal.

DIGESTION IN THE STOMACH

The esophagus opens into the stomach, a muscular bag that can stretch to store a quart or more of food at a time. This ability of your stomach to stretch means that you can eat an entire picnic

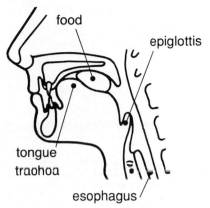

The ball of food is pushed to the back of your throat by your tongue.

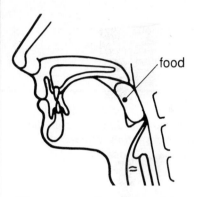

When you swallow, your epiglottis closes the opening to your windpipe.

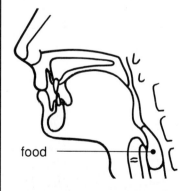

Food passes into your esophagus.

Figure 12-2 What important function does the epiglottis serve during swallowing?

	Organs or Glands	Secretions and Enzymes	Functions
Mouth	Salivary Glands	Salivary amylase	Breaks down starch into dextrins and maltose
Stomach	Gastric Glands	Pepsin	Breaks down proteins into polypeptides
		Rennin	Digests milk proteins
		Lipase	Breaks down emulsified fats into fatty acids and glycerol
		Hydrochloric acid	Kills harmful bacteria; stimulates pepsin
Small Intestine	Pancreas	Trypsin	Digests certain polypeptides to amino acids
		Lipase	Digests fats to fatty acids and glycerol
		Amylase	Digests starch to maltose
	Intestine	Peptidase	Digests polypeptides to amino acids
		Sucrase	Digests sucrose to glucose and fructose
		Maltase	Digests maltose to two molecules glucose
		Lactase	Digests lactose to galactose and glucose

Figure 12-3   Your body produces numerous chemicals that help in digestion. What is the function of lipase?

lunch at one time. If your stomach did not stretch, you would have to eat small amounts of food constantly.

The stomach walls are made of three layers of muscle, each arranged at a different angle. As food enters your stomach, muscle contractions begin to twist, turn, and churn the food. This movement of food in the stomach is part of mechanical digestion. Chemical digestion occurs as food is mixed with gastric juices. The juices help liquefy food and break it into simpler forms.

The chemical digestion of complex carbohydrates, such as whole grain bread, that began in the mouth slows down in the stomach. The gastric juices begin the digestion of proteins and fats. In Figure 12-3, which enzymes in the gastric juices break down proteins, such as those in the grilled chicken in the picnic lunch?

While it is in the stomach, the partially digested food is changed into a thick liquid called **chyme** [*KYM*]. A valve at the end of the stomach allows chyme to move into the small intestine a little bit at a time.

DIGESTION AND ABSORPTION IN THE SMALL INTESTINE

Most chemical digestion and absorption of food occur in the small intestine. The **small intestine** is a 22-foot-long coiled tube about one inch in diameter. When food leaves the stomach, it enters the duodenum [*doo uh DEE num*], the first part of the small intestine. The major chemical digestion of your picnic lunch begins here.

The pancreas and intestinal glands play important roles in completing the breakdown of your lunch. The **pancreas** [*PANG kree us*] is a long, soft gland lying behind the stomach that secretes digestive enzymes into the duodenum. The tiny intestinal glands are found in the lining of the small intestine. They release digestive enzymes and mucus. Enzymes from the pancreas and intestinal glands continue to break down proteins. They also change starch into simple sugars and change fats into fatty acids.

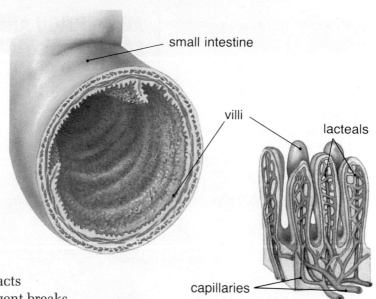

Another substance that helps in the breakdown of fats is bile. **Bile** is a yellow-green digestive juice released by the liver. It acts somewhat like a dish detergent. Just as detergent breaks down grease on dishes, bile breaks fats into little globules that the other enzymes can then break down completely. Excess bile is stored in the gallbladder, a sac attached to the liver. Stored bile is released into the duodenum as needed.

The absorption of nutrients into the blood occurs throughout the wall of the small intestine. The wall is wrinkled into millions of tiny finger-like projections called villi [*VIL eye*]. The presence of the villi vastly increases the surface area of the small intestine. This increased surface area allows the small intestine to absorb most of the nutrients that enter your body. As you can see in Figure 12-4, each villus contains a network of blood vessels (capillaries) and a lacteal containing a fluid called lymph. Fat-soluble vitamins and fatty acids are absorbed into the lymph. Glucose, amino acids, water-soluble vitamins, and minerals are absorbed into the blood. Blood carries these nutrients through the liver before it goes to the rest of your body.

Figure 12-4 *Within the villi are complex networks of blood and lymph vessels. Nutrients pass through the villi into the blood and the lymph.*

THE FUNCTIONS OF THE LIVER

When the nutrients reach the liver, some are broken down even further. Others are converted to different substances. For example, excess glucose, a sugar, is converted to a starch-like substance called glycogen and stored in the liver. Glycogen can be broken down quickly to maintain blood sugar levels between meals and to provide quick energy when your body needs it. The liver has many other functions as well. All of its major functions are listed below.

- changes surplus glucose to glycogen for storage until glucose is needed
- secretes bile, which breaks fat into smaller globules
- stores some fat
- breaks down and stores amino acids used to form proteins
- detoxifies substances such as alcohol and many drugs
- stores vitamins A, D, E, K, and B_{12}
- stores iron for use in making new red blood cells

FOR YOUR INFORMATION

Although your body can exist with only half a stomach, half a large intestine, and no gallbladder, it must have at least two thirds of a healthy liver in order to survive.

ABSORPTION AND ELIMINATION IN THE LARGE INTESTINE

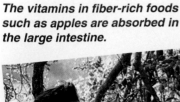

The vitamins in fiber-rich foods such as apples are absorbed in the large intestine.

The large intestine, or colon, is a five-foot-long tube that extends from the end of the small intestine to the anus. As you can see in Figure 12-1, the large intestine looks like an upside down U. Notice that the large intestine is much wider than the small intestine.

The only materials that usually enter the large intestine are water, fiber, and foods that the body is unable to break down. Which foods in the picnic lunch contained materials that would eventually reach your large intestine?

The major function of the large intestine is to reabsorb the water that was used during digestion. The remaining materials form semi-solid feces, or stools.

A second function of the large intestine is the absorption of vitamins produced by bacteria that live there. These bacteria live within the large intestine on undigested food materials such as fiber. In turn, the bacteria produce some B vitamins and vitamin K.

The third function of the large intestine is the elimination of wastes from the digestive tract. These wastes include cellulose (plant fiber), bacteria, bile, mucus, and worn-out cells. The wastes are stored in the part of the large intestine called the rectum until the body is ready to expel them. During elimination, the solid wastes leave the body through the anus, a muscular opening at the end of the rectum.

SUMMARY

Mechanical and chemical digestion begin in the mouth. Food moves down the esophagus to the stomach, where it is changed into chyme. The chyme enters the small intestine, where most chemical digestion takes place and nutrients are absorbed. Water and undigested material pass into the large intestine, where water and vitamins are absorbed. Wastes are then eliminated.

LESSON 12.1 USING WHAT YOU HAVE LEARNED

REVIEW

1. What are the functions of saliva and its enzyme amylase?
2. Why doesn't food go into the back of your nose or down your windpipe when you swallow?

THINK CRITICALLY

3. Calories are the fuel needed by the body to function. How does the body keep running without a constant fuel supply?
4. Suppose you stood on your head and sipped from a cup of water. What would cause the water to go up to your stomach?

APPLY IT TO YOURSELF

5. Imagine that you are a doctor who has just advised a 14-year-old boy living off fast foods to eat a diet rich in fiber. Why is your advice important for the health of the boy's digestive system, when fiber passes undigested out of the body?

PREVENTING DIGESTIVE PROBLEMS

According to surveys conducted by the U.S. Department of Health and Human Services, digestive problems are very common. In fact, one out of every ten people in your age group will experience some difficulty related to the digestive system at least one time during the year. Most of these problems are minor and disappear within a few days. Occasionally, digestive problems continue over several months. If this happens, the digestive system's ability to function as it should may be affected.

COMMON DIGESTIVE DISORDERS

A digestive disorder may cause pain in your chest or abdomen, vomiting, and problems in eliminating wastes. If any of these symptoms appears often or for long periods of time, you should seek medical help. Disorders of the digestive system may be caused by the following:

- eating habits such as overeating or eating foods that your body has trouble digesting
- bacteria or viruses in food
- a disease related to an organ in the digestive system

INDIGESTION Indigestion is a very common digestive problem. The term *indigestion* actually refers to a variety of different symptoms. These symptoms include an uncomfortably full feeling in the stomach, nausea, belching of gas from the stomach, and heartburn. Heartburn is a sharp pain caused by stomach acid backing up into the esophagus.

Indigestion can be caused by eating too much or too quickly, eating certain foods, or drinking too much alcohol. In most cases, indigestion occurs soon after eating. Indigestion itself is not a serious problem. However, frequent or severe indigestion may be a sign of a more serious digestive disorder. Anyone who is often troubled by indigestion should see a doctor.

NAUSEA AND VOMITING Nausea and vomiting are common symptoms of a variety of digestive problems. Skipping meals or eating too much may cause you to feel nauseated. Nausea often is a sign that you are about to throw up, or vomit.

Vomiting occurs when the digestive system forcefully expels the food in your stomach. When there is little food in your stomach, only digestive juices are expelled. In most cases, vomiting is due to infection by bacteria or viruses. Vomiting also can be a protective mechanism for your body. For example, if the food you have eaten is contaminated in some way, your body may react by vomiting. Vomiting also may be caused by eating too much, eating certain foods, or drinking too much alcohol.

Prolonged vomiting or forced vomiting, such as that practiced by people with the eating disorder bulimia, can be dangerous.

MAIN IDEAS

CONCEPTS

✔ Poor eating habits, bacteria in food, or diseases may produce a digestive problem.

✔ Many different disorders commonly affect the digestive system.

✔ Diseases of the digestive system include gallstones, ulcers, and cancer.

✔ Food poisoning is caused by bacteria in foods.

VOCABULARY

constipation	gallstone
diarrhea	ulcer
irritable bowel	cancer
syndrome	food
hemorrhoids	poisoning
appendicitis	

Digestive disorders can be very uncomfortable.

LACTOSE INTOLERANCE AND ETHNICITY

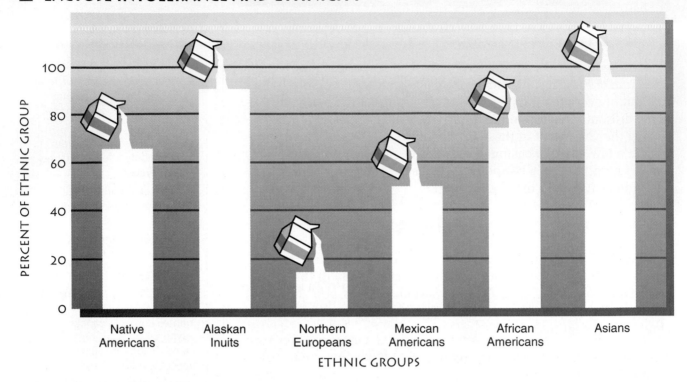

Figure 12-5 Lactose intolerance is a hereditary condition that is more common in some ethnic groups than in others. Which group has the lowest rate of lactose intolerance?

Vomiting removes nutrients and water from your system. This can result in dehydration and, in extreme cases, death. Dehydration is a severe loss of essential body fluids and salts that can be fatal if not treated.

LACTOSE INTOLERANCE Some people do not produce the enzyme needed to digest lactose, or milk sugar. If these people drink milk or eat milk products, they develop gas, cramps, and diarrhea. Although many people have some trouble digesting lactose as they grow older, lactose intolerance is usually hereditary. As you can see in Figure 12-5, many ethnic groups are unable to digest lactose efficiently. Using Lactaid™ powder to break down milk sugar or buying lactose-free milk are options for those who want to drink milk. If you cannot digest lactose, you can meet your calcium requirements by eating yogurt or aged cheeses.

CONSTIPATION AND DIARRHEA Different people have different patterns of eliminating waste. Many people have a daily bowel movement. Some people have two or three movements each day. Others have only one movement every few days. A change from your usual pattern may be a sign of a disorder.

Constipation [*kahn stuh PAY shun*] is a condition in which the stools are unusually hard and dry. Bowel movements may be difficult or painful. In most cases constipation is not a serious condition. It simply may be the result of too little exercise, a diet low in fiber and fluid, or emotional distress. However, if constipation continues for a week or more, you should check with your doctor. As a temporary measure, your doctor may prescribe a laxative, a

STRATEGIES FOR LIVING

To avoid indigestion, follow these guidelines:

- Avoid skipping meals, overeating, and wearing clothing that is too tight.
- Eat calm, relaxed meals.
- Avoid eating beans, cabbage, chocolate, or other foods that your body has trouble digesting.
- Get regular exercise.

medicine that stimulates the process of elimination. Preventing constipation may involve dietary and life-style changes.

Diarrhea [*dy uh REE uh*] is a condition that occurs when the large intestine does not absorb enough water. As a result, the feces become watery and loose and the bowels move too often. Diarrhea may cause great loss of water and other important nutrients. For this reason, a person with diarrhea should drink plenty of clear fluids, such as water and flat soda. As diarrhea improves, a soft diet of rice cereal, mashed bananas, toast, and crackers may be added. Most bouts of diarrhea respond quickly to this kind of therapy. If diarrhea continues for more than 48 hours or if you experience signs of dehydration, be sure to get medical help. Signs of dehydration include a rapid pulse, dry mouth and tongue, decrease in urination, and pale, dry skin,

IRRITABLE BOWEL SYNDROME One common disorder of the digestive system is irritable bowel syndrome. **Irritable bowel syndrome** is a chronic disorder, also known as spastic colon, that typically develops in late adolescence or early adulthood. Its symptoms can include constipation, diarrhea, abdominal cramps, bloating, and gas. Not all of the symptoms are present in all sufferers. The exact causes of irritable bowel syndrome probably vary among people. In some, the disorder may be brought on by chronic stress. In others, an inherited tendency or certain foods may be the cause. Because the pain can become quite severe, sufferers often fear that they have a more serious disease.

Lois had become really anxious about the cramps and diarrhea that she was experiencing. For a while the symptoms disappeared. When they returned just before final exams, Lois also experienced pain much like heartburn, and constipation instead of diarrhea. Lois confided to a friend that she was concerned that she might have a really serious disease such as cancer. Her friend urged Lois to talk with

FROM A CULTURAL PERSPECTIVE

Lactose Intolerance

An estimated 30 to 50 million Americans are lactose intolerant, or unable to digest milk comfortably. Of those people, 7 out of every 10 are of African, Asian, or Southern European ancestry. In fact, seventy percent of the world's population is lactose intolerant. The only population groups in which lactose intolerance is not common are people of Northern European and Western European ancestry.

Lactose is a natural sugar found in milk and in products made from milk, such as yogurt, cheese, and ice cream. During digestion, lactose is broken down by the enzyme lactase in the small intestine. If the intestine does not produce lactase at all or does not produce enough to digest milk effectively, the person experiences gas, bloating, cramps, and diarrhea after ingesting milk or milk products.

Milk is an excellent source of calcium, so giving it up entirely is not a wise diet choice for most lactose intolerant people. Some lactose-intolerant people can drink a small amount of milk along with food without feeling discomfort. Many can eat low-lactose milk products such as hard cheeses and yogurt or supplement their diet with calcium tablets. Lactose-free milk and lactase supplements that are added to food are also available. These products help lactose-intolerant people to meet their dietary needs for calcium—and to enjoy milk products such as ice cream—without suffering uncomfortable effects.

her family doctor but added that she thought the symptoms were probably caused by stress.

Lois thought about what her friend had said. She realized that if her pain was the result of a serious disorder, she needed to deal with it. Lois went to see her doctor.

After performing several tests to rule out the possibility of serious disease, food allergy, and lactose intolerance, the doctor diagnosed Lois's symptoms as irritable bowel syndrome. She assured Lois that it was natural to feel anxiety about the symptoms she experienced. The doctor also pointed out that irritable bowel syndrome is treatable and won't turn into something worse.

That night Lois slept much better. Although she realized that her condition was chronic, she had learned that there were things she could do to help herself. She would begin eating a high-fiber diet of fruits, vegetables, and whole grains, drinking plenty of fluids, and exercising regularly.

HEMORRHOIDS Hemorrhoids [*HEM uh roydz*] are swollen veins in the anal area. Hemorrhoids tend to develop in people who sit a lot, strain during bowel movements, or suffer from chronic constipation. Hemorrhoids also occur often in pregnant women and in people who are very overweight.

The signs of hemorrhoids may include itching as well as pain and bleeding. Ointments and hot baths may be used to relieve the pain and itching. In severe cases, surgery may be required.

DIGESTIVE DISEASES

You have just read about disorders of the digestive system. Some of these disorders are symptoms of more serious digestive diseases.

APPENDICITIS A small pouch located near the junction of the small intestine and the large intestine is the appendix. The appendix has no known function in people. However, it can suddenly become inflamed, swollen, and filled with pus. This condition is called **appendicitis** [*uh pen duh SYT us*]. Appendicitis usually is caused by a blockage of the channel inside the appendix, where hardened feces become trapped.

The first sign of appendicitis often is pain around the navel that moves to the lower-right side of the abdomen. Fever, nausea, vomiting, and loss of appetite are usually present as well. If appendicitis is not treated immediately, the appendix may burst. A ruptured appendix may result in a potentially life-threatening infection of the lining of the abdominal wall. Treatment for appendicitis involves both surgical removal of the appendix, as shown in Figure 12-6, and the use of antibiotics to control infection.

GALLSTONES One of the most common diseases of the digestive system is the formation of gallstones in the gallbladder. **Gallstones** are hard particles made of calcium salts, cholesterol, and pigments in the bile. The concentration of these substances becomes so high

Figure 12-6 *During surgery, the appendix is cut off and the incision is closed with stitches. What is the function of the appendix?*

site of incision

appendix

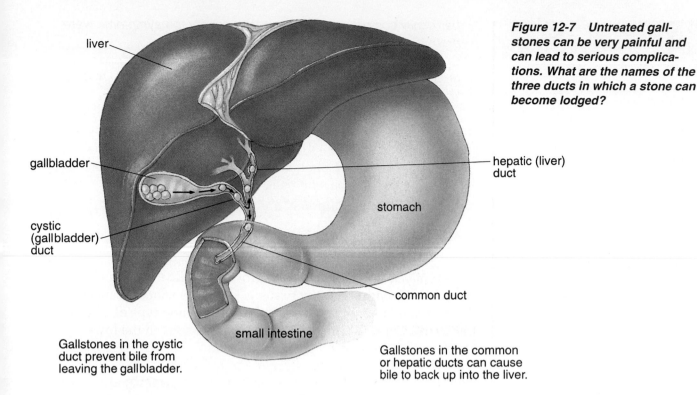

Figure 12-7 *Untreated gallstones can be very painful and can lead to serious complications. What are the names of the three ducts in which a stone can become lodged?*

liver

gallbladder

cystic (gallbladder) duct

hepatic (liver) duct

stomach

common duct

small intestine

Gallstones in the cystic duct prevent bile from leaving the gallbladder.

Gallstones in the common or hepatic ducts can cause bile to back up into the liver.

that they can no longer stay dissolved in the bile. Instead, tiny solid particles develop and enlarge over time. Gallstones can range in size from as small as sand grains to as large as gravel. Gallstones often may be present without causing any symptoms. However, sometimes they get caught in the tube leading out of the gallbladder, as shown in Figure 12-7. If the gallstones prevent bile from moving out of the gallbladder, it becomes inflamed and swollen. This causes fever and severe pain.

Before 1980, gallstones that caused symptoms were treated by surgically removing the gallbladder. In the late 1980s, a technique called lithotripsy began to be used. Lithotripsy uses a series of ultrasound waves to shatter the stones. The pieces are small enough to pass out of the tube with little or no pain. This technique may eliminate the need for surgery.

ULCERS Open sores that form on the surface of the skin or in the alimentary canal are called **ulcers.** Peptic ulcers are ulcers that form in the stomach (gastric ulcers) or in the first part of the small intestine (duodenal ulcers). The most obvious sign of a peptic ulcer is a burning or gnawing pain in the upper abdomen.

For many years, medical professionals believed that peptic ulcers were caused by an overproduction of stomach acid due to factors such as stress, eating rich or spicy food, smoking, and drinking alcoholic or caffeinated beverages. However, recent studies have shown that most peptic ulcers are caused by a specific type of bacteria that attacks and damages the lining of the stomach or duodenum. Taking aspirin, ibuprofen, or other anti-inflammatory drugs for long periods also can cause ulcers.

STRATEGIES FOR LIVING

Tips for maintaining digestive health.

- Chew food slowly and thoroughly.
- Eat in a pleasant, relaxed environment.
- Avoid eating while standing or "on the run."
- Eat moderate amounts of food, and stop eating before you feel stuffed.

The following methods are used to treat peptic ulcers:

* Take prescribed antibiotics and anti-ulcer medications.

* Take medications to neutralize or reduce the amount of acid in the stomach.

* Eat nutritious, regularly spaced meals and snacks.

* Avoid tobacco, alcohol, and drinks that contain caffeine, such as coffee, tea, and cola.

* Avoid aspirin, ibuprofen, and other anti-inflammatory medications.

COLON CANCER   An uncontrolled growth of cells that invade and destroy neighboring healthy tissue is known as **cancer**. Cancer of the colon and rectum is the second most common type of cancer in the United States. Colon cancer most often occurs in the lowest part

MAKING A DIFFERENCE

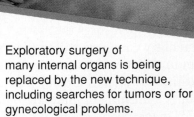

Laparoscopic Surgery

For thousands of Americans, a sharp and nagging pain after a meal used to signal the beginning of a long road toward gallstone surgery, then recovery. Today, that nagging pain can be eliminated quickly using a surgical technique known as laparoscopy.

Gallstones are often the cause of chronic pain in the stomach or abdomen, especially after a meal that is high in fats. Gallstones form in the gallbladder, a small organ that secretes bile to aid digestion. The best cure for gallstones is the removal of the gallbladder, an organ whose function is not essential to digestion.

Until recently, gallbladder surgery was an hour-long operation to remove the gallbladder. The surgeon made a six-inch incision into the abdomen, cutting through several walls of muscle to reach the organ. Recovery from surgery often took up to six weeks. But today, because of laparoscopic surgery, the same operation can be done with minimal damage to the

abdominal muscles. Additionally, the recovery period is more than cut in half.

In laparoscopy, four or five small holes are made in the abdomen. Surgical instruments are inserted in all but one of the holes. The laparoscope, which contains a tiny light and a miniature video camera, is then placed into the last hole.

While one surgeon focuses the video camera, another surgeon watches a television monitor connected to the laparoscopic camera as he or she works. In this way, the surgeon sees what he or she is doing.

The cost of laparoscopy is about the same as that of the traditional surgery, but the recovery time after the procedure is reduced. Hospital stays are shorter and therefore less expensive for laparoscopy patients, who are usually back to full activity, including work, within twelve days.

Laparoscopy is being used in areas other than gallbladder.

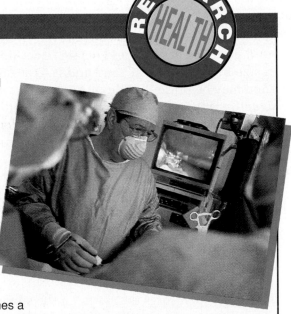

Exploratory surgery of many internal organs is being replaced by the new technique, including searches for tumors or for gynecological problems.

1. In what ways has laparoscopy revolutionized the removal of gallstones and exploratory surgery?

2. How could laparoscopic surgery help people who are very sick and unable to withstand major surgery?

Facing Surgery

José could eat anything. However, lately he had been feeling sick after meals. He would feel a sharp ache in his stomach. Sometimes the ache would move to the back. José would feel real nauseous, too. José blamed it on nerves.

One day José was watching a football game with his brother. At halftime, they made some cheeseburgers and fries. Within an hour, José felt a pain in his stomach. He walked around, hoping it would help. It didn't.

Several weeks went by and José's symptoms did not get any better. His parents decided he had better see a doctor.

As José described the pain, Dr. Russell listened carefully and asked some questions. "It's possible that you may have gallstones," said Dr. Russell. "You're awfully young to have this problem, but it's not unheard of. I'd like you to have an ultrasound to be certain." A day later, the test results were back. José did have gallstones. The doctor explained how gallstones develop and that fatty foods can cause the irritation. "There are several options," said the doctor. "You can

change your eating habits and avoid foods with fats. Or we can try to dissolve the stones with medication. This method helps some people but not everyone. Or we can go in and surgically remove your gallbladder. Laparoscopic surgery has made recovery much shorter than it used to be."

José wasn't sure what he should do. Changing his eating habits would mean eliminating many of the foods he loved. The medication was a long-term process and it wasn't a sure thing. But José didn't like the thought of surgery.

PAUSE AND CONSIDER

1. *Identify the Problem.* What is José's conflict?

2. *Consider the Options.* What are José's options?

3. *Evaluate the Outcomes.* Why might it be difficult for José to change his eating habits?

José told a friend what the doctor had said. "Well the choice seems simple. If you can avoid surgery and medication, then do it.

Change your diet by all means," said the friend. José agreed. It did seem like the best solution.

For several months, José ate nothing with fat in it. It was difficult, but he did feel better. However, some days José would eat something he thought was safe and would soon be stricken with pain.

One evening José met up with some friends. They ordered a heaping platter of nachos with cheese. José just wanted to try one chip. He hadn't had an attack for a while and felt it would be safe. He even took a chip with very little cheese on it. "A little bit won't hurt me, " he thought. An hour later, his pain was back. José barely made it home.

"This is ridiculous," he thought. "As much as I hate the thought of surgery, I just don't think I can continue this way." The next day José's father called the doctor and made arrangements for surgery.

DECIDE AND REVIEW

4. *Decide and Act.* What was José's first choice for handling his gallstone problem?

5. *Review.* Why did José change his mind? Would you have made the same choices as José?

PROJECTS

1. From a variety of materials of your choice, make a three-dimensional model of the digestive system. Use Figure 12-1 and Plate Four as a guide, or find other resources. With small file cards, make labels explaining the processes that occur at different points as food passes through your system.

2. How do you react to certain foods? Keep a log of the foods you eat for one full week. After each entry, write down how you felt immediately after eating and how you felt about an hour later. At the end of the week, note which foods led to any discomfort. Work to eliminate those foods from your diet and find healthy substitutes.

WORKING WITH OTHERS

Work with a partner to research an author, such as Adelle Davis or Anne-Marie Colbin, who wrote about nutrition and health. With your partner, role-play an interview in which one of you acts as the author and the other as the interviewer. The interviewer should ask questions to draw out information about the author's research and theories. The author should be able to explain his or her work, including the reasons for the theories.

CONNECTING TO...

MEDICAL TECHNOLOGY Kidney dialysis is a relatively recent development that can prolong the life of patients suffering from kidney failure. Do library research to find out how this technique was originally developed. What types of machines have been used in the past and are being used now? What new advances are expected? You also might want to compare dialysis with an alternative treatment such as a kidney transplant.

USING VOCABULARY

absorption	food poisoning
alimentary canal	gallstone
appendicitis	glomerulus
bile	hemorrhoids
bladder	indigestion
cancer	irritable bowel syndrome
chyme	kidney
constipation	nephron
cystitis	pancreas
diarrhea	peristalsis
digestion	small intestine
elimination	ulcer
enzyme	ureter
esophagus	urethra
excretion	

Number a separate sheet of paper from 1 to 10. Match each of the following definitions with a vocabulary term in the list above.

1. Proteins that cause a rapid chemical breakdown of complex substances.
2. A tube that connects the mouth with the stomach.
3. A yellow-green digestive juice released by the liver.
4. A long, soft gland behind the stomach that secretes digestive enzymes into the small intestine.
5. Swollen veins in the anal area that may cause itching, pain, and bleeding.
6. A serious illness caused by spoiled, infected, or contaminated food.
7. The process that collects and eliminates harmful or useless substances from the blood, tissues, and cells.
8. A tube leading from the bladder to the outside of the body.
9. A condition in which the stools are unusually hard and dry.
10. A long, winding tube made up of the organs through which food passes.

CONCEPT MAPPING

Copy and complete the concept map shown below. Information on concept mapping appears at the front of this book.

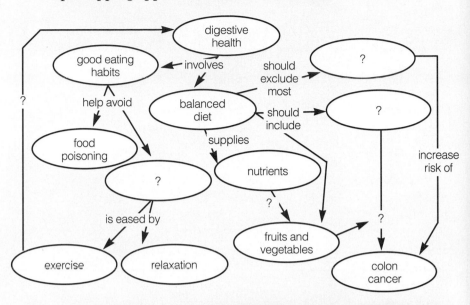

THINKING CRITICALLY

INTERPRET

LESSON 12.1

1. Name the organs of the digestive system in the order in which they function during digestion.

2. What is the difference between mechanical digestion and chemical digestion?

3. In which part of the digestive system does most chemical digestion and absorption take place?

4. Identify four functions of the liver in digestion.

LESSON 12.2

5. Identify two types of foods that help prevent colon cancer.

6. What is often the first sign of appendicitis? What other symptoms usually occur?

7. What are gallstones?

8. Why is eating food that has been left out of the refrigerator too long a potential health hazard?

LESSON 12.3

9. Identify two functions of the liver in excretion.

10. What function do the lungs serve in excretion?

11. What is cystitis?

12. Name the organs in the urinary system.

APPLY

LESSON 12.1

13. The wall of the small intestine has millions of tiny projections called villi. Why is a wall with villi an advantage over a flat, smooth wall?

LESSON 12.2

14. What causes gallstones?

LESSON 12.3

15. Why is excretion such an important process?

16. What is the difference between excretion and elimination?

COMMITMENT TO WELLNESS

FOLLOW-UP

SETTING GOALS

Review your responses to the checklist at the beginning of this chapter. Which statements accurately describe you? Which behaviors do you not engage in now?

Make a separate list of the behaviors that are now part of your daily routine. Next to each behavior, note whether it has always been a part of your routine or whether it is a recent change in habit. Next, make another list of the behaviors that are not part of your routine. What action can you take to make these practices a regular part of your routine? Refer back to your list of positive behaviors, and see if any of the changes or steps you took can be applied to the behaviors not already in your routine.

WHERE DO I GO FROM HERE?

Review your lists again in a month or two. Which *no* answers have you been able to change to *yes*? For the *no* answers that did not change, try to find some new ideas about ways to change your behavior. Many books and magazines deal exclusively with healthy eating and digestion. Ask your health teacher or a librarian to direct you to these references.

FOR MORE INFORMATION ABOUT DIGESTIVE DISEASES AND DISORDERS, CONTACT:

Digestive Diseases Education and Information Clearinghouse
Box NDDIC
7000 Rockville Pike
Bethesda, Maryland 20892

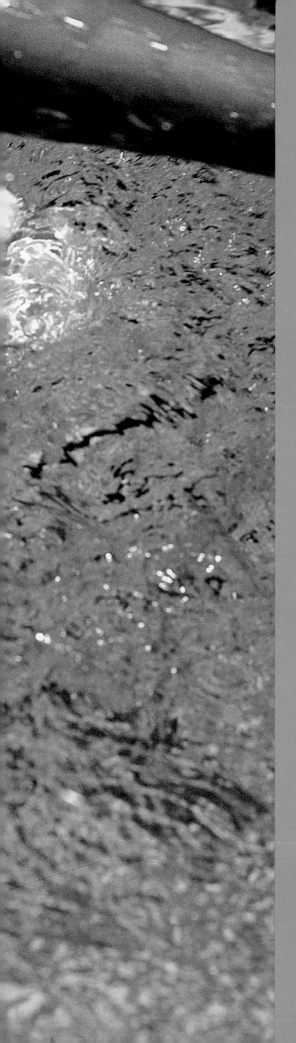

Physical Fitness

Chapter 13
Bones and Muscles

Chapter 14
Circulation and Respiration

Chapter 15
Lifelong Activity

What is the best way to avoid sprains and strains?

Does regular physical exercise really affect longevity?

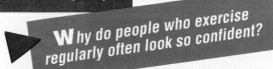

Why do people who exercise regularly often look so confident?

Bones and Muscles

"The great thing in this world is not so much where we are, but in what direction we are moving."

Oliver Wendell Holmes

Movement is the mainstay of growth. Your intellect, your emotions, and your body are growing—moving forward—every day. To be productive and healthy, you need to nurture growth by building on the strength of today. Your mind grows by being open and aware; your body grows by maintaining good nourishment and care.

The human body is an amazing machine—one that requires the cooperation and coordination of several important body systems. Your body moves because of an intricate and cooperative system made up of hundreds of bones and muscles. These bones and muscles grow stronger with use, and atrophy, or grow weaker, with disuse. Understanding how your bones and muscles work and grow is an important way to keep active and healthy and to continue "moving forward."

On a sheet of paper or in your Wellness Journal, write *yes* or *no* to respond to the following statements.

1. I exercise regularly to maintain healthy bones, muscles, and joints.

2. I eat well-balanced meals rich in calcium to ensure healthy bone formation and maintenance.

3. I wear a helmet when I cycle, play baseball, or ride a motorcycle to protect my skull from serious injury.

4. I maintain muscle tone throughout my body with exercises aimed at maintaining good posture.

5. I maintain the strength and flexibility of the muscles that surround joints to protect from injury.

6. Whenever I injure muscle or joint tissue I apply ice immediately to the injured area to prevent swelling.

7. I understand the proper way to lift heavy objects to prevent a back injury.

8. I do stretching and warm-up activities before engaging in physical activity.

9. I understand how to assist an injured person with first aid treatment for a broken bone.

10. I eat well balanced meals rich in carbohydrates, the main source of energy for muscle contraction and effective movement.

Review your responses and consider what might be your strengths and weaknesses. Save your personal checklist for a follow-up activity that appears at the end of this chapter.

BONES—LIVING ORGANS

Bones are living organs. You may find this hard to believe if you have seen bones at the dinner table. Bones are made of cells that make new bone and replace old bone. Bones also contain minerals, which are nonliving materials.

The bones in your body are different sizes and shapes. The smallest bones are the three tiny bones in your middle ear. You can see those bones in Figure 2-8 in Chapter 2, "Taking Care of Yourself." The largest bones in your body are the bones in your thighs, the upper part of your legs.

The bones in your legs and arms are long, with a cylindrical shaft and large, rounded ends. Part of a typical long bone is shown in Figure 13-1. Other bones are short, flat, or irregularly shaped.

THE FUNCTIONS OF BONES

Regardless of their size or shape, bones perform five major functions in your body. They provide support for soft tissues, protect internal organs, help produce movement, store and release minerals, and produce new blood cells.

SUPPORT   The beams in a building form a framework that supports the floors, roof, walls, windows, and other building parts. In a similar way, your bones form a supporting framework that holds your body erect and gives it shape. Without bones, your body would be a mound of soft tissue.

PROTECTION   Bones provide a hard, protective covering for some of the soft tissues and organs inside your body. For example, your ribs protect your heart and lungs. Your skull protects your brain and the delicate structures inside your eyes and ears. The bones in your lower back and your hips protect the soft organs in your lower abdomen.

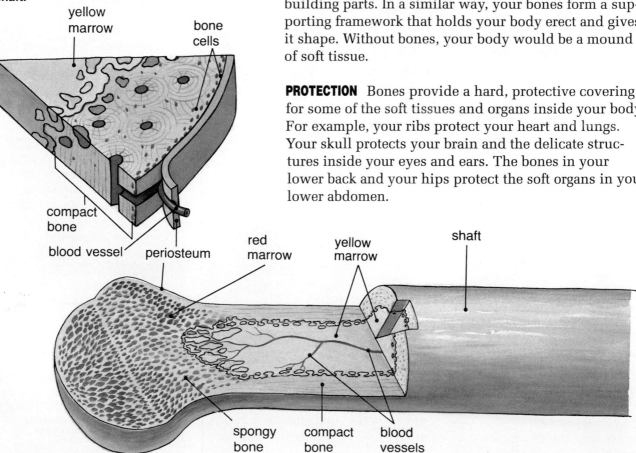

Figure 13-1   This picture shows the structure of a long bone. The wedge is taken from the bone shaft.

Joint Replacement Surgery

RESEARCH
HEALTH

Margery Beddows spent most of her almost 60 years dancing. She performed all over the world and choreographed hundreds of performances. In 1986, it was clear that Beddows' career was over. Her hips had stopped working. She had lost all mobility and the daily pain was unbearable. Margery Beddows, who knew no other work but dance, thought she would have to spend the rest of her life in a wheelchair.

Joints can be damaged in many ways. Common problems that can cause a joint to deteriorate enough to be disabling include osteoarthritis and sports injuries.

Fortunately for Beddows and for thousands like her who suffer from joint disintegration due to osteoarthritis or injury, joint replacement surgery is now available.

Joint replacement surgery, or arthroplasty, was first performed in 1962. This complicated surgical procedure uses mechanical devices to replace the hip, knee, shoulder, elbow, or wrist. Patients who undergo joint replacement surgery must be prepared for a long and possibly painful recovery that includes extensive physical therapy. Successful surgery will allow a fully recovered patient to move freely with no pain.

The replacement of a hip joint involves replacing the socket of the pelvis and the upper portion of the femur with a metal and plastic two-piece implant. Part of the implant resembles half of a tennis ball. The inside of the "tennis ball" is made of plastic and the outside is made of metal. The outside of the ball is imbedded into the pelvic bone. The other part of the implant is a shaft that is inserted into the open end of the femur. Eventually bone tissue grows into the metal, incorporating the shaft and new socket as part of the skeleton.

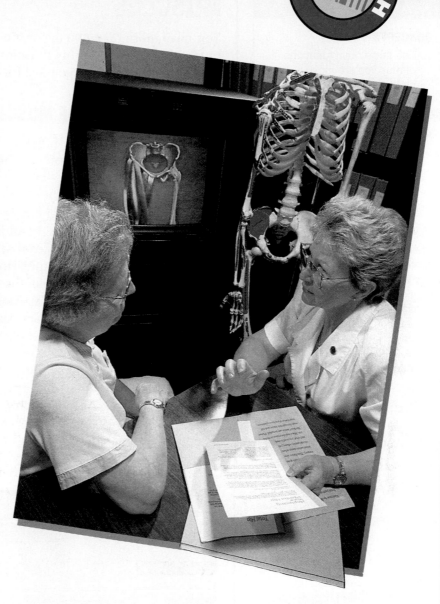

Each year, scientists are discovering new technology to increase mobility and reduce pain. Advances in joint replacement surgery are giving people a second chance to live active, vibrant lives. For Margery Beddows, joint replacement surgery saved her career—and, she says, her life.

1. Explain how a person suffering from joint disintegration would benefit from joint replacement surgery.

2. Why is it important for scientists to continue to work on new technology for joint replacement surgery?

MUSCLES

You have more than 600 major muscles in your body. Muscles range in size from the tiny muscles that make the hairs on your arm stand up, to the large muscles that move your leg at your hip.

THE FUNCTIONS OF MUSCLES

Muscles have three main functions: movement, maintenance of posture, and production of body heat. In addition, muscles help give your body its shape.

MOVEMENT You know that bones cannot move by themselves but must be moved by muscles. In addition to the muscles that move your bones, you have muscles that move other organs and tissues within your body. For example, tiny muscles in the iris contract and relax to control the size of the pupil and the amount of light that enters your eye. Other muscles pump blood through your body, mix food in your stomach, and cause many other movements that you are not aware of most of the time.

MAINTENANCE OF POSTURE Bones support your body, but your skeleton cannot balance upright by itself. To keep your body upright against the pull of gravity, muscles must continually contract, pulling against your bones. Your brain and the semicircular canals in your ears also play an important role in maintaining your posture and balance.

MAIN IDEAS

CONCEPTS

✔ The three main functions of muscles are movement, maintenance of posture, and production of body heat.

✔ All body movements are the result of muscle contraction and relaxation.

✔ Muscles use carbohydrates, fats, and oxygen to produce energy for contractions.

VOCABULARY

skeletal muscle
smooth muscle
cardiac muscle
tendon
muscle tone
cramp
strain
tendonitis
hernia

All movements, including this cartwheel, are the result of muscles moving bones.

PRODUCTION OF BODY HEAT To contract, muscles require energy, which they get from nutrients in the food you eat. Muscles convert some of this food energy to movement, but most is converted to heat. The constant muscle contractions throughout your body produce a large amount of heat. This heat helps maintain your body's normal temperature.

TYPES OF MUSCLES

There are three types of muscle tissue in your body: skeletal muscle, smooth muscle, and cardiac muscle. Each type of muscle tissue has a different function.

SKELETAL MUSCLE As its name suggests, **skeletal muscle** is attached to the bones in your skeleton. The major skeletal muscles are shown in Plates Two and Three. All movements that you can control are produced by your skeletal muscles. Because you can control them, skeletal muscles are also called voluntary muscles.

SMOOTH MUSCLE **Smooth muscle** produces movement in your internal organs. For example, layers of smooth muscle line the walls of your blood vessels. This muscle helps control the flow of blood through your body. Unlike movements caused by skeletal muscle, you do not have to think about movements of smooth muscle. In fact, you usually are unable to control smooth muscle. For this reason, smooth muscle is also called involuntary muscle.

CARDIAC MUSCLE **Cardiac muscle** [*KARD ee ak*] is a type of involuntary muscle that forms the walls of the heart. Cardiac muscle works nonstop for your entire lifetime. At rest, your heart normally beats about 60 to 80 times a minute.

HOW MUSCLES WORK

Working together, your muscles produce a great variety of movements. However, each muscle in your body is capable of only two actions: contraction and relaxation. When a muscle contracts, it gets shorter and bunches up. When it relaxes, it returns to its original length.

Muscles generally do not contract or relax on their own. Muscles—skeletal, smooth, and, under some conditions, cardiac—are controlled by nerve impulses from your brain. Different parts of your brain control different types of muscles.

All skeletal movements are the result of muscles pulling on bones. Muscles are attached to bones by tendons. A **tendon** is a cord of tissue that connects a muscle to a bone. Like the ligaments that attach one bone to another bone, tendons are made mostly of collagen.

To move a bone, a muscle must cross over a joint. One end of the muscle is attached to one bone, and the other end is attached to another bone on the other side of the joint. When the muscle contracts, it pulls one bone toward the other bone.

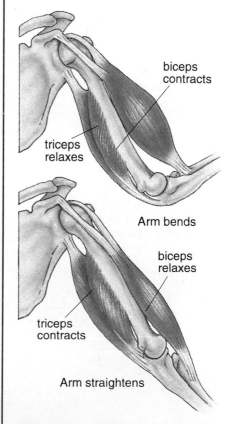

Figure 13-8 When one muscle in a pair contracts, the other muscle relaxes.

Many muscles in your body cross over two joints. An example is your biceps muscle, one of the two upper-arm muscles shown in Figure 13-8. One end of your biceps is attached to your shoulder blade. The other end is attached to a bone in your lower arm. When the biceps contracts, its shoulder end stays steady. The other end pulls your lower arm up toward your shoulder, bending your arm at the elbow. To straighten your arm, the triceps contracts while your biceps relaxes. At joints throughout your body, muscles are paired or grouped in this way to move bones.

ENERGY FOR MUSCLES

Carbohydrates and fats are the energy sources for muscle contractions. Your body breaks down carbohydrates to form glucose. If the glucose is not needed immediately, it is converted to glycogen and stored in the muscles and the liver. Excess glucose also may be converted to fat. Fats that are not needed immediately are stored in fat cells throughout your body.

As blood flows through your intestines and liver, it picks up glucose. In your lungs, it picks up oxygen. It also picks up fats throughout your body. The blood carries the glucose, oxygen, and fats to your muscles. The muscle cells use these materials in chemical reactions that produce energy.

The chemical reactions also produce waste products—carbon dioxide and water. Blood flowing through your muscles picks up these waste products and carries them to your lungs, kidneys, and skin for removal. Carbon dioxide and water vapor leave your body in the air that your lungs exhale. Water also leaves your body in urine and perspiration.

During an aerobics workout, do muscles get more energy from glucose or from fats?

PLATE ONE

Skeletal System

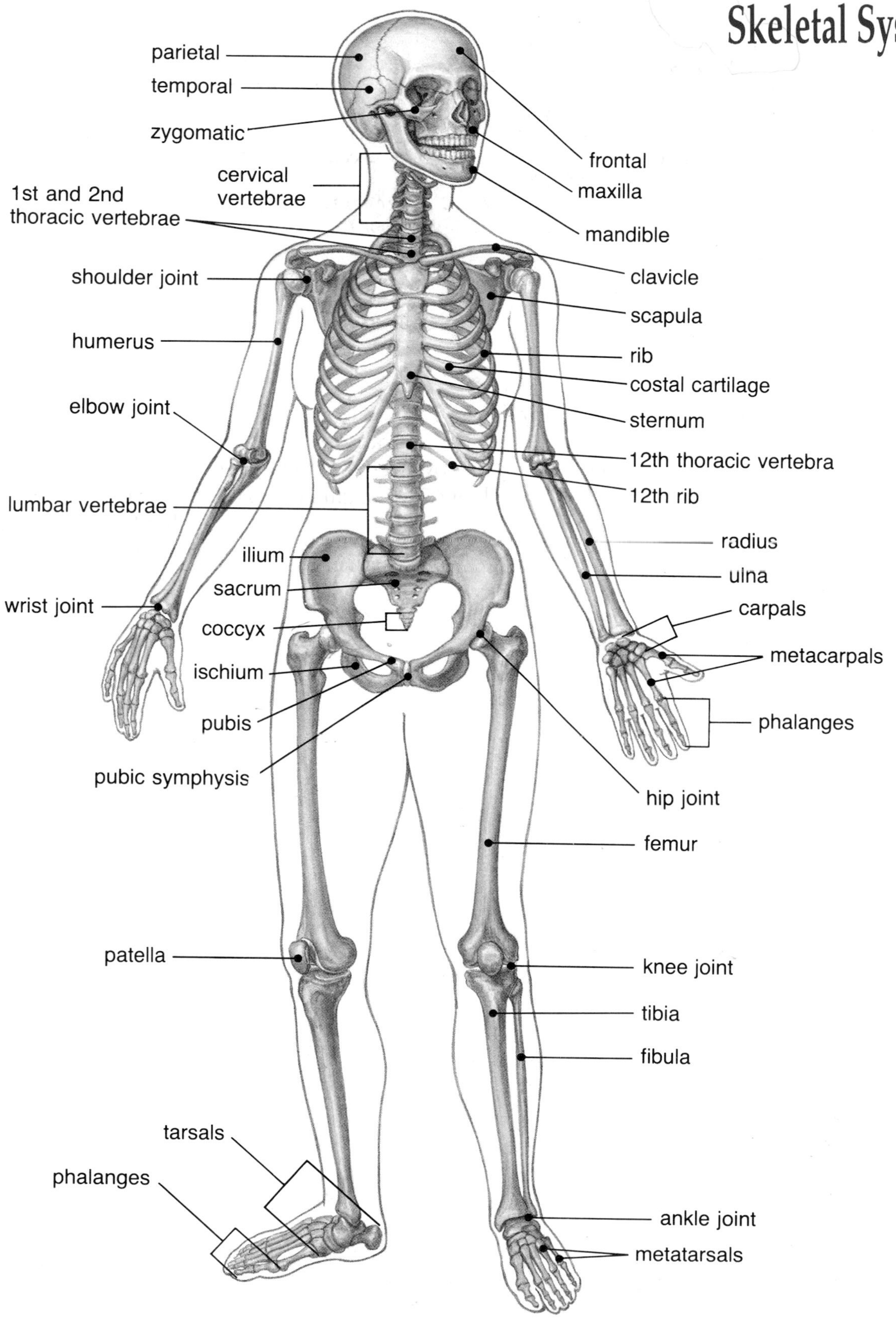

parietal
temporal
zygomatic
cervical vertebrae
1st and 2nd thoracic vertebrae
shoulder joint
humerus
elbow joint
lumbar vertebrae
ilium
sacrum
wrist joint
coccyx
ischium
pubis
pubic symphysis
patella
tarsals
phalanges
frontal
maxilla
mandible
clavicle
scapula
rib
costal cartilage
sternum
12th thoracic vertebra
12th rib
radius
ulna
carpals
metacarpals
phalanges
hip joint
femur
knee joint
tibia
fibula
ankle joint
metatarsals

PLATE TWO
Muscular System

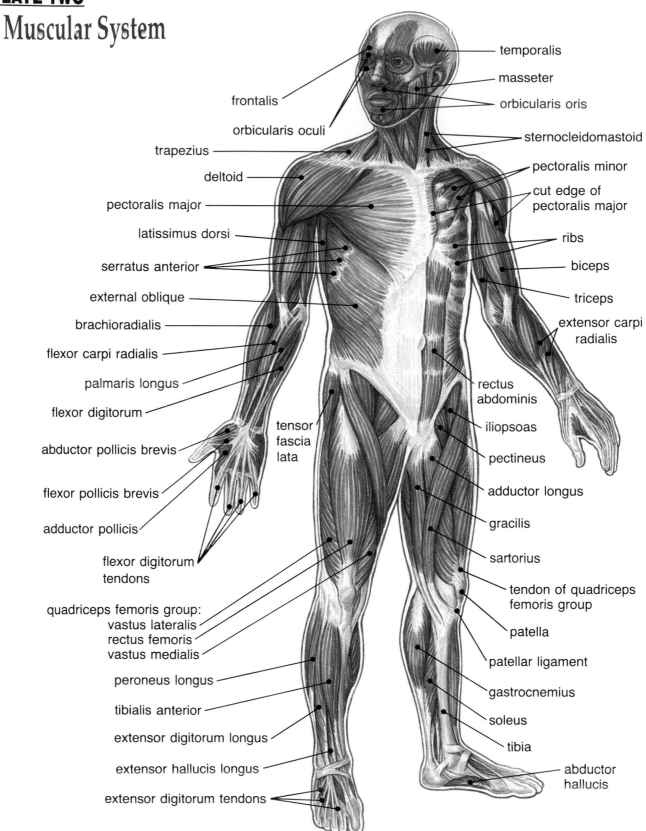

frontalis

orbicularis oculi

trapezius

deltoid

pectoralis major

latissimus dorsi

serratus anterior

external oblique

brachioradialis

flexor carpi radialis

palmaris longus

flexor digitorum

abductor pollicis brevis

flexor pollicis brevis

adductor pollicis

flexor digitorum
tendons

quadriceps femoris group:
vastus lateralis
rectus femoris
vastus medialis

peroneus longus

tibialis anterior

extensor digitorum longus

extensor hallucis longus

extensor digitorum tendons

tensor
fascia
lata

temporalis

masseter

orbicularis oris

sternocleidomastoid

pectoralis minor

cut edge of
pectoralis major

ribs

biceps

triceps

extensor carpi
radialis

rectus
abdominis

iliopsoas

pectineus

adductor longus

gracilis

sartorius

tendon of quadriceps
femoris group

patella

patellar ligament

gastrocnemius

soleus

tibia

abductor
hallucis

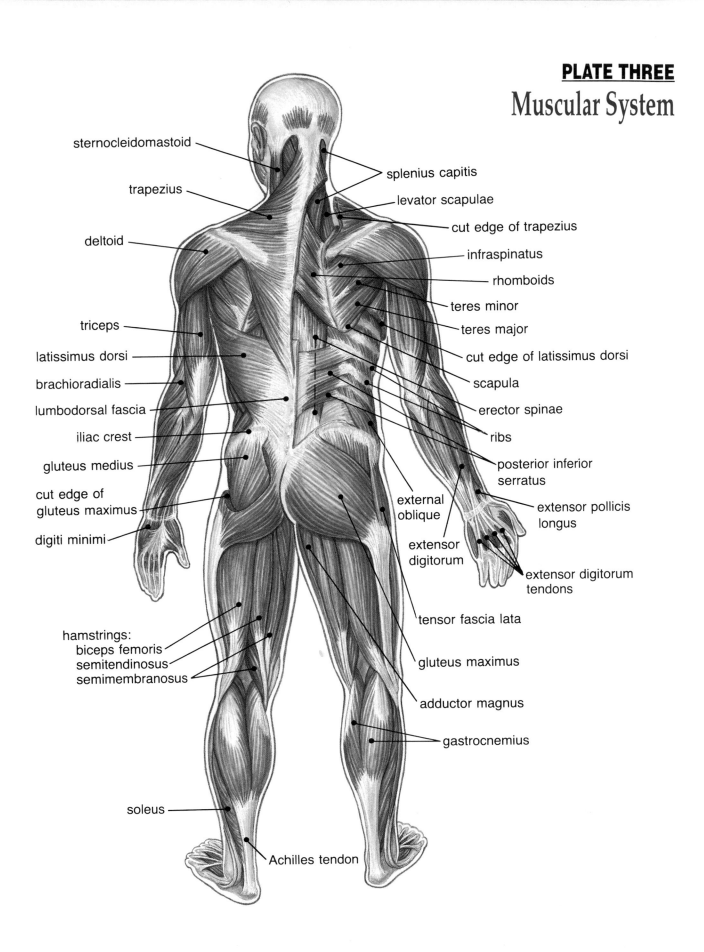

PLATE THREE

Muscular System

sternocleidomastoid

splenius capitis

trapezius

levator scapulae

cut edge of trapezius

deltoid

infraspinatus

rhomboids

teres minor

teres major

triceps

cut edge of latissimus dorsi

latissimus dorsi

scapula

brachioradialis

erector spinae

lumbodorsal fascia

ribs

iliac crest

posterior inferior
serratus

gluteus medius

cut edge of
gluteus maximus

external
oblique

extensor pollicis
longus

digiti minimi

extensor
digitorum

extensor digitorum
tendons

tensor fascia lata

hamstrings:
biceps femoris
semitendinosus
semimembranosus

gluteus maximus

adductor magnus

gastrocnemius

soleus

Achilles tendon

PLATE FOUR
Digestive System

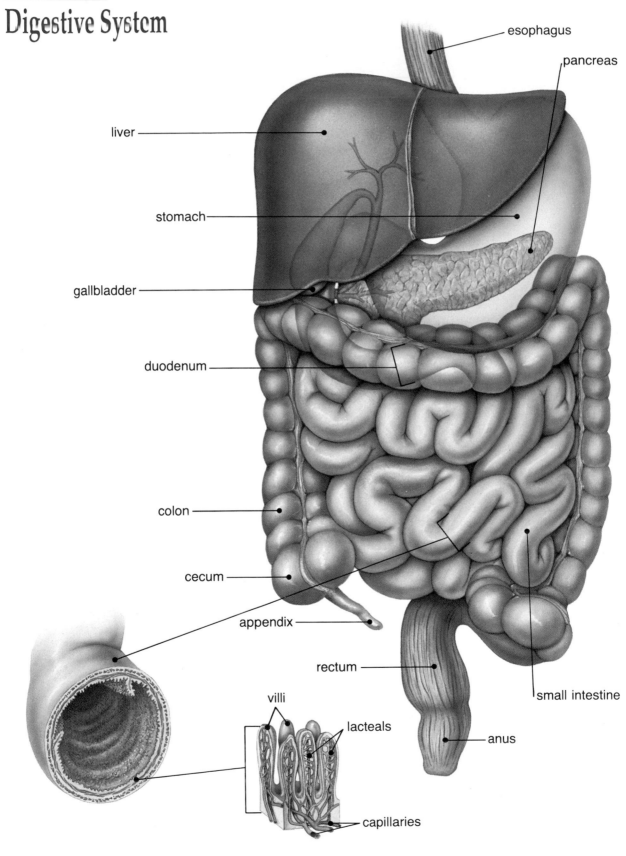

esophagus

pancreas

liver

stomach

gallbladder

duodenum

colon

cecum

appendix

rectum

small intestine

anus

villi

lacteals

capillaries

The amount of glucose and fats needed for energy varies according to your activity. When you are sitting quietly, your muscles use roughly equal amounts of glucose and fats. When you are vigorously active for a short time—as a weight lifter is, for example—your muscles use more glucose than fats. However, when you are moderately active over a longer period of time, your muscles get more energy from fats than from glucose. The longer the activity lasts, the more fats that are used. This is why 30 minutes or more of moderate exercise is better for weight control than short spurts of intense exercise.

POSTURE AND MUSCLE TONE

With good posture, the parts of your body are in balance with each other. Poor posture makes your muscles work harder. In addition, your bones, ligaments, and joints have to bear a greater load over time. This can cause pain, particularly in your lower back.

Good posture depends on muscle tone. **Muscle tone** is the slight but constant contraction of skeletal muscles. To maintain this constant contraction, some cells in each muscle contract while the other cells stay relaxed, then the contracted cells relax while other cells contract. This tightens the muscle enough to maintain posture but not enough to produce movement.

Your abdominal muscles help support your body weight. Poor tone in these muscles places additional strain on your lower back, increasing the likelihood of lower back pain and disc rupture. Moderate exercise on a regular basis and stretching exercises build and maintain muscle tone.

MUSCLE INJURIES AND DISORDERS

Muscle injuries are common. You have probably overworked or overstretched your muscles at times. Although muscles can suffer damage, they usually heal themselves. Regular exercise helps prevent muscle injuries.

CRAMP   A **cramp** is an intense and prolonged muscle contraction that causes pain. A muscle may cramp when it is overworked. Massaging the muscle and gently stretching against its pull usually helps relieve the cramp.

STRAIN   A **strain** is a tear in a muscle or tendon. Do not confuse a strain with a sprain, which is a tear in a ligament. Strains often result from overworking a muscle, such as lifting too much weight or lifting too suddenly. A large tear, which is a serious injury, can result from a sudden force or pull. Strains commonly occur in large muscles, such as the muscles in the hip and shoulder. The best way to avoid straining a muscle is to warm up and stretch before an activity.

If you strain a muscle, apply an ice pack as soon as possible, and continue using ice to keep the swelling down. Let the muscle rest

If sitting like this becomes a habit, your muscle tone and posture will suffer.

to aid healing. If the tear is small, usually no permanent damage will result. However, the muscle may continue to be sore for some time. A large tear may take a long time to heal.

TENDONITIS   Overusing a muscle may cause a tendon to become inflamed, irritated, and swollen. This painful condition is called **tendonitis** [*ten duh NYT us*]. One example is tennis elbow, which is caused by repeated turning of the hand and impacts to the arm. Tendonitis can be a troublesome condition because the injury heals slowly. Also, tendonitis tends to recur because the tendon can be injured again quite easily. Resting the tendon seems to be the only treatment.

HERNIA   Some people have a weak spot in the layers of skeletal muscle that cover the abdomen and groin area. The weak spot might be present at birth, or it could be the result of surgery or of conditions that put strain on the abdominal muscles, such as obesity or pregnancy. A **hernia** [*HUR nee uh*] occurs when part of the intestine pushes through the weak spot. A hernia requires medical treatment. In most cases, surgery is necessary.

MUSCLE DISEASES   Muscle diseases are far less common than muscle injuries. One muscle disease is muscular dystrophy [*MUS kyuh lur DIS truh fee*], a hereditary disease that slowly destroys muscle tissue. People with muscular dystrophy gradually lose muscle control and eventually may become completely unable to move. There is no cure for muscular dystrophy, but treatment helps keep the person physically active as long as possible. This treatment includes exercising to strengthen muscles, wearing braces, and in some cases, surgery.

Lifting too much weight can cause a hernia.

SUMMARY

Muscles move your bones and internal organs, maintain your posture, and produce body heat. You can control skeletal muscle voluntarily, but smooth muscle and cardiac muscle function involuntarily. All muscles work by contracting and relaxing. Carbohydrates, fats, and oxygen supply the energy for muscle contractions. Muscle injuries can be prevented through regular exercise.

LESSON 13.4   **USING WHAT YOU HAVE LEARNED**

REVIEW

1. Why are skeletal muscles also called voluntary muscles?
2. What is the difference between a ligament and a tendon?
3. Describe the treatment for a strain.

THINK CRITICALLY

4. Moderate exercise for 30 minutes or more is better for weight control than short spurts of intense exercise. In your own words, explain why this is true.
5. Suppose that in science class, your younger brother drew a picture of a muscle attached to opposite ends of the same bone. What would you tell your brother to explain why his drawing is wrong?

APPLY IT TO YOURSELF

6. Imagine that you play on a softball team. You arrive late for practice one day, and the two practice squads have already started playing. You immediately join a squad and start fielding. Why is this a bad idea? What should you do instead?

Broken Chances

Andrea was the star center of the basketball team. Her team depended on her to win. Indeed, they were undefeated, and tonight was a big playoff game against their chief rival—Madison High. The winner would go on to the state tournament. Andrea was psyched about the game and knew that it would be one of the biggest of her career. She was hoping to play ball in college, and several college coaches would be at the game.

The first half of the game was tough. Both teams were playing well. As the end of the third quarter approached, the score was 54–50 with Madison ahead. Andrea was making a move to the basket when she twisted her ankle. The referee called time-out. The crowd was hushed as Andrea's team gathered around her. Her ankle didn't appear too swollen, so it was hard to tell the seriousness of the injury. As her coach examined her ankle, Andrea saw the anxious looks on her teammates' faces. She had sprained her ankle before but somehow this felt worse than a sprain.

"There isn't much swelling. Andrea, can you put pressure on it?" asked her coach.

"Let me try," said Andrea. She got to her feet and took a few steps. It really hurt, but she could walk on it. She thought she might be able to keep going. Andrea knew that if she quit now, the chances were good that her team would lose. But she was afraid that if she kept playing, she could risk serious damage. She didn't want to be a quitter.

PAUSE AND CONSIDER

1. **Identify the Problem.** What is Andrea's conflict?
2. **Consider the Options.** What are Andrea's choices?

3. **Evaluate the Outcomes.** What could happen if Andrea kept playing? What could happen if she was unable to keep going?

As she tried to walk off the pain, her foot and ankle just didn't feel right. Andrea knew she would be crazy to keep playing. She felt as though she was letting everyone down— her teammates, her coach, her school, her parents. With tears streaming down her face, she said, "No, coach, it hurts really badly. I don't think taping it will be enough. I'm sorry."

"Hey, don't worry about it. Your health is what's important," said her coach.

Her parents and a school official then took Andrea to the hospital for X rays. While she was at the hospital, Andrea learned that her team had indeed lost the game. She also learned that she had a hairline fracture of one of the small bones in her ankle. Andrea knew she had made the right choice, difficult as it was.

DECIDE AND REVIEW

4. **Decide and Act.** Why did Andrea make the choice that she did?
5. **Review.** What were the possible consequences if Andrea had kept playing? Why would some people have continued to play?

PROJECTS

1. Imagine that you are an athlete in training for the Olympics. Pick a competition that interests you, such as swimming, running, gymnastics, or volleyball. Create a daily training program that includes exercise, a well-balanced diet, rest, and injury prevention appropriate for the sport you chose.

2. In the stories of the Trojan War, Achilles was the greatest warrior of the Greek army. According to one tale, he was invulnerable except for a certain tendon in his body. Find out the location of this tendon and how Achilles' tendon became vulnerable. Then find your own Achilles tendon, one of the largest tendons in your body. It should feel like a thick, stiff rope.

WORKING WITH OTHERS

With a partner, create the following scenario. One of you has suffered a muscle or bone injury while playing your favorite sport. You apply first aid treatment for the injury but require medical attention. The other partner acts as doctor or nurse practitioner working to heal the injury. Be sure that the injured partner describes the injury—its symptoms and the first aid treatment given. The doctor or nurse then describes the reason for the injury and the prescription for long-term care.

CONNECTING TO...

HOME ECONOMICS   One of the basic tools of home economics is learning proper nutrition. Nutrition is an essential part of maintaining healthy bones and muscles. Create a week-long eating plan for yourself that includes all of the nutrients important for building and maintaining your bones and muscles.

USING VOCABULARY

appendicular skeleton	dislocation	periosteum
arthritis	estrogen	pivot joint
axial skeleton	fracture	red bone marrow
ball-and-socket joint	gliding joint	scoliosis
	greenstick fracture	skeletal muscle
	hernia	smooth muscle
bursitis	hinge joint	spongy bone
cardiac muscle	joint	sprain
cartilage	ligament	sternum
closed fracture	muscle tone	strain
collagen	open fracture	tendon
compact bone	osteoarthritis	tendonitis
cramp	osteoporosis	vertebra/vertebrae
cranium	pelvis	yellow bone marrow

On a separate sheet of paper, write T or F to indicate whether each statement is true or false. For each false statement, change the underlined term to make the statement true.

1. <u>Red bone marrow</u> consists mostly of fat cells.

2. The spinal column is made of irregularly shaped bones called <u>vertebrae</u>.

3. The <u>appendicular skeleton</u> consists of the bones in the skull, spinal column, and chest.

4. The part of the skull that protects the brain is called the <u>sternum</u>.

5. A <u>ligament</u> connects one bone to another bone.

6. A <u>strain</u> is a tear in a ligament.

7. An inflammation of a sac near a joint is called <u>bursitis</u>.

8. <u>Osteoarthritis</u> is a thinning and weakening of bones caused by calcium loss.

9. The slight but constant contraction of skeletal muscles is known as <u>scoliosis</u>.

10. <u>Compact bone</u> is hard and dense, with few spaces.

11. <u>Cartilage</u> holds minerals together in bones.

12. In a <u>closed fracture</u>, the broken ends of the bone do not pierce the skin.

13. <u>Smooth muscle</u> produces movement in the internal organs.

14. In a <u>hernia</u>, the end of one bone is pulled out of the joint.

15. At a <u>gliding joint</u>, one bone rotates around another bone.

CONCEPT MAPPING

Copy and complete the concept map shown below. Information on concept mapping appears at the front of this book.

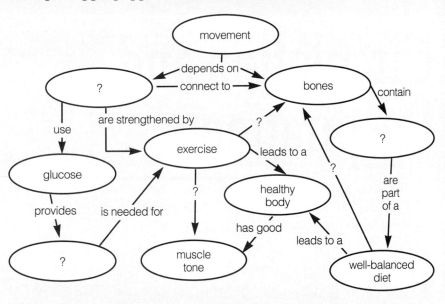

THINKING CRITICALLY

INTERPRET

LESSON 13.1
1. Identify the five functions of bones.

2. Describe how bone tissue changes from infancy through adolescence. What is the result of this change?

LESSON 13.2
3. Name the two major divisions of the human skeleton, and identify the parts of the skeleton included in each division.

4. What is the function of the curves in the spinal column?

5. Describe three functions of the pelvis.

6. Why are partially movable joints stable?

LESSON 13.2
7. Name and describe three common types of fractures.

8. Why is ice recommended as a treatment for injuries?

9. How does an adequate level of estrogen prevent osteoporosis?

LESSON 13.4
10. What are the functions of muscles?

11. Describe how a skeletal muscle moves a bone at a joint.

12. Identify two ways of building and maintaining muscle tone.

APPLY

LESSON 13.1
13. Describe how the balance between bone formation and bone loss changes from childhood through adulthood.

LESSON 13.2
14. Why is the cranium sometimes compared to a crash helmet?

15. The bones in your foot fit together to form two arches, but the bones in your hand do not. Suggest a reason for this.

LESSON 13.3
16. Describe four ways of easing the symptoms of arthritis.

LESSON 13.4
17. What kinds of problems are caused by poor muscle tone?

Circulation and Respiration

"To live is not merely to breathe, it is to act; it is to make use of our organs, senses, faculties, of all of those parts of ourselves which give us the feeling of existence."

Jean-Jacques Rousseau

To act, or "to make use of . . . all those parts of ourselves," is a vital way to participate in the world around you. Without action, "merely to breathe," you are left lifeless and unmoving.

Inside your body there is action every moment. Blood delivers oxygen and nutrients to your organs. Your heart, lungs, kidneys, skin, and reproductive and digestive systems could not act, could not keep you alive, without the circulatory and respiratory systems. These systems work together to deliver essential nutrients throughout your body and to rid your body of wastes. But your heart and lungs cannot function well without your help. You can help by eating a balanced diet and by refraining from smoking to ensure an active, healthy life.

BACKGROUND

An eighteenth century French philosopher, Jean-Jacques Rousseau was well known for his revolt against the social order of his day. He is considered to be one of the influences that began the French Revolution.

SELF-ASSESSMENT

On a sheet of paper or in your Wellness Journal, write *yes* or *no* to respond to the following statements.

1. I exercise regularly.
2. I understand how the heart and lungs function.
3. I limit saturated fats in my diet.
4. I do not smoke.
5. I try to avoid stress.
6. I would like to be a regular blood donor.
7. I eat a well-balanced diet that includes vitamins and minerals.
8. I avoid settings where people may be smoking.
9. I seek medical advice whenever I contract a serious inflammation of my throat or lungs.
10. I have my blood pressure checked at least once every year.

Review your responses and consider what might be your strengths and weaknesses. Save your personal checklist for a follow-up activity that appears at the end of this chapter.

THE CIRCULATORY SYSTEM

MAIN IDEAS

CONCEPTS

✔ The circulatory system delivers essential materials to cells and picks up wastes from cells.

✔ The contraction of the heart muscle pumps blood through arteries, capillaries, and veins.

✔ Circulation occurs in two phases called pulmonary circulation and systemic circulation.

VOCABULARY

atrium
ventricle
artery
capillary
vein
pulmonary circulation
systemic circulation

Your circulatory system—or cardiovascular system, as it is also called—is made up of your heart, your blood vessels, and the blood that circulates through them. The system is shown in Plate Six and in Figure 14-3 later in this lesson.

THE FUNCTIONS OF THE CIRCULATORY SYSTEM

The primary functions of the circulatory system are to deliver materials to cells throughout your body and remove wastes from cells. The system also plays an important role in maintaining your body temperature.

DELIVERS MATERIALS TO CELLS   Your blood picks up and carries a variety of essential materials as it circulates. These materials include nutrients from your digestive system and oxygen from your lungs. The blood releases these materials to cells throughout your body.

REMOVES WASTES FROM CELLS   As it circulates, blood also picks up waste products from cells. The blood carries the wastes to other parts of your body to be eliminated. For example, carbon dioxide is carried to your lungs to be eliminated when you exhale. Urea, water, and other wastes are carried to your kidneys to be eliminated in urine.

HELPS MAINTAIN BODY TEMPERATURE   Your circulatory system plays an important role in helping your body adapt to varying conditions of heat and cold. The system transports heat from your muscles and internal organs to the surface of your skin. When your body is

Figure 14-1   Notice the muscular wall between the right and left sides of the heart.

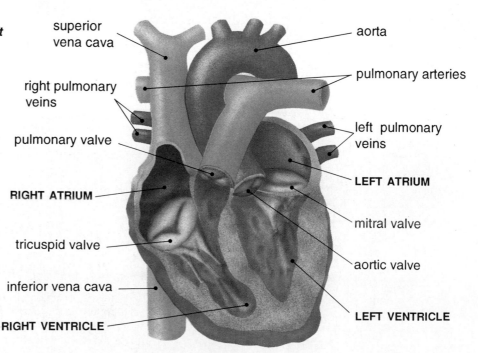

superior vena cava

aorta

right pulmonary veins

pulmonary arteries

pulmonary valve

left pulmonary veins

RIGHT ATRIUM

LEFT ATRIUM

mitral valve

tricuspid valve

aortic valve

inferior vena cava

LEFT VENTRICLE

RIGHT VENTRICLE

too warm, your brain triggers a sweating response. Evaporation of perspiration releases excess heat into your surroundings. In cold conditions, blood is directed away from your skin to the internal parts of your body. This process retains heat.

THE HEART

Your heart is a hollow, muscular pump about the size of your clenched fist. The heart's thick walls are made of strong cardiac muscles that contract and relax about 60 to 80 times every minute when you are at rest. These continuous contractions keep blood flowing throughout your body.

The inner structure of your heart is shown in Figure 14-1. You can see that a wall of muscle separates the heart into right and left sides. (The words *right* and *left* refer to your own viewpoint, not the viewpoint of someone looking at you.) Normally there is no opening between the right and left sides of the heart.

Each side is further divided into two chambers, one above the other. On both sides, the upper chamber is called the **atrium** [*AY tree um*], and the lower chamber is called the **ventricle** [*VEN trih kul*]. The atrium and ventricle on each side are connected by a one-way valve. This valve allows blood to flow in only one direction from the atrium to the ventricle and not backward from the ventricle to the atrium. Other one-way valves connect the ventricles to the two main blood vessels leading away from the heart. These valves prevent blood from flowing backward into the heart. Find all four valves in Figure 14-1.

Blood always travels the same path through the heart. Imagine you are a microscopic speck in your bloodstream. You are floating along in oxygen-poor blood returning to your heart from another part of your body. Figure 14-2 shows the path you would travel.

If you were in your bloodstream, you would experience these steps one by one. However, if you were outside your heart looking in, you would see that both sides of the heart pump at the same

Figure 14-2   Blood travels through the heart in a sequence of steps. What happens to blood when it passes through the lungs?

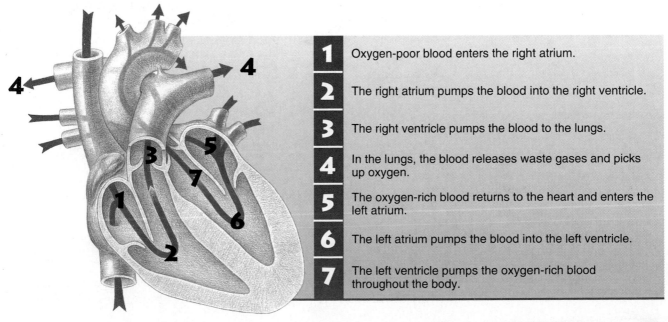

1	Oxygen-poor blood enters the right atrium.
2	The right atrium pumps the blood into the right ventricle.
3	The right ventricle pumps the blood to the lungs.
4	In the lungs, the blood releases waste gases and picks up oxygen.
5	The oxygen-rich blood returns to the heart and enters the left atrium.
6	The left atrium pumps the blood into the left ventricle.
7	The left ventricle pumps the oxygen-rich blood throughout the body.

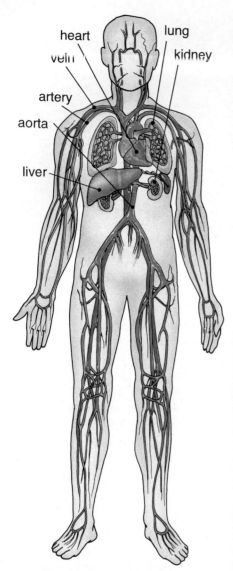

heart
lung
vein
kidney
artery
aorta
liver

Figure 14-3 *In this diagram of the circulatory system, red represents arteries, and blue represents veins.*

time. First, both atria pump blood to the ventricles (steps 2 and 6). Then both ventricles pump blood out of the heart (steps 3 and 7). The repeated "lubb-dupp" of your heartbeat is the sound of your heart valves closing—first the valves between the atria and ventricles, then the valves between the ventricles and blood vessels.

THE BLOOD VESSELS

Your circulatory system includes three types of blood vessels: arteries, capillaries, and veins. Some of the larger arteries and veins are shown in Figure 14-3.

ARTERIES   Arteries [*AHRT uh reez*] carry blood away from the heart. When the left ventricle pumps oxygen-rich blood out of the heart, the blood enters the aorta [*ay ORT uh*], the largest artery in your body. From the aorta, the blood flows through a branching system of smaller and smaller arteries. The walls of the arteries are lined with smooth muscle tissue. These muscles contract and relax to control the amount of blood flowing through the arteries and into the capillaries.

CAPILLARIES   Capillaries [*KAP uh ler eez*] connect the smallest arteries to the smallest veins. Capillaries are microscopic vessels with extremely thin walls. Oxygen, nutrients, and other materials carried by your blood pass through the capillary walls into the fluid surrounding the body's cells. At the same time, waste products from the cells pass through the capillary walls into the bloodstream. The blood then flows into the smallest veins.

VEINS   Veins [*VAYNZ*] carry blood back to your heart. Smaller veins connect to form larger and larger veins. Eventually, the blood flows into either of the two largest veins and then into the right atrium.

PULMONARY CIRCULATION

The circulation of blood between your heart and your lungs is called **pulmonary circulation** [*PUL muh ner ee*]. In this pathway, oxygen-poor blood is pumped from the right ventricle through the pulmonary arteries to a network of smaller arteries and capillaries in your lungs. The capillaries surround tiny air sacs. Blood flowing through the capillaries releases waste gases into the air sacs and picks up oxygen. The oxygen-rich blood flows through veins back to the heart and into the left atrium. In pulmonary circulation, arteries carry oxygen-poor blood away from the heart, and veins carry oxygen-rich blood back to the heart.

SYSTEMIC CIRCULATION

The circulation of blood between your heart and all other parts of your body except your lungs is called **systemic circulation** [*sis TEM ik*]. In systemic circulation, arteries carry oxygen-rich blood away from the heart, and veins carry oxygen-poor blood back to the heart. Blood leaving the heart flows through many different

FOR YOUR INFORMATION

Each time your heart beats, a wave of blood surges outward through your arteries. This wave produces the pulse that you can feel in your neck and wrist.

pathways as the arteries branch. Three important pathways carry blood to and from the kidneys, the liver, and the walls of the heart.

THE HEART   Because cardiac muscles constantly contract and relax, they need a continuous supply of oxygen and nutrients. Contrary to what you might expect, the blood passing through the atria and ventricles does not nourish the heart muscles. Instead, coronary arteries deliver nutrients and oxygen to the muscles. These arteries are the first branches from the aorta. The coronary arteries branch into smaller arteries and then into capillaries. After releasing oxygen and nutrients and picking up wastes, the blood enters coronary veins and returns to the right atrium. You can see this branching system of coronary blood vessels in the photograph at the right.

THE KIDNEYS   One fifth of the blood that leaves your heart travels to your kidneys through arteries branching from the aorta. The kidneys filter wastes from the blood and eliminate them in urine, as described in Chapter 12, "Digestion and Excretion." Passage of blood through the kidneys removes most materials not needed by your body's tissues. Needed materials—such as glucose, amino acids, and water—are reabsorbed into the blood. Veins return the blood to the heart.

THE LIVER   In the small intestine, blood picks up vitamins, minerals, water, and other products of digestion. Before returning to your heart, the blood travels through veins to your liver. The liver picks up nutrients and stores any that your body does not need immediately. The liver also removes materials that might harm your body, such as mercury, a toxic metal. The harmful materials are either detoxified or stored so they do not reach the rest of your body. The cleansed blood then flows into other veins that return it to the heart.

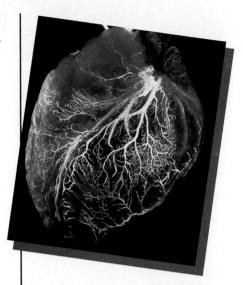

A special dye was used to highlight the coronary blood vessels for this photograph.

LESSON 14.1   USING WHAT YOU HAVE LEARNED

REVIEW

1. Name two materials that blood delivers to cells throughout the body.
2. What is the major difference between an artery and a vein?

THINK CRITICALLY

3. Normally there is no opening between the right and left sides of the heart. What would happen to the blood in the heart if there were an opening?
4. Some people think that all arteries carry oxygen-rich blood and all veins carry oxygen-poor blood. Explain why this belief is incorrect.

APPLY IT TO YOURSELF

5. Imagine you are a microscopic speck in your bloodstream. You are about to be pumped out of your left ventricle and to your small intestines. Describe the pathway you would follow before you were pumped out of your left ventricle again.

SUMMARY

The circulatory system carries essential materials to cells throughout your body and picks up wastes from the cells. The exchange of materials between the blood and the fluid surrounding the cells takes place in capillaries, the smallest blood vessels. The heart pumps constantly to maintain blood flow. Pulmonary circulation carries blood to and from your lungs. Systemic circulation carries blood to and from the rest of your body.

CIRCULATION

Every cell in your body depends on blood circulation to deliver needed materials and remove wastes. Without a continuous supply of oxygen and nutrients, your organs would be unable to carry on their life-sustaining activities. Without circulation to remove carbon dioxide, urea, and excess water and salts, cells would be poisoned by their own waste products.

REGULATING CIRCULATION

Different parts of your body need a larger or smaller blood supply at different times, depending on your activities. After a meal, for example, the blood supply to your digestive system increases while the supply to your skeletal muscles decreases. When you are physically active, the reverse is true. Blood circulation is regulated by the rate of your heartbeat and the contraction and relaxation of smooth muscles in the artery walls.

HEART RATE   In the right atrium is a small bundle of specialized cardiac tissue that function as the heart's pacemaker. The pacemaker creates electrical signals that trigger your heartbeat. The pacemaker generates signals on its own, without nerve impulses from your brain. However, the brain modifies the rate of the pacemaker's signals to meet your body's needs and to respond to different conditions. Many conditions affect the heart rate, including temperature, physical activity, stress, emotions such as fear and anger, and chemicals such as hormones, caffeine, nicotine, and drugs in the bloodstream.

If the pacemaker does not function properly, the person's heart rate will be too slow or too fast for the body's needs. An artificial pacemaker can be surgically implanted to regulate the person's heartbeat.

BLOOD PRESSURE   In Lesson 1 you learned that smooth muscle in the artery walls contracts and relaxes to control blood flow. When a part of your body needs more blood, the arteries leading to that part dilate, increasing the blood supply. When less blood is needed, the arteries constrict.

Blood pressure is the force with which blood pushes against the walls of blood vessels as it flows through them. Blood pressure is highest in the arteries, lower in capillaries, and lowest in veins. The faster and stronger your heartbeat, the higher your blood pressure. Blood

MAIN IDEAS

CONCEPTS
✔ Your heart rate and blood pressure regulate your blood circulation.
✔ Atherosclerosis and hypertension are two leading causes of heart disease and stroke.
✔ Diet is an important factor in avoiding atherosclerosis.

VOCABULARY
blood pressure
atherosclerosis
cholesterol
hypertension
stroke

The device used to measure a person's blood pressure is called a sphygmomanometer.

pressure is also affected by the contraction and relaxation of the smooth muscles in artery walls. Your blood pressure varies from place to place in your body. It also varies during the day as your level of activity changes.

If blood pressure is too high over a long period of time, the walls of the blood vessels can be weakened and the heart itself may be damaged. For this reason, blood pressure is routinely measured during any physical checkup. Two readings are taken. The first reading, called systolic pressure [*sis TAHL ik*], measures blood pressure in the artery when the ventricles contract. The second reading, called diastolic pressure [*dy uh STAHL ik*], measures blood pressure when the ventricles relax. When the measurements are recorded, the systolic reading is written above or before the diastolic reading. Blood pressure between 110/70 and 120/80 is considered normal for young adults, although some healthy people have lower blood pressure.

HEALTHY PEOPLE 2000

Increase to at least 90 per-cent the proportion of adults who have had their blood pressure measured within the preceding two years and can state whether their blood pressure was normal or high.

Objective 15.13
from *Healthy People 2000: National Health Promotion and Disease Prevention Objectives*

WHAT IS FAINTING?

Have you ever fainted or seen someone faint? A person faints when his or her brain is not getting enough oxygen. An irregular heartbeat or a sudden decrease in blood pressure may cause fainting.

Nausea, sweating, lightheadedness, and dimming vision are signs that you may be about to faint. To keep from fainting, immediately lie down, if possible, or sit down and lower your head between your knees. This position will restore normal blood flow to your brain.

If you are with someone who faints, the best thing to do is simply lay the person flat on his or her back. In most cases, the person will soon regain consciousness and will suffer no damage from the reduced oxygen supply. In fact, the most serious problem associated with fainting is not brain damage but the risk of injury from the fall.

CIRCULATORY DISORDERS AND DISEASES

Your circulatory system must be healthy and fit in order to transport materials throughout your body. If the heart does not pump efficiently or if blood does not flow smoothly, serious problems can develop.

ATHEROSCLEROSIS   Atherosclerosis [*ath uh roh skluh ROH sus*] is a condition in which fatty material builds up on the inner walls of arteries and blocks the flow of blood. Sometimes the artery walls also harden. The fatty material contains **cholesterol** [*kuh LES tuh rohl*], a waxy, fat-like substance produced by the body. You can read more about cholesterol in Chapter 10, "Understanding Nutrition." If the blockage is diagnosed early enough, it can be treated with medicine or surgery. If the blockage is not treated, the fatty material continues to build up, and the blood flow decreases further. Eventually, the tissue nourished by the arteries dies from the inadequate blood supply.

Coronary heart disease, also called coronary artery disease, occurs when atherosclerosis affects the coronary arteries supplying the heart muscle. In addition to causing pain, coronary heart disease is life-threatening because it can lead to a heart attack. In a heart attack, the blood supply to part of the heart is suddenly cut off, killing the muscle tissue in that part.

HYPERTENSION Blood pressure that remains too high for a long period of time is called **hypertension** [*hy pur TEN chun*]. In adults, blood pressure of 140/90 or more is considered to be high. Hypertension is often caused by the narrowing and hardening of arteries. The heart must work harder to pump blood, and this increases the blood pressure. Hypertension can damage not only the heart and blood vessels but other organs as well.

Why hypertension develops in some people is not fully understood, but the following risk factors are known to affect blood pressure. Are you or is anyone you know at risk?

RISK FACTORS FOR HYPERTENSION

The following risk factors are associated with developing hypertension. The more risk factors that are true for a person, the higher the person's risk.

These risk factors are hereditary and cannot be changed.

- being male
- being of African descent
- having close relatives with hypertension

These risk factors involve health habits that can be controlled.

- smoking cigarettes
- not getting enough exercise
- having too much sodium and saturated fat in the diet
- consuming more than two alcoholic drinks daily
- being overweight

STROKE A **stroke** is a sudden disruption of the blood supply to a part of the brain, killing nerve tissue in that part. Both atherosclerosis and hypertension can lead to a stroke. With atherosclerosis, a blockage in an artery can stop the blood flow. The nerve cells die without a constant supply of oxygen. With severe hypertension, artery walls that have been weakened by continuously high blood pressure can suddenly rupture. Blood leaks out of the artery and presses against nerve tissue, killing the cells.

The long-term effects of a stroke vary greatly, depending on which part of the brain is damaged and how severe the damage is. Some typical effects are paralysis of part of the body and loss of the ability to speak or to understand speech.

STRATEGIES FOR LIVING

The following guidelines can help you avoid circulatory diseases.

Diet

- Limit your intake of foods high in fats, particulary saturated fats. Saturated fats raise the blood cholesterol level.
- Eat foods that contain polyunsaturated and monounsaturated fats. These fats lower blood cholesterol.
- Limit your intake of foods high in cholesterol, such as fatty meats, butter, and eggs.
- Eat foods that are high in fiber, such as beans, grains, fruits, and vegetables.
- Limit your sodium intake. Use salt sparingly, and substitute sodium-free spices.

Other Factors

- Do not smoke. Smoking constricts the smaller arteries in your body and contributes to atherosclerosis.
- Avoid being overweight. Excess weight increases blood cholesterol.
- Exercise regularly. Exercise strengthens your cardiovascular system, helps control weight, and can reduce blood pressure.
- Avoid alcoholic drinks. Alcohol use can lead to high blood pressure.

PREVENTING CIRCULATORY PROBLEMS

Circulatory diseases—including coronary heart disease, heart attacks, and strokes—are the leading causes of death in the United States. You can reduce your risk of developing circulatory problems by following the guidelines on this page. Although all the guidelines are important, avoiding cigarette smoking, eating a healthy diet, and exercising regularly have the greatest effect on lowering your blood cholesterol level. By lowering your blood cholesterol level, you greatly reduce your risk of developing circulatory diseases. It is also a good health practice to have your cholesterol level tested regularly, particularly if you have a family history of circulatory problems.

LESSON 14.2 ## USING WHAT YOU HAVE LEARNED

REVIEW

1. Identify three factors that affect heart rate.
2. What happens to the walls of blood vessels if blood pressure is too high for a long period of time?
3. Why is it important to control your blood cholesterol level?

THINK CRITICALLY

4. Compare the risk factors for hypertension with the risk factors for osteoporosis on page 295. Which factors are the same?
5. Blood pressure is highest in arteries, lower in capillaries, and lowest in veins. Suggest a reason for this difference in pressure among the blood vessels.

APPLY IT TO YOURSELF

6. Imagine that you are shopping at the mall with friends. Just for fun, you decide to check your blood pressure on a do-it-yourself machine. The machine says your blood pressure is 100/65. Should you see a doctor? Explain your answer.

SUMMARY

Your heart rate and blood pressure regulate the flow of blood throughout your body. The heartbeat is triggered by the pacemaker; heart rate is modified by the brain. Atherosclerosis and hypertension are serious conditions that can cause heart disease, heart attacks, strokes, and death. Circulatory problems can be avoided through a careful diet, regular exercise, not smoking, and other healthy habits.

BLOOD AND LYMPH

Blood is not just a red liquid with cells floating in it. Blood is living tissue that transports materials, repairs injuries to blood vessels, and helps protect your body against disease.

THE PARTS OF BLOOD

Blood has four main parts: plasma, platelets, red blood cells, and white blood cells. About 55 percent of your blood is plasma; the rest is cells. You can see this proportion in Figure 14-4.

PLASMA   Plasma [*PLAZ muh*] is the liquid part of your blood. When it is separated from the cells it carries, plasma appears yellowish. Plasma is about 90 percent water and 10 percent dissolved materials. Some of the dissolved materials are needed by your cells. Other materials are waste products being transported for elimination. The dissolved materials are listed in Figure 14-4.

Notice that the word *proteins* appears twice on the list. Plasma proteins are not the same as the proteins your body uses as nutrients. Plasma proteins have other functions. Fibrinogen [*fy BRIN uh jun*], for example, plays an important role in blood clotting.

PLATELETS   Platelets [*PLAYT luts*] are the blood parts that form clots to stop bleeding. When an injury tears open a blood vessel, platelets stick to the vessel wall around the opening. Fibrinogen then sticks to the platelets, forming a tangled network of thin fibers, as you can see in the photograph below. The fibers catch more platelets and blood cells, forming a clot. The clot plugs the opening and stops the bleeding. If bleeding occurs on the surface of your skin, the clot dries to form a hard scab. The scab keeps disease-causing organisms from entering your skin while the wound heals.

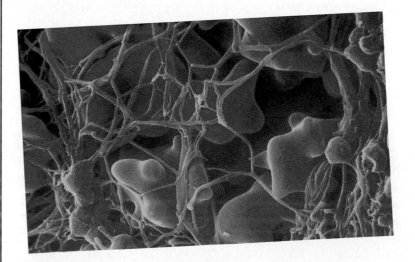

This photograph shows platelets and fibrinogen forming a blood clot. Platelets are not shown in the test tube at left because platelets disintegrate when blood is separated.

MAIN IDEAS

CONCEPTS

✔ Blood is made of plasma, platelets, red blood cells, and white blood cells.

✔ The lymphatic system is one of the body's major defenses against disease.

VOCABULARY

plasma	spleen
platelet	tonsils
red blood cell	blood
hemoglobin	transfusion
white blood	mono-
cell	nucleosis
antibody	anemia
lymph	sickle-cell
lymph node	anemia
thymus	leukemia

Figure 14-4 The blood in this test tube has been separated into its parts.

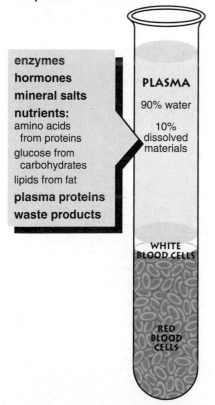

enzymes
hormones
mineral salts
nutrients:
amino acids
  from proteins
glucose from
  carbohydrates
lipids from fat
plasma proteins
waste products

PLASMA
90% water
10% dissolved materials

WHITE BLOOD CELLS

RED BLOOD CELLS

RED BLOOD CELLS **Red blood cells** transport oxygen throughout your body. They are the most numerous cells in your blood. Healthy red blood cells look like tiny saucers, as shown in the photograph at right. Their red color comes from **hemoglobin** [*HEE muh gloh bun*], an iron-rich protein that attaches to oxygen very easily.

When blood flows through your lungs, the hemoglobin picks up oxygen from the air sacs. As blood flows through your body, the hemoglobin releases oxygen to cells, and the blood picks up carbon dioxide. When it returns to the lungs, the blood releases carbon dioxide, and the hemoglobin picks up oxygen again.

The combination of hemoglobin and oxygen is what gives your blood its bright red color when it flows through arteries. When it flows through veins after releasing oxygen to cells, your blood is a dull red color. It is never blue, although it looks that way when you see veins through your skin.

A red blood cell lives about 120 days. Every day of your life, your body must produce new red blood cells to replace those that die. As explained in Chapter 13, "Bones and Muscles," red blood cells are produced by red bone marrow in spongy bone.

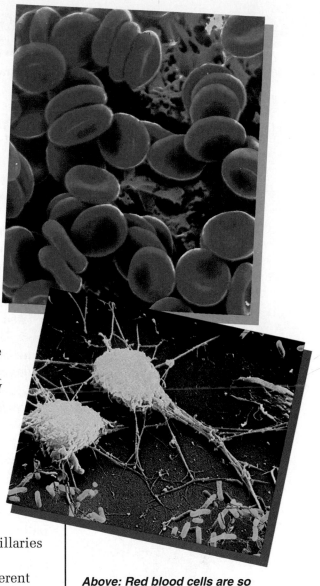

WHITE BLOOD CELLS **White blood cells** protect your body against infections. They are larger than red blood cells, but normally there are fewer of them. Unlike red blood cells and platelets, which can only float along with the blood flow, white blood cells can move by themselves. When bacteria, viruses, or other disease-causing organisms enter your body, white blood cells move through the walls of capillaries and into body tissue to attack the invaders.

Different types of white blood cells fight infection in different ways. Some white blood cells produce antibodies. **Antibodies** are proteins that attach to foreign materials that enter your body. Other white blood cells surround and digest bacteria, viruses, and other organisms. Many white blood cells function as your body's clean-up crew, surrounding and digesting dead cells, cell parts, and other useless particles.

Unlike red blood cells, most white blood cells live only a few days. During an infection, some may live only a few hours. Like red blood cells, though, new white blood cells must be continuously produced to replace ones that die. Some white blood cells are produced by red bone marrow. Others are formed in the lymphatic system.

Above: Red blood cells are so tiny that more than 3,000 could be lined up in a row one inch long. Below: Two white blood cells are attacking a type of bacteria found in your intestines.

THE LYMPHATIC SYSTEM

The lymphatic system [*lim FAT ik*], shown in Figure 14-5 on the following page, is the body's secondary system of circulation. Throughout your body, a plasma-like fluid called **lymph** [*LIMF*] fills the spaces between cells. The lymphatic system collects this lymph and carries it to the bloodstream. The system functions as

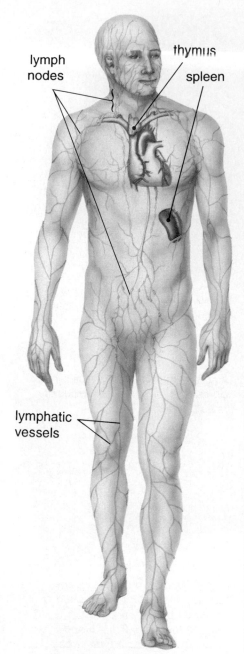

lymph nodes

thymus

spleen

lymphatic vessels

Figure 14-5 *The lymphatic system also includes the tonsils at the back of the mouth.*

one of your body's major defenses against infection. In addition, lymphatic capillaries pick up nutrients and wastes that cannot be absorbed by blood capillaries. The lymphatic system consists of lymphatic vessels, lymph nodes, the thymus, the spleen, and the tonsils.

LYMPHATIC VESSELS   The lymphatic vessels, which resemble small veins and capillaries, are distributed throughout your body. Lymph is pushed through the vessels by contractions of your skeletal muscles. Lymph from all parts of your body drains into large veins in your neck and enters the bloodstream.

LYMPH NODES   As it travels through lymphatic vessels, lymph passes through lymph nodes. **Lymph nodes** are small lumps of tissue that filter out disease-causing organisms and dead body cells. The nodes also produce some types of white blood cells. Lymph nodes are located throughout your body. Clusters of nodes are located in your neck, armpits, and groin, as you can see in Figure 14-5. The nodes vary in size from as small as a pinhead to as large as an olive. When your body is fighting an infection, your lymph nodes may swell because of their increased activity.

THE THYMUS   Your thymus is located in your upper chest, behind your sternum. The **thymus** [*THY mus*] produces specialized white blood cells, called T cells, that provide immunity against different diseases. The immune system and the function of T cells are discussed in Chapter 23, "Infectious Diseases." The thymus is active during childhood and adolescence, when the body's immunity is being developed. The thymus then becomes less active and is gradually replaced by fat.

THE SPLEEN   Your spleen is located on your left side behind your lower ribs. Besides producing white blood cells and destroying organisms that cause disease, the **spleen** has two unique functions.

- The spleen *filters blood,* destroying worn-out red blood cells and platelets and recapturing the hemoglobin for new red blood cells.

- The spleen *stores blood,* releasing it when the body suddenly needs an increased supply, such as during intense physical activity or heavy bleeding.

The spleen is not a vital organ. In fact, if your spleen were ruptured in an accident, it might have to be removed to prevent uncontrolled bleeding. You could live a healthy life without a spleen, although your risk of certain infections would increase.

THE TONSILS   Your tonsils are masses of lymph tissue located in the back of your mouth. The **tonsils** destroy disease-causing organisms and produce white blood cells. Like the spleen, the tonsils are not vital. Before antibiotics were developed, tonsillitis—inflammation of the tonsils—was routinely treated by removing the tonsils. Today, surgery is not used as frequently.

BLOOD TRANSFUSIONS AND BLOOD TYPES

When you lose some blood through an injury or surgery, your body replaces it. However, if you lose so much blood that your health or even your life is endangered, you may be given blood from another person. The process of removing blood from one person and putting it into another person is called a **blood transfusion** [*trans FYOO zhun*]. Blood transfusions are also used to treat people with certain blood diseases or disorders.

Before a transfusion is given, the patient's blood type must be identified. If the transfused blood does not match the patient's blood, antibodies in the patient's blood will attack the red blood cells in the transfused blood and make them clump together. These clumps can damage organs and cause death. Blood is classified into four major types—A, B, AB, and O—based on how the red blood cells react when blood is mixed. Figure 14-6 shows the blood types that can be mixed without causing clumping.

BLOOD DISORDERS AND DISEASES

Blood tests are one of the most common tests used to get concrete information about your health. When you have a physical checkup, you may be asked to give a blood sample. This sample is much smaller than the amount of blood donated for a transfusion. More than 30 different tests can be conducted on one blood sample. A problem in another part of the body, such as the liver, may show up in a blood test. Other problems may involve the blood itself.

MONONUCLEOSIS   Mononucleosis—or "mono" for short—is such a common disease in adolescents and young adults that you have probably heard of it, known someone who had it, or perhaps even had it yourself. **Mononucleosis** [*mahn oh noo klee OH sus*] is a virus infection that causes an abnormal increase in certain types of white blood cells.

The symptoms of mononucleosis are so varied that the disease is often difficult to diagnose. Common symptoms include fever, a sore throat, swollen lymph nodes, and prolonged fatigue. There is no cure for mononucleosis, but it is usually not a serious disease and will cure itself in time. Doctors usually recommend bed rest, drinking plenty of water and juices, taking aspirin, and soothing the sore throat by gargling with salty water.

ANEMIA   The most common blood disorders are forms of anemia. In **anemia** [*uh NEE mee uh*], the blood does not have enough red blood cells or enough hemoglobin to carry an adequate supply of oxygen. The anemic person is often weak or pale and may tire easily. Different types of anemia are caused by dietary deficiencies, destruction of red blood cells, or an inherited defect.

Not enough iron, folic acid, or vitamin B_{12} in the diet can cause nutritional anemia. This form of anemia is easily cured by increasing iron, folic acid, or vitamin B_{12} in the diet. Pernicious anemia [*pur NISH us*] is a form of anemia in which the body is unable to absorb vitamin B_{12} in the diet and use it to make red blood cells.

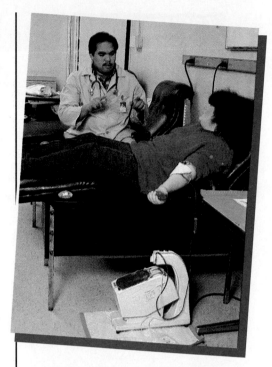

You cannot catch a disease by donating blood, and the process is not painful.

BLOOD TYPES

Blood Type	Can Donate To	Can Receive From
O	O, A, B, AB	O
A	A, AB	O, A
B	B, AB	O, B
AB	AB	O, A, B, AB

Figure 14-6   Type O blood is called the "universal donor." Can you tell why?

FOR YOUR INFORMATION

Researchers have discovered that the gene responsible for sickle-cell anemia also produces increased resistance to malaria, a serious disease that is common in Africa and other tropical areas.

Pernicious anemia can be successfully treated, although not cured, with regular injections of vitamin B_{12}.

SICKLE-CELL ANEMIA **Sickle-cell anemia** is a life-threatening hereditary disorder in which the red blood cells carry an abnormal type of hemoglobin. The cells rupture easily, which reduces the amount of oxygen carried throughout the body. Also, instead of being flexible and round, the red blood cells can become rigid and sickle-shaped. The cells' rigidity and shape makes them unable to pass through blood vessels easily. The sickled cells block vessels, causing pain and damaging the tissues supplied by the vessels. People with sickle-cell anemia also get infections more easily.

Sickle-cell anemia occurs most often in people of African ancestry. Blood tests are used to detect the disease. There is no cure for the disease itself, but antibiotics can cure or even prevent infections, and other treatments can ease the symptoms. Researchers are working on more effective treatments and trying to develop a drug to prevent the red blood cells from sickling.

LEUKEMIA **Leukemia** [*loo KEE mee uh*] is cancer of the body tissue that produces blood cells, including red bone marrow and lymph nodes. The cancerous tissue produces a large number of abnormal white blood cells. These abnormal cells interfere with the production of normal white blood cells, red blood cells, and platelets. As a result, the blood-cell functions that you read about earlier—clotting, transportation of oxygen, and fighting disease—are disrupted.

Although the causes of leukemia are not known, cure rates have been steadily improving. Leukemia is usually treated with powerful anticancer drugs. A newer technique is a bone marrow transplant, which involves replacing the patient's cancerous marrow with healthy marrow after the cancerous cells have been killed by exposure to X rays. Even if the disease is not cured, treatments can enable the patient to be healthier and live longer.

SUMMARY

Blood plasma and red blood cells transport necessary materials and wastes. Platelets are important in blood clotting. Lymph nodes and organs in the lymphatic system produce white blood cells that destroy disease-causing organisms. Blood transfusions are used to treat serious blood loss and some types of blood disorders. Blood disorders can be caused by virus infections, dietary deficiencies, inherited defects, or cancer.

LESSON 14.3 USING WHAT YOU HAVE LEARNED

REVIEW

1. Name the two elements in blood that form clots.
2. What are antibodies?
3. Identify the two unique functions of the spleen.

THINK CRITICALLY

4. White blood cells are able to move out of the bloodstream and into body tissues. Why is this movement important?
5. Researchers working on sickle-cell anemia are trying to develop a drug to prevent the red blood cells from sickling. How would this benefit people with sickle-cell anemia?

APPLY IT TO YOURSELF

6. Imagine that you are a doctor in a hospital emergency room. A patient with type B blood needs an immediate transfusion. What blood type or types could the patient be given safely?

THE RESPIRATORY SYSTEM

The word *respiration* actually refers to two separate processes. One is breathing—simply moving air in and out of your lungs. The second process is gas exchange—the exchange of carbon dioxide and oxygen between the air and the blood in your lungs and between the blood and the cells throughout your body. You learned about this gas exchange in Lesson 1. The function of the respiratory system is to deliver oxygen to the circulatory system and eliminate carbon dioxide.

THE STRUCTURE OF THE RESPIRATORY SYSTEM

The respiratory system is shown in Figure 14-7 and in Plate Seven. Scientists divide the system into two sections according to the location of the organs. The upper respiratory tract extends from the nose to the pharynx [*FAR ingks*]. The lower respiratory tract extends from the larynx [*LAR ingks*] to the lungs.

THE UPPER RESPIRATORY TRACT   When you inhale, air passes through your nose and into the nasal cavity. Hairs in your nose filter out particles in the air. Your nasal cavity warms and moistens the air. The air then passes through your pharynx. At the end of the pharynx are two openings. One leads to the larynx, the beginning of the lower respiratory tract. The other opening leads to the

MAIN IDEAS

CONCEPTS
✔ The respiratory system delivers oxygen to the circulatory system and eliminates carbon dioxide.

✔ Changes in air pressure cause air to move in and out of the lungs.

✔ Many respiratory diseases can be prevented through good health habits, particularly not smoking.

VOCABULARY
mucous membrane	tuberculosis
cilia	asthma
diaphragm	emphysema
bronchitis	cystic fibrosis
pneumonia	air pollution

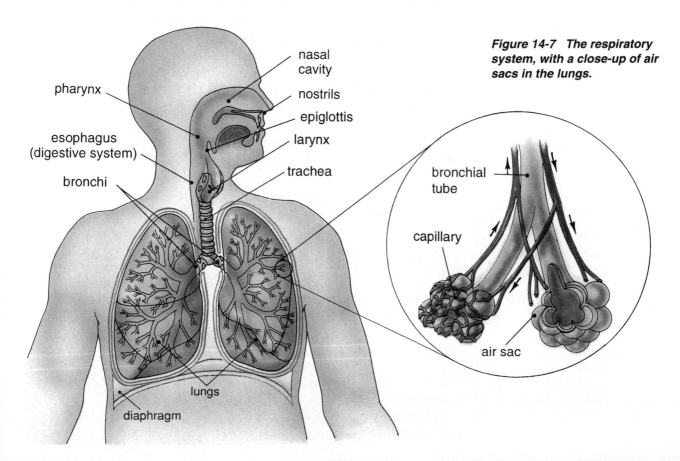

Figure 14-7   The respiratory system, with a close-up of air sacs in the lungs.

Labels: nasal cavity, nostrils, epiglottis, larynx, trachea, pharynx, esophagus (digestive system), bronchi, lungs, diaphragm, bronchial tube, capillary, air sac

esophagus, which is part of your digestive tract. When you swallow, a small flap of tissue called the epiglottis [*ep uh GLAHT us*] covers the opening to the larynx. This prevents food and liquid from entering the lower respiratory tract.

The entire upper respiratory tract is lined with mucous membrane. **Mucous membrane** [*MYOO kus MEM brayn*] is the type of tissue that lines all body passageways open to the outside. This type of tissue is found in your digestive and reproductive systems as well as your respiratory system. Mucous membrane produces mucus, a thick fluid that keeps the passageways from drying out. Mucus also traps dust, bacteria, and other foreign particles and prevents them from moving deeper into your body.

The mucous membrane in your respiratory system has tiny hairlike structures called **cilia** [*SIL ee uh*] projecting from it. The cilia trap some particles, but their major function is to eliminate mucus from your respiratory system. They do this by moving in waves that carry the mucus upward, toward your mouth and nose.

What is the major function of the cilia in your respiratory system?

THE LOWER RESPIRATORY TRACT From your upper respiratory tract, air moves into your larynx and then your trachea [*TRAY kee uh*]. These two passageways are also lined with mucous membrane and cilia. The larynx is your voice organ. It contains a pair of vocal cords that vibrate as air passes between them when you exhale. These vibrations produce sounds, which you modify and shape to form speech.

The lower end of the trachea divides into two tubes called bronchi [*BRAHNG ky*], which are also lined with mucous membrane and cilia. One bronchus enters each lung. Inside the lungs, the bronchi branch into smaller and smaller tubes. The smallest tubes end in clusters of tiny air sacs called alveoli [*al VEE uh ly*].

You learned earlier that these air sacs are surrounded by capillaries. Only the thin walls of the sacs and capillaries separate outside air from your bloodstream. When you inhale, sacs fill with fresh air. Oxygen moves from the air through the walls of the sacs and capillaries and into the bloodstream, where it attaches to hemoglobin in the red blood cells. At the same time, carbon dioxide moves from the capillaries into the air sacs. When you exhale, the carbon dioxide is eliminated from your body.

THE BREATHING PROCESS

If you have ever thought about your breathing, you probably assumed that your chest expands because your lungs fill with air. Actually, your lungs fill with air because your chest expands.

Air moves in and out of your lungs as a result of differences in air pressure. When the air pressure inside your lungs is lower than the air pressure outside your body, air moves into your lungs to equalize the pressure. When the pressure inside is higher than the pressure outside, air moves out of your lungs.

The air pressure inside your lungs is changed by the contraction and relaxation of skeletal muscles—the muscles between your ribs,

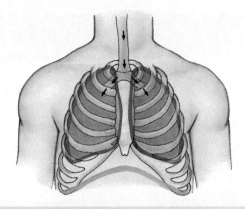

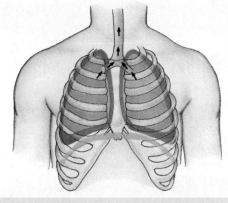

To move air into your lungs, the diaphragm contracts, which makes it move downward. At the same time, your rib muscles contract, pulling your rib cage upward and outward. These movements make your chest cavity larger, which in turn lowers the air pressure in your lungs. Because the air outside your body is at higher pressure, air moves into your lungs.

To move air out of your lungs, the diaphragm relaxes and curves upward. Your rib muscles also relax, allowing your rib cage to move back downward and inward. These movements make your chest cavity smaller, which increases the air pressure in your lungs. Because the air outside your body is at lower pressure, air moves out of your lungs.

Figure 14-8   Your diaphragm and rib muscles produce your breathing.

and a large sheet of muscle called the diaphragm. The **diaphragm** [*DY uh fram*] is the major muscle in breathing. Figure 14-8 shows how the diaphragm and rib muscles produce breathing.

RESPIRATORY DISORDERS AND DISEASES

Diseases of the respiratory system may affect the nose and throat, the bronchial tubes, or the lungs. Avoiding sources of infection or irritation and practicing good health habits can help prevent many respiratory diseases.

Henry has been a pack-a-day cigarette smoker for many years. Lately he has noticed that he catches colds very easily and recovers slowly. It's been two months since his last cold, but he still has a bad cough.

One of the most important health habits is not smoking. Smoking damages the air passages and lungs, making them more easily attacked by disease-causing organisms.

BRONCHITIS   Bronchitis [*brahn KYT us*] is an inflammation of the mucous membrane that lines the bronchial tubes. Thick mucus builds up, causing coughing, difficulty in breathing, and a heavy feeling in the chest. Bronchitis may be caused by bacteria, viruses, or irritants in the air.

Henry finally went to his doctor, who told him that he has bronchitis. The doctor said she'd prescribe an antibiotic to help clear it up, but she warned him that if he didn't give up smoking, his bronchitis would most likely become chronic.

The word *chronic* [*KRAHN ik*] means that a disease is long-lasting, recurs regularly, and requires repeated or continuous treatment. Smokers and other people who are continually exposed to harmful airborne substances often develop chronic bronchitis.

HEALTHY PEOPLE 2000

Reduce the initiation of cigarette smoking by children and youth so that no more than 15 percent have become regular cigarette smokers by age 20.

Objective 3.5
from *Healthy People 2000: National Health Promotion and Disease Prevention Objectives*

Humidifiers

The indoor heat of winter months can dry the air, which causes breathing difficulties at night and makes your throat dry in the morning. The remedy for dry air is a pot of water on the radiator or a humidifier.

Humidifiers do their jobs in many ways. Vaporizers boil water and emit the steam into the air. Cool mist vaporizers break up water particles and send them into the air. Warm mist units boil water and force air into a room. Ultrasonic humidifiers use vibrations to break liquid water into mist particles. Whatever your choice of humidifiers, follow a few guidelines in maintaining them.

- Read the manufacturer's instructions carefully and follow them.
- Keep the humidifier clean. Bacteria emitted from humidifiers can cause allergic reactions and have been linked with serious illnesses such as Legionnaire's Disease.
- Change the water in a humidifier daily, and empty the tank before filling it up again.
- Clean the tank with a scrub brush regularly.
- If you decide to use chlorine bleach to clean the humidifier, rinse the tank carefully to avoid breathing in harmful fumes.
- If you use an ultrasonic model, use only demineralized water.

When he thought about it, Henry decided that chronic bronchitis was too high a price to pay for his smoking habit. He called his doctor and asked her to recommend some groups and techniques that could help him stop smoking.

Bronchitis caused by bacteria can be treated with antibiotics. However, the infection can weaken the body and lower resistance to other infections. If not treated promptly, bronchitis can persist for an extended period of time.

PNEUMONIA   **Pneumonia** [*nyu MOH nyuh*] is an inflammation of the air sacs in the lungs. The inflammation is usually caused by infection, but it can also be caused by foreign particles that are inhaled. The air sacs fill with fluid and dead white blood cells, making breathing difficult. Symptoms of pneumonia can include shortness of breath, a high fever, chills, coughing, and chest pain. Treatment depends on the type of infection causing the inflammation. Pneumonia caused by bacteria can be treated with antibiotics. Severe pneumonia can result in death, especially among people whose bodies are already weakened by another disease.

TUBERCULOSIS   **Tuberculosis** [*tu bur kyuh LOH sus*]—or TB, as it is commonly called—is a bacterial infection that destroys lung tissue. TB also may damage other organs. Symptoms of TB usually include fatigue, weight loss, loss of appetite, a low-grade fever, and a persistent cough. TB bacteria spread in airborne droplets coughed out by someone with the disease. Poor nutrition and crowded, poorly ventilated living conditions contribute to the spread of TB. The only cure is anti-tubercular drugs taken over a period of months. Without treatment, TB is often fatal.

In the United States, cases of TB declined steadily during the early and mid-1900s with improvements in nutrition, sanitation, and medical care, particularly the development of anti-TB drugs. Since the 1980s, however, TB has been increasing in this country and has again become a serious public-health problem.

ASTHMA   Asthma [*AZ muh*] is a chronic respiratory disorder caused by inflammation and narrowing of the bronchial tubes. An asthma attack may be triggered by airborne substances, certain foods, or common bacteria or viruses that are ordinarily harmless. The reaction of the airways causes spasms, or uncontrolled contractions, of the smooth muscle in the bronchial tubes. The inflamed mucous membrane lining the tubes also swells. As a result, the person wheezes, coughs, and has difficulty breathing. Asthma attacks can be relieved with drugs that treat or prevent inflammation, relax the bronchial muscles, and open up the air passages.

EMPHYSEMA   Another chronic respiratory disease, more common in middle-aged and older people, is emphysema. In **emphysema** [*em fuh ZEE muh*], lung tissue is destroyed and air sacs are lost. The lungs become unable to deflate fully during exhaling. Normal gas exchange between the air sacs and capillaries can no longer occur.

Emphysema is caused by long-term exposure to irritants in the air—most often, cigarette smoke or air pollution. Because the lung damage is permanent, there is no cure for the disease, and it can

MAKING A DIFFERENCE

Organ Donation

Valdies Doss gave life to five people he had never met. Before he died in a car accident, Doss had specified that in the event of his death, all of his organs were to be donated so that others might continue to live. Nearly 24,000 people in the United States are waiting for a gift like the ones Valdies Doss gave. A new kidney, heart, lung, or liver may be all that stands between an ill person and death.

During the last two decades, medical advances have improved the success of organ transplantation. Successful heart transplants have become common surgical procedures, as have lung and kidney transplants. Liver transplants were once only possible by using a donated liver from a deceased person. However, in the 1980s, the first partial transplant of a liver from a living donor-parent to her dying child was successful. In the past, bone marrow transplants, used in the treatment of fatal blood diseases such as leukemia or plastic anemia had relied on bone marrow from a matching donor. Today, a new technique allows a patient to donate his or her own marrow, have it frozen and cleaned of diseased cells, and then transplanted back into the body.

Transplantation is not limited to organs. New hope is available to infertile women through the advanced technology of egg transplantation. A fertilized egg from an outside donor is implanted into the uterus of the infertile woman. The infertile woman then carries the fetus and gives birth.

Matching donors to the thousands of people who wait each year for donated organs is the biggest problem with organ donation and transplant. One effective way to make organ donation easy is to place a sticker on a driver's license, stating that person's desire to donate his or her organs in case of accidental death.

Today, because of more donors and easier transplantation, organ donation is making a difference in the quality of life for thousands of Americans.

1. How has organ donation advanced during the last two decades?

2. Have you considered becoming an organ donor? How can you arrange to donate your organs?

eventually cause death. However, emphysema can be prevented by not smoking and by avoiding long-term exposure to air pollution.

CYSTIC FIBROSIS   Cystic fibrosis [*SIS tik fy BROH sus*] is a hereditary disease that causes mucous membranes throughout the body to produce too much mucus. In the respiratory system, the excess mucus clogs the bronchial tubes and obstructs breathing. In 1992, researchers identified the gene responsible for cystic fibrosis. They hope that genetic engineering will be able to alter the defective gene and cure the disease. Until that time, improved treatments and medications are enabling people with cystic fibrosis to live longer, more active lives.

THE AIR YOU BREATHE

Air pollution [*puh LOO shun*], or harmful materials in the air, can cause inflammation of the upper and lower respiratory tracts, the eyes, and other parts of the body. Automobile exhaust, smoke from factories, and chemicals from spray cans are examples of pollutants that can harm the body. Some pollutants damage the lining of the bronchial airways by destroying the cilia. When this happens, mucus cannot be eliminated normally from the airways. Irritants and disease-causing organisms remain in the air passages, and bronchitis may result. Air pollution also worsens existing respiratory disorders and diseases.

Air pollution can damage your respiratory system.

Smoking is a form of air pollution. People who smoke suffer many more respiratory problems than people who do not smoke. In addition, nonsmokers can be harmed by breathing air that is polluted with tobacco smoke. Because of this, many restaurants, office buildings, airport terminals, and other public places restrict smoking to a separate area or ban smoking altogether. Fortunately, more people today understand that smoking can cause serious health problems for themselves and others, and are choosing not to smoke. You can learn more about the effects of smoking and techniques to stop smoking in Chapter 20, "Tobacco."

LESSON 14.4   **USING WHAT YOU HAVE LEARNED**

REVIEW

1. Name the organs of the lower respiratory tract.
2. What is the major function of the cilia in the respiratory tract?

THINK CRITICALLY

3. Emphysema is more common in middle-aged and older people. Why is this disease not as common in young people?
4. When you inhale, your nose and nasal cavity filter, warm, and moisten the air before it goes farther into your respiratory system. Suggest two possible benefits of these processes.

APPLY IT TO YOURSELF

5. Imagine that you are living with two cigarette smokers. They say they are not hurting anyone but themselves. How would you explain why their view is incorrect?

SUMMARY

The term *respiration* refers both to the act of breathing and to the exchange of oxygen and carbon dioxide between air sacs and capillaries in the lungs and between capillaries and cells throughout the body. Rib muscles and the diaphragm contract and relax to change air pressure in the lungs. These changes in air pressure move air in and out of the lungs. Respiratory diseases occur when irritants or disease-causing organisms attack the air passageways.

Medical Directives

DECISION FOCUS MAKING

Matt was working at the local hospital during his summer vacation. He wanted to get as much experience as he could before entering the pre-medical program at the university.

Matt attended some of the lectures given by doctors to the medical students. One morning he attended a lecture called "Medical Directives—the New Living Will." Matt learned that Medical Directives are intended to honor the wishes of a dying person, even when that person cannot speak for himself or herself. If he or she does not want "extraordinary measures" such as a respirator or heart pump to sustain life, then that request can be made in advance.

The rest of the day, Matt kept thinking about Medical Directives. What if something were to happen to one of his parents? "I have no idea what they would want," he thought. "For that matter, they have no idea how I feel about the use of support systems."

Matt wanted to discuss the idea of Medical Directives with his parents. He felt that it was important to know their wishes should they become sick or suffer a bad accident. But he was a little nervous about bringing up the subject. Matt didn't want them to think he was obsessing about death.

PAUSE AND CONSIDER

1. *Identify the Problem.* What is Matt's conflict?

2. *Consider the Options.* What are Matt's options?

3. *Evaluate the Outcomes.* What could happen if Matt didn't discuss Medical Directives with his parents? What might happen if he did discuss it?

Matt decided that he would bring up the subject of Medical Directives that night at dinner. As they ate, Matt and his parents discussed various topics. When his parents asked Matt about his day, he told them about the lecture.

"Hmm, I've never really thought about it," said his mother. "I guess it might be helpful to some people."

"Yeah, that's what I was thinking," Matt said. "I mean, what if one of you was in an accident? I would want to know what kind of treatment you would prefer. Knowing your wishes would help me make decisions and feel right about them."

"Oh Matt, there's no need to worry about such things now," said his father. "I don't plan on anything happening to me."

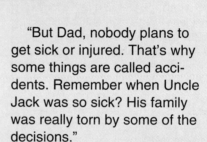

"But Dad, nobody plans to get sick or injured. That's why some things are called accidents. Remember when Uncle Jack was so sick? His family was really torn by some of the decisions."

His parents understood what Matt was saying and asked him more questions about Medical Directives. They all agreed to find out more information about them and to keep the subject open.

DECIDE AND REVIEW

4. *Decide and Act.* How did Matt introduce the subject of Medical Directives to his parents? Why was this a good strategy?

5. *Review.* How else could Matt have raised the subject with his parents? Would you feel comfortable discussing Medical Directives with members of your family?

PROJECTS

1. Make a stethoscope to listen to your heart. Attach a foot of rubber tubing to a metal kitchen funnel. Then press the funnel against your chest and listen through the tubing. What information can a doctor or nurse obtain by listening to your heart? What causes the "lubb-dupp" sound that your heart makes?

2. At your school or local library, find out about the Rh factor. How did the Rh factor get its name? How can the Rh factor affect a pregnant woman and her fetus?

WORKING WITH OTHERS

With a partner, create a list of foods considered to be high and low in cholesterol. You may want to check a book on nutrition to confirm your findings. Then make a list of all of the food items you ate yesterday. Trade lists with your partner, and assess his or her cholesterol intake. Then, if necessary, make recommendations for how your partner can improve his or her eating habits to reduce cholesterol intake.

CONNECTING TO...

SOCIAL STUDIES   Certain blood disorders are common to one group of people. For example, sickle-cell anemia occurs in people of African ancestry. At your school or local library, find out about other blood diseases that are common to one group. How can these diseases be diagnosed, treated, or cured? Do a written report, oral presentation, or bulletin board display to share your findings with the class.

USING VOCABULARY

air pollution	diaphragm	red blood cell
anemia	emphysema	sickle-cell anemia
antibody	hemoglobin	spleen
artery	hypertension	stroke
asthma	leukemia	systemic
atherosclerosis	lymph	circulation
atrium	lymph node	thymus
blood pressure	mononucleosis	tonsils
blood transfusion	mucous membrane	tuberculosis
bronchitis	plasma	vein
capillary	platelet	ventricle
cholesterol	pneumonia	white blood cell
cilia	pulmonary	
cystic fibrosis	circulation	

On a separate sheet of paper, write the vocabulary term that matches each phrase.

1. Iron-rich protein that combines with oxygen to give blood its red color.
2. The circulation of blood between the heart and all other parts of the body except the lungs.
3. Blood pressure that remains too high for a long period of time.
4. Tiny hairlike structures located in the mucous membrane of the respiratory system.
5. Upper chamber of the heart.
6. The liquid part of blood.
7. Chronic respiratory disorder caused by inflammation and narrowing of the bronchial tubes.
8. The circulation of blood between the heart and the lungs.
9. The organ that produces specialized white blood cells called T cells.
10. Fat-like material produced by the body that can build up on the walls of arteries.
11. Blood cells that protect your body against disease.
12. An inflammation of the mucous membrane that lines the bronchial tubes.
13. Lower chamber of the heart.
14. The major muscle used in breathing.
15. Small lumps of tissue that filter out disease-causing organisms.

CONCEPT MAPPING

Copy and complete the concept map shown below. Information on concept mapping appears at the front of this book.

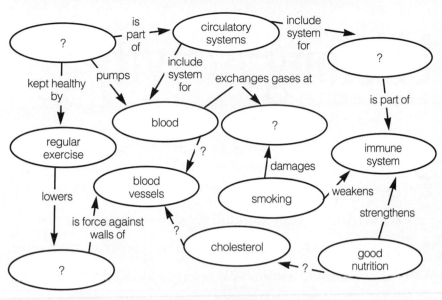

THINKING CRITICALLY

INTERPRET

LESSON 14.1 **1.** Identify the three main functions of the circulatory system.

2. Name the four chambers of the heart. Which chamber pumps blood to the lungs?

3. What happens to harmful materials in the bloodstream when they reach the liver?

LESSON 14.2 **4.** How can atherosclerosis cause a stroke?

5. Identify three hypertension risk factors that can be controlled.

LESSON 14.3 **6.** Name the four parts of blood.

7. Explain why the thymus is most active early in life?

8. Why is it necessary to match the patient's and donor's blood types before giving a blood transfusion?

LESSON 14.4 **9.** Identify two functions of the mucus produced by the mucous membrane lining the respiratory tract.

10. Why do people with pneumonia often have difficulty breathing?

11. Identify two ways to prevent emphysema.

APPLY

LESSON 14.1 **12.** Describe the exchange of materials that takes place between capillaries and body cells.

LESSON 14.2 **13.** How do arteries control blood flow?

LESSON 14.3 **14.** Describe the process by which platelets and fibrinogen stop the bleeding when a blood vessel tears open.

LESSON 14.4 **15.** Explain how your diaphragm and rib muscles produce your breathing.

COMMITMENT TO WELLNESS
FOLLOW-UP

SETTING GOALS

Look back at the Commitment to Wellness checklist that you completed at the beginning of this chapter. Review your responses to the checklist items. How many *yes* answers did you have? How many *no* answers?

Evaluate your *yes* answers. How were you able to develop those healthy practices? What might you be able to do to apply those habits to your weaker areas?

Evaluate your *no* answers. Choose one that you would like to change to *yes*. Copy the checklist item in your journal. Below it, list some specific steps that you could take to achieve your goal. For example, if you want to improve your diet to avoid circulatory disorders, you might list *Eat one banana or apple every day* and *Buy low-salt, low-fat snacks* as specific steps. Write down a target date when you will evaluate how well you are doing in reaching your goal.

WHERE DO I GO FROM HERE?

On the target date you set, look back at your list and evaluate your progress toward your goal. For each step that you did not accomplish, either revise the step or replace it with a new step that is more realistic for you.

FOR MORE INFORMATION, CONTACT:

American Heart Association
7320 Greenville Avenue
Dallas, Texas 75231

American Lung Association
1740 Broadway
New York, New York 10019

CHAPTER 15

Lifelong Activity

"This world belongs to the energetic."

Ralph Waldo Emerson

BACKGROUND

Ralph Waldo Emerson was an essayist and philosopher whose work greatly influenced American thought at the turn of the twentieth century.

Energetic people are vibrant and alive. They tend to participate actively in the world around them and they bring creative energy to almost any project. Energetic people are not just physically alive, they are emotionally strong and intellectually stimulating. The world belongs to them. They are in control of their bodies, minds, and emotions. Because of this, they create new choices and opportunities every day.

Physically fit people often describe their feelings of fitness in terms of newfound energy. Everyone has the tools to change what may be a lifetime of bad habits or to correct sedentary ways. By understanding the benefits and rewards of physical fitness and by taking the steps to become an energetic person, you can feel immediate results. Not everyone has to be an Olympic contender or a star athlete to feel physically energetic or to experience a boost in self-esteem. Even the smallest changes can bring greater energy and control, starting today.

SELF-
ASSESSMENT

How would you assess your fitness knowledge? Copy the following statements into your Wellness Journal or on a separate sheet of paper. Respond to each statement by writing a yes or no.

1. I know that keeping fit is a lifetime pursuit with many benefits.

2. I enjoy exercise.

3. I exercise on a regular basis—at least 3 to 4 times a week for 20 minutes or more.

4. I engage in activities that have aerobic benefits such as walking, running, dancing, hiking, or swimming.

5. I understand that exercise can reduce stress and tension of a day.

6. I participate regularly in some kind of sport such as basketball, softball, swimming, or tennis.

7. I walk or bike as much as I can instead of riding in a car.

8. I enlist a friend to join me in physical activity.

9. I listen to my body for signs that I may be overdoing exercise and stop as soon as I feel any pain.

10. I always stretch and warm up before beginning any exercise program.

Review your responses and consider what might be your strengths and weaknesses. Save your personal checklist for a follow-up activity that appears at the end of the chapter.

THE BENEFITS OF FITNESS

MAIN IDEAS

CONCEPTS
✔ Physical fitness allows you to meet the challenges of life without undue fatigue.

✔ A regular program of exercise contributes to physical fitness.

✔ The benefits of physical fitness include improved physical health as well as improved intellectual, social, and emotional well-being.

VOCABULARY
physical fitness
endorphins

Physical fitness is the ability of your body to handle physical, intellectual, social, and emotional challenges without undue fatigue. When you are physically fit, you are able to perform at your top level of efficiency. You are able to tolerate stress better and maintain long periods of mental alertness.

Rest, sleep, and nutritious food all contribute to your fitness. They help your body to grow and repair itself. But the primary contributor to fitness is a regular program of exercise. Research shows that people who exercise regularly tend to be healthier and live longer than people who do not. In a study of 5,000 men and women, researchers found that people who were most sedentary [*SED un ter ee*], or inactive, were five times more likely to develop heart disease than those who were most active. People who exercise regularly also develop feelings of self-confidence.

PHYSIOLOGICAL BENEFITS

Exercise makes your muscles and bones strong. It works your circulatory and respiratory systems so that they deliver needed amounts of food and oxygen to your cells with less effort. Exercise also helps to develop your coordination, balance, and reaction time—skills that come in handy as you carry out everyday activities.

THE HEART   When you exercise regularly, your heart is able to pump much more blood each minute than the heart of an inactive person. This means that more oxygen can be delivered to your muscles, and that your muscles can perform efficiently for a long period of time. If you are walking or running, you can walk or run much farther than you had before you started exercising. Regular exercise helps you perform higher workloads for much longer.

BLOOD PRESSURE   The blood pressure of people who exercise regularly is about 35 percent lower than the blood pressure of inactive people. In fact, exercise is used along with stress control, salt restriction, and weight reduction as treatment for high blood pressure.

METABOLISM   You may have heard that exercise only increases your appetite and therefore will result in a weight gain. Before you make the decision to avoid physical activity, keep in mind that the more you exercise, the more calories you will burn. Regular vigorous exercise also tends to curb the appetite. In other words, you will take in fewer calories and burn off more!

Regular exercise can help you develop a feeling of well-being.

LONGEVITY   The idea of longevity as a benefit of regular exercise may not seem particularly important at your age. You may prefer to think of exercise as a means of living better throughout life. This is because people who establish healthy exercise patterns at a young age can favorably modify the changes of aging. As people age, their muscle mass decreases and the percentage of body fat increases. Bones may lose calcium and become brittle. Muscle strength also declines, and blood pressure tends to increase. Maximum heart rate declines and the amount of blood that the heart can pump gets smaller. The lungs are also affected by the aging process. As the chest wall becomes stiffer, maximum breathing capacity decreases and oxygen delivery declines as a result. When these changes occur varies among people.

You may be surprised to learn that a regular program of exercise can reverse many of the changes associated with aging. For example, exercise can increase heart and lung capacities and lower blood pressure. As people become fit from working out regularly, muscle strength increases and a person's body fat decreases. In fact, regular physical activity can even improve reaction time, so reflexes are faster.

OXYGEN   Your "wind" improves through exercise. In other words, the body's ability to deliver and use oxygen improves. Rather than changes in your lungs, there are beneficial changes in the pumping of the heart and the ability of your muscles to generate energy.

IMMUNE SYSTEM   When you exercise vigorously, your brain produces greater quantities of **endorphins** [*en DAWR funz*], chemicals that act as natural painkillers in your body. Some research suggests that endorphins can increase immune system activity. As you exercise, your body temperature rises. Elevated body temperature has been linked to improved immune activity.

PSYCHOLOGICAL BENEFITS

Research is beginning to confirm a strong association between fitness, exercise, and psychological well-being. After a vigorous workout, the body tends to let go of all the tensions of the day. In fact, studies indicate that regular exercisers are less tired, more relaxed, more productive at work, more satisfied with their looks, and more self-confident.

STRESS REDUCTION   Sooner or later you will probably experience some stress in your life. Stress may appear as tension, anxiety, or a pounding heart. Difficulty falling asleep, compulsive eating, and perspiring heavily are other signs of stress. The important thing is figuring out an effective way of dealing with stress. Vigorous exercise is one important tool in managing stress.

Here are several reasons why exercise is so effective in managing stress:

- Exercise can remove you—at least temporarily—from the stressors of daily life.

FOR YOUR INFORMATION

For older people, exercising provides protection against osteoporosis, a disease that results in loss of bone density and poor bone strength. With stronger bones, the elderly are less likely to suffer debilitating bone fractures.

Exercising with other people can help you develop friendships with people who have similar interests.

- Exercise improves your mood. It produces both relaxation and feelings of confidence in your own abilities.
- As you exercise, you have a chance to think out problems and work out angry, hostile feelings.

SELF-ESTEEM   As you master exercise goals that may have seemed impossible for you a few months earlier, your self-esteem will soar! The fitness improvements you acquire through vigorous exercise will boost your self-image as well. The improved coordination, increased muscle tone, and better posture will give you the healthy glow of a fit individual.

SOCIAL BENEFITS   As you work out with a friend or play for a team, you will strengthen bonds of friendship and enjoy the benefits of companionship. Laughing together as you learn, and talking out problems as they arise are ways to stick with an exercise program and build friendships at the same time.

REDUCTION IN DEPRESSION   When you think of someone who is depressed, you probably have an image of a physically inactive person. Depression is often associated with a lack of physical and mental activity. Exercise is a useful way to counter mild depression. As you know, endorphins are produced in greater quantity during exercise. An increase in endorphin production may account for improvement in mood, appetite, and even memory.

SUMMARY

Physical fitness is the ability of the heart, blood vessels, lungs, and muscles to function at their best. Physical fitness results from rest, sleep, good nutrition, and regular exercise. As the primary contributor to physical fitness, exercise provides physiological benefits as well as social benefits, increases in self-esteem, and reduction in stress and depression.

LESSON 15.1 **USING WHAT YOU HAVE LEARNED**

REVIEW

1. How are blood pressure and the immune system affected by regular vigorous exercise?
2. How do endorphins affect physical fitness?

THINK CRITICALLY

3. A sedentary life-style can negatively affect a person's life span. How can a sedentary life-style lead to heart disease? What other health problems might be related to a sedentary life-style?
4. A program of regular exercise can reverse many of the changes associated with aging. Why do you think this is so?

APPLY IT TO YOURSELF

5. Imagine that you are the physical education instructor in an elementary school where each student receives only one 45-minute physical education class per week. How might this time restriction affect your ability to provide a program that keeps students physically fit? How might you overcome this restriction in order to bring about fitness?

The Easy Access Project

Each summer millions of Americans flock to the 350 national parks and historic sites to enjoy their unique beauty and opportunities to hike, boat, climb, and explore the natural and historic heritage of the United States. In many of the national park areas, miles of extensive wilderness trails, undeveloped waterways, and rugged mountain paths offer the opportunity to increase physical fitness and meet unusual physical challenges.

No one is more aware of the physical challenges of the national parks than Wendy Roth. Roth is living with disabilities caused by multiple sclerosis and moves with the use of a wheelchair. As she and Michael Tompane traveled on a recent vacation, they discovered that, while many parks do provide adequate access to people living with disabilities, much more could be done to increase accessibility so that all of the parks can be enjoyed by everyone.

Ms. Roth and Mr. Tompane have made a business out of this discovery. They began a systematic exploration of favorite tourist sites in the United States and they spent a good deal of time researching issues related to accessibility. Their vacation turned from leisurely exploration of the nation's park system to important mission: the Easy Access Project.

Roth contends that everyone at some point or another is restricted by physical disabilities. She suggests that people with disabilities form the only minority group that anyone can join anytime. Sometimes, people are members of this group temporarily, due to broken limbs, sprained ankles, and restrictions of youth or age. But for many people, membership in the group is permanent. Since having a disability does not imply that a person is uninterested in the outdoors, access to recreation areas is important.

Roth suggests that the wilderness offers unique challenges to everyone no matter what their physical ability. "They are remarkably equalizing," she says of the challenges of the wilderness. "In these astounding locales, everyone explores his or her abilities."

The results of Roth's and Tompane's travels and research is a book called *Easy Access to National Parks,* a handbook describing many of the nation's parks and their degrees of accessibility. Roth and Tompane worked diligently with park managers and park visitors analyzing inaccessible areas and areas whose accessibility could be greater.

They enlisted the support of the National Parks Foundation, who created the Easy Access Challenge, a national volunteer network to improve recreational opportunities in the parks. Together with the volunteer efforts of the Telephone Pioneers of America, the National Parks Foundation has in the words of National Park Service director James Ridenour, "Expanded hiking-

biking trails, campgrounds, boating, cross-country skiing, and swimming opportunities at a number of our national parks as a result of this initiative."

Millions of visitors each year have Roth and Tompane and their supporters to thank for expanding access to allow more Americans to experience and appreciate their national park system.

1. What kinds of barriers to wheelchair access are natural? What kinds of barriers are created by people?

2. How might an architect or engineer change plans for a building or other structure to allow for easy access?

ASSESSING YOUR FITNESS LEVEL

Muscular strength, muscular endurance, flexibility, cardiorespiratory endurance, and body composition are the five health-related components of fitness. Each component is equated with the healthy functioning of the body. Body composition, or the percentage of body fat, often is thought of as more of an outcome of fitness. However, excess body fat is known to be harmful to health. Therefore, body composition is an important component to monitor. Balance, reaction time, coordination, and a range of motor skills are sometimes included in the list of fitness components. Motor skills refer to general athletic skills.

FITNESS TESTS AND RATINGS

Testing for physical fitness is a good way to identify your physical strengths and weaknesses. The tests that follow measure the health-related components of fitness. Each test shows how well certain parts of your body are working. The tests are easy to take and need little equipment. If you are testing yourself, work with a partner. It is easier, safer, and more fun.

Each test has a rating chart. The ratings, which range from poor to excellent, are based on performance. Keep in mind that these ratings give only a rough idea of your current level of fitness. A *good* rating is within the reach of most healthy young people.

Do not worry about how you rate against others. Instead, use the test results to help you set personal goals that work best for you. After working out for a few weeks, retest yourself to see how well you have progressed.

MAIN IDEAS

CONCEPTS

✔ Fitness testing is a way to identify physical strengths and weaknesses.

✔ Cardiorespiratory endurance, muscular strength, muscular endurance, body composition, and flexibility are the five health-related components of fitness.

✔ Motor skill development encourages coordinated movement and balance.

✔ Body composition is based on how much of a person's body weight is fat.

VOCABULARY

cardiorespiratory endurance
strength
muscular endurance
flexibility
motor skills
body composition

ATHLETICS AND ACADEMICS

Athletic participation can be a wonderful way to stay fit. However, some health and fitness officials have raised concerns about what they perceive as an over-emphasis on competition. They fear that too much emphasis on the competitive side of athletics can create other problems, including the development of unrealistic expectations in young athletes.

For many young athletes, the dream of becoming a professional sparks hope for opportunities. Some may see sports as the only way to get ahead in society. What many of these young people do not recognize is that the chance of making a living playing professional sports is very slim. Only 1 in 10,000 high school athletes makes it to a professional team, and only 1 in 1,000 even competes at the college level.

Efforts are being made across the country to help young people understand that the key to opportunity rests in academic achievement. Lifelong fitness does mean regular exercise, but it is important to realize the balance between mind and body in order to grow.

CARDIORESPIRATORY ENDURANCE

The ability of your heart, lungs, and blood vessels to function efficiently at rest and during long periods of vigorous activity is called **cardiorespiratory endurance** [*kahrd ee oh RES puh ruh tawr ee*]. It is the single most important health-related component of fitness because it greatly affects your overall health. A person with high cardiorespiratory endurance has more energy. Such a person tends to have a slower, stronger heartbeat than does a less fit person.

You can get a good idea of your cardiorespiratory endurance when you take the one-mile run test. Before taking the test, be sure to warm up your muscles by walking quickly for about five minutes and stretching afterwards. Warming up properly will help you avoid injury. During the test you may only be able to run a short distance at a time. If so, alternate between running and walking. Do not push yourself to a point of potential injury.

To take the one-mile run test, use an area where distance has been measured and marked out, such as a track. Find out the number of laps it will take to complete one mile. For example, on most standard tracks, four laps are equal to a mile. For the test, use a watch with a second hand to time yourself. Begin timing as soon as you begin your run. You may be able to run only a short distance at a time. If so, take turns running and walking. Your goal is to cover the distance as rapidly as possible. Record your score in minutes and seconds.

CARDIORESPIRATORY ENDURANCE

ONE-MILE ENDURANCE RUN

Rating	Girls	Boys
Excellent	Under 8:00	Under 7:00
Good	8:01–8:30	7:00–7:30
Average	8:31–9:00	7:31–8:00
Fair	9:01–9:30	8:01–8:30
Low	9:31–10:00	8:31–9:00
Very Low	10:01 plus	9:01 plus

Figure 15-1 *The one-mile endurance run tests your cardiorespiratory endurance. How well do you think you would do on this test?*

STRENGTH AND MUSCULAR ENDURANCE

The ability of a muscle to exert force against a resistance is called **strength**. Lifting a weight and pushing against a wall are acts of strength. The greater the weight a muscle can lift, the greater its strength. You gain strength with training by using your muscles to do more than they are accustomed to doing.

Muscular endurance is the ability of a muscle to apply force over a period of time. In other words, it is the ability of a muscle to perform repeated contractions or to hold a muscle contraction over a period of time. Many day-to-day activities require muscular endurance. For example, keeping a firm grip on a screwdriver while putting up shelves requires muscular endurance. The upper body, abdominal area, and legs are most often tested for strength and endurance. Two common tests of muscular endurance are sit-ups and pull-ups. As you test your strength and muscular endurance, compare your scores with standards in Figure 15-2.

BENT-KNEE SIT-UPS The bent-knee sit-up test measures the muscular fitness of your abdominal area. To do sit-ups, lie on your back with your arms crossed on your chest and your hands placed on opposite shoulders. Bend your knees until your feet are flat on the

BENT-KNEE SIT UPS (CURL-UPS)

Rating	Girls	Boys
Excellent	47	56
Very Good	43	52
Good	39	48
Average	35	45
Fair	31	42
Low	27	38
Very Low	23	34

PULL-UPS

Rating	Girls	Boys
Excellent	5	12
Very Good	4	10
Good	3	8
Average	2	6
Fair	1	4
Low	0	2
Very Low	0	1

FLEXED-ARM HANG (SECONDS)

Rating	Girls	Boys
Excellent	40	64
Very Good	31	52
Good	23	40
Average	15	28
Fair	7	16
Low	0	4
Very Low	0	0

Figure 15-2 shows the scores for the tests for strength and muscular endurance. How might a rock climber need these two fitness components?

floor. Have a partner place one knee between your feet and hold your ankles. The assistance of a partner should be used only for testing purposes. When doing sit-ups for exercise, your feet or ankles should not be anchored down in any way. With such support, you tend to use the hip muscles more than the abdominals.

To measure your abdominal muscular fitness, begin curling up to a sitting position. Come up until your forearms touch your thighs. Return to the starting position to complete the sit-up. Keep your forearms close to your chest throughout the test. Your score is the number of complete sit-ups you can do in one minute. You may rest during the test, but only on your back with your arms and legs in the proper positions.

PULL-UPS   Pull-ups measure upper-body strength and muscular endurance. To take the test, you will need a horizontal bar that is high enough overhead that it allows the body to hang without touching the floor or ground. Grasp the bar with your palms facing away from your body. Hang with your arms fully extended. Pull your body up until your chin clears the bar. Then lower your body to the full-hang starting position. This represents one complete pull-up. Kicking your legs for momentum and resting in between pull-ups are not permitted.

Your score is the number of complete pull-ups that you can complete. There is no time limit. Have a partner help you count and hold you if you start to slip.

FLEXED-ARM HANG   The flexed-arm hang is an alternative test for people who are unable to do a pull-up. As in a pull-up, grasp an overhead bar with your palms away from you. With assistance from a partner, position your body with your chin above the bar and your elbows fully flexed. Your chest is held closed to the bar and your legs hang straight. Your score is the number of seconds your chin stays above the bar. Timing begins when you assume the flexed-arm position. Hold this position for as long as possible. Timing is stopped when your chin touches or falls below the bar.

FLEXIBILITY

The ability to bend joints and stretch muscles through a full range of motion is called **flexibility**. All movements require some degree of flexibility. When you increase your flexibility, you help prevent muscle strains and other problems, such as backache.

Since flexibility involves all of your muscles and joints, no single test can measure your overall flexibility. The sit-and-reach test measures your ability to stretch the major muscles in your lower back and the back of your legs.

Place a 3-foot piece of adhesive tape on the floor. This is your measuring line. Place a 2-foot piece of tape, called the baseline, across the measuring line at its middle point. The point where the two lines cross is the 0 point. Use a ruler to mark the measuring line at every half-inch. Numbers on one side of the 0 point should be marked with positive (+) numbers. Numbers on the other side of the 0 point should be marked with negative (−) numbers.

Now you are ready to take the test. Sit on the floor straddling the measuring line on the negative side with your legs straight and your heels up against the baseline tape. Slide your hands as far as possible along the measuring line without bending your knees. Record the farthest point touched by the tips of your fingers in the best of three tries. Do not bounce forward and back, as this can injure muscles and tendons.

FLEXIBILITY

SIT-AND-REACH TEST

Rating	Girls	Boys
Very Good	+4 to +6 in.	+3 to +4 in.
Good	+2 to +4 in.	+1 to +3 in.
Average	0 to +2 in.	+0 to +3 in.
Fair	-2 to +0 in.	-2 to 0 in.
Low	-2 to -3 in.	-2 to -4 in.

Figure 15-3 Who is expected to be more flexible, girls or boys?

Figure 15-4 *Motor skills are necessary for controlling movement. What are two tests often used to determine a person's motor skills?*

STANDING LONG JUMP (INCHES)			SHUTTLE RUN (SECONDS)		
Rating	Girls	Boys	Rating	Girls	Boys
Excellent	85	94	Excellent	10.0	9.0
Very Good	74	86	Very Good	10.4	9.3
Good	63	78	Good	10.8	9.6
Average	52	70	Average	11.2	9.9
Fair	41	62	Fair	11.6	10.2
Low	30	54	Low	12.0	10.5
Very Low	20	46	Very Low	12.4	10.8

MOTOR SKILLS

Motor skills are skills of balance and coordination. Through the development of motor skills, you are able to control movement. You see well-developed motor skills in action when you watch great athletes or dancers. The standing long jump and the shuttle run are two general tests of your motor skills.

STANDING LONG JUMP   The standing long jump is a measure of body power and coordination. Stand with both feet behind a line on the floor. Bend your knees and swing your arms backward. Then jump forward as far as you can. Swing your arms forward during the jump to help yourself go farther. Mark the spot where your heels land. Measure the distance of the spot from the starting line. Record the best of three jumps.

SHUTTLE RUN   The purpose of the shuttle run is to measure agility. Agility is the ability to stop, start, and change directions quickly. Speed, balance, and coordination all contribute to agility. To take the shuttle run test, place two blocks, or other objects you can pick up easily, at a point 30 feet away. On the command to start, run to the point 30 feet away and pick up one block, run back to the

The shuttle run is a good measure of agility.

staring point and place the block behind the starting point. Then run back to pick up the second block and return it to the starting point as well. When the second block is placed behind the starting point, the test is completed. Your score is recorded as the number of seconds it takes you to complete the test.

BODY COMPOSITION

The ratio of body fat to lean body tissue, such as muscle and bone, is called **body composition**. Your body composition is based not on how much you weigh, but on how much of your weight is fat. The most accurate measure of body fat includes weighing underwater. Bone and muscle tissue are more dense than fat tissue. Therefore, the closer a person's underwater weight is to his or her dry weight, the lower the percentage of fat on his or her body. However, the technique requires special equipment. Therefore, a common method for testing body fat uses a skinfold caliper. A skinfold caliper is a simple tool used to measure the amount of fat on the body by measuring skinfold thickness.

You will need someone experienced with calipers to measure your skinfolds. Generally two or three measurements are made at each of two sites on your body. Equations are then used to determine your percentage of body fat. Common sites on your body for testing body fat include the back of your arm (triceps), your waist, your lower leg, and one of your shoulder blades. However, you should remember that a complete test for body fat takes into consideration height, weight, circumferences, diameters, as well as skinfolds. Also, acceptable percentages of body fat differ by age and by gender.

One of the best places on the body for testing for body fat is the back of the arm.

LESSON 15.2 ## USING WHAT YOU HAVE LEARNED

REVIEW

1. What are the five health-related components that generally are used to determine physical fitness?
2. What are some of the characteristics of a person with good motor skills?
3. What is body composition? How is it measured?

THINK CRITICALLY

4. A person does not need to be an athlete in order to be physically fit. Explain how a person can be physically fit but not be very good in athletics.
5. A person can have a heavy, athletic build and have very little fat, or be slim but have relatively more fat. How can you explain the truth of this statement?

APPLY IT TO YOURSELF

6. Suppose you consistently score poorly on the test for cardiorespiratory endurance. How might your poor performance affect your ability to be on an athletic team? How might your poor cardiorespiratory capacity affect you during your daily routine?

SUMMARY

Being physically fit helps you stay healthy and carry out your daily activities with quality. Physical fitness is made up of cardiorespiratory endurance, strength, muscular endurance, flexibility, and body composition. These health-related components can be easily measured and used as a baseline to help you develop your own fitness program.

DESIGNING A FITNESS PLAN

Using the results of the tests you took in the previous lesson gives you an idea of how fit you are. Do not be discouraged if you did not score well in some areas. Instead, use the information to set some personal fitness goals.

SETTING GOALS

In order to stick with a regular program of exercise, you need to set goals that are reasonable for you. Focus on what you want to accomplish and choose the kind of exercise that will lead to your particular goal. For example, if you want to increase your endurance, choose exercises designed to improve your cardiorespiratory system. If you want to shape and strengthen your muscles, try weight-lifting and calisthenics. Before beginning, you should discuss your fitness plan with a doctor or fitness professional to be sure your plan is safe.

When setting your goals, keep in mind these guidelines.

- Set goals based on your test results. Short-term goals based on where you are now are more effective than long-term goals based on where you would like to be a year from now.

- Set goals based on the amount of time you can devote to an exercise program and how hard you are willing to work.

- Set goals that you can reach. You will continue working toward your goals if you see positive change along the way.

EXERCISE GUIDELINES

For your fitness workouts to be safe and effective, you need to follow a carefully planned training program. This means developing a program that addresses three principles of training—overload, progression, and specificity.

- **Overload** refers to working the body harder than it normally is worked, such as through repetitions of a certain exercise. The increased workload causes the body to undergo changes that result in greater muscular strength and overall fitness.

- **Progression** refers to the gradual increases in exercise overload that you need in order to continue improving your fitness. For example, you may have to run faster or longer, or increase the number of sit-ups or push-ups you do as your body adapts to each level of training.

- **Specificity** is the process of doing exercises that are specially suited to the fitness components you want to improve. For example, lifting weights will do little to improve cardiorespiratory fitness, but lifting weights will develop strength and muscular endurance.

Highly-skilled athletes follow a very strict fitness plan that helps them perform at peak efficiency.

Whatever your fitness goals, you need to determine how hard, how long, and how often you must work out. These three elements are referred to as intensity, duration, and frequency. Together, they determine the amount of overload during your workouts.

INTENSITY How hard you exercise is called the **intensity**. To improve your physical fitness, you must work your muscular and cardiorespiratory systems at higher-than-normal levels. During such an overload, your heart beats more quickly, your blood flow is increased, and your breathing is much deeper than during normal activity. These responses to the intensity are what makes your body stronger and causes it to become healthier and more fit.

You can check your exercise intensity by counting your pulse rate immediately after you exercise. To count your pulse rate, you must first find a pulse point. A pulse point is a place where you can feel your pulse easily. The pulse points most commonly used are located on your wrists and neck. The carotid arteries [*kah RAHT ud*] are located just under your jaw, slightly to the right and left of your windpipe. The pulse points on your wrists are located below the bases of the thumbs. To find your pulse rate, follow these steps.

1. With your first two fingers, find a pulse point. Do not use your thumb. It is not as sensitive as the other fingers.

2. Using a watch with a second hand, count your pulse rate for 15 seconds.

3. Multiply the number of pulses by 4 to find your pulse rate per minute.

During cardiorespiratory exercise, your heart must pump enough blood to meet the needs of your muscles. The harder your body works, the faster your heart pumps. Of course, your heart has a top speed. Your maximal heart rate, or HRmax, is your highest attainable heart rate. It is your heart rate at exhaustion. At rest, the average person's heart beats about 70 times a minute. The average HRmax for a young person is around 200 beats a minute. The difference between the heart rate at rest and the heart rate at exhaustion is your heart rate reserve. The heart rate at which you must exercise to improve your cardiorespiratory fitness is called your **target heart rate.** Your target heart rate is the sum of your resting heart rate and 75 percent of your heart rate reserve.

You can calculate your target heart rate by completing the following steps.

1. Take your heart rate at rest.

2. Subtract your resting rate from 200. This will be your heart rate reserve.

3. Multiply your heart rate reserve by 0.75.

4. Add this result to your resting rate. This number represents your target heart rate.

343

HOW DO YOU KNOW WHEN YOU'VE HAD ENOUGH OF AN AEROBIC WORKOUT?

OH, THAT'S VERY SIMPLE.

LET'S SEE... YOU TAKE YOUR AGE AND SUBTRACT IT FROM YOUR WEIGHT MULTIPLY BY YOUR HEARTRATE, DIVIDE BY TWO AND THEN YOU HAVE...

YOU'VE HAD ENOUGH WHEN YOU GET REALLY SWEATY.

© 1992 by NEA, Inc.

reprinted by permission of NEA, Inc.

There are many better ways to monitor your workouts.

For example, calculate the target heart rate of a person whose resting heart rate is 70 beats per minute.

a) Find heart rate reserve	**b)** Determine 75% of heart rate reserve	**c)** Identify target heart rate
200 (Avg. HR max)	130 (HR reserve)	98
- 70 (resting HR)	x .75	+ 70
=130 (HR reserve)	= 98	= 168 (Target HR)

Exercising at too low an intensity does not overload your cardiorespiratory system enough to improve your physical fitness. On the other hand, exercising at too high an intensity is also not necessary to improve your fitness. The key is to work out at an intensity that allows you to carry on a conversation with a friend at the same time. Working out at an intensity level near 75 percent of your heart rate reserve allows you to carry on a conversation and get a good fitness stimulus at the same time.

Your heart, lungs, and muscles need time to adjust to the increased demands you are making on them. Prolonged fatigue—one hour or more after you exercise—is a sign that the intensity level of your activity was more than was necessary. To check your heart rate (equal to your pulse rate) during a workout, take your pulse within 5 seconds after you stop exercising.

DURATION   The amount of time it takes to do your workout is called the **duration**. You will get an adequate cardiorespiratory and muscular fitness benefit if you exercise at your target heart rate for 20 to 30 minutes. However, if you are just starting a program, you may need to limit your workout duration to 10 to 15 minutes. Include several 1-minute recovery periods between periods of activity at 75 percent effort. The recovery periods should involve mild exercise, such as brisk walking, rather than complete rest.

FREQUENCY   **Frequency** refers to the number of times you exercise during a week. Although exercising regularly enables you to reach and maintain a good level of fitness, daily workouts are not necessary. Therefore, schedule three to four workouts a week with no more than two days between each workout.

TYPE OF EXERCISE

Not all exercise provides the same results. For example, if you want to develop cardiorespiratory fitness, you will need to do some form of aerobic exercise. **Aerobic exercise** involves vigorous and continuous physical activity for a duration of at least 20 minutes. When you exercise aerobically by swimming or running, your body requires more oxygen to meet the energy demands of the exercise.

Anaerobic exercise involves intense bursts of activity in which the muscles work so hard that they produce energy without using oxygen. Calisthenics, weight training, and sprinting are examples of anaerobic exercise. If you want to develop muscular strength and endurance, you will need an anaerobic program of progressive resistance training. Progressive resistance training is the systematic and progressive overloading of a muscle.

WORKOUT STAGES

Doing your workout in stages will ensure that you exercise safely. Your physical fitness workout should consist of three stages: a warm-up, a vigorous conditioning period, and a cool-down.

WARM-UP Increasing circulation to the muscles through slow, fluid motions is called a **warm-up**. Warming up properly before each workout prepares your body for the stressful activity to follow. You will avoid unnecessary injuries if you warm up first. A complete warm-up gradually builds up the heart rate and blood flow to the muscles. It also raises muscle temperature and improves the elasticity of muscles and tendons.

Start out with 3 to 4 minutes of walking, moderate jogging, or any exercise that is continuous. Then begin to stretch and tone the key muscle groups. The stretching part of the warm-up should last between 8 and 10 minutes.

CONDITIONING The segment of the workout that develops cardiorespiratory endurance or strength and muscular endurance is **conditioning**. If you are training for cardiorespiratory endurance, pace your conditioning activity so that your average heart rate is at your target level. This vigorous conditioning period should last between 20 and 30 minutes.

When you train for strength and muscular endurance, the intensity of your workout is governed by the overload of the weights being lifted. Some people follow their cardiorespiratory workout with some progressive resistance exercises for strength and endurance training. Others alternate days of cardiorespiratory training and strength training.

COOL-DOWN A tapering-off period after completion of the main conditioning workout is called a **cool-down**. The best way to cool down is to continue your conditioning activity at a lower intensity. For example, if you are jogging, jog more slowly or walk. If you are cycling, cool down with slow, easy pedaling. If you are swimming,

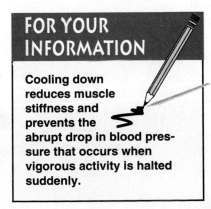

Proper stretching before a workout can help you avoid injury.

FOR YOUR INFORMATION

Cooling down reduces muscle stiffness and prevents the abrupt drop in blood pressure that occurs when vigorous activity is halted suddenly.

| Step | Rating on Endurance Run | One Set is | | Start with: | Add 1 set at a time up to: | Approximate distance run: |
		Run	Walk			
1	Very low	30–45 sec.	30 sec.	8 sets	12 sets	1/2–3/4 mile
2	Low	1–1 1/2 min.	30 sec.	6 sets	12 sets	3/4–1 1/2 miles
3	Fair	2–3 min.	30–45 sec.	6 sets	10 sets	1 1/2–2 1/2 miles
4	Average	4–6 min.	30–45 sec.	4 sets	6 sets for two days	2–3 miles
5	Good	8–12 min.	1–2 min.	2 sets	4 sets	2–4 miles
6	Very Good	12–16 min.	2–3 min.	1 set	2 sets	3 miles or more
7	Excellent	20–40 min.	5 min. or more	Run continuously, then walk until cooled down		2–4 miles

Figure 15-5   The Run-Walk-Run Program is an effective way to start a fitness plan. How might it help a person get started on the road to fitness?

do some stretching in the water or on the deck. You should keep moving until your breathing and heart rate return to near normal.

WORKOUT CHOICES

Each exercise activity has something different to offer—the speed of bicycling, the floating sensation of swimming, the joy of moving to music in dance. Whatever you do, be sure to build up gradually. Also, select activities according to your interests and skills. When you enjoy an activity and become competent at it, you are more likely to make it a lifetime activity.

At age 15, Tom was self-conscious about his thin body. He had grown taller but felt that his upper body lacked the musculature of many of his peers.
Although Tom had scored quite well on the cardiorespiratory test at school, his scores for muscular strength had been quite low. Tom spent most of his afternoons on a skateboard instead of training for one of his school's athletic teams. Tom thought about using some money from his savings for mail-order exercise equipment that promised a body bulging with muscles. Or should he take steroids for quick results?

RUNNING   To get fitness benefits fast, you may want to consider running, one of the easiest activities to take up. Running for 30 minutes 3 to 4 days a week quickly improves the fitness of the cardiovascular system. For people who are interested in exercise as a method for controlling their weight, running burns as many as 400 calories in a half hour.

If you are not used to exercising on a regular basis, you may be wondering how to start a program of running or other aerobic activity. One way is to follow the Run-Walk-Run Program in Figure 15-5. The Run-Walk-Run Program is designed to take you at your present fitness level and gradually increase your workouts. Your goal is to exercise at your target heart rate for 20 minutes or more.

To begin, check your rating on the cardiorespiratory test. For example, if you scored *fair* on the one-mile run, start with Step 3. If you rated *good,* start with Step 5.

WALKING   Of all the fitness activities, walking is the easiest and least expensive. To avoid injury, use a program of walking with gradual increases in distance and vigor. Start out walking at your normal, easy gait. At first, cover a mile if you can. Increase the distance each day until you can walk 2 miles. Check your pulse rate, but do not be concerned if you are not at your target heart rate.

Once you can walk for 2 miles easily, speed up your pace. As you become accustomed to walking briskly, gradually increase your walks to 3 miles in 45 to 50 minutes. At this point, you can consider starting at Step 1 of the Run-Walk-Run Program.

BIKING   Biking for fitness requires a lot more exertion than coasting down a hill at a leisurely pace. As a general guideline, you have to ride at twice the speed you run to get the same fitness benefits. For example, running 1 mile in 10 minutes is equivalent to biking 1 mile in only 5 minutes. Alternate high- and low-intensity exercise rides as you would in the Run-Walk-Run Program. Gradually increase the duration and frequency of your high-intensity segments. Use the steps in Figure 15-5, and bike at your target heart rate during the run segments of your workout. For example, at Step 3, bike vigorously for 2 to 3 minutes. Then bike slowly for 30 to 45 seconds. Start at an easy level and move up at a comfortable rate.

SWIMMING   Swimming is excellent exercise for overall fitness. Swimming a half mile is equivalent to running two miles. Swimming benefits people with joint problems because the water supports the body's weight. Therefore, no stress is placed on the joints.

Biking can be a fun way to get in an aerobic workout.

CONSUMER HEALTH

Athletic Shoes

As recently as ten years ago, sneakers were the cheapest, most comfortable shoes you could buy. Whether you played basketball, baseball, tennis, walked, or ran, a ten-dollar sneaker did the job.

Today, many sneakers have been replaced by athletic shoes—a whole new industry specializing in shoes for just about any sport. Each type of athletic shoe is designed for the general wear and tear of a spe-

cific sport. Aerobic shoes have firm heels and lots of cushion to absorb shock. Running shoes are light and flexible and have curved edges to help propel the runner forward. Basketball shoes are well-cushioned and usually high-topped for ankle support. Walking shoes are roomy at the toe and have a strong cushion around the ankles.

When shopping for athletic shoes, it is important to understand your needs and your budget. Are you buying the shoes to improve performance and avoid injury in a

specific sport? Or are you more interested in fashion? Do you have any special needs due to your walking style or foot structure? Can you get the same performance from a less-expensive shoe?

Of course the all-purpose athlete can buy one shoe to meet all of his or her needs. But specialists do recommend that if you engage in any sport on a regular basis, choose a shoe that is built to meet the rigorous demands of that sport.

AEROBIC DANCE Aerobic dancing and similar programs set continuous, rhythmical exercise movements to music. When done properly, these forms of exercise have good cardiorespiratory fitness benefits. Aerobic dance also improves strength, muscular endurance, and tone if the intensity and duration meet the guideline standards.

In recent years, step aerobics has become extremely popular.

KNOW YOUR AEROBICS

Aerobic dance has grown considerably over the past ten years. Many people take part in formal instruction classes. Others may purchase exercise videos and exercise in the privacy of their own homes. It is not unusual for some people to do both. The three most common types of aerobic dance are:

- high-impact: includes routines that require both feet to be off the ground at the same time
- low-impact: one foot is always in contact with the surface; often includes exaggerated arm movements to increase heart rate
- step aerobics: routines are performed by stepping up onto and down from a platform that can be adjusted in height from 4 to 9 inches

EXERCISE MACHINES Indoor fitness equipment, such as stationary bicycles, rowing machines, and treadmills, is used for cardiorespiratory exercise. This equipment provides the resistance and challenge needed to improve fitness by elevating the heart rate. Be sure you are using the machines safely and correctly.

WEIGHT TRAINING Lifting weights, either with barbells or on machines, is the best way to develop muscular strength and power. Proper strength training requires an overload resistance that is repetitious and progressive. The weight should be light enough so that no less than 10 lifts and no more than 15 lifts can be performed. However, remember that such exercises do not develop your aerobic fitness. This is why a balance of activities during your workouts is needed to address all the health-related fitness components.

Tom convinced one of his skateboarding friends to work out with Tom on the weights and exercise machines at a local gym. Tom enjoyed the workouts with his friend and began to gain confidence in his physical ability. At the gym, he also heard some disturbing stories about what happened to people who used steroids to develop muscles. Tom was glad he had chosen the natural method to develop his body, rather than use drugs. Because of the increase in his self-confidence, Tom began to realize that he could use his thin, tall body and his cardiorespiratory endurance to his advantage. No one was surprised when Tom made the track team in the spring.

ASSESSING YOURSELF

The more fun you have doing an activity, the more likely you are to stick with it and become competent at it. But how do you know when you've become competent at a particular activity or reached your fitness goal? In most exercise programs, you will notice changes in your body within 12 weeks. Your heart rate at rest may be lower and your body composition may have changed. At this point you may want to repeat the fitness tests that you took earlier. If you have been training properly, your rating for a particular fitness component should have improved. For example, suppose you are training for muscular strength by working out with barbells and weight-resistance machines. After about 12 weeks of training, you should find that your rating on the sit-ups and pull-ups or flexed-arm hang have improved.

Once you have reached a fitness goal, how can you maintain it? Maintenance is important because the benefits of a regular program of exercise are short-lived. When you stop an exercise program, you lose the benefits. The good news is that the more fit you are and the longer you've been in training, the more slowly the loss of benefits occurs. Keep this in mind when you have less time to do exercise or have restrictions because of an injury. Rather than stopping your exercise program altogether, maintain some of your fitness with a less demanding workout schedule. The intensity of your workouts is the important factor. If intensity is decreased, your body begins to detrain. However, the frequency and the duration of your workouts can be shortened without suffering the consequences of detraining.

LESSON 15.3 **USING WHAT YOU HAVE LEARNED**

REVIEW

1. What guidelines can be used to set realistic goals for an exercise program?
2. What is the difference between aerobic exercise and anaerobic exercise? Give examples of each.
3. Why is weight training not a good activity for developing cardiorespiratory fitness?
4. What are the three segments of a physical fitness workout? What takes place during each segment?

THINK CRITICALLY

5. More and more people are becoming aware of the need for physical fitness. Why is it important to learn the proper exercise techniques before beginning a workout program?
6. Swimming often is said to be the ideal form of exercise. In what ways is this true?

APPLY IT TO YOURSELF

7. Imagine that you are an aerobics instructor for high school students. What kinds of things should you be aware of in order to protect your students' health? What information would you need to convey to students in order to run safe, productive classes?

SUMMARY

When you plan an exercise program, you need to consider overload, progression, and specificity. An aerobic exercise program is one in which you exercise at your target heart rate for at least 20 minutes about 3 to 5 times a week. Aerobic exercise increases cardiorespiratory fitness and improves muscular endurance. Anaerobic exercise increases muscular strength and endurance and helps maintain flexibility. Including a warm-up, a conditioning stage, and a cool-down in your workout will ensure that you exercise safely and effectively.

Steroid Abuse

HEALTHY PEOPLE 2000

Reduce to no more than 3 percent the proportion of male high school seniors who use anabolic steroids.

It is estimated that there are over one million current or previous users of anabolic-androgenic steroids in the United States, with approximately one-half this group comprised of adolescents...studies have associated [anabolic steroid use] with changes in the physiology of organs and body systems with [the] potential for subsequent health problems.

Objective 4.11

from *Healthy People 2000: National Health Promotion and Disease Prevention Objectives*

The Terminator, Rambo, and Conan the Barbarian are heroes of fiction and the actors who play them have become models for many young men. It takes years of training to achieve a look like theirs. But recently, the abuse of anabolic steroids has created a life-threatening, health-threatening short cut to the Rambo look.

Steroids are synthetic versions of the male hormone, testosterone. In small doses, their use can help repair soft-tissue injuries, skeletal disorders, malnutrition, and some forms of anemia. Steroids increase muscular fiber and fluids and decrease the body's ability to create scar tissue. The side effects of steroid use can include edema, hypertension, conversion of latent diabetes to active diabetes, testicular shrinkage, increased cholesterol levels, jaundice, infertility, decreased sexual drive, prostate cancer, kidney disorders, hardening of the arteries, liver malfunction, and mental disorders including severe depression, aggression and violence, suicidal tendencies, and extreme moodiness. The abuse of steroids may lead to death.

Medical experts suggest that no one is exempt from these side effects. Yet steroid abuse is fast becoming a very serious problem among young athletes and non-athlete adolescent males. As members of the high-risk group, you can have a strong influence on meeting the health goals for the year 2000.

WHAT WENT WRONG

Anabolic steroids were introduced in the 1940s to help nourish and add weight to survivors of concentration camp. By the 1950s, steroids were used increasingly by athletes in the hopes of building bulk and enhancing athletic strength and performance.

The most recent and startling statistic about steroid abuse includes male non-athletes—young men who take them for cosmetic reasons. In a practice known as stacking, they take double or sometimes triple an already high dose in order to achieve huge body mass quickly. With this kind of cosmetic misuse, for many young men who are not yet fully grown, steroids may halt growth by sealing off bone development.

Researchers suggest that steroids are psychologically and physiologically addictive. Once a person has begun abusing them, he or she may find it extremely difficult to stop.

What attitudes and values are reflected in the desire for short-term good looks and long-term health risks? Teenagers need to be aware that bulk and aggression are not the ways to achieve personal acceptance and social status. A healthy approach to good looks includes balanced eating and regular exercise. For those who wish, increased body size and mass can be achieved through a weight lifting and body building program.

WHAT YOU CAN DO

These guidelines may help you to prevent steroid abuse.

1. Rather than choose steroids, work with a certified weight trainer to find ways to increase bulk.

2. Evaluate your heroes. Make a list of the qualities that you admire in another person. What healthy steps can you take to acquire some of the same good qualities? What qualities do you already possess that give you strength?

3. If body building is a goal for you, enlist a friend to join you as you train. Keep a weekly log of your progress. You will be amazed at how quickly you will achieve results without the use of steroids.

4. Practice self-acceptance. Understand that not all body types are alike. Some bodies are better suited for endurance or stamina than for bulk. Be comfortable with your body as it is before you begin any type of body-altering routine.

WHAT DO YOU THINK?

1. Skim through the advertising section of a favorite magazine. What messages do the ads convey about body image? Write a paragraph that describes your own feelings about how your body fits into the norms of the messages in magazines.

2. Interview a coach or athlete engaged in a sport that you enjoy. Ask him or her what steps were taken to achieve a strong physique. If you are interested in building your own body, ask about ways you can work toward your goals.

3. Why do you think there is a growing preoccupation with

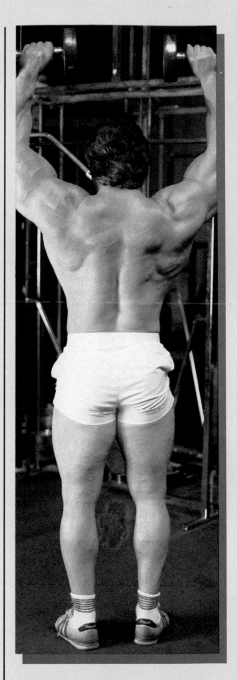

size and mass in males? Why do you think that characters such as Rambo and the Terminator are appealing?

MAIN IDEAS

CONCEPTS

✔ There are many things you can do to reduce risks during exercise.

✔ Choosing clothing and equipment that are appropriate for a particular exercise activity increases both comfort and safety.

✔ Exercising safely in extremes of weather requires proper clothing, adequate fluid intake, and good judgment about the intensity of the workout.

SENSIBLE PLANNING

Your workout should be designed to meet your immediate goals and to help you live a healthy life. Do not worry about keeping up with your friends. Remember, you are working with your body, not theirs. Your fitness will increase in time, but you must be sure to work within your capabilities, starting from your present level of fitness. Whatever type of activity you choose, follow the intensity, duration, and frequency guidelines to get the best results. Remember to progress at a reasonable rate and choose activities that are specific to the fitness components you want to improve.

REDUCING RISKS

For most people who exercise regularly, a life without injury is probably an unrealistic goal. However, you can reduce the risk of injury. Sensible planning based on your present level of fitness and known medical limitations is one way. An awareness of the kinds of injuries that are most likely to occur is another. Finally, there are several relatively simple measures that you can take to protect yourself.

KNOW YOURSELF   If you have a medical limitation such as asthma or knee problems, discuss the condition with your doctor before you begin your program. Usually, there is a way to modify an exercise program and still achieve your goals.

Begin your program with low-intensity activities if you are overweight or have a medical problem. You may need to exercise for longer periods of time at a slower pace. You will gain cardiorespiratory benefits even if your heartbeat does not reach your target rate.

Sensible planning and learning to listen to your body can help you reduce the chances of injury during your workouts.

GAIN WITHOUT PAIN   Many people believe that if exercise does not hurt, it will not help. That is not true. If you feel pain while you are exercising, you are either working too hard or you have not warmed up adequately. On the other hand, it is normal to experience some muscle soreness a day after exercising. This soreness usually occurs when your body has not been accustomed to a particular type of exercise. Soreness may be reduced by investing 5 to 10 minutes in stretching the muscles before exercising.

Too much exercise can lead to fatigue and injury. When you become tired, your judgment and muscle control decrease, which may cause an injury. Rest helps to restore your strength after periods of activity. It gives your muscles and tissues time to rebuild and adapt to the training stimulus.

For people beginning an exercise program, doing too much too soon often leads to unnecessary injuries. Injuries also result from overtraining, from poor exercise techniques, and from muscle or skeletal imbalances.

Many injuries cause swelling. This is due to bleeding or tissue inflammation in and around the injured area. If swelling occurs, elevate the injured part, wrap the area with a wet elastic bandage, and apply ice to reduce swelling. If the problem continues after a few days' rest, seek the help of a doctor.

WHEN AND WHERE TO EXERCISE

Finding a regular time to exercise can be difficult. According to one survey, people who exercise regularly fit their workouts into their existing schedule. For example, you might walk or bike to school rather than ride. Instead of watching television or playing video games after school, take an aerobic dance class or follow an aerobic routine on a pre-produced videotape. Take the stairs instead of elevators or escalators.

The time of day that you exercise can affect what you do afterwards. Fitness experts suggest that you plan to work out just before doing activities that require your greatest concentration. Also, try to schedule your workouts at least two hours before you plan to go to sleep.

Fortunately, many communities now have places for people to work out, such as gyms and indoor swimming pools. School gyms and pools often schedule open hours as well. You may want to consider exercising outdoors. If so, avoid jogging or working out in isolated places. Increase your security by having friends join you. Not only is it safer to work out with friends, but it is also more fun.

COPING WITH THE WEATHER

To make exercising in extremes of weather safe and enjoyable, it is important to use good judgment. For example, if you like to jog in cold weather, plan to dress in layers of clothing that trap air. Air is an excellent insulator that allows you to retain your body heat. Also, be sure to wear mittens, a hat, and warm socks. These garments protect you against cold better than any others because they cover the places—fingers, head, and toes—that contain the most sensitive nerve receptors for cold.

Winter exercise also holds the risk of a serious fall on icy surfaces. Generally, exercising on ice or snow is not worth the risk. The one exception may be hard, packed snow. If you decide to run on this kind of surface, be sure to slow your pace, take smaller steps, and wear running shoes with good traction.

Occasionally, exercising during hot, humid weather causes the body to overheat. To reduce your chances of overheating, drink at least one to two 8-ounce glasses of water about an hour before exercising. As you exercise, take rest breaks and continue to drink water. Taking in water is important in order to replace the fluids lost through perspiration. It will not lead to bloating or cramping during the exercise session.

STRATEGIES FOR LIVING

Keys to Avoiding Injury

- Start any new exercise at a lower level of intensity and increase the level over several weeks.
- Halt your exercises when you experience pain.
- Avoid bouncing as you stretch. Bouncing shortens muscles and increases the risk of muscle tears.
- Do low-impact aerobics rather than high-impact aerobics.
- Always warm up and cool down.
- Work out regularly—a minimum of three 20-minute workouts a week.

Cold weather does not mean exercising has to stop. But don't bundle up too much.

CLOTHING AND EQUIPMENT

Proper clothing and equipment can make a difference in your comfort and safety. For example, always wear a helmet when you set out on your bike. The safest helmets are fully enclosed on top with a foam liner inside to absorb blows in case of a fall. When skateboarding or rollerblading, make sure your knees and elbows have protective padding as well.

Be sure to choose equipment that is appropriate for the activity. For example, if you are running track, don't rely on your well-worn sneakers, regardless of how comfortable they are. Wearing improper shoes places stress on your hips, knees, ankles, and feet—places where most sports injuries occur.

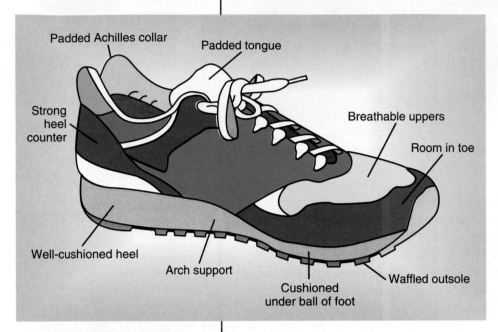

Padded Achilles collar

Padded tongue

Strong heel counter

Breathable uppers

Room in toe

Well-cushioned heel

Arch support

Cushioned under ball of foot

Waffled outsole

It is important that your shoes provide you with proper support during physical activity. How can your shoes affect your enjoyment during physical activity?

For most activities, clothing should be light and loose-fitting. Cotton shorts and T-shirts are good for warm weather. For outside activity in cold weather, wear mittens, a hat that covers your ears, and several thin layers of clothing. You can then peel off layers as you start to sweat.

If you exercise outdoors at night, be sure to wear bright, reflective clothing. If you are biking, use a headlight.

SUMMARY

Keeping fit for a lifetime means choosing a well-balanced program that will build and maintain your overall fitness. Whenever you exercise, consider your own safety. Avoid unnecessary injury by warming up and cooling down and by not doing too much too soon. If you exercise outdoors, take sensible safety precautions and watch weather conditions. Be sure to wear clothing and shoes that are appropriate for your chosen activity.

LESSON 15.4 USING WHAT YOU HAVE LEARNED

REVIEW

1. What steps can you take to reduce the risk of injury?
2. How can swelling from an injury be treated?
3. How can the soreness associated with exercise be prevented?

THINK CRITICALLY

4. Exercise authorities often advise people to wear several layers of clothing when they exercise in cold weather. Why is this way of dressing more sensible than wearing a single heavy outer garment?
5. In cold weather, will your hands stay warmer in mittens or in unlined gloves? Explain your answer.

APPLY IT TO YOURSELF

6. Imagine that you are the parent of a 15-year-old girl who regularly delivers papers on her bike before sunrise. How would you help her to take adequate safety measures in terms of equipment, clothing, and rules of the road?

Fitness For Life

Helcio's first year of college was going well. His classes were challenging but manageable, and the social life was great. There always was something to do—a party, a concert, or a lecture. A lot of times, Helcio and his friends would stay up late watching TV and snacking the entire time.

On weekends, Helcio usually rolled out of bed around 11:00 A.M. after having been up late the night before. He'd get up just in time to join other guys on his dormitory floor to watch football. They often sent out for pizza and would snack on chips during the games. Helcio never worked out anymore.

One Friday in November, Helcio went to the student health center to get something for a cold. He had a paper due on Monday and there was a BIG home football game on Saturday. There would be something going on all weekend. Helcio figured he'd need to pull an all-nighter on Sunday to finish the paper.

The doctor checked Helcio's vital signs, including his blood pressure. "Helcio, this reading is too high for a person your age. Has anyone in your family had problems related to high blood pressure?"

"My uncle died from a stroke when he was 40, and my dad takes medication to control his blood pressure," said Helcio.

"Well," said the doctor, "unless you take care of yourself, you're going to be in the same shape. You need sleep, a balanced diet, and regular exercise. Otherwise you will have to start on medication." As Helcio and the doctor spoke, Helcio realized that he needed to modify his life-style.

Helcio thanked the doctor and went back to his room. He thought about his uncle and his father. Then he thought about the good times he had been having. He really didn't want to miss them, but if he continued at the same pace, Helcio knew he was risking his health.

PAUSE AND CONSIDER

1. ***Identify the Problem.*** What dilemma does Helcio face about treating his high blood pressure?

2. ***Consider the Options.*** What choices does Helcio have?

3. ***Evaluate the Outcomes.*** What could happen if Helcio waited until later to deal with his high blood pressure? What might happen if he begins to modify his life now?

Helcio thought about what the doctor had said. "You don't have to give up all fun. But adopting a healthy life-style can be fun, too."

The more Helcio thought about his options, he realized there was only one option—good health. He decided to cut back on some of his social life. He didn't need to do everything this weekend. "Tomorrow," he said, "I start eating better and working out again. I was in great shape in high school!" He made a plan to work out at least three times a week. He had been missing his time in the gym. "A lot of other people are managing to take care of themselves, so why not me?"

DECIDE AND REVIEW

4. ***Decide and Act.*** What plan did Helcio develop that would help him deal with his high blood pressure?

5. ***Review.*** What else could Helcio do to take care of his high blood pressure?

PROJECTS

1. You are a fitness instructor and a client has come to you for help. You learn that she is 42 years old, a smoker, and she is overweight. She has not exercised regularly for 20 years. Create a fitness plan that will help your client get into shape. What exercises will be best for her to improve flexibility, endurance, strength, and aerobic functions?

2. Pick one fitness activity such as rowing, tennis, swimming, aerobic dancing, weight lifting , cycling, or calisthenics and find out what services and products are available to help people engage in that activity. Find out the approximate cost of each service or product, the possible safety issues they may raise, how easy they are to use, and the effectiveness of each piece of equipment. Present your findings as a "consumer report."

WORKING WITH OTHERS

As a class, develop a survey that investigates the fitness knowledge of students in your school. Use the information in Chapter 15 to develop test questions about important aspects of physical fitness. One group of students in class should be responsible for developing the questionnaire. Another group should be responsible for administering the survey. The final group is responsible for evaluating the results.

CONNECTING TO...

SOCIAL STUDIES   On a world map, find the places where the Olympics have been held during the last century. Use push pins to locate the Olympic sites and use different colors to mark summer or winter Olympics. Then find out how the Olympic committee chooses where the Olympics will be held.

USING VOCABULARY

aerobic exercise	intensity
anaerobic exercise	motor skills
body composition	muscular endurance
cardiorespiratory endurance	overload
conditioning	physical fitness
cool-down	progression
duration	specificity
endorphins	strength
flexibility	target hart rate
frequency	warm-up

On a separate sheet of paper, make a list from 1 to 10. Match the words from above with the following definitions. Keep in mind that there are more words than matching definitions.

1. the ability of the heart, lungs, and blood vessels to function efficiently both at rest and during vigorous activity

2. the ability to apply strength over a period of time

3. the ability to bend joints and stretch muscles within a full range of motion

4. the ratio of body fat to lean body tissue

5. the act of performing exercises designed especially for target fitness components

6. the act of working the muscles harder than they normally work to improve fitness

7. the rate at which the heart must be exercised to improve cardiorespiratory fitness

8. intense bursts of activity where the muscles work so hard that they produce energy without using oxygen

9. the tapering off period after completing a physical work-out

10. a period during a work-out that develops cardiorespiratory endurance or strength and muscular endurance

CONCEPT MAPPING

Work by yourself or with others to create a concept map for *exercise*. In your map, use as many of these concepts as you can: *aerobic exercise, cardiorespiratory endurance, conditioning, cooldown, exercise, flexibility, injury, muscle endurance, physical fitness, strength, stress, warm-up*. You may include other concepts related to *exercise* in your map. Information about concept mapping appears in the front of this book.

THINKING CRITICALLY

INTERPRET

LESSON
15.1
1. What are the overall benefits of good physical fitness?

2. How does exercise affect heart function?

3. How does the immune system benefit from regular exercise?

4. How might the production of endorphins affect depression?

LESSON
15.2
5. What role does cardiorespiratory endurance play in health?

6. Why is flexibility an important component of physical fitness?

7. Why is body fat an important factor for a person to monitor?

8. What is the difference between muscular strength and muscular endurance?

LESSON
15.3
9. Why is it important to establish a carefully planned training program to improve physical fitness?

10. Why is it important to exercise muscular and cardiovascular systems at a higher than normal rate to increase fitness?

11. How can a person cool down after exercising?

12. Why might swimming be a good exercise for someone who has arthritis?

LESSON
15.4
13. What is the best way to avoid injury during a workout?

14. If a person does not have the time to exercise, what is one way to increase fitness levels?

15. How can exercising in extreme heat be dangerous?

APPLY

LESSON
15.1
16. Why might an exercise program be easier to follow if you do it with another person?

LESSON
15.2
17. Why is body composition more important in physical fitness assessment than weight?

18. When you do sit-ups, why is it important to curl your back up rather than coming up with a straight or arched back?

LESSON
15.3
19. Why do you think it is important to exercise at least three times a week to attain and maintain physical fitness?

20. George and his friend Sally decided to start a running program for physical fitness. The day they started, George set out ahead of Sally boasting that he could run four miles in the time it took her to run one. He finished the course faster than Sally but the next day complained of sore muscles and a pulled hamstring. Why did this happen to George?

LESSON
15.4
21. Jason and Rich joined a weight-lifting club whose instructor had a reputation for getting results. The club's motto was "No Pain, No Gain." Why do you think many people believe in this approach? Why is this approach incorrect?

22. Tito wants to keep in shape during the winter to be ready for baseball practice in the spring. What safety precautions should he take during the icy conditions of winter?

COMMITMENT TO WELLNESS FOLLOW-UP

SETTING GOALS

Look back at your completed Commitment to Wellness checklist. Out of the ten items on the checklist, pick one behavior you would most like to change. Write the statement in the center of a page in your Journal or on a separate sheet of paper. Then under the heading, write down the following questions, leaving room to fill in the answers.

1. What is my ultimate goal in regard to this fitness behavior?

2. What is the first step I need to take to change this behavior?

3. How can I make time in my life for this change?

4. Whom can I ask to help me change this behavior?

5. What, if any, equipment will I need?

6. What are some intermediate goals I can set that will help me?

When you have finished answering these questions, write yourself a "contract." In it include the statement, "I want to accomplish a change in this behavior no later than (identify a date)." Refer back to your contract from time to time to check on your progress.

WHERE DO I GO FROM HERE?

As you work toward your fitness goal, you may want to investigate various methods of fitness training.

FOR MORE INFORMATION ABOUT
PHYSICAL FITNESS, CONTACT:
American Fitness Association
820 Hillside Drive
Long Beach, CA 90815

UNIT 6

The Human Life Cycle

Chapter 16
Reproduction and Heredity

Chapter 17
Growth and Development

Chapter 18
Understanding the Aging Process

Why are people concerned about personal care during pregnancy?

What does old mean to you?

What kind of changes are you experiencing as a teenager?

Reproduction and Heredity

"In every child who is born, under no matter what circumstances, and of no matter what parents, the potentiality of the human race is born again."

James Agee

Birth is a remarkable process. A birth is the result of many complex events changing a single fertilized egg cell into a complete human being. Within each fertilized egg are a set of instructions that are inherited from each parent. These instructions strongly influence everything from the development inside the womb to the physical characteristics such as height and hair color that will be carried through to adulthood.

All of the instructions that are needed to grow into a healthy baby are present in the fertilized egg. However, proper care is needed during pregnancy to improve the chances of the birth of a healthy baby. By maintaining a healthy diet, avoiding harmful substances such as tobacco, alcohol, and other drugs and getting regular medical check ups, a pregnant woman can take important steps toward ensuring that the new baby will be able to lead a healthy life.

BACKGROUND

James Agee was an American writer whose home town served as the setting for some of his novels. Where was Agee from? Can you identify some of the works Agee is known for?

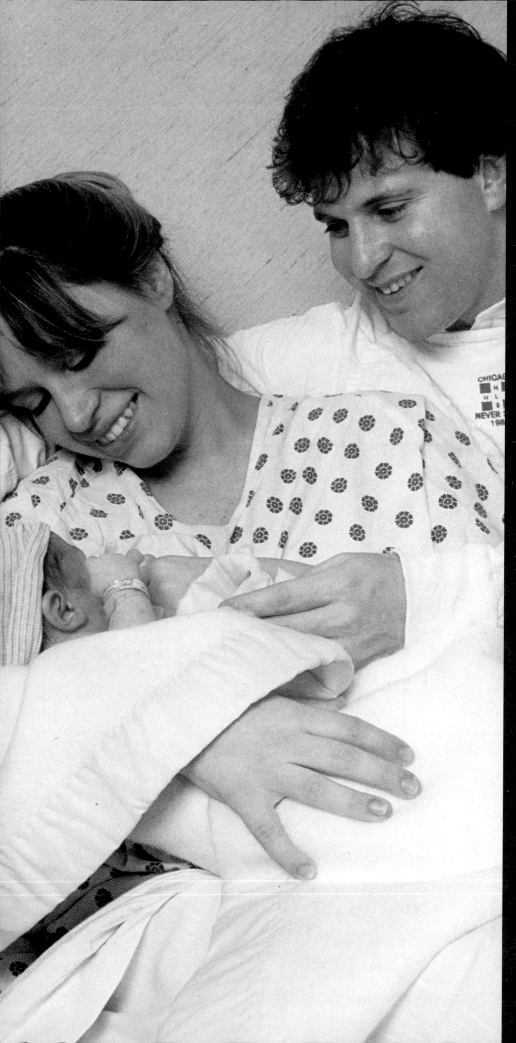

How much do you know about reproduction and heredity? Use the following checklist to take a closer look. Number a separate sheet of paper from 1–8 and respond to the items below by writing a *yes* for each item that describes your knowledge about that health issue.

1. I am aware that proper medical care is necessary for a healthy pregnancy.

2. I understand the importance of eating a healthy diet throughout pregnancy.

3. I know why the use of tobacco, alcohol, and other drugs during pregnancy can be dangerous.

4. I know the importance of staying physically fit throughout pregnancy.

5. I am aware of the dangers that teenage pregnancy poses to both the mother and the baby.

6. I understand how traits are passed from parents to their children.

7. I am aware of the responsibilities that go along with parenthood.

8. I thoroughly understand the process of fertilization.

Review your responses and consider what may be your strengths and what may be your weaknesses. Save your personal checklist for a follow-up activity that appears at the end of the chapter.

BEGINNING OF LIFE

The development of a new individual is a complex process that begins when a sperm cell from a man and an egg cell from a woman unite. The resulting cell contains all the information needed to make a new person. By making good health decisions throughout pregnancy, the parents can increase the chances that a healthy baby will be born.

FERTILIZATION

The joining of an egg cell and a sperm cell is called **fertilization** [*furt il uh ZAY shun*]. Fertilization occurs in a narrow tube called the **Fallopian tube** [*fuh LOH pee un*] that connects an ovary and the uterus. The process begins when an egg is released from one of the woman's ovaries and enters the Fallopian tube. The egg remains in the Fallopian tube for approximately two days. In order for fertilization to occur, sperm also must be in the Fallopian tube during this time. In Chapter 17, you will learn more about the role of the male and female reproductive systems in the process of fertilization.

The final step in the fertilization process is the joining of the egg cell and the sperm cell. Millions of sperm cells surround the thin wall of tissue that covers the egg cell, trying to break through to the egg. Only one sperm cell will be successful. When the sperm enters the egg, fertilization occurs. Within the next thirty hours, the egg splits into two cells. These two cells divide into four; these four become eight, and so on. What starts as one fertilized cell develops in nine months into a baby made of trillions and trillions of cells.

MAIN IDEAS

CONCEPTS

✔ The growth of a single cell into a new baby is a very complex process that requires proper care.

✔ Nutrients pass from the mother to the baby through the placenta.

✔ Proper nutrition is critical for healthy development.

✔ Problems during pregnancy and childbirth can be minimized with proper medical care.

VOCABULARY

fertilization
Fallopian tube
embryo
placenta
umbilical cord
amniotic sac
fetus
labor
identical twin
fraternal twin
breech birth
cesarean section

Figure 16-1 After fertilization, the fertilized egg is implanted in the endometrium. In which organ does fertilization occur?

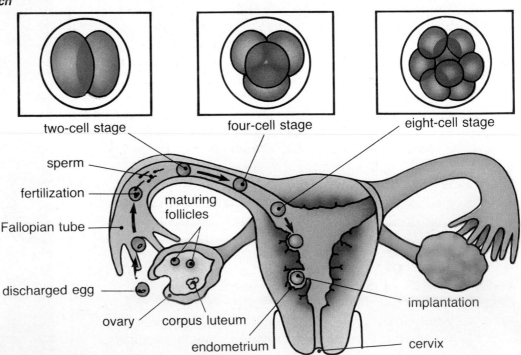

two-cell stage
four-cell stage
eight-cell stage
sperm
fertilization
maturing follicles
Fallopian tube
discharged egg
ovary
corpus luteum
endometrium
implantation
cervix

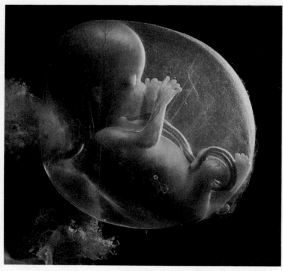

This woman is carrying a fetus at approximately 3 months (left). A fetus at 3 months (right) is slightly over an inch long and has a recognizably human form.

THE EMBRYO

As the fertilized egg begins to divide, it travels down the Fallopian tube. By about the fourth day, it reaches the uterus. Soon after, the mass of dividing cells attaches to the inner lining of the uterus. At this stage, it is slightly larger than the size of the period at the end of this sentence. During its first two months, the rapidly dividing mass of cells is called an **embryo** [*EM bree oh*].

By the time it reaches the uterus, the embryo is surrounded by a layer of cells that develops into an organ called the placenta. The **placenta** [*pluh SENT uh*] provides nourishment to the embryo by absorbing nutrients and oxygen from the mother's bloodstream. Nutrients and oxygen are passed from the placenta to the embryo through a thick cord called the **umbilical cord** [*um BIL ih kul*]. The placenta also serves as a filter, screening out many harmful substances. However, some harmful substances, including alcohol, nicotine, and other drugs, as well as the AIDS-causing virus (HIV), can be absorbed through the placenta. As you will learn later, these substances can cause permanent harm to the developing baby.

The placenta also receives the waste products from the embryo and passes them into the mother's bloodstream. These wastes are eliminated through the mother's kidneys. Although substances are exchanged between the mother and the embryo through the placenta, each has a separate circulatory system. Therefore, the blood from the mother and the embryo do not mix.

The embryo is also wrapped in a protective covering called the **amniotic sac** [*am nee AHT ik*]. The amniotic sac is filled with fluid that helps cushion the embryo from jolts and bumps.

During the first two months, the embryo grows rapidly. The placenta and amniotic sac grow along with it. After four weeks, the embryo's heart begins to beat. By the seventh week, the embryo is

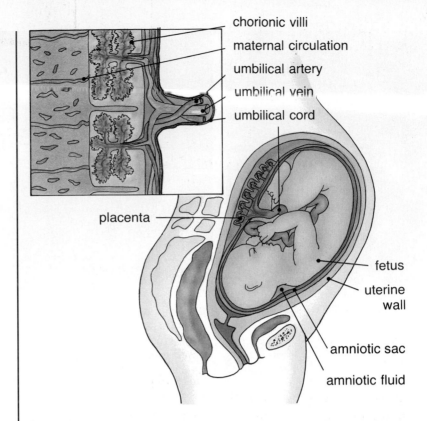

chorionic villi
maternal circulation
umbilical artery
umbilical vein
umbilical cord
placenta
fetus
uterine wall
amniotic sac
amniotic fluid

about an inch long. The eyes, the ears, and the mouth have developed, and limbs are beginning to grow. At this stage, the largest part of the embryo is the head, which is curled over the stomach. During these critical two months, when all the organs of the body are developing, the embryo is particularly sensitive to chemicals such as alcohol, nicotine, and other drugs. These chemicals, as well as diseases such as rubella (German measles), can prevent the organs and limbs from developing properly.

THE FETUS

From the third month until birth, the embryo is called a **fetus** [*FEET us*]. The fetus is still surrounded by the amniotic sac and the placenta has formed along the uterine lining as shown in Figure 16-2. The fetus continues to grow rapidly, and bone starts to replace the cartilage in its skeleton. The fetus begins to use its muscles, and the mother can feel it stretching and rolling. By the end of the sixth month, the fetus is about one foot long and weighs slightly over one pound.

In order to develop properly, the fetus requires the right nutrition. Fetal nutrition depends on the mother's eating nutritious foods and avoiding foods that could be harmful to the fetus.

Roberta is three months pregnant. Recently, she had fallen behind in her work and the deadline for a report was approaching. In the past, when faced with similar stressful situations, Roberta would work straight through lunch, only taking time to go to the vending machine to buy peanut butter crackers, chips, and a ginger ale. This day, as Roberta gathered her loose change, she suddenly remembered

The Cost of Raising a Child

At some point in your life, you may want to have a child. Before deciding to have a child, it is important to consider the costs and plan your budget for the changes a child will bring.

The cost of raising a child includes far more than the basic needs of food and shelter. Early childhood brings expenses such as medical check-ups, diapers, clothing, toys, and safety equipment.

You can save money by choosing baby equipment carefully—many baby items are unnecessary or are used for only a few months. Consider borrowing equipment and clothing if possible, and sharing child care with other parents. If both parents work or attend school, the cost of day care in the early years can be hundreds of dollars each month.

As children grow older, they continue to need regular medical care. The cost of clothing increases as children grow but sturdy, depend-

able clothing does not have to cost a fortune. For school-age children, the cost of outside activities such as dance classes, music lessons, or sports camps can be prohibitive. Often, however, worthwhile extracurricular activities are available at low cost within the community.

Having a child is rewarding and challenging. By planning ahead, you will be better able to meet the challenges without the extra worry that inadequate finances bring.

---

how sick she had felt three days earlier after she had quickly eaten a bag of greasy potato chips. Roberta reminded herself that she was eating for her baby as well as for herself. Roberta knew that in order for the fetus to receive the necessary nutrients, she needed to eat well. Roberta decided to take a half hour of relaxed time to eat a sandwich and a salad with her friends in the cafeteria.

Eating a wide variety of good foods each day, particularly foods rich in protein, calcium, iron, and vitamins, is the best way to make certain that the mother and the fetus are getting all the nutrients they need. Eating slowly and avoiding greasy foods can help prevent heartburn—a frequent source of discomfort among pregnant women.

The fetus gains most of its weight during the last three months of pregnancy—increasing from just over one pound to an average of seven and a half pounds at birth. At this time, the fetus may change position several times. Just before birth, it is usually situated with the head against the cervix, ready for birth to begin.

BIRTH

Approximately 40 weeks after fertilization, the baby is ready to be born. Birth occurs in three stages. The process of birth is called **labor**.

The nutritional needs of a woman are very important during pregnancy because she is feeding her baby by what she feeds herself.

STAGE ONE During the first stage of labor, there are usually mild muscle contractions in the mother's abdomen as muscles in the uterus begin to push the baby against the cervix, which is the lower portion of the womb. The pushing gradually causes the cervix to dilate, or open.

At first, the contractions occur about every 15 to 20 minutes and only last a few seconds. As the first stage of labor continues, the time between contractions decreases to one every few minutes and the contractions are much stronger. The contractions come every minute and are even stronger just before birth. The first stage of labor ends when the cervix is completely stretched so that the baby's head can move into the birth canal.

STAGE TWO   During the second stage of labor, the baby passes through the cervix and moves into the birth canal. The head appears first, pushing its way through the outer opening of the birth canal. The baby turns slightly and its shoulders and the rest of its body slip out.

STAGE THREE   After the baby is born, the muscles of the uterus continue to contract, causing the placenta to separate from the lining of the uterus. The delivery of the placenta, often called the afterbirth, takes between 5 and 10 minutes. Although the length of labor differs from one person to the next, on the average, the entire birth process takes about 14 hours for the first baby and 8 hours for second and later births. Some studies indicate that a routine, doctor-approved exercise program during pregnancy may help shorten and ease some of the stress of labor.

THE NEWBORN INFANT

Several important events occur immediately after the baby is born. The baby's lungs fill with air and the baby takes its first breath. This first breath is accompanied by a loud cry which is a healthy sign that the lungs are working.

Since the baby no longer needs the umbilical cord, it is cut by the doctor. There are no nerves in the umbilical cord, so this procedure is painless. The spot on the infant's abdomen where the umbilical cord is attached will become its navel. The baby then is weighed and examined to make sure it is healthy.

REFLEXES   At birth, the baby has several natural reflexes, or involuntary responses to stimuli. The stimulus can be pressure or light. For example, touching the bottom of the foot will cause the baby's toes to curl. It is also a natural reflex for a baby to grab a finger placed in its palm. These and other reflexes are signs that the baby is alert and that its nervous system is working properly.

NUTRITION   The infant soon wants food and is able to suck from a bottle or its mother's nipple immediately after birth. In most cases, the best food for a newborn baby is milk from its mother's breast. The mother's milk provides nutrition as well as temporary immunity to certain diseases. However, bottle-feeding may be necessary in some cases and can provide the infant with needed nutrients. Breast-feeding also has benefits for the mother. It contracts the muscles of the uterus, helping it return to its normal size. Additionally, the mother's weight may return to normal more quickly when breast-feeding.

Women who breast-feed should be aware that they continue to eat for their babies. It is recommended that they eat an extra 500 Calories a day, get plenty of calcium and drink

Bonding between the parent and child usually begins at the moment of birth.

extra fluids. Nursing mothers should continue to avoid alcohol, caffeine, tobacco, and other drugs. These substances, as well as HIV and certain foods that may irritate the infant, can be passed on to the baby through the mother's milk.

MULTIPLE BIRTHS

Women usually give birth to one baby per pregnancy. However, multiple births do occur, as in twins, triplets, and quadruplets. There are two ways in which multiple births can occur.

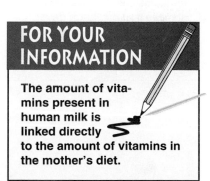

SINGLE EGG   The first type of multiple birth occurs when the small group of cells that develops from the fertilized egg splits into two or more groups. Each group develops into a complete embryo. The embryos share the same placenta, although they have separate amniotic sacs. Since the embryos first came from the same egg cell and sperm cell, each baby will be the same gender, or sex, and will look almost exactly alike. Twins that develop from the same fertilized egg are called **identical twins**. If the egg splits into three groups, the babies will be identical triplets.

Fraternal twins do not inherit the same traits, and are no more alike than non-twin brothers and sisters.

MULTIPLE EGGS   A second type of multiple birth occurs when an ovary releases more than one egg at one time and each egg is fertilized by a different sperm. The fertilized eggs develop as separate embryos in the uterus—each with its own placenta. The babies will be no more alike or different than brothers and sisters, although they will be the same age. Twins that develop at the same time but from different fertilized eggs are **fraternal twins**.

Being one of many developing embryos can cause problems for some of the babies. There may not be enough room in the uterus for the fetuses to develop normally. It is important for the physician to determine early in the pregnancy whether there will be multiple births so that the health of the fetuses can be monitored.

MANAGING DIFFICULT DELIVERIES

Most births are normal, but the presence of a doctor or health professional is necessary to help the mother have a smooth delivery and to take quick action if there are problems. With every birth, there is the chance of something going wrong. One possible problem is the failure of the baby to turn head down before delivery. This results in a breech birth. A **breech birth** is one in which the feet or buttocks of the baby enter the birth canal first. During the final weeks of pregnancy, doctors check to see if the baby will be born in the breech position. If so, the doctor may try to turn the fetus during labor so that it is in the right position.

FOR YOUR INFORMATION

The amount of vitamins present in human milk is linked directly to the amount of vitamins in the mother's diet.

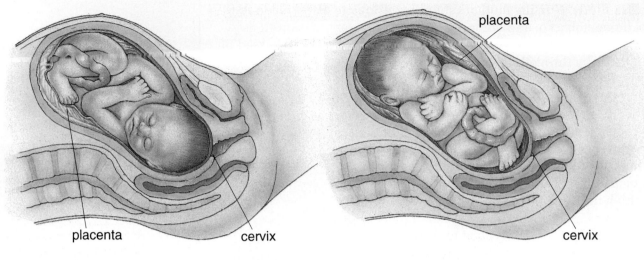

placenta

placenta   cervix   cervix

Normal birth   Breech birth

Figure 16-3   In a normal delivery (left), the fetus is born head-first. The baby's feet or buttocks enter the birth canal in a breech birth (right). How may a breech birth be prevented?

If labor has started and the fetus cannot be turned, the doctor may decide to make an incision in the abdomen and uterus and lift out the baby. This method of delivery is called a **cesarean section** [*si ZAR ee un*]. Doctors perform cesarean sections whenever they feel that the mother or the baby would be at risk during a normal delivery. Cesarean sections are now performed in over 20 percent of all births in the United States.

There is still a lot that we do not understand about how a single fertilized egg develops into a healthy baby. Scientists continue to research how cells and chemicals interact to ensure normal development. Clearly, however, the mother can play a major role in making sure that a healthy baby is born by making wise health decisions throughout her pregnancy.

SUMMARY

Reproduction begins with an egg cell and a sperm cell. As the fertilized egg develops from an embryo to a fetus, a human life takes shape. To ensure healthy development, the mother needs to maintain a nutritious diet and avoid substances that can harm development. Proper medical care is essential to guard against problems.

LESSON 16.1   USING WHAT YOU HAVE LEARNED

REVIEW

1. Describe what happens to the egg during the first week following fertilization.
2. What is the role of the placenta in the developing fetus?
3. What is a breech birth? What action can a physician take to prevent a breech birth?

THINK CRITICALLY

4. Compare the process leading to the birth of fraternal twins with the process leading to the birth of identical twins.
5. Explain what effects the mother's dietary habits can have on her and on the developing fetus.

APPLY IT TO YOURSELF

6. Imagine that you are a developing fetus. Write a brief description (1-2 paragraphs) about how it feels (a) inside the womb as you are growing, (b) during birth, or (c) as a newborn infant.

PRENATAL CARE

Beginning a new life is not without risks for both mother and child. However, proper medical care and nutrition before and during pregnancy, called **prenatal care**, helps increase the chance that a baby will be born healthy and that the mother will have no serious health problems.

PREPARING FOR PREGNANCY

The decision to have a baby is one that will bring about tremendous changes in the lives of both parents and will bring on an entirely new set of responsibilities. The impact of these changes can be lessened if the couple prepares well before the woman becomes pregnant.

CHOOSING A PHYSICIAN   One decision is the choice of a physician who will care for the pregnant woman and the fetus during pregnancy and delivery. Recommendations from friends, relatives, and other doctors can be helpful in identifying possible physicians. However, no final decision should be made until after the couple has talked with each physician. The following list shows a few of the important issues that should be considered when choosing a physician.

• The physician's qualifications
• The physician's philosophy regarding nutrition and use of medications during pregnancy and birth
• The feeling of open communication with the physician

Once a physician is selected, the woman should have a medical checkup to ensure that she is in good physical condition. The physician may review the medical histories of both parents to determine whether there might be any problems.

CHOOSING A LOCATION   Although most couples choose to have their babies in hospitals, couples have other choices of settings where childbirth can take place. One alternative is a birthing center. A birthing center is a health-care facility which is administered by a hospital but is located in a separate building. It can offer a more comfortable environment than the traditional hospital delivery room. Other couples may choose to have their baby born at home under medical supervision. Couples should discuss with their physician which option is best for them.

OVERCOMING ANXIETY   As with any major life change, both the pregnant woman and her husband will experience many different emotions, ranging from joy to anxiety. The couple may worry

MAIN IDEAS

CONCEPTS

✔ A pregnant woman should choose a physician with whom she and her husband feel comfortable.

✔ Prenatal care can help prevent many of the problems that may occur during pregnancy and childbirth.

✔ Abstaining from alcohol, tobacco and other drugs can decrease the risks of premature birth.

✔ Teenage pregnancy can pose physical risks to both the mother and the baby.

VOCABULARY
prenatal care
human immunodeficiency virus
anemia
toxemia
miscarriage
stillbirth
premature
incubator
birth defect
Fetal Alcohol Syndrome

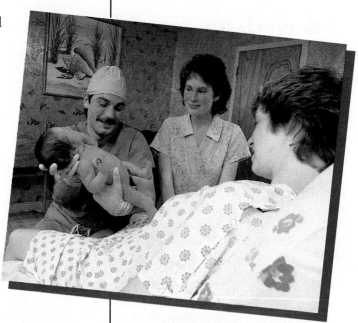

Some parents choose a birthing center, which offers comfortable, homelike surroundings.

Dietary suggestions for pregnant women.

- Carbohydrates: 4 servings a day of bread, pasta, rice, and potatoes.
- Protein: 2-3 servings a day of lean meat, poultry, fish, eggs, milk, dried beans.
- Calcium: 3-4 servings a day of milk and milk products such as cheese, yogurt, and cottage cheese.
- Vitamins: 4-5 servings a day of fruits and vegetables
- Iron: present in meat, poultry, fish, fortified cereals, fruits, and vegetables. Your physician may recommend an iron supplement.

Figure 16-4 *A pregnant woman should change her diet to provide the extra protein, minerals, and vitamins needed by the developing fetus. By what percent should a pregnant woman's folate intake increase?*

about whether the baby will be healthy or about whether they are prepared to be good parents. They may also worry about the physical changes the mother is experiencing. By working together, a couple can overcome some of these anxieties. Open communication helps the mother and the father become aware of the changes and feelings each other is experiencing.

CARE DURING PREGNANCY

If a woman suspects that she is pregnant, she should visit a doctor. One of the early signs of pregnancy is a missed menstrual period. Other signs may include swollen and tender breasts, nausea, fatigue, and frequent urination. Although home pregnancy tests are available without a doctor's prescription, a woman should always see a doctor for a more reliable pregnancy test. Tests can be given in a doctor's office, a hospital, or a health clinic.

If the woman is pregnant, her doctor will usually recommend a change in her diet to provide extra protein, calcium, and certain vitamins. Proper nutrition is essential for the development of the fetal brain, bones, and teeth. It is recommended that a pregnant woman eat between 2,200 and 2,400 Calories a day. Under normal conditions, a woman will gain between 20 and 30 pounds during pregnancy. This extra weight includes the weight of the baby, the placenta, and extra body fluids.

Doctor's visits are normally scheduled once a month for the first seven months. After that, more frequent visits are scheduled. The doctor checks the mother's urine, blood pressure, weight, and the general health of the fetus. After the third month, the doctor also checks the heartbeat of the fetus.

■ INCREASED NUTRIENT NEEDS OF PREGNANT WOMEN

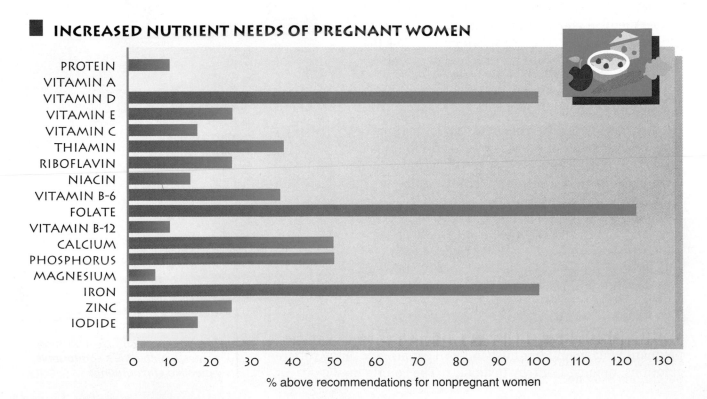

% above recommendations for nonpregnant women

The doctor will also discuss with the woman the importance of avoiding exposure to infectious diseases. Viruses, which are the cause of many infectious diseases, can pass from the mother to the fetus through the placenta. Some diseases, such as rubella, may not cause serious health problems for the mother, but they can be very dangerous to the fetus. The **human immunodeficiency virus (HIV)**, which causes AIDS, can cross the placenta to the fetus. You can learn more about AIDS and HIV in Chapter 24.

POTENTIAL CONCERNS

Most women experience some discomfort during pregnancy. Many of these discomforts are temporary and pose no danger to the pregnancy. Some of the more serious problems that pregnant women may experience can be prevented through proper prenatal care or can be successfully treated. Occasionally, however, a problem can occur which is beyond the control of the mother or the doctor.

PROBLEMS DURING PREGNANCY   Approximately half of all pregnant women suffer from morning sickness during the first few months of pregnancy. Morning sickness ranges from mild feelings of nausea to frequent vomiting. Despite these discomforts, morning sickness poses no danger to the pregnancy. Other discomforts, including heartburn and trouble with digestion and bowel movements, may last throughout pregnancy. Eating small meals at frequent intervals and avoiding greasy or spicy foods may help lessen these discomforts.

Many doctors recommend that pregnant women maintain a mild exercise program. Exercise may reduce or prevent back pain associated with pregnancy. It also can aid in the ease of delivery and recovery of muscle tone after birth. Exercises that are safe and that emphasize low impact and endurance, such as walking, swimming, and riding a stationary bicycle, often are recommended.

Many pregnant women have a lower than usual number of healthy red blood cells—a condition called **anemia** [*uh NEE mee uh*]. Anemia may be caused by insufficient iron in the blood and often causes the woman to feel tired and weak. Pregnant women become anemic when the fetus takes iron from the mother's bloodstream to make its own red blood cells. If the anemia cannot be corrected by increasing the amount of iron in the diet, iron pills are usually prescribed.

A potentially dangerous condition that develops in some women during the final three months of pregnancy is toxemia. Symptoms of **toxemia** [*tahk SEE mee uh*] include retention of toxic body wastes, rapid weight gain, high blood pressure, and swelling in the face and hands. If untreated, toxemia can lead to convulsions and coma. The cause of toxemia is not understood; however, teenagers, women over 40, and women who have gained excess weight during pregnancy may be at higher risk than others.

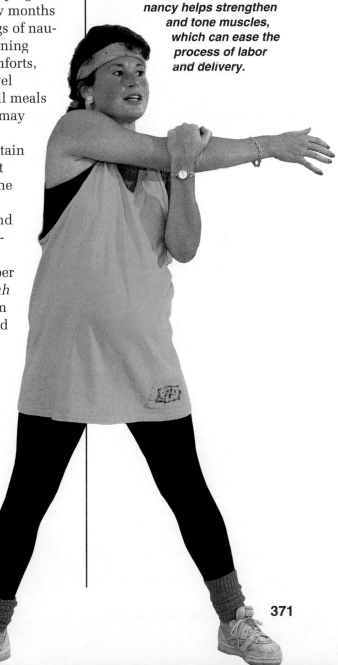

Regular exercise during pregnancy helps strengthen and tone muscles, which can ease the process of labor and delivery.

MISCARRIAGE AND STILLBIRTH   For various reasons, some pregnancies end unsuccessfully. A **miscarriage** occurs when the muscles of the uterus contract and force a nonliving embryo from the body. Although a miscarriage can occur anytime during a pregnancy, most occur during the first three months. Many miscarriages occur before the woman even realizes that she is pregnant. A **stillbirth** occurs if the mother gives birth to a nonliving fetus after a full term of pregnancy.

Most miscarriages are caused by problems in the development of the embryo over which the mother has no control. Other miscarriages can result from infections such as rubella, from preexisting conditions in the mother such as diabetes, or from a defect in the uterus. Miscarriages can also result from drug abuse. The risk of miscarriage is increased for women who do not receive regular prenatal care.

PREMATURE BIRTHS   Babies who are born before they are fully developed are said to be **premature** [*pree muh TYOOR*]. Although

MAKING A DIFFERENCE

CAREERS HEALTH

Midwives

Joyce Harding doesn't say she delivers babies, she says, "It's the mothers who do all the work, I just offer a little support, a little guidance, and some medical care when I'm needed."

Harding, a midwife, has helped at the births of over 1,000 babies. When a woman is pregnant, she needs medical care, support, and encouragement because pregnancy and childbirth are life-changing events. Midwives try to make these experiences truly happy events.

For many years in the United States, midwives were rare and not highly regarded. But today midwifery is a growing career. While it is still important for a woman to see an obstetrician during her pregnancy, many doctors recognize the important role a midwife can fill. For a mother anxious about the birth and health of her child, a midwife may be able to offer more hand-holding than a doctor can.

Midwifery is a demanding profession, requiring personal qualities such as sensitivity, flexibility, and dedication, plus medical ability. A person entering the profession can choose to be either a certified nurse-midwife (C.N.M.) or a lay-midwife. A C.N.M. has an R.N. degree, status, and a specialist qualification that gives her or him certain medical rights, while a lay-midwife either serves an apprenticeship or goes to a lay midwife school. Only 10 states permit lay-midwives to practice in a hospital.

1. Why do you think there is a new trend toward obstetricians working with midwives during pregnancy and delivery?

2. In what ways is a midwife different from an obstetrician?

the causes of premature births are not fully understood, the health of the mother can be a major factor. Mothers who have poor nutritional habits, who smoke or use drugs, or have some type of infection increase their risk for premature births. In some cases, a doctor will intentionally cause a woman to go into labor early because he or she has found some problem with the fetus that needs immediate care.

Premature babies are almost always smaller than average, generally weighing less than five pounds. They usually are placed in a special container called an **incubator** [*IN kyuh bayt ur*] that keeps the baby at the right temperature and protects it from disease. The baby is fed on a regular schedule and is closely monitored. Protected in the incubator, the baby can develop and grow strong.

TEENAGE PREGNANCY

After a decrease in the rate of teenage pregnancies during the 1970s and early 1980s, teenage pregnancy rates are once again on the rise. By the early 1990s, over one million teenage females became pregnant each year. Over 500,000 of these mothers were between 15 and 19 years of age. Although teen pregnancy affects all groups, the rate is especially high among urban populations and lower socioeconomic groups. Based on the trends shown in Figure 16-5, many people consider teenage pregnancy to be one of the nation's most serious health problems.

Teenage pregnancy can be dangerous to both the mother and the baby. Because women in their teens are still growing, their bones and muscles may not be ready for the physical stress of pregnancy. Approximately 25 percent of the babies born to teenage mothers are born prematurely. Many other babies have a low birthweight. Medical problems are often compounded because teenagers may not seek proper prenatal care.

Concern about increasing rates of teenage pregnancy go far beyond the immediate medical problems. Many teenagers are unprepared for the tremendous commitment involved in raising a family. Two thirds of teenage mothers drop out of school. Emotional support from family and friends is essential; however, some pregnant teenagers may be afraid to face the situation or feel that they cannot turn to their parents or friends for support. Many pregnant teenagers receive little or no emotional or financial support from the baby's father. Most couples do not get married, but if they do, teenage marriages often end in divorce.

Many communities offer programs for helping teens think more carefully about teenage pregnancy. These programs provide information about avoiding pregnancy and provide counseling for teenagers who are searching for advice. If a teenager is already pregnant, the programs offer prenatal care and classes on childbirth and parenting. Many also offer classes for teenage fathers.

MEDICINES AND DRUGS

As you have learned, many substances that a mother-to-be takes into her body can pass through the placenta. When a pregnant

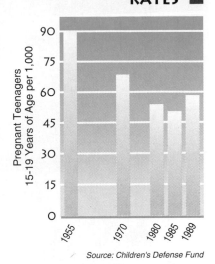

Figure 16-5 *According to the graph, what trend do you see in the rate of teenage pregnancy?*

What are some of the risks for pregnant women who are exposed to tobacco smoke?

woman smokes, drinks, uses drugs, or takes medicine that is not prescribed by a doctor, she threatens the health of her fetus.

Pregnant women who smoke or are exposed to tobacco smoke are at greater risk of having premature deliveries and underweight babies than are women not exposed to smoke. Women who smoke suffer twice as many miscarriages as women who do not smoke.

When a pregnant woman drinks an alcoholic beverage, the fetus also receives the alcohol through the placenta. Alcohol can harm the developing fetus, resulting in physical or mental disorders called **birth defects**. Also called congenital defects, birth defects are physical or mental disabilities that are present at birth. Alcohol consumption during pregnancy can result in a series of birth defects known as **Fetal Alcohol Syndrome**, or FAS. In fact, the leading known cause of birth defects in the United States is FAS. Babies with FAS may have low birthweight, mental retardation, heart defects, and unusual facial characteristics. Even small amounts of alcohol consumption are considered unsafe for pregnant women.

Other addictive drugs, such as cocaine, crack, and heroin can pass to the fetus through the placenta. Babies born to mothers who used cocaine are more likely to be born prematurely, and to have malformations of the skull and other organs. In addition, the fetus may become addicted to the drug just as the mother is, and may suffer withdrawal from the drug after birth. Drug withdrawal is very hard physically for an adult and can be fatal for a newborn baby. Even prescription medicines and over-the-counter medicines may put the fetus at risk. Pregnant women should consult a doctor before taking any medicine.

Advances in medical care have helped increase the likelihood that babies born with health problems will recover and lead normal, healthy lives. However, these advances alone cannot lower the risks to pregnant women and their fetuses. These risks will be lowered primarily through efforts in prevention, including careful preparation and planning before pregnancy, and healthy choices throughout pregnancy.

LESSON 16.2 **USING WHAT YOU HAVE LEARNED**

1. When should a woman have a medically-prescribed pregnancy test?
2. Describe the benefits a pregnant woman can receive from a moderate fitness program.

THINK CRITICALLY

3. Using examples, explain how the mother's health can be a major factor leading to premature births.
4. Describe two factors that you feel are important when choosing a site where the baby should be born.

APPLY IT TO YOURSELF

5. Imagine that you are a pregnant woman who is used to either jogging or swimming every day. Would you continue both forms of exercise during your pregnancy? Explain your answer.

SUMMARY

One of the first decisions a couple who is planning to have a baby needs to make is to choose a physician and a location where the baby will be born. Problems of pregnancy range from occasional nausea to life-threatening conditions that require medical treatment. To be sure that her baby has the best chance of being born healthy, a pregnant woman should choose to live a healthy life-style and refrain from the use of tobacco, alcohol, or other drugs.

HEREDITY

Every baby is born with its own special characteristics. Physical traits, such as skin color, hair color, and eye color are determined largely by instructions inherited from each parent. Occasionally traits can be passed down that have a negative effect on the health of the baby. For this reason, it is important that couples understand how these traits can be passed to their children.

CHROMOSOMES, GENES, AND HEREDITY

Almost every cell of the body contains tiny threadlike structures called **chromosomes** [*KROH muh sohmz*]. Chromosomes carry hereditary information from generation to generation. Each chromosome is divided into many smaller units called **genes** [*jeenz*]. A single gene contains instructions that help determine a particular characteristic in an individual. For example, one pair of genes controls whether you are born with five fingers or six fingers on each hand. A different pair of genes determines whether or not you have a cleft chin. Complex characteristics such as height and eye color are influenced by many different sets of genes.

Genes are composed of a chemical substance called deoxyribonucleic acid, or **DNA**. The structure of DNA can be likened to a complex code. It is this code that provides the instructions for each characteristic.

HOW CHROMOSOMES ARE INHERITED   Except for sperm cells or egg cells, the cells in the human body contain 23 pairs of chromosomes, or a total of 46 chromosomes. Each chromosome pair consists of one chromosome that was inherited from the mother and one that was inherited from the father. These chromosomes come together during the fertilization process when a sperm cell from the father and an egg cell from the mother unite. Unlike the other cells in the body, the sperm from the father and the egg from the

MAIN IDEAS

CONCEPTS

✔ Instructions for all physical traits are passed from parents to their children on chromosomes.

✔ Some traits that are inherited from parents may be harmful to the health of the baby.

✔ Medical advances have made it possible to detect genetic disorders while the fetus is still in the womb.

VOCABULARY

chromosome
gene
DNA
X chromosome
Y chromosome
dominant
recessive
genetic disorder
sickle-cell anemia
sex-linked disorder
Down syndrome

Inheritance of physical traits, such as skin color, hair color, and eye color results in resemblances among family members.

mother contain only one of each type of chromosome, or a total of 23 chromosomes. When the sperm and the egg unite, the result is a fertilized egg with 23 chromosome pairs, or 46 chromosomes.

HOW GENDER IS DETERMINED   The gender of the embryo is determined by a single pair of chromosomes called sex chromosomes. Each egg contains one **X chromosome**. About half of the sperm cells also contain an X chromosome. The other half of the sperm cells contain a **Y chromosome**. Because all egg cells contain an X chromosome, the gender of the embryo depends on whether it inherits an X chromosome or a Y chromosome from the father. If the egg is fertilized by a sperm carrying an X chromosome, the embryo will carry two X chromosomes in each cell, and therefore be female (XX). If the egg is fertilized by a sperm carrying a Y chromosome, the embryo will carry one X chromosome and one Y chromosome in each cell, making it a male (XY). Thus, the father's sperm determines the sex of the embryo.

DOMINANT AND RECESSIVE GENES

When the egg and the sperm cells unite, they bring together the genetic information from two different people who may have different physical characteristics such as height, hair color, and eye color. What determines how the baby will look?

Figure 16-6   Inheritance of the ability to roll one's tongue is a dominant trait. Will a child who inherits the recessive gene from both parents be a tongue roller?

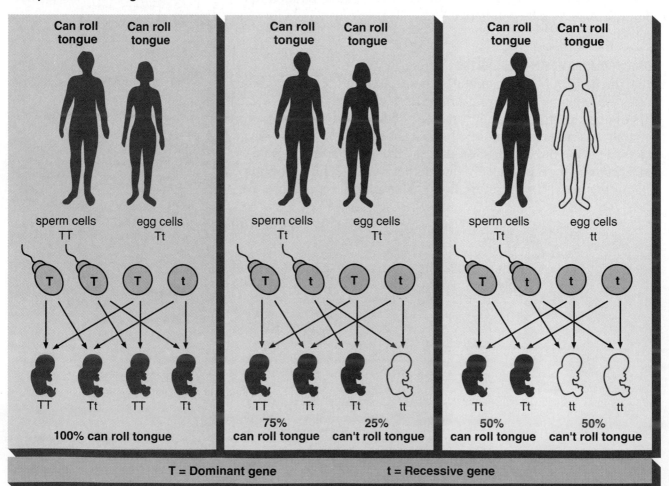

Like the chromosomes on which they are located, genes occur in pairs. Each gene of a pair is inherited from a different parent. With some genes, the person will show the trait coded for by the gene even if only one gene is present. Such genes are said to be **dominant**. With other genes, the person will only show the trait if the dominant gene is not present. These genes are said to be **recessive**. For example, the ability to roll one's tongue into a U-shape is a dominant trait. If the child inherits the recessive gene from both parents, the child will not be able to roll his or her tongue. However, if the baby inherits the dominant gene from one parent and the recessive gene from the other parent, the child will be able to roll his or her tongue. Figure 16-6 illustrates how the ability to roll the tongue can be inherited.

GENETIC DISORDERS

Sometimes children inherit genes that have mistakes in the genetic code, often resulting in severe health problems. Conditions caused by defective genes are called **genetic disorders**. Although many of the genetic disorders currently have no cure, progress is being made in treating them. Other genetic disorders can be successfully treated if detected early. By learning how genetic disorders are

Figure 16-7 Most genes that are responsible for genetic disorders are recessive. What are some examples of sex-linked genetic disorders?

COMMON RECESSIVE GENETIC DISORDERS

Disorder	Symptoms	Cause
Albinism	Very pale skin, eyes, hair.	Inability to produce the pigment melanin.
Tay-Sachs disease	Mental retardation, blindness, deafness, convulsions. Usually fatal in childhood.	Inability to produce a protein necessary for nervous system to function properly. Most common among people of eastern European and Jewish descent.
Cystic fibrosis	Breathing problems and digestive disorders. Usually fatal by early adulthood. New research may provide a cure.	Production of thick mucus in lungs and digestive system. Most common among people of northern European descent.
Phenylketonuria	Severe mental retardation if untreated.	Inability to break down phenylalanine, an amino acid common in many foods. If detected early, can be treated by keeping phenylalanine out of child's diet.
Duchenne muscular dystrophy	Muscle weakness, severe paralysis. Usually fatal by early twenties.	Sex-linked trait. Important type of protein missing in muscle cells. Deterioration of muscles.
Hemophilia	Severe bleeding from minor cuts and bruises.	Sex-linked trait. Inability to produce a protein necessary for blood to clot. Can be treated with transfusions of clotting substance.

Cystic Fibrosis

Cystic fibrosis, or CF, is a hereditary disease that afflicts more than 25,000 children in the United States. Cystic fibrosis causes problems in the respiratory and digestive systems of children who have it. As of the early 1990s, there was no cure. Until recently, most victims of CF died while still in their teens. But during the 1980s, the discovery of new treatments lengthened the expected lifespan of CF victims until their late twenties and beyond. In 1989, the gene that causes cystic fibrosis was discovered. This discovery has led to further gene and drug therapies that may, eventually, lead to a cure.

Cystic fibrosis is a disease found almost exclusively in children of Northern European descent. It is caused by a missing protein in the cells of the respiratory and digestive organs. With the discovery of the gene, called CFTR, that carries cystic fibrosis, scientists now hope to cure the disease by replacing the protein while the respiratory and digestive organs are still being formed. Scientists have discovered that there are various mutations of the CF gene. This discovery has delayed the search for a single cure but is presenting more and more options for treatment. It is believed that some time in the 1990s, CF will become a treatable, curable disease.

---

passed from one generation to the next, couples can evaluate their risk of giving birth to a child with a genetic disorder.

RECESSIVE DISORDERS   The genes responsible for genetic disorders can either be dominant or recessive, but the majority are recessive. One such recessive disorder is **sickle-cell anemia**, a sometimes fatal condition that is found primarily among people of African descent. People with sickle-cell anemia produce red blood cells that have a curved, sickle shape instead of normal disk-shaped red blood cells. These abnormal cells clog up tiny blood vessels which cuts off oxygen to certain tissues. Because the gene for sickle-cell anemia is recessive, only people who have inherited the gene from both parents will suffer the severe symptoms. People who inherit only one defective gene will not get sickle-cell anemia, but they are able to pass the gene to their children.

SEX-LINKED DISORDERS   Conditions that are caused by genes on the X chromosome are called **sex-linked disorders**. Remember, all women carry two X chromosomes and all men carry one X chromosome and one Y chromosome. Therefore, women carry two copies of each sex-linked gene, but men carry only one copy. Because men carry a single X chromosome, they will show the trait if they inherit only a single recessive sex-linked gene. However, women would need to inherit two recessive sex-linked genes, one from both parents, in order to show the trait. Therefore, men are more likely than women to inherit sex-linked disorders.

The most common sex-linked disorder, colorblindness, is a condition in which a person cannot distinguish certain colors, usually red and green. Colorblindness is much more common in men than in women.

A more serious sex-linked disorder is hemophilia [hee muh FIL ee uh], in which the blood lacks a substance that is necessary for normal clotting. For people with hemophilia, the smallest cut or bruise can be very dangerous, as it can lead to uncontrolled bleeding. Hemophilia is treated by transfusions of blood plasma or injections of the blood clotting substance.

CHROMOSOMAL DISORDERS

Some disorders are caused by errors in entire chromosomes or in chromosome number rather than in individual genes. Sometimes a piece of a chromosome will break off. Other times the baby will inherit the wrong number of chromosomes. Most chromosomal disorders result in the death of the embryo and miscarriage. A few chromosomal disorders cause birth defects and mental retardation.

The most common chromosomal disorder is **Down syndrome**, a disorder in which the person inherits one extra chromosome, giving the person 47 chromosomes instead of the normal 46. Down syndrome usually causes mental retardation and slowed physical development. The abilities of people with Down syndrome vary tremendously. Most people with Down syndrome lead very active and meaningful lives.

GENETIC COUNSELING

Couples who have a history of genetic disorders in one or both of their families may want to consider genetic counseling when deciding to have children of their own. A genetic counselor reviews the couple's family history to determine which relatives have had genetic disorders. The genetic counselor then may be able to determine the statistical risk of the couple's child inheriting a genetic disorder.

Couples are also encouraged to seek genetic counseling if any of the following situations apply.

- The couple has already had a child with a genetic disorder and is planning to have more children.
- The woman has had two or more miscarriages or early infant deaths.
- The couple wants information about specific genetic disorders that occur frequently in their ethnic group.

PRENATAL DIAGNOSIS

If a couple feels that the woman is at risk of having a baby with a birth disorder, the physician or genetic counselor may recommend prenatal diagnosis. Many recent medical advances have made it possible to monitor the health of the fetus during pregnancy. By diagnosing problems during pregnancy, parents can prepare themselves in advance to care for any special needs the baby may have. Sometimes surgery can be performed on the fetus to correct heart defects and other developmental problems.

The following techniques are commonly used to diagnose problems with the fetus during pregnancy.

- *Amniocentesis [am nee oh sen TEE sus]* A long needle is used to take a sample of the amniotic fluid surrounding the fetus. Doctors can detect chromosomal disorders such as Down syndrome and many developmental disorders by studying the amniotic fluid. Although amniocentesis is generally safe, it increases slightly the risk of miscarriage.

Genetic counselors can explain to couples the statistical chances that they will pass on a genetic disorder to a child.

HEALTHY PEOPLE 2000

Increase to at least 95 percent the proportion of newborns screened by State-sponsored programs for genetic disorders and other disabling conditions...

Objective 14.15

from *Healthy People 2000: National Health Promotion and Disease Prevention Objectives*

Ultrasound provides valuable information about fetal development and possible fetal abnormalities.

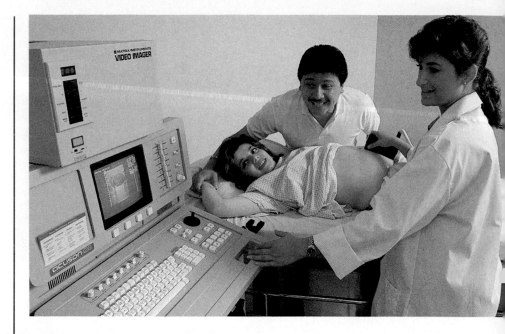

- *Ultrasound* Sound waves above the range of human hearing are used to produce an image of the fetus on a screen. Physicians can use ultrasound to monitor the development of the fetus and to check for signs of genetic disorders and potential birth defects. Ultrasound is also used to determine whether the mother is carrying more than one fetus. The technique causes no harm or discomfort to the mother or fetus, and can be an important diagnostic tool.

Genetics, or the study of genes and heredity, is one of the fastest growing areas in science. New information about the specific genes causing genetic disorders may someday lead to prevention or cures for these diseases. In the meantime, knowledge about how genetic disorders are passed from one generation to the next can help couples better prepare for the risks involved in having children.

LESSON 16.3 USING WHAT YOU HAVE LEARNED

REVIEW

1. How many chromosomes does each human egg cell or sperm cell carry? How many chromosomes does a fertilized egg carry?
2. What is the cause of Down syndrome?

THINKING CRITICALLY

3. Explain the process of amniocentesis and why it is used.
4. Some couples seek genetic counseling even when nobody in each immediate family has a genetic disorder. Explain why, based on how genes are inherited.

APPLY IT TO YOURSELF

5. What advice would you give to a pregnant woman who is considering whether or not to have ultrasound or amniocentesis performed to determine the sex of the child? To diagnose a genetic disorder in the fetus? Explain your answers.

SUMMARY

When the genetic material carried by the egg cell and the sperm cell unite, the chromosomes in the fertilized cell determine the characteristics of the baby. Chromosomes carry genes for traits. Genetic counselors can help couples understand their risks of having a child with a genetic disorder. Doctors can now detect and sometimes treat birth defects before the child is born.

Becoming a Family

When Becky and Jim first were married, they tried to have a baby, with no success. They went to a specialist and found out that Becky would have difficulty conceiving. For several years, Becky and Jim went to specialists who suggested numerous solutions to their problem. Nothing worked.

Becky and Jim finally gave up. They were exhausted from the anxiety. Their whole life had been on hold. Although they were both very disappointed, Becky and Jim eventually accepted that they would remain childless.

One evening, years later, Jim brought up the subject of adopting a child. At first Becky said no. They were both in their late 30s, and Becky didn't think she could go through a long waiting period or a lengthy background check. More than anything, she was concerned that she wouldn't make a good adoptive parent. Jim asked her to think about it. She promised she would.

PAUSE AND CONSIDER

1. *Identify the Problem.* What decision do Becky and Jim face? Why is Becky worried about adopting a child?

2. *Consider the Options.* What are their options?

3. *Evaluate the Outcomes.* How might Becky and Jim feel if they didn't have a child? How might adoption help them realize their dreams?

A few weeks after their initial discussion, Becky told Jim that she would be willing to look into adoption. She felt she could deal with the issue of waiting for a child. But she was still concerned about the uncertainty of the adoption process. She wanted to know what would happen. Jim reassured her that he too needed to know a lot more about the process. They decided to talk to an adoption counselor about some of their feelings.

During the discussion, Becky expressed her worries about being a good adoptive parent. The counselor reminded Becky that all parents enter parenthood with uncertainty. But the counselor also observed that Becky and Jim had a lot of love to offer.

After their first meeting with the counselor, Becky felt better about the idea of adopting a child. She knew that together she and Jim could face every obstacle they encountered. If they didn't try, she and Jim would never know the joy of raising a child.

A year later, one-year-old Danielle came into their lives. Becky felt a sense of warmth the minute she saw Danielle. Becky knew that she and Jim had made the right decision.

DECIDE AND REVIEW

4. *Decide and Act.* What did Becky and Jim decide to do about adoption? What made them choose as they did?

5. *Review.* What other choices might Becky and Jim have had? Why is it important that couples be well-prepared for adoption?

PROJECTS

1. Do a survey of the various programs in your community that are designed to heighten teen awareness of pregnancy issues. Investigate each program to determine what types of information it provides for teenagers. Are the programs free? Do they offer classes on prenatal care, childbirth, and parenting? Are there classes for teenage fathers as well? Is there a counselor on staff with whom a teenager can discuss issues of teenage pregnancy? Report your findings to your classmates.

2. Collect information about organizations in your community that assist parents of children with the following disorders. Down syndrome, cystic fibrosis, and sickle-cell anemia. Create a chart showing the type of treatment available for each disorder as well as new treatments being researched.

WORKING WITH OTHERS

With a partner, research statistical data about birth rate, infant mortality, and low birthweight babies in the United States. Include in your research any information that suggests a difference in rates based upon socioeconomic status or race. Together, develop a visual of charts or tables that show your findings.

CONNECTING TO...

SOCIOLOGY Investigate the birthing or parenting practices in another country. How are the country's customs similar to practices in the United States? How are they different? Prepare a one-page report that explains your findings. Explain which custom or tradition you like best and why.

USING VOCABULARY

amniotic sac
anemia
birth defect
breech birth
caesarean section
chromosome
DNA
dominant
Down syndrome
embryo
Fallopian tube
fertilization

Fetal Alcohol Syndrome
fetus
fraternal twin
gene
genetic disorder
human immunodeficiency virus
identical twin
incubator
labor
miscarriage

placenta
premature
prenatal care
recessive
sex-linked disorder
sickle-cell anemia
stillbirth
toxemia
umbilical cord
X chromosome
Y chromosome

On a separate sheet of paper, identify the vocabulary word that matches each of the following phrases.

1. The term used for the stage of development during the first two months of pregnancy.
2. The special organ through which the fetus receives nutrients from the mother's bloodstream.
3. The series of birth defects that can result from the drinking of alcohol by the pregnant woman.
4. A condition caused by too little iron in the blood that often occurs in pregnant women.
5. A special container in which premature babies are placed for care and protection.
6. The term used for muscle contractions that occur when the mother is giving birth.
7. A procedure during childbirth in which a doctor makes an incision in the woman's abdomen and lift out the baby.
8. Thread-like structures in cells that carry genetic information.
9. A chromosomal disorder caused by the baby inheriting 47 chromosomes instead of 46.
10. The term used for the birth of a nonliving baby after a full term of pregnancy.

CONCEPT MAPPING

On a separate sheet of paper, create a concept map for a concept that you learned in this chapter. Include at least six concepts in your map. You may use terms from the vocabulary list above and other terms as appropriate. Information about concept mapping appears at the front of this book.

THINKING CRITICALLY

INTERPRET

LESSON 16.1

1. Describe the fertilization process. In what part of the woman's body does fertilization occur?

2. What is the function of the amniotic fluid?

3. List three nutrients that need to be increased in a pregnant woman's diet. In what foods can these nutrients be found?

4. Explain the difference in the fertilization processes of identical and fraternal twins.

5. What events mark the end of the second part of labor? What occurs during the third part of labor?

LESSON 16.2

6. List two exercises that are safe for pregnant women. Why are these exercises safe?

7. Explain why teenage mothers are at higher risk of giving birth to a premature baby or a baby with a low birth weight than mother's in their twenties and thirties.

8. What are birth defects? What actions can mothers take to decrease the risk of giving birth to a baby with birth defects.

9. What is toxemia and what are its symptoms? Why should a pregnant woman and her doctor watch for signs of toxemia?

LESSON 16.3

10. Explain why chromosomes from the father rather than chromosomes from the mother determine the gender of the baby.

11. What is the function of prenatal diagnosis? Name two methods of prenatal diagnosis.

12. Is it possible to inherit a genetic disease even if both parents do not have the disease? Explain your answer.

13. Explain why sex-linked disorders are inherited more often by men than by women.

APPLY

LESSON 16.1

14. Your sister has known that she has been pregnant for over a month yet she still is prone to skipping meals. Write a paragraph in which you explain to your sister why it is important for her to change her eating habits.

LESSON 16.2

15. Carla is pregnant for the first time. She has trouble sleeping due to anxieties about giving birth and the health of the baby. She is especially concerned about pain involved in giving birth. What steps can Carla take to calm her fears?

16. During a lively discussion with friends about parenthood, Bill dismissed the notion that the husband can play a useful role during prenatal care. Write a paragraph in which you explain why the support of the husband is essential for a healthy pregnancy.

LESSON 16.3

17. Jonathan and Kate are planning to have a family, however John just learned that a great uncle of his had Tay-Sachs disease. Explain how a genetic counselor can help the couple evaluate the risk of having a child with a genetic disorder.

COMMITMENT TO WELLNESS
FOLLOW-UP

SETTING GOALS

Look back at your responses to the Personal Commitment to Wellness checklist in the Chapter Opener. Identify two of the items about which you feel you need to know more information.

Now consider how you can become better informed about the two items you have identified. First, write two goal statements as headings of two columns on a separate sheet of paper or in your Wellness Journal. For example, if you would like to know more about fitness concerns during pregnancy, you might write the following statement: *Learn more about about pregnancy and fitness.* Under each heading, write at least three questions that you will want answered. Then make a list of possible sources where information may be found. As you search out answers to your questions, you may wish to add more questions and update your source lists.

WHERE DO I GO FROM HERE?

A tremendous amount of research is being conducted to understand genetics and human development.

FOR MORE INFORMATION, CONTACT:

National Maternal and Child Health Clearinghouse
38th and R Streets, N.W.
Washington, DC 20057

Growth and Development

"I think that one's art is a growth inside one. I do not think one can explain growth. It is silent and subtle. One does not keep digging up a plant to see how it grows."

Emily Carr

BACKGROUND

Emily Carr was a Canadian artist and painter who was born in 1871 and died in 1945. She is best known for her paintings of Native American village scenes and the forests of British Columbia.

Every day there are silent and subtle changes taking place in your mind and body. Your mind is expanding to meet the challenges of the adult world while your body quietly, subtly, is developing from its childhood form to its adult form.

Every person's growth is indeed "art," as each individual grows in a unique and powerful way. The way that you grow has to do with your heredity, your unique system of hormones and glands known as the endocrine system, and the ways in which you care for your body.

The development into adulthood is most dramatically felt during adolescence when a myriad of changes occur in young women and men. This is a time to celebrate the "art" that is your growth—safe in the knowledge that soon you will be a fully developed adult, thanks to the intricate and perfect developmental system silently at work in your body.

SELF-ASSESSMENT

On a sheet of paper or in your Wellness Journal, write *yes* or *no* to respond to the following statements.

1. I know and understand the changes occurring in my body.
2. I have learned how to cope with the anxieties that change can bring.
3. I have learned to accept my emerging identity.
4. I respect my maturing body and will keep it healthy.
5. I accept responsibilities that accompany maturity.
6. I practice health behaviors that enhance my maturity.
7. I try to understand and respect changes in my friends.
8. I understand that not all people change at the same rate.
9. I avoid putting down other teenagers who are not yet mature.
10. I respect the maturity of those older than I am.

Review your responses and consider what might be your strengths and weaknesses. Save your personal checklist for a follow-up activity that appears at the end of this chapter.

THE ENDOCRINE SYSTEM

From infancy through adulthood, the human body goes through many remarkable changes. When you were an infant you could not even sit up. As you grew and entered childhood, you became stronger and heavier. Some of the most profound physical changes occur during adolescence. This is the time when the reproductive system matures and you physically become an adult. Many of these changes are regulated by a network of organs that release specific chemicals into the bloodstream. This group of organs is collectively known as the **endocrine system** [*EN duh krun*].

GLANDS AND HORMONES

The organs of the endocrine system are called **endocrine glands**. Each endocrine gland produces and releases hormones into the bloodstream. The major endocrine glands are shown in Figure 17-1. A **hormone** is a chemical substance that travels from an endocrine gland through the bloodstream to other organs and tissues to regulate growth or activity.

BODILY FUNCTIONS   The endocrine system controls many important functions that keep your body in balance even under changing conditions. For example, the endocrine system is responsible for maintaining the body at a constant temperature whether you are exercising heavily or relaxing in the shade. The endocrine system also controls appetite and thirst, the rate at which food is digested, the elimination of waste through the kidneys, and a person's sleeping cycle. Even heart rate and blood pressure are partially controlled by the endocrine system. Finally, the endocrine system controls the rate at which you grow and develop, and it controls the changes that occur that make reproduction possible.

HYPOTHALAMUS AND PITUITARY GLANDS   Because hormones can exert such powerful effects, even in small amounts, it is critical for the body to be able to regulate the amount of each hormone that is released by the glands. The key to controlling the release of hormones is by close coordination between the nervous system and the endocrine system. The nervous system senses whether hormones are needed and signals the endocrine system to release hormones. One of the most important connections between the nervous system and the endocrine system is the link between a part of the brain called the **hypothalamus** [*hy poh THAL uh mus*] and a pea-sized gland located just below the hypothalamus called the **pituitary gland** [*puh TYOO uh ter ee*].

The hypothalamus plays a key role in keeping track of many bodily functions. The hypothalamus monitors body temperature, blood pressure, and controls hunger and thirst. It also monitors the levels of many different hormones circulating in the blood. If the hypothalamus senses low levels of a particular hormone, it signals

MAIN IDEAS

CONCEPTS
- ✔ Hormones released by the endocrine system control many bodily functions.
- ✔ Hormones trigger many of the physical changes that occur during adolescence.
- ✔ Endocrine disorders can result in serious health problems.

VOCABULARY

endocrine system
endocrine gland
hormone
hypothalamus
pituitary gland
pancreas
insulin
diabetes mellitus

thyroid gland
adrenal gland
adrenaline
puberty
estrogen
testosterone
ovary
testes

Figure 17-1   The endocrine glands are located throughout the body. Which gland is in the brain?

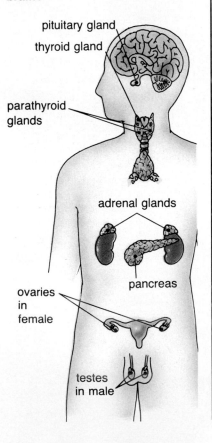

pituitary gland
thyroid gland
parathyroid glands
adrenal glands
pancreas
ovaries in female
testes in male

FEMALE DEVELOPMENT

For girls, puberty not only brings about changes in physical appearance, but it is also the time when the reproductive system matures and the reproductive cycle begins. Often these changes can seem unsettling. However, by understanding the changes that are taking place, a teenage girl can begin to come to terms with the changes that are occurring, and she also can take steps toward keeping her reproductive system healthy.

CHANGES DURING PUBERTY

As you learned in the previous lesson, hormones released by the pituitary gland and the ovaries trigger a growth spurt and the maturation of a girl's reproductive organs. The hormone estrogen is largely responsible for changes in the reproductive system; however it is also responsible for a number of other physical changes known as **secondary sex characteristics**.

SECONDARY SEX CHARACTERISTICS
As puberty begins, a girl will start to notice changes in the shape of her body. One of the most notable changes is the development of breasts. The breasts start as a small concentration of fat and gradually develop to their full size over several years. A girl's hips will also begin to widen.

Other secondary sex characteristics begin to develop at various times during puberty. The girl's voice will become richer. Coarse hair called **pubic hair** begins to grow around the external sex organs, or genitals. Hair also begins to grow under the arms and on the legs. There also may be some growth of a small amount of facial hair. The pores in the skin become larger and glands in the skin produce more oil and sweat. Some effects of increased oil and sweat production include acne and increased body odor.

STRESSES OF PUBERTY
The rapid changes that occur during puberty can often be a source of tension, particularly for girls who develop earlier or later than others their age. A girl who matures early may sometimes feel isolated because none of her friends are at the same stage of development. On the other hand, a girl who develops later than her friends may feel anxious about her slower development and worry that something is wrong with her. In most cases, anxious feelings will disappear once everybody has reached a similar stage of development.

THE FEMALE REPRODUCTIVE SYSTEM

During puberty, the female reproductive system matures to the point where the teenager is physically able to have a child. A healthy female reproductive system is able to produce egg cells that are capable of being fertilized and also is physically able to support a developing fetus.

Rapid physical changes during adolescence often can make teenagers feel uncomfortable with their appearance.

PRODUCTION OF EGG CELLS   As you can see in Figure 17-4, egg cells are produced and stored in each ovary—the same organs that produce estrogen. Next to each ovary is a narrow tube called the **Fallopian tube** [*fuh LOH pee un*]. Egg cells that are released from the ovary travel through the Fallopian tube. If sperm cells are also present in the Fallopian tube, fertilization of the egg may occur.

THE UTERUS   After traveling through the Fallopian tube, the egg cell reaches the uterus. The **uterus** [*YOOT uh rus*], or womb, is the muscular organ in which the fetus develops. The uterus is lined with a thick, spongy tissue called the **endometrium** [*en doh MEE tree um*], which provides the fertilized egg with nourishment during the early stages of development.

The lower portion of the uterus is called the **cervix**. Normally the opening to the cervix is quite small, but during childbirth the cervix stretches to allow the baby to pass through. The cervix opens into the **vagina**. The vagina, also called the birth canal, serves as a passageway for the baby during childbirth.

THE MENSTRUAL CYCLE

Once the reproductive organs have become mature, a woman's body begins a monthly reproductive cycle that is known as the **menstrual cycle** [*MEN strul*]. Girls usually experience their first menstrual cycle at about 12 years of age. However, the age at which the first menstrual cycle occurs varies from person to person and can start anytime between 9 and 16 years of age.

OVULATION   During each menstrual cycle, an egg cell is released from one of the ovaries. The release of an egg cell from the ovary is called **ovulation**. The egg cell travels down the Fallopian tube to

Figure 17-4   In which part of the female reproductive system are the egg cells produced?

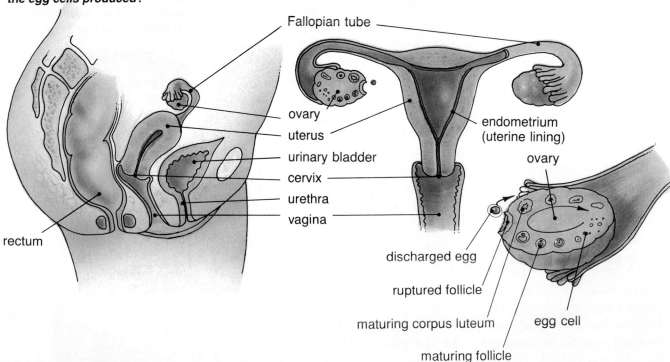

Fallopian tube

ovary
uterus
urinary bladder
cervix
urethra
vagina

rectum

endometrium (uterine lining)

ovary

discharged egg

ruptured follicle

maturing corpus luteum

egg cell

maturing follicle

the uterus. In the meantime, the endometrium begins to thicken, preparing the uterus in case fertilization occurs. If the egg cell becomes fertilized, it will become implanted in the wall of the uterus and begin to develop.

MENSTRUATION   If the egg cell does not become fertilized, the endometrium breaks down into a fluid. This fluid, which also contains blood, flows out of the body through the vagina. The breakdown and loss of the endometrium is called **menstruation**. The menstrual period usually lasts from three to seven days. Women either wear sanitary pads and/or tampons to absorb the blood flow from menstruation.

HORMONAL CONTROL   Figure 17-6 shows how changing levels of different hormones released by the pituitary glands and by the ovaries affect each event of the menstrual cycle. The entire menstrual cycle typically lasts about 28 days. However, the length of the menstrual cycle will vary from one woman to the next, especially during the first few years of menstruation. Poor nutrition, low body fat, abnormally strenuous exercise, and mental stress can delay menstruation or stop the menstrual cycle altogether.

Menstruation usually occurs each month for as long as a woman has a healthy reproductive system or until she stops producing egg cells. At some point, often between 45 and 55 years of age, the ovaries stop producing estrogen, the hormone that controls menstruation, and menstruation ends. The time of life during which a woman stops menstruation is called **menopause**.

CONCERNS ABOUT MENSTRUATION

Although it is fairly uncommon for a woman to experience medical problems resulting from menstruation, it is common for some women to experience temporary discomfort during menstruation. Typical discomforts include mild soreness in the breasts, mood changes, and muscle cramps in the abdomen and back caused by the uterus contracting to get rid of the endometrial lining. Because

Figure 17-5   What are the first physical changes teenage girls can expect to notice?

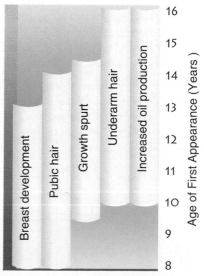

the discomforts experienced during menstruation vary from one woman to the next, different remedies work for different women. Some find that getting more rest and using relaxation techniques help while others find that exercise helps.

PREMENSTRUAL SYNDROME   Some women experience physical and emotional symptoms up to two weeks before menstruation begins. These symptoms are known as **premenstrual syndrome (PMS)**. Physical symptoms may include nausea, headaches, fatigue, a bloated feeling, and weight gain. Emotional symptoms may include mood swings, irritability, feelings of depression, and the inability to sleep or concentrate. Although these symptoms do not

Figure 17-6   In which stage of the menstrual cycle are estrogen levels the highest?

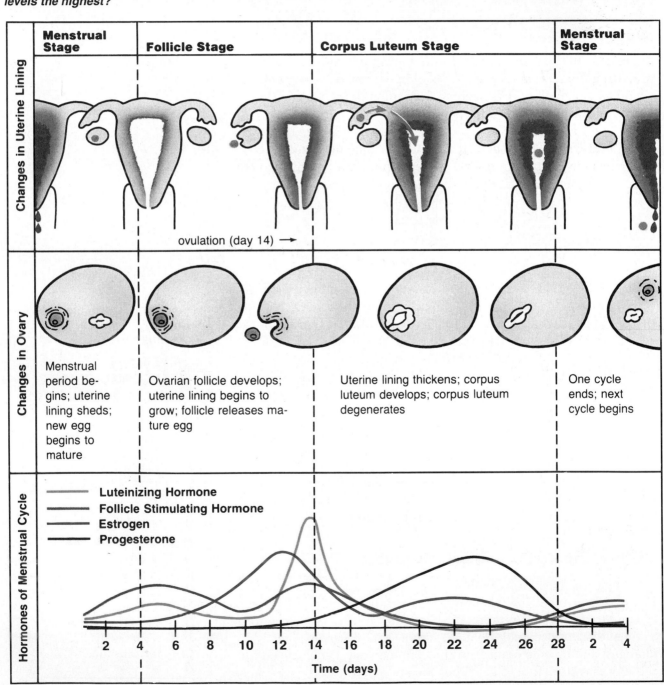

Changes in Uterine Lining

| Menstrual Stage | Follicle Stage | Corpus Luteum Stage | Menstrual Stage |

ovulation (day 14) →

Changes in Ovary

Menstrual period begins; uterine lining sheds; new egg begins to mature

Ovarian follicle develops; uterine lining begins to grow; follicle releases mature egg

Uterine lining thickens; corpus luteum develops; corpus luteum degenerates

One cycle ends; next cycle begins

Hormones of Menstrual Cycle

Luteinizing Hormone
Follicle Stimulating Hormone
Estrogen
Progesterone

2 4 6 8 10 12 14 16 18 20 22 24 26 28 2 4

Time (days)

signify any underlying medical problems, for many women PMS can be disruptive.

It is not clear what causes PMS, although some studies suggest the symptoms may be connected with the rise and fall of hormone levels during the course of the menstrual cycle. The treatment for PMS varies by individual. Medications have been helpful for some women. A diet low in salt can reduce the bloated feeling. The avoidance of caffeine has been reported by some women to reduce some of the emotional symptoms associated with PMS. An exercise program may also reduce some of the symptoms associated with PMS. Also, in most cases, the severity of the symptoms will diminish as a woman becomes older.

TOXIC SHOCK SYNDROME Many women choose to use tampons during menstruation. However, the misuse of tampons can result in a potentially fatal bacterial infection called **toxic shock syndrome**. If a tampon is kept in for too long, it can provide an ideal environment for the growth of bacteria. The toxin produced by these bacteria causes a sudden high fever, a rash on the hands and feet, a sudden drop in blood pressure, and kidney and liver damage. If detected early, toxic shock syndrome can be effectively treated with antibiotics. A woman should contact a doctor at once if she has any of these symptoms. Toxic shock syndrome can be avoided by limiting the use of tampons, especially the super absorbant tampons. If tampons are used, they should be changed every four to eight hours.

Physical exercise, such as swimming, can help relieve some of the symptoms of PMS.

FEMALE REPRODUCTIVE DISORDERS

Women are susceptible to a number of disorders of the reproductive system. Many disorders, such as those that are caused by infections, can be prevented through good health practices. Other disorders, if discovered early, can be cured.

OVARIAN CYST A fairly common problem among women is the development of an ovarian cyst. An **ovarian cyst** is a fluid-filled sac on an ovary. Small cysts may develop as a result of regular changes in hormone levels and often disappear without treatment. Cysts that are large may cause severe pain in the abdomen and may need to be surgically removed.

CANCER Cancer is the uncontrolled growth of abnormal cells. In women, cancer sometimes occurs in the endometrium, cervix, or ovaries. Many times, cancer is curable if detected early. A routine pelvic exam in which a Pap test is given can often detect cancer of the cervix. A **Pap test** is an examination in which a doctor takes a smear of cells from the cervix. The cells are studied for any sign of cancer. A Pap test should be done every one or two years after a woman has reached 18 years of age or has become sexually active.

STRATEGIES FOR LIVING

Tips for lessening the effects of PMS:

- Eat a balanced diet, avoiding caffeine and salt.
- Have a regular exercise program.
- Get plenty of rest.
- Keep a diary of symptoms. A diary will allow a woman to predict the onset of symptoms and determine whether or not they are due to PMS.

INFERTILITY

A woman who is unable to become pregnant because of physical complications is said to be **infertile**. Infertility affects as many as eight percent of all women of childbearing age. The following are some of the most common causes of infertility.

FAILURE TO OVULATE   In some women, the ovaries are unable to release an egg cell. The failure to ovulate regularly may be due to problems in the development of the ovaries or due to the under-production of hormones which trigger ovulation. In some cases, women with this problem can be treated by giving them the hormone that stimulates ovulation.

BLOCKAGE OF THE FALLOPIAN TUBE   The most common cause of infertility is a blockage of one or both of the Fallopian tubes, which prevents the egg cell from reaching the uterus. The blockage may be the result of an infection, a tumor in the Fallopian tube, or problems in the development of the Fallopian tube. In some cases, the blockage can be removed through surgery.

MAKING A DIFFERENCE

RESEARCH HEALTH

Hormone Replacement Therapy

All at once, when Theresa Gorman turned 50, she began to feel old. She began to have sweats at night and hot flashes during the day. Her skin grew flaky and wrinkled, and she was very depressed.

Gorman was experiencing menopause—a hormonal phenomenon that affects all women. Menopause occurs when a woman's body stops producing the hormones estrogen and progesterone, usually between the ages of 45 and 50. Some women experience severe changes. Other women hardly notice menopause.

If a woman decides that the changes she experiences during menopause are seriously affecting her life and happiness, she can talk with her doctor about the benefits and risks of Hormone Replacement Therapy (HRT). HRT is administered orally or through a skin patch. Today HRT includes a combination of estrogen and progestin—a synthetic progesterone.

Supporters of HRT swear by its ability to counteract some of the changes brought about by menopause. HRT, when begun within three years after the onset of menopause, can significantly reduce the incidence of osteoporosis. Recent studies also indicate that HRT may reduce heart disease. Other studies suggest that the risk of cancer associated with HRT may be reduced if the hormones are taken for short periods, such as six years.

Opponents of HRT suggest that hormone treatment is an example of society's lack of acceptance of aging as a natural process of life. Some scientists, concerned that HRT might increase the risk of cancer, find that many women who are experiencing an uncomfortable menopause can do just as well on a treatment plan that includes vitamins, good nutrition, and exercise.

Some women should not even consider HRT. These are women who have had breast cancer or now have migraine headaches,

diabetes, asthma, heart disease, or other illnesses. But the quality of life for women like Theresa Gorman, who have been helped by hormone replacement therapy, has vastly improved.

1. Explain what is meant by menopause.

2. What are the positive and negative aspects of hormone replacement therapy?

Many couples who have been unable to have children have turned to adoption.

OTHER CAUSES   Sometimes infertility can be traced to problems in the uterus. **Endometriosis** [*en doh mee tree OH sus*] is a condition in which the endometrium grows outside of the uterus, sometimes blocking one or both of the Fallopian tubes. Endometriosis usually can be corrected by surgery. Infections, such as those caused by sexually transmitted diseases, can result in permanent damage to the reproductive system. One very serious condition resulting from bacterial infection is **pelvic inflammatory disease (PID)** which is an infection in the Fallopian tubes or other reproductive organs. PID can usually be treated with antibiotics.

Although there are many specific steps women can take to prevent reproductive disorders, maintaining one's general health is also important. Following a good nutrition plan, exercising regularly, and managing stress effectively can contribute to the health of the reproductive system.

LESSON 17.2   USING WHAT YOU HAVE LEARNED

REVIEW

1. Describe the events of the menstrual cycle. What is the average length of the menstrual cycle?
2. Describe two causes of infertility in women.

THINK CRITICALLY

3. During puberty, females undergo many physical changes. What do you think are the purpose of these changes?
4. As females reach puberty, the ovaries begin to produce fluctuating levels of the hormones estrogen and progesterone. Explain the function of these fluctuating hormone levels.

APPLY IT TO YOURSELF

5. You have been put in charge of writing a public service announcement about the health concerns of teenage girls. What do you think is the best way of presenting this information?

SUMMARY

During adolescence, girls reach sexual maturity and menstruation begins. Menstruation may cause discomfort for some women, but there are a variety of methods women can use to cope with the discomfort. Many disorders of the female reproductive system can be prevented with sensible health practices. Most disorders of the female reproductive system can be cured.

MALE DEVELOPMENT

During puberty, boys experience many of the same emotional changes as girls. Like girls, boys go through a phase of rapid growth as well as experiencing changes to the shape of their bodies. Often these changes cause a teenage boy to feel awkward. Although boys and girls may have many of the same types of anxieties as they go through puberty, there are important differences in their development.

CHANGES DURING PUBERTY

Puberty in males generally begins between 11 and 15 years of age. During puberty, growth hormone from a boy's pituitary gland triggers a very rapid growth spurt. At the same time, testosterone released from the testes causes the development of secondary sex characteristics. Finally, the reproductive system matures to the point that a boy is able to produce healthy sperm cells.

SECONDARY SEX CHARACTERISTICS Some of the secondary sex characteristics that occur in a girl also occur in a boy. The voice gradually becomes lower. Pubic hair begins to appear. Hair begins to grow under the arms and on the arms and legs. The skin starts to produce more oil which often results in acne. Other secondary sex characteristics are unique to boys. Secretion of the hormone testosterone triggers the growth of some facial hair and chest hair. In boys, muscles begin to develop rapidly and the amount of body fat decreases.

COPING WITH CHANGES Puberty can be an awkward time for many boys. The rapid growth of arms and legs may cause a boy to feel clumsy. While the voice is becoming deeper, it is common for the voice to crack, or to switch back to higher tones. However, these periods of transition will pass over time, and the boy will usually begin to feel more comfortable about his body as his coordination adjusts to his rapid changes in size.

A boy who develops later than other boys his same age may have negative feelings about himself. Sometimes these negative feelings can last into adulthood. In order to avoid feelings of self-doubt, it is important that the teenage boy remember that his development will eventually catch up with that of his friends. It is also important for him to remember that his delayed development does not mean that he is not normal, but rather that he is just developing at a different pace.

THE MALE REPRODUCTIVE SYSTEM

The male reproductive system is composed of both internal and external organs. Each structure is shown in Figure 17-8. During puberty, these organs mature to the point where the male can produce sperm cells.

MAIN IDEAS

CONCEPTS

✔ During puberty, hormones trigger the maturation of the male reproductive system.

✔ The age at which puberty occurs differs from one boy to the next.

✔ Many reproductive disorders can be prevented or cured if detected early.

VOCABULARY

scrotum
vas deferens
prostate
 gland
semen
urethra
ejaculation
penis
foreskin
circumcision
erection
nocturnal
 emission
inguinal
 hernia
testicular
 cancer

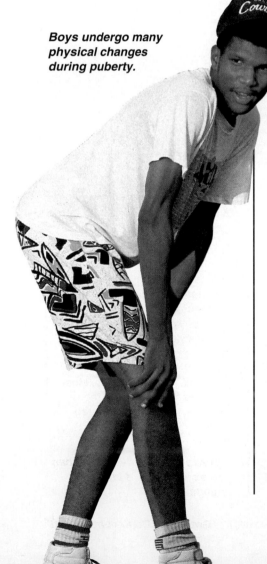

Boys undergo many physical changes during puberty.

These sperm cells shown in the photo have been magnified over 5,000 times.

SPERM-PRODUCING STRUCTURES   Sperm cells are the cells that fertilize the egg cells of the female. They are composed of a head, a body, and a whip-like tail. The sperm cell uses the tail to swim toward the egg cell once the sperm cell enters the female.

Sperm cells are produced in the testes—the same glands that produce the hormone testosterone. Each male has two testes. After puberty, the testes can produce up to 300 million sperm cells a day. The testes are originally formed inside the body near the abdomen. However, just before birth, they descend into a pouch of loose skin called the **scrotum** [*SKROHT um*], which hangs outside the body. The testes hang outside the body where the temperature is a few degrees cooler than inside the body. The testes need this lower temperature to produce active, healthy sperm.

INTERNAL STRUCTURES   Once sperm cells leave the testes, they travel to the penis through a series of tubes as shown in Figure 17-8. The first tube that the sperm cells enter is the **vas deferens** [*VAS DEF uh runz*], which connects the testes to the prostate gland. The **prostate gland** is a small, walnut-sized gland located below the bladder. As the sperm cells pass through the prostate gland, they combine with a thin, milky fluid produced by the prostate gland and fluids produced by another set of glands called the seminal vesicles. The combination of these fluids and the sperm cells is called **semen**. The final tube through which the semen travels is the **urethra** [*yu REE thruh*]. The opening of the urethra is at the tip of the penis. The process by which sperm leaves the penis is called ejaculation. **Ejaculation** [*ih jak yuh LAY shun*] is caused by muscle contractions that push the semen through the urethra and out of the penis. The urethra also carries urine from the bladder out of the body. Valves near the location where the urethra leaves the urinary bladder prevent urine from mixing with the semen.

MALE SECONDARY SEX CHARACTERISTICS

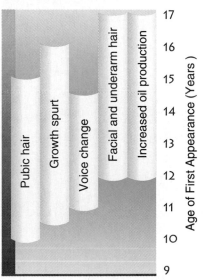

Figure 17-7   At which ages can you expect a boy's voice to change?

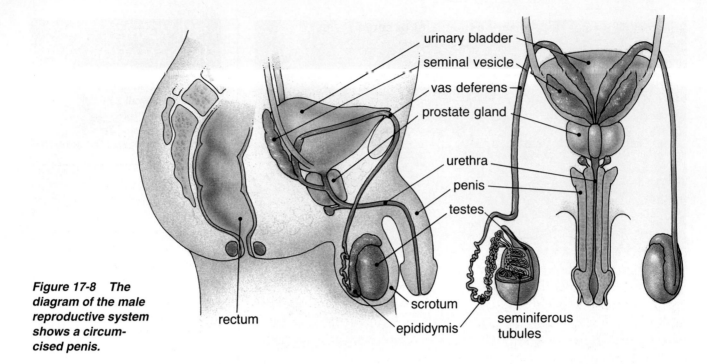

Figure 17-8 The diagram of the male reproductive system shows a circumcised penis.

Labels on diagram:
urinary bladder
seminal vesicle
vas deferens
prostate gland
urethra
penis
testes
scrotum
epididymis
seminiferous tubules
rectum

PENIS   The **penis** is the external, cylinder-shaped organ through which urine and sperm pass out of the body. At birth, the end of the penis is covered by a flap of skin called **foreskin**. For social and religious reasons, parents sometimes choose to have the foreskin removed from the infant shortly after birth. Surgical removal of the foreskin is called **circumcision**. If the penis is not circumcised, it is important to clean around the foreskin regularly while bathing. Otherwise a build-up of fluid from small glands in the foreskin will develop and may cause infection.

Normally the penis is limp. However, during certain states of arousal the spongy tissue and blood vessels of the penis will fill with blood, causing an erection. An **erection** is a stiffening of the penis that causes it to point up and away from the body.

One of the first signs that the reproductive system is maturing is the occurrence of **nocturnal emissions**, or wet dreams. A nocturnal emission is the normal ejaculation of semen during sleep, and does not mean that anything is wrong.

MALE REPRODUCTIVE DISORDERS

Although there are many types of disorders that can affect the male reproductive system, many can be prevented or effectively treated. Infections, including those that are a result of sexually transmitted diseases, usually can be prevented if proper precautions are taken. Other serious problems such as cancer often can be treated if detected early. However, many disorders can result in permanent damage if not treated early.

DEVELOPMENTAL DISORDERS   Some male reproductive disorders result from developmental problems. Occasionally one or both testes may fail to descend from the abdomen into the scrotum before birth. This condition usually corrects itself within the boy's first year. If it does not, hormone treatment or surgery can correct the problem. If untreated, undescended testes can lead to infertility and an increased risk of testicular cancer.

Sometimes the opening between the abdomen and the scrotum does not close properly after the testes have descended. Later in life, a part of the intestine may push through the opening into the scrotum or the groin area, causing an **inguinal hernia** [*ING gwuhn ul*]. An inguinal hernia can be corrected through surgery.

TESTICULAR CANCER   One of the most serious reproductive disorders in men between 15 and 35 years of age is cancer in the testes which is called **testicular cancer**. Testicular cancer accounts for over 20 percent of all cancers of men in this age group. If detected during its early stages, it can be cured over 95 percent of the time. Testicular cancer can be detected by doing a simple monthly self-examination of the testes. A self-examination is performed by grasping the testicle and gently rolling it between the thumb and forefingers. Unusual lumps or other changes in the testes that are detected during a self-examination don't necessarily indicate cancer, but they should be examined by a physician.

DISORDERS OF THE PROSTATE GLAND   As men get older, the prostate gland may become enlarged. In most cases, an enlarged prostate gland is not serious. However, if it gets too large, it can block urination. If the blockage is not treated, infection of the bladder and kidneys may occur. Medicine or a simple surgical procedure can be used to decrease the size of the prostate gland.

Cancer also can occur in the prostate gland. Unlike testicular cancer, prostate cancer is most common in men over 65 years of age. Like all cancers, prostate cancer is most easily treated if detected during its early stages. The American Cancer Society recommends that all men over 40 years of age receive a yearly examination for any signs of prostate cancer.

STRATEGIES FOR LIVING

Monthly self-examination for testicular cancer

- The best time to do a self-examination is after a warm bath or shower.
- Examine one testicle at a time.
- Roll testicle gently between thumb and forefinger.
- Feel for any unusual lumps on surface of testicle.
- Note any enlargement or hardening of testicles.
- Report any changes in testicles to your doctor.

CONSUMER HEALTH

Hair Loss

In much of the American culture, a thick, luxuriant head of hair is considered a sign of health, beauty, youth, and vitality. Advertisers have capitalized on these images—much to the dismay of those experiencing hair loss or baldness.

Baldness and thinning hair are due mainly to heredity. Hereditary hair loss is gradual and in most cases irreversible. Factors that can cause temporary hair loss are preg-

nancy and nursing, severe emotional stress, malnutrition, anorexia nervosa, anemia, and various medications, particularly chemotherapy for cancer patients.

Although many people find thinning hair or baldness attractive, many men and women feel uncomfortable with their thinning hair. For these people, there are many treatments for hereditary hair loss, most of them unreliable and all of them costly.

Hair implants cost about $10,000 and only work for some people.

Cosmetic remedies, such as sprays and gels, hair dye, hair weaves, or a short haircut are less expensive than implants and mask the symptoms of thinning hair. Over-the-counter lotions, oils, or vitamin supplements do nothing to reverse hair loss. The best, least expensive remedy for hair loss is accepting yourself the way you are.

INJURIES TO THE TESTES

Because the testes are located outside of the body, they are prone to injuries. All blows to the testes can be very painful and can occasionally result in permanent damage. In extreme cases, damage to the testes can cause infertility. For these reasons, it is important that males wear protective gear when participating in contact sports. If a man receives a blow to the testes and the pain and swelling persist for more than a few hours, he should seek medical care.

INFERTILITY

Many reproductive disorders in men can affect their general health, and can also cause infertility, or the inability to fertilize an egg cell. The most common cause of infertility in men is the inability to produce enough sperm cells. Sperm production can be impaired by sexually transmitted diseases or other infections. Infections may also cause a blockage in the vas deferens, preventing sperm from passing through. Hormonal problems also might cause a decrease in sperm production. Hormonal disorders can sometimes be treated by using medication. Occasionally surgery can repair problems in the testes.

The health of the reproductive system often can be traced to health behaviors. The use of some drugs, both legal and illegal, has been linked to the decreased production of sperm. Exposure to toxic chemicals also may damage the male reproductive system. Because the health of the reproductive system is linked to one's overall well-being, maintaining a nutritious diet, avoiding alcohol and other drugs, and watching for any signs of problems are the best precautions one can take.

LESSON 17.3 USING WHAT YOU HAVE LEARNED

REVIEW

1. Which changes during puberty does testosterone stimulate?
2. Why is the early detection of testicular cancer so important?

THINK CRITICALLY

3. The teenage years are sometimes marked by mood swings and periods of irritability. Why might these moods be a result of the physical changes teenagers are experiencing?
4. The rate of testicular cancer among young men is much higher than the rate of breast cancer among young women. Yet young women are more likely to receive regular examinations—by a doctor or self. Why do you think this difference in behavior exists?

APPLY IT TO YOURSELF

5. You are the teacher of a health class. Why do you think it is important for everybody to learn about the development of both males and females?

Preventive Care

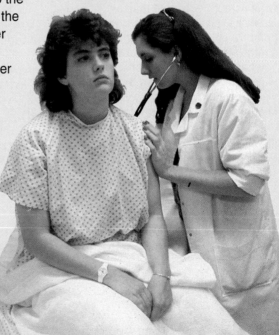

DECISION FOCUS MAKING

Shelly was excited about going to college. There were all kinds of things she wanted to get for school in the fall. One day her mother asked Shelly to have a complete medical checkup before she left for school. "Just so that our doctor has a recent medical history on file," her mother explained.

Shelly called Dr. Loy and set up an appointment. During the exam, the doctor recommended that Shelly have a routine Pap test and pelvic examination. "I, or our nurse practitioner, could perform the examination," said Dr. Loy, "Or you could begin regular checkups with a gynecologist." The doctor explained that a gynecologist is a doctor who specializes in female health care.

"Every woman of reproductive age should be examined regularly. It's good preventive care," explained Dr. Loy. "I can give you a couple of names if you'd rather see a gynecologist. Think about it."

Shelly wasn't sure what she should do. She didn't know much about the tests. Shelly wondered whether she really needed the tests. She was young and healthy. What could possibly be wrong?

Shelly also wondered whether she should have the examination done by a gynecologist, if she decided to have

it at all. She had always liked Dr. Loy, but now she felt a little awkward about having him do the exam. "But he did say that his nurse practitioner could do the exam."

PAUSE AND CONSIDER

1. *Identify the Problem.* Why is Shelly hesitant about having a Pap test and pelvic exam?

2. *Consider the Options.* What are Shelly's options?

3. *Evaluate the Outcomes.* What could happen if Shelly has the test and examination? What might happen if she doesn't make the appointment?

Shelly decided that she wanted to find out more information about a Pap test and pelvic examination. She went to the library and read more on the subject. Then she told her mother what Dr. Loy had suggested. "Have you ever been to a gynecologist?" Shelly asked.

Shelly's mom smiled, "Yes I have, dear. It's not unusual to feel nervous. There really is nothing to worry about. Dr. Loy has given you some very good options."

Shelly and her mom talked a while longer.

Shelly decided to have the examination. She would have it done by the nurse practitioner at Dr. Loy's office.

When Shelly went for her exam, Ms. Day made Shelly feel very relaxed. She answered all of Shelly's questions and explained the entire procedure before the examination. On the way home, Shelly wondered why she had been scared. It had been so simple.

DECIDE AND REVIEW

4. *Decide and Act.* What was Shelly's decision?

5. *Review.* What did Shelly do to help her make an informed decision? Why was it important that Shelly feel comfortable about the person who would be doing the examination?

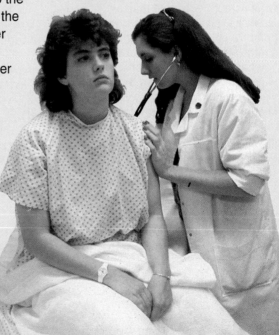

PROJECTS

1. At your school or local library, research the new ways that natural and synthetic hormones are being used in the medical field.

2. On a bulletin board or a sheet of poster board, create a simple drawing of the human body. Mark the locations of the endocrine glands. Using small file cards, make a label for each gland with its name and function.

WORKING WITH OTHERS

Choose a partner and describe to him or her the symptoms that you felt the last time you were nervous—before a test or a big game, for example, or before you had to make an oral presentation. Together with your partner, write a description of the sensations you remember. Then write an explanation of what was going on in your body to cause these sensations.

CONNECTING TO...

ENGLISH American literature has a wealth of books devoted to young people "coming of age." J.D. Salinger's *Catcher in the Rye* and Betty Smith's *A Tree Grows in Brooklyn* are two examples. Undoubtedly, you have read at least one book that depicts a young person's passage into adulthood. Create a report based on a book you have read that tells about the ways in which a character deals with the emotional and physical changes during adolescence. You may want to present your report to the class.

USING VOCABULARY

adrenal gland	inguinal hernia	prostate gland
adrenaline	insulin	puberty
cervix	menopause	pubic hair
circumcision	menstrual cycle	scrotum
diabetes mellitus	menstruation	secondary sex
ejaculation	nocturnal emission	characteristic
endocrine gland	ovarian cyst	semen
endocrine system	ovary	testes
endometriosis	ovulation	testicular cancer
endometrium	pancreas	testosterone
erection	Pap test	thyroid gland
estrogen	pelvic inflamma-	toxic shock
Fallopian tube	tory disease	syndrome
foreskin	penis	urethra
hormone	pituitary gland	uterus
hypothalamus	premenstrual	vagina
infertile	syndrome	vas deferens

On a separate sheet of paper, write the headings "Endocrine System," "Female Development," "Male Development," and "Reproductive Disorders." Under each heading, write the vocabulary terms from the above list that belong in that category. Then choose one category, and write a paragraph using as many of its vocabulary terms as you can.

CONCEPT MAPPING

Copy and complete the concept map shown below. Information on concept mapping appears at the front of this book.

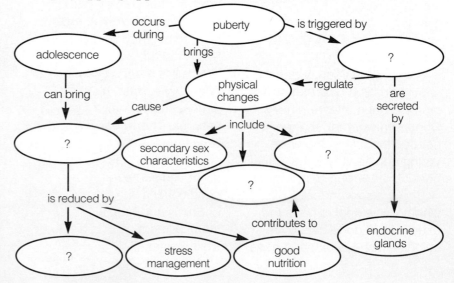

THINKING CRITICALLY

INTERPRET

LESSON 17.1

1. What is a hormone?

2. What controls the release of hormones by the endocrine system?

3. What role does insulin play in the control of blood sugar? What happens when the pancreas is unable to produce enough insulin?

4. Describe the thyroid gland—its shape, its location, and the function of the hormones it produces.

5. What function do the adrenal glands serve in reacting to stress?

6. Describe the functions of estrogen in females and of testosterone in males.

LESSON 17.2

7. Identify two secondary sex characteristics that develop only in females during puberty.

8. What other conditions besides pregnancy can delay or stop a woman's menstrual cycle?

9. Describe four ways to alleviate the symptoms of PMS.

10. What is a Pap test, and what is its purpose?

11. Identify four causes of infertility in females.

LESSON 17.3

12. Identify three secondary sex characteristics that develop only in males during puberty.

13. What causes ejaculation?

14. Why is it important that the testes descend into the scrotum?

15. What is the most common cause of infertility in males?

APPLY

LESSON 17.1

16. Identify four functions of the endocrine system.

17. A 14-year-old girl suddenly grew four inches in the past year. She feels awkward because she is now taller than all her classmates, both girls and boys. No one in her family is unusually tall. Why should the girl not be worried about her greater height?

LESSON 17.2

18. Describe the process of ovulation. What happens if the egg cell is fertilized? What happens if it is not fertilized?

19. What physical and emotional symptoms are characteristic of premenstrual syndrome?

LESSON 17.2

20. Identify four conditions that can cause a decrease in sperm production in males.

21. What secondary sex characteristics develop in both girls and boys during puberty?

COMMITMENT TO WELLNESS

FOLLOW-UP

SETTING GOALS

Look at your responses to the checklist you completed at the beginning of this chapter. Which statements reflected your strengths? Which reflected your weaknesses?

Choose one checklist statement that you would like to change from no to yes. Copy the statement in your Wellness Journal, or on a separate sheet of paper. Below the statement, list three specific actions you could take to achieve that goal. In a month or two, review your objectives and evaluate your progress. As you achieve your goal, choose another checklist item to work on, and develop an action plan for that goal.

WHERE DO I GO FROM HERE?

Many books on the male and female reproductive systems are available for teenagers. If you would like more information, ask your health teacher or a librarian to recommend some specific books.

FOR MORE INFORMATION, CONTACT:

National Institute of Child Health and Human Development
Building 31, Room 2A 32
Bethesda, Maryland 20892

Understanding the Aging Process

BACKGROUND

Nineteenth-century writer Ralph Waldo Emerson is famous for encouraging independent thinking and democratic ideals.

"Life is a succession of lessons, which must be lived to be understood."

Ralph Waldo Emerson

From the day you were born, your life has been and will continue to be a succession of lessons about your changing self. As an infant and young child, you learned to walk, talk, and interact with others. Later, you started school, where you learned to read, write, and reason logically. Now, as a teenager, you are learning new skills, exploring new interests, and considering your future.

This rapid change will continue for a few more years as you enter young adulthood. You will learn to form adult relationships, develop a mature self-concept, and choose your life's work. Many people continue to experience rapid change well into their twenties and thirties. For most people, however, change becomes more gradual as they grow older.

Aging is a process of gradual change. Some of the changes of adulthood are choices people make as they pursue new interests or respond to new situations. Other changes are natural and are common to everyone. To maintain wellness, people must learn to adapt to all changes in their lives.

Aging provides a great range of choices and challenges. Learning positive ways to adapt to change will affect both your physical and your mental well-being throughout your life.

THINKING CRITICALLY

INTERPRET

LESSON
18.1

1. Why do many people expect to be less physically active as they grow older?

2. Why might the average life expectancy be steadily increasing in much of the world?

3. Why do many young adults change their minds several times when making decisions about work and family?

4. How might a mid-life crisis be a positive transition?

5. What choices might indicate an interest in generativity?

6. Why is retirement a difficult transition for many people?

7. What can people do to achieve integrity in older adulthood?

LESSON
18.2

8. How might the trend toward telling people that they have terminal illnesses have changed the experience of dying?

9. Why do dying people sometimes try to bargain by changing negative health habits that have led to illness?

10. What is the purpose of a funeral?

11. Why might deciding to donate organs or tissues for transplantation give someone a good feeling?

APPLY

LESSON
18.1

12. Ted has been winning track events all through high school. Now he has to decide whether to continue training for competitive sports. His coach thinks he should delay going to college and devote at least a year to training. His coach thinks Ted might even make the Olympic team. Why might his coach give Ted this advice? What advice would you give him?

13. Ken has just retired, after forty years as a high school teacher. At first, Ken was delighted when September came and he didn't have to return to school. As the months went by, however, he became increasingly unhappy. Now he wonders whether he made the right decision by retiring. You've suggested that he volunteer at the local youth center, but Ken says he isn't interested. Why might Ken be unhappy at this time? What else might he consider doing?

LESSON
18.2

14. Charles is 55 years old and had a very close relationship with his father, who died two months ago after a long illness. Since his father's death, Charles has been thinking about becoming involved in a local boys' and girls' club. He has also been thinking about volunteering at a local hospice. Why might Charles want to volunteer his time in these ways? Would you advise him to do so? Why or why not?

15. Ellen has just been diagnosed with a terminal illness. Although she is still healthy enough to see her friends, she expects to spend more time in the hospital during the next months. As her friend, you notice that people are beginning to avoid her. What could you do to help Ellen? What would you tell her? What would you tell some of her other friends?

COMMITMENT TO WELLNESS
FOLLOW-UP

SETTING GOALS

Look back at the Personal Commitment to Wellness checklist in the chapter opener. Review your responses to each of the items on the checklist.

Now consider the ways in which these areas are useful to you now and will be useful as you grow older. For example, knowing that some adults find middle adulthood a time of responsibility for aging parents, you might talk to your parents or grandparents about aging. Find out how they would like to spend their older adulthood. What needs might they have as they grow older? How could you help them meet those needs?

Now review the areas you consider weaknesses. Describe a time in your future when each of these areas might be important. What might you be able to do to make these areas strengths?

WHERE DO I GO FROM HERE?

As researchers learn more about the needs of people with terminal illnesses, more communities are opening hospices for people of all ages. Many hospices depend on trained volunteers.

FOR MORE
INFORMATION ABOUT
HOSPICES, CONTACT:

National Hospice Organization
1901 North Moore Street,
Suite 901
Arlington, VA 22209

427

Preventing Substance Abuse

Chapter 19
Coordination and Control

Chapter 20
Tobacco

Chapter 21
Alcohol

Chapter 22
Psychoactive Drugs and Steroids

What's the big deal about alcohol and teenagers?

How do you feel about cigarette smoke?

Why do some people abuse certain substances?

CHAPTER 19 〜

Coordination and Control

"There is a great deal of unmapped country within us."

George Eliot

For centuries, scientists have acted as great explorers in search of the secrets that lie within the human body. As each decade passes, more discoveries are made that reveal unknown territories of the human body. Yet, many scientists believe that we have barely scratched the surface in our quest for more information about the power center of human life—the brain.

The brain is the center of every thought, action, word, and emotion. Everything you feel and everything you do is processed in the brain—the hub of the complex and amazing nervous system. Like an array of intricate roads, the nervous system contains many pathways that run side-by-side and cross over each other. By following the pathways in the nervous system, we can begin to understand how we are able to maintain both physical and emotional balance.

Your nervous system is at work every waking and sleeping moment. Although it has built-in protection, your nervous system needs to be cared for carefully. As you begin to understand the workings of the human nervous system, you will begin to create your own map about yourself—one that will tell you which paths to take and which to avoid.

How well do you take care of your nervous system? Number a page in your Wellness Journal or on a separate sheet of paper from 1–10. Respond to the following items by writing *yes* or *no* next to each statement below that describes you all or most of the time.

1. I understand the basic functions of the nervous system.

2. I protect my head by wearing a helmet when riding a bicycle or motorcycle, or when playing contact sports.

3. I always wear a safety belt when riding in a car.

4. I know and practice safe, simple ways of treating sleep problems.

5. I am aware of the foods that can affect my nervous system.

6. I always read the labels on over-the-counter medicines so I am sure to take the proper dosage.

7. I avoid all substances that can affect my nervous system negatively.

8. I never take drugs that are not prescribed for me by my doctor.

9. I get 7 to 9 hours of sleep each night.

10. I understand the factors that can cause headaches.

Review your responses and consider what might be your strengths and weaknesses. Save your personal checklist for a follow-up activity at the end of the chapter.

THE NERVOUS SYSTEM

The complex group of organs and nerves that control all your actions and thoughts is your **nervous system.** The human nervous system is a remarkable arrangement of complex structures. The nervous system drives the other systems of the body. It is a network that transmits signals—both electrically and chemically—from and to the tissues of the brain and the body's many organs. A detailed illustration of the human nervous system is shown in Plate Eight.

Your nervous system serves many vital functions.

- *Processes information*   The brain is the control center of the nervous system. Nerve cells in the brain receive messages from and transmit messages to every part of the body.

- *Stores information*   Your nervous system stores information to be used days, months, or even years later. It stores facts, responses you have learned, and past experiences, including events seen, heard, and felt.

- *Controls voluntary movements*   Your nervous system is in charge of your body's voluntary muscle movements. Billions of nerve cells throughout your body send signals to each other and to muscles to respond to the task at hand.

- *Controls involuntary processes and actions*   Control of your heart rate, breathing changes, and digestive responses are examples of the involuntary aspects of your nervous system.

NEURONS

The basic units of the nervous system are cells called **neurons.** They are too small to be seen without a microscope. Neurons make up the machinery of the nervous system that is dedicated to controlling and monitoring all of your thoughts, movements, and responses to everyday living. Neurons carry messages from one part of your body to another. These messages of sensation and information are called **impulses.** Neurons form the communication system that controls the body's many functions and stores information. Although there are different types of neurons, there are certain features that are similar in all types.

MAIN IDEAS

CONCEPTS

✔ Nerve impulses travel through the body by way of a complex array of neurons.

✔ The nervous system includes the central and peripheral nervous systems.

✔ Coordinated movement requires efficient transmission of impulses through a healthy nervous system.

VOCABULARY

nervous system
neuron
impulse
nerve
synapse
neurotransmitter
sensory neuron
interneuron
motor neuron
central nervous system
cerebrum
cerebral cortex
thalamus
hypothalamus
cerebellum
brainstem
engram
reflex
reflex arc

Figure 19-1   In a neuron, which structure carries the impulse away from the cell body?

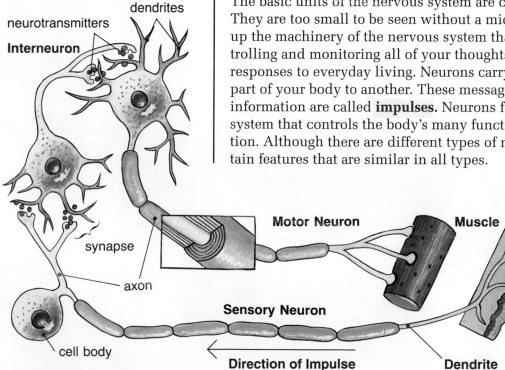

STRUCTURE OF NEURONS   A neuron has three parts: a cell body, an axon, and dendrites. The cell body with structures leading to and from it is shown in Figure 19-1. The structures consist of one axon and one or more dendrites.

The axon is a long structure that carries impulses away from the cell body to other neurons. Axons that reach through your body to distant neurons may be over one yard long. A **nerve** is actually a bundle of axons from many neurons. One nerve may have more than 1,000 axons, with each axon acting independently of the other axons.

The dendrites are branching structures that look like tiny trees. They receive impulses and send them to the cell body. Dendrites are extensions of the cell body that carry nerve impulses toward the cell body. Because dendrites have many branches, one neuron can receive messages from hundreds of other neurons.

NERVE IMPULSES   The impulse that travels along a neuron is similar to a tiny electrical charge. Nerve impulses may travel as fast as 360 feet per second along an axon. At that speed, an impulse could cover the length of a football field in less than one second.

Between the end of the axon of one neuron and the dendrite of another neuron is a space, or gap, called a **synapse** [*SIN aps*]. As an impulse arrives at the end of an axon, it is passed across the synapse to a dendrite by neurotransmitters. **Neurotransmitters** [*nur oh TRANS mit urz*] are natural chemicals located at the synapse that assist in the transmission of impulses.

KINDS OF NEURONS   There are three kinds of neurons: sensory, motor, and interneurons. Figure 19-1 illustrates the relationships among the kinds of neurons. **Sensory neurons** detect changes in the environment, both outside and inside your body. They carry nerve impulses from the sense organs, the skin, the muscles, and the internal organs to the spinal cord or brain. For example, when you touch an ice cube, the neurons that sense cold send this message to your brain.

The **interneurons** are neurons that receive sensory messages and send responses. They are found only in the brain and spinal cord. In the example of the ice cube, many interneurons in your brain act together to form an awareness that you are touching the cube. They then send messages to motor neurons to produce actions.

The **motor neurons** are neurons that carry a response from the interneurons to the muscles, glands, and internal organs of the body. Every movement of the body, from a blink of the eyes to a jump through the air, is controlled by messages carried by motor neurons to the muscles. In the example of the ice cube, the message being carried by the motor neurons might be to stimulate the hand's muscles to pick up the ice cube and place it in a glass.

THE CENTRAL NERVOUS SYSTEM

People once thought that the heart controlled the body. Scientists now know that the brain is the master control unit for the body. The ability of this three-pound mass of spongy tissue to receive,

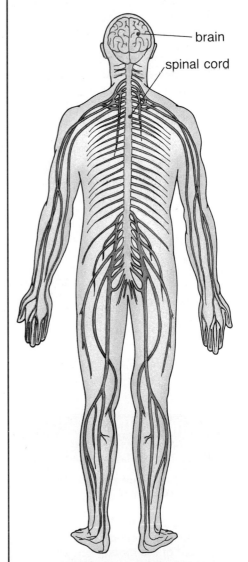

Figure 19-2   *The central nervous system (yellow) and the peripheral nervous system (brown) work together to send messages throughout your body.*

Figure 19-3 What structure of the brain is located directly behind the midbrain?

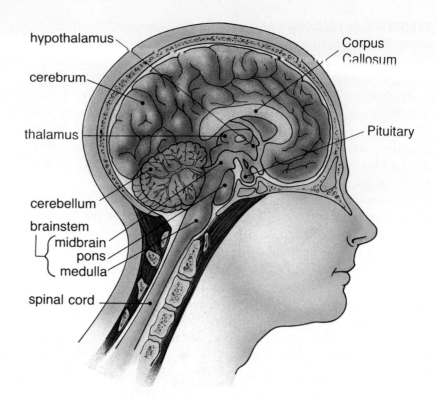

hypothalamus
Corpus Callosum
cerebrum
thalamus
Pituitary
cerebellum
brainstem
  midbrain
  pons
  medulla
spinal cord

store, and send information is fascinating, but is still not fully understood. The brain and spinal cord together make up the **central nervous system,** shown in Figure 19-2. Although the brain and the spinal cord have many parts, they all must work together as a unified whole.

PROTECTIVE COVERINGS   Because the brain and spinal cord are so vital, they have several protective coverings. The outer covering is bone. The skull surrounds and protects the brain. The vertebrae protect the spinal cord. Under the skull and vertebrae, three membranes, called meninges [*muh NIN jeez*], provide even more protection. In addition, a protective fluid fills the spaces between the middle and inner membranes and certain spaces within the brain. This fluid helps cushion the brain and spinal cord in the event of an impact or a sudden change of direction.

THE CEREBRUM   The largest and uppermost part of the brain, which regulates your thoughts and actions, is the **cerebrum** [*SER uh brum*]. The cerebrum's outer layer is called the **cerebral cortex** [*suh REE brul*]. It is made up mostly of interneuron cell bodies. About three-fourths of all the nerve cell bodies in your nervous system are in the cerebral cortex. Buried deep within the cerebrum are the thalamus and the hypothalamus. The **thalamus** relays sensory impulses to the cerebral cortex. The **hypothalamus** regulates some of your body's most basic needs, such as body temperature, sleep, digestion, and the release of hormones. You can see these structures in Figure 19-3.

The cerebrum is responsible for the highly developed intelligence of human beings. The surface of the cerebrum looks like a wrinkled walnut with many grooves that form patterns. The patterns can be used to identify specific regions of the brain. Some regions receive messages about what you see, hear, and smell or how you move. Other parts control your ability to think, write, talk, and express emotions.

The cerebrum is divided in half from front to back. The two halves, or hemispheres, of your cerebrum control opposite sides of your body. The right side of your brain actually controls the muscles of the left side of your body. The left side of your brain controls the muscles of the right side of your body. Each hemisphere is divided into four lobes: the frontal, temporal, parietal, and occipital. Figure 19-4 identifies the lobes of the brain and some of the different regions.

THE CEREBELLUM   The part of the brain that coordinates the muscles that you use for action, such as running, walking, or playing the piano, is the **cerebellum** [*sehr uh BEL um*]. The cerebellum is under and behind the cerebrum and coordinates a constant flow of nerve impulses from the body and cerebrum. The cerebellum puts this information together to help your muscles coordinate and perform the way you want. It also helps control your balance and maintain posture.

THE BRAINSTEM   The structure that connects the cerebrum with the spinal cord is the **brainstem.** It consists of three parts that have specialized functions: the medulla, the pons, and the midbrain.

- The medulla [*muh DUL uh*] is found just above the spinal cord. It controls some of the most important functions of life, such as breathing, blood pressure, heart rate, and swallowing. When you get excited or frightened, the emotional centers of your brain and sense organs stimulate the medulla.
- The pons is a bundle of nerve fibers that link the spinal cord with the brain. It also connects the cerebrum with the cerebellum.
- The midbrain is a group of nerves that control certain involuntary actions such as blinking.

THE SPINAL CORD   Within the vertebral column is the spinal cord. It extends from the medulla to just below the ribs. The average spinal cord is about 18 inches long and about the diameter of a finger. The nerve fibers in the spinal cord reach out to connect all of the nerves in your body to the central nervous system. If the spinal cord is damaged, the body may be unable to feel or move from the point of injury downward.

THE PERIPHERAL NERVOUS SYSTEM

The system that carries messages between the central nervous system and the rest of the body is the peripheral nervous system. Impulses constantly travel between the two nervous systems. This happens through 31 pairs of large nerves branching from the spinal cord and 12 pairs of nerves branching from the

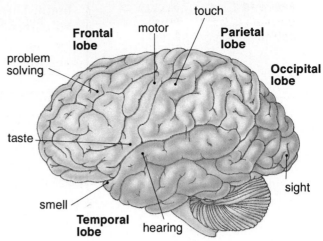

Figure 19-4   Which section of the brain is responsible for higher level thinking?

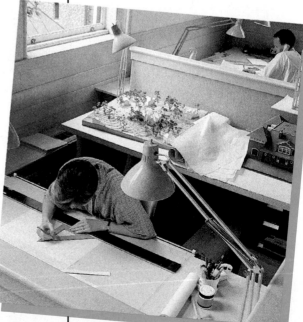

Many areas of the brain are involved in coordinating a task as complex as this one.

brain. These nerves contain thousands of nerve fibers that reach to all parts of the body. The peripheral nervous system consists of two subsystems—the autonomic nervous system and the somatic nervous system.

THE AUTONOMIC NERVOUS SYSTEM   The part of the peripheral nervous system that controls involuntary responses is called the autonomic nervous system [*aw tuh NAHM ik*]. For example, your breathing and digestion are controlled by involuntary responses. The autonomic nervous system plays a major role in emotions. It affects many of the body's organs, including the heart, lungs, stomach, intestines, liver, kidneys, sweat glands, salivary glands, and pupils of the eye. The autonomic nervous system also consists of two subsystems. Each subsystem reaches and affects the same organs, but produces opposite effects.

Figure 19-5   Which part of the autonomic nervous system is working when you see something that makes your mouth water?

- The parasympathetic nervous system is the subsystem of the autonomic nervous system that generally slows down the body's functions. For example, when you are sleeping, it slows the heartbeat and rate of breathing.

- The sympathetic nervous system is the subsystem of the autonomic nervous system that works when you are active or under

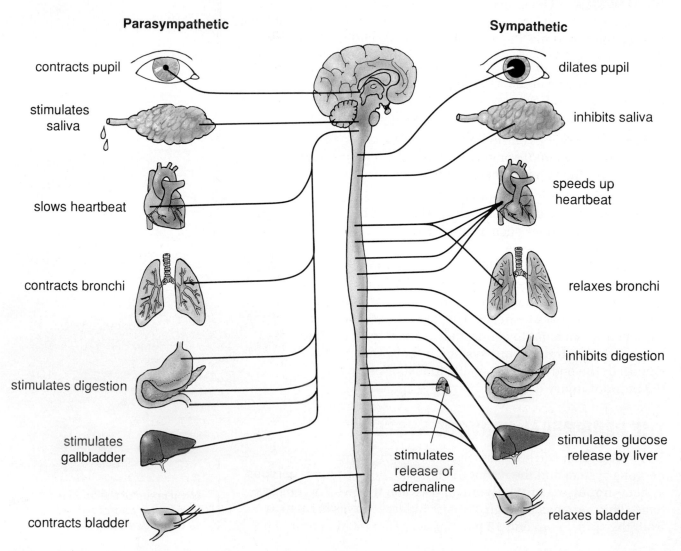

Parasympathetic

contracts pupil

stimulates saliva

slows heartbeat

contracts bronchi

stimulates digestion

stimulates gallbladder

contracts bladder

Sympathetic

dilates pupil

inhibits saliva

speeds up heartbeat

relaxes bronchi

inhibits digestion

stimulates glucose release by liver

relaxes bladder

stimulates release of adrenaline

emotional stress. As you read this, you are probably calm and sitting still. Parasympathetic impulses are regulating your heart rate, keeping it slow and steady. If something were to excite you or if you were to move quickly, your sympathetic nervous system would take a stronger role. Your heart rate would speed up and your breathing rate would increase. Blood flow would decrease in organs such as the stomach and the intestines. At the same time, blood flow would increase to active muscles.

The interplay between the two parts of the autonomic nervous system keeps your body working properly in all situations. It is done without your conscious control. Figure 19-5 illustrates the relationship of the sympathetic and parasympathetic nervous systems.

SOMATIC NERVOUS SYSTEM   The other division of the peripheral nervous system is the somatic nervous system [*soh MAT ik*]. It carries sensory information about external stimulation and controls voluntary action of the muscles. The somatic nervous system processes information about your skin, muscles, and joints. It makes you aware of sensations such as pain, pressure, temperature, and movement of your body.

MOVEMENT

Every day, you perform many activities. You brush your teeth, comb your hair, and tie your shoes. Most of the time you do not even think when you perform these activities. Your body is carrying out the tasks of routine movement without the need for your conscious thought.

VOLUNTARY BODY MOVEMENTS   Your nervous system coordinates voluntary body movements in several ways, each as simple or complex as the movement itself. Your spinal cord, brainstem, cerebellum, and cerebrum each play a role in that control.

Blushing is an involuntary response that is more obvious in some people than in others.

FROM A CULTURAL PERSPECTIVE

Tea

A tea is a drink made from steeping certain plants in water. What we normally call tea is made by steeping the leaves of a variety of the tea plant, but teas can be made from many other plants.

For the Japanese, green tea has long been an important element in the culture as well as the diet. While the cultural importance attached to the ritual of preparing, serving, and drinking tea has long been understood, even in the west, recent research has led to the discovery that green tea has some beneficial effects of its own. At the University of California, a Japanese research team recently discovered that green tea reduces the bacteria in the mouth, inhibiting cavity formation. They also discovered that green tea can help relieve some symptoms of acne and stomach cramps.

For many years, people in some western cultures have made a ritual of the afternoon tea, where the usual tea served is black tea. In the late 1980s, researchers at Johns Hopkins University in Baltimore, Maryland, pinpointed a number of physiological effects of drinking regular tea. They found that some of the compounds in tea actually do provide a soothing effect. Beyond that, they found that tea may inhibit various bacteria that produce tooth decay and a number of gastrointestinal problems.

Teas made by steeping local herbs have been an important part of many cultures. Researchers are continuing to explore the positive and negative health-effects of these teas.

Your nervous system does more than control all of your individual movements. It causes them to work together smoothly. The ability to make many movements work together smoothly is called coordination. As you read the words on this page, your nervous system coordinates the movement of your eyes so that they both focus to see each word as one image. In addition, your nervous system helps your body adjust to varying demands. For example, playing the piano requires more delicate control than throwing a ball as far as you can.

BALANCE AND SMOOTH MOVEMENT Much of your muscle control occurs without your conscious direction. When you walk down the stairs, you do not think about which muscles to contract to keep your balance. The brainstem and the cerebellum control your balance and the smoothness of your movements. Impulses from your inner ear constantly go to the brainstem. The brainstem sends impulses to your muscles, making them tighten just enough to keep you balanced. When you are standing or sitting, the muscles in your legs, abdomen, and back receive signals. The constant slight contractions of these muscles keep you upright.

Your cerebellum perfects all of your movements. Sensory neurons are located in your muscles, tendons, and joints. These neurons send impulses to your cerebellum and tell it how much your muscles are contracting and the angle of each joint. Your cerebellum combines this information with signals from your inner ears and eyes to coordinate your movements. It makes sure that you move the way you want to move.

The graceful movements of this dancer require careful coordination of information throughout her nervous system.

SKILLED MOVEMENTS You can learn many tasks by practicing the motions involved over and over. Learning to tie your shoes is a simple example. Once you mastered the task, you could tie your shoes without thinking. You had developed memories of the different motions that were needed. Your brain developed a special code, or **engram,** about how to perform the task. An engram records the pattern of a skilled movement. When activated, the engram directs the body in repeating the pattern of movement. Now when you want to tie your shoes, you call forth an engram that sets the proper motor nerves into action. Sensory nerves let your brain know how the body is actually moving. The sensations are compared to the engram memories, and minor adjustments are made as needed.

REFLEXES

Not all patterns of movement are controlled. A rapid, automatic response to the environment that occurs without action from the brain is called a **reflex.** You were born with reflexes. Reflexes are involuntary, although sometimes you can overrule them. Most reflexes protect you

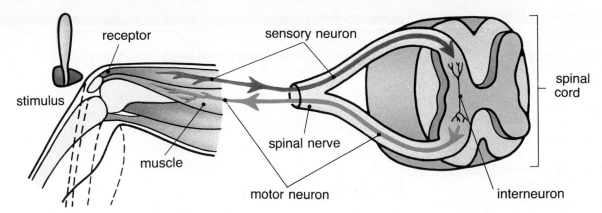

Figure 19-6   *What three neurons are involved in the knee-jerk reflex arc?*

from harm. For example, coughing and sneezing are reflexes that help to remove objects from your throat and air passages. Blinking is a reflex that helps protect your eyes. A doctor may check your reflexes during a routine medical examination. The tests help determine whether your reflexes are working properly.

When you accidentally touch a hot pan, your muscles quickly pull your arm away from the heat. This involuntary jerking movement is called a reflex action. When you touched the hot pan, nerve endings sent a message through a sensory neuron to the spinal cord. Here the impulse passed by way of an interneuron to a motor neuron. The motor neuron, in turn, passed the impulse along its axon to muscles in the arm, which tightened to pull the hand away from the pan. This entire reflex response took less than 1/50 of a second.

The route the impulses travel during a reflex action is called a **reflex arc**. This reflex arc is illustrated in Figure 19-6. The reflex arc is the simplest response pattern in the body. This kind of response does not involve the brain. It involves only the coordination of sensory and motor neurons. Because a reflex is not processed by the brain, it can happen quickly.

LESSON 19.1 USING WHAT YOU HAVE LEARNED

REVIEW

1. List and describe the role of the three kinds of neurons.
2. What two parts of the brain are responsible for controlling your balance and coordination?

THINK CRITICALLY

3. The synapse plays an important role in the transmission of an impulse. What might happen if an impulse is unable to travel across a synapse for some reason?
4. List three feelings you might experience and describe what part of the autonomic nervous system will be most involved with each feeling. Examples might be fear, being relaxed, and worry.

APPLY IT TO YOURSELF

5. As a parent, you always insist that your children wear helmets when they ride their bicycles. Why is your concern for safety appropriate for the protection of your children's nervous systems?

SUMMARY

Your nervous system is a remarkable system of nerves and organs. It drives and controls all the systems of the body. It not only controls your everyday movements, it controls all of your feelings and thoughts. The two main parts of the nervous system work together to send impulses to all parts of the body through a complex array of neurons. Your nervous system coordinates your body functions and thoughts in a way that allows you to live to your fullest.

BRAIN ACTIVITY AND SLEEP

No matter what you are doing, neurons in your brain constantly transmit and receive impulses. This activity varies depending on what you are doing. Whether you are thinking, running, sleeping soundly, or dreaming, your brain continues to work.

BRAIN ACTIVITY

Regardless of whether you are awake or asleep, your brain is continually collecting sensory information. It uses this information along with stored information to determine your body's response to stimuli. A **stimulus** is anything that is capable of producing a response. Scientists feel that very little is known about the true power of the human brain.

TRANSMITTING AND PROCESSING INFORMATION Three-fourths of all the nerve cell bodies in your nervous system are located in your cerebral cortex. Just as a computer is able to store information for later use, your brain stores your memories of past experiences in the cerebral cortex. However, the main function of your brain is to transmit and process information. It receives thousands of bits of information from the different sensory organs and then determines your response.

RECORDING BRAIN ACTIVITY Changes in the electrical activity of the brain can be measured and recorded by a special instrument called an **electroencephalograph (EEG)** [*ih lek troh en SEF uh luh graf*]. An EEG gives a visual record of the impulses being processed by the brain. An EEG printout is shown in Figure 19-7. When you are actively thinking, waves of electrical activity occur more often and

MAIN IDEAS

CONCEPTS

✔ Brain activity varies, depending on what you are doing.

✔ There are five stages of sleep, one of which is a dreaming stage.

✔ The amount of sleep that is needed for good health differs from person to person.

✔ Sleep is important for maintaining a healthy mind and body.

VOCABULARY

stimulus
electroencephalograph
rapid eye movement
insomnia
narcolepsy
sleep apnea

Figure 19-7   On the average, how many times each night do you dream? Which stage is characterized by the slowest brain waves?

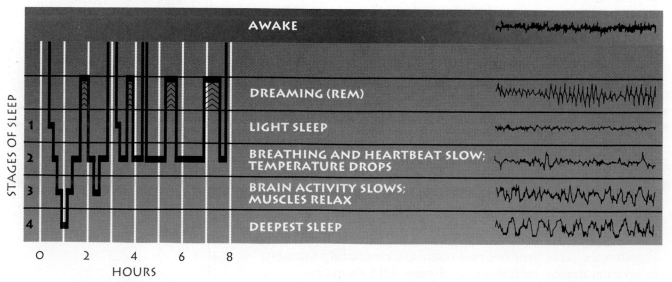

STAGES OF SLEEP   BRAIN WAVES

AWAKE

DREAMING (REM)

LIGHT SLEEP

BREATHING AND HEARTBEAT SLOW; TEMPERATURE DROPS

BRAIN ACTIVITY SLOWS; MUSCLES RELAX

DEEPEST SLEEP

STAGES OF SLEEP

1
2
3
4

0   2   4   6   8

HOURS

do not vary much in height. During sleep, the waves occur more slowly, but may vary greatly in height. In certain types of brain dis-orders, the waves show other changes. Changes in your brain activ-ity depends a great deal upon the health of your nervous system and on the kind of activity in which you are involved.

SLEEP

Sleep is a time when the body is actively restoring its energy and repairing itself. Sleep is an important aspect of wellness. Sleep refreshes the body and mind. Research suggests that sleep serves two functions—physical and psychological restoration. People feel and work better if they get a regular amount of sleep every night. Extended periods of time without sleep can cause a person to feel confused, unable to concentrate, and irritable.

People have different ways of coping with the inability to sleep.

Through the use of recorded brain waves, scientists have studied the activity of the brain during sleep. These studies indicate that as you sleep your brain progresses through sev-eral distinct stages. These stages occur in cycles with each cycle lasting about 90 to 100 minutes. Figure 19-7 shows the various stages of sleep. When you first fall asleep, your brain waves slow down. They get slower in the second and third stages of sleep as you relax. In these stages, you become more unaware of the surrounding world. The fourth stage is the deepest stage in the cycle. After that, you drift into a lighter sleep. This stage is the time when most people dream. This dream stage is called **rapid eye movement (REM)** sleep. One feature of REM sleep is the back-and-forth movement of your eyes under your eyelids. After ten or more minutes of REM sleep, the sleep cycle repeats four or five times.

Sleep research indicates that dreaming also is good for your health. Although you may not remember your dreams, it is thought that everyone dreams. People are most likely to remember their dreams when they wake up during REM sleep.

Have you ever felt like this after a sleepless night? Most teenagers require 8 to 10 hours of sleep to avoid this look.

SLEEP PROBLEMS

Most people sleep between 7 and 9 hours each night. However, not all people are able to realize the benefits of normal sleep. A great number of people suffer from one or more sleep disorders.

INSOMNIA   The inability to fall or stay asleep is called **insomnia** [*in SAHM nee uh*]. Insomnia is a problem for an estimated 75 million Americans. Insomnia often results from worry, stress, depression, pain, discomfort, or changes in pre-sleep routine. Everyone occasionally is unable to sleep. However, chronic insomnia is serious and should be treated by a doctor. To get a good night's sleep, doctors often advise the following.

- Avoid foods that keep you awake, such as spicy foods or foods that contain caffeine, such as chocolate and cola drinks.
- Exercise during the day often helps people sleep better.
- Establish a regular bedtime.
- Engage in a relaxing activity before bedtime, such as reading or listening to soothing music.

NARCOLEPSY   Some people may have problems staying awake during the day, even though they get a full night's sleep. Extreme daytime sleepiness may indicate a disorder called narcolepsy. People affected by **narcolepsy** [*NAHR kuh lep see*] experience a recurrent uncontrollable desire to sleep and a loss of muscle tone. People with narcolepsy fall asleep suddenly even while doing something such as talking or driving. Recent studies suggest that narcolepsy may be the result of a genetic disorder.

SLEEP APNEA   **Sleep apnea** [*ap NEE uh*] is a condition in which breathing stops periodically during sleep. It may stop because of a blockage of the upper airway or when the brain interrupts its signals to breathe. When this happens, the sleeper partly awakes, gasps for breath, and then falls back to sleep. This may happen many times during the night, leaving the person feeling very tired by day.

SUMMARY

Your brain transmits and processes a multitude of informational messages. Although the activity of the brain slows down when you sleep, the brain continues to process information. Sleep is a vital part of wellness. While everyone has difficulty sleeping at times, some people will experience more serious problems.

LESSON 19.2   USING WHAT YOU HAVE LEARNED

REVIEW

1. What is an electroencephalograph?
2. Describe the cycles and stages of sleep and how people dream.

THINK CRITICALLY

3. What information might the brain process during sleep?
4. Episodes of narcolepsy can occur at any time without warning. How might this affect the person's day-to-day life?

APPLY IT TO YOURSELF

5. Your son has been studying late every night for an important test coming up at school. What would you say to him to help him understand that studying for shorter periods and getting a full night's sleep would be a better study strategy?

NERVOUS SYSTEM DISORDERS

The nervous system is subject to many disorders. Signs of a nervous system disorder may include pain, numbness in the limbs, or slurred speech. However, these symptoms also may be caused by other ailments. Because your nervous system controls and receives input from all parts of your body, it can warn you of many disorders. For example, a pain in the lower jaw that also runs down the left arm may be a symptom of a heart problem. Disorders of the nervous system can be grouped based on the cause or symptoms of the disorders.

HEADACHES

A headache is a common problem that affects most people. The level of pain from a headache varies from mild to severe. Headaches may be caused by muscle tension, stress, eyestrain, or sinus problems due to allergies or infections. Headaches also may be caused by a brain tumor, disease, or head injury. Few headaches are caused by problems in the nervous system, even though the pain of a headache is felt through the nervous system. Since your brain does not have sensory neurons for feeling pain, headaches do not arise from the brain itself. The actual pain you experience during a headache arises from the tissues surrounding your brain.

TENSION HEADACHE Muscle tension is a common cause of headaches. A tension headache can happen when the muscles of your neck or scalp tighten. This usually causes a dull, squeezing pain in your forehead, temples, or the back of your head and neck. A tension headache may be due to a physical problem, such as muscle strain, or it may be the result of stress, anxiety, or depression. It is best treated by removing the cause of the strain or tension. Rest or medication also may be used. If a headache lasts for several days, you should see a doctor.

MIGRAINE A **migraine** [*MY grayn*] is a severe headache caused by changes in the blood vessels in the brain. Before the pain begins, some people see bright spots or experience other unusual sensations. Pre-pain symptoms are referred to as the aura. This is followed by intense, throbbing pain, sensitivity to light, and often nausea. A migraine may come on quickly or it may build over several hours. It may occur repeatedly or very rarely.

There are many causes of migraines. This type of headache may be brought on by stress, drinking alcohol, smoking, eating particular foods, or changes in your daily routine. Treatment for migraines ranges from prescription medicines to relaxation techniques.

A headache may be caused by a variety of factors.

MAIN IDEAS

CONCEPTS
- ✔ The causes of many nervous system disorders are unknown.
- ✔ Most headaches are caused by tension.
- ✔ Some nervous system disorders are the result of serious accidents.

VOCABULARY

migraine	paralysis
concussion	paraplegia
contusion	quadriplegia
coma	degenerative
tumor	disorder
seizure	

Tips for protecting yourself against head injuries.

- Wear protective headgear during sports, when riding bike, and when working in dangerous places.
- Wear a safety belt when driving.
- Be careful when swimming or diving. Do not dive into shallow water, or where the bottom is rocky.

When Tai got home, she went straight to her room. All day long a terrible headache had been building in her. Now she felt really sick. She just wanted to lie down and rest, but even lying down caused nausea. Tai thought about taking some really strong medication that her mother had for migraines. "Anything to get rid of this pain," she thought. But Tai really didn't like taking pills, especially someone else's prescription. She decided to try to get rid of the migraine through relaxation. She pulled the shades in her room, propped up pillows on the bed to keep her at a 45° angle, and then closed her eyes and focused on pleasant thoughts.

STRUCTURAL DAMAGE

The tissue in your central nervous system is very delicate. Most of the time, your central nervous system is protected by the skull and vertebrae. However, any blow to the head or serious fall can cause an injury to the nervous system. Structural damage to the brain can be suspected after a doctor's evaluation and confirmed by using specialized technology. Magnetic resonance imagers and CT scans can take cross-sectional pictures of the brain and spinal cord, which helps identify the specific causes of problems.

HEAD INJURIES A brief loss of consciousness after a hard blow to the head is called a **concussion** [*kun KUSH un*]. Rest usually brings recovery. A very hard blow to the head may result in a contusion. A **contusion** [*kun TOO zhun*] is a bruise, which is a collection of blood in a damaged area.

A contusion of the brain tissue can be very serious, depending on the extent of the damage and on the amount of bleeding inside the brain. If a contusion creates a great deal of swelling on the brain, the person may be in serious danger. Because the brain is enclosed in the bony skull, any swelling causes internal pressure. Surgery may be necessary to drain some of the blood and relieve the pressure.

Severe damage may cause a coma that lasts for days or weeks. A **coma** [*KOH muh*] is a deep unconsciousness from which a person cannot be awakened. A coma also may be caused by a drug overdose, alcohol or carbon monoxide poisoning, or disease.

BRAIN TUMOR A **tumor** is an abnormal growth of cells. Brain tumors may develop for a variety of reasons and can occur at any age. Most brain tumors originated in another part of the body. The tumor cells moved through the bloodstream and settled in the brain. Symptoms of brain tumors include recurrent headaches, unexplained vomiting, sensory difficulty, problems with speech or movement, such as in the use of an arm or leg, or seizures. A **seizure** is a convulsive action caused by disorganized brain activity.

Wearing a helmet when riding a bike is one of the best safety precautions you can take.

SPINAL CORD INJURIES

An injury to the spinal cord can cause paralysis. **Paralysis** [*puh RAL ih sis*] is a loss of the ability to move a part of the body due to nerve or muscle damage. It may affect one little muscle or most of the body. **Paraplegia** [*par uh PLEE jee uh*] is the paralysis of the lower body and legs. **Quadriplegia** [*kwahd ruh PLEE jee uh*] is the paralysis of the body from the neck down.

Accidents are the most common causes of injuries to the spinal cord. Many injuries result from auto and work-related accidents. However, many spinal injuries are the result of accidents during recreational activities or carelessness around the home. You can prevent some of these injuries by following safety rules at work, at play, at home, and when riding in or driving a vehicle.

INFECTIONS

Infections of the nervous system are less common than infections of other systems of the body. Unlike the lungs and skin, the brain and spinal cord are well protected from the outside environment.

MAKING A DIFFERENCE

RESEARCH HEALTH

The Miami Project

Former Miami Dolphin football star Nick Buoniconti is back on the playing field—this time around, it's the corporate playing field. Buoniconti is the founder of the Miami Project to Cure Paralysis, a private research foundation dedicated solely to the research of new ways to treat—and possibly cure—paralysis due to spinal cord injuries. Buoniconti co-founded the Miami Project after his son was paralyzed during a college football game.

As few as ten years ago, injury to the spinal cord meant certain paralysis. Researchers working toward treatment and cure of spinal cord injury victims were told by other scientists that they were wasting their time. But today, because of the research conducted at the Miami Project and at similar institutions, there is evidence that nerves in the spinal cord and brain may indeed regenerate. Such news offers new hope to victims of spinal cord injuries.

The Miami Project is focusing on recent studies that show that dam-aged spinal cords are missing a coating of a fatty substance known as myelin. By replacing the myelin, there is hope that nerves may eventually regenerate and restore movement to previously paralyzed spinal cords.

Most of the research that is being conducted at the Miami Project and at research centers around the world involves laboratory animals rather than human subjects. There have been some promising results, and there is hope that some experimental procedures may work in humans in the not-so-distant future.

Spinal cord injuries afflict nearly 10,000 people each year in the United States. Fortunately, the number of spinal cord injuries is decreasing because of enforced speed limits on highways and increased safety awareness for high-risk sports. But with the efforts of research centers like the Miami Project, those whose injuries have restricted their movement may well

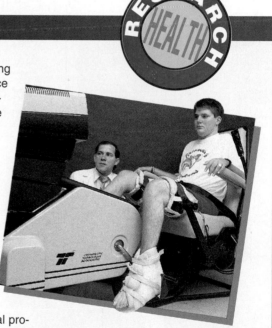

regain something they once thought was lost for good.

1. Why did Nicholas Buoniconti found the Miami Project?

2. Why do you think scientists continued their research of treatment and cure for spinal cord injuries when their scientific colleagues told them it was a waste of time?

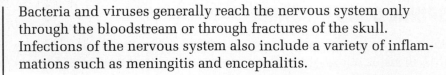
Physical therapy can help some people with nervous system disorders retain some control.

Bacteria and viruses generally reach the nervous system only through the bloodstream or through fractures of the skull. Infections of the nervous system also include a variety of inflammations such as meningitis and encephalitis.

MENINGITIS   An inflammation of the membranes around the brain and spinal cord is called meningitis [*men in JY tis*]. It may be caused by a bacterial or viral infection. Some types of meningitis spread from person to person, most commonly among children and teenagers. The signs are fever, severe headache, nausea, and vomiting. Other signs of meningitis include a stiff neck and being bothered by bright lights. Although most children recover, some types of meningitis can cause deafness, mental retardation, or death. When left untreated, bacterial meningitis can be fatal.

A vaccine is now available to protect against one form of bacterial meningitis. It is given at three different times during the first six months of life. Except for some older people, most adults are immune to this infection.

ENCEPHALITIS   An inflammation of the brain itself is called encephalitis [*en sef uh LY tis*]. It is caused by a viral infection of the central nervous system or another part of the body. In mild cases, the common signs are a headache, fever, loss of energy, and sometimes a stiff neck. In severe cases, victims feel drowsy and weak, may run a high fever, and may become unconscious. Brain function may be permanently affected, even after recovery.

POLIO   Polio, or infantile paralysis, is a highly contagious viral infection that attacks the central nervous system of its victims. The virus infects nerve cells in the brainstem or spinal cord, causing paralysis and muscle weakness. Ninety percent of all polio victims, mostly children, recover completely. However, adult polio can be very severe. Fortunately, polio can be prevented with vaccines.

DEGENERATIVE DISORDERS

Some nervous system disorders are caused by a progressive deterioration of vital tissues. Such disorders are called **degenerative disorders.** The causes of several nervous system disorders are unknown or only partly understood. These disorders may have long-lasting effects. In some cases, the disorders can be disabling.

MULTIPLE SCLEROSIS   A disease in which the tissue that surrounds and protects many nerve fibers is destroyed is called multiple sclerosis [*skluh ROH sis*]. It causes the patients to lose nervous system control over the body, especially the muscles. Patients develop a variety of symptoms that may affect coordination, vision, speech, and energy level. Symptoms may disappear and never return, or they may return years later. The cause of this condition is unknown.

Although there is no known cure for multiple sclerosis, its symptoms may be helped by exercise therapy to keep muscle tone. Certain medicines and lots of rest are also helpful to some people. Many people with multiple sclerosis are able to carry out normal activities.

CEREBRAL PALSY A general term for various disorders that result from brain injury during birth is cerebral palsy [*suh REE brul PAWL zee*]. Infections suffered by the mother or the presence of toxic substances in her blood during a fetus's development also may cause this disabling condition in the baby.

The effects of cerebral palsy range from a slight problem in coordinating the muscles to major handicaps. The symptoms may range from jerky movements to poor balance and speech problems. Special exercises help some people overcome the disability to some extent. In severe cases, braces and other supportive devices are helpful.

People with disabling disorders find ways to pursue their interests.

EPILEPSY

A disorder marked by sudden surges of electrical impulses in the brain is called epilepsy [*EP uh lep see*]. An attack of epilepsy is called a seizure. Some types of epilepsy may cause violent body shaking and loss of consciousness. Other types may cause just a brief clouding of consciousness, during which the person stares into space.

There are many causes of epilepsy. These include a chemical imbalance, an infection, a brain injury, a very high fever, or a tumor in the brain. In many cases, the cause is never known. Certain medicines can control the seizures and allow most epileptics to lead normal lives. Epilepsy in children often is a mild form of the disorder. It usually ends by adolescence.

 LESSON 19.3 USING WHAT YOU HAVE LEARNED

REVIEW

1. Describe a migraine headache and its symptoms.
2. What are concussions and contusions?

THINK CRITICALLY

3. Many head injuries occur during car accidents. Why do you think this happens? How can such injuries be prevented?
4. Degenerative disorders are the result of neural deterioration over a period of time. Why might it be very difficult for people to adjust to such disorders?

APPLY IT TO YOURSELF

5. Whenever you ride your bike, you wear a helmet. Some of your friends have been giving you a hard time about this practice. What would you say to your friends to explain how wearing a helmet protects you from a serious injury?

SUMMARY

Because the nervous system controls and receives input from the entire body, it often sounds the warning signal for many disorders. Disorders in the nervous system itself range from minor to major problems. The nervous system should be guarded as much as possible against injury.

HOW DRUGS AFFECT THE BODY

As you learned in the first lesson, neurotransmitters play a key role in the transmission of nerve impulses. Without these important natural body chemicals, you would be unable to feel, hear, think, speak, or move. Some disorders of the nervous system are the result of a natural deterioration of particular neurotransmitters. For example, Parkinson's disease—a disease that affects muscle movements—is caused by the absence of a neurotransmitter called dopamine.

The most subtle way in which neurotransmitters can be affected is through substances that are absorbed into your body. Because your body contains a unique chemical balance, any substances absorbed into your system will interact with your body's natural chemicals. Just as the wrong combination of chemicals can cause an explosion in the chemistry lab, so too can it cause a reaction within your body.

A chemical that causes changes in your body, your brain, or sometimes both is called a drug. The caffeine in a cola drink and the nicotine in a cigarette are commonly used drugs. Drugs that are used to treat or prevent illness are medicines. The ways in which a certain drug affects your body are determined by the nature of the drug, how the drug enters your body, and how the drug acts on your body or brain or both.

THE NATURE OF DRUGS

The chemicals that make up drugs may come from plants, animals, or minerals. Today many of the chemicals in drugs also are created artificially in a laboratory. These drugs are called synthetic drugs. All drugs are identified as legal or illegal.

LEGAL DRUGS The Food and Drug Administration (FDA) regulates the use of drugs. Legal drugs are those that are approved by the FDA for sale and use. Except for caffeine, nicotine, and alcohol, most legal drugs contain a chemical or chemicals designed to treat a medical problem.

Legal drugs that may be purchased without a doctor's prescription, or written order, are called **over-the-counter drugs**. Over-the-counter drugs include such items as mild pain relievers, cough syrups, and sleep aids. Although over-the-counter drugs are available to anyone, they are safe only when the instructions on the labels are followed.

Drugs available only with a doctor's written order for their preparation and use are called **prescription drugs**. The manufacture and sale of prescription drugs are regulated by laws to ensure the purity and safety of the drugs. These drugs are controlled more closely than

MAIN IDEAS

CONCEPTS

✔ The ways in which a drug affects the body are determined by the nature of the drug, how it enters the body, and how it interacts with the body chemistry.

✔ Many drugs can have dangerous effects on the body.

✔ Psychoactive drugs affect the mind and behavior of the user.

VOCABULARY

over-the-counter drug
prescription drug
psychoactive drug
side effect
dose

Figure 19-8   A close-up of the synaptic gap shows the importance of neurotransmitters in synaptic activity. What causes an impulse to cross over the gap?

neuron

receptor

neuro-
transmitter

synaptic
gap

neurotransmitter
vesicle

axon

over-the-counter drugs because they have more dangerous effects if used incorrectly. Before prescribing a drug, a doctor takes into consideration the condition of the patient and the particular medical problem being treated.

ILLEGAL DRUGS   Illegal drugs are those whose use or sale have been forbidden by law. Such drugs have been forbidden because their harmful effects outweigh any useful purposes. Illegal drugs are especially dangerous because there is no control over their manufacture or sale. Therefore, the user has no way of knowing exactly what is in an illegal drug. In spite of government efforts, illegal drugs have become a serious public health problem.

HOW DRUGS ENTER THE BODY

Drugs may be chewed, swallowed, injected, inhaled, sniffed, or applied to the skin. Most drugs are taken orally, or into the mouth, as capsules, tablets, or liquids. Drugs that are taken orally usually dissolve in the stomach and are absorbed through the small intestine. Because the breakdown and absorption of a drug by the digestive system takes time, it sometimes may be possible to remedy a dangerous or unexpected effect.

Some drugs can be absorbed into the bloodstream more rapidly than drugs taken orally. For example, drugs that are inhaled into the lungs are absorbed by the blood of the capillaries in the lungs. The speed with which an inhaled drug acts on the body depends on the size of the particles taken into the lungs and how readily they are absorbed into the blood. The effects of drugs that enter the bloodstream rapidly are hard to reverse.

DRUG ACTION

Drugs that are able to enter the brain and affect the mind and behavior of the user are called **psychoactive drugs** [*sy koh AK tiv*]. These include alcohol and nicotine, as well as all illegal drugs. Inside the brain, psychoactive drugs react with various neurotransmitters to speed up, slow down, or stop certain brain activities. Most psychoactive drugs can be grouped into five categories using the following classifications.

- Stimulants are drugs that speed up nerve activity.
- Depressants are drugs that slow down nerve activity.
- Narcotics are strong painkillers that produce a relaxed and dreamy state.
- Hallucinogens [*huh LOOS un uh junz*] are drugs that distort users' perceptions of their surroundings and their own bodies.
- Cannabis [*KAN uh bus*] includes drugs, such as marijuana, that come from the cannabis plant. These drugs create a euphoric, relaxed state.

When a drug interacts with the neurotransmitter in a synaptic gap, it alters the ability of the neurotransmitter to relay an impulse across the gap. For example, alcohol is a depressant. When a person

HEALTHY PEOPLE 2000

Increase the proportion of high school seniors who associate risk of physical or psychological harm with the heavy use of alcohol, regular use of marijuana, and experimentation with cocaine....

Objective 4.10
from *Healthy People 2000: National Health Promotion and Disease Prevention Objectives*

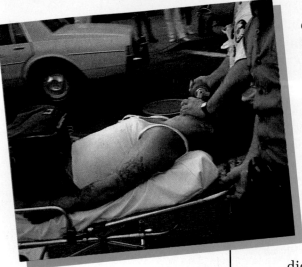

Your body's reactions to drugs sometimes can have deadly consequences.

drinks, the chemical compound in the alcohol slows down the action of certain neurotransmitters present at the synapse. This is the reason for the slowed reflexes of a person who has been drinking. Overuse of a psychoactive drug can permanently affect neurotransmitter activity.

Drugs rarely affect only one part of the body. A drug's chief effect is the physical or mental change for which it is taken. A different, unknown, or undesirable reaction to a drug is called a **side effect**. For example, two people may take aspirin for their headaches. The chief effect for both will be relief from pain. One person, however, may suffer a side effect of an upset stomach. The upset stomach may be the result of the aspirin irritating the lining of the stomach. Not all side effects can be predicted. For example, some drugs first thought to be safe have caused birth defects.

When a doctor prescribes a drug, she or he is very careful to consider the age and condition of the patient in determining the appropriate amount, or **dose**, of a drug that is prescribed. The doctor may warn the patient to watch for side effects. Because illegal drugs are not prescribed by a medical professional, the side effects can be unpredictable and very dangerous.

DRUG INTERACTIONS

When two or more drugs act on each other as well as on the body, the combined drugs may produce different effects, called synergistic effects [*sin ur JIS tik*], than either drug by itself. Synergistic effects often are unpredictable. Synergistic effects differ from person to person and depend on the amounts and qualities of the drugs involved.

LESSON 19.4 USING WHAT YOU HAVE LEARNED

REVIEW

1. Why are prescription drugs available only with a doctor's written order?
2. What is meant by a drug's side effect?

THINK CRITICALLY

3. The human body has its own unique blend of chemicals. Why is this important to remember when taking medication or eating certain foods?
4. All legal drugs are carefully tested before they are put out on the market. Why does a person still need to be very careful when taking a drug for the first time?

APPLY IT TO YOURSELF

5. One evening, before you went to bed, you drank a cola drink. That night you were unable to sleep. How might the cola have affected your ability to sleep?

SUMMARY

The way a drug affects your body is determined by the nature of the drug, how it enters your body, and how it interacts with your unique body chemistry. All drugs affect your body in some way. Over-the-counter and prescription drugs are strictly regulated. Illegal drugs are not regulated and therefore create a great problem. Psychoactive drugs affect the bodies and minds of users. Mixing drugs can cause unexpected, and sometimes dangerous, effects.

Burning the Candle

George had always had an unusual talent for music. He knew he wanted to pursue music as a career. As far as George was concerned, the first step toward that goal was to get into the School for Performing Arts in New York City. For several months before his audition, George had been spending every spare hour at the piano. In order to get his schoolwork done, he sometimes was up after midnight.

After several weeks, the long practice hours and late nights began to take their toll on George. He stopped caring about how he looked each day, he was irritable with friends and family, and his schoolwork was slipping. He had even fallen asleep in class a couple of times. George kept saying to himself, "I just need to get through these last few weeks."

Shortly before the audition, George's music teacher asked him to play for a group of other students. George was exhausted but he agreed to play. The first note he hit was wrong. From there he just couldn't find his way through the piece. He started again and again. Finally, overwhelmed by embarrassment, George stopped and left the room.

George knew that the reason he had done so badly was that he was tired. But now more than ever, he felt as though he needed the practice to do well for his audition. Three nights before the audition, George stayed up until 3:00 A.M. finishing a paper for school. The next night, as he sat down to practice, George's hands began to shake. "I'm so tired," he thought. "I don't know if I can keep going. But I've got to get this right if I want to be accepted."

PAUSE AND CONSIDER

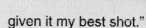

1. **Identify the Problem.**
   What is George's problem?

2. **Consider the Options.**
   What are George's options about preparing for the audition?

3. **Evaluate the Outcomes.**
   What could happen if George stays up late rehearsing? What might happen if he decides to get some sleep instead?

Torn by his desire to keep practicing and his need for sleep, George decided that he just had to sleep in order to be fresh and alert. He wasn't going to get anywhere if he was exhausted, and he certainly didn't want to repeat what happened at music class.

"I just can't do it," George decided. "I've been practicing for months. If I'm not ready now, I'll never be ready. A few more hours isn't going to make a difference. If I make it, I make it. If I don't, at least I will have given it my best shot."

George went to bed early for the first time in months. The next day he was still a little tired but much more refreshed. That evening, he ran through his audition piece a couple of times and then went to bed early again.

The morning of the audition, George felt better than he had in weeks. When he performed, the notes seemed to flow from his fingers. He felt that he had done well. George knew that he had given it his best effort.

DECIDE AND REVIEW

4. **Decide and Act.** What decision did George make about practicing for his audition? What action did he take?

5. **Review.** What other options might George have considered? Have you ever missed sleep in order to prepare for an important event? How did your sleeplessness affect your performance?

PROJECTS

1. Sleep apnea is a condition that can affect many areas of the body other than the brain. In fact, some forms of arthritis are thought to be related to sleep apnea. Research sleep apnea and its treatments, and present your findings in a report.

2. Many psychologists and psychiatrists throughout the years have tried to interpret the meaning of dreams. Some say that dreaming is a way of relieving anxiety. Others say that it is the voice of the unconscious. Research a theory about dream interpretation. Write a brief report that explains the theory and how it was developed. Include some examples of how the theory could be applied.

3. There are several different types of epilepsy. Do further research into epilepsy and identify the different types. Create a table that includes the following headings: *Type, Characteristics, Treatment.* Fill in the table with information you have collected.

WORKING WITH OTHERS

With a partner, choose two of the following neurotransmitters: acetylcholine, norepinephrine, dopamine, serotonin, and endorphins. Research the actions of each neurotransmitter. Find out as much as you can about how each is affected by different drugs and what kind of damage, if any, to the nervous system can result. Create a chart to illustrate your findings.

CONNECTING TO...

SCIENCE   Scientists are working to understand degenerative nerve disorders such as cerebral palsy and multiple sclerosis. Pick a nervous system disorder or disease, and find out about the scientific research taking place to treat or cure it.

USING VOCABULARY

brainstem
central nervous system
cerebellum
cerebral cortex
cerebrum
coma
concussion
contusion
dose
degenerative disorder
electroencephalograph
engram
hypothalamus
impulse
insomnia
interneuron
migraine
motor neuron
narcolepsy
nerve
nervous system
neuron
neurotransmitter
over-the-counter drug
paralysis
paraplegia
prescription drug
psychoactive drug
quadriplegia
rapid eye movement
reflex
reflex arc
seizure
sensory neuron
side effect
sleep apnea
stimulus
synapse
thalamus
tumor

Match each definition below with its vocabulary term above.

1. The stage of sleep during which dreams occur.
2. A different, unknown, or undesirable reaction to a drug.
3. The part of the brain that coordinates the muscles that are used for action.
4. Chemicals that trigger an impulse to pass across a synapse.
5. A severe headache that is caused by changes in the blood vessels in the brain.
6. The outer layer of the cerebrum.
7. Messages of sensation and information carried from one part of the body to another.
8. A hard blow to the head that causes unconsciousness.
9. A rapid, automatic response that does not involve the brain.
10. A condition in which a person stops breathing during sleep.
11. Drugs that enter the brain, affecting the mind and behavior.

CONCEPT MAPPING

On a separate sheet of paper, create a concept map for the *nervous system*. In your map, use as many of these concepts as you can: *disease, drugs, impulse, injury, interneuron, motor neuron, movement, nervous system, neurons, paralysis, polio, sensory neuron, stimuli.* You may use additional concepts related to the nervous system in your map. Information about concept mapping appears at the front of this book.

THINKING CRITICALLY

INTERPRET

LESSON 19.1
1. Identify four involuntary responses that are controlled by the nervous system.

2. Name the three parts of a neuron.

3. Which parts of the brain control balance?

4. How do you know how to repeat tasks such as tying shoes?

LESSON 19.2
5. Identify four possible causes of chronic insomnia.

6. How many stages of sleep are there? How many sleep cycles does a person usually experience each night?

7. When is a person most likely to remember a dream?

LESSON 19.3
8. Where does a headache actually arise?

9. Identify three possible causes of migraine headaches.

10. What is the most common cause of spinal cord injuries?

11. What is the difference between meningitis and encephalitis?

LESSON 19.4
12. Why are prescription drugs controlled more closely than over-the-counter drugs?

13. Identify five categories of psychoactive drugs. In which category is alcohol classified?

14. What factors help a doctor determine the dose of a medication?

APPLY

LESSON 19.1
15. As you cook dinner, you accidentally touch a hot pan. Describe your body's reaction to this event.

16. What part of the brain might be damaged if a person is suffering from loss of speech and memory? Loss of balance and coordination? Loss of control of eye movement?

LESSON 19.2
17. The average person needs between 7 and 9 hours of sleep each night. Why might some doctors recommend that teenagers get between 8 and 10 hours of sleep each night?

18. Tomás had stayed up late three nights in a row studying for an upcoming exam. The day after the third night, Tomás was very irritable at school and had a difficult time concentrating. How did Tomás's study habits affect his behavior?

LESSON 19.3
19. Why is a contusion potentially life-threatening?

20. Dorothy suddenly developed a stiff neck, severe headaches, nausea, and muscle weakness. When she went to see her doctor, he asked to see the record of her immunizations. Why would Dorothy's immunization record be helpful to her doctor?

LESSON 19.4
21. Why are the use and sale of illegal drugs forbidden by law?

22. Why is it important to undersand the effects that various drugs can have on your body?

Tobacco

"It's easy to stop smoking. I've done it thousands of times."

Mark Twain

BACKGROUND

Mark Twain was a writer and humorist considered by many to be the first truly American writer. His wit and wisdom are reflected in numerous essays and books, most notably *Tom Sawyer* and *Huckleberry Finn*.

Quitting smoking is *not* easy, as Mark Twain would have agreed. Each year, millions of Americans quit smoking—an act that results in a longer, healthier life. However, each year about one million young people start smoking, and thousands more begin using smokeless tobacco. As these young people soon learn, tobacco use is a fiercely addictive habit.

At one time, tobacco use was considered glamorous and sophisticated. Today, it is recognized as socially unacceptable, offensive, and dangerous—dangerous not only to the user but to other people as well. Each year, hundreds of thousands of people die from diseases related to tobacco use, including cancer, heart disease, and chronic lung disease. People who smoke have more colds, flu, and respiratory ailments than those who do not smoke. People who use smokeless tobacco have even higher rates of oral cancer than smokers do. Nonusers who breathe other people's tobacco smoke also suffer.

Clearly, there are no good reasons to use tobacco and many excellent reasons not to use it.

How aware are you about the dangers of tobacco use? Use the following checklist to take a closer look at your behavior and attitudes. On a sheet of paper or in your Wellness Journal, respond *yes* or *no* to each of the following statements.

1. I do not smoke or use smokeless tobacco.

2. I know that breathing other people's tobacco smoke is dangerous to my health.

3. I know that tobacco use contributes to chronic illness and life-threatening diseases.

4. When someone offers me a cigarette or some smokeless tobacco, I feel comfortable refusing.

5. I encourage people who are trying to stop using tobacco.

6. I discourage tobacco use among my friends who are beginning to try it.

7. I avoid places and situations where I'd have to breathe other people's tobacco smoke.

8. I practice healthy ways of dealing with stress.

9. I know that low-tar, low-nicotine cigarettes are not safer than regular cigarettes.

10. I know that using smokeless tobacco is not safe.

Review your responses, and try to decide which statements might be your strengths and weaknesses. Save your personal checklist for a follow-up activity that appears at the end of this chapter.

TOBACCO AND PEOPLE

All tobacco products are made from the dried and treated leaves of the tobacco plant. Cigarettes and pipe tobacco are made from crumbled tobacco leaves. Rolled tobacco leaves are used to make cigars. Leaves are ground up to make **smokeless tobacco** —tobacco that is inhaled or chewed rather than smoked. **Snuff** is finely ground tobacco that is sniffed or dipped, which means put into the mouth and held against the gums. **Chewing tobacco** is coarsely ground tobacco that is chewed and held in the mouth. Using any tobacco product, regardless of the form, is dangerous to your health.

TOBACCO'S POPULARITY

Until the late 1800s, chewing tobacco was widely used. Tobacco was also smoked in pipes or hand-rolled cigarettes. When a machine to make cigarettes was invented in 1891, cigarette smoking became more popular.

The popularity of smoking reached its height in 1964, when nearly 50 percent of all adults in the United States smoked. In that year, the Surgeon General's Report on Smoking and Health linked smoking to heart disease, lung cancer, and other diseases. Since 1964 the percentage of adult smokers in the United States has declined steadily and is now about 28 percent.

HEALTH WARNINGS

In 1966 the federal government began requiring cigarette manufacturers to clearly label all packages with this caution: *Cigarette smoking may be hazardous to your health.* In 1970 the caution was changed to a warning: *The Surgeon General has determined that cigarette smoking is dangerous to your health.* Today, even stronger warnings are required. One of the following warnings must appear on every cigarette package and in every printed advertisement for cigarettes:

- *Smoking causes lung cancer, heart disease, emphysema, and may complicate pregnancy.*
- *Cigarette smoke contains carbon monoxide.*
- *Smoking by pregnant women may result in fetal injury, premature birth, and low birth weight.*
- *Quitting smoking now greatly reduces serious risks to your health.*

A federal law also prohibits ads for tobacco products on television and radio. In addition, state and local laws now ban smoking in many public areas. Smoking also is banned on all airline flights within the 48 contiguous United States. These bans are designed to protect nonsmokers from the harmful effects of breathing other people's tobacco smoke.

What is this 1920s cigarette ad saying about smoking?

In 1986, in response to concerns about the use of smokeless tobacco, Congress passed a law requiring these warnings on all smokeless tobacco products.

- *This product may cause mouth cancer.*
- *This product may cause gum disease and tooth loss.*
- *This product is not a safe alternative to cigarettes.*

Most states have laws to protect young people from the risks of using tobacco. These laws prohibit tobacco products from being sold to or purchased by children and teenagers. Unfortunately, many communities do not strictly enforce these laws. As a result, many young people find it easy to obtain tobacco products.

WHY PEOPLE DO NOT USE TOBACCO

As you can tell from reading the warnings, tobacco use causes serious health problems. For this reason alone, many people choose not to use tobacco, and millions of users have given up the habit.

For most people today, tobacco use has become socially unacceptable. According to recent surveys, most teenagers and young adults prefer to date people who do not smoke. Most also think that becoming a smoker shows poor judgment. More and more people now recognize that tobacco use is unattractive, not glamorous and sophisticated. Tobacco use stains users' fingers and teeth and causes bad breath. It leaves a foul odor on clothes and in smokers' homes and cars. Smoking also causes premature wrinkling of the skin. Tobacco use is an expensive habit, too.

Smokeless tobacco products must carry warnings about their health risks.

TOBACCO IN HISTORY

Tobacco use was unknown to Europeans until the voyages of Christopher Columbus. As Columbus found, Native Americans used tobacco in religious and social ceremonies. They smoked it in pipes, chewed it, and also used snuff. Columbus brought tobacco samples back with him when he returned to Europe, but few people there used it.

In 1580, Sir Walter Raleigh started a smoking fad in Europe. Raleigh was a popular person in the English court of Queen Elizabeth I. When Raleigh started smoking tobacco in a pipe, many people copied him. Smoking soon spread to other European countries and to English colonies in Africa and Asia.

Tobacco growing and processing is one of the oldest industries in the United States. Tobacco's popularity in Europe helped the English colony at Jamestown, Virginia, survive. Jamestown was almost abandoned in 1614, but tobacco crops sold to England soon brought prosperity.

Although cigarette smoking is decreasing among all segments of the population, studies have shown that the smoking habit is usually established at an early age. It is a very difficult habit for young people to break. Teenagers often overrate their ability to quit.

- One study of high school seniors who smoked found that most of them began smoking in junior high school or in their early high school years.

- When people who had smoked a half pack a day as seniors were questioned five years later, they said they had tried to quit smoking but were unsuccessful.

- Of those people who had been daily smokers in high school, nearly 75 percent were still daily smokers—even though most of them had said in high school that they would *not* be smoking five years from then.

WHY PEOPLE START USING TOBACCO

Despite the decreasing popularity of tobacco, there are still more than 50 million users in the United States today. The reasons people start to use tobacco are many and complex. Studies have shown that stress, social pressures, and advertising are important influences on teenagers.

STRESS If you have already studied Chapter 5, "Managing Stress," you know that **stress** is the body's response to a physical or mental demand or pressure. Many young people start using tobacco as a way of coping with stress or uncomfortable feelings, such as depression, anger, frustration, boredom, anxiety, and nervousness. For example, people who are nervous or shy in social situations may begin smoking cigarettes because it gives them something to do with their hands. One key to avoiding tobacco use is to develop healthy ways of dealing with stress.

How might this smoker influence other teenagers to smoke?

SOCIAL PRESSURES People often start using tobacco to be like someone they admire—a friend, a parent, or a famous person. Many young people view tobacco use as a sign of adulthood. They think that using tobacco will make them appear sophisticated or in control of social situations. If a teenager's parents or other adult role models use tobacco, it may seem natural for

the teenager to try tobacco products. On the other hand, some children of nonsmokers try to show their independence by smoking.

Most young people start to use tobacco when it is offered to them by a friend. Peer pressure is a very strong force. If your friends use tobacco, refusing to try it may be difficult. Many young people know the dangers of tobacco use but think they will not be affected. They also underestimate the power of tobacco and think they can give it up anytime they want.

ADVERTISING In an effort to gain new customers, tobacco companies target some advertisements toward young people. In the early 1990s, for example, one company began using a sophisticated-looking animal cartoon character to promote smoking as a "smooth" thing to do. A study found that young children recognized this character as easily as they recognized Mickey Mouse. Thousands of parents and other adults voiced their outrage. The company denied that they were targeting the ads toward youngsters and continued using the character.

Whatever the age of the target audience, tobacco ads always show users as healthy, happy, attractive people. These images imply that if you use tobacco, you will be like those people—slim, calm, mature, glamorous, sophisticated, rugged, independent, or tough. The ads do not show coughing smokers with discolored teeth, prematurely wrinkled skin, and stained fingers. They do not show tobacco chewers spitting and dribbling tobacco juice. They do not show long-time smokers who suffer from lung disease having to breathe oxygen through a nasal tube while they do ordinary activities. In fact, tobacco companies deny that there *is* a direct connection between tobacco use and poor health.

Many long-time smokers with lung disease must breathe oxygen from a tank. Cigarette ads never show this result of smoking.

HOW PEOPLE BECOME ADDICTED

Tobacco use is not just a bad habit, like biting your nails. Tobacco use is an addiction. An **addiction** [*uh DIK shun*] is a strong physical and psychological craving for a substance. The addictive substance in tobacco is **nicotine** [*NIK uh teen*]. Nicotine addiction causes tobacco users to progress from experimentation and occasional use to regular use.

EXPERIMENTATION The first few times people try using tobacco, they may experience very unpleasant effects. The main effects are dizziness and nausea. Inhaling makes beginning smokers cough as their bodies try to reject the foreign material. Many first-time users react to these unpleasant effects by deciding not to use tobacco again. Others keep trying tobacco until they overcome the unpleasant effects. Once the user's body becomes conditioned to nicotine, each dose produces a brief "lift." This feeling of well-being and pleasure reinforces the desire to use tobacco again—and the user is hooked.

HEALTHY PEOPLE 2000

Reduce the initiation of cigarette smoking by children and youth so that no more than 15 percent have become regular cigarette smokers by age 20.

Objective 3.5
from *Healthy People 2000: National Health Promotion and Disease Prevention Objectives*

OCCASIONAL USE   A small percentage of people who use tobacco use it only at certain times, such as at a party, after a meal, or when going out with friends. Occasional use may seem harmless, but using tobacco in *any* amount can have serious health consequences. Also, for many young people, occasional use leads to regular use.

REGULAR USE   Most people who use tobacco do so every day, usually in a set pattern. Whenever the nicotine level in the brain and bloodstream drops, the user craves another dose. Regular users become accustomed to their daily pattern of nicotine intake. They use tobacco without even thinking about it.

Regular users are physically addicted to nicotine. They have a great need to satisfy their craving. They also find it extremely difficult to get through the day without tobacco. Regular users also are psychologically addicted to the behaviors associated with tobacco use. For example, cigarette smokers say that they enjoy the act of smoking. Lighting the cigarette, inhaling and exhaling the smoke, and even watching the exhaled smoke are relaxing to them.

CIGARETTES: THE "BUSY" DRUG

No other drug keeps a user as busy taking it as does tobacco. In an average day, for example, a two-pack-a-day cigarette smoker spends three to four hours with a cigarette in his or her mouth, hand, or ashtray and takes about 400 puffs of smoke.

Often, when regular users try to quit or to reduce their tobacco use, they become irritable, depressed, anxious, restless, and tired. These are all common symptoms of withdrawal from nicotine. A major reason that regular users continue using tobacco is to avoid these symptoms.

SUMMARY

Tobacco use has steadily declined since 1964, when the Surgeon General's report linked smoking with serious health problems. However, each year many young people start using tobacco to cope with stress or in response to social pressures and advertisements. Because the nicotine in tobacco products is addictive, people who use tobacco regularly have trouble quitting, even when they want to stop.

LESSON 20.1   USING WHAT YOU HAVE LEARNED

REVIEW

1. Identify four health problems caused by tobacco use.
2. Describe three reasons that many people choose not to use tobacco.
3. Why is quitting so difficult for regular users of tobacco?

THINK CRITICALLY

4. Look through some entertainment or sports magazines to find ads for cigarettes. What strategies have the advertisers used to present a positive image of smoking? What messages are being communicated by the ads?
5. One warning on smokeless tobacco products is *This product is not a safe alternative to cigarettes.* Why is that true?

APPLY IT TO YOURSELF

6. Imagine you are a parent who has just found a pack of cigarettes hidden in your 13-year-old daughter's laundry bag. What would you say to her?

TOBACCO'S EFFECTS ON THE BODY

Medical research has shown over and over again that tobacco has many harmful effects on the body. Tobacco leaves contain more than 2,500 different chemicals. Tobacco smoke contains more than 4,000 chemicals. Many of these chemicals are toxic. In fact, over 40 chemicals in tobacco smoke and an even greater number in smokeless tobacco have been identified by scientists as known carcinogens. **Carcinogens** [*kahr SIN uh junz*] are substances that cause cancer.

CIGARETTES

Tobacco smoke is a combination of hot gases and tiny particles. The three most dangerous substances in tobacco smoke are nicotine, carbon monoxide, and tars.

NICOTINE   As you learned earlier, nicotine is the addictive substance in tobacco. Inhaling tobacco smoke is the fastest way of getting nicotine into the blood and to the brain. For this reason, cigarette smokers absorb nicotine more quickly than people who use smokeless tobacco. They also absorb it more quickly than pipe and cigar smokers, who usually do not inhale.

In its pure form, nicotine is a deadly poison. Heavy smokers absorb enough nicotine in a day to kill them if it were put into their bloodstream all at once. Nicotine poisoning causes dizziness, nausea, faintness, clammy skin, and sometimes vomiting and diarrhea. Any smoker may suffer from nicotine poisoning by smoking too many cigarettes too quickly.

From the first puff, cigarette smoke changes the way the body works. Nicotine causes certain glands to release **adrenaline** [*uh DREN ul un*], the hormone that prepares your body to fight danger or flee from it. Usually only an emergency releases adrenaline into the bloodstream. When a person smokes, however, adrenaline is released after every dose of nicotine. This rush of adrenaline makes the smoker feel more alert.

Adrenaline speeds up the heart rate and makes the blood vessels constrict. This combination increases the smoker's blood pressure. The constricted vessels also prevent blood from flowing easily to the hands, feet, and skin. The reduced blood flow lowers the skin temperature.

CARBON MONOXIDE   Cigarette smoke contains several gases. One is carbon monoxide, the same deadly gas contained in automobile exhaust. What makes carbon monoxide so dangerous? It is picked up by the body's red blood cells more easily than oxygen. As a result, carbon monoxide takes the place of oxygen in the blood, so the smoker's body does not receive enough oxygen. Lack of oxygen can affect the smoker's vision, hearing, and judgment. It also may cause shortness of breath.

MAIN IDEAS

CONCEPTS

✔ The most harmful substances in tobacco smoke are nicotine, carbon monoxide, and tars.

✔ Smoking low-tar, low-nicotine cigarettes does not reduce the risk of serious health problems.

✔ People who use smokeless tobacco are exposed to more cancer-causing substances than people who smoke.

VOCABULARY

carcinogen	tars
adrenaline	cilia

The unpleasant effects that beginning smokers experience are actually a mild form of nicotine poisoning.

Costs of Smoking

A lot of people have trouble saving money regularly for something special—a vacation, a car, a house, a college education. But for those who smoke, quitting may be the first step toward getting something they really want.

Smoking costs around $2,000 a year for the average smoker. The cost is climbing each year as the price of cigarettes and the taxes on them increase. But smoking takes other financial tolls. Smokers generally spend more money on personal care services and products such as breath mints and throat lozenges, and more frequent trips to the dentist for teeth cleaning. Smokers' medical costs are generally higher due to more frequent colds, bronchitis, and more serious diseases such as cancer and heart disease.

Smokers tend to dirty their clothes, their furniture, and their houses much more than their non-smoking neighbors. The costs for repairing a burnt coat, couch, or car seat or cleaning or repainting walls, ceilings, or furniture can add up.

The dangers of smoking to your health are inarguable. But the financial costs are prohibitive as well. The answer, of course, is never to start the habit or to quit now before the costs dip more deeply into your pocket.

TARS Tars are tiny particles in cigarette smoke that form a sticky mixture in the air passages and lungs. This mixture interferes with normal air flow, making it harder for a smoker to breathe. In addition, tars contain carcinogens that cause lung cancer. Researchers have estimated that a pack-a-day smoker inhales about one cup of tars each year.

As explained in Chapter 14, "Circulation and Respiration," your air passages are lined with mucous membrane. This membrane traps bacteria, dust, and other foreign particles. Projecting from the membrane are tiny hairlike structures called **cilia** [*SIL ee uh*]. Cilia move in waves to eliminate the trapped particles and keep your air passages clean.

In smokers, tars stick to the mucous membrane and paralyze the cilia, eventually killing them. Without the wave-like action of the cilia, mucus and foreign particles build up in the air passages. This buildup produces a chronic cough as the smoker's body tries to eliminate the mucus. Also, bacteria and other disease-causing organisms remain in the air passages. Because of this, a smoker is more vulnerable to infections.

Are low-tar, low-nicotine cigarettes safer than regular cigarettes?

LOW-TAR, LOW-NICOTINE CIGARETTES   As the health risks of smoking became widely known, tobacco companies reacted by developing low-tar, low-nicotine cigarettes. These cigarettes are promoted as being safer than regular cigarettes, but they are not. Studies have shown that smoking low-tar, low-nicotine cigarettes does *not* reduce the risk of heart disease, chronic lung disease, oral cancer, and other diseases.

These cigarettes are made with denser filters, thinner paper, and air holes. These methods do not reduce the amount of tar and nicotine in the tobacco. They simply reduce the amount of smoke that reaches the smoker. Just as important, filters cannot remove toxic carbon monoxide or other gases from the smoke. Also, smokers who switch to low-tar, low-nicotine cigarettes often do not reduce their intake of nicotine, carbon monoxide, and tars.

 Rosita knew that her pack-a-day cigarette habit was the cause of her bad cough. She decided to switch to a low-tar, low-nicotine brand, thinking it would be less irritating. After a few weeks, though, she noticed that her cough wasn't clearing up. She also realized that she was smoking close to two packs a day now.

"This is foolish!" Rosita thought. "The only way I'm going to get rid of this cough is to get rid of cigarettes!" She called her doctor to find out about stop-smoking programs.

ARE CLOVE CIGARETTES SAFE?

Since the early 1980s, Indonesian clove cigarettes, called *kretek*, have become quite popular among young people in this country. Users think that these cigarettes are safer than regular cigarettes. The truth is, they are not.

Contrary to what many people think, clove cigarettes do contain tobacco. About 60 percent of each clove cigarette is low-grade tobacco. This tobacco produces a high level of toxic gases and tars when smoked. In fact, clove cigarettes deliver *twice as much* nicotine, carbon monoxide, and tars as regular cigarettes.

Clove cigarettes have been directly linked to severe illness and even death in some otherwise healthy young adults. Because of these risks, some states are working to ban the purchase and sale of clove cigarettes.

PIPES AND CIGARS

Pipe and cigar smokers rarely inhale the tobacco smoke. As a result, these smokers are generally at lower risk for developing lung cancer. However, they are at very high risk for developing oral cancer. Also, pipe and cigar smokers who do inhale are at higher risk of lung cancer than cigarette smokers. This is because pipe and cigar smoke contains more tars than cigarette smoke.

Some cigarette smokers believe that switching to cigars or a pipe will be better for them because they will smoke less often. However, cigarette smokers who switch are likely to smoke more often and inhale more deeply than pipe and cigar smokers who have never smoked cigarettes. Thus, the health risks to smokers who switch are not reduced.

SMOKELESS TOBACCO

Although smoking is steadily declining in this country, the use of smokeless tobacco is steadily increasing. The majority of new users each year are preteen and teenaged males.

Some advertisements for snuff and chewing tobacco suggest that smokeless products are safer than cigarettes. This claim is not true.

HEALTHY PEOPLE 2000

Reduce smokeless tobacco use by males aged 12 through 24 to a prevalence of no more than 4 percent.

Objective 3.9
from *Healthy People 2000: National Health Promotion and Disease Prevention Objectives*

■ SMOKELESS TOBACCO USE BY TEENAGE MALES

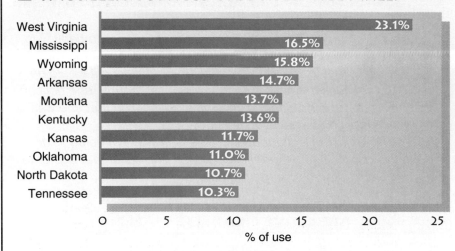

West Virginia — 23.1%
Mississippi — 16.5%
Wyoming — 15.8%
Arkansas — 14.7%
Montana — 13.7%
Kentucky — 13.6%
Kansas — 11.7%
Oklahoma — 11.0%
North Dakota — 10.7%
Tennessee — 10.3%

% of use

Source : Office on Smoking and Health, Department of Health and Human Services

Figure 20-1   This graph shows the ten states with the highest use of smokeless tobacco by teenage males age 16 and older. In what ways are these states similar?

Smokeless tobacco users do not inhale carbon monoxide and tars. They do, however, take in nicotine and are exposed to carcinogens. In fact, as you learned earlier, smokeless tobacco contains an even greater number of known carcinogens than does tobacco smoke. Because of these higher levels of carcinogens, smokeless tobacco users have a greater risk of developing cancer of the mouth and throat than smokers do. Smokeless tobacco users also experience dental problems such as gum disease and tooth loss more often than smokers.

When smokeless tobacco is chewed, sniffed, or dipped, nicotine is absorbed through the mucous membrane in the nose and mouth and enters the bloodstream. This process is more gradual than the absorption of nicotine in a smoker's lungs. However, the nicotine in smokeless tobacco has the same physical and psychological effects—and is just as addictive—as the nicotine in tobacco smoke.

SUMMARY

There are no safe forms of tobacco. The most dangerous substances in tobacco smoke are nicotine, carbon monoxide, and tars. Nicotine causes increased heart rate, constricted blood vessels, and higher blood pressure. Carbon monoxide reduces the amount of oxygen carried by the blood. Tars obstruct air passages and cause cancer. People who use smokeless tobacco are exposed to nicotine and to even higher levels of carcinogens than tobacco smokers.

LESSON 20.2 USING WHAT YOU HAVE LEARNED

REVIEW

1. What are tars?
2. Why are low-tar, low-nicotine cigarettes unsafe alternatives to regular cigarettes?
3. Identify two health risks associated with smokeless tobacco.

THINK CRITICALLY

4. Tars paralyze and kill cilia in the air passages. Why is this damage to the cilia harmful to the smoker?
5. Suppose a new type of tobacco were developed that did not contain nicotine. Would this make tobacco use safer? Explain your answer.

APPLY IT TO YOURSELF

6. Imagine you are a dentist working on the teeth of a teenaged boy who has started to dip snuff. What would you say to try to convince him to stop this habit?

TOBACCO'S LONG-TERM RISKS

The harmful effects of tobacco use worsen and multiply over time. If you are healthy, using tobacco can make you sick. If you are sick, using tobacco can make it harder for you to recover. Nonsmokers are harmed when they are exposed to secondhand smoke. Even fetuses are affected by tobacco use.

RISKS FOR TOBACCO USERS

Smoking is the major cause of premature, preventable death in the United States. Smoking causes heart disease, different types of cancer, and chronic lung disease. Smoking is also a contributing factor in other serious health problems. Smokers require medical care and hospitalization more often than nonsmokers.

People who use smokeless tobacco are not immune from health risks. In fact, smokeless tobacco users have even higher rates of some types of cancers than smokers do.

HEART DISEASE   The majority of tobacco users smoke cigarettes. For this reason, most of the known long-term risks relate to cigarette smoking. It is well established that cigarette smoking is a primary cause of coronary heart disease. In this disease, the coronary arteries supplying the heart become blocked by atherosclerosis. **Atherosclerosis** [*ath uh roh skluh ROH sus*] is a buildup of fatty material on the artery walls. Eventually the blockage cuts off the blood supply to the heart tissue, resulting in a heart attack.

Smoking contributes to atherosclerosis in several ways. It damages the lining of the arteries. It raises total blood cholesterol while lowering "good" cholesterol. It also makes blood platelets stickier so they clot more easily. As you learned in the previous lesson, nicotine raises blood pressure. Also, carbon monoxide reduces the amount of oxygen in the blood.

All of these effects of smoking place a great strain on the heart. Heredity, stress, diet, and exercise also play important roles in heart disease. However, according to the Surgeon General, smoking is the most controllable risk factor.

CANCER   Tobacco use is the leading cause of deaths due to cancer in the United States. **Cancer** is an abnormal, uncontrolled growth of cells that invade and destroy healthy tissue. As you learned earlier, both smoking tobacco and smokeless tobacco contain a large number of carcinogens. The most common types of cancer caused by tobacco use are lung cancer, oral cancer, and throat cancer.

Most cases of lung cancer are a direct result of smoking cigarettes. Lung cancer is difficult to detect in its early stages. Its primary symptoms are shortness of breath and coughing up mucus, sometimes with blood in it. These symptoms are so similar to a

MAIN IDEAS

CONCEPTS

✔ Smoking causes heart disease, different types of cancer, and chronic lung disease.

✔ People who use smokeless tobacco have an even greater risk of oral cancer than do smokers.

✔ Passive smoking causes serious health problems for nonsmokers.

VOCABULARY

atherosclerosis
cancer
leukoplakia
larynx
bronchitis
emphysema
stroke
passive smoking
mainstream smoke
sidestream smoke

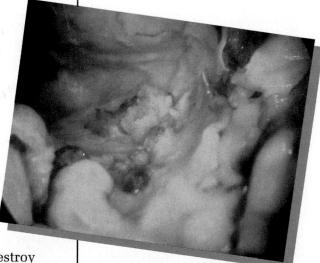

This is a highly magnified view of the inside of an artery. The yellowish material is fatty buildup from atherosclerosis.

Compare the lung tissue from a smoker (left) with the lung tissue from a nonsmoker (right). What differences can you see?

smoker's usual health problems that many smokers ignore the symptoms. By the time the patient consults a doctor, the cancer may be too far advanced and may have spread to other parts of the body.

If lung cancer is discovered in its early stages, it is treated by surgically removing all or part of the diseased lung. If the cancer is discovered too late or recurs after surgery, the patient's chances for recovery are poor. Anticancer drugs and radiation therapy can be used to help prolong the patient's life and ease pain.

Oral cancer is cancer of the mouth, including the tongue and lips. All tobacco users risk developing oral cancer. However, smokeless tobacco users are at a greater risk than smokers because of the higher level of carcinogens in smokeless tobacco. Smokers and smokeless users who also drink alcohol have an even higher risk. Oral cancer may occur anywhere that tobacco or its smoke has come in contact with the delicate tissues of the mouth. Most often, the first warning sign is **leukoplakia** [*loo koh PLAY kee uh*], white patches on the lips, gums, tongue, or inner cheeks. Leukoplakia itself is not a form of cancer. However, it can lead to cancer, especially in tobacco users.

Another type of cancer commonly associated with smoking is cancer of the larynx. The **larynx** [*LAR ingks*] contains your vocal

SMOKING: THE GRIM STATISTICS

Every day in the United States, more than 50 million smokers consume 80 million packs of cigarettes—almost 30 *billion* packs every year.

- Every year more than 360,000 premature deaths occur due to smoking: 130,000 premature deaths from cancer, 170,000 from heart disease, and 60,000 from chronic lung diseases.

- Smokers are twice as likely as nonsmokers to suffer a heart attack and four times as likely to die from it.

- Smokers are 14 times more likely to die from lung, throat, and mouth cancer than nonsmokers.

- About 85 percent of all deaths from lung cancer are caused by smoking.

- Cigarette smoking is a major cause of stroke, the third leading cause of death in the United States.

- Every year smoking-related diseases kill more Americans than cocaine, heroine, alcohol abuse, auto accidents, homicide, and suicide *combined*.

Every year an estimated one million young people—3,000 every day—start smoking.

cords and is your voice organ. The main symptom of this type of cancer is persistent hoarseness. If cancer of the larynx is diagnosed early enough, it can be cured by radiation therapy or by removing part of a vocal cord. If the cancer is more advanced, the entire larynx must be removed. The patient then must learn to speak with air burped from the esophagus or with an electronic voice aid.

In addition to the above types of cancer, smoking increases the risk of cancer of the esophagus, stomach, pancreas, kidneys, and bladder. In women, smoking has been linked with an increased risk of cancer of the cervix.

CHRONIC LUNG DISEASE   A chronic disease is one that is long lasting, recurs regularly, and requires repeated or continuous treatment. Cigarette smoking is the major cause of chronic lung disease in the United States. These diseases include chronic bronchitis and emphysema.

If you have already studied the respiratory system in Chapter 14, "Circulation and Respiration," you know that **bronchitis** [*brahn KYT us*] is an inflammation of the mucous membrane that lines the air passages, or bronchial tubes. Tobacco smoke irritates the mucous membrane, and the air passages become clogged with mucus. The accumulation of mucus causes coughing, difficulty in breathing, and a heavy feeling in the chest. The only effective treatment for chronic bronchitis caused by smoking is to stop smoking.

Smoking also causes **emphysema** [*em fuh ZEE muh*], a disease in which lung tissue is destroyed and air sacs are lost. The lungs become unable to deflate fully during exhaling. As a result, normal gas exchange in the lungs cannot occur, and the person has great difficulty in breathing. Even the smallest effort causes shortness of

A smoker whose cancerous larynx must be removed can learn to speak with an electronic voice aid.

SMOKELESS TOBACCO: THE GRIM STATISTICS

More than 12 million people in the United States use smokeless tobacco regularly. Of those users, about 3 million are under age 21.

- Smokeless tobacco delivers 10 times as many cancer-causing substances to the bloodstream as do cigarettes.
- The risk of oral cancer is four times as high in smokeless tobacco users as in nonusers. The risk increases to *50 times as high* with long-term use.
- About 30,000 new cases of oral cancer occur each year.
- Because oral cancer is often discovered too late, only about 50 percent of oral cancer patients survive 5 years.

Adolescent males are the fastest-growing group of smokeless tobacco users.

breath. Emphysema has no cure. Quitting smoking will keep the disease from getting worse, but the damage that has already been done is permanent.

OTHER HEALTH PROBLEMS   Both smoking and smokeless tobacco use are associated with a range of health problems. As you learned earlier, smoking contributes to atherosclerosis and high blood pressure. Both of these conditions can cause a stroke. A **stroke** is a sudden disruption of the blood supply to a part of the brain. The lack of blood kills nerve tissue in that part. A stroke can cause severe physical and mental disabilities or even death.

Smokers in general are not as healthy as nonsmokers. Smoking damages the body systems that protect a person from disease. Smoking also triggers allergies and may lead to inflammation and swelling of the sinuses. Smokers suffer from the common cold more often than nonsmokers. Smokers' colds are often more serious than those of nonsmokers. Smokers are also more likely to get infectious lung diseases such as influenza and pneumonia.

Other health problems caused by tobacco use are noncancerous diseases that affect the gums and teeth. Smoking and smokeless tobacco use contribute to tooth loss, gum disease, and delayed healing after dental surgery. Smoking, chewing, and dipping stain the teeth and give the user chronic bad breath. Chewing tobacco contains grit that wears away the surfaces of the teeth.

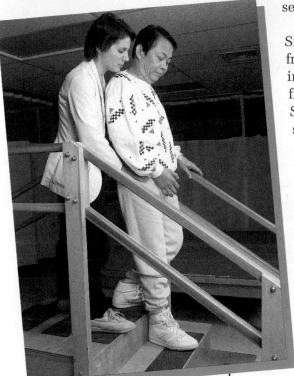

This stroke patient is learning to walk normally again. How can smoking lead to a stroke?

RISKS FOR NONSMOKERS

Smokers are not the only people who suffer negative effects from smoking. Each year hundreds of nonsmokers die in fires ignited by the careless handling and disposal of cigarettes. Many of the innocent victims are infants and children. Smokers also harm family members, friends, and co-workers with their smoke.

PASSIVE SMOKING   **Passive smoking** means breathing air that has been contaminated with tobacco smoke. Passive smoking has serious health consequences for nonsmokers. In fact, about 50,000 nonsmokers die each year from health problems caused by passive smoking. Nonsmokers who suffer from asthma, emphysema, heart disease, or other serious conditions are particularly vulnerable, as are infants and young children. Because of the harmful effects of second-hand smoke, more than 30 states have passed laws that limit or prohibit smoking in certain public areas.

A passive smoker breathes two types of smoke: mainstream smoke and sidestream smoke. **Mainstream smoke** is smoke that has been inhaled and then exhaled by the smoker. **Sidestream smoke** is smoke from the burning end of a cigarette, cigar, or pipe. Sidestream smoke is more harmful than mainstream smoke. Sidestream smoke contains twice as much tar and nicotine and five times as much carbon monoxide as mainstream smoke. It also contains much higher levels of other harmful substances.

Children of smoking parents are especially at risk from passive smoking. These children tend to have more infections, miss more time from school, and need more days of hospital care than the children of parents who do not smoke.

PREGNANCY AND SMOKING   The fetus of a pregnant woman who smokes is a passive smoker. Obviously, a fetus does not inhale contaminated air. However, nicotine, carbon monoxide, and other harmful substances pass from the mother's bloodstream to the fetus's bloodstream through the placenta.

Since carbon monoxide competes with oxygen, smoking reduces the oxygen supply to the fetus. For example, a pregnant woman who smokes two packs of cigarettes a day cuts her fetus's oxygen supply by 40 percent. Nicotine increases the fetus's heart rate and blood pressure. It also upsets chemical balances, interferes with vitamin use, and delays development of the fetus.

Pregnant women who smoke double their risk of miscarriage. They also experience more stillbirths and premature births than nonsmokers. In general, babies born to women who smoke weigh less than babies born to women who do not smoke. The babies of smokers also have a higher rate of birth defects and a lower survival rate. Because nicotine is excreted in breast milk, a baby can receive nicotine when breast-fed by a mother who smokes.

Most women who use tobacco are cigarette smokers. For this reason, smokeless tobacco's effects on fetuses have not been well studied. It is likely that the nicotine in smokeless tobacco has the same general effects on fetuses as the nicotine in cigarettes.

What term describes the child in this situation?

LESSON 20.3 USING WHAT YOU HAVE LEARNED

REVIEW

1. Name three long-term health problems that are associated with tobacco use.
2. Name and describe the two types of tobacco smoke inhaled by passive smokers.

THINK CRITICALLY

3. Sidestream smoke contains higher levels of nicotine, carbon monoxide, and tars than mainstream smoke. Why do you think this is so?
4. Many women who become pregnant decide to give up smoking until after the baby is born. Explain what is wrong with this approach.

APPLY IT TO YOURSELF

5. Imagine you are a high school health teacher. Despite your efforts to educate students about the risks of tobacco use, many student athletes use smokeless tobacco. What might you be able to do to stop this behavior?

SUMMARY

Tobacco use greatly increases the risk of developing heart disease, lung cancer, oral cancer, and chronic lung disease. Smokers suffer from these and other diseases on a much greater scale than nonsmokers. Smokeless tobacco users have an even higher risk of developing oral cancer than smokers do. Nonsmokers also suffer the harmful effects of tobacco smoke. Pregnant women who smoke may harm their fetuses.

QUITTING TOBACCO USE

Every year over one million people in the United States stop using tobacco. For most users, quitting is not easy. Because nicotine is an addictive substance, a user must go through a period of physical and psychological withdrawal before feeling comfortable as a nonuser. Regardless of how difficult quitting may be, however, the benefits are well worth the effort.

THE BENEFITS OF QUITTING

Many tobacco users are not aware of the positive aspects of quitting. They think of "giving up" tobacco as a negative action that will deprive them of something desirable—which tobacco *is* to the addicted user. Often, understanding the benefits of quitting helps people start trying to quit.

HEALTH BENEFITS   When someone stops using tobacco, the body immediately begins to clean itself. During the first 24 hours, the levels of nicotine and carbon monoxide in the bloodstream rapidly drop. Without repeated doses of nicotine, the heart rate decreases, blood vessels no longer constrict unnaturally, and blood pressure is lowered. Without carbon monoxide, the amount of oxygen in the bloodstream increases.

Within a few days, a smoker's chronic cough begins to clear up, although coughing may continue for a few weeks. With the source of irritation from smoke removed, cilia in the air passages begin to recover. The lungs slowly clear, and breathing is easier—even for someone with permanent damage from emphysema. Colds and lung infections occur less often.

In time, much of the damage caused by tobacco is reversed, even in heavy users. Long-term studies of smokers who quit show a steady decline in their risk of heart disease, chronic lung disease, lung cancer, oral cancer, and other types of cancers. Within two years, the ex-smoker's risks of heart and lung disease are about the same as those of someone who never smoked.

OTHER BENEFITS   People who quit soon discover that food tastes better. Their sense of smell improves, and the bad taste in their mouth disappears. They sleep more soundly and feel more alert and rested when they wake up. Quitting improves ex-users' appearance, too. Tobacco stains on their teeth and fingers fade. Their breath and clothing smell fresher. Their skin looks healthier as their blood circulation improves. Ex-users also save money when they stop buying tobacco products.

Some of the most satisfying benefits of quitting are psychological. Ex-users feel a great sense of pride when they break their addiction. Succeeding at such a difficult task makes ex-users feel very good about themselves. They also feel great relief to be finally free of tobacco.

Breaking free of the tobacco habit is rewarding in many ways.

WHAT TO EXPECT

Tobacco users typically experience certain withdrawal symptoms when they quit. **Withdrawal symptoms** are uncomfortable reactions that occur when a person stops using an addictive substance. Figure 20-2 lists common withdrawal symptoms associated with tobacco use. Keep in mind that these symptoms are typical, not universal. Different tobacco users experience withdrawal in different ways.

Two or three days after quitting, most of the nicotine in the ex-smoker's body is gone. Within a week the remainder disappears. Once nicotine is eliminated, physical dependence is broken. However, psychological dependence may continue for some time.

BJ paced nervously as he waited for his turn in the roping competition. He'd quit using snuff three months ago, but now he wanted some. When he noticed another competitor taking a pinch, BJ's craving suddenly became intense. "Maybe just one," he thought. "It'll calm me down so I can concentrate."

The other competitor noticed BJ watching and held the tin out to him. "Want some?" he asked.

BJ almost took the tin, but then he thought, "Wait a minute! I've been practicing for weeks. If I'm not good enough by now, a pinch won't make me any better."

"No, thanks," BJ answered with a smile. "I don't use it any more."

Figure 20-2   These withdrawal symptoms are common, but not every ex-user experiences every symptom.

◆ WITHDRAWAL SYMPTOMS

Symptom	Duration	Cause
Craving for tobacco*	Most frequent during first 2 or 3 days, then tapers off; may recur occasionally for weeks, months, or years	addiction to nicotine
Dizziness	1 or 2 days	more oxygen in bloodstream
Coughing, dry throat, postnasal drip	a few days	body getting rid of accumulated mucus
Tight feeling in chest	a few days	physical tension; sore muscles from coughing
Trouble sleeping*	1 week	nicotine affects brain function and sleep patterns
Constipation, gas, abdominal pain	1 or 2 weeks	intestinal movements decrease briefly
Irritability*	2 to 4 weeks	addiction to nicotine
Tiredness*	2 to 4 weeks	body no longer being stimulated by nicotine
Difficulty concentrating*	a few weeks	body needs to adjust to lack of nicotine
Hunger*	up to several weeks	nicotine craving confused with hunger; desire for something in the mouth

*These symptoms are typical for both smokers and smokeless tobacco users.

HOW TO QUIT

If you are a tobacco user who wants to quit, this section should help you reach your goal. If you have a friend or family member who is quitting, this section should help you understand what that person is going through so you can be supportive.

ON YOUR OWN Quitting under any conditions is not easy. Quitting is particularly difficult if you have no idea of how to go about it. The strategies listed on this page have proven successful for thousands of people.

Keep in mind that there is no right way or best way to quit. For many people, quitting suddenly—"cold turkey," as it is called—has been very successful. For other people, gradually cutting down works best. With the "cold turkey" approach, withdrawal symptoms are more intense but last for a shorter period of time. With a gradual approach, withdrawal symptoms are milder but last for a longer period.

If you do not succeed the first or second or third time you try to quit, remember this: Most people who have quit and stayed off tobacco had to try several times before they were finally successful.

GROUP PROGRAMS In the past 20 years, many group programs have become available to help people stop using tobacco. These programs provide information, supportive materials, and a structured quitting plan. Most importantly, they provide an opportunity for

STRATEGIES FOR LIVING

These techniques have helped thousands of people quit the tobacco habit.

- **Set a quit date.** Pick a realistic date not too far in the future. Before that date, you might want to switch to a milder or even distasteful brand of tobacco so using is not as satisfying to you.

- **Keep track of your tobacco use.** Before you quit, note how often you use tobacco, what types of situations trigger your desire, and what types of activities keep your mind off tobacco. When you quit, this information can help you.

- **List your reasons for quitting.** Review your list from time to time before and after you quit. This will help keep you focused on your positive goals.

- **Tell other people.** Don't keep quitting a secret. Tell your friends and family that you plan to quit and when, and ask for their support.

- **Stop *completely* on your quit date.** Don't keep any tobacco of your own, and don't let yourself have "just one" if someone offers it to you.

- **Quit one day at a time.** Focus your effort and attention on not using tobacco *today*. Don't worry about tomorrow or next week.

- **Change your tobacco-related habits.** During the most difficult quitting period, avoid activities and places that you associate with using tobacco, such as parties or bowling. Once you feel more comfortable and secure as a nonuser, you can resume your normal activities and routines.

- **Substitute other activities.** Get involved in activities that take your mind off using tobacco. If you were a smoker, do things that make smoking impossible, such as swimming or taking a shower.

- **Learn and use relaxation techniques.** A number of relaxation techniques are suggested in Chapter 5, "Managing Stress."

- **Reward yourself.** With the money you save by not using tobacco, do something satisfying. For example, buy yourself a new CD, make a donation to your favorite charity, or start a savings account for a trip you've wanted to take.

- **Think positively.** Remind yourself that quitting is something you are doing *for* yourself, not *to* yourself. Review your list of reasons to quit. Picture yourself in the future as a comfortable and healthy nonuser.

Nicotine Patch

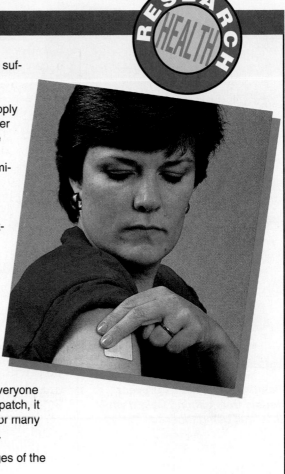

Larry Martin loved to smoke. He smoked at home. He smoked at work. He smoked in the car, and he smoked after he ate. But Larry Martin knew he had to quit smoking. He tried over a dozen times, but each time he found himself lighting up again.

Then Martin heard about the Patch. The Patch, actually called a transdermal nicotine patch, is a palm-size bandage applied to the upper body that releases nicotine slowly into the system. Martin decided to give the patch a try. Two months later he was off cigarettes for good.

Quitting cigarette smoking cold turkey is tough even for the most determined quitter. First, he or she must fight off the chemical addiction to cigarettes. Then, the smoker must break a habit that she or he has been doing twenty or thirty times a day for years. The patch offers a gradually reduced dose of nicotine to the would-be quitter. Using the patch, smokers can concentrate on the psychological issues of smoking without suffering intense withdrawal symptoms.

The patch is easy to apply and is not easily seen. After a number of weeks on the patch, the user usually is ready to let go of the chemical addiction.

People are finding that the nicotine patch is an effective way to quit smoking. However, the patch must be used properly and under the direction of a doctor. It should never be worn while the person is smoking. High amounts of nicotine in the body from both the patch and smoking may cause serious health problems. Although not everyone will quit smoking with the patch, it does promise new hope for many who want to quit smoking.

1. What are the advantages of the nicotine patch?
2. Why do you think the patch is so effective?

participants to talk together and provide each other with suggestions and moral support.

Some group programs are sponsored by hospitals, clinics, and health organizations such as the American Lung Association and the American Cancer Society. These programs generally charge only a very small fee or no fee at all. Other programs are run as self-supporting businesses and charge higher fees. To find a program in your area, check with your doctor, a hospital, or the local chapter of a health organization. In some areas, group programs are listed in the Yellow Pages under "Smokers' Information and Treatment Programs."

NICOTINE SUBSTITUTES   Some people have particular difficulty breaking their addiction to nicotine. These people may find it helpful to use a nicotine substitute. A **nicotine substitute** is a manufactured form of nicotine that is used as a temporary replacement for the nicotine in tobacco. Two nicotine substitutes are currently available: nicotine gum and nicotine patches. Both of these products require a doctor's prescription.

Nicotine gum is kept in the mouth and chewed whenever the user begins to feel uncomfortable. Chewing delivers periodic doses

QUITTING AND WEIGHT GAIN

Many people worry that they will gain weight if they quit smoking. Actually, whether you gain weight depends on your eating and exercise habits. Studies have found that in general, one third of the people who quit smoking gain weight, one third lose weight, and one third stay the same.

Healthy eating habits prevent people from gaining weight while they quit using tobacco.

of nicotine, much like smoking cigarettes. The user gradually tapers off and finally stops using the gum completely. Nicotine patches—a fresh one each day—are worn on the user's skin. With the patch, nicotine is released continuously. Over a period of weeks, patches with weaker nicotine dosages are used. The person finally stops using patches entirely.

The nicotine in these products is as addictive as the nicotine in tobacco. However, users generally find it easier to taper off and finally stop. Also, using a nicotine substitute does not involve the pleasurable habits associated with using tobacco, such as lighting up or watching exhaled smoke. Users do not develop a psychological dependence. These substitutes have mostly been used by smokers. It is not known whether they are as effective with smokeless tobacco users.

Neither of these nicotine substitutes is risk-free. With nicotine gum, heavy long-term use can irritate the tissues in the mouth. Also, some people have not been able to taper off and have become addicted to using the gum. With the patches, some people develop contact dermatitis, which is red, swollen, itchy areas on the skin. They have to stop using the patches. There have also been a few reports of patch-wearers suffering heart attacks. As yet, no one knows whether the patch actually helped cause the attack. As with any prescription drug, the use of nicotine gum or patches should be closely supervised by a doctor.

LESSON 20.4 USING WHAT YOU HAVE LEARNED

REVIEW

1. List three health benefits that both smokers and smokeless tobacco users can expect after quitting.
2. In your own words, explain the term *withdrawal symptom.*
3. How do group programs help people quit?

THINK CRITICALLY

4. Sometimes when people quit smoking, their cough becomes worse for a few days. Suggest a reason why this happens.
5. Nicotine gum and nicotine patches are expensive. How could a tobacco user justify spending that money?

APPLY IT TO YOURSELF

6. Imagine that you have just quit smoking and are extremely irritable and short-tempered. Identify some techniques you could use to cope with those feelings.

SUMMARY

Quitting tobacco is a positive action. Immediately after quitting, the ex-user begins to notice health benefits. In time, an ex-smoker's health risks approach those of someone who never smoked. The ex-user also experiences financial and psychological benefits. A number of simple but proven techniques can help users quit. For some people, group programs and nicotine substitutes are helpful.

In a Pinch

Jamie hung around with a good group of guys. They all got along well and had the same interests. Jamie and his friends often hung out together on Saturday nights. A lot of Jamie's friends used smokeless tobacco, or snuff. Often somebody in the group would pass around the tin, and they'd all have a pinch. Jamie usually took a pinch, but he wasn't sure why. He didn't like snuff very much. It was just kind of the thing to do.

At first, Jamie would just take a pinch when his friends would pass the tin. Soon Jamie was using snuff regularly whenever he went out with his friends, so he started carrying his own. Jamie had been afraid that the guys would think he was cheap if he didn't have his own tin. He was sure it wasn't a habit, and he wasn't worried about hurting his gums. Jamie only used snuff when he was with his friends.

One day during finals week, Jamie had had a tough day. He was sure that he had just flunked his English Comp. test. "I fail that, and I'm ineligible for at least four weeks!" Jamie thought. The coach of Jamie's swim team had a strict rule about grades.

Jamie felt really tense as he paced around his room. He walked over to his desk. When he opened the top drawer to put away his keys, he noticed the tin of snuff. He grabbed for it without even thinking. Just as

Jamie was about to put a pinch of snuff into his mouth, he stopped and looked at the tin. "Wait a minute. What am I doing?" Jamie stood looking at the tin for a long time. "Am I developing a habit?"

PAUSE AND CONSIDER

1. **Identify the Problem.** Why do you think Jamie stopped before he put the snuff into his mouth?

2. **Consider the Options.** What are Jamie's options at this point?

3. **Evaluate the Outcomes.** What might happen if Jamie goes ahead and puts the snuff in his mouth? Do you think Jamie is developing a habit? What might happen if Jamie puts the tin away?

"I really don't want to get addicted to this stuff," Jamie thought. But he realized that might be exactly what was happening. He had gotten used to the taste and to the feeling he got from it. Although he felt as though the snuff was just what he needed to relax, Jamie knew that using it would be a big step toward dependence.

"No way," Jamie said to himself. "That's it. I'm not going to get addicted to this stuff." Jamie dumped the contents of the tin into the trash and threw away the container as well.

When Saturday came around, Jamie was out with his friends as usual. One friend, Frank, pulled out his tin and offered it to Jamie. "No thanks," said Jamie. "I'm quitting."

"You're quitting?" laughed Frank. "I didn't know you had really started."

"Well, I felt as though I had," said Jamie. He told his friends what had happened. "When it was a once-in-a-while thing, I didn't think anything of it. But the fact that I felt I needed the stuff to feel better kind of scared me. I have no interest in developing cancer." Jamie's friends seemed to understand. That night, he noticed that some of the guys didn't dip as often as they used to.

DECIDE AND REVIEW

4. **Decide and Act.** What choice did Jamie make about using snuff? What were his reasons for his decision?

5. **Review.** Why was it easier for Jamie to quit when he did rather than wait until he had developed more of a habit?

PROJECTS

1. Find some magazine advertisements for smokeless tobacco. What images do the ads use to promote smokeless tobacco use? What messages are being communicated by the ads? Write a short paragraph about each ad, rebutting the advertiser's message with factual information about the effects of using smokeless tobacco.

2. People use various methods to quit smoking, including hypnosis, acupuncture, and self-help groups. Pick one of these methods of quitting smoking. Research its success rate as a stop-smoking aid.

WORKING WITH OTHERS

With a partner, interview someone who stopped smoking or using smokeless tobacco. Find out why the person began using tobacco, how much the person used and for how long, and how many times the person tried to quit before being successful. Ask the ex-user to suggest some strategies that he or she found effective in quitting. Present your findings to the class in a role-playing situation, with one partner acting as the ex-user and the other acting as the interviewer.

CONNECTING TO...

MATH   Find out the price of a pack of cigarettes in your area. Use that price to calculate the yearly cost of cigarettes for a two-pack-a-day smoker. Develop a list of several other things that the smoker could buy or do with that amount of money. Next, suppose that the person keeps smoking for another 20 years and that the price of a pack of cigarettes increases 10 percent each year. Calculate how much the smoker would spend on cigarettes over 20 years. Develop another list of things the smoker could buy or do with that amount of money.

USING VOCABULARY

addiction	emphysema	smokeless tobacco
adrenaline	larynx	snuff
atherosclerosis	leukoplakia	stress
bronchitis	mainstream smoke	stroke
cancer	nicotine	tars
carcinogen	nicotine substitute	withdrawal
chewing tobacco	passive smoking	symptom
cilia	sidestream smoke	

Use vocabulary terms from the above list to complete the sentences in the following paragraph.

All tobacco products contain __1__, the substance that causes the intense physical and psychological craving known as __2__. Tobacco smoke also contains carbon monoxide and tiny particles called __3__. These particles paralyze and eventually kill the __4__ in the smoker's air passages. Continued exposure to tobacco smoke causes serious respiratory diseases such as __5__ and __6__. Because smokeless tobacco contains a greater number of __7__ than does tobacco smoke, smokeless tobacco users have an even higher rate of oral __8__. When tobacco users quit, they typically experience __9__. Some users find it helpful to use a(n) __10__ while they quit.

CONCEPT MAPPING

Copy and complete the concept map shown below. Information on concept mapping appears at the front of this book.

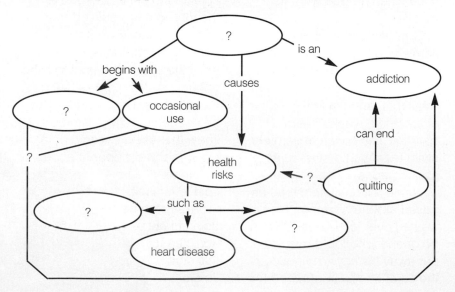

THINKING CRITICALLY

INTERPRET

LESSON 20.1

1. Name two forms of smokeless tobacco.

2. Why do federal, state, and local laws ban smoking in many public places?

3. Identify three important factors that influence teenagers to begin using tobacco.

4. According to the warnings on smokeless tobacco products, what health problems do these products cause?

LESSON 20.2

5. Name the three most dangerous substances in tobacco smoke. Which of these substances also is contained in smokeless tobacco?

6. Identify the effects of nicotine poisoning.

7. Why are low-tar, low-nicotine cigarettes just as dangerous as regular cigarettes?

8. Why does using smokeless tobacco carry an even greater risk of mouth and throat cancer than smoking does?

LESSON 20.3

9. Why is lung cancer in smokers difficult to detect early?

10. What is the difference between mainstream smoke and sidestream smoke? Which is more harmful to passive smokers?

11. How can smoking lead to a stroke?

LESSON 20.4

12. How quickly are an ex-smoker's risks of heart and lung disease reduced to the level of someone who has never smoked?

13. Why do some smokers feel dizzy when they first quit smoking?

14. What are the differences between the "cold turkey" approach and the gradual approach to quitting tobacco use?

15. Define the term nicotine substitute.

APPLY

LESSON 20.1

16. Despite the health warnings, cigarette smoking is still a serious problem among teenagers. Identify three possible reasons why teenagers continue to smoke.

17. Why do you think tobacco ads always show users as healthy, happy, and attractive?

LESSON 20.2

18. How does the carbon monoxide in cigarette smoke affect the smoker's body?

19. Many smokers suffer from a chronic cough. What causes this "smoker's cough"?

LESSON 20.3

20. How does smoking contribute to heart disease?

21. Identify three risks of smoking during pregnancy.

LESSON 20.4

22. Describe the immediate effects of quitting tobacco use.

23. Within a week of quitting tobacco use, all nicotine is eliminated from the body. Why do most ex-users still experience withdrawal symptoms for weeks afterward?

Alcohol

"It is not who is right, but what is right, that is important."

Thomas Huxley

Every day, voices come at you from all directions. Parents offer advice about what is best. Teachers and advisors work to guide you and open the doors of awareness. Friends share their experiences, hoping that you will enjoy doing what they have done.

Often, these voices offer conflicting messages. Who is right? There are few absolutely right answers, but there are many right choices. One of those choices is the path of healthy and responsible decisions.

You can choose to listen to the healthy voices, the voices that strive to nourish and nurture the best that you are. You can choose to say "No" to the voices that encourage you to hurt yourself or impede your growth. Among the hurtful voices are those that tell you it's okay to drink alcohol even though you are not of legal drinking age. For teenagers, alcohol use is illegal and it is dangerous. It invites life-threatening risks, such as driving while under the influence of alcohol. Used to excess, alcohol slowly destroys the drinker's mind and body.

Some voice in your life might say, "It's okay to drink." But, as Huxley said, the truth lies not in who is right, but what is right. And what is right is not drinking while you are a teenager and using alcohol responsibly if you choose to drink when you are of legal drinking age.

SELF-ASSESSMENT

Number a page from 1 to 10 in your Wellness Journal or on a separate sheet of paper. Respond *yes* or *no* to each of the following statements. Answer *yes* for each statement that describes you all or most of the time.

1. If a driver who was going to give me a ride has been drinking, I find someone else to drive me home.

2. I know how to get help if someone I care about is a problem drinker.

3. I do not try to buy alcoholic beverages illegally or get someone else to buy them for me.

4. I never use alcohol to relieve boredom, loneliness, anxiety, or other uncomfortable feelings.

5. If someone pressures me to have a drink, I can say No with confidence.

6. When I feel nervous at a party, I do not take an alcoholic drink to loosen up.

7. I do not take part in drinking contests or drink a lot on a dare.

8. I do not use alcohol with another drug, even a prescription or over-the-counter medicine.

9. I do not try to cover up for someone else's drinking.

10. I use healthy techniques for dealing with stress.

Review your responses, and try to decide which statements might represent your strengths and weaknesses. Save your personal checklist for a follow-up activity that appears at the end of this chapter.

ALCOHOL, THE PROBLEM DRINK

Alcohol consumption in the United States is at its lowest level in 30 years. Despite this decline, alcohol abuse remains the number one drug problem among teenagers and young adults. Over three million adolescents between the ages of 14 and 17 experience problems as the result of alcohol use. These problems include poor performance at work and in school, illness, and automobile accidents. Because alcohol impairs judgment, its use is also linked with teenage pregnancy, violence, crime, and infection with sexually transmitted diseases.

WHAT IS ALCOHOL?

Alcohol is a psychoactive drug. As you may recall from Chapter 19, "Coordination and Control," a **psychoactive drug** [*sy koh AK tiv*] is a chemical substance that acts on the brain, affecting a person's mind and behavior. Alcohol is a **depressant** [*dih PRES unt*], a drug that slows down nervous system activity.

Alcohol also may function as a gateway drug. A **gateway drug** is a psychoactive substance that leads the user to try other drugs. Research studies suggest that for some young people, alcohol use may lead to the use of illegal drugs.

ALCOHOLIC BEVERAGES   There are several different types of alcohol. Only one type, ethanol [*ETH uh nawl*], is found in alcoholic beverages. Beers and wines are labeled with the percentage of their alcohol content. Distilled spirits are labeled with their proof. **Proof** is a measure of alcohol content that is two times the percentage of alcohol. For example, whiskey labeled 80 proof is 40 percent alcohol.

ALCOHOL CONTENT

The three types of alcoholic beverages—beer, wine, and distilled spirits—contain different percentages of alcohol.

- Beer is usually 3 to 5 percent alcohol.
- Wine is usually 9 to 14 percent alcohol. Wine coolers are made of wine mixed with carbonated water and flavorings. Wine coolers are about 4 to 6 percent alcohol.
- Distilled spirits such as whiskey, gin, scotch, and vodka are usually 35 to 50 percent alcohol.

NO NUTRITIONAL VALUE   Alcohol contains no nutrients and interferes with the body's ability to absorb key vitamins and nutrients from other sources. Even though alcohol contains no nutrients, it is high in Calories. Therefore, those people who drink alcohol regularly may gain weight as a result of their alcohol use.

Which of these three drinks contains the most alcohol?

WHY PEOPLE DO NOT DRINK ALCOHOL

There are many reasons people choose not to drink alcohol. Some people do not like the taste of alcohol. Others do not drink alcohol because of religious beliefs or social customs. People who are weight-conscious may avoid alcohol because it is high in Calories. Some people do not like the feeling of losing control that alcohol causes. Others are concerned about the health risks associated with its use. Many ex-drinkers avoid alcohol completely because they know they cannot control their drinking.

WHY PEOPLE START DRINKING ALCOHOL

Social pressures, stress, and advertising are important factors that influence people to begin drinking alcohol. In addition, many young people drink as a way of rebelling against their parents or other adults.

SOCIAL PRESSURES　Many young people first experience alcohol use in their homes. Adults in the family may drink at meals, at special occasions such as parties and weddings, or simply while sitting at home reading or watching TV. The children in the family may come to view drinking as part of being an adult.

Peer pressure is the main reason many young people start drinking. Some teenagers may find it difficult to refuse a drink if it is offered by friends who are drinking. Many young people ignore their own better judgment because they fear disapproval or rejection by their friends.

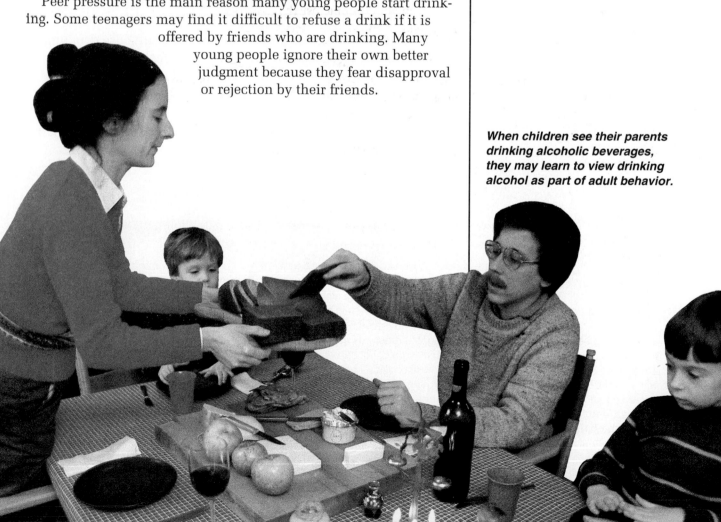

When children see their parents drinking alcoholic beverages, they may learn to view drinking alcohol as part of adult behavior.

STRESS   Many young people drink to cope with stress and to change the way they feel. The pressures of school, work, or family obligations can feel overwhelming. Drinking may seem to offer an escape. People also use alcohol to deal with depression, boredom, anxiety, and other uncomfortable feelings. Many people use alcohol to overcome their nervousness and tension when they are in social situations.

ADVERTISING   Ads for alcoholic beverages appear on television, in magazines, and on billboards. Wherever they appear, these ads always portray drinkers in a positive way. Drinkers are shown as healthy, attractive, strong, glamorous, adventuresome, athletic, fun-loving, or sophisticated. These images are meant to appeal to your emotions, to make you want to be like the people in the ads. The ads also imply that drinking is an important part of having a good time.

   In addition to the ads themselves, alcoholic beverages are often shown being used in movies and TV shows. Whenever an actor pours a drink or takes a sip from a beer bottle or wine glass, alcohol use is being portrayed as an ordinary and acceptable aspect of everyday life. Many times, people are shown reaching for a drink when they are under stress or facing a problem. In recent years, public pressure on networks and advertisers has reduced casual alcohol use in TV shows.

A WAY TO REBEL   Some teenagers and young adults use drinking as a way of rebelling against authority. They feel that drinking shows their independence from parents and other adults. Becoming independent is a healthy and normal part of growing into adulthood. However, alcohol use does not contribute to maturity and healthy independence. In fact, alcohol use can interfere with normal development.

CONSUMER HEALTH

Alcohol Advertising

You know the dangers of alcohol. But everywhere you look—at sports arenas, at concerts, on television, in magazines, and in newspapers—advertisers are presenting the public with images that alcohol is fun and rewarding and leads to glamour, success, and fortune. People are shown skiing, surfing, climbing, and partying with alcohol. If you didn't know better, you'd think alcohol was more fun than anything else.

A significant few advertisers are beginning to balance their fun ads with a warning that alcohol may be dangerous in certain situations. These advertisements are increasing, but most ads still imply that drinking alcohol carries no risk.

   With millions of Americans joining organizations like Alcoholics Anonymous (AA), it is clear that alcohol addiction is a problem in our culture. Lately more people under the age of 30, including a record number of teenagers, are joining AA than ever before. Some experts believe that advertising is partly responsible for the rise in alcohol addiction among teenagers. For this reason, it is especially important for young consumers to think critically about advertisements for alcohol and then behave responsibly. What you have learned about alcohol and its inherent dangers is true. Don't let the advertisements fool you.

Many people drink alcohol only at parties and other social occasions.

TYPES OF DRINKING BEHAVIORS

Two out of three adults in the United States drink alcoholic beverages. Their alcohol use ranges from occasional light drinking to regular heavy drinking. For some people, alcohol use becomes a serious addiction. As you may recall from earlier chapters in this unit, **addiction** [*uh DIK shun*] is a strong physical and psychological craving for a substance.

SOCIAL DRINKING   Of the adults who drink, half are light drinkers. A **light drinker** is someone who consumes an average of less than one drink (one half ounce of alcohol) per day. Most light drinkers are social drinkers. That is, they drink only at social occasions such as parties, family get-togethers, or special meals. For young people, however, occasional use can quickly lead to regular use because of alcohol's psychoactive effects.

MODERATE DRINKING   According to the National Institute on Alcohol Abuse and Alcoholism (NIAAA), a **moderate drinker** is someone who consumes no more than one ounce of alcohol per day on average. One ounce is the amount contained in two drinks.

1 ounce of alcohol
{
two 12-ounce cans of beer
or
two 5-ounce glasses of wine
or
two 1.5-ounce shots of distilled spirits

Moderate drinkers use alcohol regularly but usually do not drink to excess. They also may drink alone, unlike social drinkers. Moderate drinkers may use alcohol, but they can stop drinking without difficulty. They consider alcohol use to be a part of their

In the United States,
10 percent of
heavy drinkers
consume 50
percent of the alcoholic
beverages sold.

lives but not a necessary part. Moderate drinking has not been scientifically linked to serious health problems.

HEAVY DRINKING   A person who consumes more than two drinks per day on average is a **heavy drinker,** according to NIAAA. Heavy drinkers often use alcohol as a social crutch. They also use it to cope with stress, worry, and unhappiness. Heavy drinkers find it difficult to limit their drinking. They also may experience discomfort and feel deprived when they go without alcohol.

Drinking more than four drinks per day on average is considered excessive drinking. For people who drink to excess, alcohol use has become an addiction. These drinkers are physically and psychologically dependent on alcohol. To addicted users, drinking is not a pleasurable activity but a necessity and an obsession. Anyone who drinks regularly risks becoming addicted to alcohol.

People who drink heavily may experience blackouts. **Blackouts** are periods of time when drinkers cannot remember what happened or what they did while they were intoxicated. Blackouts are considered a serious warning sign of excessive drinking.

When addicted drinkers try to stop drinking, most of them suffer severe withdrawal symptoms. **Withdrawal symptoms** are uncomfortable reactions that occur when a person stops using an addictive substance. The symptoms of withdrawal from alcohol include

IDENTIFYING PROBLEM DRINKING

How can you tell if someone has a drinking problem? The following behaviors are some important warning signs. It is not necessary for someone to show all of these behaviors to be considered a problem drinker.

- Drinking alone.
- Hiding alcohol use from family and friends.
- Relying on alcohol to get through stressful situations.
- Feeling uncomfortable when alcohol is not available in social situations.
- Drinking in the morning or at other unusual times.
- Drinking in inappropriate or risky situations, such as while at work or in school or before driving.
- Switching from a stronger alcoholic beverage to a weaker one to keep from getting drunk.
- Getting drunk regularly or more frequently than in the past.
- Experiencing blackouts.
- Suffering hangovers frequently.
- Missing time from work or school because of drinking.
- Getting annoyed or angry when others criticize the drinking.
- Feeling guilty about drinking.
- Trying to cut down or stop drinking but being successful for only a few days.

uncontrollable trembling, nausea, vomiting, hallucinations, and seizures. Like addicted tobacco users, addicted drinkers continue their drug use partly to avoid withdrawal symptoms.

ALCOHOLISM

As you read the previous section, you may have wondered why the terms *alcoholic* and *alcoholism* were not used. Some experts define alcoholism as a disease, not a type of drinking behavior. To them, **alcoholism** [*AL kuh haw liz um*] is a chronic disease characterized by physical and psychological dependence on alcohol and an inability to control one's drinking.

The description of addicted alcohol users in the previous section applies to alcoholics as well. All alcoholics are addicted to alcohol. However, there is some question whether all addicted drinkers are alcoholics. According to many doctors and other medical professionals, alcoholics have an inborn tendency to abuse alcohol and become addicted.

Researchers have found that a large number of children of alcoholics become alcoholics themselves, even when they are raised by adoptive parents who are not alcoholics. This finding suggests that a tendency toward alcoholism is genetically passed from parent to child. However, no one has yet found a specific genetic factor that might explain alcoholism.

Some medical professionals contend that alcoholism is simply a learned behavior. As they point out, parents who drink moderately tend to raise children who drink moderately. Heavy drinkers tend to raise children who drink heavily. Researchers have also tried to identify a personality trait common to all alcoholics, but none has been found.

Most alcoholics are ordinary men and women in all kinds of jobs and from all kinds of backgrounds. Some alcoholics are teenagers.

LESSON 21.1 **USING WHAT YOU HAVE LEARNED**

REVIEW

1. Identify four symptoms of withdrawal from alcohol.
2. What is the main reason many young people begin drinking alcohol?
3. Why is alcohol considered a gateway drug?

THINK CRITICALLY

4. All alcoholics are addicted to alcohol, but every addicted drinker is not necessarily an alcoholic. Explain this statement.
5. Young people tend to think that their peers use alcohol more than they actually do. Explain how this belief could influence a teenager to start drinking.

APPLY IT TO YOURSELF

6. Studies indicate that alcohol use by teenagers is a serious problem today. Is drinking a problem among the teenagers you know? What evidence do you have for your answer?

SUMMARY

Alcohol is a depressant that slows down nervous system activity, affecting the drinker's mind and behavior. Social pressures, stress, advertising, and a desire to rebel influence young people to begin drinking alcohol. The pleasant effects of alcohol can quickly lead to regular use and addiction. Alcoholism is a disease characterized by alcohol addiction and an inability to control drinking.

Staying Clean

HEALTHY PEOPLE 2000

Provide to children in all school districts and private schools primary and secondary school educational programs on alcohol and other drugs, preferably as part of quality school health education.

A quality school health education program should provide factual information about the harmful effects of drugs, support and strengthen students' resistance to using drugs, carry out collaborative drug-abuse prevention efforts with parents and other community members, and be supported by strong school policies as well as services for confidential identification, assessment, referral to treatment, and support groups for drug users.

Objective 4.13

from *Healthy People 2000: National Health Promotion and Disease Prevention Objectives*

Alcohol and drug abuse are the number one health problems among teenagers today. Illegal use of alcohol and drugs accounts for most of the crimes committed by people between the ages of 12 and 20. Nearly 50 percent of all academic problems of high school students stem from alcohol abuse. Twenty-eight percent of students who drop out of college do so because of alcohol or drug abuse.

Surgeon General Antonia Novello said drinking and drug abuse are out of control among teenagers in the United States. She added, "We're going to lose a whole generation if we don't pay attention."

Prevention seems to be the best solution to drug and alcohol abuse among school-age people.

Every teenager must do his or her part to prevent further damage to the generation. As a member of your generation, you can contribute to a "cleaner" society—that is, a society with less drug abuse—by evaluating your own goals and by working toward the goals for the year 2000.

REBELLING WITHOUT A CAUSE

Drinking alcohol has been a rite of passage during the twentieth century. Your parents and grandparents may have tried it to mark their emergence into adulthood. In the days when they were first experimenting with alcohol, far less was known about its dangers than is known today.

Most researchers agree that there are six reasons for alcohol and drug abuse—boredom, peer pressure, escape from psychological pain, a search for community, rebellion against authority, and a desire to feel good.

The simplest way to prevent alcohol and drug abuse is to stop the behavior before it starts. The in-school prevention programs that seem to work best are those that foster a support network among peers. Groups talk about the problems that face the group and the individuals in the group. In times of stress, boredom, or frustration, many group members find they can turn to people instead of to alcohol or drugs. These groups emphasize action and offer concrete strategies for staying clean.

Programs such as Alcoholics Anonymous (AA) boast a high recovery rate for the 21 percent of their members who are under 30 years old. Groups like AA can help anyone who has a problem with drinking.

Recovery from abusive behavior usually means overhauling many areas of a person's life. It means finding new friends among non-using allies and changing social patterns and habits. These changes are challenging. However, getting clean and staying clean is the first priority for the abuser.

CLEANING UP THE ACT

Staying clean has its own set of challenges. The following strategies may provide ways to work toward staying clean.

1. Get the facts. Attend the alcohol and drug prevention program in your school. Gather as much information as you can about the effects of alcohol and drug abuse on physical and emotional health, and find out about the legal consequences of alcohol and drug use.

2. Say *no*. If friends pressure you to indulge in abusive behavior, respond simply and clearly, for example, "I don't drink. I don't use drugs. I don't need them."

3. If your friends are abusers, find another set of friends. Establish friendships with people with whom you have other things in common.

4. Acknowledge that boredom, stress, and a desire to rebel are part of everyday emotions. Find ways to react to each feeling—take up a hobby, or do something a bit out of the ordinary, such as doing volunteer work.

5. Stop, look, and listen for the signs of alcohol or drug abuse among the people that you know. If you see such signs, encourage the person to attend prevention workshops or to seek help through a program such as Alcoholics Anonymous or Narcotics Anonymous. Set an example by staying clean.

WHAT DO YOU THINK?

1. Why do you think that alcohol and drug abuse are problems among teenagers?

2. Read about adults or young people who are currently in

recovery from alcohol or drug abuse. What reasons do they give for their abuse? What steps did they take to recover? What tips can you learn from them for staying clean and avoiding abusive behavior?

3. What issues do researchers say cause drug and alcohol abuse? Which of these issues affect you the most? What steps do you take to alleviate the stress of these issues and stay clean?

ALCOHOL'S IMMEDIATE EFFECTS

MAIN IDEAS

The short-term effects that alcohol and other psychoactive drugs have on the mind and body are called **intoxication** [*in tahk suh KAY shun*]. Intoxication is not the same as being obviously drunk. Alcohol intoxication can be caused by as little as one drink. The process of becoming intoxicated begins with the first sip.

INTOXICATION

Unlike foods, alcohol does not have to be digested, or broken down into simpler substances, before it can enter the bloodstream. Alcohol is absorbed directly into the bloodstream through the lining of the stomach and the small intestine. Because it does not have to be digested, alcohol enters the bloodstream quite rapidly, especially when there is no food in the stomach. Once in the bloodstream, alcohol is carried to all parts of the body, including the brain.

EFFECTS ON THE BRAIN   Alcohol depresses neuron activity in areas of the brain that control attention, memory, and inhibitions. **Inhibitions** [*in huh BISH unz*] are psychological checks on emotions and actions. At first, alcohol's depressant effect makes people feel more relaxed and gives them a sense of well-being.

Shameeka's boyfriend, Al, took her to a party where she didn't know anyone else. While Al talked with friends, Shameeka stood there feeling like an outsider. "I'd better have a drink and loosen up," she thought. Soon Shameeka felt less nervous and was talking with other people. "This isn't so bad," she thought as she opened another can of beer.

As inhibitions become more depressed, people have less self-control. Buried feelings may come out, sometimes in sudden bursts of anger or crying.

Later, Shameeka noticed Al sitting with another girl, deep in conversation. Shameeka's eyes filled with tears. "He brings me here, and then he dumps me!" Shameeka stormed over to Al and the girl. "You're a—" she began.

Al cut her off with a smile. "Sheek! Meet Lilly, my cousin from Florida." Al got up. "Can I get you guys another beer?"

Shameeka felt so ashamed. She was glad that she hadn't made a scene. "Lilly! I've heard a lot about you," she said to the girl. Then she turned to Al. "No more for me, thanks. But get me a soda, would you?"

People are also less capable of judging what is inappropriate or unsafe when they are intoxicated. If drinking continues, alcohol affects the areas of the brain that control speech, vision, and coordination. Speech becomes slurred, and vision becomes impaired.

MAIN IDEAS

CONCEPTS

✔ Alcohol affects areas of the brain that control memory, attention, and inhibitions.

✔ Someone who drinks a large amount of alcohol in a short period of time risks death from alcohol poisoning.

✔ Using alcohol with other drugs is extremely dangerous because alcohol may increase their effects.

VOCABULARY

intoxication
inhibitions
reflex
blood alcohol content (BAC)
tolerance
multiplier effect
hangover

The drinker also may have trouble walking. In addition, the drinker may feel nauseated and start to vomit. If the person continues to drink, alcohol depresses the areas of the brain stem that control heartbeat and breathing. Heartbeat and breathing may become irregular and even stop. A drinker who reaches this point is suffering from alcohol poisoning. Emergency medical treatment is necessary, or death may result.

Drinking a large amount of alcohol in a short time—as in "binge" drinking, a drinking contest, or on a dare—carries a great risk of death from alcohol poisoning. Usually, drinkers pass out before they can drink a fatal amount of alcohol. Sometimes, however, drinkers consume a fatal amount just before passing out. Even if the amount of alcohol is not fatal, drinkers may pass out, vomit while unconscious, and suffocate in their own vomit.

EFFECTS ON REFLEXES By interfering with nerve impulses, alcohol slows the body's reflexes and reaction time. Recall that a reflex is an automatic muscle response to pain or danger. Jamming on the car brakes when someone suddenly steps out into the street is a learned behavior that requires a quick reaction time. A driver who has been drinking cannot respond quickly in such an emergency. Even an ordinary response to a red light or a stop sign takes longer when the driver has been drinking.

EFFECTS ON TEMPERATURE REGULATION Alcohol makes blood vessels relax. This causes more blood to flow to the skin's surface. The increased blood flow produces a feeling of warmth. At the same time, though, blood near the skin's surface releases body heat through the skin. This release of heat lowers the body's internal temperature. The body loses heat rapidly during drinking. It therefore can be fatal to drink when you are exposed to the cold.

EFFECTS ON BODY FLUIDS Alcohol prevents the release of the hormone that controls how much urine the body produces. Without

What might happen in this situation if the driver's reflexes were slowed?

BAC Levels*						Effects on Mind and Behavior	
	Number of Drinks in Two Hours					BAC Level	Effects
Body Weight	2	4	6	8	10	0.02–0.05	Relaxation; good feeling. Decreased alertness, impaired judgment.
120 lbs.	0.06	0.12	0.19	0.25	0.31		
140 lbs.	0.05	0.11	0.16	0.21	0.27	0.08	Lowered inhibitions; exaggerated feelings. Slowed reaction times; impaired coordination; less caution. Person is considered legally drunk in some states.
160 lbs.	0.05	0.09	0.14	0.19	0.23		
180 lbs.	0.04	0.08	0.13	0.17	0.21	0.10	Difficulty with balance; clumsy movement and speech; impaired vision. Person is considered legally drunk in most states.
200 lbs.	0.04	0.08	0.11	0.15	0.19		
						0.20	Very drunk; staggering movement; slurred speech. Loud and difficult to understand. Blurred vision or double vision; impaired depth perception. Outbursts of feelings; mood shifts.
SOURCE: THE WELLNESS ENCYCLOPEDIA, UNIVERSITY OF CALIFORNIA, BERKELEY							
						0.30	Conscious but not aware of surroundings; loss of control over voluntary movements.
*Food in the stomach, the drinker's emotional state, and other factors also affect the blood alcohol level.						0.35 and above	Unconscious; coma and death possible.

Figure 21-1 *Alcohol begins to affect a drinker's mind and behavior at a BAC level of 0.02 to 0.05. At 0.10, a drinker is considered legally drunk in most states.*

this hormone, urine is made continuously, and body fluids become depleted. As a result, the drinker becomes very thirsty. More importantly, the drinker's body loses the fluids that are needed for normal functioning. This is why it is risky to drink alcoholic beverages on a very hot day or when exercising heavily.

MEASURING INTOXICATION

A drinker's level of intoxication from alcohol is measured by his or her **blood alcohol content (BAC).** BAC is the number of grams of alcohol per 100 milliliters of blood, expressed as a percentage. The higher the BAC percentage, the greater the effect on the drinker's mind and behavior. Figure 21-1 lists the behavioral effects of different BAC levels.

FACTORS INFLUENCING INTOXICATION

Alcohol's effects differ from one person to another and from one time to another in the same person. These differences are determined by several factors: the characteristics of the drinker, the rate of alcohol intake, and the rate of alcohol elimination.

THE DRINKER Once it is absorbed into the bloodstream, alcohol is evenly distributed throughout the tissues of the body. In general, after drinking the same amount of alcohol, a larger, heavier person will have a lower BAC level than a smaller, lighter person. The drinker's emotions and overall state of health also affect the level of intoxication. In addition, alcohol's effects on a drinker decrease as he or she builds up tolerance over a period of time. **Tolerance** [*TAHL uh runts*] is a reduced sensitivity to a drug as the result of regular use.

THE RATE OF INTAKE   The rate of intake is the *amount* of alcohol taken in *during a given period.* The rate of intake also affects the drinker's level of intoxication. The presence of other substances in the stomach can increase or decrease the rate at which alcohol enters the bloodstream. For example, foods that contain fats and proteins slow the rate of alcohol absorption. Diluting alcohol with plain water also slows the absorption rate. On the other hand, carbonated water speeds up the absorption rate. As you learned in Lesson 1, wine coolers contain carbonated water.

A breathalyzer can detect a tiny amount of alcohol in a drinker's exhaled breath. The amount of alcohol indicates the drinker's BAC level.

THE RATE OF ELIMINATION   Most of the alcohol in a drink is broken down in the liver. The liver normally takes about three hours to break down one ounce of alcohol. Recall that one ounce of alcohol is the amount contained in two drinks. If the drinker takes in alcohol faster than the liver can break it down, the drinker's BAC level rises.

TESTING A DRINKER'S BAC LEVEL

Police officers and medical professionals can use three different tests to measure a drinker's BAC level: a breathalyzer test, a urine test, and a blood test.

Most of the alcohol in a drinker's bloodstream is broken down in the liver. Some alcohol, though, is eliminated in the drinker's breath and urine. By measuring the amount of alcohol in the breath or the urine, the drinker's BAC level can be determined. However, the most accurate measure of the drinker's BAC level is a blood test, which directly measures the blood's actual alcohol content.

The results of any of these tests can be used as evidence to prosecute a drinker for drunk driving and for any damage or injury caused by the drinker. In some states, a driver can have his or her driver's license taken away if he or she refuses to take a breathalyzer or urine test. Many states now require a blood test for anyone suspected of driving under the influence of alcohol.

USING ALCOHOL WITH OTHER DRUGS

Using alcohol with other drugs is extremely dangerous. The danger lies in the fact that alcohol increases the effects of many other drugs. The process of one drug increasing the effects of another

While someone is experiencing a hangover, it's easy to vow never to drink again!

drug is called the **multiplier effect.** For example, alcohol greatly increases the effects of prescription tranquilizers, which are also depressants. Many accidental deaths have resulted from a person drinking and taking tranquilizers at the same time.

Using alcohol with another drug can distort your senses and thinking, cause coordination problems, and seriously disrupt heart and liver function. Young people who use alcohol along with other psychoactive drugs have higher-than-average rates of irreversible coma and death.

Even some over-the-counter drugs and nonpsychoactive prescription medications can be dangerous when combined with alcohol. Drug interactions are not always predictable. For this reason, alcohol should never be used with *any* other drug without first consulting a doctor.

RECOVERING FROM INTOXICATION

About 95 percent of the alcohol in a drinker's bloodstream is broken down and converted by the liver. The other 5 percent is eliminated in urine, perspiration, and exhaled air. Depending on the drinker's BAC level, it can take anywhere from two to ten hours, or even longer, for all of the alcohol to be eliminated.

As long as some alcohol remains in the bloodstream, the drinker is still intoxicated to some degree. Normal coordination, reaction time, and reasoning ability return only when all the alcohol has been removed. Some people think that black coffee, cold showers, exercise, or fresh air can cure intoxication. However, none of these "cures" reduces the drinker's blood alcohol level.

A **hangover** is the unpleasant physical effects that follow the heavy use of alcohol. A hangover may include an upset stomach, a headache, tiredness, dizziness, and thirst. Drinkers also may suffer from worry, sadness, and guilt about their behavior while drinking and about the drinking itself.

SUMMARY

Alcohol initially makes the drinker feel happy and relaxed. If drinking continues, alcohol affects the drinker's judgment, speech, vision, and coordination. In later stages, alcohol depresses heartbeat and breathing. Alcohol's effects depend on the drinker's physical characteristics and mental state and on the rates of intake and elimination. Because alcohol increases the effects of many other drugs, combining alcohol with another drug is extremely dangerous.

LESSON 21.2 ## USING WHAT YOU HAVE LEARNED

REVIEW

1. What is intoxication?
2. Why does alcohol enter the bloodstream more quickly than foods do?
3. Why is it dangerous to use alcohol with another drug?

THINK CRITICALLY

4. Alcohol depresses the drinker's inhibitions. Describe one example of something inappropriate that the drinker might do as a result of being intoxicated.
5. Use Figure 21-1 to answer this question. Suppose a 180-pound man drank six beers in two hours. What signs of intoxication might other people notice?

APPLY IT TO YOURSELF

6. Imagine that you are at a party, and someone challenges you to a drinking contest. How would you explain your refusal?

ALCOHOL'S LONG-TERM EFFECTS

Used in moderation and responsibly, alcohol can be a source of relaxation and social pleasure for adults. However, used to excess and under the wrong conditions, alcohol causes serious harm. The damaging effects of alcohol become worse with long-term use. For people who experience problems with drinking and want to stop, medical treatment, support groups, and therapy are available.

DAMAGE TO THE DRINKER

Heavy drinkers cannot escape damaging their own bodies. Some types of damage are irreversible and even fatal. Studies have shown that the life expectancy of heavy drinkers is 10 to 12 years shorter than the average life expectancy.

BRAIN   Heavy drinking permanently damages the brain. In fact, long-term alcohol abuse actually causes the brain to shrink. Memory and intelligence damaged by alcohol abuse can never be fully recovered. Heavy drinking also has been linked with depression and suicide.

LIVER   Second to the brain, the liver suffers most from alcohol abuse. Alcohol interferes with the liver's ability to break down fats, so they collect in the liver. Over time, fat accumulation and the high alcohol level destroy liver cells. Scar tissue grows in place of the dead cells. This scarring of the liver is called **cirrhosis** [*suh ROH sus*]. With fewer functioning cells, the liver begins to fail. Unless the person stops drinking, cirrhosis can be fatal.

Cirrhosis of the liver is a leading cause of death among heavy drinkers. Cirrhosis is painless in the early stages. For this reason,

MAIN IDEAS

CONCEPTS

✔ Brain damage, cirrhosis of the liver, and oral cancer are serious health consequences of heavy drinking.

✔ Pregnant women who drink risk harming their fetuses.

✔ Alcoholics Anonymous, Al-Anon, and Alateen are self-help support groups for addicted drinkers and their families.

VOCABULARY

cirrhosis
hepatitis
fetal alcohol syndrome
detoxification

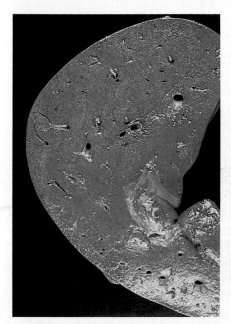

Compare the healthy liver (left) with the liver that has been damaged by heavy drinking. What differences do you see?

its progress often goes undetected until a later stage. Fortunately, a blood test can detect the liver damage at a very early stage. Early detection improves the drinker's chances of survival, provided that he or she stops drinking.

Heavy drinkers also risk contracting a form of **hepatitis** [*hep uh TYT us*], a liver inflammation caused by infection or toxic substances. Alcoholic hepatitis is caused by the toxic effects of alcohol in large amounts. Someone suffering from hepatitis has little energy because important chemical activity controlled by the liver does not occur. Liver cancer, too, is more common among heavy drinkers than among nondrinkers and light or moderate drinkers.

MOUTH AND THROAT   Alcohol damages the delicate tissues of the mouth and throat. This constant irritation increases the risk of oral cancer, particularly if the drinker also uses tobacco. Drinkers who smoke are 10 times more likely to develop oral cancer than nondrinkers who do not smoke. Heavy drinkers also have a higher risk of developing cancer of the esophagus.

STOMACH AND INTESTINES   Alcohol irritates the stomach lining by causing it to produce too much acid. The excess acid also irritates the lining of the small intestine, causing indigestion and even ulcers. Long-term alcohol use also interferes with the small intestine's ability to absorb nutrients, particularly vitamins and minerals. In addition, heavy drinkers usually do not have healthy eating habits, so they often suffer from malnutrition.

HEART   Heavy alcohol use weakens the heart muscle, causing scar tissue to build up in the muscle fibers. As a result, heavy drinkers have an increased risk of high blood pressure, stroke, coronary artery disease, and heart attack.

DAMAGE DURING PREGNANCY

A pregnant woman who drinks risks harming her fetus. Alcohol in the mother's bloodstream enters the fetus's bloodstream through the placenta. The alcohol disrupts normal development of the fetus's brain and other organs, resulting in mental retardation, delayed growth, and abnormal facial features. This pattern of mental and physical birth defects caused by alcohol use during pregnancy is known as **fetal alcohol syndrome (FAS).**

Studies have found that pregnant women who drink just one or two drinks a day have a 14 percent risk of bearing a baby with FAS. With six or more drinks a day, pregnant women increase the risk of FAS to 75 percent. Even one bout of heavy drinking during the important early stages of fetal development can cause birth defects. In addition, pregnant women who drink have an increased risk of miscarriage and stillbirth. Not drinking any alcohol at all is the only safe course for an expectant mother. Unfortunately, a woman may drink and cause harm before she even knows she is pregnant.

Small eyes, a flattened upper lip, and a flattened bridge of the nose are typical facial features of children with fetal alcohol syndrome.

RECOVERY FROM ALCOHOL ADDICTION

Recovering from alcohol addiction is difficult. The drinker must first admit that he or she has a problem. Then the drinker must be determined to stop drinking and be willing to accept help. Many organizations offer medical care and emotional support to addicted drinkers and their families.

SUPPORT GROUPS   The most effective long-term treatment for alcohol addiction has been group programs. Hospitals, clinics, health agencies, family service organizations, churches, and private organizations offer group programs for addicted drinkers.

Perhaps the best known group is Alcoholics Anonymous (AA). AA is a voluntary association of addicted drinkers who help each other stop drinking and stay sober. All AA members are either recovering alcoholics—alcoholics who no longer drink—or alcoholics who want to stop drinking. The group support and fellowship offered by AA have been very effective in fighting alcohol addiction. AA is listed in the Yellow Pages under "Alcoholism Information and Treatment."

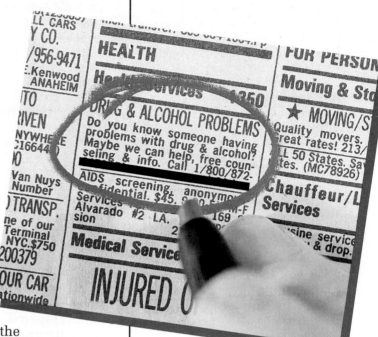

Many organizations operate 24-hour helplines that alcoholics and their family members can call for advice.

ALCOHOLICS ANONYMOUS (AA)

AA was started in 1935 by a businessman and a doctor who had been "hopeless drunks" (as they called themselves) for many years. After the men helped each other stop drinking and stay sober, they founded AA to help other alcoholics. Since that time, AA has spread throughout the world. Today there are over 40,000 AA groups and more than 835,000 AA members throughout the United States. AA meetings are open to anyone who wants to attend. There are no fees or dues for AA membership. Members remain anonymous by using only their first names in the group.

Alcohol addiction also affects the drinker's family. Family members may spend a great deal of time and effort covering up for the drinker. They often try to solve the problems that are caused by the drinker's behavior.

For the second time in a month, Jenny called her father's boss to tell him that her father was sick and couldn't come to work that evening. Actually, her father had passed out after drinking heavily all day. Jenny felt like a failure. "It's my fault," she thought. "It's too hard for him to raise me all by himself. If he didn't have me to worry about, he wouldn't drink so much."

Alateen

All across the United States, thousands of teenagers feel imprisoned by the alcoholism of a parent or loved one. For those teenagers, Alateen is available to help.

Alateen is a national support organization dedicated to helping teenaged children and teenaged friends of alcoholics understand the disease of alcoholism. In a group setting, which is free of charge or dues, Alateen promises a safe place for teenagers to talk about living with an alcoholic parent, sibling, or friend. For some teenagers, living with an alcoholic parent means taking over the responsibilities of a household. For others, it means living in constant fear of public embarrassment, or worse, of physical abuse. For most, living with an alcoholic produces feelings of isolation and loneliness.

Alateen follows the format of its parent organization, Al-Anon, a support group for the families and loved ones of alcoholics. Both organizations are based on 12 principles that were first developed by

Alcoholics Anonymous, the support group that has helped millions of alcoholics recover. Teenagers in Alateen find the support and love that they may be missing at home. At Alateen, no one judges or talks back or makes fun of the feelings of those suffering from the effects of alcoholism. Everything that is said within the group stays within the group—there is no fear of reporting. Alateen is a safe haven.

Alateen also can help teenagers understand that they are not responsible for a drinker's behavior. Many start attending Alateen meetings in the hope of finding a miracle cure for the drinker in their lives. But they discover that they cannot fix the alcoholic. Instead, they learn that they have choices about ways to deal with the alcoholic. By focusing on themselves instead of on the drinker, teenagers learn that their behavior and outlook are all that they can control. The teenagers learn that only the alcoholic can make the choice to recover.

Through Alateen, the teenaged relatives and friends of alcoholics can learn ways to cope with the problem of alcoholism while leading productive and happy lives.

1. Why do you think a group setting is important in helping friends or family members work out their feelings about the way alcoholism affects them?

2. Whose behavior is the focus of change in the format of Alateen? Why might this focus be effective for the attendees?

Family members often feel responsible for the drinker's behavior. This unrealistic and unhealthy view is called codependency. Instead of feeling responsible, family members must learn to separate themselves psychologically from the addicted drinker.

Jenny stayed awake most of the night, trying to figure out how she could help her father. As she got ready for school the next morning, she suddenly thought, "Maybe I can't do anything for him. Maybe the only person I can help is me." She decided to go to her guidance counselor when she got to school to see if he knew of any groups that could help her.

Separate support groups are available for those who are affected by the drinker's addiction. Al-Anon is a group for relatives and friends of alcoholics. Alateen is for teenaged children of alcoholics. Al-Anon and Alateen are also listed in the Yellow Pages.

INDIVIDUAL COUNSELING   Some addicted drinkers abuse alcohol as a way of avoiding problems in their lives. For these drinkers, individual counseling can be very helpful once they have stopped drinking. Beginning to understand oneself and the behavior patterns that led to heavy drinking can result in a more positive outlook and increased self-esteem. Counseling also helps the ex-drinker develop new behaviors and learn healthy ways of dealing with problems.

DRUG THERAPY   Doctors sometimes use drug therapy to help addicted users stop drinking. One drug, called Antabuse, blocks the enzymes that enable the drinker's body to process alcohol. If the person uses alcohol while taking Antabuse, he or she suffers effects similar to a severe hangover—a headache, nausea, vomiting, difficulty in breathing, and other unpleasant reactions. In this way, drinking becomes associated with getting sick, so the drinker avoids alcohol. Drug therapy is not a permanent solution to alcohol addiction. However, it can be useful as one part of a treatment program.

DETOXIFICATION   For an addicted drinker who has used excessive amounts of alcohol over a long time, the first step in treatment is usually detoxification. **Detoxification** [*dee tahk suh fuh KAY shun*] means allowing the body to rid itself of all alcohol. Detoxification involves withdrawal from the physical dependence on alcohol under medical supervision, usually in a hospital or an alcohol treatment center. Drugs are sometimes given to make withdrawal less dangerous. Withdrawal usually lasts about three or four days.

After detoxification, continued medical treatment is required, and a healthy nutritional program is established. Then counseling and support groups such as AA can be used to help the ex-drinker learn to live an alcohol-free life.

Counseling can help the ex-drinker learn constructive ways to deal with problems.

LESSON 21.3   **USING WHAT YOU HAVE LEARNED**

REVIEW

1. What is fetal alcohol syndrome?
2. Why should a drinker go through detoxification only with medical supervision?
3. In your own words, describe how alcohol causes cirrhosis.

THINK CRITICALLY

4. The family members of an addicted drinker often assume responsibility for the drinker's behavior. Give one example of something a family member might do to cover up for the drinker.
5. Members of Alcoholics Anonymous use only their first names in the group. Why do you think they do not tell each other their last names?

APPLY IT TO YOURSELF

6. Imagine that you are a high school guidance counselor talking with a girl whose mother is a heavy drinker. The girl's schoolwork has been suffering because she has to take over her mother's work at home. What would you say to help the girl?

SUMMARY

The harmful effects of alcohol abuse become worse over time. Alcohol abuse permanently damages the brain and liver, increases the risk of oral cancer and heart disease, and contributes to digestive problems. Alcohol also harms the fetuses of pregnant women who drink. Addicted drinkers who are motivated to stop drinking can be helped by support groups, counseling, and medical treatment.

ALCOHOL AND SOCIETY

Alcohol abuse affects not only the drinker but the drinker's family, friends, and co-workers. Also affected are the innocent victims of alcohol-related accidents, violence, and crime. Even mildly intoxicated drinkers can injure others in the home, on the job, in the classroom, and on the highway.

Alcohol abuse plays a major role in accidental deaths. It is also linked with suicide, homicide, rape, and robbery. Alcohol abuse increases medical and insurance costs for everyone. It creates a need for social services to treat problem drinkers and the people they affect.

ALCOHOL IN THE HOME

Alcohol abuse destroys one of the most important aspects of family life: trust. An addicted drinker thinks only about the need to drink. The drinker cannot be depended on as a parent or spouse. He or she may use money needed for food, rent, clothing, or medical expenses to buy alcohol. Family members may live in constant fear of the drinker's sudden mood changes.

Two thirds of all child abuse cases involve alcohol abuse. In some cases, abuse is in the form of neglect, with children not being adequately cared for and fed. Children in such a home feel helpless. They often have behavior problems in school and with their peers. In other cases, the abuse involves physical and psychological injury to the children. The damaging effects of such abuse can last well into adulthood.

Family members often feel ashamed of the drinker's behavior. They also may feel guilty because they no longer respect the alcoholic. Often, family members start avoiding their friends and rela-

MAIN IDEAS

CONCEPTS

✔ Alcohol abusers harm not only themselves but the people around them.

✔ Anyone who is planning to drive should not drink any alcohol at all.

✔ The legal drinking age in all states is 21.

VOCABULARY

driving while intoxicated (DWI)

minor

Figure 21-2   Which of these consequences of alcohol use involve crimes of violence?

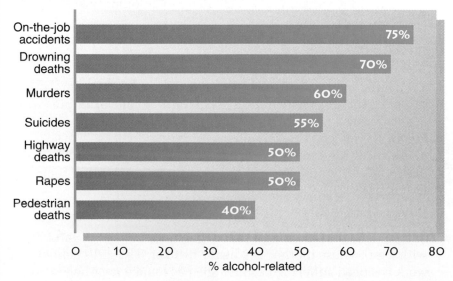

■ SOCIAL CONSEQUENCES OF ALCOHOL USE

Source: U. S. Department of Health and Human Services.

tives, trying to hide the problem. They may begin to lie and make excuses for the drinker. This behavior does not solve the drinker's problem. Instead of being protected by their family, alcohol abusers must come to the realization that they have a problem and accept responsibility for their own behavior.

Alcohol also contributes to safety hazards in the home. The risk of home accidents such as falls and fires is increased when alcohol is abused. For example, heavy drinkers who smoke may doze off or pass out and start a fire with a smoldering cigarette.

ALCOHOL ON THE JOB AND IN SCHOOL

Alcohol abuse leads to absences, poor concentration, poor performance, and accidents in school and at work. As a result, heavy drinkers often drop out of school or lose their jobs. To help prevent this outcome, many schools and businesses offer counseling and treatment programs for their students or employees with drinking problems.

According to one research study, 4,000 of the 20,000 students at a major university tested poorly or skipped class at least once a month due to heavy drinking. Another study found that students with lower grades tended to be heavier drinkers than students with higher grades. Because alcohol affects memory and concentration, heavy use impairs a student's ability to study and learn.

Alcohol is involved in over 50 percent of home fire deaths.

ALCOHOL AND DRIVING

Every year, 20,000 people are killed and 500,000 are injured by drunk drivers. Drunk drivers between the ages of 16 and 24 cause more fatal accidents than drunk drivers of any other age group.

Anyone who is planning to drive should not drink at all. Signs of intoxication can appear with a BAC level as low as 0.02. Drivers who have been drinking cannot concentrate as well as if they had not been drinking. They also may underestimate dangers and take careless risks. Because reaction time is slowed, the drinking driver takes longer to respond to road signs, traffic lights, or dangerous conditions. The driver's eyes also move more slowly and take longer to adjust to the glare of lights at night. At higher levels of intoxication, the driver's vision is blurred and coordination is impaired.

DRIVING WHILE INTOXICATED   In every state, it is illegal to drive while under the influence of alcohol. It is also illegal to drink alcohol while driving. In some states, it is illegal simply to carry an open container of any alcoholic beverage in the car. A majority of states have enacted a mandatory jail sentence as the immediate consequence for anyone who is caught driving while intoxicated. In most states, **driving while intoxicated (DWI)** is legally defined

STRATEGIES FOR LIVING

If you are driving and notice someone else driving erratically, the other driver might be drunk. Use the following strategies to protect yourself.

- Make sure seat belts are fastened and car doors are locked.
- If the drunk driver is coming *toward* you, pull over to the side of the road and honk your horn or blink your lights.
- If the drunk driver is *behind* you, pull over to the side of the road and wait for the driver to pass you.
- If the drunk driver is *ahead* of you, don't pass. Stay behind the other car, and leave a safe distance between it and your car.
- Watch carefully and be prepared for the driver to do something unexpected.

as driving with a BAC level of 0.10 or higher. A movement is now underway to lower the standard to 0.08 percent nationwide, and some states have already done so.

ALCOHOL AND BOATING

In most states, it is against the law to operate a boat while under the influence of alcohol. The National Safe Boating Council estimates that alcohol is involved in more than half of all boating accidents. Many states consider a boating DWI conviction to be the same as a motor vehicle DWI conviction.

DRINKING AND THE LAW   In recent years, public pressure against drunk driving and alcohol-related accidents has increased. As a result, more limits have been placed on the sale of alcoholic beverages. Many states now outlaw "happy hours" in which bars offer drinks at lower prices to encourage drinking after work. In many states, bar owners and bartenders are legally responsible for any damage or injury caused by a drunk driver they have served. People who serve alcoholic beverages in their homes are also considered responsible for their guests.

The legal drinking age is 21 in all states. Anyone under the age of 21 is a **minor.** In several states, any minor who is caught driving while intoxicated can have his or her driver's license taken away on the spot. In most states, it is illegal for minors to buy alcoholic beverages and to pretend they are older in order to buy them. It is also illegal for anyone to sell alcoholic beverages to a minor. In some states, a minor can drink at home or at a private social function if the minor is with a parent or legal guardian. National groups are working to make laws uniform in all states.

LESSON 21.4 USING WHAT YOU HAVE LEARNED

REVIEW

1. Who is a minor?
2. Identify two ways in which a drinker's alcohol abuse might affect people whom he or she doesn't even know.

THINK CRITICALLY

3. Suppose you live in a state that uses a BAC level of 0.10 as the standard for DWI. What could you say to convince legislators to lower the standard to 0.08?
4. In many states, bartenders and bar owners are legally responsible for damage or injury caused by a drinker whom they have served. Do you think this law is fair? Explain your answer.

APPLY IT TO YOURSELF

5. Imagine that you are a 25-year-old clerk in a liquor store. Your best friend's teenage brother comes in late one night and asks you to sell him a six-pack of beer on the sly. What would you say to refuse him?

SUMMARY

Problem drinkers harm not only themselves but the people around them. Alcohol abuse destroys trust among family members and causes problems in school and at work. Driving while under the influence of any amount of alcohol is dangerous. In recent years, new laws have been enacted in an effort to curb drunk driving and alcohol-related accidents. However, laws often vary from state to state.

MAKING RESPONSIBLE CHOICES

Although teenagers are legally prohibited from drinking alcohol, laws do not stop them from drinking. Young people often underestimate the power of alcohol's effects. They think they will be able to control their drinking but then find that they cannot.

DECIDING NOT TO DRINK

There is no scientific evidence that complete abstinence from alcohol is necessary for good health. On the other hand, there is a great deal of evidence that heavy alcohol use can damage your health, interfere with your development, and impair your relationships with others. If you choose to drink when you become of legal drinking age, it is critical that you use alcohol moderately and responsibly. While you are still a minor, you must be mindful of the legal consequences of underage drinking.

TEENAGERS AND DRINKING

There is no good reason for teenagers to drink, and many good reasons for them not to drink.

- People who begin drinking heavily as teenagers have a high risk of becoming addicted to alcohol as adults.

- The addicted drinkers who are the most successful in quitting alcohol are those who began drinking after age 20.

- According to a 1991 survey, 2.6 million teenagers don't know that a person can die from an overdose of alcohol. About 35% of these teenagers think that black coffee, a cold shower, or fresh air can sober up an intoxicated drinker.

- The majority of young people who use illegal drugs first used alcohol. Moreover, they continue using alcohol along with regular use of other drugs. As a result, these young people have higher-than-average rates of alcohol-related injury and death.

- Alcohol-related accidents and violence kill more American teenagers than all other factors combined.

- Almost 50 percent of all deaths among teenagers 15 to 19 years old occur in alcohol-related auto accidents.

Even if you do not try to buy or drink alcohol illegally, you still may be faced with situations in which alcohol will be made available to you—at a friend's party, a neighborhood cookout, or a wedding, for example. There may be times when taking a drink will seem like a natural and even comforting thing to do. Learning ways to resist peer pressure, develop social skills, and cope with stress will enable you to avoid becoming a drinker.

MAIN IDEAS

CONCEPTS

✔ Teenagers can resist pressure to drink alcohol by refusing calmly, firmly, and confidently.

✔ Alcohol use interferes with normal development of social skills.

✔ It is important to develop techniques for dealing with intoxicated drivers.

✔ Alateen provides support for teenaged children of alcoholics.

VOCABULARY

designated driver

STRATEGIES FOR LIVING

These techniques can help you refuse a drink when someone is urging you to take one.

- **Say, "No, thanks."** Make your refusal calmly, firmly, and confidently.

- **Keep it brief.** Don't give excuses, explanations, apologies, or arguments. This is not the time to discuss your reasons.

- **Expect others to respect your choice.** When you are firm and confident of your choice, your "No, thanks" will be more likely to be respected by others. If you seem hesitant or unsure of yourself, you give others an opening to tease you or argue with you.

- **Don't make fun of the drinker's choice to drink.** Criticizing the drinker's choice opens the door to further discussion and arguments. Focus on your own refusal.

- **Consider another group of friends.** If you continue to be pressured by friends who are drinking, consider developing other friendships. People who try to push alcohol on someone who refuses a drink generally are using alcohol irresponsibly themselves. If they base the friendship on your drinking behavior, it may be best to look elsewhere for friendship.

RESISTING PEER PRESSURE Resisting peer pressure is very difficult, particularly when you are being pressured by friends or other people you like and admire. You need to be prepared to refuse the urgings of others. The strategies suggested above can help you deal with such a situation. Remember, refusing a drink is a personal decision that requires no apology or explanation on your part.

DEVELOPING SOCIAL SKILLS Some people feel that drinking makes them more sociable and outgoing. In reality, however, drinking prevents people from developing honest, undistorted relationships with others. Learning how to relax and be comfortable in different social settings is part of growing up. Using alcohol to ease you through such situations interferes with this learning process. If you are somewhat shy and anxious in social situations, remind yourself that other people are, too—and not only teenagers. Instead of drinking when you feel shy and anxious, work on developing social skills, and allow yourself time to grow.

Learning how to relax and be comfortable in social situations takes practice.

COPING WITH STRESS   In movies and on TV, adults are often shown taking a drink when they are under stress or trying to cope with a problem. In reality, drinking does not solve problems but creates other problems. Everyone experiences stressful times. Learning and practicing healthy techniques for dealing with stress will enable you to avoid using alcohol as an escape.

Being able to share feelings with friends often helps put a problem in perspective. Maintaining close, honest relationships with others is an important part of developing your self-esteem and confidence. Learning constructive ways to relax—such as doing fitness workouts or listening to music—helps relieve stress.

AVOIDING INTOXICATED DRIVERS

Every 20 minutes, a teenager dies in an alcohol-related highway accident. Not all of those teenagers are intoxicated drivers. Many are passengers in cars driven by teenagers who have been drinking. If you know that a driver has been drinking, or if you smell alcohol on the driver's breath, find another ride. If you are already in the car when the driver starts drinking, insist that the driver stop the car in a safe place and let you out. Offending and inconveniencing a friend is far better than risking serious injury or death.

You may have heard the slogan "Friends don't let friends drive drunk." If you are with a friend who is intoxicated but who still intends to drive, insist that your friend ride with you or with another driver who has not been drinking. If you cannot convince your friend not to drive, take his or her car keys. Your friend may get angry with you, but this is far better than letting your friend risk serious injury or death.

In recent years, two organizations—Mothers Against Drunk Driving (MADD) and Students Against Driving Drunk (SADD)—have increased public awareness of the tragedies caused by drunk driving. MADD has successfully lobbied state and local officials to enact stricter drinking-and-driving laws and to increase penalties against drunk drivers. SADD works within schools and communities to educate students and their parents about the risks of driving while intoxicated and to suggest alternatives to this dangerous and sometimes deadly behavior.

> ### HEALTHY PEOPLE 2000
>
> *Reduce deaths caused by alcohol-related motor vehicle crashes to no more than 8.5 per 100,000 people.*
>
> Objective 4.1
> from *Healthy People 2000: National Health Promotion and Disease Prevention Objectives*

CONTRACT FOR LIFE

One important tool developed by SADD is the Contract for Life. The contract is a printed form with written agreements between a student and his or her parents.

- *The student promises* to call his or her parents for a safe ride rather than drive while intoxicated or ride with an intoxicated driver.

- *The parents promise* to pick up the student or provide a taxi—at any time, no questions asked, and with no argument. The parents also promise not to drive when intoxicated themselves.

What support groups for problem drinkers and their families are listed in the Yellow Pages in your area?

Friends who are going out together can avoid risky driving situations by choosing one person beforehand to be the designated driver. A **designated driver** is a person who agrees not to drink at all so that he or she can safely drive the others home. An added benefit of this technique is that the designated driver finds it less uncomfortable to refuse drinks. In fact, there is some prestige in saying, "No, thanks. I'm the designated driver tonight." Of course, any minors in the group also should not drink.

GETTING HELP

If someone in your family is a problem drinker, or if you are concerned about your own drinking, help is available to you. Sources of help are listed in the Yellow Pages under "Alcoholism Information and Treatment" and "Drug Abuse and Addiction." Don't be afraid to call any of these groups. Anything you tell them will be kept strictly confidential, and you won't even have to give them your name. You might prefer to contact a local helpline or teen referral service or to discuss your situation with a teacher, guidance counselor, neighbor, or other trusted adult.

If someone in your family is a problem drinker, get help *for yourself.* One source is Alateen, the group described in *Making a Difference* earlier in this chapter. The key is to realize that the drinker's problem is not your responsibility. You cannot solve the problem, change it, or assume responsibility for it. You have a right to develop as a healthy person regardless of a family member's drinking problem.

SUMMARY

Drinking and drunk driving take a heavy toll on teenagers. It is therefore particularly important for teenagers to learn how to resist peer pressure, develop social skills, and cope with stress so that drinking can be avoided. Teens also should learn how to protect themselves against intoxicated drivers. Help is available for teenagers who have a family member with a drinking problem or who are concerned about their own drinking.

LESSON 21.5 USING WHAT YOU HAVE LEARNED

REVIEW

1. Who is a designated driver?
2. Identify three healthy ways to cope with stress.
3. What is the focus of Alateen?

THINK CRITICALLY

4. When you refuse a drink, you shouldn't make fun of the drinker's choice to drink. Why would this approach be more effective than criticizing the drinker?
5. This lesson suggests several ways to avoid riding with an intoxicated driver and to prevent an intoxicated friend from driving. Suggest another technique you might use in either one of these situations.

APPLY IT TO YOURSELF

6. Imagine that you are a police officer who has just arrested a 17-year-old boy for driving while intoxicated. This is the boy's first offense, and he's obviously very frightened. How would you handle this situation? As you decide, think about the positive and negative outcomes of each action that you could take.

Making a Contract

Kira and her parents were always arguing about her friends. "They're not the kind of people we want you hanging around with," said her mother. "They smoke and they drink."

Some of her friends did drink, and yes, a couple of them smoked. But Kira didn't smoke or drink. She felt as though her parents didn't trust her to make the right decisions.

One day, the president of Students Against Driving Drunk spoke to the whole school about the organization. At the assembly, Kira learned about the Contract for Life. It is a signed agreement between a student and his or her parents. It states that if a student is ever in a situation where he or she cannot get home for any reason, one of the parents would come pick up the child with no questions asked. The second part of the Contract stated that the parents would agree never to drive if they have had any alcohol to drink. Kira was impressed by the idea of a contract, but she couldn't imagine asking her parents to sign one. "That would just raise the same old arguments," she thought. "They would use it as

proof that my friends are bad." But Kira also knew that not asking them to sign the Contract could leave her in a difficult situation at some point.

PAUSE AND CONSIDER

1. ***Identify the Problem.*** Why is it difficult for Kira to discuss the Contract for Life with her parents?

2. ***Consider the Options.*** What are Kira's options?

3. ***Evaluate the Outcomes.*** What does Kira think might happen if she tells her parents about the Contract for Life? What could happen if she does not discuss the Contract with her parents?

The next day at school, Kira spoke with the S.A.D.D. president about her dilemma. Hal reassured her that a lot of students had similar concerns. Kira had an idea. "Hal, would you consider coming over to my house for dinner one night? Maybe you can tell them

about S.A.D.D., and you can bring up the Contract for Life."

"That's a good idea. When should I come over?"

When Hal came to dinner, Kira told her parents that he was the president of S.A.D.D. at school. "Really," said Kira's father. "I'm not familiar with that group." Hal explained about S.A.D.D. and about the Contract for Life. Kira's father said, "You know, that's a good idea. Maybe we should do something like that. At least then we won't have to worry about you riding home with those wild friends of yours."

"Oh Dad, they're not wild. Were your parents always happy about your friends?" Kira's father laughed. "No, I guess not. I remember once my father saying to me..." Kira laughed. She was glad he hadn't forgotten what it was like to be a teenager.

DECIDE AND REVIEW

4. ***Decide and Act.*** What was Kira's decision? How did Kira solve her dilemma?

5. ***Review.*** How else might she have brought up the Contract for Life with her parents?

PROJECTS

1. In 1919 an amendment was added to the U. S. Constitution banning the sale and consumption of alcoholic beverages. In 1933 the amendment was repealed. The period during which the amendment was enforced is called Prohibition. Find out more about Prohibition. Who supported the amendment? Who opposed it? What happened during Prohibition? Present your findings in an oral or written report.

2. Alcoholics Anonymous, Al-Anon, and other support groups have been very effective in helping problem drinkers and their families. Find out more about a group in your area or one that you think should be started in your area. What principles and techniques does the group use? Why do you think the group has been effective?

WORKING WITH OTHERS

With a partner, role-play a situation in which one of you is trying to persuade the other to take an alcoholic drink. When you role-play the situation, be realistic. What might a teenager who is trying to convince another teenager to drink really say? What might the other teenager actually say to refuse the drink without risking ridicule or rejection?

CONNECTING TO...

SOCIOLOGY Gather information about alcohol-related problems in your own community. Arrange to talk with an officer in your local police department or with a staff member in an alcohol treatment center or hospital. Try to find out how many alcohol-related accidents, injuries, deaths, and crimes occur in your community. Prepare a classroom display or oral report to share your findings with the class.

USING VOCABULARY

addiction
alcoholism
blackouts
blood alcohol
  content (BAC)
cirrhosis
depressant
designated driver
detoxification
driving while
  intoxicated (DWI)

fetal alcohol
  syndrome
gateway drug
hangover
heavy drinker
hepatitis
inhibitions
intoxication
light drinker

minor
moderate drinker
multiplier effect
proof
psychoactive drug
reflex
tolerance
withdrawal
  symptom

Number a separate sheet of paper from 1 to 9. Use terms from the vocabulary list to complete the sentences in the following passage.

Alcohol is a(n) __1__ that acts on the brain, affecting a person's mind and behavior. For some young people, alcohol may function as a(n) __2__ that leads them to try other drugs. Because alcohol slows down nerve activity, it is classified as a(n) __3__. Alcohol's short-term effects on a person's mind and behavior are called __4__. The unpleasant physical effects that follow heavy alcohol use are known as a(n) __5__.

A person who consumes more than two drinks per day on average is considered a(n) __6__. For people who drink more than four drinks per day, alcohol use has become a(n) __7__. Heavy drinkers risk developing serious diseases such as __8__ and __9__.

CONCEPT MAPPING

Copy and complete the concept map shown below. Information on concept mapping appears at the front of this book.

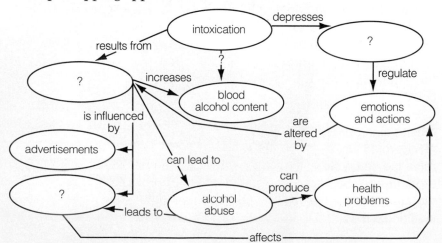

THINKING CRITICALLY

INTERPRET

LESSON 21.1
1. What does "proof" mean?

2. According to NIAAA, what amount of alcohol use characterizes a moderate drinker?

3. How many ounces of alcohol are contained in six 12-ounce cans of beer?

4. What is alcoholism?

LESSON 21.2
5. Why does alcohol enter the bloodstream so rapidly?

6. What happens when a person drinks alcohol more quickly than the liver can break it down?

7. Identify three physical characteristics of a hangover.

8. How long does it take the liver to break down the amount of alcohol contained in two drinks?

LESSON 21.3
9. Why is cirrhosis often not detected until its later stages?

10. Why do heavy, long-term drinkers often suffer from malnutrition?

11. Why do heavy drinkers have an increased risk of high blood pressure, stroke, coronary heart disease, and heart attack?

12. What birth defects are associated with fetal alcohol syndrome?

13. What type of long-term treatment has been most effective for alcohol addiction?

LESSON 21.4
14. How does heavy alcohol use impair a student's ability to study and learn?

15. What is the legal definition of driving while intoxicated in most states?

16. If you are driving and you suspect that the driver behind you is drunk, what should you do?

LESSON 21.5
17. Who is a designated driver?

18. How could someone easily and quickly find sources of help for a drinking problem?

APPLY

LESSON 21.1
19. Why do advertisements for alcoholic beverages always portray drinkers in a positive way?

LESSON 21.2
20. Briefly describe the stages of alcohol intoxication.

21. Explain why cold showers, black coffee, and other "cures" for alcohol intoxication actually do not work.

LESSON 21.3
22. Describe how cirrhosis of the liver develops.

23. In what ways can individual counseling help an addicted drinker once he or she has stopped drinking?

LESSON 21.4
24. Describe alcohol's effects on drivers who have been drinking.

LESSON 21.5
25. In SADD's Contract for Life, what agreements are made between a student and his or her parents?

COMMITMENT TO WELLNESS

FOLLOW-UP

SETTING GOALS

Review your responses to the checklist at the beginning of this chapter. Which statements accurately describe you? Which behaviors do you not engage in now? Which do you most want to change? Write those items in your Wellness Journal. Think about specific actions that you can take to change the behaviors, and outline a plan.

If there are other behaviors that were not included in the assessment checklist but that you would like to work on, include them in your plan as well. At the end of the plan, establish a target date for changing the behavior. On that date, review your plan and evaluate your progress toward your goals.

WHERE DO I GO FROM HERE?

There are numerous organizations that can help you if you or someone you know has a problem with alcohol abuse. Contact Alcoholics Anonymous, Al-Anon, Alateen, or your local chapter of SADD, or talk with a guidance counselor or adjustment counselor.

FOR MORE INFORMATION ABOUT ALCOHOL ABUSE, CONTACT:

Alcoholics Anonymous World Services
475 Riverside Drive
New York, New York 10163

Al-Anon/Alateen Family Group Headquarters
P.O. Box 862 Midtown Station
New York, New York 10018

Alcoholism Helpline
1-800-527-5344

CHAPTER 22 ≈

Psychoactive Drugs and Steroids

"No one can safely expose himself [or herself] to danger. The man [or woman] who has often escaped is caught at last."

Seneca

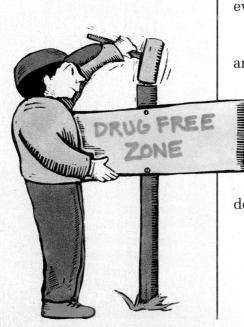

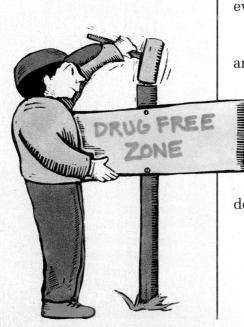

BACKGROUND

Lucius Seneca was a Roman statesman and philosopher during the heyday of the Roman empire. His numerous philosophical works reflect a sharp wit and a learned mind. He was responsible for introducing financial and judicial reform in the Roman senate.

Every day, people take risks. Some risks are healthy. They stretch the imagination and open the door to new horizons. Other risks are dangerous. One of the most dangerous risks a person can take is to begin using a drug illegally. Drug abuse is not merely dangerous but often life-threatening.

No one can long escape the consequences of drug abuse. Sooner or later, abusers get caught. Sometimes they are caught by the law. Other times, they are caught in the nightmare of addiction. Some are caught by a serious disability or disease or even by death.

Drugs rob users of the ability to think clearly, to feel honestly, and to meet the challenges and opportunities the world has to offer. By learning all that you can about drugs—especially, how to avoid and refuse them—you will not be robbed of your health and your friendships. Instead, you will continue to grow and to nurture relationships, free of a demanding and dangerous habit.

Use the following checklist to take a closer look at yourself. Number a page from 1 to 10 in your Wellness Journal or on a separate sheet of paper, and respond *yes* or *no* to each of the following statements. Answer *yes* for each statement that describes you all or most of the time.

1. I avoid places where drugs might be used.
2. I know several warning signs that indicate someone might be using drugs.
3. I do not drink alcohol or smoke cigarettes.
4. I do not use a prescription drug unless it has been prescribed for me, and I follow my doctor's instructions on how to take it.
5. I do not associate with people who use drugs.
6. I am involved in activities that interest me.
7. I exercise regularly, eat a healthy diet, and get enough sleep.
8. I know techniques for refusing drugs when other people offer them to me.
9. I never use a drug, including alcohol, to relax or to help me sleep.
10. I use healthy strategies for dealing with stress and with uncomfortable feelings.

Review your responses, and try to decide which responses might represent your strengths and which would represent your weaknesses. Save your personal checklist for a follow-up activity that appears at the end of this chapter.

MAIN IDEAS

CONCEPTS

✔ Drug abuse includes misusing legal drugs and household products as well as using illegal drugs.

✔ For some young people, alcohol and tobacco function as gateway drugs to illegal drug use.

✔ Using alcohol with another psychoactive drug can be deadly.

VOCABULARY

drug abuse
psychoactive drug
gateway drug
addiction
tolerance
withdrawal symptom
overdose

Figure 22-1   In which category is marijuana classified? (Hint: Marijuana is made from the cannabis plant.)

WHAT IS DRUG ABUSE?

When someone mentions the term *drug abuse,* you may at first think of illegal drugs such as marijuana, heroin, crack, and LSD. Certainly, any use of an illegal drug, even occasional light use, is drug abuse. However, the term *drug abuse* also includes intentionally using legal drugs and substances—prescription medicines, over-the-counter medications, alcohol, and even some common household products—in an inappropriate or unsafe manner. Thus, **drug abuse** is any use of an illegal drug or the misuse of any legal drug or other psychoactive substance.

As you may recall from earlier chapters, a **psychoactive drug** [*sy koh AK tiv*] is a chemical substance that acts on the brain, affecting a person's mind and behavior. Depending on the type of drug that is used, a psychoactive drug may make you feel elated, relaxed, more energetic, more excited, or simply *different* from the way you normally feel. These mind-altering effects are a major reason that psychoactive drugs are abused.

Because of their damaging effects, psychoactive drugs are controlled by federal and state laws. Federal law classifies psychoactive drugs in five categories, as you can see in Figure 22-1. The drugs with the highest potential for abuse and addiction and no accepted medical use are classified in Category I.

WHY DO YOUNG PEOPLE TRY DRUGS?

The most common reason that teenagers and young adults start using drugs is to be accepted by their peers or "fit in." In addition, many young people try drugs because they are curious about the

CATEGORIES OF PSYCHOACTIVE DRUGS

Category	Characteristics	Drugs
Category I	Highest potential for abuse and addiction. No accepted medical use.	Cannabis, heroin, LSD, mescaline, methaqualone
Category II	High potential for abuse and addiction. Restricted medical use.	Amphetamine, cocaine, codeine, methadone, methamphetamine, morphine, opium, phencyclidine (PCP), some barbiturates
Category III	Some potential for abuse and addiction. Accepted medical use.	Nonamphetamine stimulants, some barbiturates and narcotics
Category IV	Low potential for abuse and addiction. Accepted medical use.	Nonbarbiturate sedatives; minor tranquilizers; some barbiturates, narcotics, and nonamphetamine stimulants
Category V	Lowest potential for abuse. Accepted medical use.	Over-the-counter medications with low amounts of codeine or other narcotics

SOURCE: NATIONAL INSTITUTE ON DRUG ABUSE

effects. Other reasons for trying drugs include wanting to relax, to relieve boredom or depression, and to escape personal problems and believing that drugs can help achieve these goals.

A study done in the 1970s found that there is a typical sequence of stages leading to drug abuse among teenagers. Most begin their drug use with beer or wine. In the second stage, many begin using liquor or cigarettes or both. In the next stage, they start using marijuana. It is only after going through these three stages that some young people try other illegal drugs. A psychoactive substance that leads the user to try other drugs is called a **gateway drug.** Thus, for some young people, alcohol and tobacco function as gateway drugs to illegal drug use. Fortunately, the majority of young people who use alcohol and tobacco do *not* go on to use illegal drugs.

HOW DOES DRUG ABUSE DEVELOP?

The powerful effects of psychoactive drugs quickly lead users from experimentation to regular use and addiction. **Addiction** [*uh DIK shun*] is a strong physical and psychological craving for a substance.

EXPERIMENTATION Many psychoactive drugs produce unusual feelings in the users. These feelings may be so attractive to experimenters that they want to use the drug again. Soon, the experimenters find themselves using the drug regularly. Regular use produces tolerance.

TOLERANCE **Tolerance** is reduced sensitivity to a drug that results from regular use. As tolerance develops, the person must use increasingly larger amounts of the drug to get

There are many constructive ways to make yourself feel good, to relax, to relieve boredom, and to deal with personal problems.

HEALTHY PEOPLE 2000

Reduce drug-related deaths to no more than 3 per 100,000 people.

Objective 4.3
from *Healthy People 2000: National Health Promotion and Disease Prevention Objectives*

the same effect. With most psychoactive drugs, tolerance quickly leads to physical dependence.

PHYSICAL DEPENDENCE   With repeated use of a psychoactive drug, the body becomes physically dependent on its effects. When addicted users stop taking the drug, they experience withdrawal symptoms. **Withdrawal symptoms** are uncomfortable reactions that occur when a person stops using an addictive substance. Depending on the type and amount of drug used, withdrawal symptoms may include depression, anxiety, chills, sweating, diarrhea, nausea, and trembling. One reason that addicted users continue their drug abuse is to avoid withdrawal symptoms.

PSYCHOLOGICAL DEPENDENCE   When a psychoactive drug is used repeatedly, the user becomes psychologically dependent on its mind-altering effects. The effects reinforce, or strengthen, the drug-taking behavior. For many drug abusers, psychological dependence is even stronger than physical dependence as a motivation to keep using drugs.

THE DANGERS OF DRUG ABUSE

Drug abuse involves two overall dangers: the damaging effects of combining drugs, and severe injury or death from an overdose. When psychoactive drugs are combined, their effects can seriously disrupt heart rate, breathing, and other body processes. The psychoactive drug most often combined with another drug is alcohol. This combination causes hundreds of accidental deaths every year.

Drug abusers also risk taking an overdose. An **overdose** is a drug dose high enough to cause serious injury, coma, or death. The purity and strength of illegal drugs are not controlled, so users can never be sure of what they are taking. By the time a user discovers that a drug—or a drug combination—is far more potent than he or she expected, it is too late.

LESSON 22.1 **USING WHAT YOU HAVE LEARNED**

REVIEW

1. What is a psychoactive drug?

2. Identify two reasons that drug abusers continue taking drugs.

THINK CRITICALLY

3. The majority of teenagers who use alcohol and tobacco do not use other drugs. Suggest one reason why some teenagers do go on to use illegal drugs.

4. Suppose someone who is taking prescribed sleeping pills becomes confused and takes too many. Is this an example of drug abuse? Explain your answer.

APPLY IT TO YOURSELF

5. Imagine that you are a doctor talking with a new patient. He asks you for a prescription for a strong painkiller. You wonder whether he might be abusing the drug. What would you do?

SUMMARY

Drug abuse includes using illegal drugs and misusing prescription drugs, over-the-counter drugs, alcohol, and psychoactive substances in household products. The effects of psychoactive drugs lead to physical and psychological dependence. Most teenagers who abuse drugs began their drug use with alcohol and tobacco. Combining psychoactive drugs or taking an overdose can cause coma or death.

LESSON 22.2

COMMONLY ABUSED DRUGS

Based on their effects on the mind and body, psychoactive drugs are classified into four major groups: stimulants, depressants, narcotics, and hallucinogens. Three other types of drugs—cannabis (marijuana), inhalants, and designer drugs—have the same effects as some drugs in the four major groups. Steroids are discussed in the last section of this lesson. Steroids are not considered psychoactive drugs but are abused for other reasons.

MAIN IDEAS

CONCEPTS

- ✔ Stimulants, depressants, narcotics, and hallucinogens have different effects on the mind and body.
- ✔ Marijuana is not a harmless drug.
- ✔ Long-term use of inhalants causes severe damage to the body.
- ✔ The damaging effects of steroids far outweigh their muscle-building benefits.

VOCABULARY

stimulant
euphoria
paranoia
depressant
narcotic
hallucinogen
cannabis
inhalant
designer drug
anabolic steroid

STIMULANTS

Stimulants [*STIM yuh lunts*] are drugs that stimulate, or speed up, nerve activity. Two weak stimulants that you already know about are nicotine and caffeine. Figure 22-2 lists the characteristics of stimulants. The most commonly abused stimulants are amphetamines, methamphetamine, and cocaine.

AMPHETAMINES Like other stimulants, amphetamines [*am FET uh meenz*] make users feel more energetic and alert. One side effect of amphetamines is loss of appetite. Because of this effect, doctors used to prescribe amphetamines for a short period to help patients lose weight.

Amphetamines and other stimulants produce **euphoria** [*yu FOR ee uh*], a feeling of intense happiness and well-being. However, when amphetamines are used in large amounts or for a long time, they can make users feel nervous and jumpy or even cause paranoia. **Paranoia** [*par uh NOY uh*] is a mental disorder in which the person is abnormally suspicious and fearful of other people. Amphetamines cause strong psychological dependence as well as physical dependence.

Figure 22-2 Which stimulant can cause aggressive behavior?

STIMULANTS

Drugs (nicknames): **amphetamines** (speed, uppers), **methamphetamine** (ice, glass, crank, crystal meth), **cocaine** (coke, snow, crack)

Physical effects: increased heart rate, blood pressure, and breathing rate; increased energy; restlessness; loss of appetite; prolonged wakefulness and difficulty sleeping. **Long-term use:** damage to brain, lungs, liver, and kidneys

Psychological effects: euphoria; perceived increase in alertness; depression; paranoia; hallucinations; effects of methamphetamine also include aggressive behavior

Effects of overdose: extreme nervousness, hallucinations, paranoia, convulsions, heart and lung failure, coma, death

Withdrawal symptoms: lack of interest in normal activities, fatigue, irritability, depression, mental confusion

METHAMPHETAMINE Methamphetamine [*meth am FET uh meen*] is an amphetamine-like stimulant that also was used legally for weight control. Methamphetamine produces euphoria that lasts from 12 to 24 hours. During this time, the user cannot sleep and has no appetite. Methamphetamine users may experience paranoia and become aggressive and violent. As you can see in Figure 22-2, the drug causes serious damage to the brain and body.

Crack, a smokable form of cocaine, is highly addictive.

COCAINE Cocaine [*koh KAYN*] is a white powder that is made from the leaves of the South American coca plant. Cocaine is sometimes used as a local anesthetic in nose and throat surgery. Cocaine is a highly addictive drug that causes serious physical and psychological problems, including hallucinations and paranoia. Cocaine is usually inhaled, or "snorted." Cocaine's effects are felt quickly but do not last very long. When the high ends abruptly, the user feels irritable, anxious, and depressed.

Crack is a smokable form of cocaine. Crack's effects are more intense than cocaine's but last for an even shorter time. The user then has an intense craving for another dose. Physical and psychological dependence develop quickly with crack. The addiction is extremely difficult to break. In addition, crack's rapid and intense effects on the heart can be extremely dangerous, even deadly. Despite these risks, crack use has become a serious problem nationwide. This is partly because crack is less expensive than powdered cocaine.

DEPRESSANTS

Depressants [*dih PRES unts*] are drugs that depress, or slow down, nerve activity. Alcohol, the most commonly abused psychoactive drug, is a depressant. Other commonly abused depressants are barbiturates, tranquilizers, and methaqualone. The characteristics of depressants are listed in Figure 22-3.

BARBITURATES Barbiturates [*bahr BICH uh ruts*] are strong depressants that are prescribed to relax people or help them sleep. People abuse barbiturates because of the drugs' lethargic effects. As tolerance increases, abusers find that they cannot sleep without taking barbiturates. Psychological and physical dependence follow.

Because barbiturates cause mental confusion, users sometimes take an accidental overdose. When barbiturates are used in combination with alcohol, they can completely stop the user's breathing. Also, barbiturates have severe withdrawal symptoms that can cause convulsions and death.

TRANQUILIZERS People who suffer from anxiety may be treated medically with tranquilizers [*TRANG kwuh ly zurz*]. Long-term use of these drugs causes physical and psychological dependence. Tranquilizers are particularly dangerous when combined with alcohol. This combination causes hundreds of fatal drug overdoses every year.

Figure 22-3   Notice that alcohol is included on this chart.

DEPRESSANTS

Drugs (nicknames): **barbiturates** (downers), **tranquilizers**, **methaqualone** (ludes, quads, sopers), **alcohol**

Physical effects: decreased heart rate, blood pressure, and breathing rate; sleepiness; drunken behavior; poor coordination; blurred vision; slowed reaction time

Psychological effects: calmness, reduced anxiety, relaxed inhibitions, lowered alertness, mental confusion, mood changes, impaired reasoning and judgment

Effects of overdose: shallow breathing; cold, clammy skin; weak, rapid heartbeat; coma; death

Withdrawal symptoms: restlessness, nausea, blurred vision, difficulty sleeping, trembling, hallucinations, paranoia, convulsions, possible death

METHAQUALONE   Methaqualone [*meh THAK wuh lohn*] produces a sudden rush of euphoria. Physical and psychological dependence develop rapidly with this drug. Its side effects include headaches, nosebleeds, dizziness, and diarrhea. Methaqualone has severe withdrawal symptoms. Combining methaqualone with alcohol carries a high risk of a fatal overdose.

NARCOTICS

Narcotics [*nahr KAHT iks*] are strong painkillers that produce a relaxed, dreamy state. Narcotics are also called *opiates* because they are derived from the opium plant. Narcotics include codeine, opium, morphine, and heroin. Figure 22-4 summarizes the characteristics of narcotics.

Narcotics act like chemicals called endorphins that occur naturally throughout your body, particularly in your brain. Endorphins control pain and regulate your emotions. Physical activity raises your endorphin levels. When your endorphin levels are high, you feel euphoric. Narcotics produce this same effect. However, narcotics also cause nausea, vomiting, and other unpleasant reactions.

Figure 22-4 Narcotics are made from the opium plant. Here you can see raw opium oozing from shallow cuts in the unripe seed pods of opium poppies.

CODEINE   Codeine [*KOH deen*], the least potent narcotic, is prescribed for mild pain. It is also used in some prescription cough medicines for its calming effect. Codeine is abused because it produces euphoria. Codeine is not as addictive as other, more potent narcotics, but it does cause physical and psychological dependence.

OPIUM   Opium [*OH pee um*], a stronger narcotic than codeine, may be prescribed to relieve pain or control diarrhea. Opium produces an initial rush of euphoria followed by a prolonged dreamy state. This narcotic is highly addictive and causes severe withdrawal symptoms.

NARCOTICS

Drugs (nicknames):   **codeine** (school boy), **opium** (blue velvet, black stuff), **morphine** (white stuff, morf), **heroin** (horse, smack, junk)

Physical effects: pain relief; sleepiness; decreased heart rate, blood pressure, and breathing rate; nausea and vomiting; constipation; slurred speech; poor coordination

Psychological effects: euphoria; relaxation; perceived reduction of anxiety; inability to concentrate; dulled senses; lack of interest in surroundings; lack of response to frustration, hunger, and sexual stimulation; mood changes

Effects of overdose: clammy skin, constricted pupils, slow and shallow breathing, convulsions, coma, death

Withdrawal symptoms: flu-like symptoms such as watery eyes, runny nose, chills, sweating, stomach cramps, nausea, and diarrhea; loss of appetite; dizziness; muscle twitches and trembling; irritability; feeling of panic

MORPHINE   Morphine [*MOR feen*] is more potent than opium. In fact, it is one of the strongest painkillers known. Because morphine is so addictive, its medical use is strictly limited by law. It is prescribed to relieve severe pain, such as after major surgery or with cancer patients. People abuse morphine for its euphoric effect. They quickly become physically and psychologically dependent. Withdrawal from morphine is extremely difficult.

HEROIN Heroin [*HER uh wun*] is a white powder made from morphine. It is more potent than morphine and acts more quickly. Because it is so addictive, heroin is prohibited from medical use in the United States. Heroin is the most widely abused narcotic in this country.

People use heroin for the intense euphoria it produces. Heroin dulls the senses and eases the user's fears and worries. Users appear to be in a daze that lasts for hours. Physical dependence develops rapidly. Addicted users must take several doses each day to avoid the drug's withdrawal symptoms. These include the flu-like symptoms listed in Figure 22-4.

Accidental overdoses are common, with many ending in death. In addition, the drug's mind-numbing effects make users careless about their health. As a result, they frequently suffer from poor nutrition. More importantly, heroin users often share dirty hypodermic needles. This practice carries a high risk of infection with hepatitis and the virus that causes AIDS, which is fatal.

HALLUCINOGENS

Hallucinogens [*huh LOOS un uh junz*] are drugs that distort users' perceptions of their surroundings and their own bodies. People who are experiencing hallucinations see, hear, or otherwise sense things that actually do not exist.

Commonly abused hallucinogens are LSD, mescaline, and PCP. Figure 22-5 summarizes the characteristics of these drugs.

Figure 22-5 Which of these hallucinogens causes aggressive and possibly violent behavior?

HALLUCINOGENS

Drugs (nicknames): **LSD** (acid), **mescaline** (DOM, STP, TMA, MMDA), **PCP** (angel dust)

Physical effects: **LSD and mescaline:** dilated pupils; increased heart rate, blood pressure, body temperature, salivation, and perspiration; muscle twitches; nausea. **PCP:** decreased heart rate, blood pressure, and breathing rate; drunken behavior; slurred speech; poor coordination; insensitivity to pain; increased aggression; possible violence

Psychological effects: euphoria or extreme fear; hallucinations; distortion of senses; altered perception of time, distance, and own body; mental confusion; impaired memory. **LSD:** flashbacks

Effects of overdose: panic; long periods of mental confusion and distorted perception resembling severe mental illness. **PCP:** violent behavior; drastic drop in blood pressure; convulsions; coma; death

Withdrawal symptoms: none known

LSD LSD (lysergic acid diethylamide) is an extremely powerful drug. Just a tiny amount causes vivid and strange visions. These visions, called a "trip," can last six to eight hours. During a "trip," users may become terrified and believe they are in danger. In some cases, users have died because they lost touch with reality and tried to do something impossible, such as fly out a window or walk on water. Weeks or months after taking LSD, users may experience flashbacks, which are times when the drug's effects return without warning. LSD is not known to cause physical dependence, but users may develop psychological dependence.

MESCALINE Mescaline [*MES kuh lun*] is a psychoactive substance found in peyote [*pay OHT ee*], a type of cactus that grows in the southwestern United States and northern Mexico. Peyote's only legal use is in religious ceremonies and spiritual practices of the

Native American Church of North America and some other Native American groups.

When mescaline is eaten, it at first produces nausea and vomiting. Users then begin to experience visions. Mescaline is not known to produce physical dependence, but psychological dependence may develop. Laboratory-made forms of mescaline are sold as the street drugs DOM, STP, TMA, and MMDA. These drugs are highly toxic in even small amounts.

PCP PCP (phencyclidine) was originally developed as a surgical anesthetic. However, when the drug was first tried with people, many had severe reactions such as hallucinations, paranoia, depression, and intense anxiety. As a result, PCP was prohibited from being used with people. Its only accepted medical use is as an anesthetic for animals.

PCP's effects can last for three or four days. Low doses make some people tipsy, confused, aggressive, and at times violent. Users seem to be awake, but they do not talk and have little or no sense of pain. Some users may hallucinate. Larger doses of PCP cause violent rages. PCP rages have caused some users to injure themselves or even commit suicide or murder.

CANNABIS

Cannabis [*KAN uh bus*], the Indian hemp plant, is the source of marijuana and hashish. The characteristics of these drugs are summarized in Figure 22-6 on the next page. Compare that chart with Figures 22-2, 22-3, and 22-5 earlier in this lesson. Notice that cannabis has some of the same physical and psychological effects as stimulants, depressants, and hallucinogens.

THC: MARIJUANA'S ACTIVE INGREDIENT

The main active ingredient in marijuana is a chemical called delta-9 tetrahydrocannabinol, or THC for short. The strength of a sample of marijuana depends on how much THC it contains. In turn, the amount of THC depends on which parts of the cannabis plant were used to make the marijuana. Some parts of the plant contain more THC than other parts.

Some people say that the marijuana available in the United States today is 10 times stronger than the marijuana that was available in the 1960s. It may be true that illegal marijuana growers in this country today are producing more high-grade marijuana with higher THC content. However, the overall THC content of marijuana in this country still ranges from 1 to 8 percent, with an average of 2 to 5 percent—the same range and average as 25 years ago.

It is the THC in marijuana that produces the medical effects described in "Could Marijuana Be a Prescription Drug?" on page 519. In fact, since 1986 THC has been legally available in capsules as a prescription medicine for chemotherapy patients.

MARIJUANA Marijuana [*mar uh WAHN uh*] is the most widely used illegal drug in the United States. Marijuana is the dried and shredded leaves and flowers of the cannabis plant. Marijuana is most often smoked in a hand-rolled cigarette, called a "joint," or in a pipe. It also has been mixed with food and eaten. Marijuana's effects are felt within minutes and may last for several hours.

Look again at the psychological effects listed in Figure 22-6. People try marijuana because they think it will make them feel good. Actually, most of marijuana's effects feel strange and uncomfortable to new users.

When Keri tried a joint for the first time, she was disappointed. For a while, she didn't feel anything at all. Then she began to feel floaty and disconnected . . . and she started having a hard time following her friends' conversation . . . and the MTV video seemed to go on forever. "This is weird!" she thought. "I don't like this!"

Keri didn't want to smoke pot again, but her friends pressured her to give it another try. This time, though, something else happened. Her heart began pounding, and she started thinking that her friends really didn't like her very much. When they giggled, she thought they were laughing at her. Keri put her head down and closed her eyes. "Get me out of this!" she thought. "Never again! It's no fun!"

CANNABIS

Drugs (nicknames): **marijuana** (pot, grass, dope, weed, mary jane), **hashish** (hash)

Physical effects: increased heart rate; increased appetite; reddening of eyes; dry mouth and throat.

Long-term use: lung damage, possible damage to reproductive system and immune system

Psychological effects: mild euphoria, relaxed inhibitions, slowed sense of time, difficulty concentrating, impaired memory, rapid mood changes

Effects of overdose: fatigue, paranoia, panic, possible mental confusion and distorted perceptions resembling severe mental illness

Withdrawal symptoms: irritability, restlessness, difficulty sleeping

Figure 22-6 *The leaves and flowers of the cannabis plant are dried and shredded to make marijuana.*

Users may unknowingly purchase stronger marijuana or marijuana that has been mixed with another substance, perhaps another drug. Many users have had "bad trips" as a result.

A major reason for marijuana's widespread use is that many people think it is a harmless drug. This is not true. Marijuana use has serious physical and psychological consequences. For example, the long-term physical effects of smoking marijuana are the same as smoking tobacco, only more severe. Marijuana contains many of the cancer-causing agents contained in tobacco, but some are present in larger amounts in marijuana. Thus, smoking marijuana increases the risk of lung disease and some types of cancer. Marijuana also lowers the levels of hormones needed for normal sexual development and functioning.

Marijuana's effects on the mind seriously impair a user's ability to drive safely. People who drive while affected by marijuana have great difficulty concentrating on what they are doing and what is happening around them. They also cannot react quickly in an emergency. Driving while under the influence of marijuana is extremely dangerous to the driver, his or her passengers, and other people on the road.

Marijuana use interferes with the social and mental development of teenagers and young adults. Regular use can cause young people to lose interest in their usual activities. Heavy users often find it difficult to set goals and work toward them. Because marijuana impairs concentration and memory, heavy users may have difficulty learning new things. These problems improve when the person stops using marijuana.

COULD MARIJUANA BE A PRESCRIPTION DRUG?

For many years, researchers have been studying marijuana's possible value as a medication. Studies have found that smoking marijuana reduces the fluid pressure that builds up inside the eyes of patients with glaucoma. Smoking marijuana also relieves the severe nausea caused by drugs that are used to treat cancer.

Some doctors, patients, and other people are working to convince government regulators to reclassify marijuana as a Category II drug instead of Category I. Reclassification would allow doctors to prescribe marijuana for these medical uses.

HASHISH   Hashish [*HASII eesh*] is an oily liquid taken from the cannabis plant. It has more intense effects than marijuana because its psychoactive substances are more concentrated. Hashish is much more expensive than marijuana and so is less widely used in this country.

INHALANTS

Inhalants [*in HAY lunts*] are psychoactive gases that produce euphoria when they are inhaled. Some inhalants are prescription drugs with valid medical uses. Others are common household products such as those listed in Figure 22-7. Inhalants generally function as depressants.

PRESCRIPTION DRUGS   At one time, amyl nitrite [*AM ul NY tryt*] and butyl nitrite [*BYOOT ul*] were commonly prescribed for heart patients to relieve chest pain. Nitrous oxide [*NY trus AHK syd*], or "laughing gas," is a painkiller used by

Figure 22-7   Notice the severe effects of sniffing glue and other inhalants.

INHALANTS

Drugs (nicknames):   **amyl nitrite** and **butyl nitrite** (locker room, rush, poppers), **nitrous oxide** (laughing gas), **household products** such as model glue, solvents, paint thinner, lighter fluid, aerosol sprays, kerosene, and gasoline

Physical effects: dizziness, headaches, slurred speech, slowed reaction time, poor coordination. **Long-term use:** severe damage to brain, kidneys, liver, and bone marrow; increased risk of cancer

Psychological effects: giddiness, euphoria, mental confusion, impaired judgment, aggression, hallucinations

Effects of overdose: heart or lung failure, suffocation, unconsciousness, coma, death

Withdrawal symptoms: not known

This athlete relies on his own hard work, not steroids, to build muscles.

dentists. These drugs make people feel relaxed, light-headed, or giddy. Side effects include dizziness, nausea, and severe, long-lasting headaches. People who abuse these drugs can become psychologically dependent.

HOUSEHOLD PRODUCTS   Many different kinds of household products give off fumes with psychoactive effects. These inhalants are attractive to many teenagers because they are inexpensive and because they produce a rapid, intense high. These inhalants are, however, extremely dangerous.

Notice the physical effects listed in Figure 22-7. As you can see, long-term use causes severe damage to the body. This damage is permanent and cannot be reversed. Even first-time users risk serious consequences. Because users cannot measure the amount they are inhaling, taking an overdose is very easy. The results of an overdose can be deadly.

DESIGNER DRUGS

Each of the psychoactive drugs that you have read about so far has a specific chemical makeup that is known to scientists. In contrast, **designer drugs** are new chemical combinations that are created to imitate the effects of controlled drugs. Designer drugs are included in the federal drug-control categories, and states also regulate them.

The most common types of designer drugs imitate stimulants, narcotics, and hallucinogens. As one example, the designer drug called Ecstasy, or XTC, imitates the effects of amphetamines and LSD. The effects of these new drugs are often more powerful and less predictable than the effects of the drugs they imitate. This presents enormous risks to users. Many cases of permanent brain damage and paralysis have been reported.

ANABOLIC STEROIDS

Anabolic steroids [*STIR oydz*] are laboratory-made drugs that function like the male hormone testosterone [*teh STAHS tuh rohn*] to increase muscle mass. Steroids may be prescribed for young people who are not growing normally. They are also used occasionally with people who are anemic or are being treated for cancer or other conditions.

Steroids are not considered psychoactive drugs, although they may have stimulant-like effects for some users. Steroids are abused not because they make the users feel good but because they build muscles. Men and women who compete in athletics or play sports that require strength are the most common abusers. In addition, some young men take steroids simply because they want to be more muscular.

Steroids alone do not make people stronger. Steroids make muscles bulkier, but the users have to work their muscles to build strength. Athletes who take steroids have more muscle tissue to work with than athletes who train without these drugs. The steroid-using athletes thus may have an advantage over other athletes. To prevent this unfair practice, organizations that control athletic competitions, including the Olympics, have banned steroid use and administer screening tests to identify athletes who are using them to enhance performance.

More important than an unfair athletic advantage is the terrible physical damage that may be caused by steroid abuse. Notice the long-term risks listed in Figure 22-8. People who take steroids may *look* strong and healthy, but inside their bodies dangerous changes are taking place. Some changes may be permanent.

Because of these dangers, in 1988 the U.S. Congress began to consider adding steroids to the federal categories of controlled drugs. However, this has not yet been done. In the meantime, young people continue to damage their bodies with these powerful an dangerous drugs.

ANABOLIC STEROIDS

Physical effects: increased muscle mass, increased calcium deposits in bones

Psychological effects: a stimulant-like high, feeling of energy, increased aggressiveness, possible violent behavior

Long-term risks

For all users: mental disorders such as paranoia; liver damage; infertility; atherosclerosis, high blood pressure, and heart disease; acne; baldness

Additional risks for young people: stunted growth if used before reaching adult height

Additional risks for males: reduced sperm production, shrinking of testes

Additional risks for females: development of masculine characteristics such as increased facial hair and deeper voice; delayed puberty; menstrual irregularity

Withdrawal symptoms: depression, mood changes

Figure 22-8   What are the long-term risks of steroid use for teenagers?

LESSON 22.2   USING WHAT YOU HAVE LEARNED

REVIEW

1. What is a hallucinogen?
2. Identify three reasons teenagers should not use marijuana.

THINK CRITICALLY

3. Crack is a smokable form of cocaine that produces rapid, intense effects. Why is crack such a dangerous drug?
4. Combining alcohol with tranquilizers can cause coma and death from an overdose. Why is this particular drug combination so dangerous?

APPLY IT TO YOURSELF

5. Imagine that you are the coach of a college wrestling team. One of your athletes tells you that he wants to try steroids to "bulk up" and improve his performance in competitions. What would you say to convince him not to use steroids?

SUMMARY

The four major types of psychoactive drugs are stimulants, depressants, narcotics, and hallucinogens. Cannabis has some of the same effects as stimulants, depressants, and hallucinogens. Inhalants generally function as depressants. Designer drugs imitate the effects of other controlled drugs. Abuse of any of these drugs causes physical and mental damage. An overdose may cause death. Using anabolic steroids to build muscles carries a risk of permanent physical harm.

DRUGS AND SOCIETY

MAIN IDEAS

CONCEPTS

✔ Federal and state drug laws are designed to protect the public.

✔ A pregnant woman who uses drugs can seriously harm her developing fetus.

✔ Drug use interferes with a teenager's emotional and social development.

✔ Different types of services are available to help abusers recover from drug dependence.

VOCABULARY

drug trafficking
domestic violence
detoxification
therapeutic community
outpatient program
after-care program
methadone

Drug abuse is a serious problem not only for individuals but for society as a whole. Our nation's courts, prisons, and jails are crowded with people who have violated drug laws or who have committed drug-related crimes. Every year, billions of taxpayer dollars are spent on law enforcement, health care, and social services related to drug abuse. Clinics and hospitals struggle to meet the medical needs of drug abusers and of victims of drug-related crimes and accidents.

People who abuse drugs risk other people's lives and well-being through their poor work performance and unsafe behavior. Pregnant women who abuse drugs endanger the health and lives of their fetuses. For drug abusers who want to break their addiction, help is available.

DRUGS AND THE LAW

To protect the public, federal and state governments have enacted laws to control psychoactive drugs. An important federal law—the Controlled Substances Act of 1970—established the drug-control categories that you learned about in Lesson 1. This law also set penalties for manufacturing, distributing, selling, using, or possessing any controlled drug. Distributing and selling drugs illegally is called **drug trafficking.** In 1986, another federal law—the Anti-Drug Abuse Act—replaced the 1970 law. The 1986 law increased the penalties for drug offenses and expanded the categories to include designer drugs.

Violations of drug laws carry serious penalties.

PENALTIES FOR DRUG VIOLATIONS

Under the 1986 federal law, a first-time offender convicted of possessing *any* controlled drug faces a possible one-year prison sentence and a $5,000 fine. In some cases, first-time offenders are instead put on probation for one year. During probation, a convicted person is allowed to remain free, with court supervision, so long as the person does not do anything illegal and follows the court's rules. On a second offense for possession, the penalties increase to a two-year prison sentence and a $10,000 fine. Penalties are much more severe for people convicted of drug trafficking.

DRUGS AND CRIME

Many serious crimes are related to drug abuse, including murder, assault, robbery, and burglary. The high cost of drugs and the craving to keep taking them make abusers desperate for money. Drug abusers steal from family members, friends, classmates, co-workers, employers, businesses, and complete strangers.

Hiep met his friends at the variety store. "Did you hear about Mrs. Chu?" David asked. "Some crackhead grabbed her purse yesterday. Knocked her down, too. Broke her arm."

Hiep thought of the small, elderly woman and got mad. "Those jerks are making it real hard for all the old people in the neighborhood," he said. "We should do something about it!"

"Like what?" Yen asked. "Go after them? We don't even know who they are."

"I know what," said Hiep. "How about if we start an escort service for the old people? When they want to go to the store or something, they call us, and one of us walks with them."

"Yeah!" said David. "Maybe if word gets around, the heads will know the old folks aren't alone any more."

To support their habit, some users turn to selling drugs. In many American cities, some gangs are involved in drug trafficking. These gangs often are heavily armed and violent. Many cities have experienced an alarming increase in drug-related shootings in recent years. Besides the gang members themselves, many innocent people have been injured or killed by drug-related violence.

Domestic violence, violence toward another family member, is often drug-related. As you learned in the previous lesson, some drugs—methamphetamine and PCP, for example—cause aggressive behavior. Someone who is under the influence of such a drug may physically attack another family member, perhaps even a child. Many other drugs cause mental confusion, paranoia, hallucinations, or impaired judgment. These effects may lead a user to strike out at others verbally or physically. States and communities generally consider domestic violence to be a crime. The abuser can be arrested and prosecuted.

DRUGS AND DISEASE

In the previous lesson, you learned that users who share dirty needles risk becoming infected with hepatitis and with the virus that causes AIDS. Sharing needles is not the only way that drug users spread disease. People who use drugs often do not protect themselves against sexually transmitted diseases, including AIDS. As a result, other sexual partners of these drug users may then become infected as well, even though they do not use drugs themselves. A pregnant woman who is infected with the virus that causes AIDS can pass the virus to her fetus.

In addition to the people close to the drug user, all of us are affected by drug-related health problems. Do you work at a part-time job after school or on weekends? If so, some of the taxes taken out of your paycheck are used to fund programs that provide medical care for drug abusers and their victims. These programs also include drug-treatment programs, which you will read about later in this lesson.

Babies who are born prematurely need special care, particularly if they are born addicted to a drug.

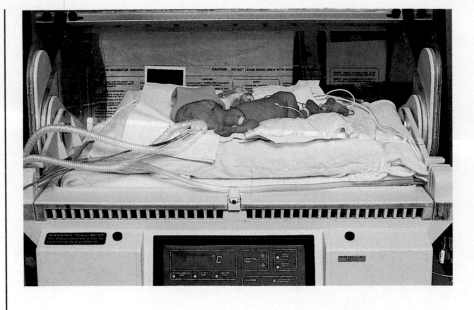

DRUGS AND PREGNANCY

When a pregnant woman uses a drug, it passes from her bloodstream into the fetus's bloodstream through the placenta. Psychoactive drugs can damage a developing fetus mentally, physically, or both. For example, researchers have studied babies born to women who used crack during pregnancy. These studies have found that the babies' emotional and mental development is not normal. Other problems caused by drug use during pregnancy include brain damage, heart defects, and deformities.

Some psychoactive drugs—particularly narcotics, barbiturates, cocaine, and crack—cause the fetuses to become addicted. When these babies are born, they must go through drug withdrawal. Withdrawal is very risky for infants. Addicted babies require close medical supervision and careful treatment to survive the difficult withdrawal process.

Pregnant women who use marijuana have a higher risk of stillbirth or miscarriage. They also risk having babies who are born prematurely or who have abnormalities. Some babies born to marijuana users have facial features similar to the features of babies born with fetal alcohol syndrome. This syndrome is described in Chapter 21, "Alcohol."

DRUGS AND RELATIONSHIPS

In many ways, drug abuse interferes with the emotional growth and social development that normally occur during adolescence. Psychoactive drugs change a person's feelings, thoughts, and behavior. Because of these changes, drug abuse distorts a user's relationships with other people, including family and friends. In school, a drug user's disruptive behavior can make learning difficult for everyone. In addition, many schools experience violence related to drug use. Other students cannot relax and enjoy the company of their friends when they fear for their personal safety. This is true in neighborhoods as well.

FOR YOUR INFORMATION

In 1989, almost 9,000 crack babies were born in eight major cities in the United States, including New York, Los Angeles, Chicago, and Miami.

Like all people, teenagers associate with others who share their interests. For teenagers who are drug users, those interests tend to focus on the drug use itself. For example, the teenagers get together with friends to use drugs and go to parties or events where drugs are available. For some teenagers, drug-sharing with friends also involves problem behaviors such as truancy, vandalism, or fighting.

DRUG TESTING

Several years ago, two trains collided at high speed, killing 16 people and injuring many others. Investigators later found that the engineer and the brakeman on one train had been sharing a marijuana joint shortly before the crash. Although there was no proof that the marijuana use caused the crash, many people assumed that it did.

Incidents like this one have convinced many Americans that routine testing for drug use is a good idea, particularly for workers whose jobs involve public safety. In fact, many employers now use drug-screening tests for job applicants before hiring anyone and also test their employees from time to time. The U.S. Navy and other armed forces have used random drug screening for many years.

People who oppose drug testing say that it violates a person's constitutional right to privacy. (A drug test requires a urine sample from the person being tested.) Opponents also point out that these tests are not always accurate. Some people have been identified as having used drugs when in fact they had not. Also, until recently, drug tests could not differentiate between amphetamines and some over-the-counter asthma medications or between marijuana and ibuprofen, a common ingredient in over-the-counter medications for headaches and other mild pain. Newer tests, however, are more accurate.

Do you think that train engineers should be tested for drug use?

TREATING DRUG DEPENDENCE

Breaking the physical and psychological dependence on a drug, *any* drug, is difficult. To overcome drug dependence, abusers first must admit that their drug use is a problem to themselves and others. Abusers who quit must go through withdrawal. They then have to change their thinking, habits, and goals and adopt a drug-free life. Recovered users also must adjust to the everyday conditions that led them into drug abuse. Success depends heavily on the abuser's determination to change.

DETOXIFICATION   The first step in drug treatment is detoxification. **Detoxification** [*dee tahk suh fuh KAY shun*] means allowing the body to rid itself of a drug. Medications may be used to ease the discomfort or pain of withdrawal. The length of time needed to complete detoxification depends on the type of drug used and the amount of the drug in the user's body.

COUNSELING Detoxification is usually followed by counseling. Specially trained drug counselors work with recovering users individually and in small groups. The goal of counseling is to help recovering users overcome psychological dependence, explore their reasons for using drugs, and find other ways to handle problems. Counseling frequently involves the user's family.

THERAPEUTIC COMMUNITIES Therapeutic communities [*ther uh PYOOT ik*] are treatment centers where recovering drug users live together in a drug-free setting. These programs are often directed by recovered users who also work as peer counselors. Therapeutic communities treat all types of drug abuse. The programs offer many types of services, including individual and group counseling, peer support, job training, and recreational activities. During the early stages of treatment, recovering users follow a set schedule of planned and supervised activities. As treatment progresses, they assume more responsibility and independence. The treatment program in a therapeutic community may take as long as two years to complete.

MAKING A DIFFERENCE

CAREERS **HEALTH**

Employee Assistance Counselor

Not very long ago, an employee with personal problems that affected his or her work, or an employee suspected of abusing drugs or alcohol, would most certainly be fired from his or her job. Today, many employers know that firing employees does not solve personal or substance abuse problems among their employees. More and more businesses are turning to employee assistance counselors to help them help employees who, when not suffering personal or substance abuse problems, are often highly productive at work.

Employee Assistance Programs (EAPs) arose out of the recognition that an employee's personal problems or problems with drugs or alcohol have a direct impact on performance, morale, and company success. Such problems cost American businesses over 60 billion dollars each year in low productivity, absenteeism, and poor morale. With the help of employee

assistance counselors, businesses can save money and, in some cases, save lives.

Employee assistance counselors are usually hired directly by businesses. Some work as consultants to groups of small businesses. Often, the employee assistance counselor acts as a mediator between management and employees to work out disputes. Counselors also can train managers to deal with the personal problems of employees. Counselors can help managers spot the signs of alcohol or drug abuse and teach managers tools to use with individuals who need help.

Employee assistance counseling is a new and rapidly-growing field of work. The qualifications of the field vary with the needs of the businesses served. At present, state regulations for qualifications or certification have not been established. In most areas, however, employee assistance counselors are college graduates who have had courses in

counseling and psychology, human resource management, and business administration. Because they often act as referral sources, employee assistance counselors must have an excellent working knowledge of both private and community services.

1. Why did the need for employee assistance counselors arise?

2. What do you think would be the most important qualification for a position as an employee assistance counselor?

OUTPATIENT PROGRAMS   Some hospitals and treatment centers offer programs for people who do not live there. **Outpatient programs** allow recovering users to live at home and come in for treatment and counseling. In addition, some hospitals and centers offer after-care programs for people who have completed the treatment program. In an **after-care program**, recovered users return regularly for group counseling to help them maintain a drug-free life.

METHADONE   Users who are addicted to heroin or other illegal narcotics may be treated with a legal narcotic called methadone. **Methadone** [*METH uh dohn*] is a laboratory-made narcotic that blocks the withdrawal symptoms of opiate narcotics. Instead of using illegal narcotics, users go to a clinic once or twice a day to receive a free dose of methadone. However, methadone is not a cure for narcotics addiction. In small doses, methadone does not produce euphoria and other mind-altering effects, but it is physically addictive. To be drug-free, users must break their physical dependence on methadone.

Methadone treatment has two major benefits for its users and for society as a whole. First, the drug is readily available and free of charge, so methadone users generally do not get involved in the criminal behaviors that are characteristic of narcotics abusers. Secondly, methadone does not make users high, so they can hold jobs and function normally.

What is your opinion of methadone treatment for people who are addicted to narcotics?

LESSON 22.3 **USING WHAT YOU HAVE LEARNED**

REVIEW

1. How does using psychoactive drugs distort a user's relationships with other people?
2. Identify three risks to the fetus of a woman who uses marijuana during pregnancy.

THINK CRITICALLY

3. Some people say that treating narcotics abusers with methadone is not a good idea because it just replaces one addicting drug with another addicting drug. Do you agree with this view? Explain your answer.
4. During the early stages of treatment in a therapeutic community, recovering users follow a set schedule of planned and supervised activities. Suggest a reason for using this approach to treatment in the early stages.

APPLY IT TO YOURSELF

5. Imagine that you have started a company that supplies security guards to businesses. Would you test job applicants for drug use? Explain your answer.

SUMMARY

Federal and state laws control psychoactive drugs in order to protect society. Drug users harm other people through serious crimes, acts of violence, the spread of disease, and the effects of drugs on unborn children. Teenagers who use drugs deprive themselves of normal opportunities for emotional and social growth. Support services can help abusers break their dependence if they are determined to change.

PREVENTING DRUG ABUSE

If you have read Chapter 21, you know that the most commonly used psychoactive drug is alcohol. You also know that alcohol use is not harmful or unhealthy so long as the drinker is of legal drinking age, drinks only lightly or moderately, and uses alcohol responsibly. This is not true of the psychoactive drugs you have read about in this chapter. There is no such thing as "responsible" use of marijuana, crack, someone else's tranquilizers, or model glue for sniffing. With the drugs discussed in this chapter, your only healthy, responsible choice is *no* use at all.

REFUSING DRUGS

Refusing drugs can be uncomfortable or difficult if they are offered by friends or other people you admire. You should be prepared to resist peer pressure to try drugs. The strategies that are suggested on page 502 for refusing alcohol are also effective for refusing marijuana, crack, or any other drug.

The best way to avoid drugs is to avoid people who are using them. If you choose friends who do not use drugs, peer pressure will work for you in a positive way. Also choose activities that will not expose you to drug use. Staying drug-free will give you a sense of pride and accomplishment.

ALTERNATIVES TO DRUG ABUSE

As you learned earlier, people use drugs because they want to change the way they feel—to relieve boredom, loneliness, or depression, to feel more relaxed or more energetic, or to escape anxiety and stress caused by personal problems. There is nothing unusual or unhealthy about wanting to feel good. However, using

MAIN IDEAS

CONCEPTS

✔ There are many healthy alternatives to using drugs.

✔ The best way to avoid drugs is to avoid people who use them.

✔ Changes in behavior may indicate that a person is using drugs.

VOCABULARY

helpline

The best way to avoid drugs is to be involved in drug-free activities with drug-free friends.

IF YOU WANT . . .	DO THIS INSTEAD OF TAKING DRUGS.
To feel more calm and relaxed	Learn relaxation techniques.
	Exercise regularly (walking, playing sports, aerobics, dancing, hiking).
	Avoid caffeine (cola drinks, chocolate, coffee, tea, cocoa).
To feel more alert and energetic	Exercise regularly.
	Get enough sleep.
	Eat a healthy diet.
	If you are overweight or underweight, see a doctor to plan a diet program to achieve a healthy weight.
	Try new activities from time to time, such as learning a new sport or skill.
To solve personal problems	Learn techniques for dealing with stress.
	Talk with your family, your friends, or a professional counselor.
	Contact a helpline or a support group. (You can find one in the Yellow Pages.)
	Read books about how to handle the types of problems you are having.
To relieve loneliness, depression, or boredom	Get involved in group activities such as sports or clubs.
	Start a physical fitness group with some friends.
	Take a course in something you would like to learn.
	Do volunteer work in your school or community.
To explore new sensations	Get involved in something artistic and creative—music, theater, photography, movie-making.
	Go to art museums and art shows in your area.
To find thrills and adventure	Learn a flashy sport such as gymnastics or fencing.
	Take part in a competitive sport or hobby.
	Try an exciting and challenging hobby such as rock climbing, juggling, or building model rockets.
	Read about adventuresome activities such as white-water canoeing and sky diving.
	Find out about far-off places you would like to visit some day, and plan your trips.

drugs to change your feelings *is* unhealthy. There are many healthy and responsible alternatives to drug use. A variety of alternatives are suggested above.

SIGNS OF DRUG ABUSE

How can you tell if someone you know has started to abuse drugs? There are a number of common warning signs that indicate possible drug abuse. Those signs are listed in Figure 22-9 on the next page. Keep in mind that one sign alone does not mean that someone is abusing drugs. Several signs together, though, are a warning. Also remember that signs can vary from one person to another and from one drug to another.

GETTING HELP

If you have a friend or family member who abuses drugs, or if you have a drug problem yourself, do not hesitate to contact a source of help. Sources are listed in the Yellow Pages under "Drug Abuse and Addiction" and "Alcoholism Information and Treatment

Changes in Behavior

- Any unexplained changes in behavior at home, with friends, or in school
- Lack of interest in usual activities, including school, hobbies, and sports
- Unpredictable behavior, temper tantrums, or mood swings
- Switching to different friends suddenly
- Spending more time away from home
- Being secretive with family or friends
- Seeming confused or unable to concentrate and pay attention
- Borrowing money frequently, or stealing money or valuables

Physical Changes

- Sleep disturbances—either having difficulty sleeping or sleeping for abnormally long periods
- Loss of interest in eating, or unexplained loss of weight
- Bloodshot eyes
- Dazed, dreamy, or blank look on face
- Excessive sweating
- Flushed skin
- Unexplained rash
- Runny nose or irritated nostrils

Figure 22-9 One sign alone does not mean that someone is using drugs. Several signs, though, are a warning.

Centers." You also could contact a helpline. A **helpline** is a confidential telephone service that provides information and advice to people with personal problems. Many treatment centers operate a helpline, or you may find one listed in the White Pages under "Drug Abuse and Alcohol 24-Hour Helpline."

Don't be afraid to call for help. Anything you say will be kept strictly confidential. You won't even have to give your name. Whether the person with a drug problem is yourself or someone you know, it is important to seek help as soon as possible to prevent the terrible physical, mental, and social damage that drug abuse causes.

SUMMARY

Using refusal strategies, avoiding drug users, and avoiding settings where drugs are used will help you stay drug free. Changes in a person's behavior and physical condition may be warning signs of drug use. You can call a treatment center or helpline if you or someone you know needs help with a drug problem.

LESSON 22.4 USING WHAT YOU HAVE LEARNED

REVIEW

1. What is the best way to avoid getting involved with drug use?
2. Why should someone not be afraid to call a helpline?

THINK CRITICALLY

3. Choose one change from the "If you want . . ." column in the chart on page 529. Suggest another alternative for that change.
4. Suddenly switching to new friends may be a sign that someone has started using drugs. Suggest a reason why switching friends might be a sign of drug use.

APPLY IT TO YOURSELF

5. Imagine that you are at a party at your older cousin's house. One of her friends lights a joint and starts passing it around. You don't want to share the joint, but you also don't want your cousin's friends to think you are childish. What would you do to refuse the joint in a way that is comfortable for you?

Talk It Out

Tanya had broken up with Keenan, her boyfriend of three years, and she was feeling pretty low. Plus, her parents had been arguing a lot lately. Tanya was afraid that they might be considering a divorce. She felt really helpless. Tanya felt as if she didn't have a friend in the world.

One day, Tanya was cleaning out the top drawer of her dresser. She found a few letters from Keenan that she had saved. As she read them again, Tanya began to cry. She had thought that they would always be together. In tears, Tanya tried to slam her dresser drawer shut. But something caught.

As Tanya dug around in the drawer to see what was in the way, she found a prescription bottle. "What's this?" she asked out loud. She looked at the label. It was a pain reliever she had taken the year before when she

had broken her arm. "I remember this stuff," she thought. "These pills were heavy duty! They sure took away the pain of my broken arm."

Then Tanya had an idea. She remembered that the pills also had made her feel a little numb to the outside world. "That's what I need right now—to feel a little numb," she thought. Maybe they would take some of the edge off her anxiety and worry. She knew that it was bad to take a prescription drug for any reason other than that for which it was prescribed. "But," she thought, "what's the harm in just taking a couple?" Deep down, however, Tanya knew that she would be taking the pills for the wrong reason.

PAUSE AND CONSIDER

1. *Identify the Problem.* What is Tanya considering doing?

2. *Consider the Options.* What options does Tanya have to help her resolve her problem?

3. *Evaluate the Outcomes.* What could happen if Tanya takes the pills? What might happen if she does not take the pills?

Tanya held the pills for a long time. As she looked up in the mirror of

her dresser, she could see how bad she looked. Her face was stained from her tears. She was holding the bottle of pills so tightly that her knuckles were white.

"I'm a mess," she thought. "These pills aren't going to do me any good." She started to cry again. Tanya realized that the pills weren't the answer. She dumped them into the toilet and flushed them away.

An hour later, Tanya went to bed. It was early but she was really tired. As she lay in bed, she began thinking of what she could do to feel better. She knew that what she really needed was to talk to someone. But she wasn't sure she could tell her parents right now. Then she remembered the time when her friend Danna had some problems. She had gone to Ms. Cooper, the guidance counselor. Danna had said that Ms. Cooper had been helpful. "She really listened to what I had to say, and helped me find some solutions," were Danna's words. As Tanya drifted off to sleep, she decided that she would talk to Ms. Cooper. "If she helped Danna, maybe she can help me."

DECIDE AND REVIEW

4. *Decide and Act.* Why did Tanya not take the pills?

5. *Review.* What are some other options that were available to Tanya? How did Tanya's emotional condition make her vulnerable?

PROJECTS

1. At one time, LSD was not an illegal drug. For what purposes was it used? Do research on LSD or another drug. Trace the drug's development or discovery, its use, and its abuse until it was controlled by federal law.

2. The actress and comedienne Lily Tomlin is strongly opposed to the use of illegal drugs. She has said, "The best mind-altering drug is truth." What does she mean by this? Write a paragraph that describes your reaction to her statement.

WORKING WITH OTHERS

With a partner, research the pros and cons of marijuana use as a medicine to relieve the symptoms of glaucoma or the side effects of chemotherapy in the treatment of cancer. Choose sides, and present your findings as a debate.

CONNECTING TO...

PERFORMING ARTS   Many famous musicians, actors, singers, and other performers have suffered from the effects of drug abuse. Some have died as the result of a drug overdose. Choose a performer who interests you and whose life and career were affected by drug abuse. Find out how the performer's life and career were affected by their drug use. Present your findings in an oral or written report or in a classroom display.

USING VOCABULARY

addiction	drug trafficking	overdose
after-care program	euphoria	paranoia
anabolic steroid	gateway drug	psychoactive drug
cannabis	hallucinogen	stimulant
depressant	helpline	therapeutic
designer drug	inhalant	community
detoxification	methadone	tolerance
domestic violence	narcotic	withdrawal
drug abuse	outpatient program	symptom

Number a separate piece of paper from 1 to 12. Write the missing vocabulary term for each of the following sentences.

1. _____ is a laboratory-made narcotic that blocks the withdrawal symptoms of opiate narcotics.

2. A(n) _____ is a psychoactive substance that leads the user to try other drugs.

3. Some drugs can cause _____, a mental disorder in which the person is abnormally suspicious and fearful of other people.

4. The plant known as _____ is the source of marijuana.

5. _____ involves allowing the body to rid itself of a drug.

6. Drugs that slow down nerve activity are called _____.

7. Uncomfortable reactions that occur when a person stops using an addictive substance are called _____.

8. A(n) _____ is a chemical substance that acts on the brain, affecting a person's mind and behavior.

9. A treatment center where recovering drug users live together in a drug-free setting is called a(n) _____.

10. Drugs that distort users' perceptions of their surroundings and their own bodies are called _____.

11. _____ are new chemical combinations that are created to imitate the effects of controlled drugs.

CONCEPT MAPPING

On a sheet of paper, create a concept map for *drug abuse*. In your map, use as many of the following concepts as you can: *addiction, community, counseling, detoxification, drug abuse, experimentation, family relationships, health and life, refusal.* You may use additional concepts in your map. Further information about concept mapping appears at the front of this book.

THINKING CRITICALLY

INTERPRET

LESSON 22.1 1. What is the complete definition of drug abuse?

2. What is the most common reason that teenagers and young adults start using drugs?

3. Why is it not uncommon for drug users to take an overdose?

4. What must users do as they develop tolerance for a drug?

5. Which psychoactive drug is most often used in combination with another drug?

LESSON 22.2 6. Name the four major groups of psychoactive drugs.

7. Identify three possible effects of an overdose of cocaine.

8. Name two drugs that may cause users to become aggressive and violent.

9. Why is it particularly dangerous to combine alcohol with barbiturates or tranquilizers?

10. What is a flashback? Which drug is known to cause flashbacks?

LESSON 22.3 11. What motivates drug abusers to steal money from family members, friends, and others?

12. Identify three ways in which drug abusers can spread disease.

13. What are the goals of counseling in a drug treatment program?

14. What is the purpose of after-care programs?

LESSON 22.4 15. How could someone find a helpline to call for advice about a drug problem?

16. Identify three ways to feel more calm and relaxed without using drugs.

APPLY

LESSON 22.1 17. Describe the typical sequence of stages that lead to drug abuse in teenagers.

LESSON 22.2 18. Identify three major risks of using crack.

19. Which of marijuana's physical and psychological effects (Figure 22-6, page 518) are the same as the effects of stimulants (Figure 22-2, page 513), depressants (Figure 22-3, page 514), and hallucinogens (Figure 22-5, page 516)?

20. Identify *all* of the long-term health risks for teenaged males who use anabolic steroids.

LESSON 22.3 21. Under the 1986 federal drug law, what are the penalties for the first and second offenses for possession of a controlled drug?

22. Explain how drug abuse can contribute to domestic violence.

23. Identify three risks of marijuana use during pregnancy.

LESSON 22.4 24. Which physical changes listed in the chart on page 530 could be warning signs that someone is using cocaine? (Hint: Use Figure 22-2 on page 513 and the information about cocaine on page 514.)

COMMITMENT TO WELLNESS

FOLLOW-UP

SETTING GOALS

Look at your responses to the checklist you completed at the beginning of this chapter. Which responses reflected your strengths? Which reflected your weaknesses?

Choose one response that you would like to change from *no* to *yes.* Copy the statement in your Wellness Journal. Below the statement, list three specific actions you could take to achieve that goal. For example, if you decided to work on getting more involved in activities that interest you, and you are interested in dance, you might list actions similar to these: (1) Get a list of all the clubs that are sponsored by the school. (2) If there's a dance club, join it. If there isn't, start one with some friends. (3) Look in the newspaper every week to find dance performances in the area.

In a month, review your objectives and evaluate your progress. As you achieve your goal, choose another checklist item to work on, and develop an action plan for that goal.

WHERE DO I GO FROM HERE?

Various resources at school and in a library can provide you with information about psychoactive drugs and steroids.

FOR MORE INFORMATION ABOUT DRUG ABUSE, CONTACT:

National Clearinghouse for Alcohol and Drug Information
P.O. Box 2345
Rockville, MD 20852
1-800-729-6686

National Institute on Drug Abuse Hotline
1-800-662-HELP

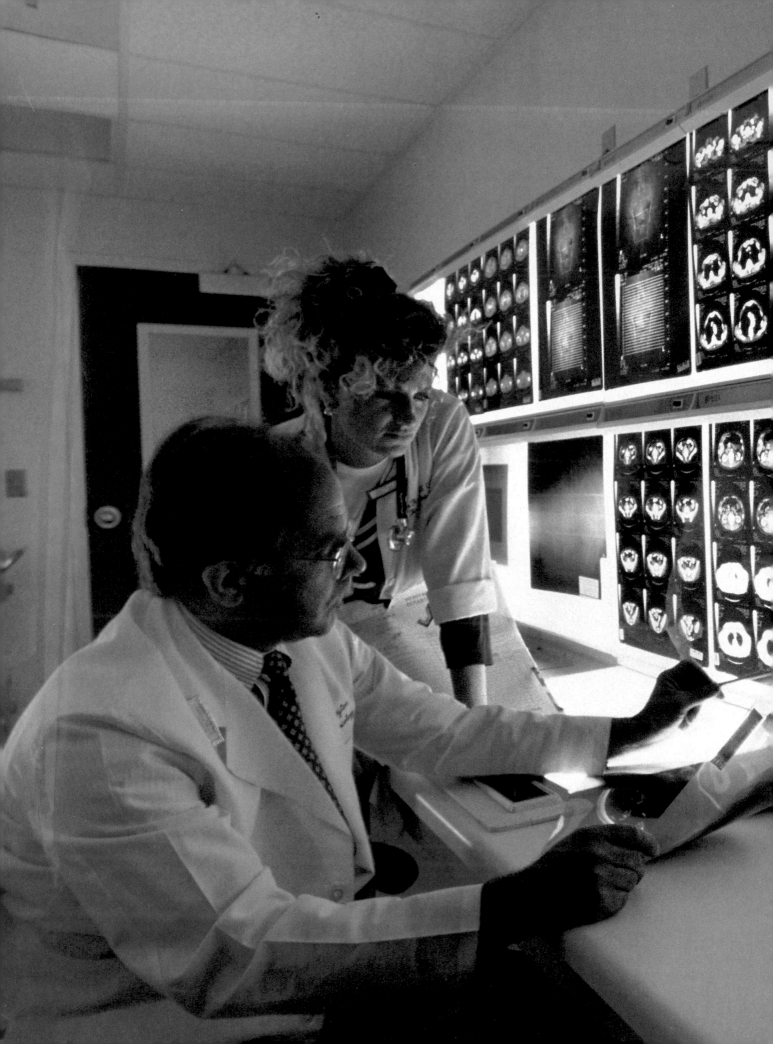

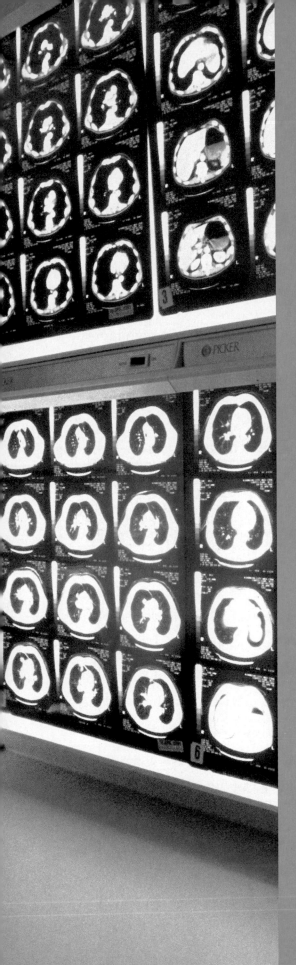

Diseases and Disorders

Chapter 23
Infectious Diseases

Chapter 24
Sexually Transmitted
Diseases/AIDS

Chapter 25
Noninfectious Diseases

Chapter 26
Selecting Health Care

Why is there so much concern over HIV infection among teens?

What can you do now to avoid serious illness as an adult?

Why is it important to know how diseases are transmitted?

Infectious Diseases

"Who would not give a trifle to prevent what he would give a thousand worlds to cure?"

Edward Young

The words of Edward Young may call to mind a modern adage with the same meaning: *An ounce of prevention is worth a pound of cure.* Both sayings point out the wisdom of practicing preventive behavior.

Most of us practice prevention in a variety of ways every day without giving these actions too much thought. For example, we look both ways before crossing streets, obey traffic regulations, get regular medical and dental check ups, complete homework and study for tests, and dress appropriately for the weather.

Your body acts preventively, too. It can ward off both mild and serious diseases through the action of its agents, which all work together to keep you healthy and vibrant. From time to time, however, even the healthiest among you can be invaded by a virus or bacteria that makes you ill. Inside the body, the immune system gears up to knock out the disease. You prevent complications by seeing a doctor or other health professional and you may get needed relief from symptoms through appropriate medication.

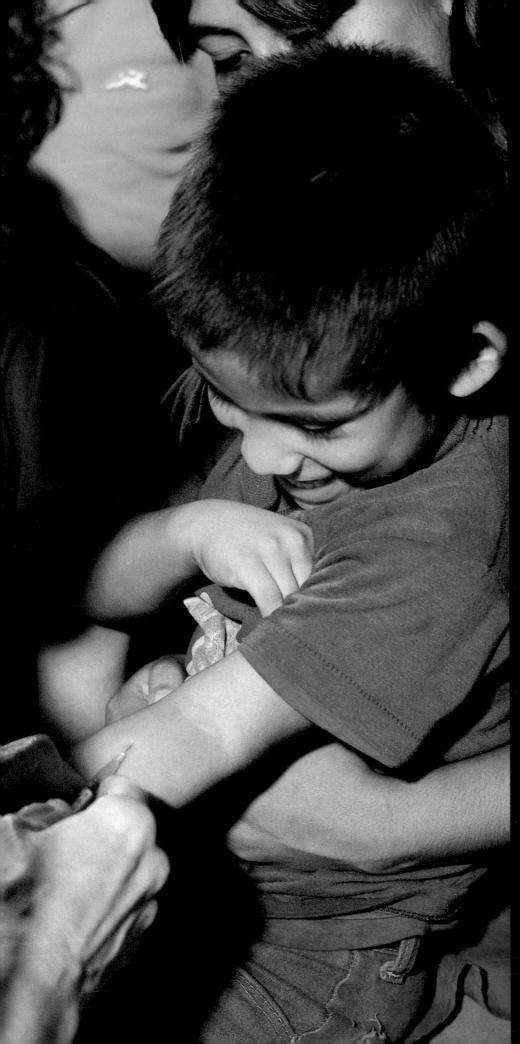

How much do you know about the causes of infectious diseases? On a sheet of paper or in your Wellness Journal, write *yes* or *no* to respond to the following statements.

1. When I am sick, I avoid spreading my disease to others.

2. I avoid close contact with others who are sick.

3. I wash my hands before eating or handling food.

4. I pay attention to signs or symptoms of a disease.

5. When I'm feeling sick, I seek appropriate medical help.

6. I follow the doctor's directions when being treated for a disease or taking medicine.

7. I read labels and follow directions on medicines I take.

8. I never take any medicine intended for someone else.

9. I never take more than the prescribed medicine to "give my system a boost."

10. I know my immunization record and keep it up to date.

11. I do not share drinking containers or personal items such as combs and brushes with others.

12. When I'm sick, I get plenty of rest.

Review your responses and consider what might be your strengths and weaknesses. Save your personal checklist for a follow-up activity that appears at the end of this chapter.

CAUSES OF DISEASE

When you become sick, whether it is a minor cold or a major case of the flu, you may find yourself doing some detective work. First, you and a physician discuss your symptoms to determine what might be causing the illness. In order to determine how you became sick, you may try to reconstruct the events leading up to your illness. Did you catch the illness from somebody at school? Did you get sick because of something you ate? An understanding of the causes of your illness and how you might have become sick in the first place can help you avoid getting sick again.

PATHOGENS

Everywhere you go, you are surrounded by billions of organisms that are too small to be seen with the human eye. These organisms are present in the air, in the soil, and on every surface. They are even present on your skin and in your intestinal tract. Most of these organisms are harmless. Others are even beneficial to your health. However, some organisms are able to invade your body and make you sick. Even normal flora—those organisms that are normally present in your body—can make you sick if, under certain conditions, they become pathogens. **Pathogens** [*PATH uh junz*] are organisms or other agents that cause disease. Diseases that are caused by pathogens are known as **infectious diseases**. Pathogens can be organized into six major groups.

VIRUSES **Viruses** are the smallest of the pathogens. They are so small that millions of them can fit on the head of a pin. Viruses are the only pathogens that are not cells. Instead, viruses are single units of genetic material in a protein shell. Viruses invade living cells, forcing the cells to create new viruses. The new viruses break out of the cell, killing it, and invade other cells in the body. Many common respiratory diseases such as the common cold and the flu are caused by viruses. More dangerous diseases caused by viruses include polio and AIDS.

BACTERIA The most numerous organisms on Earth are **bacteria**, which are simple, one-celled organisms. Only a small percentage of bacteria are pathogens. Millions of beneficial bacteria live in the human digestive tract, where they aid in digestion and discourage the growth of pathogens. However, some bacteria can cause dangerous diseases including food poisoning, pneumonia, tetanus, and tuberculosis. Some bacteria produce **toxins,** or poisons, that harm human cells. For example, bacteria that cause tetanus produce toxins that damage the nerves controlling your muscles.

MAIN IDEAS

CONCEPTS
✔ Infectious diseases are caused by six major types of infectious organisms.
✔ Preventive health practices can help reduce the spread of infectious diseases.

VOCABULARY
pathogen
infectious disease
virus
bacteria
toxin
rickettsia
protozoan
fungi
parasites

Viruses, such as those that cause the flu (top), can only multiply inside living cells. Under the right conditions, bacteria, such as the bacteria that cause tuberculosis (bottom), can double their number every 30 minutes.

RICKETTSIAS   Rickettsias [*rik ET see uhz*] are organisms that are larger than viruses but smaller than bacteria. Like bacteria, rickettsias are one-celled organisms. Most rickettsias can survive only in other living cells. They usually attack the cells of small blood vessels. In the United States, one of the most common diseases caused by rickettsias is Rocky Mountain spotted fever. This disease is passed to humans through the bite of ticks.

PROTOZOA   Protozoa [*PROHT uh zoh uh*] are also one-celled organisms. However, protozoa have many more specialized internal structures than either bacteria or rickettsias. Some of the most dangerous protozoa live in an infected person's blood stream. Diseases caused by protozoa, including malaria and African sleeping sickness, are most common in tropical countries.

FUNGI   Fungi are plantlike organisms which can be either single-celled or multicelled. Very few types of fungi cause diseases. Those that do usually attack the skin, mucous membranes, or lungs. Some of the most common fungal infections include athlete's foot, ringworm, and yeast infections.

PARASITES   Parasites are multicelled organisms that get their energy and nutrients by feeding on other living things. Parasites that affect humans include mites, lice, and parasitic worms. Parasitic worms usually infect the intestines of their hosts, although some types infect other organs such as the liver and lungs. Humans usually become infected with parasitic worms by consuming contaminated water or food, such as contaminated meat that has been undercooked.

TRANSMISSION OF PATHOGENS

In order to take preventive measures against getting an infectious disease, you need to understand how pathogens are spread. Food, water, animals, and other people are some of the places where pathogens can be found. A pathogen commonly invades the body through the air you breathe, food you eat, or through cuts.

HUMAN TRANSMISSION   One of the most common sources of pathogens is other infected people. Many viruses and bacteria can pass from person to person during close physical contact such as touching, kissing, or intimate sexual contact. For example, you can become infected with a virus that causes the common cold if you put your hand to your mouth after shaking hands with someone who has just used their hand to cover a sneeze.

Often viruses and bacteria can be passed from person to person even when there is no direct contact.

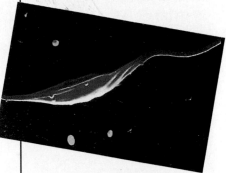

FOR YOUR INFORMATION

Many bacteria that live in your body protect you from infectious diseases by crowding out harmful bacteria.

The protozoan shown in the photo causes African sleeping sickness.

When large groups of people are crowded together, viruses and bacteria easily can be transmitted from person to person.

Staying Healthy While Traveling

If you are planning a trip outside the United States, it is important to check with your local health department about any diseases that may be a problem at your destination. Travel to some parts of the world requires inoculations against infectious diseases such as yellow fever, hepatitis, and typhoid fever.

Another complaint, traveler's diarrhea, can greatly reduce your enjoyment of any trip. Its symptoms include severe diarrhea, cramps,

nausea, bloatedness, and general discomfort. Avoiding this common illness requires a few simple but necessary precautions.

- Never eat raw foods. Cooking destroys the food-borne bacteria that can cause traveler's diarrhea.
- Do not eat unpasteurized dairy products such as milk or cheese. Pasteurization kills bacteria that can cause illnesses like traveler's diarrhea and more severe illnesses such as tuberculosis and cholera.

- Always drink bottled water, preferably carbonated water. Carbonation kills water-borne microorganisms which can cause infections. If you do not have access to bottled water, be sure to boil the water you do have for at least 20 minutes.
- If you are unsure about the quality or preparation of a food, a good guideline is "when in doubt, throw it out."

Rick could tell he was coming down with a cold. He had been sneezing and coughing but thought he was well enough to go to school. As the day went on, Rick began to feel much worse and he was coughing and sneezing a lot more. He remembered that last week in one of his classes another student was sneezing uncontrollably. Rick wondered whether he had caught his cold from that other student. Rick decided he was probably putting other students at risk of being infected and wasn't doing himself much good either. After class, Rick went to the main office to be excused to go home and rest.

When you are infected with a cold virus or flu virus and you cough or sneeze, you spray thousands of pathogen-carrying droplets into the air. If somebody breathes in these droplets, this person may become infected as well. Pathogens also can be transmitted indirectly in other ways. For example, if you use a drinking glass or eating utensil that has been used by an infected person, you risk becoming infected.

FOOD AND WATER   A potential source of pathogens is contaminated food and water. Foods can provide an ideal environment for the growth of bacteria. Meat from infected animals may contain the eggs of parasitic worms. Although government regulations require food processing plants to inspect meats and follow procedures that keep pathogens out of food, it is very important that proper precautions are taken at home. Proper cooking of food kills bacteria and parasitic worms. Refrigeration and freezing slows or stops the multiplication of most bacteria in food. To prevent pathogens from being introduced to the food, always wash your hands before handling food and prepare the food on a clean surface.

Pathogens also can be transmitted through drinking water. Water may become contaminated if it is exposed to untreated sewage or animal wastes. All public water supplies in the United States are treated to kill pathogens. Therefore, illness due to infected tap water is rare in the United States. However, untreated water from lakes, rivers, and streams may contain pathogens even if the water appears clean.

ANIMALS Some pathogens are present in other animals. These pathogens can be passed to humans through the bites of infected animals. For example, mammals including dogs, raccoons, and skunks can carry the virus that causes rabies—a deadly viral disease that attacks the central nervous system. Ticks can carry the rickettsia that causes Rocky Mountain spotted fever and the bacteria that causes Lyme disease. In tropical countries, mosquitoes can carry the protozoa that cause malaria or the viruses that cause yellow fever. If you live in an area where an animal-borne disease is common, you should take steps to avoid contact with these animals. For example, avoid all animals that are behaving strangely, and wear long pants or use a safe insect repellant to limit exposure to mosquitoes and ticks.

Explain how a salad bar can help to spread viruses that cause the common cold.

Despite the many precautions you can take to prevent becoming infected, avoiding pathogens can often be difficult. Contact with infected people is inevitable. If you are in an enclosed area where ventilation is poor, the chances increase that you will inhale airborne pathogens. People who live, work, or go to school in areas where sanitation is poor are more likely to be exposed to pathogens. As you will learn, your body is usually able to fight off pathogens before you become sick. However, your body's ability to do so depends a great deal upon your overall health.

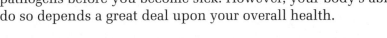

LESSON 23.1 ## USING WHAT YOU HAVE LEARNED

REVIEW

1. What are pathogens and how can they be transmitted?
2. What is the main difference between a virus and the other five types of pathogens?

THINK CRITICALLY

3. Infectious diseases can range from mild to very serious illnesses. Why is it so difficult to completely avoid pathogens?
4. When many people travel to other countries, they often are very careful about the foods they eat. Why might this be a good precaution for a traveler?

APPLY IT TO YOURSELF

5. Identify at least two precautions you can take to try to avoid pathogens and remain healthy.

SUMMARY

Everywhere you go, you are surrounded by billions of microscopic organisms. Pathogens can be organized into six major groups and can be transmitted in several ways. You can become ill as a result of the air you breathe, the objects you touch, or even the people with whom you come in contact. You can avoid serious illness by understanding how diseases are spread and by following safe health practices.

THE BODY'S RESPONSE TO PATHOGENS

MAIN IDEAS

CONCEPTS
✔ Your body has several lines of defense to protect you against serious illness.
✔ Your immune system is your most powerful line of defense against disease.
✔ Infectious diseases pass through several stages.

VOCABULARY
sebum	immunity
mucous membrane	memory cell
inflammation	incubation stage
phagocyte	prodromal stage
lymphocyte	
macrophage	illness stage
helper T cell	recovery stage
antibody	
killer T cell	relapse

Your skin acts like a suit of armor, keeping pathogens out of your body.

Even though you are constantly exposed to millions of pathogens, most of the time you remain healthy. Much of the credit for keeping the pathogens in check goes to your body's defenses. Your body has several lines of defense that prevent pathogens from entering your body or fight pathogens that do enter your body.

PHYSICAL AND CHEMICAL DEFENSES

Consider what happens when you cut yourself. Some of the bacteria from the surface of your skin and from the surface on which you cut yourself are pushed into the wound. In order to keep as many bacteria out of the wound as possible, you wash the wound with soap and water. But your actions are not always enough to keep pathogens out of your body. Your body's first lines of defense are a number of physical and chemical barriers.

THE SKIN   One of the most effective barriers against pathogens is your skin. Pathogens can move past the skin only when the skin has been damaged by a tear or a burn. In addition to providing a physical barrier, the skin also produces chemicals that fight pathogens. Glands in the skin produce an oily substance called **sebum** [*SEEB um*] that stops the growth of bacteria and fungi. Chemicals present in sweat also slow the growth of pathogens.

MUCOUS MEMBRANES   Skin does not cover all of your body openings that may come in contact with pathogens. However, these openings—your eyes; your respiratory tract including your nose, mouth, throat, and lungs; your digestive tract; and your reproductive tract—are still protected. Each opening is lined with moist coverings called **mucous membranes**. Because mucous membranes are much thinner than skin, they are not as effective as a physical barrier. The mucous membranes are washed by bodily fluids containing chemicals that kill many pathogens. For example, tears wash pathogens from the eyes and saliva contains chemicals that destroy some bacteria in the mouth.

Your respiratory tract also has mechanisms which remove pathogens before they can pass through the mucous membranes. Mucous produced in your respiratory tract traps pathogens that you inhale. The trapped pathogens are then removed by hairlike cilia that line your throat and trachea. The constantly waving cilia move the mucous and other debris up to the mouth where they are sneezed, coughed out, or swallowed.

INFLAMMATION

Sometimes pathogens are able to get past your physical and chemical defenses. For example, when you cut yourself, bacteria can move past your skin and into your bloodstream. Bacteria that enter the body through the wound begin to multiply and may start to release toxins. After a while, you may notice that the area around the cut turns red and begins to swell. The redness and swelling are signs that your body is fighting the infection. This local response to the invasion of pathogens is called **inflammation**.

Inflammation begins almost immediately after bacteria move into your body. Cells called mast cells release chemicals around the site of the invasion. These chemicals attract specialized white blood cells called **phagocytes** [*FAG uh syts*] that engulf and destroy the bacteria. Other chemicals cause the small blood vessels around the wound to expand, making it easier for the phagocytes to move quickly to the site.

The battle that occurs between the phagocytes and the bacteria can cause the infected area to turn red and become warm. Fluid composed of dead bacteria and phagocytes accumulates, causing swelling. In most cases, the phagocytes bring the infection under control, and the tissue damaged by the bacteria begins to heal.

THE IMMUNE SYSTEM

At times, physical and chemical defenses and inflammation are not enough to keep pathogens from making you sick. However, if you have ever been sick with the flu, you know first hand that your body will soon defeat the virus and you will recover. Your recovery is due to the presence of your body's most powerful and complex line of defense, the immune system.

An important part of the immune system is a group of cells called lymphocytes. **Lymphocytes** [*LIM fuh syts*] are specialized white blood cells that are able to recognize different types of pathogens and to produce chemicals that can fight these pathogens. There are two groups of lymphocytes—B cells and T cells. Both B cells and T cells are produced in the bone marrow and stored in the organs of the lymphatic system. Before T cells enter the lymphatic system, they are modified in the thymus, which is located in your upper chest. Despite the similarities in appearance of B cells and T cells, these two types of cells differ in their functions. To understand the different functions, consider what happens if you become infected with the flu virus.

Your immune system responds to the flue virus in four stages: recognition, mobilization, disposal, and immunity.

RECOGNITION   Imagine that while you are at school, you inhale droplets floating in the air that contain flu viruses. The viruses get past the mucous membranes in your throat and lungs, infect cells in the area, and begin to multiply. Eventually some of the viruses will encounter large white blood cells called **macrophages** [*MAK ruh fayj uhz*]. Like phagocytes, the macrophages engulf and destroy pathogens. However, a macrophage also takes a piece of the flu virus and uses it to signal the immune system that your body has been invaded.

The next step for the immune system is to recognize which pathogen is present. Special T cells called **helper T cells** serve

How to prevent a minor cut from becoming infected:

1. Swab wound gently with a clean, wet cloth or hold under cold running water.
2. Clean around cut with mild soap.
3. Remove any debris such as dirt from wound with a pair of clean tweezers.
4. Apply bandage to wound if wound is likely to get dirty again or reinjured.

Figure 23-1   Your body has many defenses against pathogens. Which organs are part of your immune system?

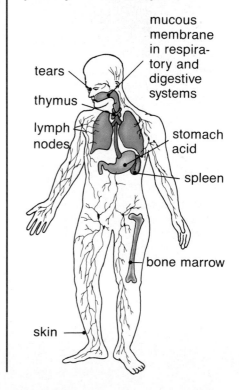

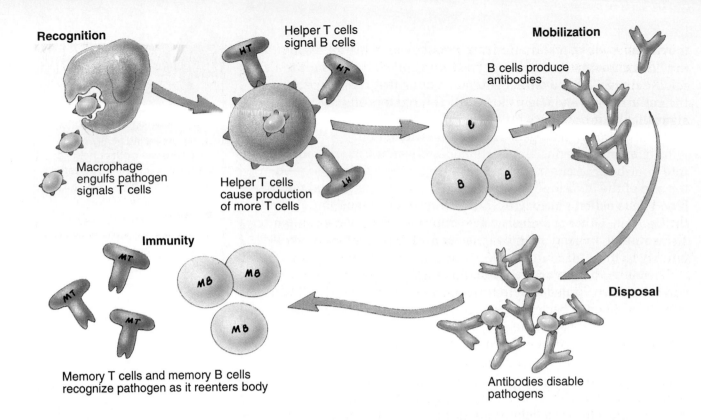

Recognition

Helper T cells
signal B cells

Mobilization

Macrophage
engulfs pathogen
signals T cells

Helper T cells
cause production
of more T cells

B cells produce
antibodies

Immunity

Disposal

Memory T cells and memory B cells
recognize pathogen as it reenters body

Antibodies disable
pathogens

*Figure 23-2 Your immune
system's response to pathogens
can be divided into four stages.
In which stage are antibodies
produced?*

several important functions, one of which is to recognize different
pathogens. There are millions of different kinds of helper T cells in
the body. Each kind is able to recognize a different pathogen.
Eventually a macrophage carrying a piece of the flu virus will
encounter a helper T cell that is able to recognize the flu virus.

MOBILIZATION   Just as there are millions of kinds of helper T cells
in the body, there are also millions of kinds of B cells. The function of B cells is to produce **antibodies**, which are proteins that
attach themselves to pathogens and their toxins and disable them.
One type of B cell is able to produce antibodies that attach themselves to the flu viruses. Helper T cells stimulate these B cells to
multiply and produce antibodies when the flu viruses are present.

DISPOSAL   As the number of antibodies increases, the antibodies
bind to the flu viruses, disabling them and making them easy tar-
gets for macrophages. Helper T cells also stimulate the production
of a second type of T cell called a **killer T cell**. Killer T cells produce chemicals that destroy cells that are infected by the flu viruses, preventing the flu viruses from reproducing. The combined
actions of the antibodies, macrophages, and killer T cells rid your
body of the flu viruses, and your body begins to recover.

IMMUNITY   Usually it takes over a week to produce enough antibodies to fight off an infection. However, if the same pathogen
returns, the immune system is able to respond much more quickly.
This ability of your body to resist and fight off a pathogen before it
makes you sick is called **immunity** [*im YOO nut ee*].

Your body develops immunity to a pathogen in the following way. After your immune system has fought off an infection, B cells and T cells capable of recognizing and responding to that pathogen remain in your body. These cells, called **memory cells**, will recognize quickly the pathogen if it ever enters your body again and will defeat the pathogen before it makes you sick.

STAGES OF DISEASE

Your body's defenses are extremely effective against most pathogens. However, occasionally pathogens are able to establish themselves in your body before they can be fought off successfully. During the week or so it takes for your immune system to respond to the infection, the damage caused by the pathogens to your body results in many of the symptoms associated with being sick. Most infectious diseases progress through four predictable stages.

INCUBATION STAGE   The **incubation stage** is the period between the time the pathogen enters your body and the time you begin to feel sick. During this period, the pathogen begins to multiply and establish itself in your body. The incubation stage usually lasts from two days to two weeks, depending on the specific disease and your overall health. However, for some pathogens, it can be as short as a few hours and as long as several years.

PRODROMAL STAGE   Your immune system often is able to defeat the infection during the incubation stage, especially if you have an immunity to the disease. Occasionally the infection progresses to the stage where you develop mild symptoms. This period is called the **prodromal stage** [*proh DROH mul*]. Symptoms that occur in the prodromal stage are similar for most infectious diseases and may include a slight fever, general aches and pains, and fatigue.

Even though the symptoms are only mild during the prodromal stage, this stage can be the most contagious. Infectious diseases are often spread during the prodromal stage because the infected person usually does not feel sick enough to stay away from others.

ILLNESS STAGE   Following the prodromal stage, the infection reaches its peak, producing its most severe symptoms. This period is known as the **illness stage**. The infection has progressed to the stage where often it is possible to identify the cause of the disease based on the symptoms and on laboratory tests. By now, the immune system has become fully involved in fighting the infection.

FEVER

One sign that pathogens have entered your body is that your body temperature begins to rise above the normal 97-99° F. A mild fever is thought to help you fight off infections by weakening the pathogens and stimulating the production of more white blood cells. However, you should contact your doctor if you have a sustained fever over 101° F.

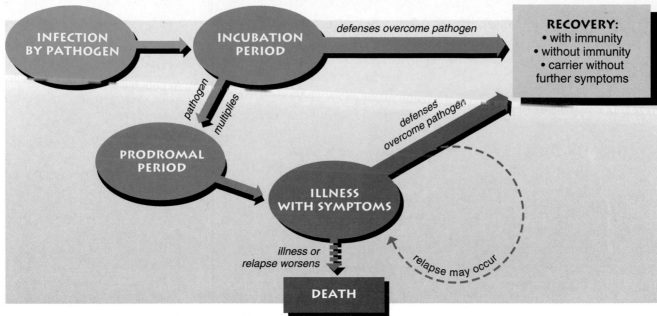

Figure 23-3   Most infectious diseases progress through four
stages. At which stage might a
person have a relapse?

RECOVERY STAGE   The time when a disease is finally overcome by the body's defenses is called the **recovery stage**. Although most of the symptoms begin to subside, your body has spent a lot of energy fighting the infection and is in a weakened state. Therefore, your body may be susceptible to a **relapse**—a return of the infection. A relapse can be more serious than the original infection because your body has not had time to recover from the first infection. Your body also may be more susceptible to other types of infections during the recovery stage. To avoid a relapse or the onset of other infections, it is important that you get plenty of rest during the recovery period and continue to take any medications that your doctor has prescribed.

LESSON 23.2   USING WHAT YOU HAVE LEARNED

REVIEW

1. What are the differences among phagocytes, lymphocytes, and macrophages?
2. During which stage of an infectious disease is a person usually the most contagious?

THINK CRITICALLY

3. Why might a disease that weakens the immune system be particularly dangerous to a person?
4. Many toxic chemicals carry warning labels that advise users to wear special goggles and air filters as precautions against severe illness. What could possibly happen to the users to require such a warning?

APPLY IT TO YOURSELF

5. Your overall well-being is important in helping your immune system fight diseases. What steps can you take to strengthen your fight against infections?

SUMMARY

Your body has several built-in defenses against infectious diseases. Some are more powerful than others. The most powerful line of defense in your body is the immune system. Most infections are easily fought without causing you much harm or discomfort. However, there are times when the pathogens that cause infection break through the lines of defense and you become ill. Diseases can pass through four different stages once they enter your body. Your body's ability to fight the pathogens at each stage determines how sick you become.

FIGHTING DISEASES

Since the early 1900s, medical advances have made infectious diseases seem less threatening. Diseases such as strep throat and whooping cough, which used to cause many deaths, can now be prevented easily or treated. Yet, despite the substantial progress that has been made, infectious diseases are still a cause of concern. Diseases such as measles and tuberculosis that were once thought to be under control are making a comeback. Diseases such as cholera and malaria are still claiming many lives in developing countries. Deadly diseases such as AIDS still have no cure. Continued research may lead to effective treatments against many diseases. However, it is important to remember that even minor infections can become dangerous. Therefore, you need to be aware of the precautions you can take to decrease your risk.

PREVENTIVE BEHAVIOR

As you read in Lesson 1, one of the keys to prevention of major illness is avoiding the sources of pathogens. Avoidance includes trying to stay away from infected people and engaging in sanitary practices such as washing your hands before handling food. A second important step in prevention of disease is to keep your body healthy. Resisting and fighting infections is hard work for your body. Therefore, life-style choices that improve your overall wellness such as proper nutrition, the right amount of sleep, and a routine fitness program will also improve your immune system's ability to respond to pathogens.

VACCINATIONS

You can give your immune system a head start against many dangerous diseases. As a child, you most likely received a series of special shots, or vaccinations, during visits to the doctor. A **vaccination** [*vak suh NAY shun*]—also called an immunization—is a treatment in which the body is injected with a small dose of disabled or dead pathogens or weakened toxins from bacteria. The pathogens and toxins in the vaccine are unable to cause you any harm. However, their presence in your body stimulates your immune system to form antibodies against the active pathogens you may come in contact with in the future. For example, a vaccine against measles will stimulate your immune system to form antibodies against measles. Remember that once your immune system has responded to a pathogen, memory cells allow your body to respond quickly if these pathogens ever invade your body again. What vaccinations did you receive as a child?

MAIN IDEAS

CONCEPTS

✔ There are many precautions that you can take to help prevent contracting an infectious disease.

✔ Vaccinations are critical for maintaining the overall health of the people of our nation.

✔ There are both benefits and dangers in using medicines to fight infections.

VOCABULARY

vaccination
booster
antibiotic
side effect

over-the-counter medicine

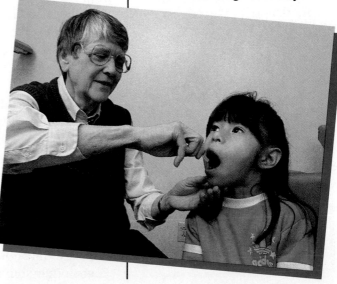

Not all vaccinations are administered by injection. The polio vaccine can be given orally.

RECOMMENDED IMMUNIZATION SCHEDULE

Age	Type of Immunization
birth	hepatitis B
2 months	Diphtheria-tetanus-pertussis (whooping cough) vaccine (DTP), oral polio vaccine (OPV), Haemophilus influenza type b (HbCV), hepatitis B
4 months	DTP, OPV, HbCV
6 months	DTP
8–9 months	hepatitis B
15 months	HbCV, Measles-mumps-rubella (MMR)
15–18 months	DTP, OPV
4–6 years	DTP, OPV
11–12 years	MMR
14–16 years	Tetanus-diphtheria (Td)
every 10 years	Td booster
when recommended	Influenza, pneumococcus

SOURCE: AMERICAN ACADEMY OF PEDIATRICS

Figure 23-4 At what ages does the American Academy of Pediatrics recommend that you receive an oral polio vaccine?

HEALTHY PEOPLE 2000

Improve the financing and delivery of immunizations for children and adults so that virtually no American has a financial barrier to receiving recommended immunizations.

Objective 20.15
from *Healthy People 2000: National Health Promotion and Disease Prevention Objectives*

Figure 23-4 shows the recommended vaccination schedule for babies and children. For some infectious diseases, a single vaccination will protect you for the rest of your life. However, some vaccinations protect you for only a limited time. Once the effect of a vaccination has worn off, you may need to be given a revaccination called a **booster**.

Because of vaccinations, dangerous diseases that were common when your grandparents or great grandparents were children are no longer considered serious threats. For example, the development of vaccinations is responsible for the elimination of the virus that causes smallpox—a deadly disease that killed many people through the early 1900s.

Outbreaks of diseases such as measles, mumps, and rubella appear periodically in different communities. One reason for periodic outbreaks is that vaccinations for diseases that have been brought under control are sometimes thought of as unnecessary and therefore may be overlooked. The rising cost of health care is another factor that can lead to the outbreak of a disease that was once under control. In communities where the availability of health care is minimal, people may not be aware that vaccinations are available, leaving a substantial number of people unprotected against many dangerous but preventable diseases. Health care providers in poor communities often cite this lack of awareness as one of their greatest challenges.

Each state has its own vaccination requirements and most schools require that children be properly vaccinated before they can attend. You can protect yourself by making sure you are up-to-date on all the vaccinations listed in Figure 23-4. The recommendations for vaccinations change frequently as improved vaccinations are developed. Therefore, it is important that you check with your doctor about the latest recommendations. Information about your state's vaccination requirements and on places where vaccinations are available can be obtained from any doctor, health care facility, or your local health department.

PRESCRIPTION MEDICINES

Sometimes, despite your best efforts to reduce the risk of becoming infected, pathogens are able to overcome your body's defenses. If you catch an infectious disease, medical attention may be necessary. In most cases, medicines are available that can kill the pathogen directly—unlike vaccines, which work by stimulating the immune system. Most of these medicines are available only through a doctor's prescription.

ANTIBIOTICS One of the most significant breakthroughs in the fight against infectious diseases was the development of medicines that can cure bacterial infections. The most widely used group of antibacterial medicines is **antibiotics** [*ant ih by AHT iks*]. Antibiotics are medicines that kill or inhibit the growth and reproduction of bacteria or other organisms. The use of antibiotics weakens the bacteria, enabling the body's defenses to take over. The first antibiotic developed was penicillin. Before penicillin was discovered, diphtheria and strep infections commonly caused serious illness or death in babies and children. Penicillin is now used to treat these and many other bacterial infections.

Today there are many antibiotics like penicillin available. Some are effective against only one or two diseases. Others, called broad-spectrum antibiotics, are effective against a wide range of bacterial infections. Because antibiotics can be very powerful drugs, you should always use caution when taking them. Antibiotics can be dangerous when combined with other medications or drugs.

STRATEGIES FOR LIVING

Questions you should ask a physician about your prescription medicine.

- Can this medication cause an allergic reaction?
- Are there any health conditions that might be aggravated by the medication?
- When during the day should the medication be taken?
- Should the medication be taken on a full or empty stomach?
- For how long should the medication be taken?
- What are the possible side-effects?

BACTERIAL RESISTANCE

If one type of antibiotic is used too often to fight a specific bacterial infection, the bacteria may become resistant to that antibiotic. When bacteria become resistant to an antibiotic, that antibiotic can no longer be used to treat the infection. Some bacteria have developed resistance to many different antibiotics. Therefore, infections caused by these bacteria can be difficult to cure.

You can reduce the risk of bacterial resistance by observing the following steps.

- Avoid using antibiotics to treat minor infections that can be taken care of by your body's immune system.
- Don't use an antibiotic to treat viral infections such as the common cold or flu.
- Always follow the prescription exactly. Skipping doses or failing to finish the prescription may allow antibiotic-resistant bacteria to develop.

If you are taking an antibiotic in order to cure a bacterial infection, you should follow your doctor's instructions carefully. If you do not finish taking the antibiotics, the infection may return. As you have learned, a relapse often is more severe than the original illness. If you do not finish the antibiotic, there is also a danger that the bacteria can spread to other parts of the body. Your doctor can answer your questions about when to take the antibiotic.

ANTIVIRAL MEDICINES　　Antibiotics do not kill viruses, and therefore, they are not effective against viral diseases. For example, an antibiotic cannot cure a cold or the flu. A few antiviral medicines have been developed that can relieve signs and symptoms or slow the progress of some viral infections. However, no medicine has been developed that actually cures viral diseases.

One promising approach that is being developed to combat viruses is to use chemicals that the body manufactures. One such chemical is interferon. Interferon is a chemical that is released by cells after the body has been invaded by viruses. The chemical helps cells resist some viruses.

MAKING A DIFFERENCE

RESEARCH HEALTH

Animal Viruses and Bacteria

Dr. Hartwick, a veterinarian at the Iowa State Extension Service, keeps track of over 3,000 diseases that can affect livestock. His job is an important one. In the past, infectious diseases in animals were sometimes transmitted to people who ate animal products such as poultry, beef, pork, or dairy milk. Today, thanks to new regulations and advances in technology, the meat you eat or the milk you drink is virtually disease-free.

It is impossible to check every animal that produces the food that you eat or drink. However, new techniques allow scientists to check milk and tissue from living animals for the presence of disease. An infected animal then can be treated by a veterinarian before a disease can spread to other animals or to humans.

Another way to prevent food products from spreading disease is through government regulation. The Food Safety and Inspection Service rejects any animal product that shows even the slightest sign of disease. The Food and Drug Administration regulates all drugs that are used to treat animals with diseases, and the Environmental Protection Agency regulates the use of pesticides to strictly limit pesticide contamination of food products.

Today, the biggest concern among animal scientists is salmonella—a bacterium transmitted through undercooked meats. To protect yourself, do not eat raw or undercooked chicken or other meats. Scientists think that salmonella, like other prevalent animal diseases, will soon be eliminated.

1. Why is it important to eliminate disease among livestock?

2. How is government regulation helping to wipe out animal diseases?

REYE'S SYNDROME

Many people have used aspirin to reduce a fever or relieve aches and pains. However, children 16 years of age or younger who take aspirin for a fever increase their risk of getting a rare yet potentially fatal disease called Reye's syndrome [RYZ]. The exact cause of Reye's syndrome is not known, but it usually occurs after a viral infection such as flu or chicken pox. Symptoms include nausea, vomiting, and swelling in the liver and brain. You can reduce your risk of getting Reye's syndrome by not using aspirin to reduce a fever when the source of the fever is unknown.

SIDE EFFECTS   Despite the many benefits provided by prescription medicines, they can also cause side effects. **Side effects** are unwanted reactions to a medicine ranging from a headache and sleepiness to more serious conditions such as kidney failure or internal bleeding. You can minimize the risk of side effects and maximize the effectiveness of the medicine by closely following the directions. Any questions about possible side effects of a medicine or about the instructions can be answered by your doctor or pharmacist.

OVER-THE-COUNTER MEDICINES

Everywhere you look—on television, in magazines, in store windows—you may notice many advertisements that describe medicines you can buy that do everything from relieving your headache to curing athlete's foot. The medicines that you see advertised on television or in magazines are known as **over-the-counter (OTC) medicines**. OTC medicines are medicines that can be purchased without a doctor's prescription.

Although a few OTC medicines, such as shampoos that kill head lice and ointments for skin wounds, help to cure infections, most OTC medicines do not cure anything. Instead, these medicines relieve the symptoms of mild illnesses and perhaps make you feel better while your immune system is at work. Therefore, it is important that you do not rely solely on OTCs when you are sick.

Like prescription medicines, OTC medicines have to be taken with caution. OTC medicines are dangerous if taken incorrectly, and many cause unwanted side effects. For example, aspirin, the most popular OTC pain reliever, can irritate mucous membranes lining the stomach. This irritation can cause indigestion and bleeding in the stomach, a serious condition.

Consumers are often faced with many choices of over-the-counter medicines.

Often, the best way to recover from an infectious disease is by resting and drinking plenty of fluids.

Lu had been fighting an infection for several days. When she finally went to the doctor, she was given a prescription for an antibiotic.

Within a few days, Lu could tell that the antibiotic was working, but now she had a cold as well.

Before bed one evening, Lu's brother suggested that Lu take some liquid cold medication that would help her sleep through the night. As Lu was about to drink the cold medicine, she noticed a warning label on the bottle. "CAUTION: May cause vomiting and dizziness when taken with other medication." Lu hesitated, remembering the antibiotic she was taking. "Oh, it's probably no big deal," she thought. But then she remembered her brother saying that the cold medicine was pretty strong and really knocked him out for the night. Lu decided not to take a chance with it and put the bottle back in the medicine cabinet. If she still felt bad in the morning, she would call the doctor to see if combining the two medicines would be safe.

TAKING CARE OF YOURSELF

When you don't feel well, you have to make a decision about how to take care of yourself. Should you take an OTC medicine to feel better and go about your usual activities? Should you stay home in bed and rest? Should you see a doctor?

Proper rest is part of treating any infectious disease. Rest allows your immune system to operate at its peak. Staying home from school and work also prevents you from passing the disease on to others. Continue to rest even after you begin to recover to avoid a relapse. Proper nutrition and plenty of liquids are also important.

If you feel sick for more than a day or if you develop a fever, a rash, or swelling, you should call or visit a doctor. A doctor can help you determine the cause of your illness, can prescribe any medications, and can advise you on ways to speed your recovery.

SUMMARY

Advances in medicine have made it possible to prevent and cure many life-threatening diseases. Vaccinations give your immune system a head start against many infections. However, dangerous but preventable diseases continue to break out in communities where people have not been properly vaccinated. Prescription medicines are only effective if they are used correctly. Full recovery from infectious diseases requires proper rest and nutrition.

LESSON 23.3   USING WHAT YOU HAVE LEARNED

REVIEW

1. What is a booster shot? When is a booster needed?
2. How do antibiotics help treat an infection?

THINK CRITICALLY

3. When used incorrectly, over-the-counter medicines can be very toxic. Why do you think OTCs are often underestimated and misused?
4. It is not unusual for certain regions of a state to require additional vaccinations than those already required by the state. Why is this sometimes necessary?

APPLY IT TO YOURSELF

5. With the discovery of vaccines and medications, health officials have been able to prevent many unnecessary deaths. How have these discoveries affected you personally?

COMMON INFECTIOUS DISEASES

Although substantial progress has been made in the fight against infectious diseases, millions of people still get sick every year. Often the diseases are minor, just causing a temporary inconvenience. For diseases such as the common cold, there is nothing you can do but get plenty of rest and wait out the infection. More serious infections often can be prevented by vaccination or treated with prescription medicines before the infection causes too much harm. However, in order to successfully treat an infectious disease, it must be properly diagnosed by a doctor. If you are sick, ignoring the illness or using the wrong type of treatment can be dangerous.

RESPIRATORY INFECTIONS

Some of the most common types of infections are those that affect the respiratory system. Most respiratory infections are caused by viruses or bacteria that infect the nose, throat, bronchi, and lungs. Anyone who is exposed to the pathogens that cause respiratory infections is at risk of becoming infected. However, smokers—and those who live with or spend a lot of time with smokers—tend to get more respiratory infections than nonsmokers.

THE COMMON COLD   The common cold results in more absences from school or work than any other infectious disease. The common cold is a mild but very contagious viral illness that can cause one or all of the following symptoms—a runny nose, a sore throat, coughs, and sneezes. A cold affects your upper respiratory tract rather than your lungs. There is no cure for a cold except bed rest. It is also important to drink plenty of liquids. Moisture helps keep your sinuses open. Many over-the-counter medicines are available to treat the symptoms of a cold. However, these medicines can sometimes cause unpleasant side effects.

INFLUENZA   Influenza [*in floo EN zuh*], or the flu, is a serious respiratory infection caused by a virus. It is spread from person to person by direct contact and by airborne droplets from infected people. The flu causes fever, aches, coughing, tiredness, weakness, and shortness of breath. Some flu sufferers may even experience depression. Major outbreaks of the flu tend to occur every three or four years, usually in the winter. Like the common cold, the best treatment for the flu is bed rest. It is also important to maintain proper nutrition and drink plenty of fluids. Although the flu will usually run its course in a week, occasionally it can be dangerous, sometimes leading to pneumonia and even death. The flu is especially dangerous for elderly people or people who already have heart or lung disorders. Vaccines have been developed for different virus strains that cause the flu. Health officials study worldwide health patterns in an effort to predict which strain of flu virus will cause the next major influenza outbreak. They then can develop vaccines to prevent a major outbreak.

MAIN IDEAS

CONCEPTS

✔ The best remedy for many infectious diseases is rest.

✔ New cases of diseases once thought to be under control are increasing at a disturbing rate.

✔ Careful health practices can help to prevent the spread of infectious diseases.

VOCABULARY

influenza
strep throat
tuberculosis
measles
mononucleosis
hepatitis

FOR YOUR INFORMATION

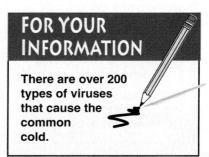

There are over 200 types of viruses that cause the common cold.

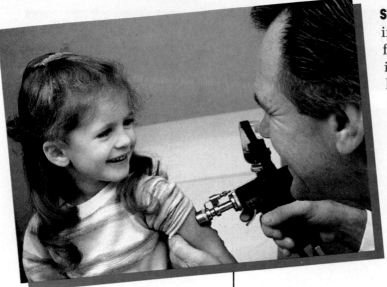

Influenza vaccinations are often recommended for children, the elderly, and for people with heart and lung conditions.

STREP THROAT **Strep throat** is a bacterial infection of the throat. It can be transmitted from an infected person much like a cold or influenza. A strep infection can make swallowing, speaking, and even breathing difficult and painful.

Strep throat can be cured using antibiotics, but the infection can return if you stop taking the medication before your prescription is used up. If not treated, the bacteria that causes strep throat can cause more serious illnesses including rheumatic fever. Rheumatic fever can cause the heart valves to become inflamed, sometimes resulting in permanent heart damage. Because of antibiotics, rheumatic fever is rare today.

TUBERCULOSIS **Tuberculosis** [*tu bur kyuh LOH sus*], or TB, is caused by bacteria that primarily infect the lungs. The first symptom of TB is usually long coughing spells. As the disease develops, the infected person may cough up blood, develop a fever, and lose weight. If untreated, the bacteria can spread to other organs.

Until the 1940s, TB was a major cause of death in the United States. Better public health, improved nutrition, and the development of antibiotics brought TB under control. However, since the late 1980s, the number of cases has continually risen. This increase is especially evident in urban areas where the rates of new cases are anywhere from 5 to 7 times greater than the national average of 10 cases per 100,000. The rates increase even more when the numbers are broken down by race and socioeconomic status. Health officials suggest that the increase in TB cases is directly related to the reduced health care available to the poor and the homeless and to the increase in the number of people living with AIDS—a group particularly susceptible to TB.

An estimated ten million people in the United States carry TB bacteria in their bodies. In healthy people, the body's immune system can usually keep the bacteria in check, so few of these people actually become sick. However, people who are already in poor health, such as those who lack adequate food and housing, or people who abuse alcohol are more likely to succumb to the bacteria.

TB usually can be cured with antibiotics, but the cure can take as long as two years. Recently, new strains of antibiotic-resistant TB were discovered, making traditional treatments ineffective. New medicines have been developed that can successfully treat some new strains of TB.

STOMACH AND INTESTINAL INFECTIONS

At some time in your life, you have probably felt a sudden rush of nausea that has resulted in diarrhea or vomiting. Illnesses that cause such a reaction are often called the stomach flu, intestinal flu, or simply "the bug." These illnesses differ from influenza because they are the result of an inflammation of the stomach or

HEALTHY PEOPLE 2000

Increase to at least 85 percent the proportion of people found to have tuberculosis infection who completed courses of preventive therapy.

Objective 20.18
from *Healthy People 2000: National Health Promotion and Disease Prevention Objectives*

Culturally Sensitive Medicine

Today, physicians find that they are treating people of different cultures regularly. For this reason, a few physicians are opting to combine their medical degrees with a study of social anthropology to better understand the emotional and cultural needs of their patients.

Practicing culturally sensitive medicine has come of age only recently, due to a growing awareness of the need to be respectful of the traditions and practices of other cultures. In the past, for example, if a patient protested a blood transfusion due to religious or cultural conviction, a doctor may have believed the protest was silly or unfounded. Today, a doctor who is culturally sensitive can better explain the technique or work with the patient to seek an alternative treatment if available.

Some diseases, like sickle cell anemia or Tay-Sachs disease, only affect a portion of the population. A doctor who has studied the social and cultural backgrounds of his or her patients with these diseases can work with them to seek the most effective treatment. By knowing more about the groups at risk for a disease, scientists can better research ways to treat the disease. By exploring the cultural as well as the medical backgrounds of their patients, culturally sensitive practitioners can help provide insight into the causes and possible cures for many diseases and provide better care.

---

intestines that is caused by viruses or bacteria. Many intestinal infections are the result of eating or drinking contaminated food or water. Contamination can occur if food is handled improperly or if the water supply is not purified properly.

Most illnesses caused by intestinal infections begin suddenly and last between 12 and 72 hours. Intestinal infections usually clear up by themselves and pose little danger. The usual treatment consists of bed rest and drinking plenty of fluids. It also is important that you start eating solid foods as soon as you comfortably can. Sometimes intestinal infections can lead to severe diarrhea. If you have diarrhea lasting longer than two days, you should be treated by a doctor. Severe diarrhea can cause your body to lose fluids and become dehydrated. Dehydration reduces the amount of plasma in your blood, which lowers blood volume and pressure. In extreme cases, dehydration can lead to shock or even death.

MEASLES

Measles is a very contagious viral disease characterized by a red, spotty rash that covers the entire body. The virus that causes measles can spread very quickly from person to person. You can become infected with measles by breathing droplets containing the virus from an infected person's sneeze or cough. The first symptoms of measles include a cough, runny nose, and high fever. The red rash usually appears about three days later. A person with measles is most contagious to other people just before the rash appears. The rash usually begins to fade after about a week, and recovery begins. Once you have had measles, you are immune to the virus for the rest of your life.

Reprinted by Permission of UFS, Inc.

OTHER INFECTIOUS DISEASES

Disease	Characteristic	Method of Transmission	Prevention/ Treatment
Chicken pox	Viral infection; causes mild fever and itchy skin rash with blisters	Close contact with infected person; airborne spread of virus	Avoid contact
Cholera	Bacterial infection of intestines; causes severe diarrhea and vomiting	Ingestion of food or water contaminated with sewage	Drinking treated water; antibiotics
Malaria	Caused by protozoan that lives in blood; causes fever, headache	Carried by mosquitoes	Preventive medication; drug therapy
Mumps	Viral infection of salivary glands; causes headache, fever, vomiting, swelling of glands in front of ears.	Direct contact with saliva or contaminated articles; highly contagious	Vaccine; bed rest
Pneumonia	Viral or bacterial infection of lungs; causes inflammation of lungs, fever, chest pain, and coughing	Airborne spread by droplets	Vaccine and antibiotics for bacterial pneumonia
Poliomyletis	Viral infection of nerves; causes fever, muscular stiffness, and weakness; can lead to paralysis and respiratory failure	Direct contact; eating contaminated food	Vaccine; no specific treatment
Rabies	Viral infection of the brain; causes convulsions, paralysis, restlessness, fever, and excessive salivation; fatal if not treated in time	Contact with saliva from bite of infected animal (dog, cat, fox, skunk, raccoon, bat, or rat)	Vaccine; see physician immediately for antirabies injections
Rocky mountain spotted fever	Caused by rickettsia; results in high fever, body rash, and severe muscle weakness; if untreated, liver, lungs, and blood can be damaged	Bite of infected dog tick	Tick repellent; antibiotics
Tetanus	Toxin from bacterial infection affects nerve cells in spinal cord; causes painful tightening of muscles	Bacteria enter body through wounds	Vaccine; antitoxin
Whooping cough	Bacterial respiratory infection; mild fever, hacking cough followed by violent coughing episodes	Airborne spread by droplets	Vaccine; antibiotics

Figure 23-5 Which infectious diseases listed in the table can be transmitted through contaminated food?

Although measles usually runs its course without any problems, it can cause complications that sometimes can be fatal. The death rate for measles is about 1 in every 3,000 cases. Effective measles vaccines have been developed, and at one time they raised hopes that measles could be eliminated from the United States. Although the number of cases has decreased dramatically since the vaccines were introduced, measles continues to occur among children and young adults who have not been vaccinated properly.

MONONUCLEOSIS

A common viral infection among teenagers and young adults is mononucleosis. **Mononucleosis** [*mahn oh noo klee OH sus*] is caused by a virus that invades the lymph nodes, causing T cells to multiply abnormally. The virus is spread by direct contact with an infected person and can be passed through his or her saliva. The incubation period is usually four to seven weeks, but it can be shorter in children. Symptoms include fatigue, loss of appetite, sore throat, and swelling of the lymph nodes and the spleen.

Although mononucleosis is not life-threatening, it can sometimes disable a person for months. There is no medical cure for mononucleosis, although medicine can help relieve some of the symptoms. The illness stage of mononucleosis lasts from three to six weeks. A tired feeling may continue during the recovery stage, which can take a few days or a few months.

LYME DISEASE

In 1975, an outbreak of a newly discovered bacterial disease occurred in Lyme, Connecticut. This new disease, later named Lyme disease, was found to be caused by bacteria that are carried by a species of deer tick. The bacteria are spread to people through the bite of the tick. Although Lyme disease was initially thought to be unique to the eastern part of the United States, today cases have been identified throughout the country.

Lyme disease is transmitted through the bite of the tiny deer tick. What measures can you take to prevent yourself from becoming infected?

The first sign of Lyme disease is a circular rash around the bite. Between three days and three weeks after the bite, you may develop flu-like symptoms including fever, chills, headaches, achy muscles and joints, tiredness, and a stiff neck. These symptoms are followed two or three weeks later by pain and swelling of the joints. Complications of untreated Lyme disease include heart and lung problems and nerve and joint disorders. Because the first symptoms of Lyme disease are similar to symptoms of the flu, it is important that you tell your doctor if you have been in a tick-infested area or have been bitten by a tick. A blood test taken two to three weeks after the bite will determine if you have Lyme disease. If you do, your doctor will prescribe an antibiotic that usually cures the disease. The antibiotic will be most effective if the disease is diagnosed and treated during its early stages.

The ticks that carry Lyme disease are about the size of a poppy seed and are commonly found in wooded areas and in tall grasses. Preventive measures include using insect repellants and wearing long pants with the cuffs tucked into your socks to prevent ticks from crawling onto your legs. When undressing in the evening, check your body for ticks. If you find one, remove it by grasping it gently but firmly with tweezers and slowly pulling it off. Then watch the area on your skin for any signs of infection.

VIRAL HEPATITIS

Hepatitis is another infectious disease that is on the increase in the United States, especially among young adults. **Hepatitis** is caused by viruses that infect the liver, causing the liver to become inflamed. Symptoms of hepatitis include jaundice (yellowing of

FOR YOUR INFORMATION

You can become infected with hepatitis A by eating raw shellfish that have come from sewage-contaminated water.

the skin), nausea, fever, and pain in the abdomen. In severe cases, hepatitis can result in permanent liver damage. There are three main types of hepatitis.

HEPATITIS A   The most common type of hepatitis is hepatitis A. It is spread through infected food or water. The incubation period lasts three to six weeks. Recovery takes about six weeks.

HEPATITIS B   Hepatitis B is the most dangerous form of hepatitis and can result in death. Hepatitis B spreads by contact with infected blood or through intimate contact with an infected person. Intravenous drug users who share needles are at high risk for hepatitis B because the needles may carry infected blood. Hepatitis B can take months to run its course.

HEPATITIS C   A third, less severe type of hepatitis, called hepatitis C, is becoming more common. Like hepatitis B, hepatitis C is transmitted through infected blood. Until recently, hepatitis C was the leading type of hepatitis transmitted through blood transfusions. However, a test has been developed that can detect the hepatitis C virus in the blood supply. Medical scientists have also identified other strains of the hepatitis virus, including hepatitis D and hepatitis E. Scientists suspect that there are still more strains that have not yet been identified.

The treatment for all types of hepatitis is rest and proper nutrition. Like most other viral infections, there is no cure for hepatitis. Recently, a vaccine has been developed for hepatitis B. Because of its high cost, the vaccine until recently was only recommended for people at high risk for hepatitis B. However, several prominant medical organizations, including the Centers for Disease Control, the American Academy of Family Physicians, and the American Academy of Pediatricians, have now recommended that all infants, children, and teenagers get vaccinated for hepatitis B.

LESSON 23.4   USING WHAT YOU HAVE LEARNED

REVIEW

1. What is the difference between influenza and intestinal flu?
2. Why is it important that a person being treated for an infectious disease take all of the prescribed medication?

THINK CRITICALLY

3. The increase in the rate of new cases of tuberculosis poses a serious health risk to the nation. Why is this increase a greater problem in poor communities than in wealthy communities?
4. People who have had hepatitis are restricted from donating blood. What might be the reason for this restriction?

APPLY IT TO YOURSELF

5. Imagine you are the only doctor working in an area of the country where you have difficulty reaching many of your patients. How might this affect your ability to prevent the outbreak of a disease?

SUMMARY

Despite the substantial progress that has been made in the fight against infectious diseases, millions of people still get sick every year. Although many diseases such as the common cold are minor, others can cause serious complications and should be treated by a doctor. Some diseases including tuberculosis, Lyme disease, and hepatitis, are actually increasing in frequency. You can help prevent the spread of many of these diseases by taking care of yourself while you are sick.

At the Beach

DECISION FOCUS MAKING

Since April, Sally and Britt had been planning a weekend trip to the beach in June. Their parents had agreed to the plan provided another adult was along. The girls convinced Sally's older brother and his wife to go. Sally and Britt were excited.

When the month of June arrived, so did the hot weather, perfect for a weekend at the beach. But about ten days before they were to go, Britt started to feel sick. She had swollen glands, a fever, and felt tired all the time. She also did not have much of an appetite. When Sally called Britt to see how she was doing, Britt said not to worry. Nothing would get in the way of this trip.

Britt missed a week of school. The doctor told her she had mononucleosis. Chances were, said the doctor, that Britt would be sick for a while. Britt was told to get plenty of rest and not to push herself. Mono could be very serious and the symptoms could linger a long time if care was not taken. When Britt told Sally about it over the phone, she said, "I'm still going. I feel okay most of the time. I'll just be careful and try to get plenty of rest while we're there." Sally didn't know what to do. "Is mono contagious?" she thought. "If it is, I can't afford to get sick. Finals are coming up. I've got a job this summer. I need the money." But she didn't want to miss the trip either. "Britt did say she thought she'd be okay."

PAUSE AND CONSIDER

1. *Identify the Problem.* What is Sally's conflict?

2. *Consider the Options.* What are Sally's options about going on the trip with Britt?

3. *Evaluate the Outcomes.* What might happen if Sally goes on the trip with Britt? What might happen if Sally doesn't go?

Two days before they were scheduled to go on the trip, Sally called Britt and asked her how she felt. "I've felt better," said Britt. "But I'm still going." Sally asked Britt what her doctor had said about going. "Well, he didn't think it was a good

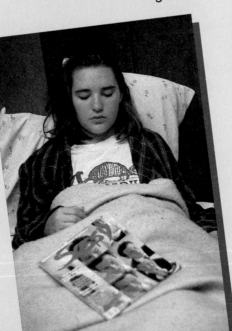

idea. In fact, he told me I should stay home. I didn't tell my parents that though."

Sally really wanted to go away to the beach, but she didn't think it was wise. She had read about mononucleosis in a health book. It was contagious, but mostly through close contact. Sally figured she would be safe. But the book also said that if care was not taken, an infection could set in. There could be more serious complications. Sally didn't feel Britt was doing the right thing. She decided to say something. "Britt, you know I really want to go, but it's okay if we don't. You need to take this seriously."

Britt paused. "You're kidding. You are really thinking about not going?" She laughed. "I was determined to go because I thought you'd be too mad if I didn't."

"No way," said Sally. "We can do it another time. Let's postpone the trip. We can go in July or August. You should be better by then. Besides, if we go later in the summer, we can go for several days instead of a weekend."

DECIDE AND REVIEW

4. *Decide and Act.* What did Sally decide about going on the trip? Why was her decision so difficult?

5. *Review.* What other choices could Sally have made about going on the trip? How would you have handled the same situation?

PROJECTS

1. Investigate the progress in the development of vaccines for hepatitis, AIDS, and the common cold. What problems have thwarted the development of a vaccine for these diseases?

2. Create a chart that lists the most commonly used antibiotics. On your chart, list the diseases the antibiotics are used to treat and some of their common side effects. You may want to consult a medical dictionary for your information.

WORKING WITH OTHERS

Throughout history, individuals and organizations have been working to discover the causes of common diseases. Scientists such as Marie Curie, Jonas Salk, and Linus Pauling are among those well noted for their research on diseases. With a partner, choose a scientist who has contributed to the cure of a disease and trace his or her progress in finding that cure.

CONNECTING TO...

SOCIAL STUDIES   As you may have discovered in social studies class, a national system of health care has been debated in the United States. Countries such as Great Britain and Sweden have what is called "socialized medicine" where taxes pay for medical care for everyone. Proponents of national health care have said that maintaining the health of every individual is an essential social service. Opponents suggested that national health care would cost taxpayers too much and endanger quality of care. Find articles that reflect the two views about national health care. Then prepare an argument for or against a nationalized system of health care to present orally to the class.

USING VOCABULARY

antibody	killer T cell	protozoan
antibiotic	lymphocyte	recovery stage
bacteria	macrophage	relapse
booster	measles	rickettsia
fungi	memory cell	sebum
helper T cell	mononucleosis	side effect
hepatitis	mucous membrane	strep throat
illness stage	over-the-counter	toxin
immunity	medicine	tuberculosis
incubation stage	parasite	vaccination
infectious disease	pathogen	virus
inflammation	phagocyte	
influenza	prodromal stage	

Number a separate piece of paper from 1-13 and complete the following sentences using vocabulary words from the list above.

1. A _____ is the smallest pathogen. These pathogens cause colds, the flu, polio, and AIDS.

2. Malaria is caused by one-celled organisms called _____.

3. _____ is characterized by redness and swelling around a cut.

4. The function of B cells is to produce _____ that disable pathogens.

5. A disease is most likely to be contagious during the _____.

6. _____ can be taken to relieve the symptoms of a disease but do not offer a cure.

7. _____ are prescribed to cure bacterial infection.

8. If you suffer sleepiness while taking a medication, you are most likely experiencing _____.

9. _____ is a disease which, if left untreated, can cause a serious illness such as rheumatic fever.

10. A virus that invades the lymph nodes can cause _____ which is characterized by swollen lymph nodes, fatigue, and loss of appetite.

11. Poisons produced by harmful bacteria are called _____.

12. You can contract _____ by eating shellfish.

13. _____ is the ability to fight off pathogens before getting sick.

CONCEPT MAPPING

On a separate sheet of paper, create a concept map for the *immune system*. In your map, include as many of these concepts as you can: *antibodies, B cells, helper T cells, immune system, infected cells, killer T cells, lymphocytes, macrophages, pathogens.* You may use additional concepts in your map. Information about concept mapping appears at the front of this book.

THINKING CRITICALLY

INTERPRET

LESSON 23.1
1. What is a pathogen? Describe the six major groups of pathogens.

2. In what ways are pathogens transmitted to humans?

3. What is the difference between a virus and bacteria?

LESSON 23.2
4. What role does your skin play in protecting you against pathogens?

5. Describe the major function and components of the immune system.

6. What are the four stages of an illness?

7. Why do some people suffer a relapse of a disease? How can you avoid a relapse?

LESSON 23.3
8. What are some behaviors that can help you prevent infectious disease?

9. Why is overusing antibiotics risky?

10. What is the best thing to do when you start to feel as if you might be getting sick?

LESSON 23.4
11. What is the treatment for the common cold?

12. What are the potential dangers of strep throat?

13. What are some causes of stomach infections?

14. How can you protect yourself from measles, mumps, or rubella?

15. What is Lyme Disease?

APPLY

LESSON 23.1
16. Pathogens can be transmitted in several ways. How can an understanding of this information help you avoid illness?

LESSON 23.2
17. Why do you think researchers can cure a disease such as smallpox but cannot come up with a cure for the common cold?

LESSON 23.3
18. The warning on your antibiotic medication says, "Be sure to finish all medication unless otherwise prescribed by the doctor." Why is finishing a medication so important?

19. How do you think it was possible to eradicate a major disease such as smallpox from the world?

LESSON 23.4
20. How might you be able to tell the difference between a cold and the flu?

COMMITMENT TO WELLNESS

FOLLOW-UP

SETTING GOALS

Look back at the Commitment to Wellness checklist that you created at the beginning of this chapter. Review your answers to assess your behaviors that help to prevent the spread of infectious diseases.

Identify your *yes* responses. How were you able to develop those healthy practices? What might you be able to do to apply those habits to areas that might be weaknesses for you?

Look at your *no* responses. Choose one that you would like to change to *yes.* Copy the checklist item in your journal, or in another place that offers easy reference. Below the item, list at least four specific steps that will help you improve your behavior. For example, if you do not take precautions to protect others when you are sick, you might list *Be careful to avoid close contact with others* and *Wash my hands before handling food* as specific steps. Awareness of proper behavior will help you take healthy precautions when the time arises.

WHERE DO I GO FROM HERE?

The following organization offers more information about the spread and prevention of many different diseases. Please be specific about the type of disease in which you are interested.

FOR MORE INFORMATION, CONTACT:

The Centers for
Disease Control
1600 Clifton Road, NE
Atlanta, GA 30333
Attention: Publications

Sexually Transmitted Diseases/AIDS

"They that will not be counseled, cannot be helped. If you do not hear reason, she will rap you on the knuckles."

Benjamin Franklin

Ben Franklin, of course, knew nothing about AIDS, though many STDs were common in his day. His message is especially relevant today, when the consequences of an unhealthy decision, a failure to listen to reason, can be so devastating. Hundreds of thousands of Americans—men and women, teenagers and children—are infected with HIV, the virus that causes AIDS. HIV, like all sexually transmitted diseases, does not discriminate on the basis of race, religion, sexual preference, or gender. Everyone who is sexually active is susceptible, and the incidence of sexually transmitted diseases is on the rise. Some STDs are curable with antibiotics. Others are, as yet, incurable. Abstinence, education, and responsible behavior can prevent the spread of STDs, including AIDS.

Talking about sex and sexually transmitted diseases is often embarrassing due to their intimate nature. But being sexually active requires responsibility and the maturity to discuss their consequences. Anyone, even you, can become infected with HIV or another STD if you do not make responsible decisions about your sex life.

Number a sheet of paper or a page from your Wellness Journal from 1-8. Respond to the following statements by writing *yes* or *no* to indicate your understandings about sexually transmitted diseases.

1. I believe that a healthy choice for me is abstinence from sexual activity before marriage.

2. I understand that many STDs do not exhibit symptoms for a long time.

3. I know that AIDS and other STDs can affect anybody, even me.

4. I never join in discrimination or jokes about people living with AIDS.

5. Whenever I hear someone make an incorrect statement about ways to contract AIDS, I speak up.

6. I understand that many STDs can affect fertility if left untreated.

7. I understand that most STDs can only be contracted through bodily fluids such as blood or semen.

8. I am not afraid to discuss sex and sexually transmitted diseases.

Review your responses and consider what might be your strengths and weaknesses. Save your list for a follow-up activity that appears at the end of this chapter.

THE STD EPIDEMIC

Throughout history, many infectious diseases have taken their toll on human society. However, even though modern medicine has helped to conquer most of these diseases in the United States, one group of infectious diseases has continued to rise, especially among teenagers and adults who are in the prime of their lives. This group of infectious diseases is the sexually transmitted diseases. A **sexually transmitted disease** (STD) is an infectious disease that is spread from person to person by sexual contact such as during sexual intercourse.

The impact of sexually transmitted diseases has been unique in modern society. Although their cause and prevention are well understood, there is still widespread fear and misinformation about STDs. Fear of contracting an STD such as the virus that causes AIDS has often led to discrimination against those who are infected. While the public debate over how to fight these diseases can be emotionally charged, many people find that sexually transmitted diseases are difficult subjects to discuss. The key for you is to learn as much as possible about sexually transmitted diseases. Once you do, you can make decisions that can reduce your risk of becoming infected.

WHAT ARE SEXUALLY TRANSMITTED DISEASES?

There are over 35 different STDs. Many of these diseases may cause only mild discomfort. Others can be life-threatening. Most STDs can be cured if treated early. However, if left untreated, many STDs can leave a person unable to have children, or lead to blindness, neurological damage, and even death. Some STDs—such as genital warts, genital herpes, and AIDS—have no cure at this time.

Like all other infectious diseases, STDs are caused by pathogens, including viruses, bacteria, protozoa, fungi, and even animal parasites. You can review these pathogens in Chapter 23, "Infectious Diseases." Compared with pathogens that cause the flu or measles, which are passed through the air, the pathogens that cause STDs are more difficult to transmit. You can be infected only through intimate skin-to-skin contact or through the exchange of certain bodily fluids—semen, vaginal fluid, breast milk or blood. With very few exceptions, the pathogens that cause STDs cannot survive

CONCEPTS
✔ The number of cases of sexually transmitted diseases is increasing in the United States.
✔ If untreated, many sexually transmitted diseases can cause permanent disability and death.
✔ Most sexually transmitted diseases can be prevented by practicing responsible behavior.

VOCABULARY
sexually transmitted disease
epidemic
asymptomatic

Unlike many infectious diseases, STDs cannot be transmitted through casual contact.

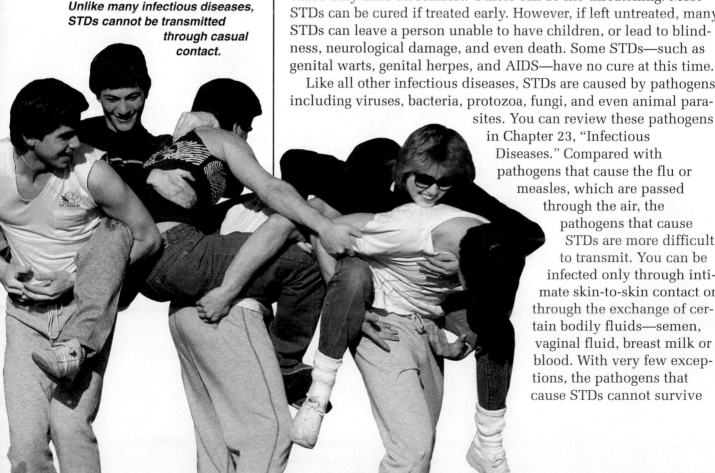

outside of the human body. For example, the vast majority of pathogens that cause STDs cannot be transmitted through kissing, holding hands, sharing eating utensils, or using public toilets. However, if you have intimate sexual contact with a person infected with an STD, your chances of becoming infected increase dramatically.

WHO HAS STDs?

STDs are considered to be an epidemic in the United States today. An **epidemic** is the outbreak of a contagious disease that spreads rapidly within a certain population. STDs have infected people of every age, gender, ethnic origin, and socioeconomic status. According to the Centers for Disease Control (CDC), over 33,000 new STD cases occur every day. That means that over 12 million Americans, including hundreds of thousands of teenagers, will be infected with an STD each year. It has been estimated that if current trends continue, one out of every four individuals between 15 and 55 years of age will become infected with at least one STD within their lifetime.

What are your chances of becoming infected with an STD? As you will learn, your chances depend not on your gender, age, ethnic origin or socioeconomic status, but on whether you choose responsible behaviors.

THE SPREAD OF STDs

Despite the fact that most STDs can be treated or cured, many of these diseases are on the rise. Why are STDs still a problem? Some of the reasons have to do with people's behaviors and attitudes toward STDs. Other reasons have to do with the nature of the diseases themselves.

BEHAVIOR   You can decrease significantly your risk of becoming infected with an STD by practicing responsible behavior. Responsible behavior starts with abstaining from sexual activity until you are involved in a mutually exclusive relationship with a person who is not infected with an STD. Unfortunately, many people put themselves at risk by practicing irresponsible behaviors.

NEWBORN BABIES WITH STDs

If a woman who is pregnant has an STD, including HIV infection, there is a good chance that the baby will become infected. Certain STDs will infect the fetus while it is still developing in the womb. Some cause birth defects or even miscarriages. Other STDs, including HIV infection, are caused by pathogens that can be transmitted to the baby during childbirth as the baby passes through the birth canal. If diagnosed early during pregnancy, the mother can be treated and cured of some STDs before the fetus becomes infected.

These behaviors include sexual activity with many partners and not using a latex condom correctly and consistently during intercourse. Despite the epidemic of STDs, many teenagers are engaging in sexual activity. People are staying single longer than they used to and are getting divorced more frequently. As a result, more and more people are engaging in sex outside of marriage and are exposing themselves to STDs.

KNOWLEDGE OF STDs Despite the clear connection between irresponsible sexual activity and the risk of becoming infected with an STD, people continue to put themselves at risk. One part of the problem is that many people do not understand how STDs are transmitted, how their transmission can be prevented, or how they can be treated or cured. Many people who become infected are unaware of the signs and symptoms of STDs. As a result, these people are unlikely to realize they are infected and therefore may fail to seek the necessary medical help. By not seeking medical help, infected people remain carriers of serious infections that can be transmitted to other people.

ATTITUDES TOWARD STDs Knowledge of how STDs are transmitted is not always enough to prevent people from becoming infected. Many people may know how to prevent STDs, but mistakenly believe that they are invulnerable. Other sexually active people do not think they can get STDs. They often believe that only certain types of people can become infected.

Some people believe that the mass media do not address some of the harmful consequences of promiscuous sex.

This sense of invulnerability may have its roots in how sex is portrayed in our culture. Interest groups, including parents, religious leaders, political leaders, and social scientists have questioned whether the mass media, which includes television, radio, movies, recorded music, and printed material such as magazines, have portrayed sexual intimacy too casually and as being risk-free. Rarely are individuals portrayed in the mass media as having an STD. Do the media make sexual experimentation appear to be safe? If so, for millions of people in the United States, this misconception can be harmful.

Many people hold negative attitudes toward people who have an STD. However, these attitudes can actually encourage the spread of STDs. Some individuals who think that they have an STD may be too ashamed to seek medical help. Others may deny that they have an STD because they are afraid of what people might think of them. Should these people fail to abstain from sex, they face the risk of infecting others.

THE NATURE OF STDs   The nature of STDs themselves is another reason for the current epidemic. The early signs and symptoms of some STDs may be so mild that they are overlooked. A person with no obvious signs or symptoms of a disease is said to be **asymptomatic**. People who are asymptomatic usually do not realize that they are infected and therefore may unknowingly pass an STD on to others.

Unlike diseases such as measles or mumps, your body does not develop an immunity to most STDs, even if you have already recovered from one. There are also no vaccines available against most STDs. Therefore you can become infected by one or more STDs over and over again. You can also become infected with more than one STD at a time. A person who has several STDs can pass any or all of them to another person during one instance of sexual contact.

INCURABLE STDs   A final reason that the number of cases of STDs is increasing is that some STDs do not yet have a cure. AIDS, genital herpes, and genital warts are three rapidly spreading STDs for which there are no cures at the present time. Each will be discussed in greater detail in Lesson 2 and Lesson 3. People with these diseases are able to transmit the infection to others for the rest of their lives.

There is a wealth of information about STDs and their prevention.

SOLVING THE PROBLEM

STDs are easy to prevent and in most cases easy to cure. Yet more and more people are becoming infected. Where does the solution to the problem lie? The first step you can take is to learn as much as possible about STDs. The correct information can help you make decisions that may reduce your risk of becoming infected. Finally, many STDs can be treated or cured. Anyone suffering from an STD should abstain from sexual intimacy and seek medical treatment immediately. Seeking medical help and abstaining from sexual activity are socially responsible behaviors.

LESSON 24.1   **USING WHAT YOU HAVE LEARNED**

REVIEW

1. What behaviors are linked to the spread of STDs?
2. How can embarrassment about STDs actually encourage the spread of STDs?

THINKING CRITICALLY

3. Given the potential seriousness of many STDs, why are so many people unwilling to seek medical help?
4. The mass media is often accused of helping the spread of STDs. Identify one way you think the mass media can help educate people about the dangers of STDs.

APPLY IT TO YOURSELF

5. As a health professional, how would you make people infected with STDs more comfortable about seeking treatment?

SUMMARY

Sexually transmitted diseases are infectious diseases that are passed from person to person by intimate sexual contact. Although most STDs are curable, the number of cases of STDs continues to increase. Reasons for the increase include lack of understanding about the diseases themselves and the nature of the STDs. By understanding the facts about STDs and the behaviors that lead to the spread of STDs, you can reduce your risk of becoming infected.

MAIN IDEAS

CONCEPTS

✔ Most sexually transmitted diseases infect the reproductive organs—often resulting in sterility.

✔ Many people with sexually transmitted diseases have no symptoms.

✔ Many complications due to sexually transmitted diseases can be prevented with early treatment.

VOCABULARY

lesion	syphilis
vaginitis	primary stage
pelvic inflammatory disease	chancre
	secondary stage
infertility	latent stage
urethritis	tertiary stage
chlamydia	genital herpes
gonorrhea	genital warts

COMMON SEXUALLY TRANSMITTED DISEASES

During the past decade, AIDS has been the sexually transmitted disease that has dominated the headlines. However, other dangerous STDs, many of which were thought to be under control, are once again reaching epidemic proportions. The majority of these STDs can be treated or cured if detected early. Not only is it necessary to understand and avoid the factors that put you at risk for becoming infected, it is also important to recognize the symptoms of common STDs so you can seek treatment if necessary.

The increase in STD cases has caused great concern among local, state, and national health officials. With the exception of AIDS, which will be discussed in greater detail in Lesson 3, most cases of STDs are one of five types: chlamydia, gonorrhea, syphilis, genital herpes, and genital warts.

HOW DO STDs HARM THE BODY?

All of the STDs discussed in this lesson infect the skin or mucous membranes of the reproductive organs. To review the structure and function of the reproductive organs, refer to Chapter 17, "Growth and Development." Most STDs cause a lesion on the skin or mucous membrane at the site of infection. A **lesion** [*LEE zhun*] is an injured or abnormal area in a tissue. Typically the lesion will be in the form of a blister, open sore, rash, wart, or inflamed area. Often the lesions are painless and may go unnoticed, particularly if they occur on an area that cannot be seen. Often lesions caused by STDs will disappear without treatment. However, the disappearance of the lesions does not mean that the disease has gone. There also are other symptoms that are common to many STDs that can help alert the person to the presence of an infection. If you experience any of the following symptoms, seek medical help.

VAGINITIS   Two of the most frequent sites of STD infection in women are the vagina and cervix. An inflammation of the vagina due to infection is called **vaginitis**. Some of the common signs of vaginitis may include burning or itching and a yellow, white, or frothy discharge from the vagina. Often the discharge has an unpleasant odor. Signs of vaginitis do not automatically indicate that a woman has an STD. Although vaginitis can be caused by an STD, it also may result from other factors, including other types of infections, such as yeast infections, that may not be transmitted by sexual contact. A doctor can diagnose the cause of the vaginitis and prescribe the proper treatment.

Jenny suspected that she might have a yeast infection. She had had some mild yeast infections in the past, but this time the symptoms were a bit worse. She started to wonder whether the infection might be

something more serious. Jenny had always felt uncomfortable discussing medical problems of this nature with other people and was nervous about seeing a doctor.

After a couple of days the infection had not gotten any better. Jenny decided that she needed to get over her embarrassment and have a doctor examine her. The doctor was very understanding, and Jenny realized that there was no reason to be embarrassed. As it turned out, medicines that Jenny had been taking for a strep infection had led to the yeast infection.

PELVIC INFLAMMATORY DISEASE A more serious condition in women that can result from an STD is pelvic inflammatory disease. **Pelvic inflammatory disease** (PID) occurs when pathogens infect the uterus, Fallopian tubes, and/or ovaries, causing inflammation. If not treated, PID can damage the reproductive organs, and cause infertility. **Infertility** is the inability to bear children due to physical complications.

URETHRITIS STD pathogens often infect the urethra of men and women. Inflammation of the urethra due to an infection is called **urethritis** [*yur ih THRYT us*] or nongonococcal urethritis. Symptoms of urethritis include an unusual discharge that varies in color and a burning sensation during urination. In men, untreated urethritis can lead to inflammation of the prostate gland, swelling of the testes, and perhaps infertility. In women, the infection may eventually move to the uterus, Fallopian tubes, and ovaries, causing pelvic inflammatory disease.

CHLAMYDIA

Chlamydia [*kluh MID ee uh*] is a bacterial infection that attacks the cervix and Fallopian tubes in females and the urethra in both males and females. Today, chlamydia is the most common STD in the United States. According to the Centers for Disease Control (CDC) in Atlanta, Georgia, an estimated four million new cases of chlamydia occur every year. Health officials fear that the concern over the growing AIDS epidemic has distracted public attention from the seriousness of chlamydia.

The symptoms of chlamydia begin to appear 7 to 14 days after infection. Males may have an unusual discharge from the penis and females may have an unusual discharge from the vagina. Both males and females may experience a burning sensation during urination. If untreated, chlamydia can lead to severe urethritis, inflammation of the prostate gland in men, and PID in women. These complications often lead to infertility.

Once chlamydia is diagnosed, it is easy to cure with antibiotics. However, chlamydia is often asymptomatic, especially in women. Therefore many people with chlamydia are unaware that they have been infected and do not seek medical treatment. Those who believe that they might have been exposed to chlamydia should consult a doctor or other medical professional.

Each person in a couple has a responsibility to the other person as well as to him- or herself.

HEALTHY PEOPLE 2000

Reduce Chlamydia trachomatis infections, as measured by a decrease in the incidence of nongonococcal urethritis, to no more than 170 cases per 100,000 people.

Objective 19.2
from *Healthy People 2000: National Health Promotion and Disease Prevention Objectives.*

Federal and state laws require doctors to report certain STDs to local public health officials. The diseases are reported by case number or code rather than the patient's name. This is done to protect the privacy of the individual. The medical reports provide valuable information about which groups of people are being infected and how rapidly the disease is spreading.

Despite the serious nature of the STD epidemic, it has been difficult to accurately determine the number of people infected. Because people with STDs are often asymptomatic, many do not seek treatment, and the disease goes unreported. Other people may simply ignore the symptoms. Even when people do seek treatment, doctors are only required to report syphilis, gonorrhea, and AIDS. Despite these problems, based on the number of cases that are reported to health officials, it is clear that STDs infect millions of people every year.

GONORRHEA

A second major STD that is in many ways similar to chlamydia but is caused by different bacteria is gonorrhea. **Gonorrhea** [*gahn uh REE uh*], like chlamydia, infects the vagina, cervix, uterus, and Fallopian tubes in women and the urethra in men. It can also infect the throat and rectum. The CDC estimates that over one million new cases of gonorrhea occur every year. The number of cases is rising very rapidly among urban adolescents between 15 and 19 years of age.

The symptoms of gonorrhea begin to appear two to seven days after infection. Men and women can experience an unusual discharge from the penis or vagina and an intense burning sensation during urination. However, most women are asymptomatic and may not realize that they are infected until the disease progresses. If untreated, gonorrhea can lead to PID in women and possibly can lead to infertility. In men, untreated gonorrhea can lead to urethritis, inflammation of the testes and prostate gland, and infertility. If the bacteria get into the bloodstream, the disease can spread to other parts of the body causing a fever, skin rash, and painful swelling of the joints.

Gonorrhea can be treated and cured with antibiotics. Recently, new types of gonorrhea bacteria have developed resistance to some antibiotics. However, these infections will still respond to other antibiotics. Because people with either chlamydia or gonorrhea often do not have any symptoms, regular screening is recommended for people who think that they may be at risk. People at risk include those who are sexually active, particularly those who have had more than one partner during the past year, and those who suspect that their partners might be infected.

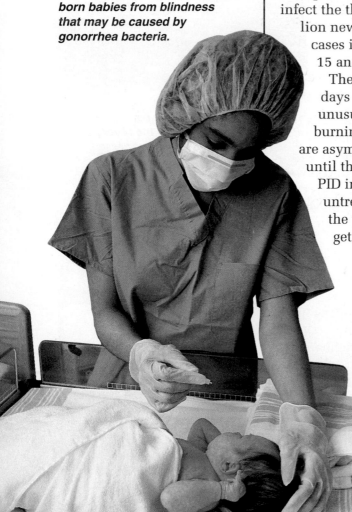

Silver nitrate drops protect newborn babies from blindness that may be caused by gonorrhea bacteria.

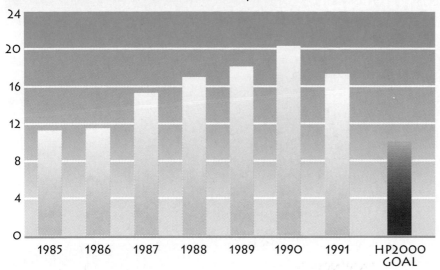

RATES OF SYPHILIS PER 100,000

Figure 24-1 Describe the general trend in the number of syphilis cases from 1985 to 1991.

SYPHILIS

One of the potentially most dangerous STDs is syphilis. **Syphilis** [*SIF lus*] is a bacterial infection that initially attacks the mucous membrane at the site of infection. If left untreated, it can spread to other organs in the body. Although the number of cases of syphilis has declined dramatically over the past forty years, it is once again on the rise—especially among young adults living in urban areas. The CDC now estimates that 134,000 new syphilis cases occur every year. The progression of syphilis is characterized by four distinct stages.

PRIMARY STAGE   The first or **primary stage** of syphilis begins about 10 to 21 days after infection. During the primary stage, a painless open sore called a **chancre** [*SHANG kur*] appears on the skin or

---

FINDING THE ANSWERS

As you learn more about the consequences of sexual behavior, you may have questions. Sometimes the new information can be frightening. You may wonder how it applies to you. Or you may question yourself unnecessarily. Often, the most difficult obstacle you face is knowing who can give you the answers you need.

Discussing sex-related concerns with someone else may make you uncomfortable but it is important that you seek out information that will help you make good decisions about issues that affect your health. When your questions pertain to sexually transmitted diseases, you can get information anonymously and confidentially. The Centers for Disease Control and the American School Health Association have established a national hotline. Trained volunteers are available Monday through Friday to answer your questions about STDs. Call the helpline at 1-800-227-8922.

OTHER SEXUALLY TRANSMITTED DISEASES

Disease	Characteristic	Treatment
Chancroid	Bacterial infection; Causes a single painful sore/ulcer and swelling in nearby lymph nodes.	Antibiotics
Chlamydia	Bacterial infection; *In women*, a thin vaginal discharge, and a burning sensation during urination. However, most women have no symptoms. *In men*, causes thin, white discharge from penis, and discomfort during urination.	Antibiotics
Genital Herpes	Viral infection; Causes small, painful blisters around genital area.	Antiviral medication
Genital Warts	Viral infection; Causes painless, pink growths resembling cauliflowers on the genitals.	Surgical removal, medication
Gonorrhea	Bacterial infection; *In women*, causes vaginal discharge, some pain during urination, and mild discomfort in pelvic area. However, most women have no symptoms. *In men*, causes foul-smelling, thick, yellow discharge from penis, painful urination. Can cause sore throat or rectum if present there.	Antibiotics
Pediculosis pubis	Pubic lice; causes severe itching in genital area.	Insecticidal powder or shampoo
Scabies	Mites; Causes severe itching in genital area and small bumps on skin surface.	Insecticidal powder or shampoo
Syphilis	Bacterial infection; Causes hard, round, painless lesion around genital area.	Antibiotics
Trichomoniasis	Protozoan infection; In women, causes vaginal itching with thin, foamy, yellowish discharge.	Antiprotozoa medication
Viral Hepatitis B	Viral infection of the liver; Causes nausea, vomiting, yellowing of skin and eyes, liver failure.	Adequate intake of calories; no intake of alcohol

Figure 24-2 Which STDs have symptoms that include painful urination for both males and females?

mucous membrane where the pathogen entered the body. The chancre is firm and rounded, and has a ragged edge. Chancres usually range from one-quarter to one-half inch in diameter. During the time that a chancre is present, the disease is highly contagious. After three to six weeks, the chancre heals on its own. However, the disease has not disappeared.

SECONDARY STAGE The **secondary stage** of syphilis begins from one to several months after the chancre disappears and can last for two to ten weeks. The secondary stage is characterized by flulike symptoms and a red rash that can occur on any part of the body but does not itch. The infected person may also have raised white patches on the mucous membranes of the mouth or throat, large moist sores around the mouth or genital area, and pain in the joints. Syphilis is highly contagious during the secondary stage.

LATENT STAGE   If syphilis is not treated during the secondary stage, all symptoms of the disease will disappear on their own. However, the disease has not disappeared. The next stage, during which no symptoms are present, is called the **latent stage**. The latent stage can last for many years, even for life. During this time, the bacteria remain present throughout the body. Although syphilis is not as contagious as it is during the primary and secondary stages, the disease can still be transmitted to others during the latent stage.

TERTIARY STAGE   The final and most serious stage of syphilis is the **tertiary stage** [*TUR shee er ee*]. During the tertiary stage, the bacteria can attack any organ of the body, including the heart and brain. Eventually, tertiary syphilis can lead to permanent damage to the heart and nervous system, including blindness, paralysis, mental disorders, and death.

As frightening as syphilis sounds, syphilis can be cured easily with penicillin, especially during the primary and secondary stages. Although syphilis also can be cured during the latent and tertiary stages, the damage to organs such as the heart and brain cannot be corrected.

GENITAL HERPES

Genital herpes [*HUR peez*], or herpes simplex, is a viral disease that causes painful blisters in the genital area. The virus is similar to the virus that causes the painful cold sore you may get around your mouth. Both types of herpes viruses can cause cold sores or genital herpes, depending on which part of the body first becomes infected. The CDC estimates that between 500,000 and 1 million new cases of genital herpes occur each year. One major reason this disease keeps spreading is that there is no cure. Therefore, sexually active people who have this diseasee can continue to transmit it to their sexual partners.

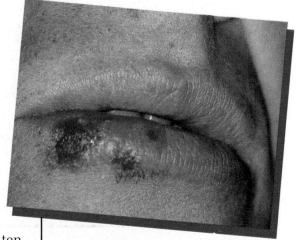

This is a cold sore. Cold sores should NOT be mistaken for genital herpes.

The first symptoms of genital herpes occur between two and ten days after infection. They include pain and itching in the infected area. If the infected area is the cervix or vagina, there may be no symptoms other than vaginal discharge. Soon afterward, many small fluid-filled blisters develop where the virus entered the body. The blisters eventually break, forming painful sores. The sores usually heal after two or three weeks, but can recur at any time. Some people have two or three outbreaks per year. Genital herpes is most contagious while sores are present. However, it is often possible for both men and women to be unaware that they have sores. For example, women can have sores on the cervix or vagina that they cannot see or feel. Even the presence of small sores means that the infection can be passed to another person.

In adults, genital herpes is not life-threatening. However, newborns also can become infected as they pass through the birth canal of mothers who have open sores. Often a herpes infection can lead to blindness, brain damage, and death in newborn babies.

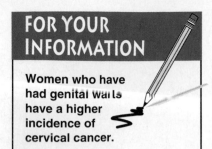
Currently there is no cure for herpes. However, medicines have been developed that reduce the pain and speed up the healing of the blisters. These medicines also reduce the number of times the blisters reappear.

GENITAL WARTS

Genital warts are soft, cauliflower-like growths that occur on the genital areas. The warts are caused by a virus that is transmitted during sexual contact. Genital warts do not cause much physical discomfort but are a risk factor for cervical cancer and probably cancer of the penis.

Because many people do not seek treatment, the estimates of the number of people in the United States who become infected with genital warts each year vary widely—ranging up to almost four million cases. Genital warts need to be examined by a physician. What appears to be a wart might be a lesion of secondary syphilis or a type of skin cancer. The doctor may take a scraping from the warts to make sure they are not caused by another disease. Treatment may consist of surgical removal of the warts or application of a medication that makes them heal.

RISK OF REINFECTION

Although many STDs can be cured, you can easily become reinfected. If you are taking medicines such as antibiotics to treat an infection, it is important that you take all of the medicine. As you learned in Chapter 23, "Infectious Diseases," infections can return if all the medication is not taken. Even after you have been cured of an STD, you can become reinfected. For example, many people who recover become reinfected because their partners did not seek treatment. The best way to avoid becoming reinfected is to avoid behaviors that led to your initial infection.

LESSON 24.2 USING WHAT YOU HAVE LEARNED

REVIEW

1. During which stages of a syphilis infection are you most likely to be contagious?
2. Describe the symptoms of genital herpes.

THINK CRITICALLY

3. Chlamydia is easy to cure, yet it is the most common STD in the United States. What action is needed to lower the incidences of chlamydia?
4. Why is it important for someone who may have been exposed to an STD to seek treatment, even if there are no symptoms?

APPLY IT TO YOURSELF

5. Imagine that a new type of STD has just been identified. As a public health official, what information would you want to find out about this new disease?

HIV INFECTION AND AIDS

Of the many STDs infecting Americans today, none has drawn as much attention and generated as much controversy as AIDS. AIDS, which stands for **acquired immune deficiency syndrome**, is a fatal disease of the immune system. It is caused by a virus called the **human immunodeficiency virus** or HIV. Currently there is no cure for AIDS, although scientists are learning more every day about the disease that is killing so many people. Since 1981, over 249,000 people in the United States have been diagnosed with AIDS. Of that total, over 171,000 people had died by 1993. However, these numbers are only the tip of the iceberg. The CDC estimates that over 1.5 million people in the United States have been infected with HIV and have the potential for developing AIDS.

The AIDS epidemic has had a unique impact on our society that goes beyond the tragedies realized by the people living with HIV infection and AIDS and the friends and families of the people living with AIDS. Widespread fear and misunderstanding about the disease and how it is spread has led to discrimination and even violence against those living with AIDS and groups perceived to be carriers of HIV. By learning about the causes of AIDS and how it is transmitted, you will learn not only how to protect yourself from this fatal disease, but you may also be able to help correct the misperceptions of others.

OUR UNDERSTANDING OF HIV INFECTION

AIDS is a relatively new disease. Prior to 1981, only 108 cases had been reported in the United States. However, as the number of cases began to rise, an intensive research effort was initiated to determine the cause of AIDS. It was not until 1984 that research teams from France and the United States identified HIV, the virus that causes AIDS. Although many questions still remain, much progress has been made in understanding the actions of HIV.

ACTIONS OF HIV   HIV is an extremely fragile virus that cannot survive outside the human body. Therefore, the only way that HIV can be passed from person to person is through the exchange of certain bodily fluids. These fluids are blood, vaginal fluid, semen, and breast milk. HIV cannot be transmitted through saliva or casual contact. Once inside the body, the virus attacks cells of the immune system. One type of cell that is attacked by HIV is the T cell. T cells are white blood cells that circulate through your body's lymphatic and circulatory systems and stimulate your immune system to fight pathogens that

MAIN IDEAS

CONCEPTS
✔ AIDS is a new disease that has reached epidemic proportions in the United States and the world.

✔ The virus that causes AIDS is transmitted mostly through sexual contact and the sharing of needles used for injecting drugs.

✔ Although there is currently no cure for AIDS, there are drugs available that can slow the progress of the infection.

VOCABULARY
acquired immune deficiency syndrome
human immunodeficiency virus
opportunistic diseases
AIDS dementia complex
ELISA
HIV positive
false positive

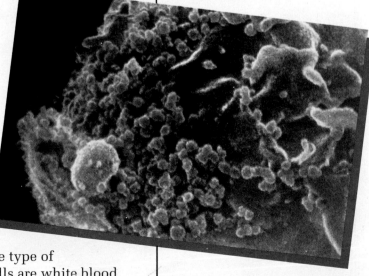

HIV (orange dots) are shown in the photo attacking and destroying a T cell.

CHAPTER 24 SEXUALLY TRANSMITTED DISEASES/AIDS   **575**

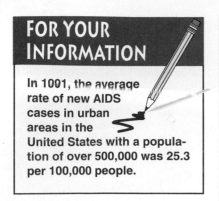
enter your body. Refer to Chapter 23, "Infectious Diseases," for a detailed explanation of the immune system. However, it is not the AIDS virus that causes the death of a person with AIDS. Once enough T cells have been destroyed by HIV, your body no longer is able to resist other pathogens that enter your body. It is the diseases caused by other pathogens that lead to the AIDS patient's death.

OPPORTUNISTIC DISEASES   After your body's immune system has been crippled by HIV, pathogens that would normally be resisted by a healthy immune system infect your body. Since the immune system helps destroy cancer cells that may develop in your body, people with AIDS are more prone to developing certain types of cancer. Diseases that occur as the result of a weakened immune system are called **opportunistic diseases**. It is the opportunistic diseases, not HIV infection, that are fatal to people with AIDS.

PROGRESSION OF HIV INFECTION

Once someone has become infected with HIV, it can take many years for the person to develop the diseases associated with AIDS. For most people infected with HIV, the infection goes through several phases, ending in AIDS. Doctors monitor the progress of the infection by counting the number of T cells in the bloodstream. As the HIV infection progresses, the number of T cells in the bloodstream drops.

ASYMPTOMATIC PHASE   After becoming infected with HIV, the person may not develop symptoms for many years. The virus can lie

Figure 24-3   The map shows the distribution of AIDS cases in the United States. How many states reported at least 16 cases of AIDS per 100,000 people in 1991?

■ **AIDS ANNUAL RATES PER 100,000 POPULATION: 1992**

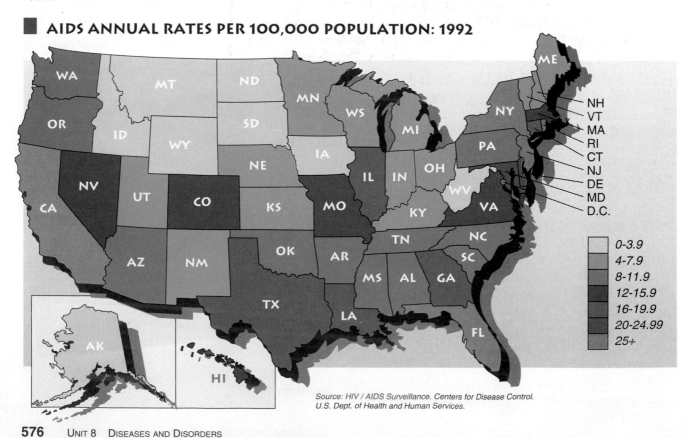

	0-3.9
	4-7.9
	8-11.9
	12-15.9
	16-19.9
	20-24.99
	25+

Source: HIV / AIDS Surveillance. Centers for Disease Control.
U.S. Dept. of Health and Human Services.

in the bloodstream for up to ten years before the first symptoms develop. During this period, the presence of HIV can only be determined through blood tests. These blood tests detect antibodies to HIV. However, antibodies may not be present until three or four months after infection. Antibodies are special proteins produced by your immune system that fight pathogens. Even when the person is asymptomatic, he or she is still capable of infecting others.

DECLINING IMMUNITY As the HIV infection progresses, the number of T cells in the body begins to drop. At the same time, the infected person may begin to develop various symptoms including a flulike illness, swollen lymph nodes, chronic fatigue, severe diarrhea, rapid unexplained weight loss, or a dry cough. Eventually the number of T cells drops to only one quarter the number of T cells that a healthy person has. This low T-cell count allows the first opportunistic diseases to appear.

AIDS The most severe form of HIV infection is AIDS. At this point, the T cell level is only one eighth that of healthy individuals. Many people living with AIDS have developed one or more opportunistic diseases.

Over thirty different opportunistic diseases have been associated with AIDS. One common opportunistic disease is a parasitic lung infection called pneumocystis carinii pneumonia (PCP). Although PCP can be treated with medicines, the immune system is unable to prevent the infection from returning. Another common opportunistic disease is a rare form of cancer of the skin and connective tissues called Kaposi's sarcoma. Kaposi's sarcoma is characterized by the presence of brownish lesions on the skin. Other opportunistic infections include tuberculosis and a severe form of herpes.

Once a person has AIDS, HIV may infect the central nervous system. The damage to the brain and other parts of the nervous system caused by HIV is called AIDS dementia complex. People with **AIDS dementia complex** may experience disorientation, loss of memory, depression, and partial paralysis.

WHO IS SUSCEPTIBLE TO HIV INFECTION?

Because AIDS first appeared primarily among homosexual males and drug abusers, many people mistakenly thought that only these groups were susceptible to the disease. This perception is far from accurate. Anybody who practices high-risk behaviors is susceptible to contracting HIV. Recent CDC reports indicate that the percentage of new AIDS cases among homosexual males has decreased, while the percentage of new cases among heterosexual men and women and teenagers has increased.

Although many people think otherwise, HIV can be transmitted only in very specific ways. The virus must enter the bloodstream. Infection can occur when specific bodily fluids are exchanged. For example, an infected mother can transmit the virus to her infant during breastfeeding. However, sexual intercourse and the exchange of blood through shared needles and syringes are the two most common modes of transmission.

You do not have to resort to extreme measures to avoid becoming infected with HIV.

HOW PEOPLE GET HIV - BY GENDER

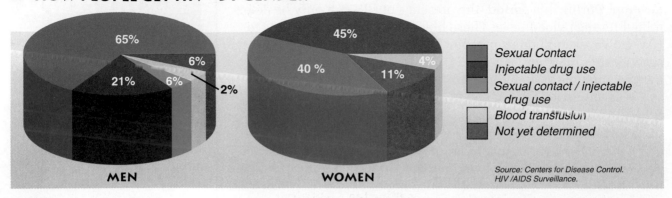

MEN
65%
21%
6%
6%
2%

WOMEN
45%
40 %
11%
4%

Sexual Contact
Injectable drug use
Sexual contact / injectable drug use
Blood transfusion
Not yet determined

Source: Centers for Disease Control.
HIV /AIDS Surveillance.

Figure 24-4 These data are for people diagnosed with AIDS between July 1991 and June 1992. What is the leading cause of HIV infection in women?

SEXUAL CONTACT The most common way in which HIV is transmitted is through sexual intercourse. The virus is carried in the semen in males and the vaginal secretions in females. In all sexual relationships, either of the people involved in the relationship can pass the virus to his or her partner during sexual intimacy.

The best way to reduce your risk of becoming infected is to abstain from sexual intercourse. People who are sexually active are at even greater risk if they are involved with people who have had multiple partners or with people who have used injectable drugs. By having sexual intercourse with one person, you still risk becoming infected with an STD that your partner may have gotten from previous partners. Although the use of a latex condom along with a spermicidal gel can reduce the risk of infection, it is no guarantee against infection. The safest practice is to abstain from any sexual relationships until marriage. However, even during marriage, if one partner is infected, the other is likely to get infected as well.

EXCHANGE OF BLOOD The second most common way to transmit HIV is through infected blood. Transmission may occur through the sharing of needles used for body piercing, including tatooing, or syringes used for injecting illegal drugs. When an infected per-

TEENAGERS AND AIDS

According to statistics from the CDC, HIV infection is spreading faster among teenagers and young adults than in any other age group. In the early 1990s, the number of AIDS cases rose by 77 percent among people between 13 and 24 years of age. Of the new cases reported in 1991 among teenagers and young adults, 57 percent were a result of sexual contact and 20 percent were a result of injectable drug use. The remaining 23 percent of the cases were a result of blood transfusions or of causes that have not yet been determined. Because the symptoms of AIDS usually take 5 to 10 years to develop, most of the people who first developed symptoms while they were in their twenties actually became infected as teenagers.

son uses a needle or syringe, blood containing HIV will often remain on or in the needle or syringe. If other people use the same needle or syringe, they can become infected. Currently, 25 percent of all new AIDS cases are a result of the sharing of needles by injectable drug users. As of 1993, the sharing of syringes was the leading cause of transmission among women in the United States.

Prior to 1985, before tests were developed that could detect the presence of HIV antibodies in blood, some people became infected through transfusions of infected blood. Blood transfusions are administered to replace blood lost during an accident or during surgery. Many of the infections occurred in people being treated for hemophilia. Hemophilia is a genetic blood disorder that requires periodic blood transfusions. Today the chance of getting the AIDS virus through a blood transfusion is extremely small. All blood donors are carefully screened to try to exclude those who have engaged in any high-risk behaviors. All blood and blood products are tested thoroughly before they are used. Acceptable blood products are then treated to kill any virus the test might not have detected. As another precaution, many people donate their own blood prior to planned surgery. It is stored and used if needed during their hospital stay.

MAKING A DIFFERENCE

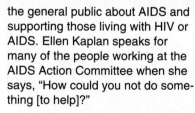

AIDS Action Committee

Ellen Kaplan never thought that AIDS would touch her life. Then, a few years ago, a close friend was diagnosed with the disease and died a short time later. Her experience made her want to know more about AIDS and to do what she could to help people who are living with AIDS. She found what she was looking for at the AIDS Action Committee, based in Boston, Massachusetts.

Founded in 1983, the AIDS Action Committee was formed to help educate and support the 13 people in the area who were then diagnosed with AIDS and assist their families and friends. By the early 1990s, the AIDS Action Committee, with over 75 paid employees and 2,200 volunteers, was helping to reach thousands of people, teaching them about AIDS and HIV—the virus that causes AIDS.

Ellen Kaplan volunteers on the toll-free helpline that receives close

to 50,000 calls a year. These calls come from people with all kinds of questions about AIDS—from how it is transmitted to concerns over health insurance. People from all walks of life are served by the helpline.

Most of the AIDS Action resources are used for prevention and education. Teenagers are among the largest group targeted for education. "Twenty percent of the people living with AIDS are [in their] 20s and 30s," says Pete Erbland, a staff member at the AIDS Action Committee. "That means that many of them, the majority of them, were infected as teenagers. Teenagers think they're immortal," says Erbland. "They're not....Education is the key. Kids have got to understand that [AIDS] can happen to them."

The AIDS Action Committee is one of a number of organizations in the country dedicated to educating

the general public about AIDS and supporting those living with HIV or AIDS. Ellen Kaplan speaks for many of the people working at the AIDS Action Committee when she says, "How could you not do something [to help]?"

1. In what ways could an organization like the AIDS Action Committee help someone living with AIDS or infected by HIV?

2. Why is it important to provide educational services to the general public about AIDS?

MYTHS ABOUT HIV INFECTION AND AIDS

Because AIDS is a fatal disease for which there is no cure, the spread of the disease has spawned a great deal of fear. Instead of driving people to learn more about AIDS and its prevention, this fear has caused some people to direct their anger and frustration against those people who have become infected. The following examples demonstrate how misconceptions about AIDS have led to the mistreatment of those infected with HIV.

- Because AIDS was first identified largely among homosexual groups in the United States, AIDS was initially labeled as a "gay disease." The association made between AIDS and the homosexual community has triggered thousands of incidents of anti-homosexual violence. However, AIDS has spread through all segments of the population.

- In one incident, three boys from the same family tested positive for HIV and were blocked from attending school even though there was little possibility that they could infect others. Eventually, violence occurred in an effort to pressure the family to leave town.

- Fear of infection has led to discrimination in the workplace as well. Countless people have been fired from their jobs after revealing that they had tested positive for HIV, although they were still capable of doing their jobs and there was little danger that they would infect others. Such a practice by employers is both illegal and unethical.

Figure 24-5 lists many of the misconceptions about the transmission of AIDS which have led to some of the extreme actions described above.

The Red Cross blood drive was being held in Ellis' neighborhood. Ellis was finally old enough to donate blood and he felt it was something he wanted to do. However, when Ellis mentioned it to his friends, they told him that people can get AIDS by giving blood. Ellis began to have second thoughts. He had heard that the virus that causes AIDS can be transmitted through infected blood. However, he also was quite sure that the Red Cross only used sterilized needles. Ellis decided that the best thing to do was to call the Red Cross and ask whether it was possible to get AIDS while giving blood. They assured him that only sterilized needles are used and that he would never come in contact with other people's blood. Therefore, it was impossible to become infected. Ellis was reassured by that information and signed up to give blood.

IDENTIFICATION AND TREATMENT OF HIV

If you have never engaged in any behaviors that can put you at risk for AIDS, there is no reason to worry about being infected. However, if you have engaged in high-risk behavior, a simple blood test is available that can determine whether you are infected. The test, named **ELISA** (enzyme-linked immunosorbent assay),

Everyone is susceptible to HIV and AIDS, but infection can be avoided.

MYTHS ABOUT HIV/AIDS

Myth	Fact
Only homosexuals and intravenous drug users get HIV.	Anybody who engages in certain high-risk behaviors can get HIV.
HIV can be spread by casual contact such as shaking hands, kissing, coughing, or sharing eating utensils.	HIV is known to be transmitted through the exchange of bodily fluids such as semen, blood, vaginal secretions, and breast milk .
People infected with HIV should be barred from school or work to protect other people	HIV cannot be spread through casual contact that would occur between school children or coworkers.
HIV can be transmitted through mosquito or bug bites.	There has never been a case of HIV being transmitted through an insect bite.
You can become infected with HIV by donating blood.	Only sterile needles are used to draw blood. These needles are immediately discarded after use.

Figure 24-5   Can HIV be transmitted through insect bites?

detects the presence of HIV antibodies, not the presence of HIV itself. If the ELISA test shows HIV antibodies, a second test called a Western Blot test also is given. If both tests detect the presence of the antibodies, the person is considered to be **HIV positive.**

WHO SHOULD BE TESTED?   The CDC recommends that anyone who has engaged in the following high-risk behaviors should take the ELISA test.

Anyone who has had sex with:

- more than one partner or with a person who has had more than one partner
- someone who has had any STD
- a homosexual or bisexual male
- someone who is an injectable drug user
- a prostitute (male or female)

or has:

- shared needles during injectable drug use
- had a blood transfusion between 1978 and 1985
- been treated for hemophilia between 1978 and 1985
- received medical treatment that required the transfer of tissue between 1978 and 1985

MARGIN OF ERROR   Although the ELISA test is very accurate, no test is perfect. There are two situations in which a person infected with HIV can test negative. Often people who are infected do not develop antibodies until several months after becoming infected. Therefore, people who are tested shortly after they have been infected often will test negative. Occasionally, the immune systems of people with advanced stages of HIV infection may be so overwhelmed that they are unable to produce antibodies. These people will also test negative.

It is also possible that people who are not infected with HIV will test positive due to a mistake in the test. When a person who is not infected tests positive, the result is called a **false positive**. Because there always exists the possibility of a false positive, anybody who tests positive is tested a second time. If the second test also is positive, a third, more expensive and more accurate test is given.

All testing is done confidentially. In order to prevent possible discrimination resulting from a positive test, each individual is identified only by the number of the testing center. The results are disclosed only to the person tested.

If a person tests positive for HIV, it does not mean that he or she has AIDS. However, it is almost certain that the person will develop AIDS at some point. An HIV-infected person can still participate in everyday activities including attending school or work. Local or state health centers can provide confidential counseling for those who have tested positive.

People who are HIV positive can interact with other people with little fear of passing on the virus. It is especially important, however, for these people to abstain from high-risk activities that could spread the virus.

TREATMENT AND MEDICATION

Although there is currently no cure for AIDS, there are some treatments and medications that slow the progress of the disease. So far, the most effective medicine has been azidothymidine (AZT), also known as zidovudine. Other medicines have also been developed that can further slow the progress of the HIV infection when taken in combination with AZT. Treatments are also used that prevent or slow the progress of opportunistic diseases.

Over 25 drugs are being tested for the treatment of HIV infection and AIDS. A number of vaccines are also being tested. Remember, vaccines prevent infections from occurring. However, it may be years before an effective treatment to cure AIDS is found.

LESSON 24.3 USING WHAT YOU HAVE LEARNED

REVIEW

1. What is the difference between HIV infection and AIDS?
2. What are two ways HIV is transmitted?

THINKING CRITICALLY

3. You have just found out that the cook at your favorite restaurant is HIV positive. Why should you not be concerned about this information?
4. You often see stories in the newspaper and on television about the AIDS epidemic. Why do you think the AIDS epidemic has drawn much more media attention than other infectious diseases?

APPLY IT TO YOURSELF

5. A student in your school has just been diagnosed as being HIV positive. As a teacher, what could you do to prepare to answer any questions of other students?

SUMMARY

As of the early 1990s, AIDS is an incurable disease of the immune system that has reached epidemic proportions. It is caused by a virus called HIV which attacks the T cells of the immune system, allowing opportunistic diseases to occur. Because HIV is extremely fragile, it can only be transmitted through direct contact with semen, vaginal secretions, blood, and breast milk. Your only protection against AIDS is to practice behaviors that eliminate your risk of infection.

PREVENTION AND TREATMENT OF STDs AND AIDS

In the fight against the STD and AIDS epidemics, it is important to remember that there really is no such thing as a high-risk group. STDs and AIDS have affected people from all parts of the country, from every ethnic group, and from every socioeconomic status. Instead, there are only high-risk behaviors. Only certain behaviors can lead to the transmission of the pathogens that cause STDs and AIDS. Therefore it is critical that you understand which behaviors place you at risk.

MAKING THE RIGHT DECISION

Throughout your life, you will find yourself in situations in which you must make a decision that affects your health. Some of the most important decisions you can make involve behaviors that can put you at risk for contracting an STD.

From reading this chapter, you have already learned that most STDs are potentially serious. Many can cause permanent disabilities or even death. Some STDs—such as genital herpes, genital warts, and AIDS—cannot be cured at this time. You have learned that people who have had multiple partners over their lifetime or who have used injectable drugs are at greatest risk. You also have learned that many people who are infected do not have any symptoms of the disease. Finally, you have learned that the vast majority of the pathogens that cause STDs cannot survive outside the body and that they cannot be transmitted through casual contact such as holding hands or sharing eating utensils. Armed with these facts, you not only will be able to make the proper decision about behaviors that put you at risk, you also may be able to help a friend someday who may not be aware of the facts about STDs and AIDS.

ELIMINATING RISK THROUGH ABSTINENCE

The most common way that STDs are transmitted is through sexual contact such as sexual intercourse. Therefore, the most effective way to prevent infection is to abstain from sexual contact of any kind. The conscious decision not to participate in intimate sexual activity is called **abstinence**.

Responsible decision making is essential for reducing the risk of becoming infected with an STD.

MAIN IDEAS

CONCEPTS

✔ Individual responsibility is the key to preventing the spread of STDs.

✔ The most effective way to avoid STDs is to abstain from intimate sexual contact.

✔ You can play a role in influencing others to engage in responsible behavior.

VOCABULARY

abstinence   monogamy

STD Support Groups—Finding Help

Sexually transmitted diseases can strike anyone who does not practice responsible sexual behavior, regardless of gender, sexual preference, race, or age. The experience of a sexually transmitted disease, particularly a life-threatening one such as AIDS, is frightening and can alter the course of a lifetime.

It is very important to get the facts about sexually transmitted diseases. For those who have contracted an STD, help is available. Most communities offer a telephone helpline and ongoing support groups to answer questions and offer guidance about the best treatments for the disease. For information on the STD helpline in your area, you can call the national STD hotline at 1-800-227-8922.

People living with HIV infection often require more support than a helpline. For this reason, support groups, volunteer agencies, and nationally funded organizations have grown to extend support to HIV-positive people and to AIDS patients. AIDS patients often have particular needs that arise out of high medical bills, housing problems, job loss, and, sometimes, fear on the part of family and friends. Most communities have extensive AIDS support groups. To locate the resources in your community, you can begin by calling the national AIDS hotline at 1-800-342-2437, 1-800-344-7432 (Spanish access), or 1-800-243-7889 (deaf access).

The fact that many people with STDs are unaware that they are infected makes abstinence critical. For example, people with chlamydia, gonorrhea, and HIV infection often show no symptoms. Therefore, a person's appearance or answers to direct questions are not clear indications of his or her status in regard to STDs or HIV. A person's sexual history can stay with him or her long after a relationship has ended.

REDUCING RISK

Couples can significantly reduce their risk of infection by practicing responsible behavior. The most responsible decision a couple can make is to commit to each other and delay sexual relations until marriage. The commitment to an intimate relationship with only one person is called **monogamy**. However, monogamy is an effective means of prevention only if neither person already has an STD. People who have engaged in high-risk behaviors prior to entering into a longterm monogamous relationship should receive a physical check-up that includes the test for HIV. If any STDs are detected, they can seek treatment or take necessary precautions to avoid infecting their partner. If one of the partners within the relationship fails to remain sexually monogamous, that person increases his or her chances of becoming infected. Failure to remain monogamous also puts the health of his or her partner at risk. Once one of the partners is infected, the chances of infecting the other partner increase greatly.

If there is any question or uncertainty about the health status of the individuals in a relationship—even within a monogamous relationship—the use of a latex condom during intercourse can help reduce the risk of infection. A condom is a sheath that fits over the penis and prevents the exchange of bodily fluids during sexual intercourse if used correctly. Latex condoms, along with a sperm-killing agent, may prevent viruses such as HIV or the herpes virus from passing from one person to another. However, it is

STRATEGIES FOR LIVING

How to Avoid STD Infection by Saying No

- Avoid situations that may create a risk for HIV contraction.

- Imagine situations in which you had to make a decision. Go over in your mind how you would respond.

- Do not feel pressured to give a reason for saying no.

- Explain to the other person that the situation is making you feel uncomfortable. However, do not criticize the other person.

- Remember that if you have said yes once before, you do not have to say yes again.

- If all else fails, just walk away.

important to remember that a condom only can reduce the risk of infection. The best way to reduce the risk of becoming infected with a sexually transmitted disease is through abstinence.

SUBSTANCE ABUSE AND STDs

A second high-risk behavior that can lead to the transmission of STDs is substance abuse. As you learned in Lesson 3, sharing syringes used to inject illegal drugs is the second leading cause of HIV transmission. Sharing needles can also lead to transmission of the virus that causes hepatitis B, and in rare cases, the bacteria that causes syphilis. However, substance abuse can also indirectly increase your risk of infection. Alcohol and illegal drugs such as marijuana, cocaine, crack, and heroin can severely impair your ability to make responsible decisions under pressure. People who are under the influence of alcohol or drugs are more likely to choose behaviors that put them at risk.

SEEKING TREATMENT

All STDs are potentially dangerous if not treated. It is therefore critical for people to seek treatment if they suspect they might be infected. Not treating STDs can lead to permanent disabilities and even death.

KNOWING THE SYMPTOMS   Any person who has practiced a high-risk behavior such as having sexual contact with multiple partners—more than one sexual partner over time—or sharing syringes should be alert for the symptoms of STDs. Symptoms that may indicate the presence of an STD include any unexplained changes in overall health, painful urination, unusual genital discharges, itching around the genitals, abdominal pain, or skin rashes. However, if you know that there is the possibility that you have been exposed, you may not want to wait for symptoms to appear before visiting a doctor. As you have learned, many people with STDs can have no symptoms.

Helplines are available that can answer questions you may have about STDs.

STD AND AIDS HELPLINES

Most cities and local communities have STD and AIDS helpline telephone numbers listed in the telephone book for people who have questions about STDs or specifically about AIDS. Anyone can call these numbers for information about the diseases or for information about tests or treatment. All calls are kept confidential.

You can participate in many activities that help increase public awareness about AIDS and other STDs.

VISITING A DOCTOR   If people have any of the symptoms listed above, or for any reason suspect that they might be infected, they should cease any behavior that could spread the disease to others and should visit a doctor immediately. Even though the symptoms may not be due to an STD, only a doctor is capable of making a proper diagnosis and prescribing the right treatment.

Many people who seek treatment go to a private physician. However, hospitals and special STD clinics can also provide effective treatment. Usually the people who work in the clinics are trained to make the patient feel as comfortable as possible. All states have laws which require that visits and test results remain confidential.

HELPING OTHERS

In order to stop the spread of STDs, every individual must take responsibility for his or her actions. However, there is a lot that you can do to help others avoid becoming infected. For example, by staying informed about STDs, you can not only protect yourself, you can serve as a resource for your friends. By sharing your knowledge, you can help clear up any misconceptions they may have about all STDs and their prevention. Peer pressure can be a powerful force in shaping people's behaviors. You can set an excellent example for your friends by not practicing high-risk behaviors. Many studies have demonstrated that people are most likely to stop practicing high-risk behaviors if they see that their friends are also stopping. Finally, you can volunteer to help organizations that educate the public or assist people who are sick.

SUMMARY

Because all STDs are preventable, responsible decision making is the key to avoiding STDs. All STDs are transmitted through sexual contact, so practicing abstinence or monogamy is the most effective means of avoiding these diseases. Substance abuse can put a person at risk by impairing a person's judgment as well as through the sharing of syringes. Individuals who think that they might have exposed themselves to an STD should seek treatment as soon as possible and avoid sexual contact until cured.

LESSON 24.4   **USING WHAT YOU HAVE LEARNED**

REVIEW

1. Why is abstinence the most effective way to avoid becoming infected with an STD or AIDS?
2. Describe two ways by which substance abuse can increase your risk of contracting an STD.

THINKING CRITICALLY

3. Explain how peer pressure can play a positive role in influencing your behavior and the behavior of others.
4. An important part of any type of relationship is communication. Why is communication between people in a relationship critical in preventing the spread of STDs and AIDS?

APPLY IT TO YOURSELF

5. As a parent of two teenagers, what steps would you take with your children to help protect them against contracting an STD or HIV?

An Open Mind

BEING **WELL, STAYING WELL**

Tobin headed for the auditorium. Today was the informational meeting about the school play. This year the school was doing a musical, and Tobin was hoping for one of the main roles. He enjoyed singing and performing, and the spring play was a big tradition.

When Tobin arrived, there already were quite a few kids in the auditorium. Tobin sat next to some of his friends. "What is she doing here?" exclaimed his friend Reece.

Tobin looked to see whom Reece was talking about. It was Tori. Tori was a very good singer. She also was HIV positive. There was a good chance that she could play one of the lead female roles.

After the meeting, Reece turned to Tobin and said, "So what are you going to do?" "About what?" asked Tobin.

"About Tori, silly! If you both end up getting the lead roles, you're going to have to kiss! The script calls for it. I'm not going to try out."

Tobin hadn't really thought about it. "I don't think you can transmit HIV through casual contact or even kissing," said Tobin. "I mean, certainly Ms. Crocker wouldn't allow Tori to try out if it wasn't safe."

The next day, Tobin learned that several students were going to boycott the play. "As long as Tori's allowed to be in this play, we're not taking part," said Reece. "Are you going to join us or not?"

Tobin was surprised by this turn of events. All year he had looked forward to the spring play, and now this. There shouldn't be any problem with Tori being in the play. She was in one of his classes and it didn't seem to matter there. Why would it matter now? Was she putting others in jeopardy?

PAUSE AND CONSIDER

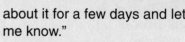

1. **Identify the Problem.** What is Tobin's conflict?

2. **Consider the Options.** What are Tobin's options?

3. **Evaluate the Outcomes.** What could happen if Tobin boycotts the play? What could happen if he refuses to join his friends?

Tobin went to speak with Ms. Crocker separately. "So are you going to join the others, Tobin?" asked Ms. Crocker.

"I don't know. I guess I really don't know much about HIV and AIDS. I'm confused. There's a lot of dancing in this play, and there is some kissing." said Tobin.

"Tobin," said Ms. Crocker, "the AIDS virus is passed through the exchange of bodily fluids such as blood or semen, not saliva or sweat. You think

about it for a few days and let me know."

Tobin did think about the situation, and he called a local AIDS information group. They confirmed what Ms. Crocker had said. After a couple of days, Tobin told Ms. Crocker and Reece that he was still going to try out for the play. He saw no risk. He also saw no reason why Tori shouldn't be allowed to try out. She had the same rights as anyone else.

DECIDE AND REVIEW

4. **Decide and Act.** What did Tobin decide to do?

5. **Review.** What did Tobin base his decision on? How did the correct information help Tobin reach his final decision?

PROJECTS

1. Investigate the progress in the development of an AIDS vaccine. A good source is Randy Shilts' book *And the Band Played On*. Look into why it took so long to allocate funds for AIDS research. Analyze the reasons that progress toward effective treatment might have been slow during the early years after the disease was identified. Assess the consequences of waiting for further research before dedicating large sums of money to battle an epidemic such as AIDS.

2. Develop a sensitive public service announcement that urges people to engage in responsible behavior to reduce the number of cases of STDs. What issues would you focus on? What issues would you steer away from? Why is it important to be sensitive when dealing with the subject of STDs?

WORKING WITH OTHERS

With a partner, look through several magazines to see how advertisers use images of sex and sexual behavior to sell products. How do you think that advertising might encourage risky behavior? What steps might advertisers take to encourage more responsible behavior?

CONNECTING TO...

HISTORY   The history of disease can tell a lot about the condition of a society. Trace an infectious disease, such as syphilis, through history. What was going on in society during the time that syphilis was most prevalent? How was the outbreak of syphilis treated during the mid-1800s? What might the current increase in the incidence of sexually transmitted diseases tell you about American society today? What steps do you think should be taken to slow the spread of STDs?

USING VOCABULARY

abstinence	infertility
acquired immune deficiency syndrome	latent stage
	lesion
AIDS dementia complex	monogamy
asymptomatic	opportunistic diseases
chancre	pelvic inflammatory disease
chlamydia	primary stage
epidemic	secondary stage
ELISA	sexually transmitted disease
false positive	syphilis
genital herpes	tertiary stage
genital warts	urethritis
gonorrhea	vaginitis
HIV positive	
human immunodeficiency virus	

Answer true or false to the following statements that use the vocabulary words above.

1. A false positive results any time a person tests positive for HIV.
2. Primary, secondary, and tertiary stages are aspects of the STD known as syphilis.
3. Monogamy means having more than one sexual partner.
4. Abstinence is the best way to prevent sexually transmitted diseases.
5. Infertility may result from STDs.
6. STDs are often characterized by lesions and chancres on the male or female genitals.
7. Genital herpes is currently incurable.
8. Sexually transmitted diseases can be contracted through casual contact.
9. Acquired immune deficiency syndrome can be contracted by anyone, regardless of age, gender, or sexual orientation.
10. Opportunistic diseases are the actual cause of death among people with AIDS.
11. Symptoms of HIV infection always appear soon after infection occurs.

CONCEPT MAPPING

Copy and complete the concept map shown below. Information on concept mapping appears at the front of this book.

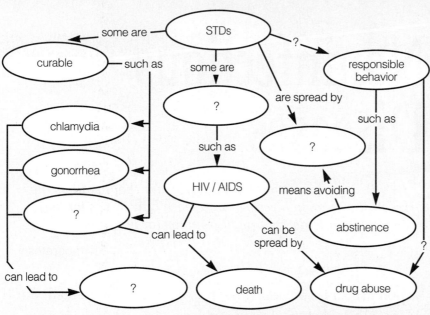

THINKING CRITICALLY

INTERPRET

LESSON 24.1

1. What pathogens cause sexually transmitted diseases?

2. Can you get an STD through casual contact? Explain.

3. How does irresponsible behavior promote transmission of STDs?

4. Give some reasons STDs may go unnoticed or unchecked.

LESSON 24.2

5. What symptoms might cause a person to suspect that she or he has an STD?

6. How can an STD affect a woman's ability to have children? A man's ability?

7. How can chlamydia and gonorrhea be treated?

8. During which two stages is syphilis most highly contagious?

LESSON 24.3

9. What is the virus that causes AIDS?

10. How do opportunistic diseases affect an AIDS-infected person?

LESSON 24.4

11. Why have misconceptions developed about people with AIDS?

APPLY

LESSON 24.1

12. Name two high-risk behaviors for contracting an STD. Why are they high-risk? Why are there so many cases of STDs?

LESSON 24.2

13. Why is it important to see a doctor if you think you have been exposed to an STD, even if you are asymptomatic?

LESSON 24.3

14. Why are the early stages of HIV infection dangerous?

LESSON 24.4

15. How can you avoid STDs?

Noninfectious Diseases

"A wise man [or woman] should consider that health is the greatest of human blessings, and learn how by his [or her] own thought to derive benefit from his [or her] illnesses."

Hippocrates

Good health is something people often take for granted. But if you ask people who have survived a life-threatening disease how they feel about good health, they will say—as Hippocrates suggested—that good health is "the greatest of blessings."

You cannot control whether you are exposed to the pathogens that cause colds, flu, hepatitis, measles, and many other infectious diseases. Similarly, you cannot control your heredity. If some of your relatives have a noninfectious disease such as diabetes or hypertension, you have a greater risk of developing that disease, too. You also cannot completely avoid agents that may cause cancer or all factors that contribute to the development of diseases associated with the aging process. However, despite all the conditions that you cannot control, there are many more conditions that you *can* control.

Poor health habits contribute to or even cause many noninfectious diseases. By avoiding risky behaviors such as using tobacco, drinking alcohol, overeating, and not getting enough exercise, you can greatly reduce your chances of developing a chronic or life-threatening noninfectious disease.

BACKGROUND

Hippocrates lived in ancient Greece from about 460 to 375 B.C. He is considered to have been the first physician. His writings and practices are as pertinent today as they were 2,500 years ago. Hippocrates established an oath of ethical medical behavior, known as the Hippocratic oath, that is still sworn to by new physicians entering medical practice.

SELF-ASSESSMENT

Assess your strengths and weaknesses in avoiding non-infectious diseases. Use the following checklist to take a closer look at yourself. Number a page from 1 to 10 in your Wellness Journal, and respond *yes* or *no* to each of the following statements. Answer *yes* for each statement that describes you all or most of the time.

1. I eat foods that are low in cholesterol, low in saturated fats, and high in fiber.

2. I wear protective clothing and use a sunscreen whenever I am going to be out in the sun.

3. I do not smoke or use smokeless tobacco.

4. I maintain a healthy weight.

5. I know the seven warning signs of cancer.

6. I have had my cholesterol level checked and know whether it is too high.

7. I do a self-examination for cancer every month.

8. I have regular medical checkups that include having my blood pressure measured.

9. I exercise regularly.

10. I am careful to avoid carcinogens as much as I can.

Review your responses, and try to decide which statements might represent your strengths and which would represent your weaknesses. Save your personal checklist for a follow-up activity that appears at the end of this chapter.

MAIN IDEAS

CONCEPTS

✔ Cardiovascular diseases are the leading cause of death in the United States.

✔ The risk of heart disease and stroke can be reduced by controlling blood pressure and cholesterol levels, refraining from smoking, and exercising.

✔ Healthier life-styles and advances in diagnosis and treatment have decreased the rate of death from cardiovascular diseases.

VOCABULARY

cardiovascular diseases
blood pressure
hypertension
atherosclerosis
cholesterol
heart attack
cardiac arrest
congestive heart failure
arrhythmia
stroke
electrocardiogram
angiogram
angioplasty
coronary bypass surgery
heart transplant

CARDIOVASCULAR DISEASES

A properly functioning heart is essential to a healthy life. As you may recall from Chapter 14, "Circulation and Respiration," the heart pumps blood. The blood transports oxygen and nutrients to all parts of the body and removes wastes. If the heart fails to function, the results are often fatal. Diseases of the blood vessels and heart are called **cardiovascular diseases (CVDs)** [*kahrd ee oh VAS kyuh lur*]. Today, CVDs are the number one killer in the United States.

WHO HAS CVDs?

Approximately 66 million Americans have one or more forms of cardiovascular disease. CVDs can strike any person at any age. However, CVDs occur most frequently among people 55 years of age or older. People whose parents and grandparents have had CVDs also may be at higher risk. Although age and heredity cannot be controlled, many other risk factors can be controlled. Understanding the risk factors and learning to control them can significantly reduce your chances of getting a CVD.

CVDs AND GENDER

Being male is considered a risk factor for developing CVDs. However, in the past few years, the number of women diagnosed with CVDs has increased dramatically. Many doctors do not believe that this increase reflects a deterioration in the health of women. Instead, they suggest that the symptoms of CVDs in women have been ignored. Today, doctors watch for signs of CVDs in women as well as men.

CONTROLLABLE RISK FACTORS

Think about the requirements for a healthy heart. First, your heart needs to be strong so that it can beat efficiently. Therefore, it is important to give your heart a workout by exercising regularly. Secondly, your heart works more efficiently when the blood vessels are clear of any type of blockage. Finally, your heart needs a steady supply of nutrients and oxygen so that it can continue to function.

In some cases, fatty material builds up on the inside of blood vessels. The vessels harden and narrow, and the fatty material completely blocks the flow of blood. The buildup of fatty material inside the blood vessels is called **atherosclerosis** [*ath uh roh skluh ROH sus*]. Atherosclerosis can eventually block the arteries that supply the heart with oxygen and nutrients. When the blood vessels become narrow, the heart has to work harder to pump blood through your body. Over many years, this added strain can cause your heart to weaken.

The American Heart Association (AHA) has identified four controllable risk factors that can significantly increase your chances of developing a CVD. These risk factors are high blood pressure, high cholesterol levels, smoking, and failure to get enough exercise.

BLOOD PRESSURE   Consider what happens when you run water through a hose. As water rushes through, pressure builds up inside the hose and it becomes stiffer. When you turn off the water, the pressure in the hose decreases. A similar action occurs every time your heart beats. As blood rushes through your blood vessels, pressure builds up inside them. Between beats, the pressure decreases. The force of the blood against the walls of the blood vessels is called **blood pressure**. Blood pressure that remains consistently too high is called **hypertension**. Over time, hypertension can damage the lining of the blood vessels.

The American Heart Association estimates that 65 million Americans have hypertension. However, because there are no noticeable signs of hypertension, many people are unaware that they have the condition. For that reason, hypertension is often known as the "silent killer." Therefore, it is important to have your blood pressure checked regularly by a doctor or other qualified health professional.

In 90 percent of the cases, the causes of hypertension are unknown. However, the following risk factors have been linked to its development.

Heredity   People who have a family history of hypertension have a greater tendency to develop the disease.

Obesity   For people who are overweight, one of the most effective ways to lower blood pressure is to lose the excess weight.

Alcohol Consumption   People who have three or more drinks a day are three times as likely to develop hypertension than those who do not drink.

Dietary Salt   For many people, excess dietary salt can cause the body to retain water, which increases blood pressure.

Lack of Exercise   Routine aerobic exercise has been shown to directly lower blood pressure.

Tobacco Use   Cigarette smoking can cause an increase in blood pressure.

For those people who are unable to control their blood pressure through life-style changes, several types of prescription medicines are available to lower blood pressure.

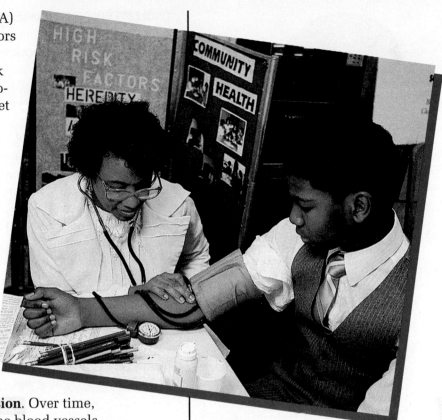

Having your blood pressure measured is simple and painless.

FOR YOUR INFORMATION

High blood pressure is 31 percent more prevalent among African-Americans than it is among Americans of European descent.

Being physically inactive increases your risk of developing CVDs.

CHOLESTEROL   **Cholesterol** is a waxy, fatlike substance that is essential to the functioning of your body. It is a very important component of cell membranes. It also is used in the formation of vitamin D and certain hormones. However, if there is too much cholesterol in your bloodstream, the cholesterol can accumulate along the inside of your arteries. The accumulation is part of the process of atherosclerosis.

According to the AHA, one out of every four adults in the United States has a cholesterol level that is considered high. People with high cholesterol levels are estimated to have twice the risk of developing atherosclerosis and heart disease as those with normal cholesterol levels. Evidence also suggests that some cases of atherosclerosis begin to develop during childhood and adolescence. Therefore, it is recommended that all teenagers get their cholesterol levels checked and take action if necessary to lower their cholesterol levels.

Your liver produces most of the cholesterol in your body from the saturated fat that you eat in your diet. However, a portion of your cholesterol comes directly from the food that you eat. Eating foods that are low in cholesterol and low in saturated fats while increasing the amount of exercise you get is the most effective way to lower your cholesterol level.

HDL AND LDL CHOLESTEROL

The National Institutes of Health recommend that all people have their cholesterol level checked at least once every five years. However, your overall cholesterol reading may not tell the whole story. Cholesterol is carried in your bloodstream on molecules called lipoproteins. There are two types of lipoproteins—low density lipoproteins (LDLs) and high density lipoproteins (HDLs). Cholesterol carried by LDLs tends to be deposited in the arteries. Therefore, a high LDL cholesterol level increases the risk of atherosclerosis. HDLs remove cholesterol from your bloodstream and transport it back to the liver, where it is stored. This removal and storage decreases the risk of atherosclerosis. Therefore, a measurement of both HDL and LDL cholesterol levels is the most accurate indicator of the risk for atherosclerosis.

STRATEGIES FOR LIVING

Follow these guidelines to lower your LDL cholesterol and raise your HDL cholesterol.

- Reduce your weight if you are overweight.
- Eat fewer foods that are high in saturated fats, including fatty meats and dairy products such as whole milk, butter, and ice cream.
- Eat fewer high-cholesterol foods, such as egg yolks, liver, and shrimp.
- Choose foods that are high in starch and fiber.
- Refrain from smoking.
- Stay physically active. Exercise raises HDL cholesterol levels.

SMOKING   Smoking can lead to the development of CVDs in several ways. Nicotine in tobacco can raise your blood pressure and speed the development of atherosclerosis. Cigarette smoke also contains carbon monoxide. This poisonous gas takes the place of oxygen in your red blood cells. As a result, your blood transports less oxygen to your body, including your heart. The good news is that within two years of quitting smoking, an ex-smoker reduces his or her risk of developing a CVD to that of a nonsmoker.

EXERCISE   Exercise can decrease your risk of developing CVDs in several ways. Exercise helps you control your weight and strengthens heart muscle so your heart works more efficiently. Exercise has also been found to lower blood pressure and to raise levels of HDL cholesterol. Vigorous exercise such as running or swimming is the most beneficial for your heart. However, even moderate forms of physical activity such as walking, doing yard work, or climbing stairs instead of using an elevator can significantly improve your cardiovascular health.

HEART DISEASE

The onset of heart disease symptoms can be sudden, often occurring when the person least expects it. However, conditions that lead to heart disease do not develop suddenly. The development of atherosclerosis can begin during childhood. By learning to control risk factors, teenagers can reduce their risk of CVDs later in life.

HEART ATTACK   In order to function, your heart needs a steady supply of oxygen and nutrients. If the blood supply that nourishes part of the heart is cut off, that portion of the heart tissue will be injured. The injury of heart tissue due to the cutoff of its blood supply is called a **heart attack**. Heart attacks are most frequently caused by a blockage in the arteries supplying the heart. Usually, the blockage is partly or entirely due to atherosclerosis. If the blockage occurs in a major artery, a large section of the heart can be damaged, causing the heart to beat erratically and then stop beating. The condition in which the heart stops beating is called **cardiac arrest**. If the blockage is in a small artery, less of the heart will be damaged, and there is a better chance that the patient will recover.

CONGESTIVE HEART FAILURE   A heart attack or years of high blood pressure, atherosclerosis, or other cardio-vascular problems can weaken the heart muscle. As a result, the heart can no longer empty its chambers when it pumps. The condition in which the heart can no longer pump blood efficiently is called **congestive heart failure**. Although the heart continues to beat, fluid from the blood accumulates in the lungs. The fluid interferes with gas exchange and causes short-ness of breath.

With proper treatment, people with congestive heart failure can live for many years. Doctors usually prescribe plenty of rest, a light exercise program if possible, and a diet low in sodium. Prescription medications are also used to help the heart pump more efficiently.

ARRHYTHMIA   The heart functions by beating in a steady, rhythmic rate. The steady beat is regulated by electrical impulses produced by special tissue in the heart. A disruption of this pattern is called an **arrhythmia** [*ay RITH mee uh*]. An arrhythmia may be caused by damage from a heart attack or by a malfunction of the heart's electrical impulse system. It can also be triggered by drugs such as

Top: This artery is partially blocked from atherosclerosis. Bottom: A special X ray called an angiogram can reveal blockage in coronary arteries.

cocaine, crack, or alcohol. Not all arrhythmias are life-threatening. However, all arrhythmias need to be monitored by a doctor. Most arrhythmias can be controlled with medication, if necessary. Some slow heart rhythms require an electric pacemaker.

STROKE

Like the heart, the brain must have a continuous supply of oxygen and nutrients. If the blood supply to the brain is interrupted, part of the brain can become damaged. The interruption of the blood supply to any part of the brain is called a **stroke**. Over 500,000 Americans suffer from strokes each year, and almost 150,000 die.

A stroke can occur when an artery in the brain becomes blocked by a clot. The clot is usually from atherosclerosis in the artery or a clot that has broken off from a site of atherosclerosis elsewhere in the body. A second and more dangerous type of stroke occurs when a blood vessel bursts. The vessel may have been weakened by years of hypertension. The bleeding damages the surrounding brain tissue.

The seriousness of a stroke depends on which area of the brain is damaged. For example, if the blood vessels leading to the speech center in the brain are blocked, the person's ability to speak or to understand speech may be affected. If the blockage is in an area of the brain that controls muscles, paralysis of a part of the body may result. If only a small area of the brain is damaged, a patient may be able to enjoy a full recovery.

TREATING CARDIOVASCULAR DISEASE

Since 1972, deaths due to coronary heart disease have decreased by over 45 percent, and deaths due to stroke have decreased by over 55 percent. Much of the decrease in mortality is due to an

Figure 25-1   Compare the stroke rates for men and women in each category. What do you notice about smokers with high blood pressure?

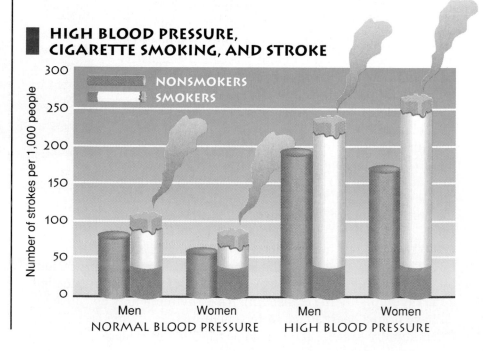

HIGH BLOOD PRESSURE, CIGARETTE SMOKING, AND STROKE

NONSMOKERS
SMOKERS

Number of strokes per 1,000 people

300
250
200
150
100
50
0

Men   Women
NORMAL BLOOD PRESSURE

Men   Women
HIGH BLOOD PRESSURE

The eating habits you acquire while you're young can affect your chances of developing CVDs. Do you eat sensibly most of the time?

increase in the number of people taking preventive measures such as controlling their blood pressure and cholesterol levels, getting regular exercise, and refraining from smoking. However, medical advances in the diagnosis and treatment of cardiovascular diseases have also made survival and recovery from cardiovascular diseases more likely.

DIAGNOSIS   The earlier a cardiovascular disease is detected, the more likely that treatment will be effective. It is therefore vital to recognize the early warning signs of a CVD, such as a heart attack or stroke, and to seek treatment immediately. Doctors now have several techniques by which they can detect damage to the heart or blood vessels due to cardiovascular diseases.

An **electrocardiogram (ECG)** measures the heart's electrical activity. This technique can detect any abnormalities in the rhythm of the heartbeat and signs of injury from a heart attack. X rays can be used to detect blockage in the arteries due to athero-sclerosis or blood clots. One common X-ray technique is called an **angiogram** [*AN jee uh gram*]. The procedure for an angiogram involves injecting a dye directly into the coronary artery so that it can be seen on an X ray. The X ray can then reveal where any blockage might occur.

MEDICATION   Many prescription medicines are now available that can control most types of CVDs. You have already learned that medications can control hypertension and arrhythmias. There also are medicines that can reduce the level of LDL cholesterol and raise the level of HDL cholesterol. Other medicines can be injected directly into the blood vessels to dissolve clots and restore blood flow in some heart attack victims.

SURGERY   Some of the biggest breakthroughs in treating CVDs are improved surgical techniques. Surgery is used to correct defects in the heart, including those present at birth. Surgery can also be

Do you think cross-country skiing would be a good form of exercise for someone who had suffered a heart attack?

used to replace damaged heart valves. Three surgical techniques commonly used to treat CVDs are angioplasty, coronary bypass surgery, and heart transplants.

Angioplasty is a technique in which a long, narrow, flexible tube with a balloon attached to the end is inserted into an artery that has been narrowed by atherosclerosis. The balloon is then inflated to widen the artery, allowing more blood to flow through.

Coronary bypass surgery is a technique used to improve the blood supply to the heart in people with coronary heart disease. A vein from a different part of the body—usually the leg—is sewn onto a coronary artery. Blood is then able to go around the blocked area.

A **heart transplant** is a procedure in which a weakened heart is replaced by a healthy heart from a person who has recently died. Heart transplant surgery began in 1968 and has proven to be successful for appropriately selected individuals.

REHABILITATION

Medication and surgery are only part of the recovery process. People who have suffered a heart attack or stroke must also reduce the risk factors that caused their illness. Risk reduction includes eating a well-planned, healthy diet, following an exercise program designed for the person's abilities, reducing stress, not smoking, and being aware of any and all signs of heart attack and stroke.

SUMMARY

Cardiovascular diseases are the leading cause of death in the United States. The risk of developing these diseases can be significantly reduced by controlling blood pressure and cholesterol levels and not smoking. A combination of behavioral changes to reduce the health risks and advances in diagnosis and treatment has greatly reduced the death rate from CVDs.

LESSON 25.1 **USING WHAT YOU HAVE LEARNED**

REVIEW

1. Describe three life-style changes that can help decrease your blood pressure.
2. Why does atherosclerosis often lead to a heart attack?

THINK CRITICALLY

3. Heart attacks occasionally occur in people who are athletic, do not smoke, and eat a healthy diet. What might cause heart attacks in such health-conscious people, and how might the attacks be prevented?
4. During the past 30 years, significant progress has been made in diagnosing and treating cardiovascular diseases. Even if all such diseases can eventually respond to treatment, why is prevention still important?

APPLY IT TO YOURSELF

5. You are the head of a research team examining the future risk of cardiovascular disease in your high school. What type of data would you try to gather?

CANCER

Cancer is a group of diseases characterized by the uncontrolled growth and spread of abnormal cells. Each year, 1.5 million Americans of all ages and ethnic groups are diagnosed with cancer. New medical treatments now cure over 40 percent of all cancer patients in the United States. Many cancers can be prevented by learning about the causes of cancer and making life-style changes.

WHAT IS CANCER?

In many body tissues, when cells become worn out or injured, healthy cells divide, replacing the old ones. This process of cell division is normally under tight control. However, if something goes wrong with the mechanism that restrains cell division, cells begin to divide uncontrollably. These abnormal cells often clump together, forming a mass of tissue called a **tumor**. Tumors may harm the body by crowding out normal tissue and using up nutrients needed by normal tissue.

Benign tumors [*bi NYN*] are confined to one area and are not cancerous. However, they can be dangerous if they interfere with normal body functions. Tumors that can invade other tissues and spread to other parts of the body are called **malignant tumors** [*muh LIG nunt*]. Cancer cells spread by breaking away from a tumor and traveling through blood vessels or lymphatic vessels. This process is called **metastasis** [*muh TAS tuh sus*].

WHAT CAUSES CANCER?

There is no single factor involved in the development of all cancers. The most promising theory is that the genes that regulate cell division somehow become damaged. As you may remember from Chapter 16, "Reproduction and Heredity," genes are sets of chemical instructions that are present in all cells. Scientists have identified many different causes, or agents, that are thought to trigger the transformation of normal cells into cancer cells by damaging genes. Agents that are linked to the development of cancer are called **carcinogens** [*kahr SIN uh junz*]. Exposure to carcinogens does not necessarily mean that you will get cancer. However, the more often you are exposed to carcinogens, the greater your risk of developing cancer later in life.

TYPES OF CARCINOGENS

Very few things actually cause cancer. So far, only about 30 different chemicals have been definitely identified as carcinogens, although many other chemicals are suspected of being carcinogens. Radiation, including X rays and ultraviolet radiation from the sun, can also increase your risk of cancer. By learning about the agents that have been most strongly linked to the development of cancer, you can take action to avoid them.

MAIN IDEAS

CONCEPTS

✔ The risk of cancer can be decreased by avoiding agents that cause cancer and by early detection.

✔ Today, over 40 percent of all cancer patients are cured.

VOCABULARY

cancer
tumor
benign tumor
malignant tumor
metastasis
carcinogens
malignant melanoma
leukemia
mammography
Pap test
biopsy
radiation therapy
chemotherapy
immunotherapy
hormone therapy

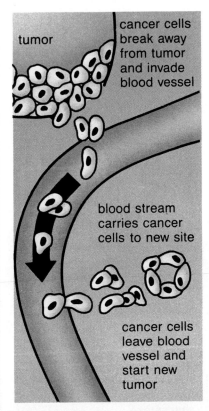

Figure 25-2   What is the name of this process?

Nelson went to his uncle's house to borrow a can of cleaning solution. When he looked at the old can, he saw that the solution contained benzene. Nelson had learned in science class that benzene is a carcinogen. When Nelson asked his uncle whether he thought the solution was safe, his uncle laughed. Nevertheless, Nelson decided to go to the hardware store to buy some new cleaning solution that did not contain any carcinogens.

VIRUSES AND CANCER

Some viruses have been linked to the development of cancer in animals. For example, a virus has been discovered that causes leukemia in cats. There is evidence that the viruses responsible for causing hepatitis B and genital warts can cause cancer in humans. For example, human papilloma virus infections are associated with cervical cancer. HIV, the virus that causes AIDS, suppresses the body's immune system so that it cannot fight cancer.

COMMON TYPES OF CANCER

There are over 100 different types of cancer. Each is named for the part of the body or the type of tissue in which the cancer originates. Some types of cancer can be detected and cured more easily than other types. Some tumors grow and spread faster than others, and some are easier to treat than others. Most types of cancer have one thing in common. The earlier they are detected, the easier they are to cure.

LUNG CANCER   Lung cancer causes more deaths among both men and women in the United States than any other type of cancer. Warning signs include a persistent cough, coughing up mucus streaked with blood, chest pain, and recurring pneumonia. The American Cancer Society (ACS) has estimated that smoking is responsible for 83 percent of all lung cancer deaths. There is growing evidence that passive smoking increases the risk of lung cancer in nonsmokers.

SKIN CANCER   A second form of cancer that is increasing rapidly in the United States is skin cancer. The most serious form of skin cancer is called **malignant melanoma** [*mel uh NOH muh*]. Malignant melanoma starts as a small, molelike growth. Because melanoma can spread quickly through the rest of the body, early detection and treatment are critical. Chapter 2, "Taking Care of Yourself," explains how to recognize the early symptoms. Skin cancer is almost always connected with overexposure to ultraviolet rays from the sun. When you are out in the sun, wearing protective clothing and a sunscreen can significantly lower your risk of skin cancer.

COLON AND RECTUM CANCER   Colon and rectum cancer are the third most common forms of cancer in the United States. If detected early, the cure rate is high. Warning signs include rectal bleeding, blood in the stool, and unexplained changes in bowel habits. There is increasing evidence that a diet low in fat and high in fiber decreases your risk of colon and rectum cancer.

BREAST CANCER   Breast cancer is the second leading cause of cancer deaths among women in the United States. The ACS estimates that approximately one out of every nine women will develop breast cancer sometime during her life. Women with a family history of breast cancer are at greatest risk of developing the disease. Recent attention has focused on the role of the hormone estrogen in the development of breast cancer. The best protection against breast cancer is early detection. The ACS recommends that women perform the monthly breast self-examination described in Figure 25-3. If breast cancer is detected early, the survival rate is high.

UTERINE, CERVICAL, AND OVARIAN CANCER   Cancer of the reproductive organs in women includes uterine cancer, cervical cancer, and

Figure 25-3   All women should do this breast self-examination every month.

1 IN THE SHOWER

With fingers flat, examine gently every part of each breast. Use the right hand for the left breast, and the left hand for the right breast. Check carefully for any lump, hard knot, or thickening.

2 BEFORE A MIRROR

Examine each breast with arms at the sides, then raise your arms high overhead. Look closely for any changes in shape of each breast, swelling, dimpling of skin, or changes in the nipple.

Next, with palms on hips, press down firmly to flex the chest muscles. Check carefully again.

3 LYING DOWN

Place a pillow or folded towel under the right shoulder. Place right hand behind the head. With the fingers of the left hand flat, press gently in small circular motions around an imaginary clock face. Begin at the outermost top, or

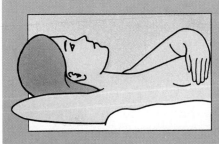

12 o'clock, position of your right breast, then move to 1 o'clock, and so on around the circle back to 12 o'clock. A ridge in the lower curve of each breast is normal. Move the hand in an inch, toward the nipple. Keep circling to

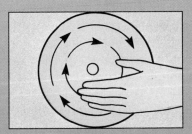

examine every part of the breast, including the nipple. Repeat for the left breast. Finally, squeeze the nipple of each breast gently between the thumb and index finger. Any discharge should be reported to a doctor immediately.

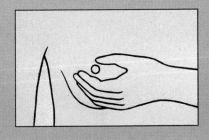

CANCER INCIDENCE AND DEATHS BY SITE AND GENDER—1994

Men			Women		
Site	Incidence	Deaths	Site	Incidence	Deaths
Prostate	200,000	38,000	Breast	182,000	46,000
Lung	100,000	94,000	Colon and Rectum	74,000	28,200
Colon and Rectum	75,000	27,800	Lung	72,000	59,000
Bladder	38,000	7,000	Uterus	46,000	10,500
Oral	19,800	5,150	Ovary	24,000	13,600
Skin (Melanoma)	17,000	4,300	Skin (Melanoma)	15,000	2,600
Kidney	17,000	6,800	Pancreas	14,000	13,500
Leukemia	16,200	10,500	Bladder	13,200	3,600
Testes	6,800	325	Leukemia	12,400	8,600
All Sites*	632,000	283,000	**All Sites***	576,000	255,000

* Figures for *All Sites* include rates for sites not listed.
SOURCE: AMERICAN CANCER SOCIETY

Figure 25-4 *"Incidence" means the number of people who developed each type of cancer. Which type of cancer kills more men and women than any other type?*

ovarian cancer. These cancers affect more than 60,000 women every year. Warning signs of uterine and cervical cancer include an abnormal vaginal discharge and bleeding outside of the normal menstrual period. Ovarian cancer rarely has any warning signs until it has spread. Like breast cancer, cancer of the uterus is partly related to estrogen levels. Certain sexually transmitted diseases, including genital warts and genital herpes, may also increase the risk of cervical cancer.

TESTICULAR AND PROSTATE CANCER   Cancer of the reproductive organs in men includes testicular cancer and prostate cancer. Testicular cancer is the most common form of cancer in males between 15 and 35 years of age. Fortunately, testicular cancer is easy to detect and curable if discovered early. The ACS recommends that all males 15 years of age and older perform a monthly testicular self-examination. The procedures for doing this self-examination are described in Chapter 17, "Growth and Development."

Prostate cancer is the second leading cause of cancer death in men. It is most common in men over 65 years of age. The American Cancer Society estimates that one out of every eleven men will develop prostate cancer. Early signs include difficulty in urinating, frequent need to urinate, especially at night, and blood in the urine. If detected early, the survival rate is high.

LEUKEMIA   Leukemia [*loo KEE mee uh*] is cancer in the tissues that produce blood cells, including bone marrow and lymph nodes. The cancer causes the tissue to produce abnormal white blood cells that crowd out normal white blood cells, red blood cells, and platelets. Leukemia is the most common form of cancer in children. The survival rates for many types of leukemia have increased dramatically over the last 30 years due to new medications and surgery that replaces the diseased bone marrow.

DETECTION OF CANCER

Despite significant advances in treating cancer, successful treatment usually depends on whether the cancer is detected before it spreads. You are responsible for learning to identify warning signs and for getting regular medical checkups.

THE SEVEN WARNING SIGNS   The warning signs of cancer are listed in Figure 25-5. Although the presence of any warning signs does not necessarily mean you have cancer, it is important to consult a doctor as soon as possible.

SCREENING   Often, cancer can become established before any warning signs appear. However, many types of cancer can be discovered early in their development through routine screening. The ACS recommends routine screening for prostate cancer in men over age 50 and for colon and rectum cancer in both men and women over age 50.

For women, a technique called **mammography** [*ma MAHG ruh fee*] can detect breast tumors that are too small to be felt. The ACS recommends that women receive a mammogram first between age 35 and 40 and then every one or two years after that.

The ACS also recommends that all women over age 18 receive a regular pelvic exam to detect any signs of cervical, uterine, or ovarian cancer. As part of the pelvic exam, a doctor will do a Pap test. In a **Pap test,** the doctor gently removes cells from the cervix with a swab and has the cells tested for signs of cervical cancer. The Pap test has been credited with reducing the number of deaths from cervical cancer by 43 percent.

CONFIRMATION   If an exam or screening finds a suspicious area, the doctor may remove a piece of the tissue. A lab examines the tissue to determine whether it is cancerous. This removal of tissue for examination is called a **biopsy** [*BY ahp see*]. If the tumor cannot be reached surgically, blood tests can sometimes be used to confirm its presence. New techniques using X rays and other forms of radiation are increasingly used instead of surgery to locate tumors and estimate the spread of cancer.

TREATMENT OF CANCER

Tremendous progress has been made in treating cancer, and new treatments continue to be developed. These treatments have increased the life expectancy of people with cancer while decreasing many of the unpleasant side effects. The type of treatment used depends on where the tumor is located and how far advanced the cancer is.

CANCER'S SEVEN WARNING SIGNS

1. Change in bowel or bladder habits
2. A sore that does not heal
3. Unusual bleeding or discharge
4. Thickening or lump in breast or elsewhere
5. Indigestion or difficulty in swallowing
6. Obvious change in wart or mole
7. Nagging cough or hoarseness

SOURCE: AMERICAN CANCER SOCIETY

Figure 25-5   If you experience one of these warning signs, see a doctor as soon as possible— just to be safe.

Computer images like this one can show cancerous tumors in patients.

SURGERY   Cancer can often be cured by surgically removing the tumor. However, surgery is only successful if all of the cancer cells are removed. Therefore, it is vital that surgery be performed before the cancer has spread. The success of surgery also depends on the location of the tumor. A tumor located in the brain or the liver is difficult to remove without causing significant damage to surrounding tissue. New surgical techniques using lasers are increasingly being used to reach such tumors.

RADIATION THERAPY   **Radiation therapy** is a cancer treatment in which a tumor is exposed to short, intense bursts of radiation. Radiation selectively destroys rapidly dividing cells. Thus, it can be used to destroy cancer cells without significantly harming normal cells. Radiation therapy is most often used to treat tumors that cannot be reached surgically.

CHEMOTHERAPY   The use of chemical medications to fight cancer is called **chemotherapy** [*kee moh THER uh pee*]. Chemotherapy slows the growth of tumors by selectively killing cancer cells. The

MAKING A DIFFERENCE

PEOPLE HEALTH

The Hole In the Wall Gang Camp

For people who are diagnosed with a serious disease, the diagnosis often signals the beginning of major life changes. Constant medical tests and treatments become part of everyday life. Adjusting to the changes can be difficult, especially for young people.

In 1988, actor Paul Newman set up a special camp for children ages 7 to 15 who suffer from cancer or blood diseases. The Hole in the Wall Gang Camp is a place where the children can enjoy themselves, free of hospital wards and free of the stares and the whispers of their schoolmates. Many of the children have spent more than half of their lives undergoing serious medical treatment, much of it painful and all of it frightening.

At the camp, the children do all the things kids at any camp do—swimming, woodworking, building campfires, fishing, riding horses, and singing. For the campers, such activities are not a regular part of

their lives. The Hole in the Wall Gang Camp gives these children a place to be just ordinary kids.

The camp is a place where campers are given unconditional love. They are accepted without exception. It provides an environment where campers feel safe to talk about their diseases with each other and with counselors who are there to listen.

Writing poetry is one activity that many Hole in the Wall Gang campers enjoy. Through their writing, they can express some of the anxiety and hurt that their diseases and treatments have caused them. Most of the poems reflect simple but thoughtful observations, such as this one, called "Bug Spray."

Bug spray is like the walls we build around ourselves to protect against fear and pain. And like these fragile walls, it never really works.

There are no protective walls at the Hole in the Wall Gang Camp—only open arms and ears that listen. The

camp has truly made a difference in the lives of hundreds of ill children.

1. Why do you think that children undergoing extraordinary medical treatment need a place like The Hole in the Wall Gang Camp?

2. How might expressing feelings in a poem or story help a person living with a serious illness?

medications are distributed throughout the body, so they can work on cancer cells that have spread. Chemotherapy is often used with surgery and radiation therapy. Despite its success, chemotherapy has many potential side effects, including hair loss and nausea.

OTHER TREATMENTS   In recent years, scientists have focused on efforts to stimulate the body's immune system to fight cancer. Treatment that uses the body's own immune system is called **immunotherapy** [*im yuh noh THER uh pee*]. Two chemicals that are naturally produced by the immune system—interleukin-2 and interferon—are now being used to fight some types of cancer. Scientists are also exploring the role of hormones in controlling the growth of tumors. Treatment in which tumors are denied hormones needed for growth or supplied with hormones that restrict growth is called **hormone therapy**.

REDUCING CANCER RISKS

You can significantly reduce your risk of getting cancer if you:

- Avoid all forms of tobacco, including cigarettes, snuff, and chewing tobacco. Chewing tobacco and snuff have been linked to cancer of the mouth, throat, and larynx.

- Limit your intake of alcohol. Heavy drinking increases the risk of developing cancers of the mouth, throat, and larynx.

- Eat properly balanced meals. Try to eat more fresh fruits and vegetables. Cut down on consumption of fats, red meats, and charcoal-broiled and smoked foods.

- Avoid overexposure to the sun. If you cannot avoid long periods in the sun, use a sunscreen to block out the harmful rays.

- Keep informed. When new carcinogens are discovered, avoid them as much as possible.

- Know your body, and recognize the warning signs of cancer. Visit your doctor immediately if you suspect a problem.

What types of foods can help you reduce your risk of developing cancer?

LESSON 25.2   **USING WHAT YOU HAVE LEARNED**

REVIEW

1. Why is it so difficult to treat cancer after it has spread?
2. Why is the rate of lung cancer so high in the United States?

THINK CRITICALLY

3. The federal government monitors the number of cases of each type of cancer in every state. How can this information help in the fight against cancer?
4. Many people have the idea that almost everything causes cancer and have decided not to bother with cancer prevention. How can you convince these people to change?

APPLY IT TO YOURSELF

5. As a teacher, you are responsible for setting up a cancer awareness program in your school. What type of information do you want to communicate to students?

SUMMARY

Cancer can start in any part of the body and spread to any other part. Cancer has been linked to agents that damage the genes controlling cell division. Over 40% of people with cancer can be successfully cured through surgery, radiation therapy, and chemotherapy. Avoiding known carcinogens and early detection through screening are your best protection against cancer.

THINKING CRITICALLY ABOUT

Cancer Prevention

HEALTHY PEOPLE 2000

Reverse the rise in cancer deaths to achieve a rate of no more than 130 per 100,000 people.

Cancer is the second leading cause of death in the United States. In 1990, an estimated 510,000 people died of the disease. Cancer strikes more frequently with advancing age, but many cancer deaths are premature. In 1987, 18 million years of potential life before age 65 were lost from cancer compared to 15 million years for heart disease.

Objective 16.1

from *Healthy People 2000: National Health Promotion and Disease Prevention Objectives*

Over two hundred types of cancer are known today. Skin cancer is the most common form of cancer and accounts for roughly one-third of all new cancer cases. Other common cancers include lung cancer, colon-rectal cancer, breast cancer, and prostate cancer.

Cancer is a life-threatening disease. However, the odds of premature death from most cancers are declining because of early detection and diagnosis, advanced medical technologies, intensive research, new drugs, and lifestyle studies. With your active participation in prevention and early detection, you will help attain the cancer reduction goals for the year 2000.

THE BILLION DOLLAR QUESTION

Each year, about one billion dollars are spent searching for the cure for cancer. Each year, scientists make progress, but they have yet to discover a cure.

Cancer is caused by abnormal cell growth inside the body. Healthy cells in the body divide through the complex process known as mitosis. They divide, then increase in size, then may divide again, in a regular cycle regulated within the cells themselves. Cancer cells do not follow the same regular cycle of division. Cancer cells divide rapidly over and over, until they eventually form a mass of cells called a tumor. In a process called metastasis, cancer cells leave the tumor and travel through the blood stream and lymph system to other organs. Cancer tumors threaten life by destroying vital organs in the body.

Several agents, called initiators, are believed to be responsible for the origin of cancers. These initiators include viruses that may have been present in a person's genetic structure since birth, environmental agents such as nicotine or asbestos, and radiation caused by the sun or overexposure to X-rays. People can protect themselves from environmental factors, such as radiation, that cause cancers.

As a teenager you are not among the highest risk group for developing cancer. However, the choices you make today can greatly affect the chances of developing cancer down the road. Many teenagers find it is easy to think that "it will never happen to me," or "they'll find a cure before it affects me." These beliefs are both unfounded and foolish.

LOWERING YOUR RISK

Prevention may indeed be the best medicine when it comes to cancer. By avoiding the behaviors that have been documented to cause cancer, a young person can avoid health risks for now and for the future. The following list of strategies can help you prevent cancer and avoid cancer-causing behaviors.

1. Avoid overexposure to the sun. Use a cream or lotion with a sun protection factor (SPF) of 15 or more, even if you have dark skin. If you are fair-skinned and tend to burn, use a sunscreen of SPF 25 or more.

2. Examine your breasts, if you are female, or your testicles, if you are male, every month. Report any change, swelling, or lump to your doctor right away. Early detection can make any treatment needed relatively easy compared with treatments that begin later.

3. Do not smoke cigarettes, pipes, cigars, or use smoke-less tobacco. These tobacco products cause lung cancer and mouth cancers.

4. Do not drink alcohol. Moderate drinking has been linked to breast cancer. Drinking alcohol greatly increases the chance of mouth, esophagus, and throat cancers.

5. Eat a high-fiber diet that includes lots of vegetables, fruits, and whole grains. Do not change your eating habits overnight. Instead, incorporate more fibrous foods into your diet over time.

6. Have regular physical examinations by your doctor. Ask your doctor questions about your body.

7. Know the seven warning signs of cancer. The acronym CAUTION may help you remember each of the signs:

   Change in bowel or bladder habits

   A sore that does not heal

   Unusual bleeding or discharge

   Thickening in the breast or elsewhere

   Indigestion or difficulty swallowing

   Obvious change in a wart or mole

   Nagging cough or hoarseness.

WHAT DO YOU THINK?

1. What is cancer and how are cancer cells different from other cells in the body?

2. Which of your behaviors might cause cancer later in your life? What can you do to avoid these behaviors?

3. Evaluate your family history. Are there any types of cancer that seem to run in your family? If so, what steps can you take to decrease the chance that this cancer will affect you?

OTHER NONINFECTIOUS DISEASES

MAIN IDEAS

CONCEPTS

✔ Diabetes, a disease that once was always fatal, can now be controlled.

✔ Arthritis is the most common noninfectious disease in the United States.

✔ Although loss of mental function is a legitimate concern for the elderly, it is not an inevitable part of aging.

VOCABULARY

insulin
diabetes mellitus
insulin-dependent diabetes
insulin shock
diabetic coma
noninsulin-dependent diabetes
arthritis
osteoarthritis
rheumatoid arthritis
Parkinson's disease
dementia
Alzheimer's disease

Noninfectious diseases can affect an enormous range of different body systems and functions. Some noninfectious diseases can strike without warning. Others develop gradually and often result from normal wear and tear or years of poor health habits. Many of these diseases cannot be cured. However, advances in treatment enable many people with these diseases to live normal lives.

DIABETES

The conversion of food to energy requires many complex steps. Carbohydrates from your food are broken down in the intestines into the sugar glucose. The glucose then enters the bloodstream, where it circulates to the rest of the body. The final critical step is the transfer of the glucose out of the bloodstream and into the cells, where it is used for energy. This process is controlled by **insulin** [*IN suh lun*], a hormone that is produced by the pancreas. If the pancreas is unable to produce enough insulin or if the body is unable to utilize insulin, the body cannot use the glucose for energy. The disease in which the body cannot properly use glucose for energy is called **diabetes mellitus** [*dy uh BEET eez MEL ut us*].

More than 600,000 new cases are diagnosed annually. Left untreated, diabetes can lead to very serious problems. The most immediate effect is that cells cannot get all of the energy they need. As a result, cells must use stored fats and proteins for energy. The breakdown of fats produces toxic chemicals called ketones. Over time, these ketones can build to dangerous levels in the blood. In addition, high levels of glucose in the blood can damage the blood vessels, resulting in poor circulation and other problems. Diabetes can eventually lead to blindness, kidney damage, nervous system damage, and heart disease. However, advances in treating diabetes have enabled most diabetics to lead normal lives. There are two types of diabetes: insulin-dependent and noninsulin-dependent diabetes.

INSULIN-DEPENDENT DIABETES   Insulin-dependent diabetes is less common but more serious than noninsulin-dependent diabetes. In **insulin-dependent diabetes,** the pancreas is unable to make insulin. People with this disease require daily injections of insulin to stay alive. Insulin-dependent diabetes usually begins in childhood and often occurs suddenly. The early symptoms include frequent urination, fatigue, excessive thirst, and rapid weight loss.

One of the greatest challenges faced by people with insulin-dependent diabetes is balancing the levels of glucose and insulin in their bodies. Therefore, they need to time their meals with their insulin doses so blood glucose levels do not get too high or too low. Illness, unplanned physical activity, or even excitement or upset may cause the body to use up glucose. If the glucose level is too low, the person can go into **insulin shock.** The symptoms of insulin shock include dizziness, rapid pulse, excessive sweating,

HEALTHY PEOPLE 2000

Reduce diabetes-related deaths each year to no more than 34 per 100,000 people.

Objective 17.9
from *Healthy People 2000: National Health Promotion and Disease Prevention Objectives*

blurred vision, a change in behavior, and paleness. People can be revived from insulin shock by eating or drinking high-sugar foods such as orange juice.

Too much glucose in the blood may cause a state of partial or complete unconsciousness called a **diabetic coma**. The person's pulse is weak and rapid, the skin is very dry, and large amounts of glucose are excreted in the urine. Someone in a diabetic coma requires emergency treatment. Such treatment usually involves injections of insulin and salt solutions to replace lost fluids. Without immediate medical attention, a diabetic coma may be fatal.

Before insulin was identified, insulin-dependent diabetes was almost always fatal. Today, people with insulin-dependent diabetes can lead long, active lives through a combination of insulin injections, diet control, and exercise.

NONINSULIN-DEPENDENT DIABETES   The noninsulin-dependent type of diabetes usually develops in adults. In **noninsulin-dependent diabetes,** the pancreas is able to produce insulin, but the body is unable to utilize it properly. People with noninsulin-dependent diabetes usually do not require insulin injections. The symptoms of noninsulin-dependent diabetes are usually less severe than those of the insulin-dependent type. Symptoms include blurred vision, fatigue, frequent infections, frequent urination, and increased thirst. If untreated, it can lead to diabetic coma, heart disease, kidney failure, and blindness.

The greatest risk factor associated with the development of this type of diabetes is obesity. Eighty percent of those diagnosed with noninsulin-dependent diabetes are overweight. The risk increases if one or both parents have diabetes. Treatment includes a diet and exercise program to maintain a normal weight. For people who are overweight, losing weight can significantly decrease the severity of the symptoms and reduce the risk of complications. Also, the risk of heart disease doubles in people with diabetes. They are therefore advised to eat foods low in saturated fats and cholesterol, reduce stress, and refrain from smoking.

ARTHRITIS

Arthritis is a group of diseases characterized by inflammation in the joints. Symptoms of arthritis can range from occasional pain and stiffness to loss of movement. More than 17 million people in the United States have some form of arthritis, making it the most common chronic disease. Most people will develop arthritis in their lifetime. Although most forms of arthritis do not develop until late adulthood, others can strike people of any age.

OSTEOARTHRITIS   Normally, the ends of bones are covered with a smooth layer of cartilage that prevents them from rubbing together. After many years, the cartilage may begin to wear away. Arthritis due to the wearing away of cartilage in a joint is called **osteoarthritis** [ahs tee oh ahr THRYT us]. Osteoarthritis is the most common form

This boy with insulin-dependent diabetes is testing his blood-glucose level.

Medical Quackery

Medical quackery is the sale of an unproven, ineffective treatment for an ailment. Each year millions of hard-earned dollars are spent on miracle cures for diseases like arthritis, cancer, and AIDS.

Con artists are ready to sell treatments from cod liver oil to coffee, packaged under different names, and some people who are living with chronic or life-threatening diseases are willing to try them.

While some miracle cures hurt only a person's wallet, others can be dangerous, especially if the person avoids proper medical care while using the product.

Some alternative medicines may offer relief but most do not. The FDA issues the following tips that can help you identify medical quackery:

• Be wary if a product's label promises immediate, effortless, or guaranteed results, or complete relief from pain.

• Don't be lured by a money-back guarantee.

• Avoid all products that claim to be effective for more than one ailment.

• Watch for misleading words on labels and in advertising such as *amazing, secret, miracle, painless, breakthrough,* or *instant.*

• Watch out for the word *natural.* It is often meaningless.

• If a product seems too good to be true, it usually is.

of arthritis, especially among people over 65 years of age. It usually affects joints in the hands and in large, weight-bearing joints such as the knees, hips, and ankles. Osteoarthritis usually results from natural wear and tear associated with aging. However, injuries, excessive use of joints, and obesity can accelerate the process.

RHEUMATOID ARTHRITIS Rheumatoid arthritis [*ROO muh toyd*] is a severe form of arthritis that can strike at any age. It is thought to be caused by an immune system response to an invading pathogen such as a virus. The body responds to the pathogen by causing inflammation in the joints. Rheumatoid arthritis occurs most frequently in people between the ages of 20 and 50. It affects twice as many women as men. In addition to having painful, swollen joints, people with rheumatoid arthritis may experience fatigue, fever, muscle weakness, and weight loss. In some cases, the disease also causes inflammation of heart muscle and blood vessels.

TREATMENT Currently, there is no cure for arthritis. However, there are ways to lessen the severity of some of the symptoms. Aspirin and other anti-inflammatory medicines can reduce some of the pain and swelling of all types of arthritis. Surgery to reconstruct or replace badly diseased joints is an option for some patients with osteoarthritis. Daily activity, including exercises supervised by a physician, can often help reduce the discomfort of arthritis and minimize the symptoms. Maintaining a proper weight can reduce some of the stress on weight-bearing joints.

DISEASES OF THE ELDERLY

The aging process does not keep most elderly people from leading active lives. Many older Americans participate in regular activities, including athletics. Aging cannot be avoided, but good health

Why is swimming an excellent form of exercise for people with arthritis?

habits, a well-balanced diet, and regular exercise can help reduce the health risks of aging. Continued physical activity and mental involvement actually reduce and slow down the effects of the aging process.

The aging process does, however, weaken many parts of the body. Among the most common problems of aging are failing eyesight and hearing, and loss of muscle tone and endurance. As the heart, lungs, and kidneys age, they do not work as well. Body temperature is more difficult to regulate, so older people often feel uncomfortable in the heat and cold. Some of the most troubling diseases associated with aging involve the degeneration of the nervous system. Two such diseases are Parkinson's disease and Alzheimer's disease.

PARKINSON'S DISEASE   **Parkinson's disease** is a slow, progressive disease of the nervous system that affects the part of the brain that controls movement. It is thought to be related to the loss of the brain's ability to produce dopamine, a chemical needed to coordinate muscle movement. Symptoms of Parkinson's disease include hand tremors, body rigidity, a shuffling gait, and muscle weakness. Parkinson's disease usually does not affect mental ability.

The cause of Parkinson's disease is not yet known, but research is examining three possibilities. These possibilities are a virus that causes inflammation of the brain, long-term exposure to carbon monoxide, possibly linked to smoking, and long-term exposure to metal poisons such as mercury, lead, and aluminum.

Parkinson's disease can develop slowly. Thus, many individuals adjust to the changes in their body and do not seek medical treatment. However, medical treatment can help. Although there is no cure yet for Parkinson's disease, some medicines can partially control many of the symptoms. Unfortunately, these are effective in only three out of four

Regular exercise helps to reduce and slow down the effects of aging.

Most elderly people remain mentally active and do not develop Alzheimer's disease.

people. Exercises that increase muscle strength can also help patients overcome many of the movement problems.

DEMENTIA   Dementia [*dih MEN chuh*] is a brain disorder characterized by severe forgetfulness, confusion, a change in personality, and an increasing tendency to become out of touch with the surroundings. The most common form of dementia in our country is Alzheimer's disease.

Alzheimer's disease [*AHLTS hy murz*] is a disorder resulting from increased loss of brain cells. This loss causes an irreversible and progressive decline in mental functioning. This decline can eventually interfere with daily life. It is estimated that Alzheimer's disease affects approximately one out of every forty people over the age of 65. It causes over 120,000 deaths each year. Although most people with Alzheimer's disease are older than 65, Alzheimer's disease may strike people earlier in life.

Very little is known about the cause of Alzheimer's disease. Currently, there are no treatments that can reverse the decline. People with this disease need constant supervision and emotional support. Often, Alzheimer's disease can place a great burden on family members who not only must care for the person with the disease but also must cope with his or her personality change. A number of support groups are available to help the families of people with Alzheimer's disease. In some communities, day-care centers have been established for Alzheimer's patients so that their family members can have some relief from constant care-giving responsibilities.

SUMMARY

Noninfectious diseases can affect a wide range of body processes. In diabetes, the body is unable to utilize the sugar glucose for energy. Arthritis is a group of diseases affecting the joints. Two nervous system diseases commonly associated with people over age 65 are Parkinson's disease and Alzheimer's disease. These diseases are not an inevitable part of growing older.

LESSON 25.3   USING WHAT YOU HAVE LEARNED

REVIEW

1. Describe the difference between the causes of insulin shock and the causes of a diabetic coma.
2. What is the cause of rheumatoid arthritis?

THINK CRITICALLY

3. People with diabetes need to be prepared for emergencies. What precautions might they need to take when they are planning a trip?
4. Alzheimer's disease is extremely difficult to diagnose. Why is it important for doctors to rule out all other possible causes of forgetfulness before telling a patient and his or her family that the patient has Alzheimer's disease?

APPLY IT TO YOURSELF

5. You work for a community-based group that provides support for the families of people with Alzheimer's disease. What would you hope that this support group would accomplish?

Have It Checked

Amy's family was busy getting ready for her older sister's wedding. Quite a few relatives were coming from throughout the United States. Amy's mother was working overtime to save money for the wedding. In her spare hours she was busy making arrangements for the wedding.

A week before the wedding, Amy had suffered from a bad sore throat. A few days after she started feeling better, Amy discovered a lump under her arm, near her left breast. Amy knew she should tell her mother, but Amy didn't feel the timing was right.

Amy waited a few days to see if the lump would disappear. She tried not to think about it, but that didn't work. "There probably is nothing to worry about," she told herself. But then Amy remembered that her grandmother had died of breast cancer at 42. Breast cancer was not out of the question, even at 18. After a few days, Amy could still feel the lump. She wanted to talk with her mother, but Amy didn't want to cause any problems this close to the wedding. She wondered if there was someone else with whom she could speak.

PAUSE AND CONSIDER

1. **Identify the Problem.** What is Amy's conflict?

2. **Consider the Options.** What are Amy's options? Who else might be able to help Amy?

3. **Evaluate the Outcomes.** What could happen if Amy tells her mother about the lump? What risks does Amy take if she remains quiet?

Amy decided that she wouldn't tell her mother about the lump until after the wedding. After school the next day, Amy went to a health clinic near school. A doctor examined Amy carefully and then asked her if she had had any swollen glands as a result of her sore throat. "Yes. I felt awful."

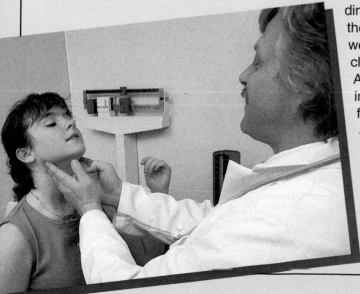

"This lump probably has to do with an infection lingering in your system. But you should watch it carefully. Especially if there is a history of breast cancer in your family," said the doctor. He suggested that she follow up with her family doctor, who could schedule tests to identify the source of infection.

Amy felt a bit relieved. She felt more confident that the lump was not serious. Just to be sure, she followed the doctor's advice and made an appointment to see her doctor.

The day after the wedding, Amy told her mother about her visit to the health clinic. "Amy," said her mother, "you absolutely should have told me about this."

"I know, Mom, but I didn't want to worry you."

"Honey, your health is important. I want to know when you're sick, no matter what else is happening. I'm very proud of you for taking the initiative to have the lump checked. It must have been scary. Would you like me to go to the doctor with you?"

"Yeah," said Amy. "I'd like that."

DECIDE AND REVIEW

4. **Decide and Act.** What did Amy decide to do?

5. **Review.** Are there other options Amy could have chosen? How would you have handled the situation?

PROJECTS

1. Many people are convinced that a cancer patient's personality and attitude can greatly affect his or her chances of recovery. Some researchers have even suggested that certain personality traits make a person more likely to develop cancer. Find out more about how personality and attitude might affect cancer risks and chances of recovery. You may want to consult Dr. Bernard Siegal's book *Love, Medicine, and Miracles* for information.

2. How has the treatment of diabetes mellitus changed over the past 30 years? Research a recent discovery or development that has helped in the treatment of diabetes. Present your findings in an oral or written report.

WORKING WITH OTHERS

With a partner, research ethnic groups and cultures around the world that have low rates of heart disease. Why is heart disease not as prevalent in those cultures? What dietary factors contribute to the low rates? With your partner, create a menu based on foods regularly found in those groups. Prepare one traditional dish from the menu, and bring it to class to share.

CONNECTING TO...

ECOLOGY What are some common types of products found in the home that might contain carcinogens? Make a list of the products and the carcinogens they may contain. Then examine your own home to see whether it contains any of those products and carcinogens. Are they stored safely? Are your family members aware of the dangers? Do any old products contain chemicals that are no longer considered safe for home use? Research the best ways to dispose of those materials.

USING VOCABULARY

Alzheimer's disease
angiogram
angioplasty
atherosclerosis
arrhythmia
arthritis
benign tumor
biopsy
blood pressure
cancer
carcinogens
cardiac arrest
cardiovascular diseases
chemotherapy
cholesterol

congestive heart failure
coronary bypass surgery
dementia
diabetes mellitus
diabetic coma
electrocardiogram
heart attack
heart transplant
hormone therapy
hypertension
immunotherapy
insulin
insulin-dependent diabetes
insulin shock

leukemia
malignant melanoma
malignant tumor
mammography
metastasis
noninsulin-dependent diabetes
osteoarthritis
Pap test
Parkinson's disease
radiation therapy
rheumatoid arthritis
stroke
tumor

Number a separate sheet of paper from 1 to 15. After each number, write the vocabulary term from the above list that matches the definition given.

1. agents that are linked to the development of cancer
2. the condition in which the heart can no longer pump blood efficiently
3. tumors that can invade other tissues and spread to other parts of the body
4. a treatment that uses the body's own immune system to fight cancer
5. a group of diseases characterized by inflammation in the joints
6. the force of the blood against the walls of the blood vessels
7. the removal of tissue for examination
8. a hormone that is produced by the pancreas
9. a slow, progressive disease of the nervous system that affects the part of the brain that controls movement
10. a waxy, fatlike substance found in your bloodstream
11. the use of chemical medications to fight cancer
12. a disease in which the body cannot properly use glucose for energy
13. cancer in the tissues that produce blood cells
14. an interruption of the blood supply to any part of the brain
15. the buildup of fatty material inside the blood vessels

CONCEPT MAPPING

Copy and complete the concept map shown below. Information on concept mapping appears at the front of this book.

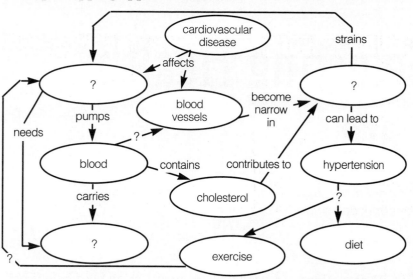

THINKING CRITICALLY

INTERPRET

LESSON 25.1
1. In which age group do CVDs occur most frequently?
2. What is the effect of hypertension over time?
3. Why should all teenagers have their cholesterol level checked?
4. What is the most effective way to lower your cholesterol level?
5. Identify two ways in which smoking can lead to CVDs.
6. What is the most frequent cause of a heart attack?

LESSON 25.2
7. How can a tumor harm the body?
8. What are benign tumors?
9. What is the most common cause of skin cancer?
10. Identify the warning signs of lung cancer.
11. Why is radiation therapy an effective treatment for cancer?

LESSON 25.3
12. What are the early symptoms of insulin-dependent diabetes?
13. How can someone in insulin shock be revived?
14. What is osteoarthritis?
15. What is Alzheimer's disease?

APPLY

LESSON 25.1
16. Name three ways exercise decreases the risk of CVDs.
17. Compare coronary bypass surgery and a heart transplant.

LESSON 25.2
18. What may cause the uncontrolled growth of cancer cells?
19. Why is a monthly self-examination for breast cancer or testicular cancer so important?

LESSON 25.3
20. Why is osteoarthritis more likely to occur in older people?

COMMITMENT TO WELLNESS

FOLLOW-UP

SETTING GOALS
Review your responses to the checklist at the beginning of this chapter. Which statements accurately describe you? Which behaviors do you not engage in now? Which behavior do you most want to change? Write that item in your Wellness Journal. Then answer the following questions about the behavior:

1. Why is it important to change the behavior?
2. What steps can I take to change the behavior?
3. Who might be able to help me change the behavior.

Then outline a specific plan for changing the behavior, using the ideas you had when you answered questions 2 and 3 above.

WHERE DO I GO FROM HERE?
Review your plan one month from now. Have you made progress in changing the behavior? If not, try to develop some new ideas to add to your plan. If you have been successful, choose another behavior that you would like to change, and develop a plan for that behavior. Review your plans and evaluate your progress from time to time.

FOR MORE INFORMATION ABOUT CARDIOVASCULAR DISEASES, CONTACT:

The National Heart, Lung, and Blood Institute
9000 Rickville Pike
Bethesda, Maryland 20205

Selecting Health Care

BACKGROUND

Harry S. Truman was the 33rd president of the United States. One of his many accomplishments as President included the institution of the Marshall Plan, a world-wide assistance program designed to help the countries that had been ravaged by World War II.

"We are a rich nation and can afford many things. But ill health is one thing we cannot afford."

Harry S. Truman

No one can afford to be sick. Good health may be more important than any other aspect of your life. All the riches or fame or popularity in the world cannot buy the happiness or satisfaction that being well provides. Treasure your health and keep it safe by selecting and keeping trusted health-care professionals to help you care for yourself.

There are many steps that you can take as you strive for wellness. Eating the right foods in moderation, following a regular exercise routine, and staying informed on health issues are a few important steps. But following a regular schedule of medical examinations and checkups is equally important.

Selecting a doctor or team of professionals that you trust takes time and careful consideration. Each time you visit a health-care professional you should act responsibly: ask questions, be sure to understand the responses you get, and share all of your symptoms and other health concerns.

SELF-ASSESSMENT

Knowing where to go for medical help is an important step in practicing wellness. How informed are you about medical care? On a sheet of paper or in your Wellness Journal, write *yes* or *no* to respond to the following statements.

1. I am happy with the doctor I am currently seeing.

2. I communicate openly with my doctor about any problems or questions regarding my health.

3. My doctor is accessible and listens well to my questions.

4. I understand the function and treatment offered by each member of my health team.

5. I keep my medical records and immunization records up to date.

6. I know where to go for help.

7. I am covered by medical health insurance and I understand exactly what it does and does not cover.

8. I do not take any medicines that have expired or that belong to anyone else.

9. I know and trust my pharmacist.

10. I avoid all medicines and services that give unbelievable guarantees.

Review your responses and consider what might be your strengths and weaknesses. Save your checklist for a follow-up activity at the end of the chapter.

YOU AND YOUR DOCTOR

Healthy behaviors, such as eating a balanced diet, exercising regularly, and avoiding high-risk situations, can go a long way in reducing your chances of becoming sick or injured. However, sometimes these behaviors are not enough. Part of staying healthy also is knowing when to seek medical help. The best time to learn about the health-care system is before an emergency arises.

THE IMPORTANCE OF HEALTH CARE

Usually a visit to a health-care provider is associated with the diagnosis and treatment of a medical condition. However, the health-care system also provides a large number of other important services that can help you to avoid illness. Often doctors can detect potentially serious medical problems long before symptoms appear. For example, many health-care providers can perform tests to determine whether you have high blood pressure or a high cholesterol count. Doctors also can screen for certain types of cancers which, if detected early, are easy to treat. Health-care providers also are an excellent source of medical information.

CHOOSING A DOCTOR

As a teenager, you likely receive care from a doctor your parents have chosen. However, as you grow older and go off on your own, you will need to begin making your own health-care decisions. One of the first decisions you will need to make is choosing a primary-care physician. A **primary-care physician** is the doctor that you will go to for medical checkups and for treatment of most medical ailments. He or she also will keep your medical records and refer you to other doctors if you need special treatments.

Omar couldn't remember the last time he had visited a doctor. He had always felt great, so he never felt the need to have a checkup. One day when he was helping his friend Randall clean out the woodshed, Randall punctured his finger with a rusty nail. Omar offered to take Randall to the hospital. However, Randall remained calm. He had just had a medical checkup and knew that he was up-to-date on his vaccination for tetanus—a dangerous disease that can be contracted from a puncture wound contaminated by soil. Randall also knew that he could call his doctor at any time so he made an appointment with his doctor to have his wound examined.

Omar began to wonder what he would have done if he had been the one to cut himself. He didn't know whether he had had a tetanus shot recently.

Clear and open communication is one key to receiving good health care.

CONCEPT MAPPING

On a separate sheet of paper, create a concept map for *health care*. In your map, use as many of these concepts as you can: *doctor, health care, medicine, medicine label, nurse, patient, pharmacist, physical therapist, side effect*. You may use additional concepts related to health care in your map. Information about concept mapping appears at the front of this book.

THINKING CRITICALLY

INTERPRET

LESSON 26.1
1. What qualifications does a person require to be a medical doctor?

LESSON 26.2
2. What should you do if you are uncomfortable with a doctor's diagnosis and prescribed treatment?

3. What are some services the health care system provides?

4. What is the difference between an RN and an LPN?

5. For what reasons might a person receive inpatient care at a hospital?

6. Why is it important to use a hospital or clinic emergency room only in case of severe emergencies?

LESSON 26.3
7. What may be the results of having no health insurance?

8. Why is it important to understand the exclusions in your insurance policy?

9. What steps has the government taken to alleviate health-care costs for low-income or elderly patients?

10. What are the characteristics of the three major health-care reform proposals?

LESSON 26.4
11. Why is it important that people can buy prescription medicine only from a pharmacist?

12. Where can you turn if you suspect medical quackery?

APPLY

LESSON 26.1
13. When Jake went for his check-up, he was sure his doctor would yell at him for his smoking. So when she asked, Jake lied and said he wasn't smoking. Why was this a bad idea?

LESSON 26.2
14. How could a visiting nurse prevent the need for a chronically ill person to go to a nursing home?

LESSON 26.3
15. The United States is one of two industrialized nations in the world without government sponsored health insurance for all citizens. Why do you think the U.S. has not chosen to provide national health care?

LESSON 26.4
16. Three years ago, Janine had a terrible backache and her doctor prescribed a strong pain reliever. Today her backache returned. Instead of calling her doctor, she took the old pills she found in her medicine cabinet. What might happen as a result?

A Safe Environment

Chapter 27
Environmental Health

Chapter 28
Safety

What are some hidden health hazards in many American homes?

What can you do to create a safer environment for yourself?

How can environmental awareness help you maintain wellness?

CHAPTER
27

Environmental Health

BACKGROUND

Margaret Mead (1901—1978) was a social anthropologist who studied the social and ethnic cultures of people throughout the world. Much of her work was based in New Guinea and Bali. She served as curator of the American Museum of Natural History for over 25 years.

"Never doubt that a small group of thoughtful, committed citizens can change the world. Indeed, it's the only thing that ever has. . ."

Margaret Mead

Your natural environment—the air you breathe, the water you drink, and the land on which you live—is the most vital element of your daily life. Without any one of these things, life on Earth would be impossible.

The environment is, in a sense, your house, just as your body houses the complex systems that run your physical, intellectual, and emotional abilities. Preserving and caring for your environment is as important as taking good care of your body. And, like caring for your body, no one else can do it for you. Government agencies can help, as can environmental organizations, but the responsibility lies with you. Each day, you can do much to tend your environment and protect it from harmful substances, much as you protect your own body.

By taking personal responsibility for your environment, you help ensure the well-being of others as well. As with any effort, you can achieve even more by working with others. Even the smallest effort can make a big difference in your lifetime and in the lives of future generations.

SELF-ASSESSMENT

Every person needs to use materials and get rid of wastes. How well do you take care of the environment in your daily activities? Number a sheet of paper or a page in your Wellness Journal from 1-10. Write *yes* or *no* to indicate how each statement describes your environmental behavior.

1. I am aware of the environmental concerns of my community and the nation at large.

2. I fill the sink instead of letting the water run when I do dishes or wash my face.

3. I walk, ride a bike, or take public transportation whenever I can.

4. I clean things with vinegar, baking soda, and other nontoxic substances whenever possible.

5. I participate in the recycling efforts of my community.

6. I reuse bags or carry my own bag when shopping.

7. I buy recycled products and products in recycled packaging whenever possible.

8. I turn off lights in rooms that are not in use.

9. I keep the heat below 68 degrees and the air conditioning above 78 degrees.

10. I place trash in a trash can and do not litter.

Review your responses and consider what might be your strengths and weaknesses. Save your personal checklist for a follow-up activity that appears at the end of the chapter.

THE GLOBAL ENVIRONMENT

The past century has seen great advancements in human health. Vaccines and medicines have controlled diseases that at one time killed many people. Advances in farming and a better understanding of nutrition have meant that people in many parts of the world are living longer. Scientists are even beginning to unlock the mysteries of diseases such as cancer and heart disease. However, despite these advancements, the quality of our health depends ultimately on the air we breathe, the water we drink, and the land on which we grow our crops. Unfortunately, as medical knowledge and technology have improved, the quality of the things we cannot live without—air, water, and land—has grown worse.

THE ENVIRONMENT AROUND US

The **environment** includes everything that is around us—air, water, and land. No matter where you are, you are interacting with the environment. Each day you breathe in about 35 pounds of air and you drink about two and a half quarts of water. To understand how the quality of the environment affects your health and why the environment is threatened, it is important to learn about the different parts of the environment.

AIR   The air you breathe is made up of 78 percent nitrogen, 21 percent oxygen, and smaller amounts of other gases. It is oxygen that the cells of your body need to carry out basic functions. As you will learn in Lesson 2, harmful substances can be released into the air by both natural and human processes. When inhaled, these harmful substances can damage your body's ability to take up oxygen by damaging your lungs, as well as other organs.

WATER   Water covers close to three quarters of the world. Most of the water is found in oceans. However, the salt in ocean water makes it unusable for drinking, farming, and home use. Fresh water does not contain salt. Most of the fresh water you see is in streams, rivers, and lakes. However, one of the biggest sources of fresh water is **groundwater,** which is water found under the ground. It is groundwater that feeds the streams, rivers, and lakes most of the year. Groundwater is also the source of drinking water for people with wells. Therefore, it is critical that the groundwater remains clean and free from toxic chemicals.

LAND   The land on which we live is incredibly varied. Land is made up of many different types of soils, rocks, and minerals. People have constant contact with the land. However, the effect that the quality of the land has on health is indirect. People depend on the land to grow food. A shortage of quality soil as well as toxic substances in the soil can limit the growing of crops. The quality of

MAIN IDEAS

CONCEPTS

✔ Clean air and clean water are essential to health.

✔ Overpopulation poses a major threat to the environment.

✔ The United States faces many difficult environmental challenges.

VOCABULARY

environment   groundwater

How does the quality of air, water, and land affect human health?

the land also has an impact on the quality of the water. If the land becomes contaminated with toxic chemicals, these chemicals can be washed into streams, rivers, lakes, and groundwater.

PEOPLE AND THE ENVIRONMENT

At one time, human societies simply moved from place to place and left their impact on the environment behind. However, as societies began to center around towns and cities, people had to live with their impact on the environment. The human impact on the environment takes two major forms: the removal of resources and the creation of wastes.

In order for societies to function, people take resources from the environment. Land is cleared for farming as well as for building. Metals are taken from the ground. Trees are used to make paper and other wood products. Sources of energy such as oil and coal are taken from the ground. Clean sources of water also are used. The taking of these resources can permanently scar the land. Often, land that has been mined or cleared of forest has been damaged so much that it can no longer be used for forest or farming or it becomes unsafe to live on.

As much as the use of resources alters the environment, it is the production of wastes that has the most immediate effect on health. Areas with big populations produce large quantities of human waste. Dangerous chemicals are produced as by-products of industry and of the burning of coal and oil for energy. Products that people have used are thrown away. Most of the wastes produced by people are released into the air and water, or are buried underground. Too often, little consideration is given to the impact of these wastes on human health.

POPULATION   People's impact on the environment has increased as the world population has increased. The number of people in the world is growing at a tremendous rate. In 1994, the world's population was estimated to be 5.7 billion people. If current rates continue, it is estimated that the number of people will be 6.3 billion by the year 2000.

As the population increases, so does the need for resources. Increased populations mean an increased need for water, food, housing, and transportation. Increased populations also produce more wastes to be released into the air, water, and land. Demands for products and services also cause shortages of clean water, energy, and even housing. Crowding caused by population increases contributes to stress, which in turn contributes to poor health.

Overpopulation is a major problem in many developing countries. Some of the fastest rates of population growth are occurring in countries in Latin America, Asia, and Africa. In many of these countries, population has increased faster than food production. The resulting shortage of food has, in many cases, led to widespread malnutrition and starvation. Shortages of clean water have led to greater risk of disease, and many of these countries lack the medical resources to care for their people.

As populations grow, so do the demands for resources and the need to dispose of wastes.

What can happen when a country ignores the health needs of its natural environment?

THE CHALLENGE AHEAD   As people continue to create problems with the environment, it is becoming increasingly clear that action must be taken. A dramatic example of the price paid for neglecting the environment can be found in the former Soviet Union. The political changes that have taken place there and in other eastern European countries have revealed widespread environmental damage. These problems were caused by rapid development with little regard to environmental consequences. Throughout these countries, damage to the environment has directly affected the health of the citizens, in many cases contributing to severe illnesses and prolonged poor health.

   The protection of the environment is just starting to be a priority in the United States, and an enormous number of difficult challenges lie ahead. The following are just a few of the challenges that the people of the United States must face.

- The United States uses more resources, including minerals and fossil fuels such as oil, coal, and gas than any other country in the world. Many of these resources will be used up eventually.
- Cities built in parts of the United States where water is scarce are beginning to experience shortages of clean water.
- Pesticides used on many farms have been found in the groundwater in many areas.
- Tremendous amounts of toxic wastes have been produced by industry.

Despite the many environmental problems the United States faces, solutions do exist. Most of these solutions involve finding ways to use resources efficiently and finding alternatives to processes that produce wastes. All of these solutions require that everybody works together.

SUMMARY

No matter where you are, you interact with the environment. Your health depends on the air you breathe, the water you drink, and the land on which you live. However, the environment has been damaged by the overuse of resources and the release of wastes into the air, water, and ground. The rapid growth of the world's population is compounding these problems. The United States faces many environmental challenges that can be addressed through cooperative efforts.

LESSON 27.1 **USING WHAT YOU HAVE LEARNED**

REVIEW

1. Why is it vital that the groundwater remains clean?
2. Describe two effects that overpopulation has on the environment.

THINK CRITICALLY

3. Many environmental problems are occurring in countries other than the United States. Explain whether or not you think that the United States should help these countries solve those problems.
4. The population in the United States is growing at a slower rate than the populations in many other countries. Explain whether or not you think that overpopulation should be a concern in the United States.

APPLY IT TO YOURSELF

5. You are speaking to a group of high school students on the state of the global environment. What would be the most important concept that you want the students to learn?

Chattanooga Cleanup

Twenty-five years ago, Chattanooga, Tennessee, was known for two things: the song depicting its "choo choo" and its filthy air—air so filthy, that it was said it could melt the stocking right off a woman's leg. Pollution from factories and manufacturing plants contributed to the fact that Chattanooga had the highest death rates from tuberculosis and respiratory ailments in the United States.

Chattanooga sits in a lovely river valley and this makes its air quality problem worse. The pollutants generated by automobiles and industry are trapped in the valley by geographic and meteorological forces that keep air from moving up or out and being replaced by clean air.

Until 1970, the citizens of Chattanooga thought of the filthy air in their city as something they just had to live with. But when a government report cited Chattanooga as the second most polluted city in the country, next to Los Angeles, suddenly the community threw itself into the business of cleaning up.

The report that finally forced the citizens of Chattanooga into action was published in 1969. It rated 60 U.S. cities in two air-quality categories: total suspended particulate (TSP) and benzene-soluble organic particles (BSO). TSP includes particles of soot and dust that are suspended in the air and BSO is very similar except that the particles are smaller. Chattanooga's air was tested between 1961 and 1965 and the 1969 report rated Chattanooga sixtieth out of 60 cities in TSP and fifty-ninth out of 60 cities in BSO (only Los Angeles had a worse BSO rating).

Chattanooga's cleanup was not the brainchild of any one person or organization. Instead, many businesses, local government, and energized citizens got together to get tough about pollution. Manufacturers who had survived for years without adhering to government

pollution standards were asked to leave the city. Other companies installed pollution filtering and scrubbing devices to cut down their emissions of toxic chemicals. Slowly but surely, Chattanooga found the pollution rates dropping and their air quality improving.

Chattanooga's river, like its air, was also laden with sludge. Broken down industrial plants and abandoned factories lined the land area near the waterfront so that many of the city's citizens never saw the river. Inspired by the change in air quality, the city made a commitment to curbing the pollution in its river as well. The city committed 750 million dollars to revitalizing the waterfront with new buildings and a clean-up of the river. A twenty-year project that includes the building of "Riverpark" will replace dilapidated buildings with walking paths, fishing piers, and picnicking facilities. A twelve-story aquarium will be the focal point along the waterfront and will house a re-created mountain forest along with a huge waterfall, trout stream, and otter pool.

Chattanooga's successful clean-up has inspired many residents of nearby Tennessee towns to do the same thing. As a model for the state and for the entire country, Chattanooga's efforts show how citizens of one city can join together to have an important and far-reaching impact on the quality of their local environment.

1. Why might Chattanooga's citizens have thought that they just had to live with polluted air and water?

2. What kinds of things are being done in your community to prevent or clean up pollution?

HEALTH AND THE ENVIRONMENT

MAIN IDEAS

CONCEPTS

✔ Outdoor and indoor air pollution can cause short-term and long-term health effects.

✔ Water pollution is difficult to control because it can come from many sources.

✔ It is becoming more difficult to find ways to dispose of solid wastes and hazardous wastes.

VOCABULARY

pollution	chlorofluoro-
carbon	carbon
monoxide	runoff
ozone	recycling
formaldehyde	radiation

Any undesirable change to the quality of air, water, or soil due to human activities is known as **pollution**. Pollution can take many forms. It can range from chemicals that are released into air or water to the creation of conditions in which disease-causing pathogens can grow. Some progress has been made in controlling the release of many pollutants and cleaning up areas that have been polluted. However, pollution still poses a health threat to people in all parts of the United States. In order to decrease these health risks, you need to protect yourself when outdoor pollution levels become high, and reduce your exposure to pollution within your own home.

AIR POLLUTION

With each breath you take, not only do you breathe in nitrogen and oxygen, you breathe in numerous tiny particles, droplets of liquid, and gases. Many of these substances are released into the air through natural causes such as wind storms, forest fires, or volcanic eruptions. However, many harmful substances are produced by the burning of coal, oil, gasoline, wood, and tobacco. There is strong evidence that exposure to many of these pollutants can cause both short-term and long-term health problems. These problems can be especially severe for the elderly, and for people who already have long-term heart and lung disorders.

OUTDOOR AIR POLLUTION Close to fifty percent of the air pollution is generated by cars and trucks. Most of the rest of the pollution comes from coal- or oil-burning power plants and from industrial processes. Air pollution has been linked to health problems such as headaches; eye, nose, and throat irritation; and asthma attacks. Pollution also can cause increased risk of illnesses such as the common cold and the flu. Some pollutants may even increase the risk of lung cancer. The following are some of the most common types of air pollution.

Sulfur oxides   Sulfur oxides are gases produced mostly through the burning of coal and oil.

Nitrogen oxides   Nitrogen oxides are gases that are produced mostly by automobiles and the burning of coal.

Particulates   Particulates are tiny particles such as dust, soot, or ash suspended in the air. Some particulates are produced by natural sources such as volcanic eruptions or forest fires. However, many are produced by automobiles, industrial plants, and wood-burning

Nearly half of all air pollution comes from vehicles like these. What are some other sources of air pollution?

stoves. Particulates often contain chemicals that are toxic to humans. Some of the most dangerous chemicals are heavy metals such as lead.

Carbon monoxide **Carbon monoxide** is an odorless, colorless gas produced mostly by cars and trucks. Tobacco smoke also contains carbon monoxide.

Ozone **Ozone** is a type of oxygen gas that is formed when nitrogen dioxide reacts with other chemicals and sunlight. Ozone is an especially big problem in large cities.

Since the 1960s, laws have been passed that put limits on the amount of pollutants that can be released by cars, power plants, and industry. Air quality has improved since these laws have been passed. However, many cities in the United States still have pollution levels that exceed what is considered safe.

FACTORS CONTRIBUTING TO AIR POLLUTION   Many factors influence the levels of air pollution on any particular day. Wind carries pollutants away from the areas where they are produced. However, these pollutants do not disappear. Instead, they can often travel hundreds of miles to other towns or to rural areas. Sometimes weather conditions prevent pollutants from being carried away. One condition that can lead to especially high pollution levels in a small area is a temperature inversion. Normally, the temperature of the air decreases the higher you go. As you can see in Figure 27-1, warm air containing pollutants rises, moving the pollutants away from the earth's surface. However, during a temperature inversion, a layer of warm air rests on top of a layer of cooler air. This condition prevents the cooler air from rising and removing the pollutants. As a result, pollutants can build up to very dangerous levels.

In order to protect the public from high pollution levels, the local Environmental Protection Agency (EPA) forecasts the levels of different pollutants and monitors the levels of existing pollutants. If

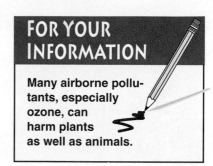
Figure 27-1   Left: Normal conditions allow pollutants to escape. Center: A temperature inversion traps pollutants near the ground. Right: the city of San Francisco under a temperature inversion

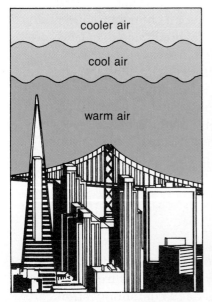

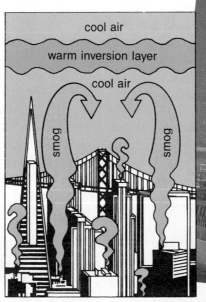

pollution reaches levels that are considered unsafe, the EPA issues a warning and recommends that all people, especially the elderly and people with heart and lung disorders, avoid any strenuous physical activity and stay indoors with the windows shut.

Inside your home, you may be surrounded by dangerous chemicals.

INDOOR POLLUTION　The pollution levels inside buildings can affect your health as much as pollution levels outside. Indoor air pollutants come from a variety of sources. Poorly-maintained coal- or oil-burning furnaces and wood-burning stoves can release dangerous levels of carbon monoxide and nitrogen oxides into the home. One of the most dangerous sources of indoor pollution is tobacco smoke. Tobacco smoke contains high levels of carbon monoxide, nitrogen oxides, sulfur oxides, particulates, and a large number of other toxic chemicals. Refer to Chapter 20, "Tobacco," for a discussion of the dangers posed by smoke inhalation.

Many home products, including furniture, carpeting, and insulation, contain dangerous chemicals that can be released into the air. One of the most common chemicals found in the home is formaldehyde. **Formaldehyde** is used as a preservative in many wood products such as countertops, paneling, and furniture. It is also used in carpeting, draperies, and foam insulation. Exposure to formaldehyde can lead to nausea, fatigue, and respiratory problems. Prolonged exposure may increase the risk of cancer.

You can limit the amount of pollutants in your home by keeping it well-ventilated and keeping your stoves and furnaces in good repair. Use household chemicals only in well-ventilated areas. Check the formaldehyde content of products before buying.

THE OZONE LAYER　As you have learned, ozone is a harmful pollutant. However, 6 to 30 miles above the ground is a layer of ozone that plays a critical role in maintaining life on the earth. This ozone layer filters out 99 percent of the ultraviolet (UV) rays from the sun. High exposure to ultraviolet rays is linked to the development of skin cancer. Years ago scientists developed chemical gases called **chlorofluorocarbons** (CFCs). Manufacturers were able to use CFCs to improve many products such as refrigerators, fire extinguishers, air conditioners, food containers, and many aerosol sprays. Scientists later discovered that when CFCs are used, they do not simply disappear. Instead, they rise up to the lower level of the ozone layer, interact with sunlight, and destroy the ozone layer. The thinning of the ozone layer allows more UV rays to reach the earth's surface. Scientists have estimated that as much as seven percent of the ozone layer has been destroyed since CFCs were developed. International treaties now exist that call for the reduction in the use of CFCs, and industries are working to produce alternative chemicals to replace them.

Pesticides applied to plants often end up in the groundwater.

WATER POLLUTION

Because water covers three quarters of the earth, it might be assumed that clean water should be plentiful. However, clean water is becoming harder to find. Many legal and community efforts are aimed at decreasing the amount of pollution and preserving the water supply. However, because there are so many sources of water pollution, the task is a difficult one.

CHEMICAL POLLUTION   The EPA has estimated that nearly 40 percent of the public water supply contains over two thousand chemicals produced by people. Many of these chemicals, including potential cancer-causing chemicals and toxic metals such as lead and mercury, are produced by industrial processes. However, industry is not the only source of pollution. Gasoline from leaking underground storage tanks and chemicals from toxic waste sites can seep through the soil and contaminate the groundwater. Pollution can also occur from runoff. **Runoff** refers to water that flows across soil or pavement after a rain. Runoff can carry chemicals such as pesticides from farms or gasoline from city streets. These chemicals are washed into lakes and rivers. Many chemicals reach the groundwater, contaminating wells and drinking water.

Old lead pipes may also be a source of pollution. If your home or school has lead pipes, lead can enter the drinking water. Consumption of lead can harm the mental and physical development of children and can lead to serious health problems in adults.

BIOLOGICAL POLLUTION   Dangerous chemicals are not the only type of pollutants that can harm the water supply. If untreated animal or human waste enters the water system, conditions can become favorable for the growth of dangerous pathogens, particularly bacteria and protozoa. In the United States, chlorine is added to the water supply to kill pathogens, making water safe for human use.

DRINKING-WATER SAFETY   Most Americans receive their water from a public water supply. All public water supplies are required to meet federal clean water standards and are therefore considered safe. People who use water from private wells should have their water tested periodically to make sure it is safe. If you have questions about the safety of the water supply, you can call state or local health officials or the local water supply company.

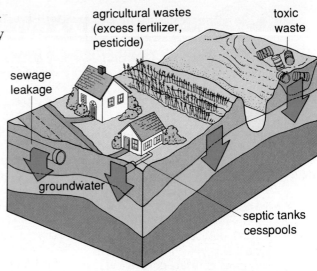

Figure 27-2 *Which of the areas in this diagram may be sources of chemical pollution? Which are sources of potential biological pollution?*

BOTTLED WATER

As concern has grown about the safety of drinking water, many people have turned to using bottled water. Bottled water can come from a variety of sources including springs, wells, and even public water supplies. In general, bottled water is no safer than public water. The safety standards are, in most cases, similar to that of public water. The EPA states that bottled water is appropriate for the protection of public health if the local water supply has somehow become contaminated. Bottled water also is recommended if you suspect you have a problem with lead in your tap water.

HEALTHY PEOPLE 2000

Increase to at least 85 percent the proportion of people who receive a supply of drinking water that meets the safe drinking water standards established by the Environmental Protection Agency.

Objective 11.9
from *Healthy People 2000: National Health Promotion and Disease Prevention Objectives*

Working Together to Preserve the Environment

Issues of pollution, hazardous waste, nuclear waste disposal, and preservation of endangered species concern the entire world. It is time to talk about creating solutions.

Until very recently, many nations did not share information about soil, air, or water contamination due to national politics. But the economic impact of imposing costly cleanup measures could be devastating to a single country without the help of others. Because one country's waste could become another country's pollution problem, no one nation has been willing to pay for environmental solutions without the help of its neighbors.

Fortunately, recognizing that preserving the environment affects not just single nations but the entire world, governments are beginning to share information and open the lines of communication. Delegations of government-sponsored environmentalists from all over the world are joining forces to discuss the successful measures they have taken in dealing with environmental issues. The United States has sent delegations to countries such as Finland, South Africa, France, Brazil, Iraq, and Turkey to explore their environmental techniques and to share resources.

Read your local newspaper to learn about current efforts at international cooperation on tough environmental problems.

STRATEGIES FOR LIVING

How to dispose of pesticides safely:

1. Never pour pesticides down the sink or into the toilet.

2. Check with your local health department to see whether there is a hazardous waste disposal program in your neighborhood.

3. If no program exists, leave pesticide in container with cap securely fastened.

4. Wrap container in newspaper and place in covered trash can.

5. Never reuse an empty pesticide container.

HAZARDOUS AND SOLID WASTE

Scientists estimate that each person in the United States produces nearly 1,300 pounds of trash each year. This trash includes paper, plastics, metals, glass, food wastes, and yard wastes. About 80 percent of this waste is buried in landfills. However, many communities are rapidly running out of space to bury their trash. One alternative to landfills is to burn the wastes at special facilities. Although burning decreases the amount of solid waste, it generates air pollution.

The most effective way to reduce the amount of waste is through recycling. **Recycling** involves the reuse of existing products such as cans or bottles or the reprocessing of old materials such as paper, plastics, or metals to create new products. Despite the effectiveness of recycling in reducing solid waste, it has been slow to catch on in the United States.

Many of the wastes produced by industrial processes are extremely toxic. These hazardous wastes are disposed of at designated sites throughout the country. However, at many of these sites, hazardous chemicals have leaked into surrounding water supplies. In one well-publicized case, a community in New York state had to be evacuated after high quantities of toxic chemicals from a nearby abandoned waste site were found in the community's water supply, sewers, and peoples' basements. These chemicals were linked to increased cases of birth defects, miscarriages, and cancer within the community.

During the 1980s, the federal government established a program to identify and clean toxic waste sites. By 1990, over 33,000 such sites had been identified. However, the cleanup of these sites is slow and costly. Laws have been passed that describe specific legal ways to dispose of hazardous chemicals. Other laws require industries to make many hazardous wastes less dangerous before disposal. Despite these laws, many industries continue to dispose of wastes illegally.

RADIATION

An environmental issue that has generated a great deal of controversy is the use of nuclear technology. Nuclear technology uses a type of energy called **radiation**. Examples of radiation include ultraviolet light and X rays. The most dangerous forms of radiation are produced by substances such as plutonium and uranium. It is these materials that are used in nuclear power plants and nuclear weapons. Exposure to large amounts of radiation is fatal. Prolonged exposure to low levels of radiation can increase the risk of cancer and can cause birth defects and miscarriages.

NUCLEAR POWER   Controversy surrounds the use of radiation in nuclear power to generate electricity. Many people view nuclear power as clean, safe, and inexpensive. Unlike coal- or oil-powered plants, nuclear power plants do not produce air pollution. However, many people question the safety of nuclear power. Two accidents, one at Three Mile Island in Pennsylvania and one at Chernobyl in the former Soviet Union, convinced many people that nuclear power plants are not safe.

NUCLEAR WASTE   One of the most difficult problems resulting from the use of nuclear technology is the disposal of radioactive waste. Radioactive waste can remain dangerous for up to 10,000 years. Therefore, it is extremely difficult to store safely. Because many communities fear the potential dangers of nuclear waste, suitable sites for storage are difficult to find. However, with over 15,000 tons of radioactive waste being generated every year, a solution will have to be found soon.

The risks associated with nuclear power have made its use controversial.

LESSON 27.2   USING WHAT YOU HAVE LEARNED

REVIEW

1. Name two sources of indoor air pollution.
2. Explain why the disposal of nuclear waste is such a difficult problem to solve.

THINK CRITICALLY

3. Many companies market products that claim to be environmentally friendly. What specific information would you need from the company to convince you that the product was indeed environmentally friendly?
4. There are many laws regulating outdoor air pollution levels but few laws regulating indoor air pollution levels. Explain whether or not you think there should be laws regulating indoor pollution levels. Why or why not?

APPLY IT TO YOURSELF

5. You are attending a public hearing on the placement of a toxic waste dump near your community. What are some of the concerns that you would want to express?

SUMMARY

Pollution can affect all aspects of the environment including air, water, and land. Air pollution, both outdoor and indoor, can result in lung disorders and greater susceptibility to infections. Toxic chemicals can enter the water from a variety of sources including industry, underground storage tanks, and runoff. Because of the tremendous amount of solid wastes, hazardous wastes, and nuclear wastes being generated each year, it is becoming more and more difficult to find safe ways of storing them.

Workers check the health of the environment through regular tests, such as this water quality test.

TAKING ACTION

You can hardly read a newspaper, watch television, or listen to a radio without being exposed to news about the environment and environmental health. The constant flow of news about the deteriorating environment can sometimes be overwhelming. Many people may conclude that there is little they can do to address the problem. However, as a responsible individual, you can have a major impact.

Improving the environment can only begin with the actions of individuals like you. In order to be an effective force for improving the environment, you first need to become educated about the environmental issues, particularly those that face your own community. Once you have learned about the issues, you can ask yourself how your behaviors may contribute to environmental problems. Then you can take action to change your behaviors.

GOVERNMENT AND ENVIRONMENTAL PROTECTION

An important part of educating yourself about environmental issues is becoming familiar with the role of government in environmental protection. As you have learned, there are many laws that set standards for clean air, clean water, and the disposal of wastes. Laws passed by the federal government in Washington, D.C. apply to the entire country. State and local governments usually pass additional laws that may address environmental problems that are unique to certain areas. The government also is in charge of enforcing environmental laws. For example, the Environmental Protection Agency is in charge of making sure pollution laws are not broken. If a company is found to have broken a pollution law, it is fined for the violation and forced to clean up the pollution it caused. If you have questions about environmental protection laws, or if you think that one of these laws has been broken, you can contact your local, state, or federal environmental authorities.

CONFLICTING PRESSURES Almost every American accepts that environmental health is an important issue. However, there is much controversy about the government's role in protecting the environment. The American government is responsible for the welfare of the country's citizens. But the country's welfare depends on several factors, and the citizens' priorities vary. Many business leaders believe that too much environmental regulation would be costly and would hurt the economy. For example, in many parts of the country, electricity is produced by burning coal. As you learned in Lesson 2, the burning of coal releases large amounts of sulfur oxides into the air.

Technology exists that can reduce the amount of sulfur oxides by 95 percent. Environmental health supporters are asking that the government require coal-burning companies to convert to this environmentally-safe technology. However, this technology is expensive. Opponents of conversion argue that the cost of using this technology would result in an increase in the price of electricity. Higher electricity costs would hurt local economies.

Because of the competing pressures on government, environmental laws try to balance a healthy environment with a healthy economy. Most environmental laws have been passed because citizens have made their concerns known. Imagine what would happen if people did not argue for environmental protection. People working in government would not have a complete picture of the needs and concerns of the citizens they serve. Therefore, by letting government officials know about your concerns, you can make a difference.

How many environmental and personal health benefits can you name that come from riding a bicycle?

BEING HEARD   As an individual, there are many ways by which you can make sure your environmental health concerns heard. However, your voice will be most effective if you are knowledgeable about the issues. You can become educated about these issues by reading the newspaper or by talking to other people who share your concerns.

Edwin had noticed that there was a strange smell in the tap water from his faucet at home. He asked his family and his neighbors whether they too had noticed the smell. Many responded that they had noticed the smell. However, they had been assured by the water department that the water was safe, and told Edwin not to worry about it. Edwin continued to be concerned, but he decided that there was not much he could do.

That week, Edwin saw a newspaper article about how the local landfill was almost filled to capacity. He had learned at school that landfills that had not been properly maintained could pollute nearby water supplies. Perhaps the landfill was the cause of the bad smell in the water. Edwin asked one of his teachers whom he could contact about his concerns. He then wrote a letter to the local water department and to the town council about his concerns. Both wrote back saying that a number of other people with similar concerns had also contacted them. As a result, they were going to look into the situation.

Writing letters to your government representatives about your concerns is one way of making your voice heard. Joining an environmental organization is another way. Environmental organizations deal with a variety of concerns ranging from local to national issues. Environmental organizations can serve several functions. They can keep you updated through newsletters on environmental issues that might concern you. They can organize activities that

HEALTHY PEOPLE 2000

Establish programs for recyclable materials and household hazardous waste in at least 75 percent of counties.

Objective 11.15
from *Healthy People 2000: National Health Promotion and Disease Prevention Objectives*

help clean up the environment and raise public awareness about environmental issues. Environmental organizations also try to influence lawmakers through a number of organized efforts.

INDIVIDUAL ACTION

Laws that protect the environment are necessary for keeping the environment clean and protecting public health. However, the most significant contributions that can be made are by individuals such as yourself. By setting an example of responsibility to the environment, you can influence others to do the same.

The united efforts of a group of individuals can accomplish a great deal. Just imagine what would happen if each person in a health class of thirty students recycled one soft drink can each school day. By the end of the school year, over 5,000 cans would be recycled. If six classrooms of thirty people recycled one can a day for the entire school year, the number of recycled cans would reach over 30,000. If this effort were extended to over 100 schools, over 3 million cans would be recycled. Now consider the potential for reducing energy consumption, reducing water use, or reducing the use of dangerous household chemicals if everyone made an effort to protect the environment.

CONSERVATION The preservation of resources is called **conservation**. As you have learned, using energy, whether it is to drive your car, heat your home, or produce electricity, is a major source of air pollution. Therefore, by conserving energy, you can help reduce pollution. Energy conservation has other advantages. By using less electricity, oil, or gasoline, you can save money. Conservation also can reduce the need to find new sources of energy or import fuels such as oil from other countries.

The best place to start when considering ways to reduce energy use is to find alternate means of transportation. Remember that close to fifty percent of the air pollution in the United States is

CONSUMER HEALTH

Safe Alternative Products

Lurking in the basement, in the garage, or under your sink may be many hazardous products that could hurt you, your family, your pets, and your environment. Many household products are full of toxic chemicals. But how do you make your house, your clothes, or your furniture shine without the use of these potentially harmful products? Here's a list of alternative products that are environmentally safe and

often less expensive than their more toxic counterparts.

- Mix white vinegar with water to clean windows.
- Use bleach to clean toilets. Bleach is safer than many commercial toilet-bowl cleaners.
- Mix washing soda with hot water to wash woodwork.
- Use olive oil or vegetable oil mixed with lemon juice to polish furniture.
- Use lemon juice mixed with salt to clean copper.

- Use baking soda as a scouring powder or mix it with water as an all-purpose cleaner.
- Mix corn starch with water to make spray starch or sprinkle corn starch with water to make a rug cleaner.

If you do choose to use a commercial product to clean your house, be sure to read the ingredients for any potentially harmful substances. Remember, you are protecting your environment as well as yourself.

generated by cars. Finding ways to reduce the use of cars is not difficult. Whenever you need to travel anywhere, consider walking or riding your bike. Not only will these alternatives reduce pollution, they also will provide you with healthy exercise. If you must travel longer distances, consider using public transportation. If you must use a car, start a car pool. You can also save energy simply by keeping your car tuned up and making sure the tire pressure is at recommended levels.

Saving energy at home can be as simple as turning out the lights when you are not using them, turning down your thermostat in the winter, and if you have air conditioning, turning up your thermostat in the summer. Other ways you can save energy at home include:

- Turn down the water heater and take shorter showers. These steps save energy used to heat water.

- Use as few pans as possible when you are cooking. Don't open the oven unnecessarily, and boil only the amount of water you need.

- Be sure your home is properly insulated and the windows have proper caulking. You reduce the amount of heat you lose in the winter and keep your house cooler in the summer.

- Purchase light bulbs that use less electricity, as well as energy-efficient appliances.

REDUCING WASTE   According to the EPA, each year Americans produce enough solid wastes to fill a convoy of trucks that can reach halfway to the moon. How can you reduce the amount of solid waste you produce? The first step you can take is to become a smart consumer. When possible, avoid buying items that have unnecessary amounts of packaging. You might even express your concern about overpackaging to the store owner. The next step you can take is to reuse as many items as you can rather than throwing

STRATEGIES FOR LIVING

Steps you can take to conserve water:

- Repair leaky faucets
- Turn off water while brushing your teeth, shaving, and soaping up in the shower.
- When doing your laundry or using a dishwasher, run full loads only.
- When hand-washing any dishes, soak all of the dishes first, then rinse them together.
- Water your lawn or garden in the morning when evaporation is lowest.
- Have water-saving devices installed on your faucets and showerheads. These devices are inexpensive and maintain a strong flow even while saving water.

Recycling conserves materials and energy and reduces pollution.

them away. For example, items such as paper and plastic bags, cardboard boxes, and bottles and jars can be reused many times. Instead of throwing away old furniture, appliances, clothing, and books, see if you can donate them to charitable organizations.

You can reduce the amounts of toxic wastes by finding alternatives to household chemicals such as pesticides, solvents and drain cleaners. Not only can these chemicals be dangerous to use, they also can be a source of water pollution. Page 713 in the Health and Safety Almanac lists some alternatives to many common household chemicals and ways to safely dispose of hazardous chemicals.

One of the most effective ways of reducing waste is through recycling. Many items, including paper, glass, metal, and some plastics, can be recycled. Even some toxic materials such as batteries and used motor oil can be recycled. Recycling saves energy and reduces pollution by reducing the need for industries to manufacture new products. The production of many products such as paper, plastic, and metal uses a lot of energy and produces many pollutants.

Despite the advantages of recycling, only ten percent of the solid wastes produced in this country are recycled. What can you do to encourage recycling? First, you should find out if there is a recycling program in your community. These programs are run either by the local government or by private community or nonprofit organizations. If there is a recycling program, find out how you can take part. Encourage your family and friends to take part as well. If there is not a recycling program in your community, see if you can help organize one. Finally, as a consumer, try to buy products that are made of recycled material or are themselves recyclable.

SUMMARY

There are many national, state, and local laws that protect the environment. Government agencies such as the EPA are charged with enforcing these laws. Despite environmental laws, a clean environment depends on individuals. You can conserve energy by driving less and by reducing energy use at home. You can reduce the amount of solid wastes you produce by reusing products, recycling, and by being a wise consumer.

LESSON 27.3 **USING WHAT YOU HAVE LEARNED**

REVIEW

1. Describe three ways you can reduce energy consumption at home.
2. Explain how, by being a wise consumer, you can reduce the amount of solid waste you produce.

THINK CRITICALLY

3. Many items such as high-efficiency light bulbs or items made out of recycled material are more expensive than standard items. Explain why these products can save you money in the long run despite the higher purchase cost.
4. Do you believe that the government should pass laws requiring recycling? Explain your answer.

APPLY IT TO YOURSELF

5. You are interviewing a candidate who is running for the town council. Write down a question that you would ask the candidate about an environmental issue that concerns you. How would you like the candidate to respond?

Cleaning Up

BEING WELL, STAYING WELL

Ben decided to clean out the garage as a birthday present to his father. He would devote the entire day to the project. Luckily, his father was gone all day, and Ben could get the project done without his dad knowing about it.

What Ben didn't know was exactly how much junk there was in the garage. It was going to be quite a project just to sort through everything, let alone straighten it out.

Ben started in one corner and sorted all of his father's tools and wood scraps. That part of the project took two hours. When he got to the cans of paint and cleaners and bags of goods to be recycled, his heart sank. "Sorting through everything and hauling it to the dump and the recycling center would take forever," he thought.

"What if he just took all of the cans, bottles, cleaners, and paint to the dump?" he thought. Ben knew he really shouldn't since many of the materials contained hazardous chemicals. He also knew he should recycle the cans and bottles. But it would take so long. Ben figured this was his only solution if he wanted to get the whole project finished on time. "Just this once," he thought, "I could dump it all. How much harm could that cause? But then what if there was something really bad in those cleaners?" He didn't want to be responsible for letting that stuff seep into the ground at the dump.

PAUSE AND CONSIDER

1. *Identify the Problem.* What is Ben's conflict about getting rid of the trash in his garage?

2. *Consider the Options.* What possible choices does Ben have about disposing of the cleaners and recyclable goods in his garage?

3. *Evaluate the Outcomes.* What could happen if Ben just took everything to the dump? What could happen if he took the time to separate everything?

Ben knew that dumping everything from the garage would be irresponsible. He couldn't do that. But he knew he couldn't possibly get everything finished in time to surprise his father. Ben decided he would try one more option before giving up on the surprise. He asked his friend Nathan to help him. "Sure," said Nathan. "But you owe me one." Ben agreed.

Together the boys worked steadily to get everything done. By four o'clock, they took their trips to the recycling center, the disposal center, and the dump. They got back by five-thirty, just as Ben's father was pulling in. "Hi guys. Staying busy?" he asked.

"Yeah, something like that," Ben laughed. "Hey Dad, do you know where your crescent wrench is?"

"Oh Ben, I haven't a clue. That garage is in such bad shape that I don't know where anything is."

"Do you mind taking a look? We kind of need it," said Ben. His father opened the garage door and couldn't believe what he saw. "Happy birthday, Dad."

DECIDE AND REVIEW

4. *Decide and Act.* How did Ben solve his dilemma about getting everything done on time and in the right way?

5. *Review.* Why would it have been wrong for Ben to dump the toxic materials, even if it was just the one time?

CHAPTER 27 ENVIRONMENTAL HEALTH 655

PROJECTS

1. The acronym "NIMBY" stands for "not in my backyard" and refers to the attitudes of many communities about hosting a disposal site for toxic wastes. Those who oppose disposal sites in their community have valid concerns about the health and safety of the people living there. However, "NIMBY" may also get in the way of conscientious waste disposal efforts. What do you think? Write an essay that evaluates the pros and cons of "NIMBY." If there are any examples from your own community, be sure to include them in your essay.

2. How many different environmental organizations exist in your area? Gather some information about each organization and make a chart that outlines the specific concerns and actions of each. Is there one particular organization you might like to join?

WORKING WITH OTHERS

With a partner, choose an environmental concern that directly affects your community such as contamination of water supplies, air pollution, or a specific factory that still exceeds federal standards for air pollution. With your partner, gather information about the nature of the problem and the steps that are being taken to solve the problem. Then write or present a report to your class about the issue. You might want to interview members of the local health department or environmental groups as part of your research.

CONNECTING TO...

HOME ECONOMICS   Create a detailed plan for how people can conserve energy at home, recycle products, and use alternative products to clean and restore their houses. Make your plan into a booklet and distribute it throughout your school.

USING VOCABULARY

carbon monoxide
chlorofluorocarbon
conservation
environment
formaldehyde
groundwater

ozone
pollution
radiation
recycling
runoff

On a separate sheet of paper, write the vocabulary words that best complete the sentences below.

1. The air, land, and water that make up the earth is called the ____.
2. The use of CFCs in products and manufacturing is being reduced because CFCs lead to damage of the ____.
3. The type of energy used in nuclear power is ____.
4. Turning in used bottles, cans, paper, and other packaging materials for reuse is called ____.
5. A colorless, odorless gas given off by automobiles, buses, trucks, and burning tobacco is ____.
6. Some wood products and household furnishings contain the chemical ____ which can affect the health of those who are exposed to it.
7. Some refrigerators, fire extinguishers, and aerosol sprays contain chemical gases called ____.
8. When rain falls on an oily surface, the resulting ____ could pollute nearby water.
9. An undesireable change to the quality of the air, water, or land due to human activity is called ____.
10. Turning down the heat, taking shorter showers, and turning off unused lights are all examples of ____.
11. The fresh water that feeds rivers, streams, and lakes most of the year is called ____.

CONCEPT MAPPING

Copy and complete the concept map shown below. Information on concept mapping appears at the front of this book.

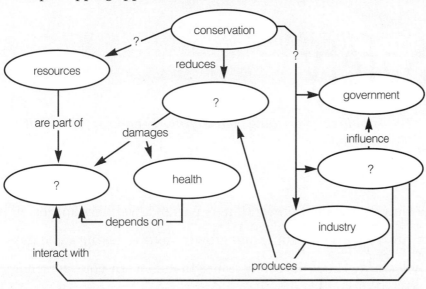

THINKING CRITICALLY

INTERPRET

LESSON 27.1
1. What are the two main ways that people leave their mark on the environment?

2. What are some of the challenges that face the global community as the twenty-first century approaches?

LESSON 27.2
3. What is one of the major sources of air pollution?

4. Why have international treaties called for a reduction in the use of chlorofluorocarbons?

5. How do many communities make sure that drinking water is free of biological pollution?

6. Why is the use of nuclear power a controversial issue?

LESSON 27.3
7. What is the role of the Environmental Protection Agency?

8. When preparing a meal, what steps can you take to conserve resources?

APPLY

LESSON 27.1
9. How could contamination of the soil of a farm in the Midwest affect a person living on the East Coast?

LESSON 27.2
10. Tim lives twenty miles away from the nearest factory, yet many mornings when he goes to work, his nose stings from the smell of sulfur. How could this factory smell be reaching his home?

11. Janelle drank bottled water because she thought it was safer than tap water. One day she found that the bottled water had a funny taste. What could be the reason for this?

LESSON 27.3
12. Why do you think the United States has been slow to respond to the idea of recycling?

Safety

"We should do everything both cautiously and confidently at the same time."

Epictetus

BACKGROUND

Epictetus was a Greek poet who was captured by the Romans and made a slave. His master saw in him a unique talent and taught him philosophy. His writings survive only through the work of one of his pupils.

Safety, or accident prevention, is part of a wellness approach to life. However, learning and growth involve taking some risks. By learning about the safety issues that concern your personal well-being at home, while traveling, working, and playing, you can become a more confident risk-taker. Accidents—one of the leading causes of death among Americans—can be avoided by planning and prevention.

Government enforces some safety regulations to ensure that its citizens remain safe on the job and within communities, but the power to prevent accidents and injuries lies with each individual. Take time to check and double-check the safety measures in your home and the equipment you use during travel or recreation. Most accidents are the result of carelessness and lack of precautions. Don't let carelessness be the cause of injury to you or your family and friends. Take the time to be safe. By doing so, you can be confident as you enjoy your everyday activities.

Think about your safety practices. Number from 1 to 11 on a sheet of paper or a page in your Wellness Journal. Write *yes* or *no* to respond to each of the following statements.

1. My home is equipped with smoke detectors.
2. I know escape routes in case of fire in my home.
3. I do not operate electrical appliances near water.
4. I make sure electrical cords are not frayed.
5. I always use a safety belt when riding in cars.
6. I always wear a protective helmet when riding a bicycle or motorcycle.
7. I never ride in a car or boat or on a motorcycle with a driver who has been drinking alcohol or taking drugs.
8. I always warm up before exercising.
9. I know the safety precautions to take during an electrical storm.
10. I know how to keep myself from drowning.
11. Before setting off for a hike or camping, I always check weather forecasts and pack accordingly.

Review your responses and consider what might be your strengths and weaknesses. Save your responses for a follow-up activity at the end of this chapter.

SAFETY AT HOME AND AT WORK

Would you be surprised to learn that accidents are the major cause of death for people under age 44? Current statistics show that every 10 minutes in the United States, 2 people are killed and 170 people suffer disabling injuries in accidents. Figure 28-1 shows the number of deaths caused by various types of accidents.

PREVENTING ACCIDENTS

Accidents are unexpected events that happen suddenly and may cause unintended loss, injury, or death. Despite what you may hear, accidents are not caused by bad luck. They are the result of unsafe acts or conditions. Many accidents can be prevented by identifying safety hazards and getting rid of them. Accident prevention, or safety, is part of your overall approach to wellness. Each person needs to choose safe ways to act and make these actions habits.

HUMAN FACTORS Decisions about ways to prevent accidents should be based on the human factors that are likely to contribute to accidents. Understanding these factors can help you develop good safety habits.

- *A person's emotional and mental state* People who are under stress, get upset, or lose their temper are more likely to have accidents than people who stay calm. When you are in a hurry, you do not concentrate well. Drinking alcohol or being overtired may be dangerous, too. Both conditions impair your judgment, and you cannot always make wise decisions and perform tasks well. People who drink and drive or people who drive when they are very tired and fall asleep at the wheel cause many automobile accidents.

■ CAUSES OF ACCIDENTAL DEATHS

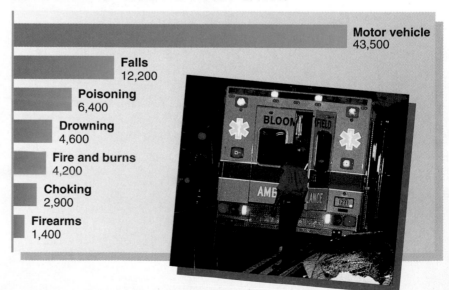

Motor vehicle
43,500

Falls
12,200

Poisoning
6,400

Drowning
4,600

Fire and burns
4,200

Choking
2,900

Firearms
1,400

Figure 28-1 *In a typical year, more people die in motor vehicle accidents than in all other types of accidents combined.*

- *Physical ability* An accident is likely to occur when a person is not able to meet the physical demands of a particular action. For example, people with a poor sense of balance are more likely than others to fall when walking or climbing stairs. Young children are not able to lift or move large or bulky objects or cross the street safely without the help of an adult.

- *Making the surroundings safe* A third factor involves keeping surroundings safe and equipment in good repair. Accidents are prevented by removing potential safety hazards from the environment.

AGENCIES THAT HELP Accident prevention is an individual responsibility. However, there are agencies that can help you learn how to prevent accidents and what to do if an accident occurs. The National Safety Council is a private agency that works to prevent accidents and collects statistics on accidental deaths and injuries. It has almost 100 state and local branches in the United States and Canada. The American National Red Cross works to increase safety throughout the United States. The Red Cross offers courses in first aid, lifesaving, and handling small water craft. The Red Cross also aids communities following disasters.

What human factor could contribute to an accident as the toddler attempts to climb the stairs?

SAFETY AT HOME

More than 24 million people are injured at home each year. Thousands of people die and many more are injured from falls, fires and burns, poisoning, and contact with electrical current. Many of these accidents can be prevented.

Claudia wanted to replace the mirror in her bathroom, but she could not find the stepladder. She could either wait for her mother to return later to help her find the stepladder or use the rocking chair from her bedroom to stand on. As she began carrying the rocking chair out of the bedroom, she sighed, put it back in place, and decided to wait for the stepladder.

FALLS Falls account for one third of all injuries and deaths at home. Many young children do not have the balance needed to go up and down stairs safely. Some elderly people cannot see well or have poor balance. Hazards such as unsteady ladders and stepladders, slippery floors, and clutter on floors and stairways are dangerous to everyone.

To prevent falls, put nonskid padding under throw rugs. In the bathroom, use nonslip bath mats and rugs. If you have an elderly family member at home, you might consider installing grab bars in the shower and tub, a seat for the tub, and an elevated toilet seat. If there are young children in the family, put a gate at the bottom and top of every staircase and keep cellar doors locked. Do not leave toys, games, books, and other articles on the floor or stairs where people might trip over them.

HEALTHY PEOPLE 2000

Reduce deaths from falls and fall-related injuries to no more than 2.3 per 100,000 people.

Objective 9.4
from *Healthy People 2000: National Health Promotion and Disease Prevention Objectives*

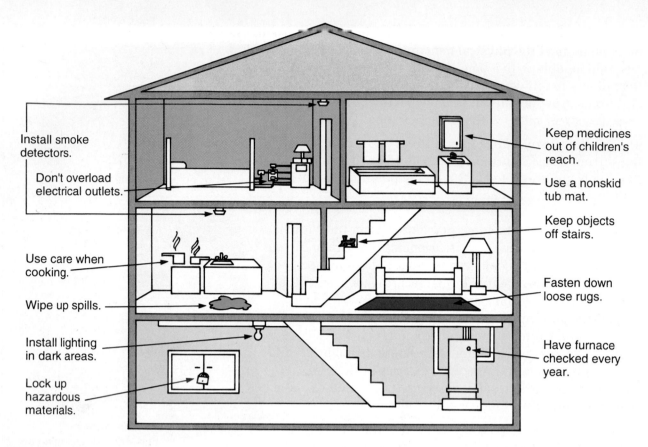

Install smoke detectors.

Don't overload electrical outlets.

Use care when cooking.

Wipe up spills.

Install lighting in dark areas.

Lock up hazardous materials.

Keep medicines out of children's reach.

Use a nonskid tub mat.

Keep objects off stairs.

Fasten down loose rugs.

Have furnace checked every year.

Figure 28-2   Accident prevention in the home is the responsibility of the whole family. What could you do to help make your home safer?

STRATEGIES FOR LIVING

To prevent poisoning:

- Keep medicines and cleaning products in their own containers and out of the reach of children.

- Buy products with child-resistant caps, or lock up medicines and poisons.

- Read the directions each time you use a poisonous product.

- Teach children to ask before taking any medicine, and never refer to medicine as candy. Avoid taking medicines in front of children.

- Dispose of all old medicines by flushing them down the toilet.

FIRES   Most burn deaths in homes are caused by careless use of matches, cigarette lighters, and cigarettes. Cooking accidents and faulty heaters and furnaces also cause home fires and burns. Early detection is your best protection from fire. Most home fire deaths happen at night when people are sleeping. Smoke detectors can give family members the warning they need to get out of the house quickly and safely.

Regular fire drills are an important part of home safety. Have a specific place to meet so that you can quickly discover if anyone is missing. In the event of fire, get everyone out of the house *immediately*. Call the fire department from a neighbor's house. Never go back into a burning building to save pets or possessions.

POISONING   Keep the number of the nearest poison control center next to your telephone. A **poison control center** is a telephone service that provides emergency medical advice about poisons. If an accidental poisoning occurs, call the poison control center immediately. Tell the person who answers what was swallowed and how much was swallowed. You may be told to make the victim vomit or to neutralize the poison with another substance. Follow exactly the directions given to you by the poison control center worker.

ELECTRICAL HAZARDS   Faulty wiring, faulty appliances, damaged cords, or outlets that are overloaded may cause fires. They also may cause serious burns or electrocution if a faulty cord or appliance is touched. **Electrocution** is death caused by electric shock.

House Inspector

CAREERS
HEALTH

John Heyn has looked at over 10,000 houses to decide whether or not to buy. He is not doing the buying, however. He is helping potential buyers determine whether the houses will be dream houses or nightmares. John Heyn is a house inspector.

When looking for a house inspector, most consumers turn to the American Society of Home Inspectors (ASHI). Most ASHI members have college degrees in construction-related disciplines such as engineering or architecture and have performed at least 250 home inspections. Members without degrees have performed 750 home inspections. All ASHI members have taken and passed three exams on home construction and mechanical systems.

House inspectors know about electricity, construction, plumbing, roofing, insect infestation, heating systems, and hazardous materials. House inspectors have two basic goals when they inspect houses. First, they evaluate the existing sys-

tems. Second, they assess needed repairs. The inspection begins at the top of the house and continues through the cellar or under the house. Inspectors' tools include an extension ladder, binoculars to inspect out-of-reach areas, and a standard form that is filled in as the inspection progresses.

The cost of a house inspection varies with the size of the house. Inspections usually take two to three hours. Many inspectors choose to work for themselves and enjoy the benefits of a freelance lifestyle. Others work for larger companies. Most inspectors get their business through real-estate broker referrals and through word of mouth.

Without the services of a house inspector, many uninformed buyers would walk into a nightmare of high repair bills and broken systems. The home inspection industry has made a difference for millions of home buyers as they approach one of the most important decisions of a lifetime.

1. What reasons might a home-buyer have for wanting an inspection before offering to buy a house?
2. Why do you think it is important for house inspectors to have professional training?

To prevent electrocution, never use electric tools or appliances in wet areas. For example, never plug in a hair dryer or radio with wet hands or use an appliance while you are in the tub or shower. Do not mow wet grass with an electric mower. Teach children not to fly kites or climb trees near power lines. Cover wall sockets with safety caps if there are young children in the house.

TOOLS AND MACHINERY   Whenever you use tools and machines, use them correctly. If you are not sure how to use them, find an experienced neighbor, friend, or professional who can help you. Any money or time saved by doing a home repair yourself may be lost if you injure yourself as you make the repair.

SAFETY AT WORK

Accidents at work affect both the worker and the employer. The employer loses a worker who often has special skills, experience, and knowledge. The worker may need medical treatment, suffer physical and mental pain, and lose his or her independence and source of income if he or she becomes disabled for life.

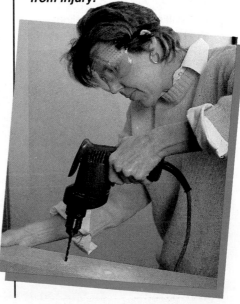

While using tools, wear safety goggles to protect your eyes from injury.

On-the-job accidents can be avoided through the use of appropriate safety equipment.

EMPLOYERS' RESPONSIBILITIES Since the early 1900s, elimination of safety hazards on the job has reduced accidental deaths in work settings by more than 75 percent. Federal and state safety regulations play a large role in job safety. One federal agency, the Occupational Safety and Health Administration (OSHA), establishes and enforces safety regulations in factories and businesses. However, OSHA regulations do not apply to farms. Because they work for themselves, farmers are free to establish and enforce their own safety rules. Unfortunately, many serious injuries are caused by careless use of farm machinery each year.

Companies that use heavy equipment, such as manufacturing and construction companies, usually have a higher accident rate than companies that do not use heavy equipment. Many companies have started safety education programs for their workers. Some workers are exposed to toxic substances or radiation whose harmful effects may take several years to appear. Many states require that workers be told about the dangers of using harmful materials on the job.

WORKERS' RESPONSIBILITIES Although employers can help safeguard workers, each worker is responsible for his or her safety on the job. Wear the protective clothing and gear required by your employer. If you notice a safety hazard where you work, tell your supervisor. If the hazard is not removed, contact OSHA. If all else fails, consider looking for another job. Your well-being is too important to risk serious injury or death.

SUMMARY

Developing good safety habits and making your surroundings as safe as possible are the best ways to prevent accidents. Try to be in a safe mental and physical state when involved in any activity. Try to make your home and work areas safe, too.

LESSON 28.1 USING WHAT YOU HAVE LEARNED

REVIEW

1. Identify three human factors that contribute to accidents.
2. Why are falls particularly common among older people?
3. What is OSHA and what are its functions?

THINK CRITICALLY

4. Martha has a summer job as a waitress. She was told to wear sturdy, closed shoes to work, but would rather wear sandals. Identify two safety reasons for wearing closed shoes while working in a restaurant.
5. You notice that an electrical outlet in your home is hot to the touch. What should you do?

APPLY IT TO YOURSELF

6. Plan a fire drill routine for your family. Draw a diagram of your home and clearly mark on it all the possible exit routes from the home. Post the diagram at home. Write a short persuasive speech to encourage your family to have fire drills regularly.

SAFETY ON THE ROAD

More people in the United States have died from automobile accidents than have died in all the wars this country has ever fought. Most safety experts say that many automobile deaths and injuries could be prevented.

AUTOMOBILE SAFETY

Drivers between the ages of 15 and 24 are the most likely to have an automobile accident, even though they generally have better reflexes and coordination than older drivers. Teenagers and young adults could have a good safety record if they followed the rules for safe driving.

DRIVING SAFELY   Driving safely begins with learning the rules of the road. Drivers' education courses are available in many states. Successful completion of such a course may lower your insurance rates. Drive only if you have a valid license, and never allow or encourage anyone without a valid license to drive. Obey traffic signs and signals and obey the speed limit.

A driver's condition is a very important factor in accidents. Alcohol is involved in more than half of all fatal accidents in this country. Safe driving means never driving when under the influence of alcohol or drugs, including over-the-counter medications. Many medicines for colds and allergies can cause you to feel dizzy or sleepy, slow your reflexes, and impair your judgment.

- *Don't tailgate.*   **Tailgating** is driving so closely behind the car in front of you that you could not stop safely or swerve to avoid a collision in an emergency. Keep a safe distance between your car and the car in front of you. If the driver behind you is tailgating, pull over and let the car pass.

- *Learn to be a defensive driver.*   A **defensive driver** is one who is prepared to respond to the driving errors of others. You can avoid accidents by being aware of traffic all around you. Be prepared for what drivers around you might do. Think about where you might see pedestrians (people on foot) and be prepared for their actions.

- *Stay alert.*   Do not let other passengers or the radio or tape deck distract you. If you stop paying attention for even a second, you could have an accident.

- *Keep your vehicle in good repair.*   Headlights or turn signals that do not work, worn brakes, and worn tires are a few of the mechanical problems that cause accidents.

- *Prepare for poor road conditions.*   Heavy rainstorms, icy roads, bad visibility, and roads in poor repair endanger your safety and the safety of your passengers. When road conditions are poor, pull off the road until conditions improve, or find another route if the roadway is hazardous.

MAIN IDEAS

CONCEPTS
✔ Both drivers and pedestrians can act wisely and prevent accidents.

✔ The rules of the road apply to all vehicles.

VOCABULARY
tailgating
defensive driver

The frequency of automobile accidents increases during bad weather. If you must drive in severe weather, be even more careful than usual.

Buckling up is a quick and easy way of reducing the risk of serious injury in an automobile accident.

WEARING A SEAT BELT More accidents happen on city streets than on highways. A crash at a speed as low as 12 miles per hour can kill. The force of a collision is usually so great and so sudden that people in an automobile or truck cannot control the movements of their bodies. Rear seat passengers usually are thrown into the front seat. Front seat passengers usually are thrown against the dashboard or through the windshield. People who are thrown free of the vehicle may scrape along the ground, be hit by other cars, or even be crushed by their own car. Wearing seat belts can help people avoid injury in almost every auto accident. Passengers can unbuckle the belt quickly and escape from the car if necessary. Wearing a seat belt may help the driver keep control of the vehicle, often reducing the seriousness of the accident.

Josef borrowed his dad's car to take friends to a basketball game. His dad had a strict rule about seat belts: everyone in the car must wear them. Josef was afraid that his friends would give him a hard time about the seat belts. He also thought that his dad's rule was good. When he picked up his friends, Josef took a deep breath and told them to buckle up. They did, without any comment.

When you are driving, you are responsible for the safety of everyone in your car. Make sure all your passengers wear seat belts. Studies show that most people are willing to wear seat belts if told by the driver. Keep children secure in safety belts or child safety seats for their own safety and to keep them from distracting the driver.

MOTORCYCLES AND BICYCLES

Motorcycles and bicycles are very dangerous if they are not ridden carefully. A two-wheel vehicle is less stable than a car or truck.

MOTORCYCLES Motorcyclists are eight times as likely to be injured or killed in accidents as are people in more-protected vehicles. The rules for safe motorcycle travel are similar to those followed by any safe driver.

Cyclists should know how to operate their vehicles and keep them in good shape. Nearly 20 percent of all motorcycle accidents are caused by problems such as brake failure or by riding a bike that is too large for the driver. Cyclists must follow all traffic laws. Many states have helmet laws to protect motorcyclists from injury during falls.

BICYCLES Bicycle riding is an inexpensive way to get around. It is also a popular recreational activity. People ride bicycles on streets, in parks, and in other recreation areas. Some communities allow people to ride bicycles on sidewalks. Keep your bicycle in good working condition. Whenever you ride, follow your community rules and the traffic rules. Be courteous to pedestrians, children at play, and those in other vehicles.

BICYCLE SAFETY

When you use a bicycle for transportation and fun, follow some simple guidelines to ensure safety and fun for everyone.

- *Obey all traffic rules.*
- *Be careful at intersections and use hand signals.*
- *Ride single file on the right side of the road.*
- *Watch out for doors opening on parked cars.*
- *Do not ride with two or more people on a bike or play games in traffic.*
- *Watch out for holes in the road that may cause falls, and report them to your local government.*
- *Wear a helmet to prevent head injuries to yourself.*
- *Always wear reflective clothing or strips, especially at night.*
- *Make sure you have front and back bicycle lights.*

Obey all traffic rules when riding your bicycle on roadways.

PEDESTRIAN SAFETY

For their safety, pedestrians need to know the laws governing traffic. As a pedestrian, you are at risk when entering a street. Use crosswalks and always look both ways before you cross. Listen for traffic, too, as you look both ways, especially at dawn, dusk, or nighttime. Do not assume that you can see all the cars approaching you, and do not count on drivers to see you.

If there is no sidewalk along your route, walk on the left side of the road so that you can watch for oncoming traffic. When walking at night, wear light-colored clothing or carry a flashlight. When jogging under low-light conditions, wear reflective clothing or strips of reflective material. Do not hitch a ride or get into a car with a stranger.

LESSON 28.2 **USING WHAT YOU HAVE LEARNED**

REVIEW

1. Identify three personal conditions under which you should not drive.
2. What is a defensive driver?

THINK CRITICALLY

3. Crossing a busy street can present many hazards. Identify three precautions that could be taken to avoid injury.
4. An important part of bicycle safety is taking precautions to avoid injury. Why is it important to wear a helmet when riding a bicycle?

APPLY IT TO YOURSELF

5. Your local community is thinking about adding bicycle lanes to the major street in town. Would you support the addition of bicycle lanes in your community? Explain your answer.

SUMMARY

The major cause of vehicular accidents is alcohol and drug use while driving. Other causes include disobeying traffic rules, faulty equipment, and poor driving conditions. When driving, biking, or walking, assume that people around you may do the unexpected. Pay attention at all times so that you will be alert enough to handle whatever situations occur while you are driving.

RECREATIONAL SAFETY

Recreational activities are fun, good exercise, and a way to relax after school or work. However, every year more and more people get hurt during recreational activities. Many recreational injuries and accidents can be prevented with a little common sense and some knowledge about safety.

SPORTS

Shin splints and tennis elbow are complaints often experienced by fitness-minded people. Many people are weekend athletes, playing a favorite sport on the weekend and doing no physical activity during the week. Sports injuries can be avoided by a regular program of fitness that develops strength. When doing any hard physical activity, remember to warm up and cool down gradually. Be sure you have the proper equipment. Learn the necessary skills and safety rules for your particular sport, and follow them.

WATER SPORTS

Swimming, fishing, boating, and waterskiing are popular forms of recreation. However, any water activity carries with it the risk of drowning. A great many of those who drown every year are teenagers, mostly teenage boys. About one third of these deaths result from swimming or playing in water. The other two thirds happen when people fall into the water from bridges, docks, or boats. Recent studies show that about one third of all recreational boating deaths are connected to alcohol use. About two thirds of all drowning victims have drunk alcohol before entering the water. Never mix alcohol and water activities.

Figure 28-3 *The steps of drownproofing: (1) Float with your face in the water, legs slightly tucked. (2) When you need to breathe, slowly raise your arms and stretch out your legs and exhale into the water. (3) Raise your head just far enough to take a breath through your mouth. (4) Slowly return to the resting position.*

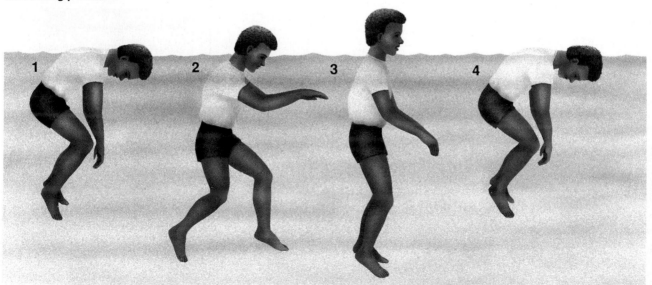

SWIMMING AND DIVING   One of the best ways to prevent drowning is to learn to swim. Even if you know how to swim, always swim with another person who could run for help if necessary. Swim only at supervised beaches and pools.

Even good swimmers can drown when they become very tired. A technique called drownproofing can help prevent drowning. **Drownproofing** is a system of rhythmic breathing and vertical floating that helps you save energy in a water emergency. You can use this technique for hours without getting tired. Do not remove your clothing. Clothing adds to your ability to stay afloat and also keeps in body heat. The drownproofing technique can be used by everyone, from good swimmers to those who cannot swim at all.

Diving accidents are the major cause of spinal cord injuries in this country. Young men between the ages of 15 and 30 have 90 percent of all diving accidents. Most diving accidents result in paralysis. To avoid injury when diving, know the water depth and test the area by jumping feet first before diving. Look for hidden rocks or currents in the water. Never dive in the shallow end of a pool.

BOATING   Boating is a popular activity. Warm weather finds shorelines, lakes, and rivers dotted with sailboats and power boats of all kinds. Safe boating requires some knowledge, care, and common sense. Before setting out, check the weather forecast and the condition of the boat. Forgo the trip if bad weather is forecast or if the boat is not in good running order. Let someone on shore know where you plan to go and when you plan to return. Have an approved flotation device aboard for each passenger. Keep a fire extinguisher on board. Know how to operate your

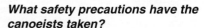

FOR YOUR INFORMATION

Even a strong swimmer should wear a flotation vest during water sports. An accident might knock the person unconscious or otherwise make the person unable to swim.

WATERSKIING SAFETY

Waterskiing is a sport enjoyed by many people. Avoid serious injuries by taking these precautions.

- Water-ski only if you know how to swim. Wear a flotation device while waterskiing.
- Never ski at night or in shallow water.
- The law requires two people to be on board a boat pulling a water-skier, one to drive and one to watch the water-skier at all times.
- If you fall, hold up a ski as a signal for other boaters. Your boat driver should stop the boat while the second person aboard assists you into the boat.

Bicycle Helmets

Each year as many as 1,000 people die as a result of injuries related to bicycling. According to some estimates, eighty-five percent of these injuries could have been prevented with the use of a bicycle helmet.

Riders who do not wear helmets complain that they are uncomfortable or that they "look funny" if they use a helmet. Today there are many styles to choose from, and manufacturers have designed helmets to be light and durable.

When choosing a helmet, it is important to check that it has been approved by the American National Standards Institute or by the Snell Memorial Foundation. Use a helmet for five years and then replace it. If you are in an accident, send the helmet to the manufacturer, who will inspect it and often replace it free of charge. Here are a few more tips for selecting and using a bicycle helmet.

- Check for shock absorbency. The liner should be at least half an inch thick and should be stiff to absorb the shock of a fall.

- Try on several helmets for comfort and fit. The helmet should be well-ventilated and should hold your head firmly.

- Buy a helmet with a hard outer shell of polycarbonate or fiberglass.

- Make sure the helmet can be fastened securely with a snug chin strap and buckle.

- Encourage children to wear helmets. Most accidents occur to children between the ages of 5 and 14.

boat and follow the rules of the waterway. Slow down when passing other boats or when near beaches. Do not bring the boat near swimming areas. Never carry more passengers than the boat allows, and enter and move about on the boat one at a time. Do not operate a boat while using alcohol or other drugs.

WATER SCOOTERS Water scooters, or jet skis, are growing in popularity. With increased use, the number of water scooter accidents has increased. Most water scooter accidents result from mistakes by the rider. Some riders go too fast and turn too quickly. Some cannot swim. Some fail to wear flotation devices. Others operate the water scooters at night or under the influence of alcohol or other drugs. Like all other recreational vehicles, water scooters can be used safely if they are used properly.

OFF-ROAD VEHICLES

Off-road vehicle use is fun but can be dangerous. To use these machines safely, follow all precautions listed on the vehicle. Learn how to ride from an experienced rider. Do not speed or turn too sharply. Wear a safety helmet. Use the vehicle as recommended by the manufacturer.

ROLLERBLADING AND SKATEBOARDING

Rollerblading and skateboarding require good balance, good vision, and quick responses. Both of these activities can be dangerous if they are done carelessly. Before you set out, know the area. Stick to smooth paved surfaces. Wear protective gear, such as helmets and knee and elbow pads. Watch for pedestrians and for children at play. Don't wear headphones that obstruct your hearing. Be courteous to others around you.

HIKING AND CAMPING

Hiking and camping are popular outdoor activities. They may seem to be risk-free activities, too. However, many people find themselves in unexpected, dangerous situations on a hike or a camping trip. In most cases, these situations can be avoided by good planning.

Know the terrain you will be covering on a hike, and know the weather forecast for the area. Bring appropriate clothing and gear and adequate food and water. Wear the proper shoes for your planned activities. Tell someone where you are going and when you plan to return. Carry a first aid kit.

HUNTING AND TARGET SHOOTING

In many parts of the country, the changing of the seasons means more than a change in temperature. It also means the arrival of a new hunting season. Hunting is a year-round recreational activity that is enjoyed by many people. Unfortunately, every year about 100,000 people are injured because of the improper use of firearms, and about 2,000 of them die. Those under the age of 24 are most likely to be involved in firearm accidents. Most accidents happen when people are cleaning weapons or playing with them carelessly.

If you use a gun, you should be trained to use it correctly. Everyone in the household of a gun owner should be taught to respect firearms and follow firearm safety rules. The rules apply to any type of gun, including air rifles and BB guns.

FIREARM SAFETY

Ownership of a gun brings with it a great deal of responsibility. Tragic accidents can be avoided by following some basic safety rules.

- Always treat a gun as if it were loaded.
- Never point a gun at anyone.
- Store guns unloaded, locked up, and out of the reach of children.
- Store ammunition separately from guns.
- When you are carrying a gun, keep the gun barrel pointed down.
- Never lean a gun against a tree, wall, or vehicle.
- When traveling, carry guns unloaded until you are ready to begin hunting or target practice.
- Keep the safety catch on until you are ready to shoot.
- Know and obey the laws for hunting in your state.

LESSON 28.3 USING WHAT YOU HAVE LEARNED

REVIEW

1. What is drownproofing?
2. List five rules for safe boating.
3. List four rules for the safe use of firearms.

THINK CRITICALLY

4. Why might nighttime waterskiing be dangerous?
5. Why do you think many people fail to take simple precautions that could prevent recreational injuries?

APPLY IT TO YOURSELF

6. Imagine that you are a parent and your teenage daughter has saved just enough money for rollerblades. What advice would you give her about whether or not to buy the rollerblades?

SUMMARY

Recreational activities are a good way to relax. Common sense and a little knowledge can prevent many of the accidents and injuries suffered during recreational activities. Learning the drownproofing technique, using vehicles and equipment properly, and planning activities carefully are three ways to reduce risk.

THINKING CRITICALLY ABOUT

Crime Prevention

HEALTHY PEOPLE 2000

Extend coordinated, comprehensive violence prevention programs to at least 80 percent of local jurisdictions with populations over 100,000.

A coordinated, comprehensive effort by State and local health, criminal justice, and social service agencies is necessary to maximize resources and ensure the availability of violence prevention strategies and information to all segments of the population.

Objective 7.17

from *Healthy People 2000: National Health Promotion and Disease Prevention Objectives*

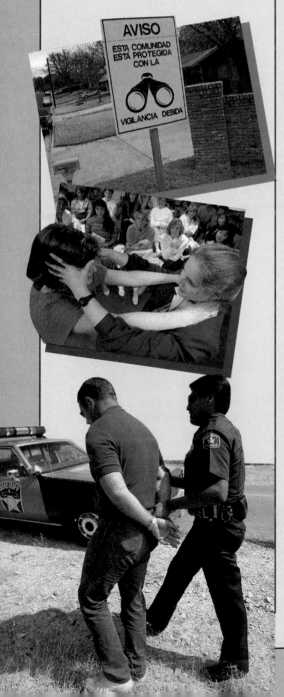

No one wants to be the victim of a crime. However, at least one member of nearly five million households in the United States has experienced some sort of violent crime.

In a recent year, there were close to six million violent crimes committed in the United States. Most crimes were committed in urban areas with populations of 250,000 to 500,000. Fewer crimes were reported in suburban or rural areas, but these areas are not crime-free. Up to 14 percent of crimes occur in the home, and most other crimes are committed near home, in cars, or at the homes of relatives or friends.

Due to stepped-up efforts by neighborhoods, police departments, and individuals, the number of crimes around the country can slowly decrease. You can help. By following safety precautions, by using good sense, and by involving yourself in your community's efforts to reduce crime, you can work with the nation to meet the health goals of the year 2000.

CRIME BEAT

The National Crime Survey reports that the overall figures on rapes, robbery, and assault dropped between 1981 and 1989. However, the incidence of some types of crimes increases each year. Assaults and robberies that take place in and around automobiles, for instance, have been on the rise. Also on the rise is acquaintance rape, or date rape. The number of crimes committed by people under the influence of drugs and alcohol is also increasing.

Some researchers suggest that date rape may not have actually increased, but rather that more and more date rapes have been reported in recent years. Rape is a violent crime, not a sexual one. Most rapes are committed by someone known by the victim. Women are the victims of most, but not all, rapes.

There are no easy solutions to the problem of crime. Community resources are helping people prevent crimes in their neighborhoods and homes. The Neighborhood Crime Watch program, for example, has increased awareness among people and encouraged them to keep an eye out for unusual activities in their neighborhoods. Police departments around the country are enlisting the help of neighborhoods and individuals to streamline reporting and implement safety programs.

SAFETY WATCH

Efforts are being stepped up to reduce the number of crimes in the United States, and you can take steps to protect yourself.

1. Travel in pairs or groups as often as you can. If you walk alone at night, walk with purpose—as if you know where you are going and as if someone is waiting for you at your destination. Stick to well-lit areas and walk near the curb.

2. If you have a breakdown on the street or highway while traveling alone in a car, put up your hood, tie a rag to the car antenna, lock the car doors, and wait for the police. If someone stops to help you, thank him or her and ask that person to call the police for you. Do not accept a ride from anyone you do not know.

3. Park in well-lit areas or garages with parking attendants on duty. Lock your car and have your keys ready upon returning to your car, so that you will not fumble to find them at the car door. Check the back seats and floor of the car before you get in. If someone approaches while you are in the car, lock the doors, honk the horn, and drive away quickly.

4. Do not go anywhere alone with someone you just met. If you are interested in pursuing a relationship with that person, agree to meet in a public place until you are completely comfortable with the person.

5. Remember, no one should touch your body without your permission. If someone makes advances toward you or makes comments that make you feel uncomfortable, make your feelings known clearly and calmly. If the person persists, remove yourself from the situation.

6. Avoid situations with people who have been drinking heavily or abusing drugs. Find a safe ride home.

7. Immediately report any crime to the police. Do not intervene in a crime, but call out from a distance or run to get help.

8. Participate in a neighborhood-watch program or a crime prevention and safety program through your school.

WHAT DO YOU THINK?

1. What actions might you be able to take to try to avoid being a crime victim?

2. What would keep a victim of date rape from reporting the crime? Why do you think more people are reporting date rape today?

3. Have you discussed a safety plan to prevent crime in the home with people in your household?

4. In addition to those mentioned in the text, what safety precautions might you take while riding on the highway?

SAFETY DURING EMERGENCIES

MAIN IDEAS

CONCEPTS

✔ Communities have plans for when disasters strike.

✔ Severe weather conditions and earthquakes are some causes of natural disasters.

✔ Planning and preparation for an emergency can increase your chances of coming through the emergency safely.

VOCABULARY

civil defense agency
tornado watch
tornado warning

Storms, floods, earthquakes, and other natural disasters cause property damage, personal injury, and death. No one can control the weather or stop an earthquake. However, people can prepare for natural disasters in order to lessen the damage they cause.

PLANNING FOR EMERGENCIES

Most communities have a disaster plan. The planners usually include representatives from the police, the fire fighters, local hospitals, the local Red Cross chapter, and members of local public health and civil defense agencies. A **civil defense agency** is an organization concerned with protecting the community. When a disaster occurs, the community can swing into action following its plan and respond quickly to those in need of help.

SEVERE WEATHER CONDITIONS

With modern weather satellites and other weather-tracking equipment, it is now possible to forecast most types of severe weather conditions. Warnings are usually given before bad weather hits so people have time to prepare. You may need to stock up on food, water, flashlights or candles, batteries, and medicines. Be ready to follow the instructions given by local or state authorities.

LIGHTNING Lightning kills about 150 people in the United States each year and injures about 250 people. To keep yourself safe during a lightning storm, go indoors and stay there. Avoid touching metal objects, and do not talk on the telephone unless absolutely necessary. Unplug electrical appliances to protect them from power surges.

LIGHTNING SAFETY

If you are outdoors when a lightning storm occurs, immediately seek shelter.

- Do not take shelter under a tree or stand in the open. Lightning often strikes the tallest or highest object in an area.

- Some automobiles offer good protection in a lightning storm because of the "skin effect." The metal frame will divert a lightning strike around you and to the ground if you are inside, surrounded by the metal frame, and not touching the outside of the car.

- Avoid tractors and other farm machines.

- If you are caught out in the open, lie down in the lowest place you can find.

- Do not enter a body of water.

FLOODS Flooding is a frequent result of severe rainstorms. Melting mountain snow in the spring may also cause floods along rivers and streams. If you are in an area that is likely to flood, have an emergency plan ready in case a flood warning is issued.

If you are in a car and it stalls because of high water, leave it immediately and get to higher ground. Pay attention to signs that warn about flooded bridges or roads. Many people have drowned because they thought they could drive through a flooded area.

Digging out after a blizzard or heavy snowfall is hard physical work. Avoid injuries while digging out by dressing warmly, using appropriate tools, and being careful not to overexert yourself.

BLIZZARDS   Blizzards are dangerous snowstorms with high winds. The snow whips around, making it difficult to see beyond a few yards. When a blizzard strikes, stay where you are. The winds of a blizzard often damage power lines, so stay indoors and prepare for a power shortage. If the heat goes off during a blizzard, there are several ways to keep yourself warm. Dress warmly using layers of clothing. Wear a wool hat, especially when sleeping. Sleep under several light-weight blankets rather than one very heavy blanket.

If you live in a state where blizzards occur, you would be wise to carry blankets, a shovel, and snacks in your automobile during the winter. If you are trapped in a car during a blizzard, stay in the car. Run the motor for brief periods a few times every hour for heat. To avoid the buildup of carbon monoxide, open the windows a little when the motor is running. Be sure the tail pipe is clear of snow so that fumes will exhaust properly. Try to move around and do not go to sleep. Turn on the light inside the car so that rescue groups will see you.

HURRICANES   A hurricane is a tropical storm with heavy rains and winds of more than 75 miles per hour. In the United States, hurricanes most often strike coastal areas between Texas and Florida and from Florida to the New England states.

TORNADOES   Tornadoes can cause great damage in seconds. Wind speeds inside their twisting clouds may reach as high as 400 miles per hour. Tornadoes

HURRICANE SAFETY

If a hurricane is forecast:

- Keep informed by listening to local weather reports.
- Secure your living area by boarding up or taping windows.
- Bring in items, such as lawn chairs, that could be tossed about in heavy winds.
- Stay away from shore areas in case they are swept by high waters.
- Do not drive if the storm is close by.
- When driving after the storm, be alert for fallen tree branches, scattered rocks, and holes in the road.

TORNADO SAFETY

If a tornado is approaching:

- *If you have a basement, go to it. Otherwise, find the smallest room with the strongest walls and no window, usually a bathroom, on the lowest level of the house.*

- *If you are in a mobile home or are not near your house, go to the nearest shelter.*

- *In open country, move at right angles away from the tornado's path. Lie down in a ditch or low area if there is no time to escape.*

have occurred in every state of the continental United States, but the central states have the most tornadoes. A **tornado watch** is issued when weather conditions are favorable for a tornado to develop. When a tornado is sighted by a person or on radar, a **tornado warning** is issued . If a tornado warning is issued for your area, seek shelter immediately.

EARTHQUAKES

In the United States, most earthquakes seem to occur along the West Coast. However, earthquakes can happen anywhere. Although they usually last only a few seconds, earthquakes can bring down buildings and bridges. Landslides may happen in areas where there are no trees or underbrush to hold the soil. If you live in an area where earthquakes occur frequently, make sure that you are prepared for an earthquake emergency.

If an earthquake strikes when you are indoors, hide under a piece of heavy furniture to protect yourself from falling materials. If you are outside, stay in the open, away from electrical wires and buildings. If you are in a car, stop the car but stay in it. After the earthquake, check your water, power, and gas lines, and report any problems. Have a battery-powered radio on hand so that you can listen to emergency bulletins. Stay out of damaged buildings until they have been inspected. The small shocks that often follow earthquakes may cause a damaged building to collapse.

SUMMARY

Although you cannot prevent natural disasters, you can increase your chances of coming through them safely. Learn and obey the procedures established for natural disasters in your community. Take all severe weather warnings seriously.

LESSON 28.4 USING WHAT YOU HAVE LEARNED

REVIEW

1. What people in the community are involved in planning for disasters?
2. Describe a hurricane.
3. Describe the dangers that result from an earthquake.

THINK CRITICALLY

4. Identify one major difference between a hurricane and a tornado.
5. After an earthquake, you should check water lines, power lines, and gas lines in your home. What could happen if these lines were damaged and left open?

APPLY IT TO YOURSELF

6. You are on the emergency planning committee in your community. Under what conditions and in what ways would you suggest that the committee make use of your school in an emergency?

Safety First

It was late Friday afternoon, and Loren wanted to bale a few more hay rows before he headed home. He was anxious. Loren had a big date that night, and he wanted to get into the house and clean up.

Everything had gone pretty well that day. Loren and his family just had one more field to finish. The old baler hadn't broken down once yet. Loren decided to speed up just a bit.

All of a sudden there was a loud noise. The baler was plugged. "I knew this was too good to be true! I do NOT have time for this!" shouted Loren. Now he would have to reach into the baler to pull out whatever was plugging the machine. He put the tractor into neutral and disengaged the power take-off (PTO) that made the baler run.

As he went to unplug the baler, Loren thought about shutting off the tractor. The power take-off had been slipping lately and sometimes it would engage on its own. Loren knew that if the PTO engaged while he was reaching into the baler, his arm could get caught and pulled in.

Loren figured it was getting close to six o'clock, and he needed to get going. "I've done it a thousand times and nothing has happened," he thought. "It shouldn't take too long."

PAUSE AND CONSIDER

1. *Identify the Problem.* What is the cause of Loren's concern?

2. *Consider the Options.* What are Loren's options?

3. *Evaluate the Outcomes.* What could happen to Loren if the machine starts running while he reaches inside of it? What might happen if he takes the time to turn off the tractor?

"Ah, it's probably okay," thought Loren. "Fortunately nothing broke."

As he started to pull out some of the hay, Loren could see that there was a rock wedged in tightly. Impatiently he went back to the tractor and got a wrench to try to pry the rock loose.

Loren jammed the wrench in between the rock and the baler head. Suddenly the head moved and snapped the wrench down. Somehow Loren got his hand out just in time. The power take-off had engaged. He ran to the tractor and shut off the motor.

When Loren got back to the baler, he saw that the sudden force of the wrench snapping against the baler had left a huge dent in the baler, right about where his hand had been. Loren could feel his heart pumping rapidly. "Never again," Loren said to himself. "I'm not taking any more chances."

Loren realized that he would not be able to finish the row and be on time for his date. He decided to take the baler back to the machine shed for the night. He would have to finish baling the next day.

DECIDE AND REVIEW

4. *Decide and Act.* What choice did Loren make?

5. *Review.* How might Loren's impatience have influenced his decision? What happened to make Loren realize that his initial decision was a mistake?

PROJECTS

1. Invite a meteorologist to speak to your class about ways of predicting weather patterns. Ask him or her if there are any tips you can use to identify signs of approaching bad weather in case you find yourself in a situation without access to current weather reports.

2. Prepare a pamphlet that describes the most common household accidents and how to prevent them.

WORKING WITH OTHERS

In some states, seat belts and helmets are not legally required to operate a motor vehicle or motorcycle. Some people feel that all states should enact laws requiring the use of seat belts and helmets. Other people feel that the use of seat belts and helmets is a personal decision and should not be mandated by government. What do you think? With a partner, prepare and present a debate that deals with both sides of this issue.

CONNECTING TO...

GEOGRAPHY   Each of the regions of the United States experiences unique weather conditions or geological events, or both, that can affect the safety of its inhabitants. For example, earthquakes are far more likely to happen in California than in Georgia. Describe the unique weather and geological conditions that contribute to natural or weather-related disasters in your region and in another, distant region in the United States.

USING VOCABULARY

accident
civil defense agency
defensive driver
drownproofing
electrocution

poison control center
tailgating
tornado warning
tornado watch

On a separate piece of paper, write the vocabulary term that best completes each of the following sentences.

1. Theresa pulled over to the side of the road because she noticed that the car behind her was _____ her.

2. When Tyrone's two-year-old brother ate a whole bottle of vitamin pills, Tyrone immediately called the _____.

3. Standing in water while plugging in or using an electrical device invites the possibility of _____.

4. Although Lakeesha already knew how to swim, she learned the technique of _____ in case of an emergency.

5. After studying weather conditions and noticing the telltale signs of a tornado, the meteorologist issued a(n) _____.

6. Peter knew that keeping his car well-tuned and the tire pressure at the right level could help prevent a(n) _____.

7. When Aaron took a driver education course, he learned how to be a(n) _____.

CONCEPT MAPPING

Copy and complete the concept map shown below. Information on concept mapping appears at the front of this book.

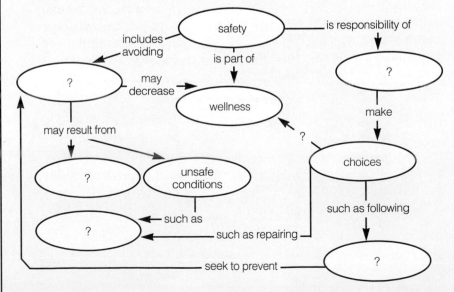

THINKING CRITICALLY

INTERPRET

LESSON 28.1

1. How might a messy home affect personal safety?
2. What safety devices and precautions can help protect a family from the dangers of fire?
3. What is the best way to dispose of old prescription medicines?

LESSON 28.2

4. Give two reasons the driver of a car should wear a seat belt.
5. Identify two common causes of motorcycle accidents.
6. In which direction should you walk along a road if there is no sidewalk? In which direction should you ride a bicycle?

LESSON 28.3

7. Why should you keep your clothes on while you do the drown-proofing technique in a water emergency?
8. The law requires two people to be in a boat when it is pulling a water-skier. What does each person in the boat do?
9. Why do you think it is important never to lean a gun against a tree, wall, or vehicle?

LESSON 28.4

10. If you are in a car that stalls in high water during flooding, what should you do?
11. Identify one way to keep warm if the power goes out during a blizzard.
12. Why should you stay out of earthquake-damaged buildings until they have been inspected?

APPLY

LESSON 28.1

13. Identify three human factors that can contribute to accidents, and give one example of each.

LESSON 28.2

14. Suggest three reasons why teenagers have a higher rate of automobile accidents than older drivers have.
15. Rhonda went to visit her relatives in New England. While she was driving north, she found herself on a road that was icy and slick. Rhonda had never driven in icy conditions before. What could she do to prevent an accident?

LESSON 28.3

16. Margaret had not been skiing for several years, so she was eager to get back on the slopes. As soon as she got off the ski lift, she headed for the hardest trail she could find. Shortly after she started down the trail, Margaret fell and broke her ankle. How might Margaret have avoided this accident?
17. Why do you think it is important to learn the drownproofing technique even if you are a good swimmer?

LESSON 28.4

18. What should you do to get ready if a hurricane is approaching your area?
19. You are driving your car to a distant city when you are unexpectedly caught in a blizzard. Snow is accumulating rapidly, and road conditions are so bad that you have to pull over to the side of the road. What should you do?

COMMITMENT TO WELLNESS

FOLLOW-UP

SETTING GOALS

Look at your responses to the Commitment to Wellness statements at the beginning of this chapter. Choose one of your *no* items. How might that behavior put your safety in jeopardy? Copy the following questions and statements on a sheet of paper or in your Wellness Journal. Next to each item, write the answers or fill in the statements to help you set goals.

1. Why is it important for me to change this behavior?
2. What further information do I need in order to change?
3. Where can I get this information?
4. What can I do to enlist the support of friends or family as I change this behavior?
5. I will change this behavior by _____.

WHERE DO I GO FROM HERE?

For almost every activity you can think of, there are safety precautions you need to take. When you begin a new activity, you should first find out the safety needs of that activity. Your local library is a good source of safety information. You can also contact the organization listed below.

FOR MORE INFORMATION, CONTACT:

National Safety Council
Public Relations Department
1121 Spring Lake Drive
Itasca, Illinois 60143

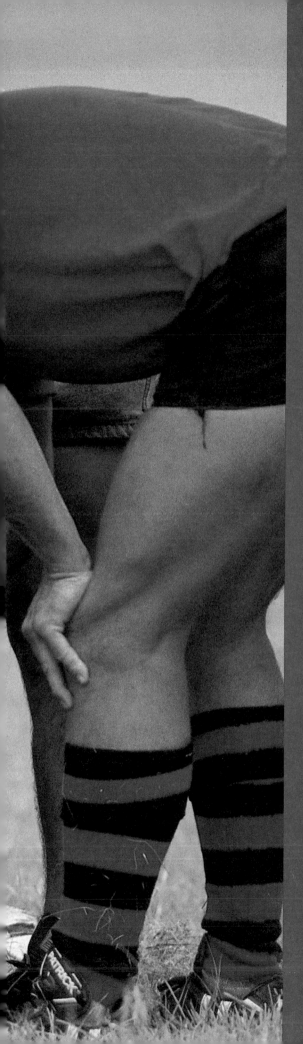

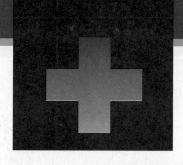

First Aid Manual

DEATHS FROM ACCIDENTS

51%
Motor vehicles

14%
Others

6%
Poisoning
solids/liquid

5%
Fire/Burns

1%
Firearms

1%
Poisoning
gases/vapors

4%
Choking/
Suffocation

5%
Drowning

13%
Falls

Source: National Safety Council

681

WHAT IS FIRST AID?

First aid is practical and immediate care for an injury or sudden illness. Such emergency care is administered until professional medical help is available.

First aid does not require elaborate training or special equipment. First aid training covers care for sudden illness and specific injuries, accident prevention, and emergency procedures. Knowing first aid is important for having the skill to handle emergencies and accidents effectively.

Any person with an injury or illness can benefit from prompt first aid. Some conditions, such as minor wounds or bruises, require only simple first aid. Other conditions, such as choking or severe bleeding, are true medical emergencies. In a medical emergency, prompt first aid can make the difference between life or death, quick or slow recovery, and temporary or permanent disability.

Although first aid requires action, the first step in an emergency is to examine the situation carefully. In this way, you can spot any conditions that may threaten your safety or that of other bystanders.

The next step is to decide what action should be taken. A thorough knowledge of first aid makes it possible for you to provide the action that is needed. It helps you to know which emergencies should be handled first. It also gives you the confidence to remain calm and to help keep others calm.

HOW TO USE THIS MANUAL

This manual is a guide to practical first aid steps to be taken until professional medical help is available. An alphabetical listing of first aid situations is found on page 683. References to other relevant topics are also given.

Cardiopulmonary resuscitation (CPR) is included at the end of this manual, rather than within the alphabetical listings, because it requires special training. This manual does NOT teach CPR. Never attempt CPR unless you have completed a course in CPR.

The major sections of the manual are identified by general types of illness or injury. Each section is then divided into specific instructions regarding specific illnesses or injuries. The information in each part consists of a description of the first aid situation followed by first aid directions. The directions are numbered and should be followed in the order presented. Illustrations are included to help make the first aid directions clear.

To use this manual, find the section in the alphabetical reference list that describes the type of illness or injury. Open the manual to the correct page for the information you will need. Remember, it is best to read and study this manual before an emergency occurs. Prompt, effective first aid is more likely if you are familiar with the procedures.

In this manual, you will find the instruction "monitor ABCs". The A stands for airway, the B stands for breathing, and the C stands for circulation. Monitoring ABCs involves three steps: (1) keeping the injured person's airway clear; (2) checking the person's breathing and using rescue breathing if the airway is blocked or breathing stops; and (3) checking circulation by feeling for a pulse and looking for signs of bleeding. If circulation has stopped, CPR should be given by someone trained in CPR.

In case of an accident or sudden illness, you should know where to call for help. Keep a list of emergency telephone numbers posted near your telephone. The emergency phone numbers should include your local emergency medical services (EMS), the police department, the fire department, a poison control center, and your family doctor. Some communities have a coordinated EMS system that can be contacted by telephoning 911.

FIRST AID REFERENCE

First aid procedures in this manual reflect the guidelines recommended by the American Heart Association and the American Red Cross.

Abdominal thrust...691

Asthma 688

Bites: animal and human 685

    insect, spiders, ticks...............................685

    snakes 685

Bleeding..686

Blisters..692

Bones, broken 696

Breathing problems 688

Bruises..692

Burns 690

Chemical: burns..690

    in the eye 693

    skin-contact poison 703

Chest pain 705

Choking 691

Cold, exposure to 695

Concussions 698

Cramps, muscle...699

Croup..688

Cuts (wounds) 686, 692

Dislocations 697

Dizziness 688, 695, 701, 704, 705

Drug overdose 701

Electric shock 694

Eye injuries 693

Exposure to cold and heat..............................695

Fainting...704

Fractures ....696 - 698

Frostbite..695

Head injuries..698

Heart attack 705

Heat cramps 695

Heat exhaustion...695

Heat, exposure to 695

Heat stroke 695

Heimlich maneuver (see Abdominal thrust)

Hyperventilation...688

Hypothermia 695

Insect bites and stings.....................................685

Mouth-to-mouth resuscitation 689

Muscle: cramps 699

    strains (tears) 699

Nosebleed 687

Poisons: inhaled 701

    in the eye 693

    on the skin..703

    swallowed 700

Poison ivy, poison oak, poison sumac.............703

Rescue breathing: for adults, children 689

    for infants 707

Scalp wounds 698

Seizures..694

Shock..702

Shortness of breath 688, 705

Snakebites..685

Splinters..693

Splinting..697

Sprains 697

Stings, insect 685

Stroke..705

Swallowed objects 691, 707

Unconsciousness 704, 705

Information about Cardiopulmonary Resuscitation (CPR) 706-707

WHAT TO DO IN AN EMERGENCY

Any sudden illness or serious injury can create a first aid emergency. First aid care is always influenced by the type of injury or illness. However, in an emergency, it is important to have first aid priorities. Observe these priorities when the facts of the situation are not known, when the extent of illness or injury is unclear, or when the injured person is unconscious or unable to explain:

1. DO NOT put yourself in danger. Examine the situation carefully and then determine the best and safest way to give help. Wash your hands, if possible. Wrap your hands in something through which blood will not soak before beginning to help the injured or ill person to prevent an exchange of blood or other fluids between you and the injured or ill person.

2. Find out if there are any problems with the airway, breathing, or circulation (ABCs) and care for them immediately.

3. Send someone else to get professional help. The person telephoning for help should state the following information: the phone number of the tele-

phone she or he is calling from, the location of the injured or ill person, the nature of the injury or illness, and the first aid being given. The person should not hang up until the other party has finished asking questions and has obtained all necessary information.

4. If there are no life-threatening conditions, examine the injured or ill person carefully in a systematic way and care for any other injuries.

5. Care for shock or act to prevent it.

6. Know your first aid limits. DO NOT attempt any procedure that you cannot do efficiently and confidently.

7. Protect the injured or ill person from further harm. DO NOT move an injured or ill person unless that person is in immediate danger.

8. Stay with the injured or ill person until professional medical help arrives.

9. In 1993, the American Red Cross began using Check, Call, Care as the three steps to follow in response to an emergency situation.

TYPES OF FIRST AID THAT REQUIRE SPECIAL TRAINING

Prompt first aid can be very effective. Most first aid care is a set of practical procedures for nonprofessionals. Such emergency care helps the ill or injured person until professional medical help arrives or the person can be taken to a hospital. These emergency techniques usually do not require special training.

Occasionally special training is required to learn a first aid procedure. Cardiopulmonary resuscitation (CPR) is a lifesaving technique that cannot be learned from a book. CPR is a method of restoring breathing and heartbeat to a person who is no longer breathing and whose heart has stopped beating. The American

Heart Association or your local Red Cross chapter can tell you where CPR instruction is offered in your area. Learn to recognize situations that require CPR, but do not attempt it without the necessary training. Individuals who attempt CPR without proper training may endanger the life of the ill or injured person.

Any additional training in first aid procedure helps to make a person confident and effective in an emergency. In addition, special programs are available in many communities to teach swimming, lifesaving, and water and boating safety. Such programs teach people to enjoy themselves, to prevent accidents, and to be prepared in case of an emergency.

FIRST AID AND GOOD SAMARITAN LAWS

Most states have some form of Good Samaritan law. These laws provide legal protection for people who aid victims of accidents or emergencies. The laws vary from state to state.

In one state, the law provides that any Good Samaritan who gives emergency aid shall not be held financially responsible for injury resulting from the emergency care. In another state, persons trained in CPR have legal protection for their rescue efforts unless their actions are deliberate misconducts of

care. In a third state, it is unlawful for a knowledgeable person to ignore a victim of an accident or emergency.

Good Samaritan laws do not protect people from being sued. These laws do protect rescuers by specifying the limits of the rescuer's legal responsibility to the victim. All states require that once the Good Samaritan has begun to give care he or she must continue to give care until more adequate help arrives.

ANIMAL BITES

When a person is bitten by another person or by an animal, an infection can result. For example, rabies infection can be transmitted through animal bites. If a person is bitten by a land mammal that may have rabies, the incident and a description of the animal and where it was last seen should be reported to the EMS, the police, and animal control. Follow these first aid directions:

1. Wash your hands. Wrap your hands in something through which blood will not soak.
2. Wash the wound with soap and water if there is not heavy bleeding.
3. Control any bleeding.
4. Apply an antibiotic ointment and clean dressing.
5. Get medical help.
6. Wash your hands with soap and water.
7. Do not attempt to capture the animal.

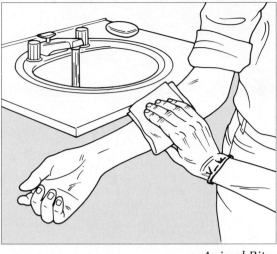

Animal Bites

INSECTS, SPIDERS, TICKS

Insect or spider bites may cause allergic reactions such as hives, wheezing, and nausea, or they may cause more serious problems like difficulty breathing or even death. Also, ticks and certain insects may transmit disease. For allergic reactions, get immediate medical help. For bites by poisonous organisms, call a poison control center or go to the hospital. Follow these first aid directions:

1. Gently scrape an insect's stinger out of the skin with the blunt edge of a table knife. With tweezers, grasp a tick as close to the skin as possible. Pull steadily, trying not to crush the tick.
2. Wash the wound with soap and water.
3. Cover it to keep it clean, and apply a cold pack.
4. Get medical help if there is an allergic reaction.

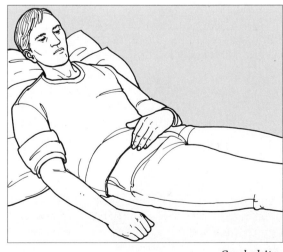

Insects, Spiders, Ticks

SNAKEBITES

In the case of a snakebite, try to notice the appearance of the snake. There are four kinds of poisonous snakes in North America: rattlesnakes, copperheads, water moccasins (cottonmouths), and coral snakes. The first three have long fangs, which may leave puncture marks. Follow these first aid directions:

1. Stay calm and keep the injured person calm.
2. Wash the wound with soap and water.
3. Keep the person lying still with the bitten area immobile and below heart level.
4. Care for shock and monitor ABCs (page 682).
5. If you think the snake might have been poisonous, get medical help as soon as possible.
6. DO NOT apply ice, remove venom, or apply tourniquets.

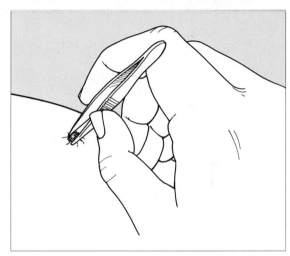

Snakebites

BLEEDING

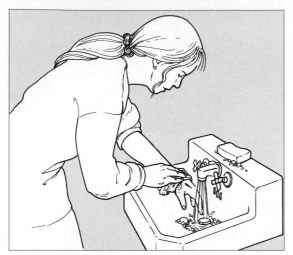

Washing a Wound

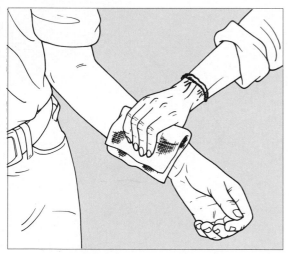

Direct Pressure

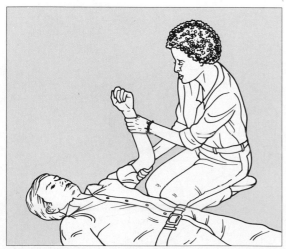

Elevation

WASHING A WOUND
In the absence of severe bleeding, washing a wound helps prevent infection. Follow these first aid directions:

1. Wash your hands with soap and water. Wrap your hands with something through which blood will not soak.
2. Rinse the injured area with clean water.
3. Put soap on a moist cloth and gently wash the wound area. Rinse again with water.
4. DO NOT try to remove material in the wound. DO NOT use antiseptics without consulting a physician.
5. Apply a clean dressing to the wound. Wash your hands.
6. Seek medical help if matter is embedded in the wound, there is severe bleeding, the wound edges do not stay closed, or the wound involves a vital structure.

DIRECT PRESSURE
Rapid loss of blood should be stopped as quickly as possible. First, apply a clean dressing to the wound. Then press down firmly with the palm of the hand. Clean towels, gauze, or clothing can be used as a dressing. If no clean material is available, apply pressure directly with the hand. Follow these directions:

1. Wash your hands with soap and water. Wrap your hands with something through which blood will not soak.
2. Apply direct pressure on a wound with a sterile pad or clean cloth.
3. Press firmly on the dressing.
4. DO NOT remove blood-soaked dressings, but keep adding dressing and applying pressure.
5. After bleeding stops, secure the dressing. Wash your hands.
6. If bleeding does not stop, get medical help.
7. Monitor ABCs (page 682).

ELEVATION
Sometimes direct pressure alone cannot control the flow of blood from an open wound. Raising an injured limb higher than the heart while continuing to apply pressure will help stop bleeding.

A bleeding open wound on the head, neck, arm, or leg should be raised above heart level and direct pressure continued. If there is any possibility of a neck injury, DO NOT move the head. If there is any sign of fracture, DO NOT elevate an injured limb. DO NOT move an unconscious person. Follow these first aid directions:

1. Wash your hands with soap and water. Wrap your hands with something through which blood will not soak.
2. Apply direct pressure to the open wound.
3. If there is no sign of fracture, elevate an injured arm or leg higher than the heart.
4. Wash your hands with soap and water.

PRESSURE-POINT TECHNIQUE

The pressure-point technique may be necessary if direct pressure and elevation are ineffective. This technique consists of applying pressure to a major artery at a point between the wound and the heart. This slows the flow of blood to the wound so that clotting can occur.

The use of pressure-point technique stops circulation within the entire limb. Stop using the technique as soon as bleeding is under control. For any case of bleeding that cannot be stopped, get medical help immediately.

The pressure points most often used to control bleeding are found on the arms and legs. These points are shown in the top illustration.

INTERNAL BLEEDING

Closed wounds can result in internal bleeding instead of blood loss through the skin. A black eye is an example. Extensive internal bleeding can be caused by the impact of a fall or a motor vehicle accident. Be alert for the following signs of internal bleeding: vomited or coughed-up blood and blood in the urine or stools, and the signs and symptoms of shock. Follow these first aid directions:

1. If the person is unconscious, vomiting, or bleeding from the mouth, place the person on her or his side to prevent choking.

2. Keep the person comfortably warm.

3. DO NOT let the person eat or drink.

4. Monitor the airway, breathing, and circulation.

5. Get medical help immediately.

NOSEBLEED

A nosebleed can be caused by an injury to the nose or head, a cold, a disease, or strenuous physical activity. A nosebleed is usually not serious. When the bleeding has been stopped, avoid activity that might start it again. Follow these first aid directions:

1. Wash your hands with soap and water. Wrap your hands with something through which blood will not soak.

2. Have the person sit down and lean forward, or if that is not possible, lie down with the head and shoulders raised.

3. Squeeze firmly the soft, flexible part of the nose for at least 10 minutes without releasing the pressure.

4. If necessary, apply cold compresses to the bridge of the nose.

5. If the bleeding continues, get medical help.

6. Wash your hands with soap and water after providing first aid.

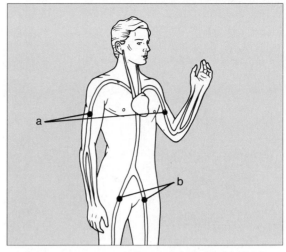

Pressure-Point Technique

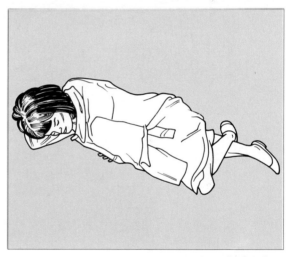

Internal Bleeding

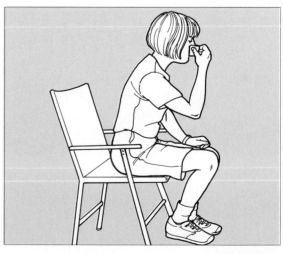

Nosebleed

BREATHING PROBLEMS

Causes of Breathing Problems

Hyperventilation

CAUSES OF BREATHING PROBLEMS
The body needs a continuous supply of oxygen to support life processes. Normal breathing supplies this oxygen. When air does not move freely in and out of the lungs, breathing problems result. Severe breathing difficulties can result in respiratory failure, a life-threatening emergency. For example, an object caught in the airway can obstruct breathing and cause respiratory failure.

Some breathing difficulties are associated with chronic medical problems. Some forms of heart disease can cause coughing and shortness of breath. Sitting upright may relieve these symptoms.

Asthma occurs when a person's airway is blocked or narrowed. Its symptoms include coughing, wheezing, and breathing difficulty. Asthma can be triggered by physical activity, an allergy, or a respiratory infection. Help the person remain calm. Give him or her an asthma medicine, if prescribed by a physician, and provide warm, moist air. If breathing difficulty continues or becomes worse, get medical help.

Croup is another type of breathing difficulty that is particularly common among young children. It causes narrowing of the larynx along with a barking cough and breathing difficulty.

Steam from a vaporizer or hot shower usually relieves the symptoms of croup. In rare cases, croup can become a life-threatening problem. If breathing becomes more difficult and exhausting, or if there is a sudden high fever or drooling, seek immediate medical help.

HYPERVENTILATION
Hyperventilation (very fast breathing) is often caused by emotional stress. It may be confused with a heart attack or a mental disorder. Symptoms include a sense of not getting enough air; sharp, short pains in the chest or stomach; dizziness; and a "pins and needles" sensation in fingers, toes, and face. In an older adult, immediate medical help should be obtained for chest pain. For a young, otherwise healthy person, follow these first aid directions:

1. Be calm and encourage slower breathing.
2. Have the person breathe into a paper bag or cupped hands to rebreathe the same air.
3. If symptoms continue, seek medical help.

RESCUE BREATHING

In some cases of severe breathing problems, normal breathing stops or is ineffective. Known as respiratory failure, this emergency is life-threatening and requires first aid.

Rescue breathing is a first aid procedure that forces air into the lungs. This mouth-to-mouth technique is considered the most practical and effective method. If rescue breathing is necessary, so is professional assistance. Send someone for immediate help. In cases of carbon monoxide poisoning, drug overdose, or electric shock, rescue breathing may be needed for a long time. Remember to monitor ABCs (page 682). Follow these first aid directions:

1. Place the person on his or her back.

2. Open the airway. Tilt the injured person's head back with the chin pointed upward. Place one hand on the person's forehead. With the other hand, place your fingertips under the bony part of his or her jaw and lift the chin gently. This procedure is known as the head-tilt chin-lift. Be careful not to close the person's mouth completely. See top illustration.

3. Check for breathing. Watch the chest to see if it is rising and falling. Listen and feel for signs of breathing at the mouth and nose. Check for about five seconds. If there is no breathing, pinch the nostrils closed. See middle illustration. Take a deep breath and seal your mouth over the person's mouth. Blow slowly into his or her mouth, taking about 1 to 1 1/2 seconds for one breath. Watch the chest rise. Raise your mouth, take a breath, and watch the person's chest fall. Repeat a second time.

4. Check for circulation by feeling gently for the pulse in the groove on the side of the Adam's apple closest to you for five to ten seconds. Use your index and middle fingers to check for the pulse. Check also for bleeding.

5. Send someone to call EMS for an ambulance.

6. For adults, if there is a pulse and no sign of breathing, give one full, slow breath every five seconds. After each breath, when the person's chest is expanded, raise your mouth, turn your head toward the chest, take a breath, and watch the chest fall. Repeat the blowing cycle for one minute and recheck the pulse. If there is no pulse and no breathing, CPR is necessary. If you have no CPR training, continue rescue breathing until qualified help takes over and administers CPR.

If the victim is a child, give one breath every four seconds. If an infant, one breath every three seconds.

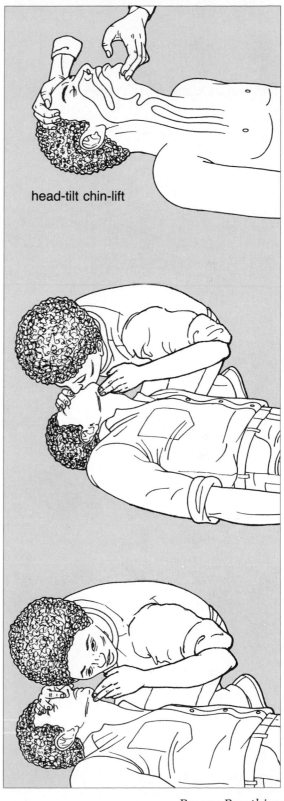

head-tilt chin-lift

Rescue Breathing

BURNS

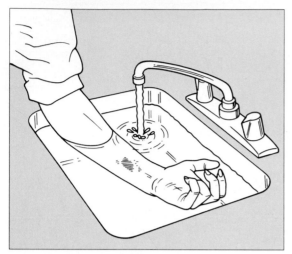

First- and Second-Degree Burns

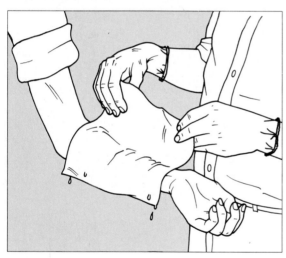

Third-Degree Burns

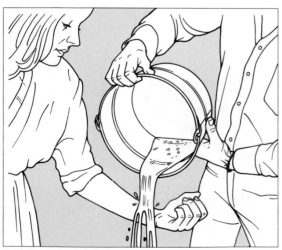

Chemical Burns

FIRST-AND-SECOND-DEGREE BURNS

Burns can result from exposure to the sun, hot liquids and objects, electricity, or chemicals. In a first-degree burn, the outside layer of skin becomes red. There may be mild swelling and pain.

In second-degree burns, the skin appears red and blotchy. Blisters and swelling often develop. Pain is more severe. Follow these first aid directions for first- and second-degree burns:

1. Cool the burned area with cold water (not ice or ice water) until pain lessens.
2. Cover the burn with a wet, clean, loose dressing.
3. DO NOT break blisters that may develop.
4. Seek medical care if burns are on the face, genitals, hands, feet, or more than one body part.

THIRD-DEGREE BURNS
Third-degree burns, which are burns that involve deep tissue and have open blisters, can be life-threatening. The skin may look leathery, white, or charred. There may be little or no pain. Burns of the face may be accompanied by respiratory burns and breathing problems. Follow these first aid directions:

1. Monitor ABCs (page 682).
2. Call EMS immediately.
3. Cool burned area with cold (not ice) water.
4. Cover burn with dry, sterile dressings or clean cloths.
5. Keep burned arms and legs above heart level. DO NOT let the person walk.
6. Help the person maintain body temperature.

CHEMICAL BURNS
Skin injury caused by irritating chemicals is called a chemical burn. Household and garden products, such as fertilizer, bleach, ammonia, and many other cleaning agents, are frequent causes of chemical burns. Before using a household or garden chemical, read all product labels carefully. The aim of first aid is to remove the irritating substance as quickly as possible. Avoid getting any of the chemical on you. Follow these first aid directions:

1. Wash the area with large quantities of water for at least 15 to 30 minutes. Remove any contaminated clothing or jewelry during the washing.
2. Cover the burned area with a sterile dressing to avoid infection.
3. Seek medical help.

UNIVERSAL CHOKING SIGNAL
A person who suddenly cannot breathe, cough, or speak may be choking. Choking occurs when an object lodges in any part of the airway. Choking can be a life-threatening emergency. The risk of choking is increased by chewing food inadequately, talking with a mouthful of food, wearing ill-fitting dentures, or drinking alcohol before or while eating. Be sure you know how to make and recognize the universal choking signal. Signs of choking include sudden collapse; bluish color of face, neck, or hands; ineffective coughing; wheezing or breathing with difficulty; inability to speak; unconsciousness; or panic.

FIRST AID FOR CHOKING
Encourage a choking person to cough. If the person coughs weakly or shows other signs of choking, give first aid immediately. For a conscious adult or child, first aid consists of abdominal thrusts (Heimlich maneuver), as described below:

1. Stand or kneel behind the choking person with both arms around the waist.
2. Place the thumb side of your fist against the person's abdomen, halfway between the navel and the tip of the breastbone. Grasp your fist with your other hand.
3. Press your fist into the choking person's abdomen with quick, hard, upward thrusts. Each thrust should be a separate, distinct motion. Continue the thrusts until the person is able to cough forcefully or breathe, or becomes unconscious.
4. If the person loses consciousness, lay him or her down face up. Visually check the mouth for objects blocking the airway. Open the airway; give two breaths. If air does not go in, do six to ten abdominal thrusts.
5. Repeat the visual check of the mouth. Give two breaths and repeat abdominal thrusts until the airway is cleared, or an ambulance arrives.

For a conscious infant

1. Turn the infant face down on your forearm, tilting downward. Support the infant's head and neck at all times.
2. Give four backblows forcefully between the infant's shoulder blades using the heel of you hand.
3. Turn the infant onto back while supporting the head and neck.
4. Tilt the infant downward. Place middle and index fingers on breastbone. Give four quick compressions.
5. Repeat the cycle until object is coughed up or infant breathes.

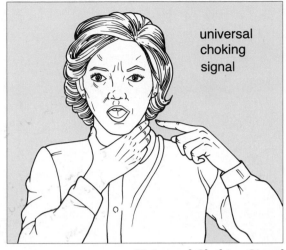

Universal Choking Signal

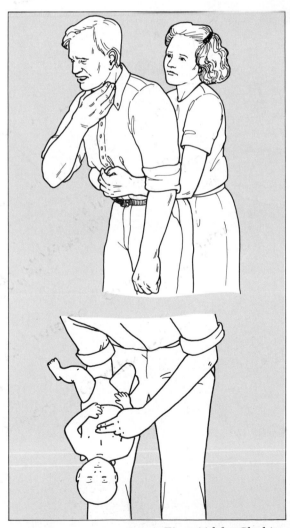

First Aid for Choking

COMMON INJURIES

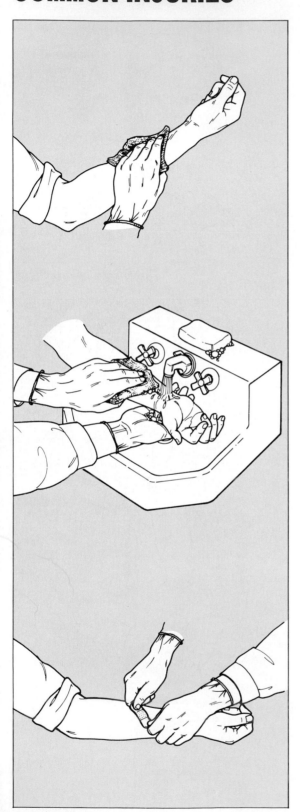

Bruises and Minor Wounds

BRUISES AND MINOR WOUNDS   Bruises and wounds are injuries of the skin and underlying tissue. Ice wrapped in a clean cloth may reduce the pain and swelling. If the bruised area is on an arm or leg, keep the limb elevated above heart level. If pain and swelling continue or if the bruise is the result of a joint injury, seek medical help.

There are several types of wounds. A laceration, in which the skin is torn, is usually more severe than a smooth cut (incision). A puncture is a hole made by a sharp object, such as a nail. An abrasion is a scrape.

For minor wounds, first aid to stop the bleeding, clean the wound, and prevent infection may be the only treatment necessary. If there is a lot of bleeding, numbness, loss of motion, or additional injury, get medical help. Puncture wounds are especially susceptible to infection, including tetanus. Follow these first aid directions:

1. Wash your hands with soap and water. Wrap your hands with something through which blood will not soak.

2. Control bleeding with direct pressure and elevation.

3. Wash the wound thoroughly with soap and water.

4. Rinse the wound with clean water and pat it dry. If bleeding recurs, control it.

5. Cover the wound with a sterile dressing.

6. Wash your hands with soap and water.

7. Watch for any signs of infection, such as pus, pain, redness around the wound, or a fever.

8. Check with the person's doctor to see whether a tetanus shot is needed.

BLISTERS   Protect unbroken blisters from pressure by applying a gauze wrap or bandage. Clean a broken blister with soap and water and cover it with a sterile dressing. Seek medical help if the blister is large, infected, or very painful. Follow these first aid directions:

1. Wash your hands with soap and water. Wrap your hands with something through which blood will not soak.

2. Wash the area with soap and water.

3. Keep the open blister clean and covered.

4. Wash your hands with soap and water.

5. Seek medical help if infection occurs.

EYE INJURIES

Causes of eye injury include a loose object in the eye, an embedded object in the eye, a chemical burn, and a direct blow to the eye. With any suspected eye injury, DO NOT rub the eye and DO NOT try to remove contact lenses. Chemical burns should be flushed with water for 30 minutes. Then close and cover both eyes and get prompt medical help. An injury caused by a direct blow, such as a black eye, should be examined by a doctor. There could be damage inside the eye. An embedded object can be a serious emergency. Do not try to remove the object. The injured person should lie down. Place an inverted paper cup over the injured eye and secure with a bandage over both eyes. Get immediate medical help.

A loose object may be a particle or an eyelash. First try to flush it out with warm water. If it will not flush out, cover both eyes and seek medical help. Follow these first aid directions to look for a loose object:

1. To examine the eye beneath the lower lid, have the person look up. With clean hands, gently pull the lower lid down.
2. To examine the eye beneath the upper lid, have the person look downward and gently pull the upper lid up.
3. If you see the particle floating on the surface of the eyeball, try to flush it out with water.
4. If you cannot flush out the particle, or if irritation, tearing, or blurred vision continues after the particle is removed, get medical help.
5. Wash your hands with soap and water.

SPLINTERS

To treat a splinter wound, follow the first aid directions for cleaning a wound. Quickly and gently, wash the area to remove any material that is not deeply embedded in the wound. If the splinter is large or deeply embedded, DO NOT try to remove it. Get professional medical help. Follow these first aid directions to remove a shallow splinter:

1. Using a clean pair of tweezers, pull out the splinter at the same angle it went in.
2. Wash the wound and cover it with a sterile dressing.
3. Wash your hands with soap and water.
4. If there is an infection or difficulty removing the splinter, get medical help.

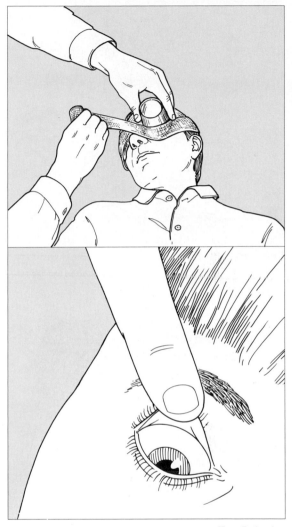

Eye Injuries

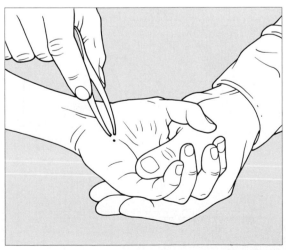

Splinters

SEIZURES/ELECTRIC SHOCK

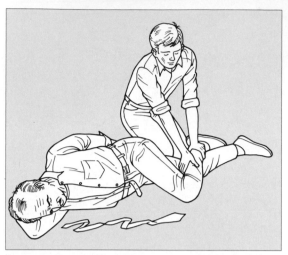

Seizures

SEIZURES

Seizures can be associated with a head injury, with epilepsy, or with a high fever or illness in young children. During a seizure, a person becomes unconscious and the body may become stiff or move violently. First aid is important to prevent injury and choking. Follow these first aid directions:

1. Protect the person from injury by clearing the area and loosening the person's clothes.
2. DO NOT restrain the person or put anything in his or her mouth. After the person's muscles relax, check breathing and pulse.
3. If the person is unconscious after a seizure, lay the person on his or her side.
4. Get medical help.

ELECTRIC SHOCK

Electric shock is the result of an electric current. Low-voltage current that passes through the body can cause burns. High-voltage current can also stop breathing and heartbeat.

Electric shock is a common danger, especially in the home. To prevent injury from electric shock at home, get electrical wiring inspected, be sure appliances are properly wired and grounded, and do not overload circuits.

In case of electric shock, avoid touching the injured person or the source of electric current until the current has been turned off. Turn off the current at the fuse box or circuit breaker. If the emergency is outside and you suspect downed power lines, call the power company first. Keep bystanders well away from any source of live current. Follow these first aid directions:

1. Call EMS immediately.
2. Check for life-threatening conditions. If the person is not breathing but has a pulse, rescue breathing is needed. If the person is not breathing and has no pulse, CPR is needed.
3. Check for additional injuries, including burns and fractures. There may be two burn sites—where electric current entered and where it left the body.
4. Cover burned areas with sterile dressings.
5. DO NOT move the person. Keep the person warm.

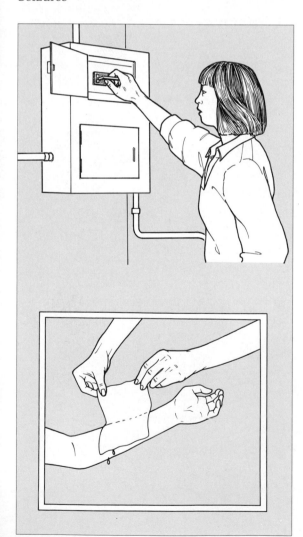

Electric Shock

EXPOSURE TO COLD AND HEAT

EXPOSURE TO COLD

Exposure to cold can result in hypothermia (lowered body temperature) and/or frostbite (frozen tissue). Avoid injury by keeping warm and rested. Drink hot, non-alcoholic drinks; wear warm, dry clothing; cover face, head, and ears. Watch for signs of frostbite, such as white or grayish-yellow skin and blisters. Follow these first aid directions for frostbite:

1. Move the person to a warm place.
2. Warm the frozen area in warm (not hot) water. DO NOT rub the area or break blisters. Handle the frozen body parts gently.
3. Bandage loosely the injured parts. Put dry, sterile gauze between injured fingers or toes.
4. Get immediate medical help.

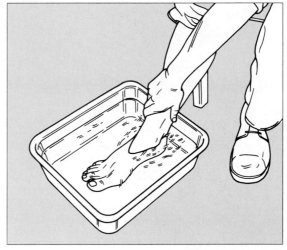

Exposure to Cold

EXPOSURE TO HEAT

Exposure to heat can result in heat cramps, heat exhaustion, or heat stroke. When more heat is produced than can be taken away by sweating, the body becomes overheated. Young children, older adults, and those who are ill are most susceptible.

Heat cramps sometimes precede heat exhaustion. Cramps are most likely to affect the muscles of the legs and abdomen. Stretch the affected muscles and massage them with the heel of the hand. Move the affected person to a cooler area. If there are no other injuries and the person can drink water, give a half glass of water every 15 minutes for one hour.

The symptoms of heat exhaustion include excessive perspiration; cool, moist, red, or pale skin; dizziness; headache; nausea; and exhaustion. Lay the person down in a cool (not cold) place and apply cool, moist towels or cold packs to the skin. Encourage the person to drink a half glass of water every 15 minutes. If the person is unconscious, get medical help.

Heat stroke is a life-threatening emergency characterized by very high body temperature; hot, dry-looking skin; lack of perspiration; and rapid pulse. Give immediate first aid to cool the body. Follow these first aid directions:

1. Call EMS for an ambulance.
2. Get the person into a cooler place. Remove tight or perspiration-soaked clothing.
3. If possible, place the person in a tub of cool water, or wrap him or her in wet sheets and fan them.
4. If the person is able to drink, have him or her drink water slowly.

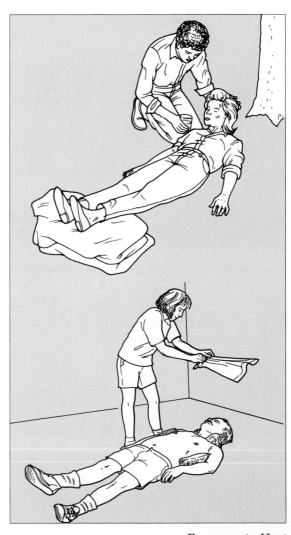

Exposure to Heat

FRACTURES, SPRAINS, AND DISLOCATIONS

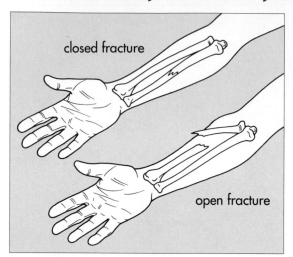

Types of Fractures

TYPES OF FRACTURES

There are different kinds of injuries to bones. One kind of bone injury is a fracture, which is a break or crack in a bone. Causes of fractures include falls, motor vehicle accidents, and accidents relating to sports and recreation.

A closed fracture occurs under the skin. An open fracture breaks the skin, often with bone protruding from the skin. Bleeding can be severe and there is always a danger of infection. An X ray is always necessary if a fracture is suspected. Signs of possible fracture include:

- painful movement
- abnormal shape
- swelling
- pain
- bruising
- numbness
- skin discoloration

PRINCIPLES FOR CARING FOR FRACTURES

Any bone in the body can be fractured. Closed fractures are the most common type. Open fractures can be more complicated because of the open wound and the danger of infection. Bone injuries must be treated promptly to minimize pain and disability.

Remember that fracture location and type determine the specific first aid procedure. However, certain first aid principles apply to all fractures, regardless of location. Be careful to keep the area and the joints above and below the broken bone from moving. Prevent shock. Follow these first aid directions:

1. Check the person's breathing and pulse.
2. Immobilize the injured part of the body.
3. Apply an ice or cold pack to the injured area.
4. Limit the person's movement.
5. Maintain normal body temperature.
6. Get medical help.

Follow these additional first aid directions for an open fracture:

1. Wash your hands. Wrap your hands in something through which blood will not soak.
2. Control serious bleeding.
3. Remove or cut away clothing if necessary.
4. DO NOT try to wash or probe the wound. DO NOT replace bone fragments.
5. If bone is protruding, cover the entire wound with a sterile dressing.
6. Treat for shock.
7. Get immediate medical help.
8. Wash your hands with soap and water.

Principles for Caring for Fractures

FRACTURES, SPRAINS, AND DISLOCATIONS

SPLINTING   A splint is used to immobilize an injured joint or bone. A splint can help decrease pain, minimize shock, and prevent further injury. A splint can be made from any rigid material, such as a board or a rolled up blanket, and held in place with rolled gauze, folded triangular bandages, or straps. Splint only if you can do it without causing more pain and discomfort. Follow these first aid directions:

1. Extend the splint past the joints that are above and below a suspected injury.
2. Pad the splint so that it conforms to the injured body part
3. Tie the splint snugly but NOT TIGHTLY, so that blood flow is not restricted.

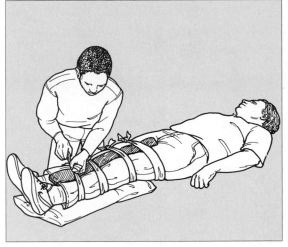

Splinting

SPRAINS   When ligaments, the strong bands of tissue that hold joints together, are stretched or partially torn, the injury is called a sprain. Ankles, knees, fingers, and wrists are the most easily sprained. Only an X ray can determine whether the injury is a sprain or fracture. Suspect a sprain if there is swelling, discoloration, and tenderness or pain when the injured part is moved or bears weight. If a sprain is suspected, follow these first aid directions:

1. Apply cold packs wrapped in towels or gauze.
2. Elevate the injured joint.
3. DO NOT let the person try to walk with an injured knee or ankle.
4. Get medical help to confirm the nature of the injury.

DISLOCATIONS   A dislocation occurs as a result of a severe sprain, usually due to a direct blow or a fall. A dislocation is an injury to a joint and the ligaments surrounding it. The end of a bone is displaced. Only an X ray can determine whether the injury is a dislocation or a fracture. Signs of a dislocation include swelling, discoloration, tenderness, pain with movement, and deformity in a joint. If a dislocation is suspected, follow these first aid directions:

1. Splint and immobilize the joint.
2. Support the limb with a sling or elevate it. Avoid putting pressure or weight on it.
3. Apply cold packs wrapped in towels or gauze.
4. DO NOT try to correct the deformity. This could injure nerves and blood vessels.
5. Get medical help.

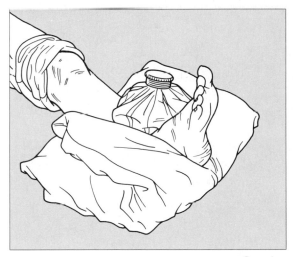

Sprains

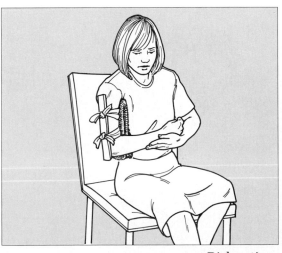

Dislocations

HEAD INJURIES

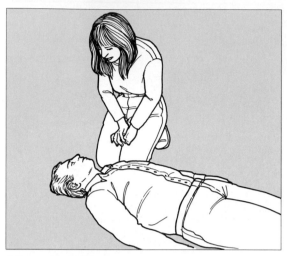

Concussions/Fractures

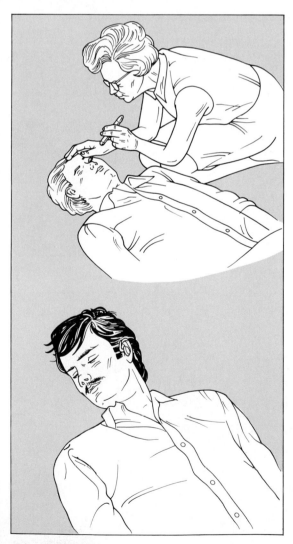

Concussions/Fractures

SIGNS OF HEAD INJURY

Head injuries require immediate medical attention. There may be internal bleeding and brain damage. There also may be a neck injury, which could cause paralysis. The signs of head injury may appear immediately or within 48 hours of an accident. A person who has received a serious blow to the head should be watched carefully for 24 to 48 hours. Signs of possible head injury include:

- drowsiness
- slurred speech
- loss of consciousness
- pupils of unequal size
- paralysis
- nausea or vomiting
- clear or bloody fluids from nose, ears, mouth
- loss of memory
- persistent headache

SCALP WOUNDS

A scalp wound is a type of head injury. Scalp wounds usually bleed a lot because of the scalp's rich blood supply. DO NOT try to remove foreign matter from a scalp wound, unless the matter is easily removed with soap and water. Get medical help as soon as possible. If there is a possible neck injury, DO NOT move the person. Follow these first aid instructions:

1. Wash your hands. Wrap your hands with something through which blood will not soak.
2. Control bleeding.
3. Clean only very minor wounds.
4. Raise the person's head and shoulders. DO NOT bend the neck.
5. Cover the wound with a sterile dressing.
6. Get medical help.
7. Wash your hands with soap and water.

CONCUSSIONS/FRACTURES

A blow to the head can cause the brain to shake against the skull. This action may result in a loss of consciousness, or a concussion. A concussion may be accompanied by a crack, or fracture, in the skull. Follow these first aid directions:

1. Keep the person lying down.
2. Call EMS for an ambulance.
3. Stabilize the injured person's head and neck as you found them by placing your hands along both sides of the head.
4. Keep the airway open.
5. DO NOT give food or drink.
6. Note the time of injury and the person's behavior just after sustaining the injury.

MUSCLE STRAINS

Muscle strains, or tears, are caused by overexertion. The muscle feels tender and may become swollen and stiff. First aid care can provide relief for the pain and promote healing of the injured tissue. Get medical help if the area is badly swollen or very painful. Follow these first aid directions:

1. Rest the muscles involved and avoid movement that causes pain.

2. Elevate the limb to minimize swelling of a strained arm or leg muscle.

3. Apply cold compresses or ice packs for 20 to 30 minutes at a time to relieve pain.

4. After 24 to 48 hours, apply warm compresses or heat to increase circulation.

MUSCLE CRAMPS

The sharp pain of a muscle cramp is caused by a sudden intense contraction of a muscle. A muscle cramp can occur during exertion or while the body is at rest. It may last from a few seconds to a few hours.

Muscle cramps are uncomfortable but rarely dangerous. They are common during pregnancy but are not significant. Leg cramps often disturb the sleep of older people.

Heat cramps are painful muscle spasms. They are most likely to affect abdominal or leg muscles. A person who experiences muscle cramps during exercise on a hot day may need to be treated for heat exhaustion or heat stroke as well as for heat cramps.

Any muscle cramp can be dangerous to a swimmer if he or she is incapacitated by pain or panic.

Most muscle cramps respond quickly to gentle massage and heat. If the cramps are not relieved by first aid or continue to occur, get medical help.

Follow these first aid directions to treat muscle cramps:

1. Gently but quickly stretch the cramped muscle. If the cramp is in an arm or leg, bend the limb gently back and forth.

2. Massage the knot in the stretched muscle with the heel of the hand.

3. For a cramp in the calf or the sole of the foot, straighten the leg while pointing the toes back up toward the body.

4. Apply a cold pack to the cramped muscle. Leave in place for 20 to 30 minutes.

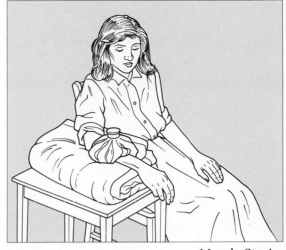

Muscle Strains

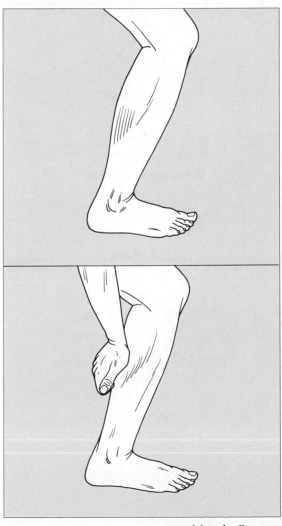

Muscle Cramps

POISONING

Common Household Poisons

most drugs

some house plants

any spoiled food

alcohol

antifreeze

cosmetics

deodorant

ink

laundry detergent

matches

mothballs

nail polish or remover

perfume

peroxide

rat or mouse poison

suntan lotion

ammonia

bleach

corn and wart removers

dishwasher detergent

drain and toilet cleaners

lye

metal cleaner

oven cleaner

quicklime

rust remover

floor polish and wax

furniture polish and wax

gasoline

kerosene

lighter fluid

liquid naphtha

paint thinner

turpentine

wood preservative

Swallowed Poisons

SWALLOWED POISONS   A poison is a substance that damages health and may cause death when it is swallowed or breathed. Many cleaning agents, house and garden plants, and garden products are very toxic when swallowed. Swallowed poison is also called poisoning by mouth. When poisoning has occurred or is suspected, first aid is needed quickly. Try to discover what product has been swallowed so that correct procedures can be followed.

Remove any poison from the person's mouth. A child may need to be prevented from eating or drinking more of the poison.

Call the local poison control center and follow their instructions. Keep the center's phone number posted near a telephone. If there is no local center, call the closest hospital emergency facility or a doctor. DO NOT rely on product labels for instructions. Be prepared to take steps to dilute the poison, maintain vital body functions, such as breathing and heartbeat, and get immediate medical treatment.

Care for shock until you have been advised by professionals. DO NOT induce vomiting if the person is unconscious or having convulsions; if the product swallowed was an acid, alkali, or petroleum product; or if it is not known what was swallowed. DO NOT give anything by mouth until you have checked with your local poison control center or EMS. Otherwise, follow these first aid directions as appropriate:

1. Assess the person's airway, breathing and circulation.

2. Care for any life-threatening conditions.

3. Look for containers that might be the source of the poison. This information will be needed when you call the poison control center.

4. Call the poison control center or other emergency number and follow their directions.

5. Save any vomited material.

Poisoning is an emergency that can be prevented. Pills and medicines should be carefully labeled and stored out of the reach of children. Household and garden products that can be poisonous should be securely closed. These items should then be safely stored out of the reach of small children.

INHALED POISONS

Inhaled poisons are smoke, gases, and fumes. Warning symptoms of poisoning include dizziness, headache, and weakness. Before you enter a place where there might be poisonous smoke, gases, or fumes, make sure it is safe for you and other bystanders. Then move the injured person to fresh air. Follow these first aid directions:

1. Send for immediate medical help.
2. Check the person's breathing. Rescue breathing or CPR may be necessary.
3. Loosen tight clothing.
4. Prevent shock and care for other injuries.
5. If the person is conscious, elevate the head and chest to ease breathing.

Inhaled Poisons

DRUG OVERDOSE

A drug is a substance that affects the function of the mind or body. Drugs include alcohol, marijuana, hallucinogens, stimulants, and tranquilizers. Even drugs that are safe when used in small amounts may be poisonous when taken in large doses or over time. Poisoning can be avoided by properly labeling and storing drugs. Keep ALL drugs away from small children.

A drug overdose can be a life-threatening emergency. Try to determine the type of drug taken, the amount, and the time it was taken. Call a poison control center or EMS and follow the instructions for specific care. If this center cannot be quickly identified, call a hospital emergency facility or a doctor. If there is no professional advice, be prepared to give general first aid.

Drug withdrawal after prolonged use can also produce severe symptoms. General first aid care is again important until professional medical help is received. In the case of drug overdose or withdrawal, get immediate medical help. Follow these first aid directions:

1. Check the person's breathing. CPR may be necessary.
2. Maintain an open airway and normal body temperature.
3. Care for a seizure if necessary.
4. Be reassuring and keep the person calm. Try to keep her or him awake.
5. Follow directions for swallowed poison, if appropriate.
6. Get medical help.

Drug Overdose

SHOCK

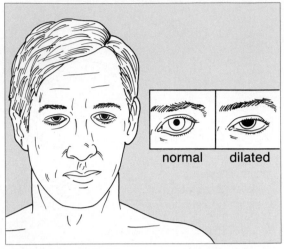

Symptoms of Shock

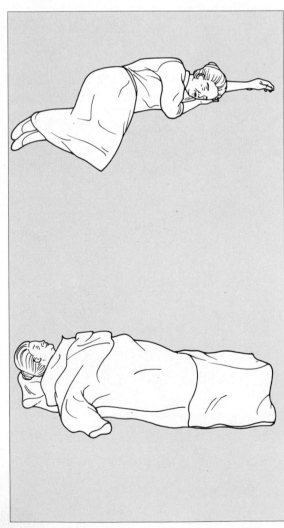

Preventing and Caring for Shock

SYMPTOMS OF SHOCK

Shock can result from any condition or injury that severely lowers blood pressure and vital body functions. Shock is not the same as electric shock, but a person can go into shock from a severe electric shock. Shock is a life-threatening emergency, even if the injury or condition that has caused it may not be fatal. Be alert for these possible symptoms of shock.

Early Symptoms of Shock:
- pale, moist, clammy skin
- rapid breathing
- weakness and nausea
- rapid, weak pulse

Advanced Symptoms of Shock:
- unresponsiveness
- unconsciousness
- vacant look, dilated pupils
- mottled skin

PREVENTING AND CARING FOR SHOCK

Prevention is an important part of treating shock. If signs of shock exist, act right away to alleviate them. Then take steps to prevent a more serious degree of shock. The injury or condition that causes shock is often severe, and may also require first aid.

Shock can be fatal, and even mild shock can become more severe without proper first aid. Improved circulation, adequate oxygen, and normal body temperature minimize the effect of shock. They are the objectives of preventing and caring for shock. Follow these first aid directions:

1. To improve circulation, keep the injured person lying down in one of these positions:

   A. Flat on the back, if there is doubt about the correct position.

   B. On the side, if the injured person may choke on vomit, is unconscious, or has serious facial injuries.

   C. On the back with head and shoulders elevated, if this improves breathing or if there is no danger of choking and no sign of head, neck, or back injury.

   D. On the back with only the feet elevated, if this improves the condition, and if there is no sign of head, neck, or back injury.

2. Monitor the ABCs (page 682) and provide care for any problem.

3. Help the person maintain normal body temperature.

4. DO NOT give anything to eat or drink.

5. DO NOT move the injured person if there is a possible neck or back injury.

6. Get immediate medical help.

POISONOUS PLANTS

Poison ivy, poison oak, and poison sumac cause allergic reactions in four out of five people. It is important to learn to recognize these plants, because they grow in suburban areas as well as in the woods.

Every part of the poison ivy plant contains oils that can cause a skin rash. A person may be exposed to the oils through contact with clothing, pet fur, or garden tools. The smoke from burning oils in poison ivy can be extremely dangerous to the lungs and eyes.

Carefully destroy poisonous plants with a chemical spray. Do not cut them down; they will grow back from the roots. After spraying, thoroughly wash all clothing.

REACTIONS TO POISONOUS PLANTS

The rash produced by the plants in the poison ivy group is characterized by redness, swelling, and itching. The rash may also produce oozing blisters and a burning sensation. The symptoms usually appear within 18 to 72 hours after contact. Follow these first aid directions:

1. Remove contaminated clothing and set aside for later washing.
2. Wash all exposed skin very well with soap and water.
3. Get medical help for a severe reaction or if there is a history of sensitivity, a rash on the face or genitals, or plant parts were chewed or swallowed .

OTHER SKIN-CONTACT POISONS

Other skin-contact poisons include harsh or corrosive chemicals often found in household and garden products. On contact with the skin, these poisons can produce a chemical burn. If the poisonous substance is a pesticide or a strong acid, emergency medical help is necessary. Otherwise, first aid for skin contact poisons is similar to that for chemical burns (page 690). Follow these first aid directions:

1. Remove contaminated clothing and jewelry.
2. Wash away the poisonous substance with large quantities of water for 30 minutes.
3. Get medical help if the chemical burn is extensive.

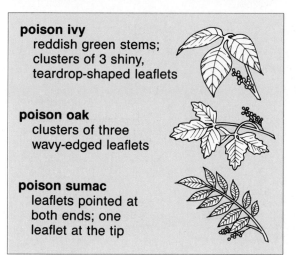

poison ivy
reddish green stems; clusters of 3 shiny, teardrop-shaped leaflets

poison oak
clusters of three wavy-edged leaflets

poison sumac
leaflets pointed at both ends; one leaflet at the tip

Poisonous Plants

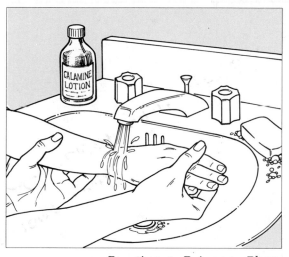

Reactions to Poisonous Plants

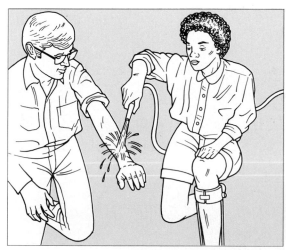

Other Skin-Contact Poisons

UNCONSCIOUSNESS

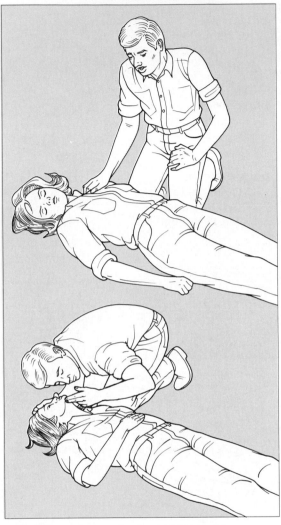

Possible Causes and First Aid Priorities

POSSIBLE CAUSES AND FIRST AID PRIORITIES

There are many possible causes of unconsciousness. Sometimes unconsciousness is brief—as in fainting—and not related to an injury. Other times, unconsciousness is related to an injury or medical problem. It can be caused by injury-related shock, respiratory failure, convulsions, drug use, head injury, or sudden illness. Unconsciousness can signal a medical emergency.

When a person is found unconscious, immediate first aid is important. Information about the events that resulted in unconsciousness may be limited or unavailable. Ask bystanders for any information they may have, and check the person's wrists or neck for tags that indicate a medical condition.

Remember the first aid priorities. Especially remember to avoid injury or danger to yourself or other bystanders and to protect the injured person from further danger or damage.

Medical treatment is always required unless the condition is very minor. Call EMS for help. Follow these first aid directions before giving care for specific injuries:

1. Confirm unconsciousness. See whether the injured person responds to a shout or a firm tap on the shoulder.

2. Open the airway. Check for any sign of breathing.

3. Check for a pulse.

4. Call EMS for help.

5. Rescue breathing or CPR may be necessary to continue first aid.

6. Prevent and care for shock (page 702).

7. Check for injuries. If there are any, care for them appropriately.

FAINTING

When the blood supply to the brain is interrupted for a short time, the result can be a momentary loss of consciousness. Fainting can occur suddenly or be preceded by symptoms including dizziness, nausea, paleness, and sweating.

A person who feels faint should lie down or sit and lean over with the head down. Follow these first aid directions:

1. Act quickly to prevent injury from a fall.

2. Keep the person lying down with legs raised. Loosen any tight clothing.

3. Monitor ABCs (page 682).

4. DO NOT give the person anything to eat or drink.

5. Get medical help if recovery is not rapid.

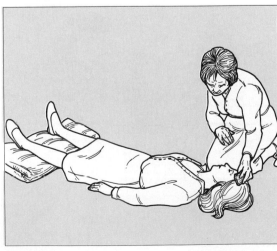

Fainting

HEART ATTACK

If sudden constant chest pain occurs, suspect a heart problem. A heart attack is caused by the blockage of a coronary artery. An attack may be mild or result in sudden death. To reduce the risk of heart attack, maintain proper weight, keep blood pressure down, get regular exercise and medical checkups, eat foods low in fats and cholesterol, and avoid smoking.

Be alert for the signs of a possible heart attack. They can include tight, crushing chest pain that can spread to arms, shoulders, or neck; severe shortness of breath; weakness; sweating; bluish color of skin or lips; and nausea. If a heart attack is suspected, the first step is to calm and reassure the person.

If there is any history of heart trouble or if the chest pain is accompanied by other danger signs, treat the condition as a heart attack. Get immediate medical help and be prepared to give prompt first aid. Follow these first aid directions:

1. Call EMS for an ambulance.

2. Have the person stop what he or she is doing and sit up or recline on pillows.

3. Loosen tight clothing and keep the person warm, NOT overheated.

4. Find out if the person has medicine for this condition. Help the person take this medicine, if he or she is conscious.

5. If the person loses consciousness, lay the person on his or her back and check for signs of breathing. CPR training may be necessary to continue first aid.

6. Stay with the victim until medical help arrives.

STROKE

A stroke occurs when an artery in the brain ruptures or a blood clot restricts circulation. The type of damage that results depends on the area of the brain affected. Symptoms of a stroke can include speech problems, weakness or paralysis on one side of the body, confusion, dizziness, or unconsciousness. Follow these first aid directions:

1. Place the person on his or her side to prevent choking.

2. Keep the person lightly covered.

3. Monitor the ABCs (page 682). Rescue breathing or CPR may be necessary.

4. DO NOT give food or drink.

5. Call EMS immediately for an ambulance.

Signs of a Possible Heart Attack

tight or crushing pain that lasts more than 2 minutes and may spread from the center of the chest to the upper abdomen, shoulder, left arm, neck, or jaw

shortness of breath

severe anxiety

weakness

sweating

pale or bluish skin or lips

nausea or vomiting

irregular pulse

Heart Attack

Stroke

CARDIOPULMONARY RESUSCITATION

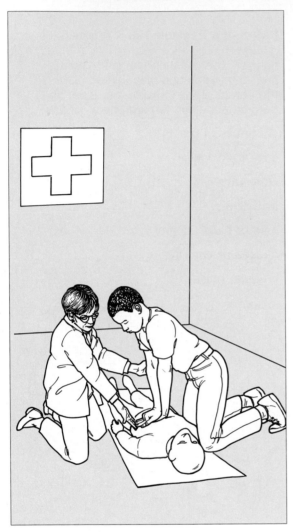

Training in chest compressions

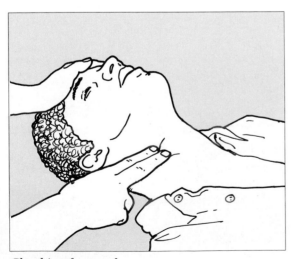

Checking for a pulse

WHAT IS CPR? CPR, or cardiopulmonary resuscitation, is a technique used to save a person who has stopped breathing and whose heart has stopped beating. CPR is a combination of rescue breathing and external chest compressions. Rescue breathing forces air into the lungs. External chest compressions circulate the blood. When the heart stops beating (cardiac arrest) and breathing stops, cardiopulmonary resuscitation is necessary. The purpose of CPR is to keep the victim alive until medical help arrives or until heartbeat or breathing return. Special training in CPR is required. CPR courses are also useful in learning to recognize the symptoms of cardiac arrest.

WHO NEEDS CPR TRAINING? CPR training can mean the difference between life and death. It is a lifesaving skill that anyone can learn. However, *the information in this manual does not take the place of CPR training.* The American Red Cross and the American Heart Association offer CPR instruction. Lectures and demonstrations by authorized CPR instructors, followed by practice sessions with manikins, are used to teach the procedure.

Cardiac arrest is a life-threatening emergency that can occur any time and any place to anyone. Medical professionals, police, fire fighters, and paramedics get CPR training. Before they arrive, you may save a life if you are trained in CPR. Who needs CPR training? You do!

WHEN IS CPR NEEDED? Follow these steps to see if CPR is needed:

1. To see whether the person can respond, tap the shoulder and shout. If there is no response, call EMS for an ambulance.

2. Check ABCs (page 682). Open the airway and monitor breathing. If the person is not breathing, give two full, slow breaths (page 689). Check for circulation by feeling for a pulse and looking for signs of bleeding.

If the person has a pulse and is breathing, watch him or her until help arrives. If the person has a pulse and is not breathing, continue by giving rescue breaths. If the person has no pulse and is not breathing, CPR is needed immediately.

THE STEPS OF CPR

CAUTION: If you have not had CPR training, DO NOT attempt to give CPR. If done improperly, CPR can cause further injury or death. If CPR is given to a person who has a pulse, it can cause cardiac arrest. CPR for children and infants is different than for adults.

A person trained in CPR checks for unresponsiveness, breathing, and pulse as described in "When Is CPR Needed." Determine unresponsiveness and remember the ABCs (page 682). Call EMS for an ambulance.

If there is no pulse, a person with CPR training finds the correct hand position and gives 15 compressions in about ten seconds. This circulates blood to the brain and other vital organs. After every 15 compressions, the rescuer stops compressing and gives two full, slow breaths. The rescuer continues cycles of 15 compressions and two breaths.

The rescuer checks the victim's pulse after the first minute (or after four sets of compressions and breaths) and again every few minutes. If there is no pulse, the rescuer continues CPR. If there is a pulse but no breathing, the rescuer gives rescue breathing. If there is a pulse and breathing, the rescuer maintains an open airway and keeps checking pulse and breathing.

RESCUE BREATHING FOR AN INFANT

The techniques effective on an infant differ from those used on a child or adult. Follow these steps to administer rescue breathing for an infant:

1. Send for medical help immediately.
2. Open the airway. Be careful not to tilt the head too far back.
3. Form a seal with your mouth tightly over the infant's mouth and nose.
4. Give breaths at a rate of one every three seconds.
5. Check for pulse on the brachial artery of the upper arm.

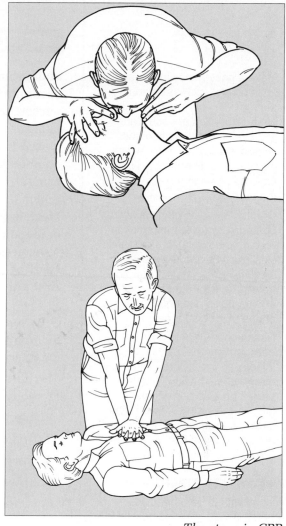

The steps in CPR

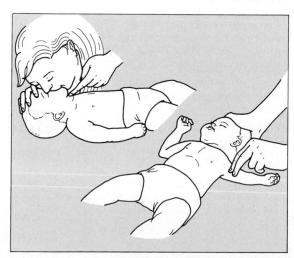

Rescue breathing for an infant

PROJECTS

1. Make a poster showing poiso-nous plants, such as poison ivy, that grow in your area. Include a brief description of each plant. Include information about the color of the leaves, their arran-gement, and whether the plants have berries and the colors of the berries.

2. Create an eye-catching bulletin board that provides information on a group of related emergen-cies, such as sports emergen-cies. Include easy-to-follow illus-trated steps for handling the emergencies and emergency phone numbers for getting help.

3. Research the differences between emergency care for infants, young children, older children, and adults. Create a packet on emergency care for infants and young children. The packet should include sketches of techniques of first aid that are unique to infants and children.

WORKING WITH OTHERS

Working with three other class-mates, organize a series of skits in which your group acts out four dif-ferent medical emergencies. Each group member is responsible for demonstrating the proper first aid technique. The following roles should be filled during each demon-stration: first-aid responder, victim, assistant (if needed), and narrator. The narrator describes the step-by-step process of the technique to the rest of the class.

CONNECTING TO...

COMPOSITION Prepare and distrib-ute a safety booklet to be used by young children. With words and cartoons, describe how to prevent accidents, including poisoning. Also show what to do if an accident happens.

USING VOCABULARY

abdominal thrust	first-degree burn	muscle strain
cardiopulmonary resuscitation (CPR)	fracture	pressure-point technique
choking	frostbite	puncture
closed fracture	heart attack	rescue breathing
concussion	heat cramp	second-degree burn
croup	heat exhaustion	seizure
dislocation	heat stroke	shock
electric shock	Heimlich maneuver	splint
emergency medical services (EMS)	hyperventilation	sprain
	hypothermia	stroke
fainting	incision	third-degree burn
first aid	laceration	unconsciousness
	muscle cramp	

On a separate sheet of paper, write the term from the vocabulary list above that matches the phrase below. Create your own phrases for those terms not used in this exercise.

1. life-threatening condition in which blood pressure and vital body functions are severely lowered

2. practical and immediate care for an injury or sudden illness

3. first aid procedure that forces air into the lungs

4. a break or crack in a bone

5. upward thrusts on the abdomen, intended to dislodge an object

6. condition caused by the blockage of a coronary artery

7. a life-threatening condition involving very high body tempera-ture, lack of perspiration, and rapid pulse

8. first aid technique for use when heart and lungs fail

9. lowered body temperature

10. type of wound in which a hole is made by a sharp object

THINKING CRITICALLY

INTERPRET

1. What are the possible causes of an eye injury? With chemi-cal burns or invisible objects in the eye, what two steps should be taken before seeking medical care?

2. Why can animal or human bites be dangerous?

3. What is the universal sign for choking? How does emergency care for a choking adult differ from emergency care for a chok-ing infant?

4. Why is it dangerous for a person without proper training to try to give CPR?

5. List five signs of head injury.

6. What immediate procedure should you follow if you discover the victim of a drug overdose?

7. What is the purpose of first aid? What are the advantages of a knowledge of first aid?

8. What steps should be followed for the removal of a splinter?

9. What are the early symptoms of shock? What are the objectives of preventing and caring for shock?

10. What are the signs of a sprain? What parts of the body are most easily sprained?

11. List three methods of controlling bleeding, in the order in which they should be tried.

12. How can you help to prevent choking during a seizure?

13. What can you do to avoid hypothermia?

14. What are the signs of a possible heart attack?

15. What directions should be followed when a child has swallowed poison? How can poisoning be prevented?

16. How can you protect yourself from the source of electricity when you are trying to care for an electric shock victim?

17. Compare the symptoms of heat exhaustion and heat stroke. Which of these conditions is more serious?

18. What is the purpose of CPR?

APPLY

19. Identify three arguments for why everyone needs CPR training.

20. Why should people like bus drivers be trained in first aid?

21. How should burns be cared for?

22. What are the differences between heat exhaustion and heat stroke? How should each be treated?

23. When frostbite occurs, why is it dangerous to rub the frozen area to help it thaw out?

24. Why do you think heat cramps are more likely to affect the muscles of the legs or abdomen first?

MAKING DECISIONS

1. Identify the correct method for handling the following situation. A child who was thought to have swallowed a household poison was promptly given syrup of ipecac in order to induce vomiting.

2. After football practice, Tom noticed swelling around one of his ankles. As he walked home, the ankle became increasingly painful. To get the swelling down, Tom applied an ice pack to his ankle. What did Tom do wrong?

3. You are a physical education instructor. During one of your classes, two of your students collide during a volleyball game. One of the students appears to be fine. You suspect that the other student may have suffered a concussion. What should you do?

4. You come upon an accident scene in which the person in one car shows the following symptoms: pale, moist skin; rapid breathing; rapid, weak pulse; nausea. What might be wrong with the person? What should you do?

MEDICINES IN YOUR HOME

It is useful to have some basic medical supplies in your home to treat minor injuries and disorders, but the family medicine chest need not be a mini drug store. Family needs will vary, but the table below lists the items that are most frequently needed.

◆ MEDICINE CABINET

Medicines	Supplies
• Pain reliever: aspirin or aspirin substitute such as acetaminophen for children and adults • Ipecac: for promoting vomiting in certain kinds of poisoning emergencies • Rubbing alcohol: for antibacterial topical use • Antidiarrheal medication • Antacid • Cough syrup • Calomine lotion or other mild lotion for itching • Sunscreen to prevent sunburn • Skin cream or lotion to treat sunburn • Insect repellant	• Bandages: adhesive strip bandages, adhesive tape and sterile gauze pads, Elastic bandages and surgical bandages • Scissors for cutting bandages • Tweezers for removing splinters • Thermometer: rectal or digital for children • Absorbent cotton

STORING MEDICINES—WHERE?

- A cool, dry place away from food and other household products
- A locked cabinet that is not in the bathroom
- A place that is not accessible to children
- Prescription drugs should be stored in a place separate from non-prescription products

MAINTAINING EFFECTIVENESS

- Buy only as much of any product as will be used in 6 to 12 months.
- Keep track of expiration dates. Discard any product that is past its expiration date.
- Discard tablets that have become crumbly. Any medicines that have changed color, odor, or consistency should be destroyed.
- Keep containers of medicines tightly closed.

PRECAUTIONS

- Keep medicines in their original containers with labels intact.
- Destroy medicines by flushing them down the toilet. Do not leave leftover drugs where they can be found by children.
- Select medicines with child-resistant caps if children are ever in your home.
- Keep the telephone numbers of your physician, hospital, rescue squad, fire and police departments, and local poison control center near your phone.

MEDICAL SPECIALISTS AND WHAT THEY DO

Medical Specialist	Description of Work
Allergist	Concerned with allergies.
Anesthesiologist	Deals with anesthesia and the administration of anesthetics.
Colon, rectal surgeon	Treats disorders of the colon and rectum.
Dermatologist	Concerned with the structure, functions, and diseases of the skin.
Practicioner in Emergency Medicine	Provides immediate treatment in emergency situations.
Practicioner in Family Medicine	Provides medical care to all members of families.
Gastroenterologist	Specializes in disorders of the digestive system.
Gynecologist	Deals with diseases of the female reproductive system and the maintenance of womens' health.
Immunopathologist	Concerned with the immune responses associated with disease.
Internist	Specializes in internal medicine.
Neurologist	Diagnoses and treats diseases of the nervous system.
Obstetrician	Deals with pregnancy, birth, and any conditions that result from the birth process.
Oncologist	Specializes in the treatment of tumors, malignant and benign.
Ophthalmologist	Concerned with the structure, functions, and diseases of the eye.
Orthopedic Surgeon	Corrects or prevents skeletal deformities.
Otorhinolaryngologist	Specializes in the treatment of disorders of the ear, nose, and throat.
Pathologist	Diagnoses the changes caused by disease in tissue and body fluids.
Pediatrician	Deals with the development, care, and diseases of children.
Physiatrist	Helps repair muscle and skeletal damage resulting from injuries and diseases.
Plastic Surgeon	Repairs, restores or improves lost, injured, or misshapen parts of the body.
Practitioner of Preventive Medicine	Devoted to preventing illness rather than curing illness.
Proctologist	Deals will disorders of the anus, rectum, and sigmoid colon.
Psychiatrist	Specializes in mental, emotional, or behavioral disorders.
Radiologist	Uses radiant energy (X rays and radium emission) for diagnosing and treating disease, particularly cancer.
Practitioner of Sports Medicine	Treats injuries and their aftermath, particularly those associated with sports.
Surgeon	Specializes in surgery.
Thoracic Surgeon	Specializes in surgery of the thorax, the portion of the body between the neck and abdomen.
Urologist	Concerned with the urinary and urogenital tract.

WARM-UP EXERCISES

ARM CIRCLE

Loosens arms and shoulders.

Starting Position Stand with your feet shoulder-width apart, knees bent, toes straight.

Movement Swing both arms in large, sweeping circles inward across your body, upward across your face, out and back down. Keep your elbows straight and swing your arms from the shoulders.

Repetitions Start with 10 and build up to 20.

TRUNK TWIST

Loosens back and shoulders.

Starting Position Stand with your feet shoulder-width apart, knees bent, toes straight. Hold your arms out at your sides.

Movement With your heels flat, twist your trunk slowly as far as you can, first to one side and then to the other. Move smoothly; do not bounce.

Repetitions Start with 6 and build up to 12.

SIDE LEG RAISE

Loosens hips.

Starting Position Lie on one side with your legs straight, head on your hand, upper arm along your thigh.

Movement Raise your upper leg as high as you can, keeping it straight. Do the repetitions for one side, then repeat on your other side.

Repetitions Start with 10 and build up to 20.

ACHILLES AND CALF STRETCH

Loosens calves.

Starting Position Stand facing a wall an arm's length away, with hands resting on the wall, feet shoulder-width apart, knees and toes straight.

Movement Lean forward, bending your elbows down slowly. Keep your legs and body straight and your heels on the floor. Do not lean so far that it hurts. Hold for 10 seconds and return to the starting position.

Repetitions Start with 2 and build up to 6.

HAZARDOUS HOUSEHOLD PRODUCT	LESS TOXIC ALTERNATIVE

Household Cleaners

Abrasive cleaners or powders	Rub area with 1/2 lemon dipped in borax. Rinse and dry. (Note: Borax is toxic to children.)
Ammonia-based cleaners	Use undiluted white vinegar from a spray bottle.
Bleach cleaners	For laundry, use 1/2 cup white vinegar or baking soda per load.
Disinfectants	Mix 1/2 cup borax with 1 gallon of boiling water, or use undiluted white vinegar. (See note above.)
Drain cleaners	Use a plunger; flush weekly with boiling water; rinse in 1/4 cup baking soda.
Floor and furniture polish	Mix 1 part lemon juice and 2 parts linseed oil. Use tooth paste to remove water stains.
Mothballs	Store cedar chips, newspapers, or lavender flowers with clothing.
Oven cleaners	Wipe oven while still warm. Use a paste of baking soda and water with steel wool to scrub.
Rug and upholstery cleaners	Clean immediately with soda water or baking soda paste, then vacuum.

Pesticides

Chemicals for controlling ants	Place boric acid in and along cracks. (Note: Boric acid is toxic for children and pets.)
Chemicals for controlling plant fungus	Do not overwater. Aerate soil.
Chemicals for controlling garden pests	Import predators (ladybugs, ground beetles, praying mantis). Use insecticidal soap.
Chemicals for killing weeds	Weed by hand. Let grass grow 2–3 inches to shade weed seedlings.
Houseplant insecticide	Mix 2 tablespoons dishwashing liquid with 2 cups water and spray on leaves.
Flea collars and sprays	Herbal collar or ointment (eucalyptus or rosemary), or Brewer's Yeast (call veterinarian for amount).
Mouse and rat poisons	Seal all holes. Use live traps or ultrasonic wave-emitting devices.

Paints and Finishes

Enamel or oil-based paints	Latex or water-based paint
Thinners and turpentine	Water with water-based paints
Paint and varnish remover	Sandpaper or scraper and heat gun
Wood preservatives	Water-based wood preservative

CALORIES, NUTRIENTS, AND MINERALS IN SELECTED FOODS

Food and Amount	Energy (Calories)	Protein (g)	Fat (g)	Cholesterol (mg)	Calcium (mg)	Iron (mg)	Sodium (mg)
Apple, 1 medium	80	tr	tr	0	10	0.2	tr
Bacon, crisp, 3 sl	110	6	9	16	2	0.3	303
Banana, 1 medium	105	1	1	0	7	0.4	1
Beans, snap,1 cup	45	2	tr	0	58	1.6	4
Beef, hamburger, 3 oz	230	21	16	74	9	1.8	65
Beef, rib roast, 3 oz	315	19	26	72	8	2.0	54
Beets, cooked, 1 cup	55	2	tr	0	19	1.1	83
Bread, white, enriched, 1 sl	65	2	1	0	32	0.7	129
Bread, whole wheat, 1 sl	70	3	1	0	20	1.0	180
Butter, salted, 1 tbsp	100	tr	11	31	3	tr	116
Candies, caramels, 1 oz	115	1	3	1	42	0.4	64
Carrot, raw, 1 ave	30	1	tr	0	19	0.4	25
Cheese, cheddar, 1 oz	115	7	9	30	204	0.2	176
Cheese, cottage, 1 cup	235	28	10	34	135	0.3	911
Cheeseburger, 1 sandwich	300	15	15	44	135	2.3	672
Chicken, batter fried, 1/2 breast	365	35	18	119	28	1.8	385
Chicken, roasted, 3 oz	140	27	3	73	13	0.9	64
Cocoa, from nonfat powder	100	3	1	0	2	0.4	3
Corn flakes, 1 cup	95	2	tr	0	1	1.4	281
Crackers, Graham, 4	120	2	2	0	12	0.8	172
Cream, sour, 1 cup	495	7	48	102	268	0.1	123
Cream, whipped topping, 1 cup	155	2	13	46	61	tr	78
Egg, omelet or scrambled	110	7	8	282	54	1.0	176
Egg, raw or cooked in shell	80	6	6	274	28	1.0	69
Frankfurter	145	5	13	23	5	0.5	504
Fruit cocktail, canned, 1 cup	185	1	tr	0	15	0.7	15
Haddock, breaded, fried, 3 oz	175	17	9	75	34	1.0	123
Ice cream, 1 cup	270	5	14	59	176	0.1	116
Macaroni and cheese, 1 cup	430	17	22	44	362	1.8	1086
Margarine, 1 tbsp	50	tr	5	0	2	0.0	134
Milk, nonfat, 1 cup	85	8	tr	12	302	0.1	126
Milk, whole, 1 cup	150	8	8	33	291	0.1	120
Orange, 1 medium	60	1	tr	0	52	0.1	tr
Orange juice, frozen, 1 cup	110	2	tr	0	22	0.2	2
Peanut butter, 1 tbsp	95	5	8	0	5	0.3	75
Peas, green, 1 cup	125	8	tr	0	38	2.5	139
Pizza, cheese, 1/8 of 15-inch pie	290	15	9	56	220	1.6	699
Pork, roasted, 3 oz	270	21	20	69	9	0.8	37
Potato, baked, 1 medium	220	5	tr	0	20	2.7	16
Potatoes, French-fried, 10 pcs	160	2	8	0	10	0.4	108
Potato Chips, 10 chips	105	1	7	0	5	0.2	94
Spaghetti from home recipe	260	9	9	8	80	2.3	955
Spinach, cooked, 1 cup	40	5	tr	0	245	6.4	126
Taco	195	9	11	21	109	1.2	456
Tuna, waterpack, 3 oz	135	30	1	48	17	0.6	468
Yogurt, plain, 8 oz	145	12	4	14	415	0.2	159

Source: U.S. Department of Agriculture, Human Nutrition and Information Service

tr=trace

COMMON NONINFECTIOUS DISEASES AND DISORDERS

Disease	Characteristics	Treatment
Acne	Overproduction of sebum causes blackheads, whiteheads, and pimples over face, upper chest, and back	Cleansing skin; medication for severe cases
Alzheimer's disease	Progressive dementia that may occur before age 60; brain cells gradually die; causes impaired language and motor functions and loss of memory and thinking ability	None yet; research underway to find effective treatments
Anemia	Disorder in which there are too few red blood cells or not enough hemoglobin; not enough oxygen reaches tissues; causes weakness	Depending on cause, iron supplements, vitamin injections, or transfusions
Anorexia nervosa	Psychological condition causing progressive weight loss; refusal to eat causes dry skin, brittle hair, dehydration, fainting, and irregular heartbeat	Counseling to change attitude toward eating and to resolve underlying conflicts
Appendicitis	Infection of appendix; causes severe pain in abdomen, vomiting, constipation, and fever	Surgical removal of appendix
Arteriosclerosis	Hardening of arteries; may cause legs to ache during physical activity, dizziness, and temporary loss of sight; may lead to stroke, heart disease, or senile dementia	Diet control; medication
Arthritis	A group of diseases in which joints in the body become inflamed, swollen, and sore	Medications; joint surgery; physical therapy
Asthma	Chronic respiratory disease; spasms of bronchi result in recurrent attacks of coughing, wheezing, and shortness of breath	Medication
Atherosclerosis	Buildup of fatty material such as cholesterol on artery walls; reduces blood flow; can lead to heart attack or stroke	Diet control; regular physical activity; quitting smoking
Bulimia	Eating disorder in which episodes of extreme overeating are followed by self-induced vomiting or use of diuretics and laxatives	Counseling to stop the binge-purge cycle and regain control over eating behavior
Cancer	Group of diseases characterized by uncontrolled growth of cells; caused by carcinogens; symptoms vary with type of cancer	Surgery; radiation therapy; chemotherapy; immunotherapy
Cerebral palsy	Disorder resulting from brain damage at or before birth; results in loss of muscle control, poor coordination, and speech and hearing problems	Exercise; supportive devices
Coronary heart disease (coronary artery disease)	Reduced flow of blood to wall of heart due to atherosclerosis; causes chest pains and possible heart attack	Diet control; regular physical activity, quitting smoking
Cystic fibrosis	Hereditary disease that affects mucus-secreting glands; causes coughing, poor digestion, diarrhea, increased susceptibility to respiratory infections	Respiratory therapy; antibiotics
Diabetes mellitus, insulin-dependent (Type I)	Hereditary condition in which the pancreas does not produce enough insulin, resulting in high blood sugar; causes frequent urination accompanied by thirst, fatigue, and rapid weight loss; if left untreated, can cause blindness, kidney failure, and death; onset usually occurs in childhood or adolescence	Insulin injections; special diet
Diabetes mellitus, noninsulin-dependent (Type II)	Condition in which the cells cannot take in glucose, resulting in high blood sugar; causes frequent urination, thirst, fatigue, blurred vision, and frequent infections; onset most common among overweight adults	Special diet; exercise; medication
Eczema	Condition of the skin; causes blisters that break leaving a raw surface to dry and crack on healing	Ointments and creams; medication, avoidance of causal irritants
Emphysema	Condition of weakened lung tissue; lungs lose elasticity, resulting in difficulty in exhaling; usually related to smoking or air pollution	Medications, hormones, air pumps, and surgery
Epilepsy	Disorder of nerve cells in brain; seizures occur when cells release a sudden burst of electric energy	Medication

Disease	Characteristics	Treatment
Glaucoma	Buildup of fluid pressure within the eye, causing the eye to become rigid; causes loss of peripheral vision and may lead to blindness if left untreated	Medication; surgery
Gout	Inflammation of joints due to buildup of uric acid; causes severe pain in elbow, knee, hand, or foot, fever, and inflamed skin; can lead to kidney disease and death if left untreated	Physical therapy; medication
Hemophilia	Hereditary disease in which blood lacks factors necessary for clotting; bleeding cannot be stopped	Avoiding injury; injections of a clotting factor
Hernia	Bulge of tissue pushing through muscle wall; a rupture; often of intestine through abdominal wall	Surgery
Hodgkin's disease	Cancer of the lymph nodes; occurs most often in young adults; produces enlarged lymph nodes, fever, weight loss, fatigue, and sweating	Radiation therapy; chemotherapy
Hypertension	High blood pressure caused by narrowing of blood vessels; no symptoms until blood pressure gets dangerously high; can lead to stroke or heart disease	Medication to control blood pressure; special diet
Leukemia	Cancer of the bone marrow in which immature white blood cells multiply rapidly and crowd out mature white cells; immune system weakens; occurs most often in children	Chemotherapy
Migraine	Severe headache accompanied by nausea and sensitivity to light	Medication; avoiding certain foods or stressful situations
Multiple sclerosis	Disease that slowly destroys nerve tissue; usually starts during childhood; causes paralysis and death	Rest and physical therapy
Muscular dystrophy	Progressive weakening of muscles usually starting during early childhood; causes deformed limbs	Physical therapy
Osteoporosis	Loss of calcium from bone; results in weakened bones and rounded shoulders; common in older women	Diet rich in calcium; exercise
Parkinson's disease	Disorder of the nervous system; results in tremors, slower body movements, weakness, stooping posture, and weak voice	Medication
Schizophrenia	Mental disorder in which a person withdraws from reality, behaves in odd ways, and has hallucinations	Psychotherapy; medication
Scoliosis	Abnormal curvature of the spine that becomes noticeable during adolescence; can cause chest infections and shortness of breath	Physical therapy; spinal brace; electrical stimulation
Sickle-cell anemia	Hereditary type of anemia in which red blood cells are deformed in shape, or "sickled;" causes severe pain, high fever, damage to body tissues, blindness, convulsions, paralysis, and loss of speech	No effective treatment yet; experimental medicines
Stroke	Blockage or rupture of blood vessel in the brain; can cause loss of physical and mental abilities or death	Physical therapy

COMMON INFECTIOUS DISEASES

Disease	Characteristics	Method of Transmission	Prevention/Treatment
Acquired immune deficiency syndrome (AIDS)	Viral disease of the immune system; causes fever, fatigue, loss of appetite, loss of resistance to infection, and swollen glands; fatal	Exchange of bodily fluids via sexual contact or breast-feeding; transfusion of infected blood; use of unsterile syringes	Screening blood donors; changing sexual behavior; medications (some experimental) prolong life
Athletes's foot	Fungal skin infection on the foot; skin becomes red and flaky, blisters develop between toes	Contact with contaminated objects such as showers and locker room floors	Cleaning and drying feet; antifungal medication
Botulism	Food poisoning caused by toxin released from bacteria; results in muscle weakness, dizziness, nausea, and paralysis of cardiac, respiratory, and central nervous systems	Eating vegetables and fruits that were canned improperly	Toxin destroyed by heating, so all canned or bottled foods should be boiled; anti-toxin
Bronchitis	Viral or bacterial infection of membranes lining bronchi; causes deep cough that brings up gray or yellowish sputum, difficulty breathing, and fever	Close contact with infected person	Bed rest; antibiotics
Chancroid	Bacterial STD; painful chancre develops in genital area	Sexual contact	Antibiotics
Chicken pox	Viral skin infection; causes mild fever and itchy skin rash with blisters that form scabs	Close contact with infected person; airborne spread of virus	Skin lotions alleviate symptoms
Chlamydia	Bacterial STD; inflammation of urethra in males and vagina in females; symptoms similar to gonorrhea	Sexual contact	Antibiotics
Cholera	Bacterial infection of intestines; causes severe diarrhea, vomiting, and dehydration	Ingestion of food or water contaminated with sewage or vomit	Drinking treated water; replacement of body fluids; antibiotics
Common cold	Viral infection of upper respiratory tract; causes coughing, sneezing, and runny nose	Close contact with infected person; airborne spread of virus	Bed rest; hot liquids
Conjunctivitis	Viral or bacterial eye infection; results in tearing, inflammation, itching, burning, and pus in eye	Contact with discharge from infected eyes	Antibiotics
Croup	Viral or bacterial infection of the voice box, windpipe, and bronchial tubes; causes a loud cough and difficult breathing	Contact with infected person	Antibiotics if the infection is bacterial; rest in a moist atmosphere
Cystitis	Bacterial infection of the bladder; causes frequent urination, burning sensation on urination, and blood in urine	Sexual activity, poor hygiene	Antibiotics
Diphtheria	Bacterial infection; results in sore throat, fever, and patches of grayish membrane on tonsils and throat; now most common in less developed countries	Direct contact with infected saliva or mucus	Vaccine; hospitalization; antitoxins; antibiotics
Genital warts	Viral infection; causes warty growths on the genitalia	Sexual contact	Medication applied to warts; surgical removal or removal by laser
Gonorrhea	Bacterial STD; males experience painful urination, puslike discharge from penis; symptoms not as obvious in females	Sexual contact	Antibiotics
Hepatitis A (infectious hepatitis)	Viral liver infection; causes fever, fatigue, loss of appetite, abdominal pain, and jaundice; sudden onset	Person-to-person contact; eating contaminated food and water	Careful attention to hygiene; isolating patients during infectious period; bed rest

Disease	Characteristics	Method of Transmission	Prevention/Treatment
Hepatitis B (serum hepatitis)	Viral liver infection; symptoms similar to Hepatitis A, but more severe and with slower onset	Contact with contaminated syringes; contact with infected blood; sexual contact	Same as Hepatitis A
Hepatitis Non-A, Non-B	Viral liver infection; symptoms similar to Hepatitis A and B, but milder	Contact with infected blood; sexual contact	Same as Hepatitis A
Herpes Type I	Viral mouth infection; causes cold sores and fever blisters that appear most often on lips and mouth	Contact with infected saliva	Heals naturally; topical medications may ease symptoms
Herpes Type II	Viral infection of the genitals; sores on genitals	Sexual contact	Antiviral medication to alleviate symptoms
Influenza	Viral respiratory infection; causes fever, chills, headache, muscle aches, runny nose, sore throat, and coughing	Person-to-person contact; contact with contaminated articles	Vaccine; bed rest; hot liquids
Legionnaire's disease	Bacterial lung infection; results in high fever, inflammation of lungs, coughing, and weakness	Contact with bacteria that grow in the water of air-conditioners	Antibiotics
Lyme disease	Caused by an organism that lives in a type of tick; results in red rash at the site of the tick bite, headache, chills and fever, body aches, and joint inflamation	Bite of a type of tick	Antibiotics and medication to relieve joint inflamation; wear long pants and long-sleeved shirt when walking in wooded areas; inspect yourself for the presence of ticks
Malaria	Caused by a parasite that lives in the blood; causes fever, chills, sweating, headache, and jaundice	Carried by mosquitoes; transfusion of infected blood	Preventive medications; drug therapy
Measles (rubeola)	Viral infection of skin and respiratory tract; results in fever, dry cough, runny nose, and rash; can lead to pneumonia and other serious complications	Contact with infected saliva or mucus; airborne spread of virus; highly contagious	Vaccine; bed rest
Meningitis	Viral or bacterial inflammation of the membranes around the spinal cord and brain; results in fever, headache, nausea, vomiting, and a stiff neck; may cause unconsciousness	Contact with infected saliva or mucus; airborne spread of virus	Vaccine or drug therapy for bacterial form; symptomatic treatment for viral form
Mononucleosis	Viral infection that spreads to many organs; causes high fever, fatigue, swollen glands, and sore throat; weakness and lack of energy noticeable for weeks	Contact with saliva, as in kissing, is suspected; other methods unknown	Bed rest; treatment of fever
Mumps	Viral infection of glands; causes headache, fever, vomiting, and swelling of glands in front of ears	Direct contact with saliva or contaminated articles; highly contagious	Vaccine; bed rest
Osteomyelitis	Inflammation of bone marrow caused by bacterial infection; causes pain and sensation of heat at site of affected bone, tenderness, swelling, and fever	Introduced through a wound, fracture, or injury	Antibiotics, bed rest and immobilization of affected bones
Pneumonia	Viral or bacterial infection of lungs; causes inflammation of the lungs, chills, fever, chest pain, and coughing	Contact with infected saliva or mucus	Vaccine and antibiotics for bacterial pneumonia
Poliomyelitis	Viral infection of nerves; results in fever, headache, vomiting, muscular stiffness, soreness, and weakness; can cause paralysis that may lead to respiratory failure and death	Direct contact; eating contaminated foods	Vaccine; no specific treatment

Disease	Characteristics	Method of Transmission	Prevention/Treatment
Rabies (hydrophobia)	Viral infection of the brain; causes convulsions, paralysis, restlessness, fever, and excessive salivation; can be fatal	Contact with saliva from the bite of an infected animal (dog, cat, fox, skunk, racoon, bat, or rat)	Vaccine; see physician immediately for antirabies injections
Rheumatic fever	Caused by streptococcal bacteria; results in severe sore throat (strep throat), fever, inflamed joints, and body rash; can cause permanent heart damage	Direct contact	Antibiotics
Ringworm	Fungal skin infection; causes ring-shaped sores	Direct contact with fungus or contaminated articles	Careful laundering of clothing; good personal hygiene; antifungal compounds
Rocky mountain spotted fever	Caused by tiny, bacterialike organisms; results in a high fever, headache, chills, rash, and muscle weakness; kidneys, liver, lungs, and blood can be damaged	Bite of an infected tick	Tick repellant; antibiotics
Rubella (German measles)	Mild viral disease; causes rash, fever, swollen glands around ears, neck, and throat; can cause birth defects if a pregnant woman contracts disease	Direct contact with saliva or mucus of infected person	Vaccine; bed rest
Salmonellosis	Bacterial food poisoning; causes acute diarrhea, abdominal pain, vomiting, and fever	Eating contaminated food such as inadequately cooked meat, poultry, and egg products	Keeping raw meats refrigerated and cooking meat thoroughly; medication
Scarlet fever	Caused by streptococcal bacteria; results in severe sore throat (strep throat), fever, vomiting, headache, rash	Direct contact	Antibiotics
Shingles	Chicken pox virus attacks nerve roots; results in fever and scabby sores	Direct contact	Skin lotions
Sinusitis	Inflammation of the mucous membranes lining the sinuses; causes pain, fever, blocked nose, and headache	Contact with pathogens	Bed rest; nasal spray to shrink swollen membranes; antibiotics
Staphylococcal food poisoning	Caused by bacterial toxin; results in vomiting and abdominal cramps; most common type of food poisoning	Eating food contaminated as a result of coughing or sneezing or handling by an infected person	Keeping food cold; medication to relieve vomiting
Syphilis	Bacterial STD; causes open sore on genitals and body rash in early stage; more serious if left untreated	Sexual contact	Antibiotics
Tetanus (lockjaw)	Bacterial infection of nerve cells in spinal cord; causes painful tightening of the muscles; can be fatal	Bacteria enter the body through wounds	Vaccine; antitoxin
Trichinosis	Caused by parasitic worms; causes diarrhea, fever, and profuse sweating	Ingestion of infected pork or game	Cooking pork thoroughly; bed rest; medication
Tuberculosis (TB)	Bacterial infection; causes coughing, weight loss, blood in phlegm, fever, and heavy perspiration at night	Contact with saliva or mucus of infected person; ingestion of infected dairy products	Antibiotics
Typhoid fever	Severe salmonellosis; causes fever, headache, weakness, loss of appetite, skin rash, and constipation or diarrhea	Ingestion of contaminated food and water	Antibiotics
Vaginitis	Yeast or protist infection of vagina; causes vaginal inflammation, soreness, discharges and itching	Yeast infection may develop with hormonal change or after use of antibiotics; protists can be spread by sexual contact	Antifungal cream; medication
Whooping cough (pertussis)	Bacterial respiratory infection; results in loss of appetite, fever, lethargy, hacking cough, then violent cough and vomiting	Contact with saliva or mucus of infected person	Vaccine; antibiotics

GLOSSARY

absorption   the process by which nutrients from digested food move into the bloodstream.

abstinence   the conscious decision not to participate in sexual activity.

accident   a sudden, unexpected event, often with undesirable results.

acquaintance   someone familiar to, but not close to, another person.

acquired immune deficiency syndrome (AIDS)   a fatal viral disease of the immune system.

addiction   a strong physical and psychological craving for a substance.

additive   a substance added to food to prevent spoilage or improve its nutritional value, appearance, texture, or taste.

adolescence   the period of human development during which children develop adult physical characteristics.

adoption   a process through which children can legally become part of a family.

adrenal glands   a pair of endocrine glands at the top of each kidney that releases several different hormones, including adrenaline, also known as epinephrine.

adrenaline   a hormone released by the adrenal glands in response to danger, excitement, or stress; the hormone that prepares the body to fight danger or to flee from it.

advertising   a method of calling attention to a product.

aerobic exercise   vigorous, strenuous physical activity that increases consumption of oxygen.

after-care program   a follow-up counseling service for recovered drug users.

AIDS dementia complex   the damage to the central nervous system caused by the human immunodeficiency virus (HIV).

air pollution   contamination of air by harmful gases or particulates.

alarm stage   the immediate physical response to stress.

alcoholism   a disease characterized by psychological and physical dependence on alcohol and the inability to control drinking.

alimentary canal   the organs of the digestive system through which food passes.

Alzheimer's disease   a serious disorder in which loss of brain cells affects a person's memory and reasoning power.

amino acid   the basic chemical unit of all proteins.

amnesia   the sudden inability to recall basic personal information.

amniotic sac   a protective membrane that surrounds the embryo and fetus.

anabolic steroid   a synthetic drug that acts like the male hormone testosterone.

anaerobic exercise   intense bursts of activity during which the muscles outstrip their oxygen supply.

anaphylactic shock   a life-threatening allergic reaction to the body's releasing too much histamine.

anemia   a blood condition caused by either too few red blood cells or too little hemoglobin to transport adequate oxygen to the cells.

angiogram   a technique used in x-raying the coronary artery.

angioplasty   a surgical technique for widening an artery by inserting a tube with a balloon attached, then inflating the balloon.

anorexia nervosa   an eating disorder marked by constant dieting, rapid weight loss, and the illusion of being overweight in spite of weight loss.

antibiotic   a prescription medicine that inhibits the growth and reproduction of bacteria and other organisms.

antibody   protein in the blood that disables pathogens or their toxins.

anxiety   a fear of the unknown.

appendicitis   a condition in which an infected appendix becomes inflamed and swollen.

appendicular skeleton   the bones in the limbs.

appetite   a desire for food that is distinct from the body's need for food.

arrhythmia   a disruption of the steady rhythmic rate at which a heart has been beating.

artery   a blood vessel with a thick muscular wall that carries blood away from the heart.

arthritis   a group of diseases characterized by the inflammation and swelling of joints.

asthma   a chronic respiratory disorder, characterized by spasms of the bronchial tubes, causing shortness of breath, wheezing, and coughing.

astigmatism   a condition in which the cornea or the lens is irregularly shaped, causing blurred vision.

asymptomatic   showing no obvious signs or symptoms of a disease.

atherosclerosis   a buildup of fatty material on the artery walls.

atrium   an upper chamber in the heart.

attitude   state of mind toward something in particular or life in general.

axial skeleton   the portion of the skeleton consisting of the bones of the skull, the chest, and the spine.

bacteria   one-celled organisms made up of a very small amount of living matter surrounded by a cell wall; some bacteria are pathogens.

ball-and-socket joint   a joint formed when the rounded end of one bone fits into a cup-shaped section of the bone joining it.

basal metabolism   the energy used by the body while at rest and fasting to carry out basic functions.

behavior modification   a form of psychotherapy that helps individuals change their personal behavior.

benign tumor a tumor that does not spread.

bile a thick yellow-green fluid released by the liver that breaks fat into smaller globules.

biopsy a medical test in which a sample of tissue is surgically removed from the body for study.

birth defect a physical or mental disorder resulting from damage to the fetus.

blackout a failure to remember occurrences or behavior during a period of intoxication.

bladder a muscular sac that stores urine.

blended family a family made up of a biological father or mother, a stepmother or stepfather, and the children of one or both of the parents.

blood alcohol content (BAC) a measure of alcohol intoxication.

blood pressure the force with which blood pushes against the vessel walls as it travels through the circulatory system.

blood transfusion the process of taking blood from one person and putting it into the circulatory system of another person.

body composition the ratio of body fat to lean body tissue, such as muscle and bone.

boomerang children mature young adults who return to their parents' home to live.

booster a revaccination against a particular disease.

brain death a condition in which the central nervous system has stopped functioning; the brain shows no electrical impulses on an electroencephalogram.

brainstem the structure that connects the cerebrum with the spinal cord.

breech birth a birth in which the baby's feet or buttocks enter the birth canal first.

bronchitis an inflammation of the mucous membrane of the bronchi.

bulimia an eating disorder characterized by episodes of extreme overeating followed by self-induced vomiting or use of laxatives.

bursitis the painful inflammation of small sacs located near joints.

caesarean section a method of childbirth in which a doctor makes an incision in the mother's abdomen and uterus, and lifts the baby out.

calculus hardened plaque on the teeth, often leading to gum disease.

Calorie a measure of the energy content of food.

cancer a group of diseases characterized by an uncontrolled growth of abnormal cells that invade and destroy healthy tissue.

canine a pointed tooth that tears food into small pieces.

cannabis the Indian hemp plant; the source of marijuana and hashish.

capillary a microscopic blood vessel with extremely thin walls.

carbohydrates nutrients containing only carbon, hydrogen, and oxygen; sugars and starches.

carbon monoxide a highly poisonous gas that is odorless and colorless.

carcinogen any substance or agent that causes cancer.

cardiac arrest the condition in which the heart stops beating.

cardiac muscle a type of involuntary muscle that forms the walls of the heart.

cardiorespiratory endurance the ability of the heart, lungs, and blood vessels to function efficiently at rest and during long periods of vigorous activity.

cardiovascular disease (CVD) disease of the heart and the blood vessels.

cartilage a tough, flexible type of bone tissue.

cataract a condition in which the lens of the eye becomes cloudy.

cavity a hole, caused by decay, in the enamel of a tooth.

cell death the ceasing of metabolism within body cells.

cemetery a burial ground where graves are usually marked by monuments or plaques.

central nervous system the brain and spinal cord.

cerebellum the part of the brain that coordinates muscular activity.

cerebral cortex the outer layer of the cerebrum.

cerebrum the largest and uppermost part of the brain, which controls thought and conscious action.

cervix the lower, neck-like, portion of the uterus.

chancre an open sore; a symptom of syphilis.

chemotherapy the use of chemical medications to fight cancer.

chewing tobacco coarsely ground tobacco that is chewed or held in the mouth.

child abuse the physical, sexual, or emotional maltreatment of children.

child neglect not providing children with proper care.

child support the payments made by one parent to the other after a divorce to help cover a child's expenses.

chlamydia a sexually transmitted disease; a bacterial infection of the cervix and Fallopian tubes in females and of the urethra in males and females.

chlorofluorocarbon a chemical gas; any of certain compounds made up of carbon, fluorine, chlorine, and sometimes hydrogen.

cholesterol a waxy, fatlike substance, part of cell membranes and nerve tissues, that may block the arteries.

chromosomes threadlike structures, found within cells, that carry the hereditary information from generation to generation.

chronic long-lasting; some illnesses are chronic diseases.

chyme the thick liquid that partially digested food becomes while in the stomach.

cilia microscopic hairlike structures that line the air passages and keep the lungs and other organs clean by trapping dust and foreign matter.

circumcision the surgical removal of the foreskin from the penis.

cirrhosis a scarring of the liver that impairs its functioning.

civil defense agency an organization concerned with protecting the community, particularly in the event of disaster.

closed fracture a simple fracture; the broken ends of the bone do not pierce the skin surface.

cochlea a spiral tube in the ear; it contains receptors that send vibrations.

cognitive appraisal the use of logic and knowledge in evaluating an event.

collagen a strong, flexible material produced by bone cells.

color blindness a hereditary disorder in which a person cannot distinguish certain colors.

coma a deep unconsciousness from which a person cannot be awakened.

communication the sharing of thoughts, feelings, and information.

compact bone a layer of hard, dense bone tissue located under the periosteum.

compatibility the ability to live, think, and act together in harmony.

compensation a defense mechanism; making up for dissatisfaction in one area of life by excelling in another.

complementary proteins a mixture of two or more sources of incomplete protein that provides all the essential amino acids.

compromise the process of settling differences in which both sides give in a little.

compulsion an urgent, repeated type of irrational behavior.

concussion an injury of the brain, resulting from a hard blow, that causes unconsciousness.

conditioning the shaping of behavior with punishment or reward; exercise that develops cardiorespiratory endurance or strength or muscular endurance.

cone a receptor that can distinguish colors but is not very sensitive to light.

congestive heart failure the condition in which the heart can no longer pump all the blood it receives.

conservation the preservation of resources such as energy.

constipation a condition in which the feces are hard and dry and the bowels do not move often enough.

consumer health the ability to make responsible decisions about products and services that can affect one's health.

contraception the prevention of pregnancy.

contusion a bruise of soft tissues; a collection of blood to a damaged area.

cool-down a tapering-off period after an exercise workout.

cooperation the act of working together.

coping dealing with a problem or difficult situation.

cornea the clear covering at the front of the eye that lets light rays into the eye.

coronary bypass surgery the grafting of an artery from another part of the body into the heart, to carry blood around a blocked coronary artery.

cramp a painful, involuntary muscle contraction.

cranium the part of the skull that protects the brain.

cremation the burning of a body so that only ashes remain.

crown the part of the tooth above the gum line.

custody the legal right of guardianship over someone.

cystic fibrosis a hereditary disease that affects the mucus-secreting glands.

cystitis an inflammation of the bladder.

date rape forcing one's dating partner to have sexual relations.

daydreaming a defense mechanism; the creation of make-believe events that seem more pleasant or exciting than the real world.

deductible a specified amount that is subtracted from an insurance reimbursement for medical expenses.

defense mechanism a method of protecting oneself against emotional pain.

defensive driver one who is prepared to respond to the driving errors of others.

deficiency having too little of a necessary substance.

degenerative disease or disorder a physical disorder that develops over several years.

dehydration the loss of water from body tissues.

delirium a mental disorder that involves confusion and loss of awareness of the environment.

delusion a strong belief in something neither true nor real.

dementia a severe, irreversible loss of mental ability.

denial a defense mechanism; the refusal to recognize reality.

dental hygienist a health care specialist who is qualified to clean and polish teeth.

dentin the substance that makes up the body of the tooth.

depressant a drug that slows down nerve activity.

depression a feeling of sadness, worthlessness, helplessness, or isolation.

dermatitis a skin condition characterized by redness, swelling, and itchiness.

dermis the thick, inner layer of the skin.

designated driver a person who agrees not to drink at a social event in order to drive others safely afterward.

designer drug a chemical combination created to imitate a legally controlled drug.

detoxification the process by which a drug abuser's body is allowed to rid itself of a drug.

diabetes mellitus   a condition characterized by high blood sugar and resulting from the body's inability to produce or utilize insulin.

diabetic coma   a state of partial or complete unconsciousness; the blood sugar level is very high and the insulin level is low.

diaphragm   the chief muscle used in breathing; it separates the chest cavity from the abdomen.

diarrhea   a condition in which the feces are watery and loose and the bowels move too often.

dietary fiber   the non-digestible part of a plant; a complex carbohydrate that cannot be digested by the human body.

digestion   the process by which the body breaks down carbohydrates, proteins, and fats into substances that cells can absorb.

disability   a condition that affects a major life activity.

dislocation   injury in which the ends of bones are pulled out of a joint.

displacement   a defense mechanism; transferring feelings about one person or situation to an object or another person.

distress   the negative use of stress.

divorce   the legal ending of a marriage.

DNA (deoxyribonucleic acid)   a chemical substance that makes up genes.

domestic violence   violence toward another family member.

dose   a safe, appropriate amount of a drug.

Down syndrome   a chromosomal disorder that usually causes mental retardation and slowed physical development.

driving while intoxicated (DWI)   the illegal act of driving a motor vehicle while under the influence of alcohol.

drownproofing   a system of rhythmic breathing and vertical floating that helps save a person's energy in a water emergency.

drug abuse   any use of an illegal drug or the misuse of any legal drug.

drug trafficking   the illegal distribution and sale of drugs.

duration   in exercising, the amount of time needed for doing a workout.

eardrum   a thin membrane across the opening to the middle ear that vibrates when hit by sound waves.

ejaculation   the process by which muscle contractions push semen through the urethra and out of the penis.

elder abuse   a family member's maltreatment of an older relative.

electrocardiogram (ECG)   a graph of the electrical impulses of the heart.

electrocution   death caused by electric shock.

electroencephalogram   an image, or tracing, of brain impulses produced by an electroencephalograph.

electroencephalograph (EEG)   an instrument that gives a visual record of brain impulses.

electrolyte   in the human body, sodium or potassium, which regulate water balance.

elimination   the process of releasing solid waste from the body.

ELISA   enzyme-linked immunosorbent assay, a blood test for HIV antibodies.

embryo   a fertilized egg during the first two months of development.

emotion   the strong, immediate reaction that a person feels in response to an experience.

emphysema   a respiratory disease caused by a weakening of lung tissue and characterized by a serious shortness of breath.

enamel   a white, compact material containing calcium that covers the crown of a tooth.

endocrine gland   an organ that produces and releases hormones.

endocrine system   a network of organs that release specific chemicals into the bloodstream.

endometriosis   a condition in which endometrium grows outside of the uterus, sometimes causing infertility.

endometrium   the lining of the uterus.

endorphin   any of several pain-relieving chemicals released by the brain.

engram   a special code a person's brain uses to remember the way to perform a task.

environment   the air, water, and land that surround an individual or community.

enzyme   a protein that speeds up the chemical activity of the body.

epidemic   the rapid spread or unusually extensive occurrence of a public health problem.

epidemiology   the study of factors that cause illness to determine their chances of occurring.

epidermis   the thin, outer layer of the skin.

erection   a stiffening of the penis.

esophagus   a muscular tube that connects the mouth to the stomach.

estrogen   a hormone produced by the ovaries.

euphoria   a feeling of intense happiness and well-being.

eustachian tube   the passageway connecting the middle ear with the throat and nose.

eustress   the positive use of stress.

evaluate   to weigh or judge information.

exclusion   a medical procedure or service not covered by an insurance policy.

excretion   the process that removes harmful or useless substances from the blood, tissues, and cells.

exhaustion stage   the stage of stress in which the body's defenses are used up.

expiration date   the date after which a medicine may no longer be effective.

extended family   a household that contains relatives who are not part of the nuclear family.

extrovert   a person who is very outgoing.

Fallopian tube   the narrow tube through which egg cells pass from an ovary to the uterus.

false positive   a test result indicating the presence of a condition, infection, or disease, when it is not present.

farsightedness   a condition in which the retina is too close to the lens; a person sees only distant objects clearly.

fertilization   the joining of egg and sperm cells.

Fetal Alcohol Syndrome (FAS)   a group of mental and physical birth defects caused by a woman drinking alcohol during pregnancy.

fetus   the name given to the developing embryo from the third month until birth.

flexibility   the ability to bend joints and stretch muscles through a full range of motion.

food allergy   a condition in which body cells, in response to certain foods, release certain substances into the surrounding tissues.

food poisoning   an illness caused by infected food.

foreskin   a flap of skin covering the end of the penis.

formaldehyde   a chemical used as a preservative in many wood products, carpets, draperies, and foam insulation.

foster children   children who receive parental care from adults without being related to or legally adopted by them.

fracture   a break or crack in a bone.

fraternal twins   twins that develop at the same time but from different fertilized eggs.

frequency   in exercising, the number of times a person exercises during a week.

friend   a person who shares another person's interests, goals, and attitudes and enjoys that person's company.

functional disorder   a mental illness induced by a person's environment rather than by a physical cause.

funeral   a ceremony in memory of someone who has died.

fungi   single-celled or multicelled plant-like organisms; some fungi are pathogens.

gallstones   hard, stone-like particles that form from cholesterol and other substances in bile.

gateway drug   a psychoactive substance that leads to the use of other drugs.

gender   the classification that refers to being male or female.

gender identification   having a sense of self that matches one's sex.

gene   the basic unit of heredity.

generativity   an interest in the welfare of others, especially of future generations.

genetic disorders   conditions caused by defective genes.

genital herpes   a sexually transmitted disease; a viral disease that causes blisters in the genital area.

genital warts   a sexually transmitted disease; a viral disease that causes soft growths in the genital area.

geriatrics   the study of aging.

glaucoma   a gradual increase of fluid pressure within the eye; it can damage the retina and lead to blindness.

gliding joint   a joint in which the bones slide over each other, such as the wrist.

glomerulus   a network of coiled blood vessels in a nephron in a kidney.

glucose   blood sugar.

glycogen   a starch stored in the muscles and liver; it maintains blood sugar levels between meals.

gonorrhea   a sexually transmitted disease that infects the vagina, cervix, uterus, and Fallopian tubes in women and the urethra in men.

greenstick fracture   a partial fracture that is common in children.

grief   a deep sorrow caused by the loss of someone or something.

groundwater   water found under the ground.

guilt   a feeling of self-reproach for having done something wrong.

hallucination   the sensation of seeing, hearing, or sensing something that does not exist.

hallucinogen   a drug that causes hallucinations.

hangover   the unpleasant physical effects that follow the heavy use of alcohol.

HDL   High Density Lipoprotein, which removes cholesterol from the body's cells.

health   a state of well-being defined as a condition of physical, intellectual, emotional, and social well-being.

health fraud   the selling of health-related products or treatments that have little or no healing power.

health insurance   an agreement in which a company agrees to pay health-care expenses of an individual in return for payment of a specified premium.

health maintenance organization (HMO)   a group of medical-care providers; it offers services to subscribers who pay a monthly fee.

heart attack   the death of heart tissue due to the cutoff of its blood supply.

heart transplant   a procedure in which a healthy heart is transferred from a person who has recently died into the body of the patient.

heavy drinker   someone who consumes, on average, more than two drinks per day.

helper T cell   a white blood cell that identifies the type of infection.

helpline   a confidential telephone service providing information and advice.

hemoglobin   an iron-containing substance in red blood cells that carries oxygen to all parts of the body.

hemorrhoids   swollen veins in the anal area.

hepatitis   an inflammation caused by toxic agents or a virus that infects the liver, causing jaundice, nausea, fever, and pain in the abdomen.

heredity   the passing of physical and mental traits biologically from parents to their children.

hernia   a loop of intestine bulging through a weak spot in the muscle wall of the abdomen or groin.

heterosexual   a person attracted to members of the opposite sex.

hinge joint   a joint in which the bones swing back and forth, such as the knee.

histamine   a substance that increases the flow of gastric juices in the stomach and dilates the walls of small blood vessels.

HIV positive   having human immunodeficiency virus (HIV) antibodies in one's blood.

homicide   the intentional killing of one person by another.

homosexual   a person attracted to members of his or her own sex.

hormone   a chemical substance that is released into the bloodstream and travels to other organs and tissues to stimulate growth and regulate activities.

hormone therapy   a treatment in which tumors are denied hormones needed for growth or supplied with hormones that restrict growth.

hospice   a medical program that provides a home-like atmosphere for patients who have a terminal illness and their families.

hostility   feeling and behaving in an unfriendly way.

human immunodeficiency virus (HIV)   the virus that causes acquired immune deficiency syndrome (AIDS).

hunger   the body's physical need for food.

hyperactivity   a condition in which a child is constantly moving and is very easily distracted.

hypertension   condition in which blood pressure remains too high for a long period of time.

hypoactivity   a condition in which a child shows signs of low activity and excessive daydreaming.

hypochondria   a strong belief that one is ill when illness is neither present nor likely.

hypoglycemia   low blood sugar; a condition caused by too much insulin being produced by the body.

hypothalamus   the part of the brain that regulates a number of basic body functions, such as temperature and the release of hormones.

idealization   a defense mechanism; exaggerating the good qualities of another person or seeing that person as perfect.

identical twins   twins that develop from the same fertilized egg.

illness stage   the stage of a disease in which the symptoms are most severe.

immunity   a resistance to a specific pathogen.

immunotherapy   a treatment that utilizes the body's immune system to fight cancer.

impulse   a message carried by neurons to one part of the body from another.

incisor   a sharp front tooth that bites and cuts food.

incubation stage   the stage of disease between the entry of the pathogen and the first appearance of symptoms.

incubator   a general container that keeps a baby warm and protects it from disease.

indigestion   the inability to digest food properly.

infatuation   a short-lived intense interest in another person.

infectious disease   disease caused by a pathogen.

infertile   unable to produce offspring.

infertility   the condition of being infertile.

inflammation   the redness and swelling in an infected area.

influenza   a serious respiratory infection caused by different viruses, all of which bring on fever, aches, tiredness, and weakness.

inguinal hernia   a condition in which tissue is pushed through an opening between the abdomen and the scrotum.

inhalant   a psychoactive gas inhaled to produce euphoria.

inhibition   a check on emotions and actions.

inpatient care   medical care given to a patient staying overnight in the hospital.

insomnia   the inability to sleep.

instinct   an inherited pattern of behavior that does not need to be learned.

insulin   a hormone produced by the pancreas that regulates the metabolism of sugar in the body.

insulin-dependent diabetes   a type of diabetes in which the pancreas is unable to make insulin.

insulin shock   a condition in which there is a very low level of blood sugar and a high level of insulin; symptoms include dizziness, rapid pulse, excessive sweating, blurred vision, a change in behavior, and paleness.

integrity   a person's sense of achievement, completeness, and importance.

intelligence   the ability to learn and to deal with change.

intensity   in exercising, a higher-than-normal level of stress that is self-imposed.

interneuron   a neuron that receives sensory messages and sends responses.

intoxication   the short-term effects that alcohol and other psychoactive drugs have on mind and body.

introvert   a person concerned mostly with his or her own thoughts.

iris   the colored circle in the eye that surrounds the pupil and controls its size.

irritable bowel syndrome   a chronic condition characterized by loose, watery feces, abdominal cramps, bloating, and gas.

joint the place at which two bones meet.

kidney an organ in the urinary system that filters wastes from the blood.

killer T-cell a white blood cell that produces chemicals able to destroy infected cells.

labor the process of birth.

larynx the voice box, located in the upper trachea.

latchkey children children whose parents let them use a house key and care for themselves after school.

latent stage the third stage of syphilis; no symptoms are present, but bacteria are spreading throughout the body.

LDL Low Density Lipoprotein, which deposits cholesterol on blood vessels' walls.

lean body mass the protein in one's muscles, organs, and bones.

legume a plant that bears seeds in pods; a member of the pea family.

lens a curved, inner part of the eye; it focuses light rays on the retina.

lesion an injured or abnormal area in a tissue.

leukemia cancer of the body tissues that produce blood cells.

leukoplakia a disease of the mouth marked by leathery white patches on the inner cheeks, gums, tongue, or lips, often associated with tobacco use.

licensed practical nurse (LPN) a nurse who is responsible for patients' basic needs.

life expectancy the measure of the average number of years that a group of people may expect to live.

ligament a thick cord of collagen fibers that binds bones together.

light drinker someone consuming, on average, less than a half ounce of alcohol per day.

lipid a substance similar to a carbohydrate but containing less oxygen and not soluble in water.

lymph the plasma like fluid that seeps out of capillaries and also fills the spaces between the cells.

lymph node tissue that produces white blood cells; tissue that traps and filters out pathogens.

lymphocyte an element of lymph; a white blood cell able to halt or fight infection.

macrophage a large white blood cell that destroys pathogens and signals the immune system.

mainstream smoke smoke that has been inhaled and then exhaled by a smoker.

malignant melanoma the most serious form of skin cancer; a small, mole-like growth that can spread.

malignant tumor a cancerous growth, capable of invading other tissue and spreading.

mammogram an X-ray image of the breasts made by mammography.

mammography the X-ray technique used to detect breast tumors.

mania a wildly elated and impulsive mood.

maturity the state of being fully grown.

measles a highly contagious viral disease characterized by a rash.

Medicaid a public health insurance program that pays for the health care of low-income people.

Medicare a federal health insurance plan for people 65 or older and others who receive Social Security benefits.

memory cell a cell that is able to recognize a particular pathogen or to produce antibodies against it after the infection.

menopause the time of a woman's life when ovulation and menstruation stop.

menstrual cycle the monthly reproductive cycle during which an ovary releases an egg cell for possible fertilization.

menstruation the monthly process in which an unfertilized egg cell and the endometrium are discharged from a woman's body.

mental trauma a violent shock that damages a person's mental health.

metabolism the processes by which the body uses food to release energy and uses the energy to build and repair body tissues.

metastasis the process by which cancer cells spread throughout the body.

methadone a legal, synthetic narcotic administered to drug addicts to block withdrawal symptoms.

mid-life crisis a transition, or major change in life, often experienced around age 40.

migraine headache a severe headache caused by changes in the blood vessels in the brain.

mineral an element occurring in non-living substances that is essential to the body's processes and structure.

minor anyone not of full legal age.

miscarriage the process in which a non-living embryo is expelled from the body.

modeling the process of learning by watching and imitating another person or role model.

moderate drinker someone consuming, on average, no more than one ounce of alcohol per day.

molar a large, flat tooth with several rounded points that grinds food into bits.

monogamy the commitment to an intimate relationship with only one person.

mononucleosis a viral disease causing a sore throat and the swelling of the lymph nodes and spleen.

monosodium glutamate (MSG) a crystalline salt used as a flavor enhancer.

motor neuron a nerve cell (neuron) that carries a response from the interneurons to the muscles, glands, and internal organs of the body.

motor skill skill of balance and coordination.

mucous membrane a layer of tissue that lines all body openings, including the respiratory, digestive, and reproductive tracts.

multiplier effect   the process of one drug increasing the effects of another.

muscle tone   the slight but constant contraction maintained by all muscles.

muscular endurance   the ability to apply strength over a period of time.

narcolepsy   a disorder in which a person falls asleep suddenly.

narcotic   a powerful drug that produces a relaxed, dreamy state; derived from the opium plant.

nearsightedness   a condition in which the retina is too far from the lens; a person sees only close objects clearly.

nephron   a main functioning unit of the kidney.

nerve   a bundle of axons (long fibers) from many neurons.

nerve impulse   electrical signal transmitted along nerves.

nervous system   the complex group of organs and nerves that controls all actions and thoughts.

neuron   the basic unit of the nervous system.

neurotransmitter   a chemical produced by nerve cells that passes across a synapse from an axon to a dendrite.

nicotine   an addictive substance found in tobacco.

nicotine substitute   a temporary substitute for the nicotine in tobacco.

nocturnal emission   the process by which semen is released from the penis during sleep.

noninsulin-dependent diabetes   a form of diabetes in which the pancreas produces enough insulin but the body is unable to utilize it.

nuclear family   a family group consisting of a mother and father and their children.

nurse practitioner   a registered nurse who has an advanced degree in a specialty.

nursing home   a health-care center that provides long-term care for those who are chronically ill or cannot care for themselves.

nutrient   a substance found within food that the body needs to function properly.

nutrition   the process by which the body takes in and uses food.

obesity   the condition of being 20 percent over one's highest recommended weight.

obsession   a persistent thought that interrupts normal thinking.

open fracture   a compound fracture; the broken ends of the bone pierce the skin surface.

opportunistic disease   any disease that occurs as the result of a weakened immune system.

organ   a body part made of different types of tissues working together to perform a function.

organic disorder   a mental illness that is the result of a physical cause, often a chemical imbalance.

osteoarthritis   a chronic condition in which the cartilage in the joints gradually wears away.

osteoporosis   the loss of calcium from bones, causing them to become brittle.

outpatient care   medical attention for patients not staying in a hospital overnight.

outpatient program   a drug recovery program in which patients live at home and visit the hospital for treatment.

oval window   the membrane-covered opening between the middle ear and the inner ear.

ovarian cyst   a fluid-filled sac that sometimes grows on an ovary.

ovary   the female reproductive organ that produces egg cells and releases sex hormones.

overdose   a drug dose strong enough to have a toxic or lethal effect.

overgeneralization   the act of drawing a broad conclusion from too little evidence.

overload   exercise performed in order to strengthen a muscle by fatiguing it.

over-the-counter (OTC) drug or medicine   a legal drug that can be purchased without a doctor's prescription.

overweight   the state of being more than 10 percent over one's recommended weight.

ovulation   the monthly release of an egg cell from an ovary.

ozone   a type of oxygen; formed when nitrogen dioxide reacts with other chemicals and with sunlight.

pancreas   a long, soft gland lying behind the stomach that secretes digestive enzymes into the duodenum and releases hormones that regulate metabolism.

Pap test   an examination for cancer in which cell samples are taken from the cervix.

paralysis   a loss of the ability to move a part of the body, due to nerve or muscle damage.

paranoia   an abnormal suspicion and fear of others.

paraplegia   the paralysis of the lower body and legs.

parasite   a multicelled organism that gets its energy and nutrients by feeding on other living things.

Parkinson's disease   a progressive disease of the nervous system, characterized by symptoms such as body rigidity and hand tremors.

passive smoking   breathing air contaminated with tobacco smoke.

pathogen   an organism or other agent that causes disease.

peer   a person who is like one or more others in age, status, or interests.

peer pressure   the strong influence of others in a person's age group.

pelvic inflammatory disease (PID)   an inflammation of the uterus, Fallopian tubes, and ovaries, due to infection by pathogens; it can result from a sexually transmitted disease.

pelvis ring of bone forming the hips; made up of pelvic girdle, sacrum, and coccyx.

penis a male reproductive structure.

periosteum a strong membrane covering the outside of the bone.

peristalsis the wave-like contraction of muscles that moves food through the digestive system.

personality the feelings, attitudes, and behavior that make each person an individual.

personalization the act of interpreting a general remark or incident as pertaining to only one person.

phagocyte a white blood cell that engulfs pathogens and disables them.

pharmacist a specialist who is qualified to prepare and sell medicines; a druggist.

phobia a constant, unreasonable fear of a situation or object.

physical fitness the ability of one's heart, blood vessels, lungs, and muscles to function at their best.

physical therapist a specialist qualified to assist in physical rehabilitation.

pituitary gland the endocrine gland that produces hormones that regulate growth rate and stimulate other glands to release other hormones.

pivot joint a joint in which one bone rotates around another, such as where the skull meets the backbone.

placenta a membrane organ that nourishes the developing embryo and fetus.

plaque a colorless material made of saliva, food particles, and bacteria, which forms on the teeth.

plasma the liquid part of the blood.

platelet one of the tiny blood cells that forms clots to stop bleeding.

platonic friendship casual or close friendship with someone of the opposite gender.

pneumonia a viral or bacterial infection that causes an inflammation of the lung tissue.

poison control center a service that provides, over the phone, emergency medical advice about poisons.

pollution any undesirable change to the quality of air, water, or soil due to human activities.

pore a tiny opening on the surface of the epidermis.

post-traumatic stress disorder a condition resulting from a traumatic event and causing extreme distress and the need for an extended period of coping.

prejudice an irrational, hostile attitude toward others.

premature born before being fully developed.

premenstrual syndrome (PMS) a group of physical and emotional symptoms that may appear before a menstrual period begins.

premium the fee paid to an insurance company in return for coverage.

premolar a flat, double-pointed tooth that tears and crushes food.

prenatal care medical care during pregnancy.

prescription drug or medicine a drug that cannot be purchased legally without a doctor's written order.

primary care physician a doctor whose caregiving includes preventive medicine, routine checkups, and the diagnosis and treatment of common problems.

primary stage the stage of syphilis beginning about 10 to 21 days after infection.

prodromal stage the stage of disease during which mild symptoms appear but are not fully developed.

progression the gradual increase needed in exercise overload to improve fitness.

projection a defense mechanism; denying an unwanted trait and assigning it to someone else.

proof a measurement of the alcoholic content of beverages: twice the percentage of alcohol.

prostate gland a male gland located below the bladder that produces a fluid that is part of semen.

protein a chemical made up of amino acids that builds and repairs body tissues.

protozoan one-celled organisms with more specialized internal structures than bacteria or rickettsias; some protozoa are pathogens.

psychoactive drug a chemical substance that acts on the brain and affects the mind and behavior of the user.

psychoanalysis a treatment process for mental disorders that tries to discover a person's unresolved conflicts.

psychologist a social scientist who studies human behavior, has a graduate degree in psychology, and is qualified to work with people who have emotional problems.

psychosomatic illness a physical disorder caused by stress rather than disease or damage to the body.

psychotherapy a method of treating mental, emotional, and nervous disorders.

puberty the period of time during which the reproductive system begins to mature.

pubic hair the coarse hair that grows at the lower part of the abdomen and surrounds the genitals.

public health the efforts to protect and improve the health of a group of people.

pulmonary circulation the pathway of blood from the heart through the lungs.

pulp a tooth's soft inner tissue that contains blood vessels and nerves.

pupil the round opening that controls the amount of light entering the inner eye.

quackery the selling of health-related products or treatments that have little or no medical value.

quadriplegia the paralysis of the body from the neck down.

quarantine   a restriction that isolates sick people from others to prevent an infectious disease from spreading.

radiation   a type of energy emitted in the form of waves or particles.

radiation therapy   a cancer treatment in which a tumor is exposed to short intense bursts of radiation.

rape   the illegal, violent act of forcing another person to have sexual relations.

rapid eye movement (REM)   the dream stage during sleep, indicated by the back-and-forth movement of the eyes under the eyelids.

rationalization   a defense mechanism; finding reasons to justify certain behaviors.

reaction formation   a defense mechanism; hiding true feelings by behaving in a manner opposite to the way one would like to act.

receptor   a nerve ending that receives or sends sensory information.

recessive gene   a gene that is expressed only if the dominant gene is not present.

recovery stage   the stage of disease in which the disease is overcome by the body's defenses.

recycling   the reuse or reprocessing of products or materials.

red blood cell   a cell that carries oxygen from the lungs to the body tissues and waste carbon dioxide from the body tissues to the lungs.

red bone marrow   bone tissue that makes red blood cells and some white blood cells.

reflex   an automatic response to the environment that occurs without action from the brain.

reflex arc   the route through the nervous system that impulses travel during a reflex.

registered nurse (RN)   a graduate of a two-year or three-year hospital program, or a four-year college nursing program.

regression   a defense mechanism; retreating into childish or immature behavior.

relapse   the return of an infection from which one has partially recovered.

relationship   a bond or connection between two persons; intensity depends on type of relationship.

repression   a defense mechanism; pushing painful thoughts or feelings away.

resistance stage   a stage of response to stress in which a person's body works against the stress.

retina   the light-sensitive tissue that lines the inner eye.

rheumatoid arthritis   a severe form of arthritis characterized by painful, swollen joints and sometimes by other symptoms, such as muscle weakness.

rickettsias   one-celled organisms that are larger than viruses but smaller than bacteria.

risk   a possibility of danger or loss.

rod   a receptor that is very sensitive to light but can only distinguish black from white.

root   the part of the tooth below the gum line that fits into the jawbone.

runoff   water that flows across soil or pavement after a rain; can wash pollutants into groundwater.

saturated fat   a fat that is solid at room temperature.

scoliosis   a condition in which there is a side-to-side curvature of the spine.

scrotum   a pouch of loose skin that houses the testes.

sebum   an oil produced by the sebaceous glands.

secondary sex characteristics   the physical changes that develop during puberty.

secondary stage   the stage of syphilis beginning one or more months after an open sore, or chancre, has disappeared.

seizure   a convulsive action caused by disorganized brain activity; an attack of epilepsy.

self-concept   one's view or image of oneself and one's role in life.

self-esteem   a person's confidence, pride, and self-respect.

self-examination   a consideration of one's own characteristics, thoughts, or emotions.

self-fulfilling prophecy   an outcome largely influenced, or caused, by the expectations of the person involved in bringing it about.

semen   a thin, whitish fluid; a combination of sperm cells with fluids secreted by the prostate gland and the seminal vesicles.

semicircular canal   a fluid-filled tube in the ear that is lined with tiny hair.

sensory neuron   a neuron that detects changes in the environment and sends messages to the spinal cord or brain.

separation   an act in which a husband and a wife agree to live apart while they try to work out their differences.

sex-linked disorder   a genetic disorder passed on by the X chromosome.

sexual harassment   subjecting someone to unwanted verbal or sexual advances.

sexually transmitted disease (STD)   an infectious disease that is spread from person to person during sexual activity.

sickle-cell anemia   a hereditary form of anemia in which abnormal hemoglobin causes red blood cells to have a long, curved shape; inhibits the transport of oxygen.

side effect   an undesirable secondary effect of a drug; a different, unknown, or undesirable reaction.

sidestream smoke   smoke that comes directly from the burning of a cigarette, cigar, or pipe.

single-parent family   a household in which a child or children live with only one parent.

skeletal muscle   a muscle connected to a bone and controlled consciously.

sleep apnea   a condition in which breathing stops periodically during sleep.

small intestine   a long, coiled digestive organ; part of the alimentary canal.

smokeless tobacco   ground-up tobacco leaves, inhaled or chewed rather than smoked.

smooth muscle   involuntary muscle that surrounds many internal organs.

snuff   finely ground tobacco that is inhaled or held against the gum.

socialization   the process of teaching behavior based on the belief and habits of the family and community.

specialist   a physician with special training in one area of medicine.

specificity   the practice of choosing exercises specially targeted to meet a particular fitness goal.

spleen   an organ near the stomach that produces white blood cells, filters blood, and stores it.

spongy bone   porous tissue found in the ends of bones.

spouse abuse   the physical or psychological harm one marriage partner does to the other.

sprain   a joint injury in which the ligament and tendons around a joint are stretched or torn.

stalking   obsessively pursuing someone either in person or by means of unwanted calls or letters; a type of harassment.

stereotyping   believing that all members of a large group share the same characteristics in a fixed way.

sternum   flat bone located in the middle and front of the chest.

stillbirth   a delivery in which the fetus is born dead.

stimulant   a drug that speeds up nerve activity.

stimulus   anything capable of producing a response.

strain   a tear in a muscle or tendon.

strength   the ability of a muscle to exert force.

strep throat   a bacterial infection that, if untreated, can cause more serious illnesses.

stress   the body's response to physical or mental demands or pressures.

stressor   an agent that causes stress.

stroke   brain damage caused by a blockage or rupture of a blood vessel in the brain.

sublimation   a defense mechanism; the replacement of undesirable impulses with acceptable behavior.

sulfites   a group of chemical substances used as food additives to prevent discoloration, mold, and spoiling.

sun block   a cream that completely blocks the sun's ultraviolet rays.

sun protection factor (SPF)   a number indicating the amount of protection provided against UVB rays.

sunscreen   a lotion that blocks out some of the sun's UVB rays.

synapse   a space between the end of the axon of one neuron and the dendrite of another.

syphilis   a sexually transmitted disease, caused by bacteria, that attacks mucous membranes and can spread to other organs if untreated.

systemic circulation   the circulatory vessels that move oxygen-rich blood to all parts of the body other than the lungs.

tailgating   driving too closely behind another car to be able to stop or swerve in an emergency.

target heart rate   the rate at which one must exercise the heart to improve cardiorespiratory fitness.

tars   particles in cigarette smoke that adhere to air passages and lungs.

tendon   a cord of collagen fibers that connects a muscle to a bone.

tendonitis   the condition in which a tendon becomes irritated and swollen.

terminal illness   an incurable disorder that eventually causes death.

tertiary stage   the final and most serious stage of syphilis.

testes   the male endocrine glands in which sperm cells are produced.

testicular cancer   a cancerous growth in the testes.

testosterone   a male sex hormone that is produced by the testes.

thalamus   the part of the brain that relays sensory impulses to the cerebral cortex.

therapeutic community   a structured, drug-free residential program.

thymus   an organ in the upper chest that produces specialized white blood cells (T cells) that provide immunity.

thyroid gland   a large gland at the front of the neck; it releases hormones that control metabolism.

tolerance   a reduced sensitivity to a drug.

tonsils   reddish masses of lymphatic tissue at the back of the mouth.

tornado warning   a warning issued when a tornado has been sighted by a person or on radar.

tornado watch   a report issued when conditions are favorable for a tornado to develop.

toxemia   a life-threatening complication of pregnancy; characterized by swelling, rapid weight gain, high blood pressure, protein in the urine, and stomach pain.

toxic   poisonous or deadly.

toxic shock syndrome   a potentially fatal bacterial infection that can result from overuse of tampons.

toxin   a poison.

transition   a time of major change in life.

transplantation   the replacement of a person's diseased organ or tissues with an organ or tissues from another person's body.

tuberculosis (TB)   an infectious disease caused by bacteria that attack the lungs and other organs.

tumor   a mass of tissue formed by abnormal cells.

Type A personality   an extreme personality type: competitive, tense, impatient, and aggressive.

Type B personality an extreme personality type: relaxed, cooperative, and satisfied with lower output.

ulcer an open sore in the lining of the stomach or other part of the digestive system.

umbilical cord a thick cord that connects the placenta to the embryo and fetus.

unconscious the part of the personality that is hidden from the person's awareness.

underweight the state of being more than 10 percent under one's recommended weight.

unsaturated fat a fat that is in liquid form at room temperature.

ureter a narrow muscular tube that connects the kidney to the bladder.

urethra the tube from the bladder through which urine, and in males, semen, passes out of the body.

urethritis a sexually transmitted disease; inflammation of the urethra due to an infection.

uterus the muscular female reproductive organ in which a baby develops.

vaccination an injection that stimulates the immune system to produce antibodies.

vagina a muscular tube that connects the uterus to the outside opening of the body; the birth canal.

vaginitis a sexually transmitted disease; inflammation of the vagina due to infection.

values beliefs and standards that an individual feels are important to live by.

vas deferens the tube that connects the testes to the prostate gland.

vegetarian a person who chooses not to eat foods that come from animals.

vein a blood vessel that carries blood to the heart.

ventricle a lower chamber in the heart.

vertebrae the bones that make up the spinal column.

violence force used so as to injure, abuse, or damage.

virus a single unit of genetic material in a protein shell.

vitamin a chemical substance that helps transform digested food into tissue and helps regulate body functions.

warm-up slow, fluid motions used to increase circulation to the muscles.

wellness a condition of physical, intellectual, emotional, and social well-being.

white blood cell a blood cell that guards the body against infection and disease.

withdrawal symptoms the reactions experienced by an addict who stops using a drug.

X chromosome a female chromosome.

Y chromosome a male chromosome.

yellow bone marrow bone tissue that consists mostly of fat cells.

Definitions are indicated by **boldface** page numbers. Plates (Pl.) follow page 300 of the text.

AA, *See* Alcoholics Anonymous.
Abdominal thrust, 691
Abortion, 163
Absorption, **259;** of alcohol, 491; in intestine, 260–262; of nutrients, 259
Abstinence, 578, **583,** 584
Acceptance, of differences, 155
Acceptance stage of grief, 87, 421
Accident, **660;** alcohol-related, 498–500, 503; fatal, 4; prevention of, 660–661; *illus.,* 660, 681; *table,* 4
Achilles and calf stretch, 712
"Acid", *See* LSD.
Acne, **30,** 33; *illus.,* 30; *table,* 715
Acquaintance, **153**
Acquired immune deficiency syndrome, *See* AIDS.
ACTH, *table,* 391
ADD, *See* Attention deficit disorder.
Addiction, **459, 483, 511**
Additives, **225,** 226, 252
Adolescent, **65, 155;** *See also* Teenager.
Adoption, 163, **171**
Adrenal gland, **390,** 401; *illus.,* 386; *table,* 391
Adrenaline, **107, 390,** 391, **461;** *table,* 391
Adulthood, 410–419; living on your own, 162; personality development in, 64–65, 70–71
Advertising, **20;** of alcoholic beverages, 20, 46–47, 482; techniques in, 20, 86; for teen markets, 46–47; of tobacco products, 46–47, 456, 459; *table,* 20
Aerobic dance, 348
Aerobic exercise, **345**
African sleeping sickness, 539; *illus.,* 539
Afterbirth, 366
After-care program, **527**
Aging, 247, 332, 410–419, 610–611; *table,* 411
AIDS, 178, 200, 516, 523, 538, 554, 567, **577;** distribution in United States, 576; among teens, 578–579; *illus.,* 576, 578; *table,* 717; *See also* HIV infection.
AIDS Action Committee, 579
AIDS dementia complex, **577**
Air, 640
Air pollution, 325, **326,** 644–646; factors contributing to, 645–646;

indoor, 646; outdoor, 644–645; reduction of, 643
Air sac, 322; *illus.,* 321
Al-Anon, 496, 507
Alarm stage of stress response, **107**
Alateen, 496, 504, 507
Albinism, *table,* 377
Alcohol, **480;** absorption of, 491; action of, 449–450; Calories in, 221, 480–481; elimination of, 491
Alcoholic beverages, 480; advertising of, 20, 46–47, 482; alcohol content of, 480
Alcoholics Anonymous (AA), 482, 487, 495, 507
Alcoholism, **485**
Alcohol tolerance, 491
Alcohol use, 271, 480; deciding not to drink, 501–503; with other drugs, 491–492; educational programs on, 486–487; effect on family, 182, 498–499; effect on immune system, 551; effect on work and school performance, 499; heavy drinker, 484; help for problem drinker, 504; hypertension and, 593; identifying problem drinking, 484; immediate effects of, 488–492; long-term effects of, 493–494; moderate drinking, 483–484; in pregnancy, 245, 373–374, 494–495; reasons for starting, 481–482; recovery from addiction, 495–497; recreational safety and, 668–671; social impact of, 191, 498–500; social drinking, 483; among teens, 191, 482, 484, 489, 494, 500–503; violence and, 97; withdrawal symptoms, 484; *illus.,* 498; *table,* 490, 514
Alimentary canal, **258**
Allergist, *table,* 619, 711
Allergy, 630; food, 246, 251–252
Alveoli, **322**
Alzheimer's disease, 132, **416,** 424, **612;** *illus.,* 129; *table,* 715
Americans with Disabilities Act, 195
Amino acids, **211,** 212
Amnesia, **137**
Amniocentesis, **379**
Amniotic fluid, *illus.,* 364
Amniotic sac, **363,** 364; *illus.,* 364
Amphetamine, **513,** 525; *table,* 510, 513
Amylase, **259;** *table,* 260

Amyl nitrite, **519;** *table,* 519
Anabolic steroids, 300, 348–351, **520,** 521; *table,* 521
Anaerobic exercise, **345**
Anaphylactic shock, **251**
Anemia, **216, 319,** 320, **371;** *table,* 214, 217, 715
Anesthesiologist, *table,* 619, 711
"Angel dust", *See* PCP.
Anger, 93; management of, 83–84; recognition of, 83–84; violence and, 96–98
Anger stage of grief, 87, 421
Angiogram, **597;** *illus.,* 595
Angioplasty, **598**
Animal bite, 541; first aid for, 685
Animal virus, 550
Ankle, 289; protection of, 293; *illus.,* Pl. 1; *table,* 289
Anorexia nervosa, **240,** 241–243, 255; *table,* 715
Antabuse, 497
Antacid, 273
Antibiotic, **549,** 550, 552; resistance in bacteria, 549
Antibody, **317, 544,** 547; *illus.,* 544
Antidepressant, 143
Anti-Drug Abuse Act (1986), 522
Antihistamine, 511
Antiperspirant, 33
Antisocial personality disorder, **136**
Antiviral medicine, 550
Anus, 262; *illus.,* 258, Pl. 4
Anvil (bone), 48; *illus.,* 49
Anxiety, **84,** 85, 90; generalized, 134
Anxiety disorder, 134–135
Aorta, **310;** *illus.,* 308, 310, Pls. 5, 6
Apnea, 442
Appendicitis, **266;** *illus.,* 266; *table,* 715
Appendicular skeleton, 285, **287–288;** *illus.,* 285
Appendix, 266; *illus.,* 258, Pl. 4
Appetite, **234,** 332, 386
Arm bones, 287
Arm circle, 712
Arrhythmia, **595–596,** 597
Arteries, **310;** *illus.,* 310, Pl. 6
Arteriosclerosis, *table,* 715
Arthritis, **294, 609,** 610; *table,* 715
Arthroplasty, 297
Artificial sweeteners, 221
Art therapy, 144
Ascorbic acid, *See* Vitamin C.
Aspirin, 511, 551
Asthma, 251–252, **325,** 398; *table,*

715
Astigmatism, **42**
Asymptomatic disease, **567**
Atherosclerosis, **313**, 314, **465, 593,** 594–598; *illus.*, 465, 595; *table,* 715
Athlete, academics and, 336; injuries to testes, 404; joint injuries, 292–293; professional, 336; sports injury, 668–671; sports nutrition, 248–249; water requirements of, 248–249
Athlete's foot, 31, 539; *table,* 717
Athletic shoes, 347, 354; *illus.*, 354
Atrium, **309**, 310; *illus.*, 308–309
Attention deficit disorder (ADD), **132**
Attitude, **75;** changes in, 75; productive, 129
Audiologist, **51**
Auditory canal, *illus.*, 49
Auditory nerve, 48; *illus.*, 49
Autism, **132**
Automobile safety, 665–666; *illus.*, 660
Autonomic nervous system, **436–437;** *illus.*, 436
Axial skeleton, 285, **286–287;** *illus.*, 285
Axon, 433; *illus.*, 432
Azidothymidine (AZT), 582

Baby, *See* Infant.
Baby teeth, 36
BAC, *See* Blood alcohol content.
Back, protection of, 293
Backache, 293–294
Bacteria, **538**, 549; antibiotic resistance in, 549; *illus.*, 538
Balance , 49–50, 438
Baldness, 403
Ball-and-socket joint, **289**, 290; *illus.*, 290; *table*, 289
Barbiturate, **514;** *table,* 510, 514
Bargaining stage of grief, 87, 421
Basal metabolism, **235,** 247
Battered women, 197
B cells, 543–545; *illus.*, 544
Beer, 480
Bee sting, 390, 685
Behavior, acceptable, 128; changes in, 16–17; classification of, 131; control over own, 129; healthy, 128–129; responsible, 74
Behavioral therapy, **141**
Behavior modification, **141**
Benign tumor, **599**
Bent-knee sit-ups, 337–338; *table,* 338
Beriberi, *table,* 214
Biceps, 300; *illus.*, 299, Pl. 2

Bicycle helmet, 670; *illus.*, 444
Bicycle safety, 354, 666–667
Biking, 347
Bile, **261,** 266–268, 272; *illus.*, 267
Biofeedback, **118**
Biopsy, **603**
Biotin, *table,* 214
Bipolar Affective Disorder, *See* Manic-depression.
Birth, 365–366; difficult deliveries, 367–368; location of, 369; midwifery, 372; premature, 372–373; *illus.*, 368
Birth canal, 366
Birth control, *See* Contraception.
Birth defect, **374,** 379, 469, 565; *table,* 4
Birthing center, 369
Birthmark, 32; *illus.*, 32
Bite, first aid for, 685
Blackhead, 30; *illus.*, 30
Blackout, **484**
"Black stuff", *See* Opium.
Bladder, **272**, 273; cancer of, 602; *illus.*, 272, 394, 402, Pl. 5
Bleeding, first aid for, 686–687
Blended family, **171**
Blindness, 42; *illus.*, 570
Blinking, 439
Blister, first aid for, 692
Blizzard, 675
Blood, disorders of, 319–320; parts of, 316–317; *illus.*, 316–317
Blood alcohol content (BAC), **490,** 491, 499; *table,* 490
Blood cells, 283
Blood clotting, 316
Blood donor, 579–580
Blood pressure, 113–114, 215, 237, **312–313,** 314, 332, 345, 386, 461, 465, 470, **593;** cardiovascular disease and, 592–593; *illus.*, 593
Blood test, 319; for alcohol, 491; for HIV, 577, 580–581
Blood transfusion, **319,** 555, 558, 579; *illus.*, 578; *table,* 319
Blood type, 319; *table,* 319
Blood vessels, 29, 310
"Blue velvet", *See* Opium.
Boating, 500, 669–670
Body building, 300, 350–351, 520–521
Body composition, 237, **341;** *illus.*, 341
Body fat, 237, 239
Body image, 240–243, 300, 350–351, 520–521
Body odor, 33
Body temperature, 386, 545; effect of alcohol on, 489; heat production, 299; maintenance of, 29–30, 308; *table,* 411

Body type, *illus.*, 235
Body weight, 10, 341; birth to five years, 246; exercise and, 236; management of, 234–241; metabolism and, 235–236; in pregnancy, 245–246, 370; reasons for eating, 234–235; smoking cessation and, 474; *illus.*, 236, 246
Bone, aging of, 411; growth and changes in, 284; prevention of injuries to, 293; problems involving, 291–296; skeleton, 285–290; structure and functions of, 282–284; *illus.*, 282
Bone cells, *illus.*, 282
Bone marrow, 283, 543; transplantation of, 320, 325; *illus.*, 543
Boomerang children, **175**
Bottled water, 540, 647
Bottle-feeding, 246, 366–367
Botulism, *table,* 269, 717
Braces (teeth), 37
Braille, *illus.*, 42
Brain, 433–435; blood flow to, 434; effect of alcohol on, 488–489, 493; organic disorders of, 129; PET scan of, 129, 138; tumor of, 444; *illus.*, 129, 138, 434–435, Pl.8
Brain activity, 440–441; *illus.*, 440
Brain death, **422**
Brainstem, **435,** 438; *illus.*, 434
Breakfast, 220–221
Breast, cancer of, 196–197, 398, 601, 603, 607; development in puberty, 393; self-examination of, 197, 601, 607; *illus.*, 601
Breastbone, *See* Sternum.
Breast-feeding, 245–246, 366–367, 469
Breathalyzer, 491; *illus.*, 491
Breathing, 321–323, 436; first aid for breathing problems, 688–689; *illus.*, 323
Breech birth, **367;** *illus.*, 368
Broad-spectrum antibiotic, 549
Bronchi, **322;** *illus.*, 321, Pl. 7
Bronchial tube, *illus.*, 321
Bronchitis, **323,** 324, 326, **467;** *table,* 717
Bruise, first aid for, 692
Bulimia, **241,** 263–264; *table,* 715
Burn, chemical, 690; first aid for, 690; *illus.*, 660, 681
Bursitis, **294**
Butyl nitrite, **519;** *table,* 519

Caffeine, 221, 237, 245, 441–442, 448, 511
Calcium, 215, 247, 265, 283–284, 295–296, 370, 390, 414; *illus.*, 370; *table,* 216

Calcium propionate, 000
Calculus (dental), **36**
Calf stretch, 712
Calories, **208;** empty, 221; food labeling, 227; *table,* 714
Calories per gram, 210; *table,* 209, 245
Cancer, **32, 268, 465, 599;** of bladder, 602; of breast, 196–197, 398, 601, 603, 607; causes of, 599–600; of cervix, 196, 397–398, 574, 601–603; of colon, 268–269, 600–603; detection of, 603; of endometrium, 397–398; of esophagus, 494; of kidney, 602; of larynx, 466–467; of liver, 494; of lung, 462, 465–466, 600, 602, 607; among men, 197; of oral cavity, 36, 463–466, 494, 602, 607; of ovary, 196, 397–398, 601–603; prevention of, 269, 605–607; progression of, 606–607; of prostate, 197, 403, 602–603; of rectum, 600–603; risk of developing, 9, 12; of skin, 32–34, 43, 600, 602, 606; of testes, 197, 403, 602; of throat, 465; tobacco use and, 465–467; treatment of, 603–605; of uterus, 196, 601–603; warning signs of, 603, 607; among women, 196–197; *illus.,* 32, 193, 466, 599; *table,* 4, 602, 715
Canine (tooth), **35;** *illus.,* 35
Cannabis, **449, 517,** 518–519; *table,* 510, 518
Capillaries, **310;** *illus.,* 29, Pl. 6
Carbohydrates, **208,** 209–210;
Carbon dioxide, exchange in lungs, 321–323; transport in blood, 308
Carbon monoxide, 461, 465, 469–470, 594, **645,** 646, 675
Carcinogen, **461,** 464, **599,** 600
Cardiac arrest, **595,** 706
Cardiac muscle, **299,** 309, 311
Cardiologist, *table,* 619
Cardiopulmonary resuscitation (CPR), 684, 706–707
Cardiorespiratory endurance, 332–333, **337,** 345; *table,* 337
Cardiovascular disease (CVD), **592,** 593–598; diagnosis of, 597; gender differences in, 592, 596; risk factors for, 592–595; treatment of, 596–598
Carotid artery, 343; *illus.,* Pl. 6
Cartilage, **284,** 290; torn, 293; *illus.,* 290
Cataract, **42,** 43; *table,* 411
Cavity, **36;** *illus.,* 36
Cell body, 433; *illus.,* 432
Cell death, **422–423**
Cemetery, **423**

Centers for Disease Control, 194, 561
Central nervous system, 433, **434,** 435; in AIDS, 577; *illus.,* 433, Pl. 8
Cerebellum, **435,** 438; *illus.,* 434
Cerebral cortex, **434,** 438, 440
Cerebral palsy, **447;** *table,* 715
Cerebrum, **434,** 435, 438; *illus.,* 434
Cervix, **394;** cancer of, 196, 397–398, 574, 601–603; *illus.,* 362, 394
Cesarean section, **368**
Chancre, **571–572**
Chancroid, *table,* 572, 717
Chattanooga Cleanup, 643
Chemical burn, 690
Chemical digestion, 259–260
Chemotherapy, 519, **604–605**
Chest, **287**
Chest hair, 400
Chewing tobacco, **456**
Chicken pox, 551; *table,* 556, 717
Child, care provider, 67; cost of raising, 365; diet of, 246; family responsibilities of, 173; mental illness among, 61; missing, 181; personality development in, 64–67; runaway, 181; toys, 179
Child abuse, **182,** 184, 498
Childbirth, *See* Birth.
Childless family, 162–163, **171**
Child neglect, **182–183,** 184
Child support, **180**
Chlamydia, **569;** *table,* 572, 717
Chlorine, 215; *table,* 216
Chlorofluorocarbons, **646**
Choking, 681; first aid for, 691; universal signal for, 691; *illus.,* 660
Cholera, 540; *table,* 556, 717
Cholesterol, **113–114, 210,** 211, 223, 252, **313,** 465, **594**
Chromosomal disorders, 379
Chromosomes, **375,** 376
Chronic, **11, 323**
Chronic disease, **414**
Chronic fatigue syndrome, **114**
Chronic lung disease, 467–468
Chyme, **260**
Cigarette smoking, air pollution from, 646; cardiovascular disease and, 315, 593–594; clove cigarettes, 463; cost of, 462; effect on body, 461–463; initiation of, 459–460; low-tar, low-nicotine cigarettes, 462–463; lung cancer and, 193, 600; osteoporosis and, 295–296; in pregnancy, 245, 373–374, 469; quitting smoking, 470–474; reducing initiation of, 323; respiratory disorders and, 323–325; risks for nonsmokers, 468–469; among teens, 198, 458, 460; warning labels, 456–457; *illus.,* 596; *See also* Tobacco

products.
Cigar smoking, 456, 463
Cilia, **322,** 326, **462,** 542; *illus.,* 322
Circulatory system, disorders of, 313–315; functions of, 308–309; prevention of disease, 315; regulation of circulation, 312–313; *illus.,* Pl. 6
Circumcision, **402**
Cirrhosis, **271, 492,** 494
Claustrophobia, 134–135, 141; *table,* 134
Clavicle, *See* Collarbone.
Clinic, **624**
Clinical depression, **133**
Clinical psychologist, **624;** *table,* 140
Clique, 155
Closed-caption television, 50
Closed fracture, **291,** 696; *illus.,* 291
Clove cigarettes, 463
Cocaine, 374, 449, **514,** 596; *table,* 510, 513
Coccyx, **286,** 288; *illus.,* 285–286, Pl. 1
Cochlea, **48;** *illus.,* 49
Codeine, **515;** *table,* 510, 515
Codependency, **182,** 496
Cognitive appraisal, **122**
Cognitive therapy, **142**
"Coke", *See* Cocaine.
Cold receptor, 29; *illus.,* 29
Cold remedy, 511, 552
Cold sore, 573; *illus.,* 573
Collagen, **283**
Collarbone, 287; *illus.,* 285, Pl. 1
Colon, 262; cancer of, 268–269, 600–603; *illus.,* Pl. 4
Color blindness, **42,** 378; *illus.,* 42
Color vision, 40
Coma, **444**
"Combat fatigue", *See* Posttraumatic stress disorder.
Combination foods, 220
Commitment, in marriage, 161
Common cold, 468, 538–540, 550, 553; *table,* 717
Communication, **154,** 176–177; breakdowns in, 176–177; effective listening, 174; in family, 173; gender differences in style, 154; in marriage, 159; open, 154
Community health, 190–194
Community mental health center, 139
Community pride, 192
Community support program, for mentally ill, 141
Compact bone, **283;** *illus.,* 282
Compatibility, **161,** 163
Compensation, **90–91**
Competence, 198

Complementary proteins, **222**
Complete proteins, 212
Complex carbohydrates, 209
Compound fracture, *See* Open
    fracture.
Compromise, **161**
Compulsion, **135**
Compulsive personality disorder,
    137
Concept mapping, instructions for,
    xviii-xix
Concussion, **444,** 698
Conditioning, **62, 345**
Condom, 578, 584–585
Cones (eye), **40**
Conflict, 110; resolution of, 96–97,
    199
Congestive heart failure, **595**
Conjunctivitis, *table,* 717
Conscience, 61, 69, 88
Conservation, **652,** 653
Constipation, 113, **264–265**
Consumer fraud, 20–21
Consumer health, **19,** 20–22
Consumer protection, 22
Consumer rights, 21–22
Contact dermatitis, 31
Contact lenses, 41–42, 45
Contact receptor, 29; *illus.,* 29
Contraception, **162**
Contract for Life (SADD), 503
Controlled Substances Act (1970),
    522
Contusion, **444**
Convenience foods, 227
Cool-down, **345–346**
Cooperation, **155**
Coordination, 438
Coping, **108**
Copper, *table,* 217
Cornea, **39;** scarring of, 43; trans-
    plant of, 43; *illus.,* 39
Coronary artery, 311; *illus.,* 311, 595
Coronary artery disease, 198, 314,
    465; *table,* 715
Coronary bypass surgery, **598**
Coronary vein, 311; *illus.,* 311
Corpus luteum, *illus.,* 362, 394, 396
Corrective lenses, 45
Cortisol, *table,* 391
Cosmetics, 31, 33
Coughing, 439, 540
Cough remedy, 515
Counseling, for alcohol abuse,
    496–497; for drug abuse, 526
Counseling psychologist, *table,* 140
CPR, *See* Cardiopulmonary
    resuscitation.
Crack, 374, 510, 514, 524, 596; *illus.,*
    514; *table,* 513
Cramp, 217, **301;** first aid for, 695,
    699

Cranium, **286**
Cremation, **423**
Cretinism, *table,* 217
Crime, drug-related, 522–523
Crime prevention, 672–673
Crisis center, 139
Croup, *table,* 717
Crown of tooth, **35**
Crying, 86
"Crystal meth", *See*
    Methamphetamine.
Cultural diversity, awareness of, 92
Custody, **171,** 180
Cuts, first aid for, 543
CVD, *See* Cardiovascular disease.
Cyst, ovarian, 397
Cystic fibrosis, **326,** 378; *table,* 377,
    715
Cystitis, **273;** *table,* 717

Daily recommended consumption,
    percentage of, 227
Dandruff, 30
Date rape, **159,** 160, 672–673
Dating, 156–160
Daydreaming, **91–92**
Deafness, 50–51
Death, 420–423; accidental, 660,
    681; alcohol-related, 498–500;
    dealing with, 86–87; definition
    of, 422–423; drug-related, 512; of
    family member, 179; leading
    causes of, 4–5; organ donation,
    423; *table,* 4
Decibel, **51;** *illus.,* 52
Decision making, 11–12; purchasing
    decisions, 22
Deductible (insurance), **626**
Defense mechanisms, **89,** 90–95;
    table, 94
Defensive driver, **665**
Deficiency, vitamin, **213;** signs of,
    214
Degenerative disorder, **129, 446**
Dehydration, **217,** 249, 264–265, 555
Delinquent behavior, 180–181
Delirium, **132**
Delusion, **136**
Dementia, **132,** 424, **612**
Dendrite, 433; *illus.,* 432
Denial, **92,** 93; *table,* 94
Denial stage of grief, 87, 421
Dental checkup, 38
Dental hygienist, **623**
Dentin, **36;** *illus.,* 35
Dentist, **623**
Deodorant, 33
Department of Health and Human
    Services (DHHS), 194
Depressant, **449, 480, 514,** 515;
    table, 514

Depression, **114,** 115, 134, 143, 334,
    416; clinical, 133; teen, 133
Depression stage of grief, 87, 421
Depth perception, 40; *illus.,* 40;
    table, 411
Dermatitis, 31
Dermatologist, **30;** *table,* 619, 711
Dermis, **28**
Descriptive terms, on food label,
    227–228
Designated driver, **504**
Designer drug, **520**
Detoxification, 311, **497, 525;** of
    alcohol abuser, 497; of drug
    abuser, 525; in liver, 272
Developmental disorder, 132–133
Diabetes mellitus, 10, **249,** 250–251,
    389, 398, **608,** 609; insulin-
    dependent, 608–609; noninsulin-
    dependent, 609; in pregnancy,
    609; *table,* 4, 715
Diabetic coma, **609**
Dialysis, **274**
Diaphragm (muscle), **323;** *illus.,* 323
Diarrhea, 113, 218, **265,** 540,
    554–555
Diastolic pressure, **313**
Diet, in adulthood, 247; athlete's,
    248–249; during breast-feeding,
    245; cancer and, 269; circulatory
    disease and, 315; in diabetes,
    249–251; fad, 237; fat intake,
    210–212, 223, 315; food choices,
    220–223; healthy, 219–224; heart
    disease and, 252; identifying
    nutritious foods, 225–228; for
    individual needs, 244–252; of
    infants and children, 246,
    366–367; non-nutritive sub-
    stances in, 221; physical reasons
    for eating, 235; in pregnancy,
    244–246, 364–365, 370; psycho-
    logical reasons for eating,
    234–235; salt in, 215, 252, 315; of
    teens, 246–247; for weight gain,
    239; for weight loss, 237–239;
    illus., 370; *See also* Nutrients.
Diet aids, 237
Dietary fiber, **209,** 262, 265, 269,
    315, 607
Dietary Guidelines, 220, 222, 244,
    246; serving size, 221
Diet pills, 237, 511
Digestion, 258, **259;** in mouth, 259;
    nervous control of, 436; in small
    intestine, 260–261
Digestive system, effect of alcohol
    on, 494; maintaining healthy sys-
    tem, 267; problems involving,
    263–270, 554–555; structure and
    functions of, 258–261; *illus.,* 258,
    Pl. 4

Diphtheria, 549; *table*, 4, 717
Disability, **199**
Disabled person, 195, 199–200; Easy
    Access Project, 335; home health
    assistance, 198
Disease, *See* Infectious disease;
    Noninfectious disease; Sexually
    transmitted disease.
Dislocation, **293;** first aid for, 697
Displacement (defense mechanism),
    94–95
Dissociative disorder, 137–138
Distilled spirits, 480
Distress, **107**
Diuretics, 237
Divorce, **163,** 171, 179–180
Dizziness, 50
DNA, **375**
Doctor, *See* Physician.
"DOM", *See* Mescaline.
Domestic violence, 182–183, **523**
Dominant genes, **376–377;** *illus.,* 376
"Dope", *See* Marijuana.
Dose, **450**
"Downers", *See* Barbiturate.
Down syndrome, **379**
DPT vaccine, *table,* 548
Dreaming, 441
Drinking age, 500
Drinking water, 647
Driving While Intoxicated (DWI),
    499–500
Drowning, 668–670; *illus.,* 660, 681
Drownproofing, 669; *illus.,* 668
Drug, **448,** 449–450; action of,
    449–450; dose of, 450; entry into
    body, 449; illegal, 449; interac-
    tions between, 450; legal,
    448–449; types of, 448–450; *See
    also* Medicine; Over-the-counter
    drug; Prescription drug;
    Psychoactive drug.
Drug abuse, **510;** AIDS and,
    578–579; alternatives to,
    528–529; commonly used drugs,
    513–523; crime and, 522–523;
    dangers of, 512; development of,
    511–512; disease and, 523; edu-
    cational programs on, 486–487;
    getting help for, 529–530; legal
    aspects of, 522; in pregnancy,
    245, 373–374, 524; prevention
    of, 528–530; reasons people try
    drugs, 510–511; refusing drugs,
    528; relationships and, 182,
    524–525; sexually transmitted
    disease and, 585; signs of,
    529–530; social impact of,
    522–527; among teens, 484, 511;
    treatment of, 525–527; violence
    and, 97; *table,* 529–530
Drug testing, 525

Drug therapy, for alcohol abuse, 107;
    in cardiovascular disease, 597; in
    mental disorders, 143
Drug tolerance, 511
Drug trafficking, **522,** 523
Drunk driving, 191, 491, 499–500,
    503, 665
Dry skin, **30,** 33
Duodenum, **260;** *illus.,* Pl. 4
Duration of exercise, **344**
DWI, *See* Driving While Intoxicated.
Dying, 420–423
Dysfunctional family, 181–183

Ear, care of, 51–52; problems involv-
    ing, 50–51; structure and func-
    tions of, 48–50; *illus.,* 48–49
Eardrum, **48;** rupture of, 51; *illus.,*
    49
Earthquake, 676
Earwax, 48, 51
Easy Access Project, 335
Eating disorders, 240–243
ECG, *See* Electrocardiogram.
"Ecstasy", 520
Eczema, 251; *table,* 715
EEG, *See* Electroencephalograph.
Egg cells, 362, 375–376, 394–395;
    production of, 394; *illus.,* 362,
    394
Egg transplantation, 325
Ego, 61; *illus.,* 61
Ejaculation, **401**
Elbow, 289, 302; protection of, 293,
    354; *illus.,* Pl. 1; *table,* 289
Elder abuse, **183**
Elderly, *See* Older adulthood.
Electrical hazard, 662–663; first aid
    for electric shock, 694; *illus.,* 662
Electrocardiogram (ECG), **597**
Electrocution, **662,** 663
Electroencephalograph (EEG), **422,**
    440; *illus.,* 440
Electrolytes, **217,** 218, 248
Electromyograph, 118
Elimination, **259,** 262; of alcohol,
    491
ELISA test, **580,** 581
Embryo, **363,** 364; *illus.,* 364
Emergency medical services, 682
Emergency medical technician, 135
Emergency medicine, *table,* 711
Emergency room, 624
Emotional appeal (advertising), 86
Emotional wellness, **7;** *illus.,* 7
Emotions, **82,** 83–88; handling of,
    74, 89–95; healthy, 128–129
Emphysema, **325–326, 467,** 468;
    table, 715
Employee assistance counselor, 526
Empty nest syndrome, 174

Emulsifier, **220**
Enamel, **35;** *illus.,* 35
Encephalitis, **446**
Endocrine gland, **386;** *table,* 391
Endocrine system, **386,** 387–392;
    coordination with nervous
    system, 386–387; *illus.,* 386
Endometriosis, 399
Endometrium, **394,** 395; cancer of,
    397–398; *illus.,* 362, 394
Endorphins, **119,** 122, **332,** 334
Energy, regulation of use of,
    388–390
Energy conservation, 652–653
Engram, **438**
Enriched foods, **226**
Environment, **640;** health and, 6;
    human impact on, 641–642; per-
    sonality and, 62–63; *illus.,* 5; *See
    also* Pollution.
Environmental health, 640–654
Environmental organizations,
    651–652
Environmental problems, govern-
    ment actions on, 650–652;
    individual actions on, 652–654;
    international actions on, 648
Environmental Protection Agency
    (EPA), 645, 650, 657
Enzyme, **259,** 260–261; *table,* 260
EPA, *See* Environmental Protection
    Agency.
Epidemic, **193, 565**
Epidemiology, **9**
Epidermis, **28**
Epiglottis, 259, **322;** *illus.,* 258–259,
    321, Pl. 7
Epilepsy, **447;** *table,* 715
Epinephrine, *See* Adrenaline.
Erection, **402**
Erikson social development stages,
    65, 410; *table,* 64–65
Esophagus, 258, **259,** 322; cancer of,
    494; *illus.,* 258–259, 321, Pl. 4,
    Pl. 7
Essential amino acids, 211–212
Estrogen, **295, 392,** 393–394, 398,
    415, 601–602; *illus.,* 396; *table,*
    391
Ethanol, 480
Euphoria, **513**
Eustachian tube, **48;** *illus.,* 49
Eustress, **107**
Evaluation, **10**
Exclusion (insurance), **626–627**
Excretion, **271,** 272; *illus.,* 272
Exercise, aerobic, 345; anaerobic,
    345; assessing your program, 349;
    body weight and, 236; cardiovas-
    cular system and, 315, 332,
    593–595; choice of activities,
    346–348; clothing and shoes for,

347, 353–354; coping with weather, 353; effect on bone, 284; guidelines for, 342–344; immune system and, 332; longevity and, 333; maintaining program, 349; osteoporosis and, 295–296; planning for, 352–354; in pregnancy, 366, 371; prevention of injury, 352–353; setting goals, 342; sports nutrition, 248–249; in stress management, 91, 119, 333–334; time and place for, 353; for weight loss, 237–239, 242; workout stages, 345–346; *illus.,* 236; *See also* Physical fitness.
Exercise machines, 348
Exhaustion stage of stress response, **108**
Expiration date, **226, 631;** *illus.,* 631
Extended family, **170–171**
External auditory canal, 48
Extrovert, **62**
Eye, aging of, 411; care of, 43–45; first aid for injuries to, 693; problems involving, 40–43; structure and functions of, 39–40; *illus.,* 39–40
Eye drops, 42
Eyeglasses, 41–42, 45
Eyestrain, 44, 443

Facial hair, 400
Fad diet, 237
Fainting, **313;** first aid for, 704
Fallopian tube, **362, 394;** blocked, 398–399; *illus.,* 362, 394
Falls, 661; first aid for, 445; *illus.,* 660, 662, 681
False positive test, **582**
Family, addition of members to, 180; death of member of, 179; functions of, 172; improving family relationships, 182; life cycle of, 174–175; responsibilities of members of, 172–173; structure of, 170 171; *table,* 175
Family crisis, 178–184; external sources of pressure, 178–179; family dysfunctions, 181–183; internal sources of pressure, 179–181; resolution of, 183–184
Family planning, 162
Family practitioner, *table,* 619, 711
Family therapy, **142,** 184
Farsightedness, **41;** *illus.,* 41
FAS, *See* Fetal Alcohol Syndrome.
Fast foods, 223; *table,* 222
Fats, **210–211;** Calories per gram, 210; in common foods, 211; dietary, 223, 315; dietary guidelines, 210–212; in fast foods,

222–223; *table,* 212; *See also* Body fat.
Fat-soluble vitamins, 213; *table,* 214
Fat substitutes, 221
FDA, *See* Food and Drug Administration.
Fear, 84–85, 93; management of, 85; violence and, 96–97
Feces, 262
Female development, 393–399
Female reproductive system, 393–394; disorders of, 397–399; *illus.,* 394
Fertilization, **362,** 375–376, 395; *illus.,* 362
Fetal Alcohol Syndrome (FAS), **374, 494**
Fetus, **364,** 365; ultrasound of, 380
Fever, **545**
Fiber, *See* Dietary Fiber.
Fibrinogen, **316;** *illus.,* 316
Fighting, *See* Violence.
Fire, 662; fire drill, 662; fire safety, 499; *illus.,* 660, 681
Firearms accident, *illus.,* 660, 681
Firearms safety, 671
First aid, **682;** training in, 684
First Aid Manual, 681–707
First-degree burn, 690
Fitness, *See* Physical fitness.
Flexed-arm hang, 338; *table,* 338
Flexibility, **339;** *table,* 339
Flood, 674
Flossing, 37–38
Flu, *See* Influenza.
Fluid intake, during exercise, 248–249
Fluoride, prevention of tooth decay, 38; *table,* 217
Folate, 319; *illus.,* 370; *table,* 214
Follicle-stimulating hormone, *illus.,* 396; *table,* 391
Food, Calories, nutrients, and minerals in, 714; contaminated, 540, 550, 555, 558
Food additives, *See* Additives.
Food allergy, 246, **251,** 252
Food and Drug Administration (FDA), 194, 224–228, 448, 632
Food choices, 220–223
Food groups, **219–220**
Food Guide Pyramid, **219–220;** *illus.,* 219
Food irradiation, 270
Food labeling, 224–228; *illus.,* 226
Food plan, 250
Food poisoning, **269–270,** 538; *table,* 269, 719
Food shopping, 227
Foot bones, 288
Foreskin, **402**
Formaldehyde, **646**

Fortified foods, **226,** 227
Foster children, **171**
Fracture, **291,** 333; first aid for, 696–697; types of, 291, 696; *illus.,* 291
Fraternal twins, **367**
Fraud, *See* Health fraud.
Freely movable joint, **289–290;** *table,* 289
Frequency of exercise, **344–345**
Freshness date, **226**
Freud psychological stages of development, 64–65; *table,* 64–65
Friendship, 82, **153,** 334
Frontal lobe, *illus.,* 435
Frostbite, first aid for, 695
Fructose, 209; *table,* 209
Frustration, 83
Functional mental disorder, **130**
Funeral, **423**
Fungi, **539**

Gallbladder, 258, 261, 266–267; removal of, 266, 268; *illus.,* 258, 267
Gallstones, **266–267,** 268; *illus.,* 267
Gangs, 180, 191, 199, 523
Gas exchange, 321
Gastric glands, *table,* 260
Gastric juice, 260
Gastroenterologist, *table,* 619, 711
Gateway drug, **480, 511**
Gender, **8, 63;** men's health concerns, 197–198; moral development and, 72; personality development and, 63; women's health concerns, 196–197
Gender differences, in communication style, 154; in cancer incidence, 602; in cardiovascular disease, 592, 596; in HIV infection, 578; in life expectancy, 410; in pelvis shape, 288
Gender identification, **67**
General Adaptation Syndrome, 107–108
Generativity, **415**
Genes, **375,** 376–377; *illus.,* 376
Genetic counseling, 379
Genetic disorders, **377,** 378; *table,* 377
Genital herpes, 567, **573–574,** 602; *table,* 572
Genital warts, 567, **574,** 602; *table,* 572, 717
Geriatrics, **416**
"Glass", *See* Methamphetamine.
Glaucoma, **42,** 45, 519; *table,* 411, 716
Gliding joint, **289;** *table,* 289
Global environment, 640–642

Glomerulus, **272;** *illus.* ???
Glucose, **209;** blood, 250–251, 388–389, 608–609
Glycogen, **209,** 248, 261, 300
Going steady, 157–158
Goiter, 216, 389; *table,* 217
Gonorrhea, **570;** *illus.,* 570; *table,* 572, 717
Good Samaritan laws, 684
Gout, *table,* 716
"Grass", *See* Marijuana.
Gray matter, 438
Greenstick fracture, **291;** *illus.,* 291
Grief, **85,** 86, **420,** 421–422; handling of, 86–87; stages of, 87, 421; *table,* 87
Groundwater, **640,** 647
Group dating, 157
Group program, for smoking cessation, 472–473
Group therapy, **142,** 143
Growth, disorders of, 388; regulation of, 387–388; variations in, 387–388
Growth hormone, 387–388; *table,* 391
Growth spurt, 387–388, 400
Guilt, **88**
Gums, disease of, 36–37, 468; *illus.,* 35
Gynecologist, *table,* 619, 711

Hair, 28; loss of, 403; *illus.,* 28–29
Hallucination, **132,** 138
Hallucinogen, **449, 516,** 517; *table,* 516
Hammer (bone), 48; *illus.,* 49
Hand bones, 287–288; *illus.,* 287
Hangover, **492**
"Hardy personality", 111
"Hash", *See* Hashish.
Hashish, 517, **519;** *table,* 518
Hazardous waste, **648,** 652
HDL cholesterol, **211, 594,** 597
Headache, 113, 398, 443–444
Headache remedy, 511
Head injury, 444, 446; first aid for, 698; prevention of, 444; signs of, 698
Health, **4;** factors determining, 5–7; leading causes of death, 4–5; medical advances and, 4–5; sociology of, 8; *See also* Wellness.
Health Almanac, 710–719
Health behavior, 5; *illus.,* 5
Health care, access to, 7–8, 192, 620; costs of, 625–629; culturally sensitive, 555; facilities, 624–625; for Native Americans, 620; reform proposals, 629; team, 622–624; *illus.,* 5

Health claims, on food labels, 228
Health concerns, men's, 197–198; women's, 196–197
Health educator, 6
Health examination, periodic, 620–621
Health fraud, **20–21,** 610, 631–632; *table,* 21
Health insurance, 8, 191, **625;** government plans, 628; insurance terms, 626–629; selection of, 625–629; uninsured persons, 628–629; *illus.,* 628
Health inventory, 14–15
Health maintenance organization (HMO), **627**
Health promotion, *illus.,* 10
Health risk, *See* Risk.
Healthy People 2000, 7–8
Hearing, 48–49; *See also* Ear.
Hearing loss, 50–51; prevention of, 51–52
Heart, 299, 309–310; aging of, 411; blood flow to, 311; effect of alcohol on, 494; transplantation, 325, 598; *illus.,* 308–309, 311, Pl. 6
Heart attack, 215, **595,** 597–598; first aid for, 705; signs of, 705
Heartbeat, 309, 312
Heartburn, 263, 273, 365, 371
Heart disease, 198, 211, 223, 398, 595–596; diet and, 252; prevention of, 315; stress and, 113; tobacco use and, 465; *table,* 4, 411
Heart rate, 312, 386; maximal, 343; reserve, 343; target, 343–344
Heart valves, 309–310; *illus.,* 308–309
Heat cramp, first aid for, 695, 699
Heat exhaustion, **249,** 353; first aid for, 695; *table,* 411
Heat receptor, 29; *illus.,* 29
Heat stroke, **249;** first aid for; 695; *table,* 411
Heavy drinker, **484**
Heimlich maneuver, 691
Helper T cells, **543–544;** *illus.,* 544
Helpline, **139, 183, 530,** 533; AIDS, 579, 584–585; alcoholism, 507; drug abuse, 530; family crisis, 183–184; health insurance, 627; personal problems, 139; sex-related concerns, 571; sexually transmitted diseases, 584–585
Hemoglobin, **216, 317**
Hemophilia, 378, 579; *table,* 377, 716
Hemorrhoids, **266**
Hepatitis, **494,** 516, 523, 540, **557**
Hepatitis A, 558; *table,* 717
Hepatitis B, 558; *table,* 548

Hepatitis B vaccine, *table,* 548
Hepatitis C, 558; D, 558; E, 558
Hepatitis Non-A, Non-B, *table* 718
Heredity, **6, 61,** 375–380; health and, 6; hypertension and, 593; personality and, 61–62; *illus.,* 5
Hernia, **302,** 403; *table,* 716
Heroin, 374, 510, **516,** 527; *table,* 510, 515
Hero-worship, 91
Herpes virus, *See* Cold sore; Genital herpes.
Heterosexual, **156**
Hinge joint, **289;** *table,* 289
Hip, 289; replacement of, 297; *illus.,* Pl. 1; *table,* 289
Hipbone, 288
Histamine, **251**
Hives, 251
HIV infection, action of virus, 575–576; asymptomatic, 576–577; from blood/blood products, 578–579; declining immunity in, 577; gender differences in, 578; myths about, 580; in pregnancy, 371; prevention of, 578, 583–586; progression of, 576–577; through sexual contact, 578; susceptibility to, 577–579; treatment of, 580–582; *illus.,* 575, 578; *table,* 4, 581; *See also* AIDS.
HIV positive person, **581**
HIV testing, 580–582; false positives, 582; margin of error in, 581–582; who gets tested, 581
HMO, *See* Health maintenance organization.
Hodgkin's disease, *table,* 716
The Hole In the Wall Gang Camp, 604
Home health care, 198, **625**
Homelessness, 190–191, 554
Home pregnancy test, 370
Home safety, 661–663; *illus.,* 662
Homicide, **96,** 100, 199; *table,* 4
Homosexual, **156;** AIDS and, 577, 580
Hormone Replacement Therapy, 398
Hormones, **386;** reproduction and, 391–392; in stress response, 390–391
Hormone therapy, **605**
"Horse", *See* Heroin.
Hospice, **421,** 422, **625**
Hospital, **624;** for mental illness, 143–144
Hostility, **83**
Hot flash, 415
Hotline, *See* Helpline.
Household products, environmentally safe alternatives to, 652, 654, 713; hazardous, 700, 703,

713; inhalants, 519–520
House inspector, 663
Human immunodeficiency virus, *See* HIV infection.
Humanistic approach, to personality development, 61
Humanitas Prize, 172
Humidifier, 324
Hunger, **235**
Hurricane, 675
Hydrophobia, *See* Rabies.
Hyoid, **286**
Hyperactivity, **132**
Hypertension, **215**, 252, **314**, 414, **593**, 596–597; among African Americans, 593; causes of, 593; risk factors for, 314; *illus.*, 596; *table*, 716
Hyperventilation, first aid for, 688
Hypoactivity, **132**
"Hypoallergic" products, 31
Hypochondria, **136**
Hypoglycemia, **251**
Hypothalamus, **386**, 387, **434**; *illus.*, 434
Hypothermia, first aid for, 695; *table*, 411

Ibuprofen, 525
"Ice", *See* Methamphetamine.
Id, 61; *illus.*, 61
Idealization, **91**; *table*, 94
Identical twins, **367**
Illegal drug, **449**, 522
Illness stage, **545**; *illus.*, 546
Immovable joint, **290**; *table*, 289
Immune system, 543–544; aging of, 411; effect of alcohol on, 551; exercise and, 332; in HIV infection, 575–577; stress and, 113; *illus.*, 543–544
Immunity, **544**, 545; *illus.*, 544
Immunopathologist, *table*, 711
Immunotherapy, **605**
Implantation, 395; *illus.*, 362
Incisor, **35**; *illus.*, 35
Incubation stage of disease, **545**; *illus.*, 546
Incubator, **373**
Indian Health Service, 194
Indigestion, **263**, 273; avoidance of, 264
Infant, 366–367; diet of, 246, 366–367; drug-addicted, 524; family crisis and, 180; low-birthweight, 244, 246, 372; personality development in, 66–67; premature, 372–373, 469; rescue breathing, 707; silver nitrate eye-drops, 570; skull of, 286
Infant formula, 246

Infantile paralysis, *See* Polio.
Infatuation, **156**
Infection, body defenses against, 317–318; of ear, 50; of eye, 42; of nervous system, 445–446; of respiratory system, 323–324, 553–554; of skin, 31
Infectious disease, **538**; in animals, 550; body's response to pathogens, 542–546; common diseases, 553–558; drug therapy for, 549–551; pathogens, 538–539; prevention of, 547–549; prevention when traveling, 540; stages of, 545–546; transmission of, 539–541, 550; *illus.*, 546; *table*, 556, 717–719; *See also* Sexually transmitted disease.
Infertility, **398**, **569**; female, 325, 398–399, 569; male, 402, 404, 569
Inflammation, **542–543**
Influenza, 468, 538, 550–551, 553; *table*, 4, 718
Influenza vaccine, 553; *table*, 548
Ingredients list, 225, 511
Inguinal hernia, **403**
Inhalant, **519**, 520; *table*, 519
Inhibitions, **488**
Inpatient care, **624**
Insect bite, first aid for, 685
Insomnia, 441, **442**
Instinct, 61, **62**
Insulin, **249**, 250, **388**, 389, **608**; *table*, 391
Insulin-dependent diabetes, **608–609**
Insulin shock, **608–609**
Insurance, *See* Health insurance.
Integrity, **416**
Intellectual wellness, **7**; *illus.*, 7
Intelligence, **61**; heredity and, 61–62
Intensity (exercise), **342**, 344
Interferon, 550
Internal bleeding, first aid for, 687
Interneuron, **433**; *illus.*, 432, 439
Internist, *table*, 610, 711
Intestinal glands, 261
Intestine, *See* Large intestine; Small intestine.
Intimate relationship, 153, 158
Intoxication, **488**, 489–491; avoiding intoxicated drivers, 503; factors influencing, 490–491; measurement of, 490–491; recovery from, 492; *table*, 490
Introvert, **62**
Involuntary muscle, *See* Smooth muscle.
Iodine, 216, 389; *illus.*, 370; *table*, 217
Iodized salt, 216

Iris (eye), **39**; *illus.*, 39
Iron, 215–217, 226, 245, 247, 319; *illus.*, 370; *table*, 217
Irradiation of food, 270
Irritable bowel syndrome, **265**, 266

Jealousy, 85
Joint, **289**; aging of, 411; prevention of injuries to, 293; problems involving, 291–296; replacement surgery, 297; types of, 289–290; *illus.*, 290; *table*, 289
"Joint", *See* Marijuana.
Joint cavity, *illus.*, 290
Joint custody, 171
"Junk", *See* Heroin.

Kaposi's sarcoma, 577
Kessler, David, 224
Kidney, **272**; blood flow to, 311; cancer of, 602; disease of, 4, 215; transplantation of, 274, 325; *illus.*, 272, Pl. 5; *table*, 4
Kidney failure, 274
Kidney stones, **273**
Killer T cells, **544**
Knee, 289; protection of, 293, 354; *illus.*, Pl. 1
Kneecap, *illus.*, 285, Pl. 1, Pl. 2
Knee-jerk reflex, *illus.*, 439

Labor (birth), **365**, 366
Lactaid powder, 264
Lactase, **265**; *table*, 260
Lacteal, 261; *illus.*, 261, Pl. 4
Lacto-ovo vegetarian, **222**
Lactose, 209, 265
Lactose intolerance, **264**, 265; *illus.*, 264
Land, 640–641
Landfill, 648, 651
Laparoscopy, 266, 268
Large intestine, 258, 262; *illus.*, 258, Pl. 4
Larynx, **321**, 322, **466**; cancer of, 466–467; *illus.*, 321, Pl. 7
Latchkey children, **170**
Latent syphilis, **573**
Laughing gas, *See* Nitrous oxide.
Laughter, 122
Launching stage, of family life cycle, 174; *table*, 175
Laxative, 237, 241, 264–265
LDL cholesterol, **211**, **594**, 597
Lean body mass, **238–239**, 247
Learned behavior, 62
Leavening agent, **226**
Leg bones, 288
Legal drug, 448–449

Legionnaire's disease, *table,* 718
Legumes, **212**
Lens (eye), **40**, 42–43; *illus.,* 39
Lesion, **568**
Leukemia, **320, 602–603;** *table,* 602, 716
Leukoplakia, **36, 466**
Licensed practical nurse (LPN), **622**
Life changes, 108, 418–419
Life change unit, 108; *table,* 109
Life expectancy, **5,** 71, 410; gender differences in, 410
Life-style, 5, 416
Ligament, **289,** 292–293; *illus.,* 290
Light drinker, **483**
Lightning, 674
Light therapy, 142
Lipids, **210–211**
Lipoproteins, 211, 594
Listening, effective, 174
"Lite" foods, 224, 228
Lithotripsy, 267
Liver, 258; blood flow to, 311; cancer of, 494; diseases of, 4; effect of alcohol on, 493–494; in excretion, 272; functions of, 261; transplantation of, 325; *illus.,* 258, 493, Pl. 4; *table,* 4
"Locker room", *See* Butyl nitrite.
Lockjaw, *See* Tetanus.
Longevity, 5, 71, 333
Love, 82–83
Low-birthweight baby, 244, 246, 372
Lower respiratory tract, 322
LPN, *See* Licensed practical nurse.
LSD, 510, **516,** 517; *table,* 510
"Ludes", *See* Methaqualone.
Lung, 310, 322–323; aging of, 411; cancer of, 193, 462, 465–466, 600, 602, 607; disorders of, 4, 467–468; in excretion, 271; transplantation of, 325; *illus.,* 193, 466, Pl. 6, Pl. 7; *table,* 4
Lyme disease, 541, **557;** *illus.,* 557; *table,* 718
Lymph, 261, **317,** 318; *illus.,* 261
Lymphatic system, 317–318, 543; *illus.,* 318
Lymphatic vessels, 318; *illus.,* 318
Lymph node, **318;** *illus.,* 318, 543
Lymphocytes, **543**

Machinery, safe use of, 663
Macrophages, **543,** 544; *illus.,* 544
MADD, *See* Mothers Against Drunk Driving.
Magnesium, 215; *illus.,* 370; *table,* 216
Mainstream smoke, **468**
Major minerals, 215–216; *table,* 216
Make-up, *See* Cosmetics.

Malaria, 320, 539, 541; *table,* 556, 718
Male development, 400–404
Male reproductive system, 400–402; disorders of, 402–404; *illus.,* 402
Malignant melanoma, **32, 600,** 602
Malignant tumor, **599**
Mammogram, **196, 603,** 627; *illus.,* 196
Manganese, *table,* 217
Mania, **134**
Manic-depression, **134,** 143
Marijuana, 449, 510–511, 517, **518,** 519, 524–525; medical uses of, 519; *table,* 518
Marriage, 160–161; children and, 162–163; delaying of, 163; failure of, 179–180
Marriage enrichment, 159
"Mary jane", *See* Marijuana.
Maslow human needs pyramid, 65; *illus.,* 65
Mast cells, 543
Maturity, **70**
Maximal heart rate, 343
Measles, 548, **555–556;** *table,* 718
Measles vaccine, 556
Mechanical digestion, 259–260
Medicaid, **628;** *illus.,* 628
Medical advances, 4–5
Medical fraud, 20–21, 610, 631–632
Medicare, **628;** *illus.,* 628
Medicine, 448; home supplies, 710; labeling of, 630–631; safety precautions, 631, 710; storage of, 710; tips for taking, 631; wise use of, 630–632; *illus.,* 630; *See also* Drug.
Medicine cabinet, *table,* 710
Medulla, **435;** *illus.,* 434
Melanin, 28
Melanoma, **32, 600,** 602
Melatonin, 142
Memory cells, **545,** 547; *illus.,* 544
Memory loss, 416, 424
Meninges, **434**
Meningitis, **446;** *table,* 4, 718
Menopause, **395,** 398, **414,** 415
Men's health, 197–198
Menstrual cycle, **394,** 395; *illus.,* 396
Menstruation, 395–396; *illus.,* 396
Mental disorder, causes of, 128–130; among children and teens, 61, 137; coping with, 74, 93; finding help for, 139–143; functional causes of, 130; organic causes of, 129; treatment of, 139–144; types of, 131–137
Mental health, **60–61;** ways to improve, 70
Mental health professionals, *table,* 140

Mentally challenged persons, 200
Mental retardation, 379
Mental trauma, **130**
Mescaline, **516–517;** *table,* 510, 516
Metabolism,235b, 236, 332; control of, 389–390
Metastasis, **599,** 606; *illus.,* 599
Methadone, **527;** *table,* 510
Methamphetamine, **513,** 523; *table,* 510, 513
Methaqualone, **515;** *table,* 510, 514
Miami Project, 445
Midbrain, **435;** *illus.,* 434
Middle adulthood, 71; diet in, 247; maintaining wellness in, 415; physical changes in, 414–415; psychological changes in, 415; social changes in, 415; *table,* 411
Mid-life crisis, **413**
Midwifery, 372
Migraine headache, 113, 398, **443,** 444; *table,* 716
Minerals, **215,** 216; deficiency of, 216–217; food labeling, 227; functions in body, 216–217; sources in diet, 216–217; storage in bone, 283; toxicity of, 216–217; *table,* 216–217, 714
Minor (legal term), **500**
Miracle cure, *See* Quackery.
Miscarriage, **372,** 379, 469, 524, 565
Missing children, 181
"MMDA", *See* Mescaline.
Modeling, **63, 141**
Moderate drinker, **482–484**
Molar, **35,** 36; *illus.,* 35
Mole, 32; *illus.,* 32
Moniliasis, *table,* 572
Monogamy, **584**
Mononucleosis, **319, 556–557;** *table,* 718
Monosodium glutamate, **252**
Mood disorder, 133–134
Moral development, 72
"Morf", *See* Morphine.
Morning sickness, 371
Morphine, **515;** *table,* 515
Mosquitoes, 541
Mothers Against Drunk Driving (MADD), 503
Motorcycle safety, 666
Motor neuron, **433;** *illus.,* 432, 439
Motor skills, **340,** 341; *table,* 341
Mouth, 258–259, 494; *table,* 260
Movement, 283, 298–299, 437–438
Mucous membrane, **322, 542;** *illus.,* 543
Mucus, 322–323, 326, 467
Multiple birth, 367
Multiple personality disorder, **137–138**
Multiple sclerosis, **446,** 447; *table,*

716
Multiplier effect, **492**
Mumps, 548; *table,* 556, 718
Muscle, action of, 299–300; energy
  for, 300–301; functions of,
  298–299; problems involving,
  301–302; types of, 299; *illus.,*
  299, Pl. 1, Pl. 3
Muscle cramp, *See* Cramp.
Muscle tension, 294
Muscle tone, **301**
Muscular dystrophy, **302;** *table,* 377,
  716
Muscular endurance, **337,** 338, 345;
  table, 338
Myelin, 445

Nails, 28
Narcolepsy, **442**
Narcotic, **449, 515,** 516; *table,* 510
Nasal cavity, 321; *illus.,* 321
National Safety Council, 661, 679
Natural disaster, 178–179, 674–676
"Natural" products, 31
Nausea, 112–113, 263–264, 519
Nearsightedness, **41;** *illus.,* 41
Neck protection, 293
Needle sharing, 516, 523, 558,
  578–579, 585
Needs hierarchy, 65; *illus.,* 65
Negative attitude, 75
Negative stress, 106–107
Negativism, *table,* 94
Neighborhood Crime Watch, 673
Nephron, **272,** 274
Nerve, **433**
Nerve impulse, **40, 432,** 433; in
  hearing, 48–49; in muscle con-
  traction, 299; transmission of,
  448; in vision, 40; *illus.,* 448
Nervous system, **432,** 433–439; cen-
  tral, 433–435; coordination with
  endocrine system, 386–387; dis-
  orders of, 443–447; peripheral,
  435–437; structure and functions
  of, 433–434; *illus.,* 433, Pl. 8
Neurologist, *table,* 711
Neuron, **432,** 433; *illus.,* 432, 439
Neurosis, **131**
Neurotransmitter, **433,** 448–450;
  illus., 432, 448
Niacin, 226; *illus.,* 370; *table,* 214
Nicotine, 448, **459,** 460–463,
  468–470, 594
Nicotine patch, 473–474
Nicotine substitutes, **473,** 474
Nightblindness, *table,* 214
Night sweats, 415
Nitrogen oxides, 644, 646
Nitrous oxide, **519;** *table,* 519
Nocturnal emission, **402**

Noise exposure, 51–52; *illus.,* 52
Noninfectious disease, arthritis,
  609–610; cancer, 599–605; car-
  diovascular, 592–598; diabetes,
  608–609; of elderly, 610–612;
  table, 715–716
Noninsulin-dependent diabetes, **609**
Nose, 321; *illus.,* 258, 321, Pl. 8
Nosebleed, first aid for, 687
Nuclear family, **170,** 171
Nuclear power, 649; waste, **649**
Nurse, **622**
Nursing home, **417,** 624
Nutrients, **208;** energy sources,
  208–212; identifying nutritious
  foods, 225–228; that regulate
  body processes, 213–218; *table,*
  714
Nutrition, **208;** through life cycle,
  244–248; for older adult, 200;
  special needs, 249–252; during
  stressful time, 119
Nutritional anemia, 319
Nutritionist, 250
Nutrition labeling, 225, 227

Obesity, **236,** 237, 240, 247, 250,
  593, 609
Obsession, **135**
Obsessive-compulsive disorder, **135**
Obstetrician, *table,* 711
Occipital lobe, *illus.,* 435
Occupational Safety and Health
  Administration (OSHA), 664
Occupational therapy, 144
Oil gland, *illus.,* 29
Older adulthood, 71; consumer
  issues in, 414; diet in, 247; health
  concerns in, 200; home health
  assistance, 198; maintaining well-
  ness in, 417; noninfectious dis-
  eases of, 610–612; physical
  changes in, 416; psychological
  changes in, 416; social changes
  in, 416–417; *table,* 411
Oncologist, *table,* 619, 711
One-mile run test, 337; *table,* 337
Open fracture, **291,** 696; *illus.,* 291
Ophthalmologist, *table,* 711
Opium, **515;** *table,* 510, 515
Opportunistic disease, **576,** 577
Optic nerve, 40; *illus.,* 39
Oral cancer, 36, 463–466, 494; *table,*
  602, 607
Organ, **28**
Organ donor, 325, 423
Organic mental disorder, **129,**
  131–132
Orthodontics, **37**
Orthopedic surgeon, *table,* 711
Orthopedist, *table,* 619

OSHA, *See* Occupational Safety and
  Health Administration.
Osteoarthritis, **294,** 297, **416,**
  609–610
Osteomalacia, **296**
Osteomyelitis, *table,* 718
Osteopathy degree, 619
Osteoporosis, **197, 215,** 247, **295,**
  296, 333, 398, **414;** *illus.,* 295;
  table, 216, 411, 716
OTC drug, *See* Over-the-counter
  drug.
Otorhinolaryngologist, *table,* 711
Outpatient care, **527, 624;** drug treat-
  ment, 527; psychiatric, 140
Oval window, **48;** *illus.,* 49
Ovary, **392;** cancer of, 196, 397–398,
  601–603; cyst of, 397; *illus.,* 362,
  386, 394; *table,* 391
Overdose, **512;** first aid in, 701
Overeating, 234–235, 240–243
Overgeneralization, **115**
Overload (exercise), **342**
Overpopulation, 641
Over-the-counter (OTC) drug, **448,**
  510–511, **551,** 552, 630; *table,*
  510
Overweight, 10, **236,** 237, 240–243
Ovulation, **394–395;** failure of, 398
Oxygen, exchange in lungs,
  321–323, 332; transport in blood,
  308, 317, 332
Ozone layer, **645,** 646

Pacemaker, heart, 312
Pain receptor, 29; *illus.,* 29
Pancreas, **261, 388;** digestive func-
  tions of, 258–261; endocrine
  functions of, 388–389; *illus.,* 258,
  386, Pl. 4; *table,* 260, 391
Panic attack, 143
Panic disorder, **134**
Pantothenic acid, *table,* 214
Pap test, **196, 397**
Paralysis, **445,** 446
Paranoia, **513**
Paranoid personality disorder, **136**
Paraplegia, **445**
Parasites, **539,** 540
Parasympathetic nervous system,
  436; *illus.,* 436
Parathyroid gland, 390; *illus.,* 386,
  390; *table,* 391
Parenthood, cost of raising child,
  365; deciding to have children,
  162–163; postponing, 162;
  responsibilities of parents,
  172–173; single, 163–164, 171;
  teen, 160
Parietal lobe, *illus.,* 435
Parkinson's disease, 448, **611–612;**

table, 716
Partially movable joint, **290**; *table*, 289
Particulates (air pollution), 643–646
Passive-aggressive personality disorder, **137**
Passive smoking, **468**, 469
Pasteurization, 540
Pastoral counselor, *table*, 140
Patella, *See* Kneecap.
Pathogen, **538**, 539, 564–565; *illus.*, 546
Pathologist, *table*, 711
Patient's rights, 621
PCP, **517**, 523; *table*, 516
Pedestrian safety, 667
Pediatrician, *table*, 619, 711
Pediculosis pubis, *table*, 572
Peer, **18, 68**
Peer counseling, 117
Peer pressure, 68–69, **155**, 199; alcohol use and, 502; drug abuse and, 528; tobacco use and, 459; violence and, 97
Pellagra, *table*, 214
Pelvic girdle, **288**; *illus.*, 285
Pelvic inflammatory disease (PID), **399, 569**
Pelvis, **288**; gender differences in, 288
Penicillin, 549
Penis, 401, **402**; *illus.*, 402
Peptic ulcer, 267–268
Periosteum, **283**; *illus.*, 282
Peripheral nervous system, 435–437; *illus.*, 433, Pl. 8
Peristalsis, **259**
Permanent teeth, 36
Pernicious anemia, 319–320; *table*, 214
Personality, **60**; environment and, 62–63; healthy, 60–63; heredity and, 61–62; mental wellness, 73–76; types of, 111–112; *illus.*, 113
Personality development, adolescent, 68–70; adulthood, 70–71; gender differences in, 72; moral development, 72; pre-adolescent, 66–67; theories of, 60–61, 64–66; *table*, 64–65
Personality disorder, 136–137
Personality traits, 62; *illus.*, 62
Personalization, **115**
Perspiration, **29–30**, 33, 248, 272, 542
Pertussis, 549; *table*, 556, 719
Pesticide, 648; *illus.*, 647; *table*, 713
PET scan, of brain, 129, 138; *illus.*, 129, 138
Peyote, **516–517**
Phagocytes, **543**

Pharmacist, 600
Pharynx, **321**; *illus.*, 321
Phencyclidine, *table*, 510
Phenylketonuria, *table*, 377
Phobia, **134–135**; *table*, 134
Phosphorus, 215, 283–284, 295; *illus.*, 370; *table*, 216
Physiatrist, *table*, 711
Physical dependence, 512
Physical environment, *See* Environment.
Physical fitness, **332**; designing fitness plan, 342–349; maintaining fitness goals, 349; physiological benefits of, 332–333; psychological benefits of, 333–334; tests and ratings, 336–341; *See also* Exercise.
Physical therapist, **623**
Physical wellness, **7**
Physician, choice of, 618–620; primary-care, 618–619, 622, 624; specialist, 619, 622; *table*, 619, 711
Physician's assistant, **623**
Piaget intellectual stages, 65; *table*, 64–65
Pica, 241
PID, *See* Pelvic inflammatory disease.
Pimples, *See* Acne.
Pinkeye, 42
Pipe smoking, 463
Pituitary gland, **386**, 387–388, 400; *illus.*, 386, 434; *table*, 391
Pivot joint, **289**; *table*, 289
Placenta, **363**, 364–366
Plaque, **36**
Plasma, **316**; *illus.*, 316
Plasma proteins, 316; *illus.*, 316
Plastic surgeon, *table*, 711
Platelets, **316**; *illus.*, 316
Platonic friendship, **153**
Play therapy, **143**
PMS, *See* Premenstrual syndrome.
Pneumococcus vaccine, *table*, 548
Pneumocystis carinii pneumonia, 577
Pneumonia, **324**, 468, 538, 577; *table*, 4, 556, 718
Poison control center, **662**, 700
Poisoning, 662; drug overdose, 701; first aid for, 700–703; inhaled poison, 701; prevention of, 662; skin-contact poison, 703; swallowed poison, 700; *illus.*, 660, 681
Poisonous plant, 703
Polio, **446**, 538; *table*, 556, 718
Polio vaccine, *table*, 548
Pollution, 192, **644**
Polyunsaturated fats, 210

Pons, **435**; *illus.*, 434
"Poppers", *See* Butyl nitrite.
Population growth, 641
Pores (skin), **28**, 30; *illus.*, 29–30
Positive attitude, 75
Positive self-talk, 121–122
Positive stress, 106–107
Post-traumatic stress disorder, **109**, 135
Posture, 298, 301
"Pot", *See* Marijuana.
Potassium, 215; *table*, 216
Poverty, 178, 190
Pregnancy, alcohol use in, 245, 494–495; cigarette smoking in, 245, 469; diabetes in, 609; diet in, 244–246, 364–365, 370; drug use in, 245, 524; exercise in, 366, 371; HIV infection in, 371; hormones in, 394; medicines and drugs during, 373–374; prenatal care, 369–374; prenatal development, 363–365; problems in, 371–373; sexually transmitted disease and, 565; teen, 160, 246, 373; weight gain in, 245–246, 370; *illus.*, 370, 373; *table*, 245
Pregnancy test, 370
Prejudice, **155**
Premature birth, **372–373**, 469
Premenstrual syndrome (PMS), **396**, 397; lessening effects of, 397
Premium (insurance), **626**
Premolar, **35**; *illus.*, 35
Prenatal care, **369**; choosing location for birth, 369; choosing physician, 369; overcoming anxiety, 369–370
Prenatal development, embryo, 363–364; fetus, 364–365
Prenatal diagnosis, 379–380
Prescription drug, **448**, 549–551, **630**; abuse of, 519–520; questions to ask doctor about, 549
Preservative, **226**
Pressure-point technique (stop bleeding), 687
Pressure-point therapy (muscle tension), 294
Pressure receptor, 29; *illus.*, 29
Preventive medicine, *table*, 711
Primary-care physician, **618**, 619, 622, 624; *table*, 619
Primary syphilis, **571–572**
Problem drinker, 484
Proctologist, *table*, 711
Prodromal stage, **545**; *illus.*, 546
Product dating, 226
Product safety, 21
Professional relationship, 153
Progesterone, 394, 398; *illus.*, 396; *table*, 391

Progression (exercise plan), **342**
Progressive relaxation, **120**
Progressive resistance training, 345
Projection (defense mechanism), **91**
Proof (alcohol), **480**
Prostate gland, **401;** cancer of, 197, 403, 602–603; disorders of, 403; *illus.,* 402
Proteins, **211,** 212, 222; Calories per gram, 210; plasma, 316; requirement for, 212; *illus.,* 316, 370; *table,* 245
Protein supplements, 249, 300
Protozoa, **539;** *illus.,* 539
Psoriasis, **31**
Psychiatric social worker, *table,* 140
Psychiatrist, *table,* 140
Psychoactive drug, **449, 480, 510;** *table,* 510
Psychoanalysis, **140;** *table,* 140
Psychoanalytic approach, to personality development, 60–61
Psychoanalytic psychotherapy, **141**
Psychological dependence, 512
Psychologist, **60,** 61, 66, 93, 624; *table,* 140
Psychosis, **131**
Psychosomatic illness, **112,** 113, 136
Psychotherapy, **140,** 141–143
Puberty, **391;** in females, 392–393; in males, 392, 400; stresses of, 393, 400
Pubic hair, **393,** 400
Pubic lice, *table,* 572
Public health, **192;** functions of health system, 192–193; international agencies, 194; levels of, 193–194; national agencies, 194; state and local agencies, 193–194
Pull-ups, **338;** *table,* 338
Pulmonary artery, *illus.,* 308, Pl. 6
Pulmonary circulation, **310;** *illus.,* Pl. 6, Pl. 7
Pulmonary vein, *illus.,* 308, Pl. 6
Pulp of tooth, **36;** *illus.,* 35–36
Pulse, 310, 343
Pulse point, 343
Pupil (eye), **39;** *illus.,* 39
Purchasing, 86
Pyridoxine, *See* Vitamin B₆.

Quackery, **20–21,** 610, 631, **632;** *table,* 21
Quadriplegia, **445**
"Quads", *See* Methaqualone.
Quarantine, **193**

Rabies, 541; *table,* 556, 719
Radiation, **649**
Radiation therapy, **604**

Radioactive waste, **649**
Radiologist, *table,* 711
Radius, *illus.,* 285, Pl. 1
Rape, **159,** 672–673
Rapid eye movement (REM) sleep, **441**
Rationalization, **90;** *table,* 94
Reaction formation, **95;** *table,* 94
Reality, perception of, 128
Receptor, **29;** *illus.,* 29, 448
Recessive genes, **376–377;** *illus.,* 376
Recessive genetic disorders, *table,* 377
Recommended amount, food labeling, 227
Recovery stage of disease, **546;** *illus.,* 546
Recreational safety, 668–671
Recreational therapy, 144
Rectum, 262; cancer of, 600–603; *illus.,* 258, 394, 402, Pl. 4
Recycling, **648,** 652–654
Red blood cells, **317,** 319; *illus.,* 316–317
Red bone marrow, **283;** *illus.,* 282
Red Cross, 661
Redress, right to, 22
Reflex, **438,** 439; effect of alcohol on, 489; of infant, 366
Reflex arc, **439;** *illus.,* 439
Registered nurse (RN), **622**
Regression, **92**
Rehabilitation, cardiovascular, 598
Reinforcement (behavioral therapy), **141**
Relapse, **546**
Relationship, **152;** formation of, 73–74, 129; healthy, 152–155; need for, 152; types of, 152–153
Relaxation, 119–120
Remarriage, 180
REM sleep, **441**
Repression, **89–90**
Reproduction, hormones in, 391–392
Reproductive system, female, 393–394; male, 400–402; *illus.,* 394, 402
Rescue breathing, 689, 707
Resistance stage of stress response, **108**
Respect for others, 155
Respiratory system, 321–322; disorders of, 323–326, 553–554; *illus.,* 321–322, Pl. 7
Responsibility, to family, 172–173; of other people, 10; to self, 9–10
Retina, **40;** detached, 42; *illus.,* 39
Retirement, 416; *table,* 175
Reye's syndrome, 511, **551**
Rheumatic fever, 554; *table,* 719
Rheumatoid arthritis, **610**

Riboflavin, 226; *illus.,* 370; *table,* 214
Ribs, 287, 290; *illus.,* 285, Pl. 1, Pl. 2, Pl. 3
Rickets, **296;** *table,* 214, 216
Rickettsia, **539**
Ringworm, 31, 539; *table,* 719
Risk, **9,** 10–11
RN, *See* Registered nurse.
Rocky Mountain spotted fever, 539, 541; *table,* 556, 719
Rods (eye), **40**
Role models, 68
Root of tooth, **35;** *illus.,* 35
Rubella, 364, 371, 548; *table,* 719
Runaway children, 181
Running, 346–347, 667
Runoff, **647**
Run-Walk-Run Program, 346–347; *table,* 346
Ruptured disc, 293–294
"Rush", *See* Butyl nitrite.

Sacrum, **286,** 288; *illus.,* 285–286, Pl. 1
SAD, *See* Seasonal Affective Disorder.
SADD, *See* Students Against Drunk Driving.
Safety, automobile, 665–666; bicycle, 666–667; at home, 661–663; with medicines, 710; motorcycle, 666; in natural disasters, 674–676; pedestrian, 667; product, 21; recreational, 668–671; toy, 179; water, 500; at work, 663–664
Saliva, 259
Salivary glands, 258–259; *illus.,* 258; *table,* 260
Salmonella food poisoning, 550; *table,* 269, 719
Salt, as preservative, 226
Salt tablets, 248
Saturated fats, **210**
Scab, 316
Scabies, *table,* 572
Scalp wound, 698
Scapula, *See* Shoulder blade.
Scarlet fever, *table,* 719
Schizoid personality disorder, **137**
Schizophrenia, **138,** 143; *illus.,* 138; *table,* 716
"School boy", *See* Codeine.
Scoliosis, **296;** *table,* 716
Scrotum, **401;** *illus.,* 402
Scurvy, *table,* 214
Seasonal Affective Disorder (SAD), 142
Seat belt, 444, 666
Sebum, **28,** 30, **542**

Secondary sex characteristics, female, 393, 395; male, 400–401; *illus.*, 395, 401
Secondary syphilis, **572–573**
Second-degree burn, 690
"Secret remedy", 632
Sedative, *table,* 510
Sedentary life-style, 247, **322**
Seizure, **444**, 447; first aid for, 694
Selenium, *table,* 217
Self-acceptance, 74–76, 129
Self-awareness, 129, 155
Self-concept, **18, 73**
Self-control, 67
Self-esteem, **17–18**, 75, 129, 198–199, 334; development of, 74; steps to improve, 17
Self-examination, **74**; of breast, 601, 607; of testes, 403; *illus.*, 601
Self-fulfilling prophecy, **122**
Self-help, family, 183–184
Self-reliance, 69
Self-talk, 121–122
Self-worth, 198
Sell/pull date, **226**
Semen, **401**
Semicircular canals, **49, 50**; *illus.*, 49
Seminal vesicle, 401; *illus.*, 402
Semi-vegetarian, **222**
Senile dementia, 132
Sensory neuron, **433**; *illus.*, 432, 439
Separation, **179–180**
Services, **19**
Serving size, 226–227; *illus.*, 221
Sex chromosomes, 376
Sex-linked disorder, **378**
Sexual abstinence, 578, **583**, 584
Sexual harassment, **159**
Sexually transmitted disease (STD), 160, 523, **564–565**; attitudes toward, 566; common diseases, 568–574; incidence of, 565, 570; incurable, 567; in infants, 565; nature of, 567; in pregnancy, 565; prevention of, 567, 583–586; reinfection, 574; spread of, 565–567; substance abuse and, 585; symptoms of, 568–569, 585; *table,* 572, 717–719
Sexual preference, 156
Sexual responsibility, 160
"Shell-shock", *See* Post-traumatic stress disorder.
Shingles, *table,* 719
Shin splint, 668
Shock, first aid for, 702; prevention of, 702; symptoms of, 702
Shoes, athletic, 347, 354; *illus.*, 354
Shoulder, 289–290; dislocation of, 293; *illus.*, 290, Pl. 1; *table,* 289
Shoulder blade, 287; *illus.*, 285, Pl. 1, Pl. 3

Shoulder girdle, 287
Shuttle run, 340–341; *table,* 340
Sickle-cell anemia, **320, 378**, 555; *table,* 716
Side effect, **450, 551, 630**, 632
Side leg raise, 712
Sidestream smoke, **468**
SIDS, *See* Sudden infant death syndrome.
Silver nitrate eyedrops, *illus.*, 570
Simple carbohydrates, 208–209
Simple fracture, *See* Closed fracture.
Single-parent family, 163–164, **171**
Single person, 164
Sinus, 286; *illus.*, Pl. 7
Sit-and-reach test, 339; *table,* 339
Sit-ups, 337–338; *table,* 338
Skateboarding, 670
Skeletal muscle, **299**
Skeleton, 285–290; appendicular, 285, 287–288; axial, 285–287; *illus.*, 285, Pl. 1
Skin, aging of, 411; cancer of, 32–34, 43, 600, 602, 606; care of, 32–34; color of, 43; defense against pathogens, 542; in excretion, 272; problems involving, 30–32, 112; structure and functions of, 28–30; *illus.*, 28–30, 32
Skinfold caliper, 341; *illus.*, 341
Skull, 282, **286**, 290, 434; *illus.*, 285–286, Pl. 1; *table,* 289
Sleep, 386, 441; disorders of, 112, 442; requirement for, 441; *illus.*, 440
Sleep apnea, **442**
"Smack", *See* Heroin.
Small intestine, 258, **260**, 261; *illus.*, 258, 261, Pl. 4; *table,* 260
Smallpox, 548
Smoke detector, 662; *illus.*, 662
Smokeless tobacco, 36, **456**, 457, 463–466; long-term risks of, 466–467; teen use of, 463–464; *illus.*, 464
Smoker's cough, 462, 467, 470
Smooth muscle, **299**
Snacking, 221, 228, 239; pre-game, 248
Snakebite, first aid for, 685
Sneezing, 439, 540
"Snow", *See* Cocaine.
Snuff, **456**, 457, 463–464
Social drinking, **483**
Socialization, **62**, 63
Social-learning approach, to personality development, 61
Social norms, 128
Social pressure, alcohol use and, 481; tobacco use and, 458–459
Social Security, 628

Social wellness, **7**; *illus.*, 7
Social worker, *table,* 140
Societal problems, 190–192
Socioeconomic status, 178, 190
Sociology of health, 8
Sodium, 215, 217–218; dietary, 215, 224, 252, 315, 593; in fast foods, 222–223; *table,* 216
Solid waste, **648**, 653–654
Solvent sniffing, 519
Somatic nervous system, **437**
Somatoform disorder, 136
"Sopers", *See* Methaqualone.
Sound, prolonged exposure to, 51–52; *illus.*, 52
Spastic colon, *See* Irritable bowel syndrome.
Specialist, **619**, 622; *table,* 619, 711
Specificity (exercise plan), **342**
"Speed", *See* Amphetamine.
Sperm cells, 362, 375–376, 401; production of, 404; *illus.*, 362, 401
Spermicidal gel, 578
SPF, *See* Sun protection factor.
Spinal column, **286–287**; *illus.*, 286
Spinal cord, 435; injury to, 293–294, 445, 669; *illus.*, 434, 439, Pl. 8
Spleen, **318**; *illus.*, 318, 543, Pl. 6
Splinter, first aid for, 693
Splinting, 697
Spongy bone, **283**; *illus.*, 282
Sports medicine, *table,* 711
Sports nutrition, 248–249
Sports psychologist, 93
Spouse abuse, **183**
Sprain, **292**; first aid for, 697
"Stacking" (steroid abuse), 351
Stalking, 158, **159**
Standard of identity, **225**
Standing long jump, 341; *table,* 340
Starch, 209
Stationary bicycle, 348
STD, *See* Sexually transmitted disease.
Step aerobics, 348; *illus.*, 348
Stereotyping, **63**
Sternum, 287; *illus.* 285, Pl. 1
Steroid abuse, *See* Anabolic steroids.
Stillbirth, **372**, 469, 524
Stimulant, 221, **449, 513**, 514; *table,* 510, 513
Stimulus, **440**
Sting, first aid for, 685
Stomach, 258; "butterflies in", 112; *illus.*, 258, 543, Pl. 4; *table,* 260
Stools, 262
"STP", *See* Mescaline.
Strain, **301–302**; first aid for, 699
Strength, **337**, 338, 345; *table,* 338
Strength training, 239–240, 249, 345, 348, 520–521

Strep infection, 549
Strep throat, **554**
Stress, **106, 458;** alcohol use and, 482; emotional signs of, 107; health and, 112–116, 119, 265–266; hormones and, 390–391; management of, 91, 113–115, 118–122, 333–334, 503; mental disorders and, 130; negative and positive, 106–107; overeating and, 234; physical signs of, 107; positive effects of, 120; recognition of reactions to, 118–119; in special populations, 110–111; stress response, 107–108; tobacco use and, 458
Stressor, **106,** 108–110; *table,* 109
Stress vitamins, 91, 119
Stroke, 215, **314, 468, 596,** 598; first aid for, 705; *illus.,* 596; *table,* 4, 716
Students Against Drunk Driving (SADD), 199, 503
Sty, 42
Subconscious, **60**
Sublimation, **94,** 98
Substance abuse, effect on family relationships, 182; violence and, 97; *See also* Alcohol use; Drug abuse.
Sudden infant death syndrome (SIDS), **420**
Sugar, 208–209; *table,* 209
Suicide, causes of, 117; depression and, 133; prevention of, 116–117; among teens, 114–117; unsuccessful, 114; *illus.,* 115; *table,* 4
Suicide peer counseling, 117
Sulfites, **252**
Sulfur, 215; *table,* 216
Sulfur oxides, 644, 646, 650–651
Sun block, **34**
Sunburn, 32–33
Sun protection factor (SPF), **33,** 43, 607
Sunscreen, **33, 34,** 607
Superego, 61, 69; *illus.,* 61
Support group, AIDS, 584; alcohol addiction, 495–496; Alzheimer's disease, 424; family in crisis, 184; sexually transmitted diseases, 584
Surgeon, *table,* 711
Surgery, in cancer, 604; in cardiovascular disease, 597–598
Swallowing, 259; *illus.,* 259
Sweat gland, 29, 272; *illus.,* 29
Swelling, 543
Swimming, 347, 669
Sympathetic nervous system, 436–437; *illus.,* 436
Synapse, **433;** *illus.,* 432, 448

Synergistic effect, **450**
Syphilis, **571,** 572–573, 585; *illus.,* 571; *table,* 572, 719
Systematic desensitization, **141**
Systemic circulation, **310–311**
Systolic pressure, **313**

Tailbone, *See* Coccyx.
Tailgating, **665**
Tampon, 397
Target heart rate, **343,** 344
Target shooting, 671
Tars, **462,** 463, 468
Tay-Sachs disease, 555; *table,* 377
TB, *See* Tuberculosis.
T cells, 543–545, 575–577; *illus.,* 544
Tea, 437
Tears, 542; *illus.,* 543
Teenager, advertising and, 46–47; AIDS and, 578–579; alcohol use among, 191, 482, 484, 489, 494, 500–503; attraction to others, 156; Calories required by, 235, 246; cigarette smoking among, 198, 458, 460; delinquent behavior by, 180–181; depression among, 133; diet of, 246–247; drug abuse among, 484, 511; family responsibilities of, 173; female development, 393–399; health concerns of, 198–199; leading causes of death, 4; male development, 400–404; mental illness among, 61, 137; parenthood among, 160; personality development in, 64–65, 69–70; pregnancy among, 160, 246, 373; runaway, 181; smokeless tobacco use among, 463–464; suicide among, 114–117; violence among, 100–101; weapon-carrying, 98
Teeth, 259; care of, 37–38; problems of, 36–38, 437; structure and functions of, 35–36; *illus.,* 35
Television, closed-caption, 50
Temperature, *See* Body temperature.
Temperature inversion, 645; *illus.,* 645
Temporal lobe, *illus.,* 435
Temporomandibular joint, *See* TMJ problems.
Tendon, **299;** *illus.,* 290
Tendonitis, **302**
Tennis elbow, 302, 668
Tension headache, 113, 443
Terminal illness, 87, **420,** 421, 625
Tertiary syphilis, **573**
Testes, **392,** 401; cancer of, 197, 403, 602; injuries to, 404; self-exami-

nation of, 403; undescended, 402; *illus.,* 386, 402; *table,* 391
Testosterone, 350, **392,** 401, 520; *table,* 391
Tetanus, 538; *table,* 556, 719
Thalamus, **434;** *illus.,* 434
THC, **517**
Therapeutic community, **526**
Therapist, **140**
Thiamin, 226; *illus.,* 370; *table,* 214
Thighbone, 288; *illus.,* 285, Pl. 1
Third-degree burn, 690
Thirst, 218, 386
Thoracic surgeon, *table,* 711
Throat, cancer of, 465; effect of alcohol on, 494; *illus.,* Pl. 7
Thumb, 288
Thymus, **318;** *illus.,* 318, 543
Thyroid gland, 216, **389,** 390; disorders of, 236; *illus.,* 386, 390; *table,* 391
Thyroid-stimulating hormone, *table,* 391
Tick, 541, 557, 685; *illus.,* 557
Time management, 120–121
"TMA", *See* Mescaline.
TMJ problems, 37
Tobacco products, addiction to, 459–460; advertising of, 46–47, 456, 459; cost of, 462; effect on body, 461–464; in history, 457; long-term risks of, 36, 193, 465–469; popularity of, 456; quitting use of, 470–474; reasons for use of, 457; reasons people start using, 458–459; warning labels on, 456–457; withdrawal symptoms, 471; *table,* 471; *See also* Cigarette smoking; Smokeless tobacco.
Tolerance, **491, 511–512;** to alcohol, 491; to drugs, 511–512
Tongue, 259; *illus.,* 258
Tongue rolling, 377; *illus.,* 376
Tonsils, **318;** *illus.,* 318
Tools, safe use of, 663
Tooth, *See* Teeth.
Tooth brushing, 37–38
Tooth decay, 36–38; *illus.,* 36
Tornado, 675–676
Toxemia, **371**
Toxicity, **215**
Toxic shock syndrome, **397**
Toxic waste, 647–648, 654
Toxin, **538**
Toys, safety of, 179
Trace minerals, 216; *table,* 217
Trachea, **322;** *illus.,* 258, 321, Pl. 7
Trait theorist, 60
Tranquilizer, 143, 492, **514;** *table,* 510, 514
Transitions, **410**

Transplantation, **423**; of bone marrow, 320, 325; of cornea, 43; of egg, 325; of heart, 325, 598; of kidney, 274, 325; of liver, 325; of lung, 325; organ donation, 325
Traumatic event, 108–109
Traveler's diarrhea, 540
Treadmill, 348
Triceps, 300; *illus.,* 299, Pl. 2, Pl. 3
Trichinosis, *table,* 719
Trichomoniasis, *table,* 572
"Trip", *See* LSD.
Trunk twist, 712
Tuberculin test, *table,* 548
Tuberculosis (TB), **191, 324,** 538, 540, **554,** 577; *table,* 4, 719
Tumor, **444, 599,** 606; of brain, 444; of pituitary, 388
Twins, 367
Type A personality, **112,** 114; *illus.,* 113
Type B personality, **112;** *illus.,* 113
Typhoid fever, 540; *table,* 719

Ulcer, **267,** 268
Ultrasound, of fetus, 380
Ultraviolet radiation, 646; protection from, 33–34, 45
Umbilical blood vessels, *illus.,* 364
Umbilical cord, **363;** *illus.,* 364
Unconscious (part of personality), **140**
Unconscious person, first aid for, 704; possible causes, 704
Underweight, **239,** 240
Unit price, 227
"Universal donor", *table,* 319
Unsaturated fats, **210**
Upper respiratory tract, 321–322
"Uppers", *See* Amphetamine.
Urea, 272
Ureter, **272;** *illus.,* 272, Pl. 5
Urethra, **272,** 273, **401;** *illus.,* 272, 402, Pl. 5
Urethritis, **569**
Urinary system, maintaining healthy system, 273; problems involving, 273–274; structure and functions of, 272; *illus.,* 272, Pl. 5
Urine test, for alcohol, 491
Urologist, *table,* 619, 711
Uterus, **394;** cancer of, 196, 601–603; *illus.,* 364, 394

Vaccination, **547,** 548–549; schedule for, 548; *table,* 548
Vagina, **394;** *illus.,* 394
Vaginitis, **568,** 569; *table,* 719
Values, **12, 69;** moral development, 72; search for, 69

Vaporizer, 324
Vas deferens, **401,** 404
VDT, eyestrain prevention, 44
Vegan, **222**
Vegetarian, **222**
Veins, **310;** *illus.,* 310, Pl. 6
Ventricle, **309,** 310; *illus.,* 308–309
Vertebrae, **286–287;** *illus.,* 286, Pl. 1
Video display terminal, *See* VDT.
Villi, **261;** *illus.,* 261, Pl. 4
Violence, **96,** 111; against women, 197; alcohol-related, 498–500; anger and, 96–98; causes of, 96–97; domestic, 182–183, 523; drug-related, 522–525; in intimate relationships, 158–160; prevention of, 97–98, 100–101, 672–673; as societal problem, 191; teen, 100–101, 199
Virus, **538,** 553, 600; *illus.,* 538
Vision, "20/20", 44; checkups, 44–45; problems in, 41–42; *See also* Eye.
Visiting nurse, 625
Visualization, **120**
Vital signs, 620
Vitamin A, 215, 284; *illus.,* 370; *table,* 214
Vitamin B$_1$, *See* Thiamin.
Vitamin B$_2$, *See* Riboflavin.
Vitamin B$_6$, *illus.,* 370; *table,* 214
Vitamin B$_{12}$, 222, 319–320; *illus.,* 370; *table,* 214
Vitamin C, 284; *illus.,* 370; *table,* 214
Vitamin D, 210, 215, 226, 284, 296; *illus.,* 370; *table,* 214
Vitamin E, *illus.,* 370; *table,* 214
Vitamin K, *table,* 214
Vitamins, **213,** 215, 262; deficiency of, 213–214; food labeling, 227; functions in body, 214; in human milk, 367; sources of, 214; stress-reducing, 91, 119; toxicity, 214–215; *table,* 214
Vocal cords, 322
Voluntary muscle, *See* Skeletal muscle.
Vomiting, 112–113, 218, 241, 263–264, 554–555

Walking, 347
Warm-up, **345,** 712
Water, contaminated, 540, 555; requirement for, 217–218, 248–249
Water conservation, 653
Water pollution, 646–647, 654; biological, 647; chemical, 647; reduction of, 643; *illus.,* 647
Water safety, 500

Waterskiing, 669
Water-soluble vitamins, 213–215; *table,* 214
Water sports, 668–670
Water supply, 640–641, 647, 651
Weapons, 97, 671; teens and, 98
Weather, severe, 665, 674–676
"Weed", *See* Marijuana.
Weight, *See* Body weight.
Weight-loss program, 237–239, 242–243
Weight training, 348
Wellness, **5;** accepting responsibility for, 16–18; consumer health, 19–22; dimensions of, 7; health inventory, 14–15; making healthy choices, 9–13; mental, 73–76; *illus.,* 7; *See also* Health.
Wellness Continuum, 10–11; neutral zone, 11; *illus.,* 10
Western Blot test, 582
Wet dreams, 402
White blood cells, **317,** 318, 320; *illus.,* 316–317
White matter, 438
"White stuff", *See* Morphine.
WHO, *See* World Health Organization.
Whooping cough, *See* Pertussis.
Widowhood, 416
Wine, 480
Wisdom teeth, 36–37
Withdrawal symptoms, **471, 484, 512;** alcohol, 484; drug, 512; tobacco products, 471; *table,* 471
Women's health, 196–197
Workout stages, 345–346
Workplace safety, 663–664
World Health Organization (WHO), 194
World population, 641
Wound care, 686, 692

X chromosome, **376,** 378
"XTC", 520

Y chromosome, **376**
Yellow bone marrow, **283;** *illus.,* 282
Yellow fever, 540–541
Young adulthood, 70–71; diet in, 247; maintaining wellness in, 413; physical changes in, 412; psychological changes in, 412–413; social changes in, 413; *table,* 411

Zidovudine, *See* Azidothymidine.
Zinc, *illus.,* 370; *table,* 217

ACKNOWLEDGMENTS

ILLUSTRATIONS

Nelle Davis: **2, 26, 33, 58, 80, 83, 90, 95, 104, 107, 120, 126, 136, 137, 150, 163, 168, 188, 206, 221, 227, 232, 234, 235, 246, 256, 263, 271, 280, 292, 302, 306, 326, 330, 337, 338, 339, 340, 353, 360, 374, 384, 393, 408, 412, 430, 437, 442, 454, 461, 470, 478, 492, 508, 536, 542, 562, 577, 590, 594, 616, 620, 632, 638, 646, 658** Laurie O'Keefe: **35, 36, 267, 286**(top), **291, 299, 323, 368, 435, 448, 544** Sue Lee: **29, 30, 49, 259, 272**(top), **310, 362, 396, 439, 599, 601, 668** Gordon Nealy: **308, 322, 390, 543** Terry Presnall: **662** Patrice Rossi: **647** Sue Solomon Seif/The Graphics Project: **258, 285, 321, 386, 394, 402, 433, 434, 436** Walter Stewart: **266, 282, 286, 290, 432** Tech-Graphics: **40**(bottom left), **41**(middle left right) Camille Venti: **5, 7, 10, 11, 52, 61, 62, 66, 113, 115, 193, 211, 236, 246, 264, 316, 354, 370, 373, 376, 395, 401, 440, 464, 498, 513-516, 518, 519, 521, 530, 546, 571, 576, 578, 596, 628, 631, 660, 667, 669, 671, 674-676** Marcia Williams: Plates One, Two, Three, Six, Eight   Charles H. Boyler, D. Patrick Russell, and Marcia Williams of the Boston University Educational Media Support Center under the direction of Jerome Glickman, Boston University School of Medicine: **261, 318,** Plates Four, Five, Seven

PHOTOGRAPHY

PHOTO COORDINATOR: Carmen Johnson   **PHOTO RESEARCHER:** Linda Finigan

Table of Contents: vi: Bob Daemmrich, The Image Works; **vii:** Spencer Grant, Monkmeyer Press; **viii:** t, Bob Daemmrich, Tony Stone Worldwide; b, Jeff Isaac Greenberg, Photo Researchers; **xi:** Frank Siteman, The Picture Cube; **xii:** Tony Freeman, PhotoEdit; **xiii:** t, Wagner, Phototake; b, CNRI/Institut Pasteur, Phototake; **xiv:** Robin Hood; **xv:** t, J. Ballard; b, Dede Hatch, The Picture Cube; **xvi:** Ellis Herwig, The Picture Cube; **xvii:** Mike Kagan, Monkmeyer Press.

Unit One: xxi - 1: Myrleen Ferguson, Tony Stone Worldwide; **3:** Lorraine Rorke, The Image Works; **5:** Bob Daemmrich, Stock Boston; **6:** Kindra Clineff, The Picture Cube; **8:** Elizabeth Crews, The Image Works; **9:** Chad Slattery, Tony Stone Worldwide; **12:** Cleo, The Picture Cube; **13:** Tony Freeman, PhotoEdit; **16, 18:** Bob Daemmrich, The Image Works; **19:** Don Smetzer, Tony Stone Worldwide; **22:** Grace Davies, Envision; **23:** John Elk III, Stock Boston; **27:** Frank Siteman, The Picture Cube; **28:** CNRI/Science Photo Library, Photo Researchers; **32:** Stephen Frisch, Stock Boston; **36:** Jim Davis, Photo Researchers; **37:** Dede Hatch, The Picture Cube; **38:** Bob Daemmrich, Stock Boston; **40:** Claude Revy, Jean, Phototake; **41:** Leonard Lessin, Peter Arnold; **42:** t, (both) Custom Medical Stock Photo; b, Photo Researchers; **43:** Bob Daemmrich, Stock Boston; **44:** Blair Seitz, Photo Researchers; **46:** t, Brent Jones, Stock Boston; m, Henry Horenstein, The Picture Cube; b, Arlene Collins, Monkmeyer Press; **47:** Bill Anderson, Monkmeyer Press; **48:** Science Photo Library, Photo Researchers; **50:** Jeff Dunn, The Picture Cube; **52:** Dean Abramson, Stock Boston; **53:** Mike Mazzaschi, Stock Boston.

Unit Two: 56-57: Webb Chappell; **59:** Bachmann, The Image Works; **60:** Bob Daemmrich, Tony Stone Worldwide; **62:** Rhoda Sidney, The Image Works; **63:** Dan McCoy, Rainbow; **67:** Tony Freeman, PhotoEdit; **68:** Rob Nelson, Picture Group; **69:** Rhoda Sidney, Monkmeyer Press; **70:** MacDonald, Envision; **72:** t, Elizabeth Crews, The Image Works; insert, Steve Crompton courtesy Harvard University Press; **73:** Pat Bruno, Positive Images; **75:** Bob Daemmrich, Tony Stone Worldwide; **76:** Ellis Herwig, The Picture Cube; **77:** Richard Hutchings, PhotoEdit; **81:** Skjold Photographs; **82:** t, Bob Daemmrich, Tony Stone Worldwide; b, MacDonald Photography, The Picture Cube; **83:** Skjold Photographs; **84:** The Image Works; **85:** Kindra Clineff, The Picture Cube; **86:** Lee Snider, The Image Works; **87:** Tony Stone Worldwide; **88:** Daniel Wray, The Image Works; **89:** Larry Lawfer, The Picture Cube; **90:** Focus on Sports; **91:** Laima Druskis, Stock Boston; **92:** Kevin Horan, Picture Group; **93:** Charles Gupton, Stock Boston; **96:** Billy Barnes, Tony Stone Worldwide; **97:** Richard Lord, The Image Works; **98:** ©1991 by NEA, Inc. Reprinted by permission.; **99:** Bob Daemmrich Photography; **100:** t, Carol Lee, The Picture Cube; m, Ogust, The Image Works; b, Skjold Photographs; **101:** Tom McKitterick, Impact Visuals; **105:** Bob Daemmrich, Stock Boston; **106:** Tony Freeman, PhotoEdit; **108:** Bob Daemmrich, The Image Works; **110:** Robert Brenner, PhotoEdit; **112:** Tony Freeman, PhotoEdit; **117:** Sybil Shackman, Monkmeyer Press; **118:** Rhoda Sidney, The Image Works; **119, 122:** Spencer Grant, Monkmeyer Press; **123:** Dennis MacDonald, PhotoEdit; **127:** Richard Hutchings, Photo Researchers; **128:** Gary Wagner, Picture Group; **129:** t, U. California, Peter Arnold, Inc.; b,deLeon, Peter Arnold, Inc.; **130:** Daily Press, Gamma-Liaison; **131:** Peter Southwick, Stock Boston; **132:** Bettina Servan; Gamma-Liaison; **135:** Edrington, The Image Works; **138:** U. California, Peter Arnold, Inc.; **139:** Bob Dammerich, Stock Boston; **141:** Bill Stanton, Rainbow; **142:** John Griffin, The Image Works; **144:** Rob Crandall, Picture Group; **145:** Owen Franken, Stock Boston.

Unit Three: 148-49: Cathlyn Melloan, Tony Stone Worldwide; **151, 152:** Ulrike Welsch; **153:** Michael Newman, PhotoEdit; **154:** John Coletti, Stock Boston; **155:** Michael Newman, PhotoEdit; **156:** Kopstein, Monkmeyer Press ; **157:** t, ©1992 Lynn Johnston Productions, Inc. Reprinted with permission of Universal Press Syndicate. All rights reserved; b, Young-Wolff, PhotoEdit; **158:** Audrey Gottlieb, Monkmeyer Press; **159:** Mark Walker, The Picture Cube; **160:** Gale Zucker, Stock Boston; **161:** Erika Stone, Peter Arnold, Inc.; **164:** Frank Siteman, Stock Boston; **165:** Bob Daemmrich, Stock Boston; **169:** Melanie Clark, Picture Perfect USA; **170:** Tony Freeman, PhotoEdit; **171:** Jim Pickerell, Stock Boston; **172:** Jon Riley, TonyStone Worldwide; **173:** Jerard Smith, Monkmeyer Press; **174:** Stephen Frisch, Stock Boston;**176:** t, Bob Daemmrich, Tony Stone Worldwide; m, Myrleen Ferguson, PhotoEdit; b, Jeff Isaac Greenberg, Photo Researchers; **177:** Charles Gupton, Tony Stone Worldwide; **178:** Scott Shaw, Texas Imprint; **180:** ©Ray Billingsley. Reprinted with special permission of King Features Syndicate; **181:** Photo Researchers; **183:** Stephen Whalen, Picture Perfect USA; **185:** Monkmeyer Press; **189:** Stock Boston; **190:** Paul Conklin, Monkmeyer Press; **191:** Jon Levy, Gamma-Liaison; **193:** Donald Dietz, Stock Boston; **194:** Hank Morgan, Rainbow; **195:** Don Smetzer, Tony Stone Worldwide; **196:** Susan Van Etten, PhotoEdit; **197:** Gale Zucker, Stock Boston; **199:** Mary Kate Denny, PhotoEdit; **200, 201:** Bob Daemmrich, Stock Boston.

Unit Four: 204-5: James Lemass, The Picture Cube; **207:** Jerry Howard, Stock Boston; **208:** Bob Daemmrich, Stock Boston; **210:** David Sams, Texas Imprint; **213:** Bob Daemmrich, The Image Works; **215:** Skjold Photographs; **218:** Ken Levinson, Monkmeyer Press; **220:** Bob Daemmrich, The Image Works; **221:** Skjold Photographs; **224:** Brad Markel, Gamma-Liaison; **228:** Bob Daemmrich, The Image Works; **229:** Ogust, The Image Works; **233:** K.B. Kaplan, The Picture Cube; **235:** MacDonald, The Picture Cube; **237:** © Jack Tippit. Reprinted with special permission of King Features Syndicate; **238:** Seitz, Photo Researchers; **239:** Walker, The Picture Cube; **240:** Gene Trindl, Shooting Star International; **242:** t, Dan Burns, Monkmeyer Press; m, Ellie Beranger, Photo Researchers; b, David Conklin, Monkmeyer Press; **243:** Tony Freeman, PhotoEdit; **245:** Dollarhide, Monkmeyer Press; **246:** Peter Southwick, Stock Boston; **247:** Cleo, The Picture Cube; **248:** Tilley, Tony Stone Worldwide; **250:** Nathan Benn, Stock Boston; **251:** Yoav Levy, Phototake; **253:** George Goodwin, Monkmeyer Press; **257:** Warren Morgan, Focus on Sports; **262:** Myrleen Feruson, PhotoEdit; **268:** Sarah Putnam, The Picture Cube; **274:** Dan McCoy, Rainbow; **275:** John Coletti, The Picture Cube.

Unit Five: 278-9: David Lissy, The Picture Cube; **281:** Barbara Lewis, Monkmeyer Press; **283:** Will & Deni McIntyre, Photo Researchers; **284:** John Coletti, Stock Boston; **287:** CNRI, Phototake; **288:** Cameramann, The Image Works; **295:** Manfred Kage, Peter Arnold; **297:** Charles Gupton, Stock Boston; **298:** Richard Hutchings, Photo Researchers; **300:** Charles Gupton, Stock Boston; **301:** Mimi Forsyth, Monkmeyer Press; **303:** Bob Daemmrich, Stock Boston; **307:** Dr. Dennis Kukel, Phototake; **311:** Lou Lainey; **312:** Bob Daemmrich, The Image Works; **316:** Phillips, Visuals Unlimited; **317:** t, Dr. Dennis Kukel, Phototake; b, Manfred Kage, Peter Arnold, Inc.; **319:** Yoav Levy, Phototake; **322:** Manfred Kage, Peter Arnold, Inc. **325:** Ken Hoge, Phototake; **327:** Mary Kate Denny, PhotoEdit; **331:** Mike Powell, Allsport USA; **332:** Nathan Bilow, Allsport, USA; **334:** Bob Daemmrich Photography; **335:** Gale Zucker, Stock Boston; **339:** Walter B. Silver Photography; **341:** Bob Daemmrich, The Image Works; **342:** Vandystadt, Allsport USA; **343:** Frank Siteman, Monkmeyer Press; **344:** Reprinted by permission of NEA, Inc.; **345:** Indiana University Natatorium, Indianapolis, Indiana; **347:** Focus on Sports; **348:** David Young-Wolff, Tony Stone Worldwide; **350:** t, Hugh Rogers, Monkmeyer Press; m, The Image Works; b, John Coletti, The Picture Cube; **351:** Donna Jernigan, Monkmeyer Press; **352:** Bob Daemmrich, The Image Works; **355:** David Young-Wolff, PhotoEdit.

Unit Six: 358-9: Suzanne Murphy, Tony Stone Worldwide; **361:** Custom Medical Stock Photo; **363:** l, Yoav Levy, Phototake; r, Lennart Nilsson from Behold Man, Little Brown & Co., Boston; **365:** Arlene Collins, Monkmeyer Press; **366:** Peter Menzel, Stock Boston; **367:** Lawrence Migdale, Stock Boston; **369:** Jim Pickerell, The Image Works; **371:** Julie Marcotte, Stock Boston; **372:** Doug Goodman, Monkmeyer Press; **375:** Lawrence Migdale, Photo Researcher; **379:** Julie Houck, Tony Stone Worldwide; **380:** David Joel, Tony Stone Worldwide; **381:** Joe Sohm, The Image Works; **385:** John Elk III, Stock Boston; **387:** Bob Daemmrich, The Image Works; **389:** l, Joe Sohm, The Image Works; r, Bob Daemmrich, Stock Boston; **392:** Gerald Smith, Photo Researchers; **395:** Hazel Hankin, Impact Visuals; **397:** Larry Lawfer, The Picture Cube; **398:** Bob Daemmrich, Stock Boston; **399:** Crystal Images, Monkmeyer Press; **400:** Bob Daemmrich, Stock Boston;